ULTIMATE GUIDE SERIES

ULTIMATE GUIDE TO THE HOLY LAND

HOLMAN®

REFERENCE

NASHVILLE, TENNESSEE

Ultimate Guide to the Holy Land
© 2022 by Holman Bible Publishers
Nashville, Tennessee
All rights reserved

Maps © 2000 and 2019 by Holman Bible Publishers
Nashville, Tennessee.
All rights reserved.

978-1-0877-5140-5

Dewey Decimal Classification: 220.91
Subject Heading: HOLY LAND / PALESTINE / BIBLE—STUDY AND TEACHING

Articles previously published in *Biblical Illustrator* magazine and are used by permission. A majority of the images and captions come from the same publication as well. See pages 657 for a listing of photographers.

The interior of the *Ultimate Guide to the Holy Land* was designed and typeset by 2K/DENMARK, using Bible Serif created by 2K/DENMARK, Højbjerg, Denmark.

Printed in China
1 2 3 4 5 6 7 8 9 10 · 28 27 26 25 24 23 22
RRD

TABLE OF CONTENTS

Introduction VII
List of Articles... IX
Contributors XIII

People.. 1
Places 211
Artifacts 455

Acknowledgements 657

INTRODUCTION

We all benefit from the efforts and work of those who have gone before us. My dad understood that; he used to say that we all enjoy sitting in the shade of trees that we did not plant. Many products and gadgets that increase our comfort and make our lives easier and better are available because of other people's visions, plans, and hard work. The Bible you hold in your hand is the product and result of many people's dedication to years of hard work and perseverance in fulfilling God's call on their lives.

In 1973, some people had a vision for a resource that would offer in-depth information for the serious student of the Word. After a time of planning and research, a new magazine was birthed, the *Sunday School Lesson Illustrator*. In its first issue, A.V. Washburn who was at the time the secretary of teaching and training of what is now Lifeway Christian Resources said: "Now we are taking a bold step to express a dream. The *Sunday School Lesson Illustrator* will contain a new world of biblical information for the Sunday School pupil and teacher. . . . It is for those Bible students who are interested in more in-depth information about persons, places, and things."

Nobel Brown, the magazine's first editor, expressed his appreciation to the first contributors: "The most noticeable attribute common to those involved in producing the *Illustrator* has been an enthusiasm translated into a determination to create a significant magazine. Our writers have put aside other demanding duties in order to spend hours of research in preparing each article."

The magazine's name was later changed to *Biblical Illustrator*, yet the purpose of the magazine never changed. Using words and images, maps and charts, *Biblical Illustrator* helped Bible teachers and students gain a deeper understanding into God's Word.

What is the significance of a particular location? How does this event fit in the larger context of Scripture? What was going on in the world at that time? Was there a significance that the initial readers would have understood that we miss, now centuries later? The *Ultimate Guide to the Holy Land* is filled with helpful articles and images that appeared in the magazine and addressed these questions and more.

As the year 2020 drew to a close, the magazine ceased publication. With this Bible, though, you have the opportunity to continue sitting at the feet of scholars, to enjoy the shade of men and women who have invested their lives as life-long learners of Scripture. Through their efforts, you will discover the culture, customs, people, and practices of the biblical day. The information on these pages can help you understand the message as the original audience did, deepen your understanding of Scripture, and increase your appreciation for the biblical world.

The intent is not to give you minutia or additional tidbits of obscure information. Instead, it is to help you grow in your relationship with both the Word of God and the God of the Word. The Lord promises, "my word that comes from my mouth will not return to me empty, but it will accomplish what I please and will prosper in what I send it to do" (Isa. 55:11).

We invite you to pore over these pages. Bask in what the Father has to say to you. Allow the articles to draw you into the biblical world. And as you do, we pray you will find yourself refreshed, spiritually renewed, and confident in your growing knowledge of God's Word. So please, find yourself a place in the shade and prepare to be blessed.

G. B. Howell
Content Editor, *Biblical Illustrator*
2002-2020

LIST OF ARTICLES

People 1
  Agrippa II 2
  Amos 5
  Who Were the Arameans? 7
  The Archaeology of David
    and Solomon 10
  Armor-Bearers 12
  Babylonian and Persian Kings 14
  Caesar Augustus 18
  The Chaldeans 22
  Cyrus the Great 26
  David and the Philistines 30
  Elijah 34
  Elisha 36
  Ezekiel and Jeremiah 38
  Ezra 42
  Felix and Festus 45
  First-Century Priesthood 48
  Fishermen in the First Century 51
  From Nebuchadnezzar to Cyrus II 54
  Haggai the Prophet and
    His Ministry 57
  The Historical Setting of Habakkuk . . . 60
  The Hittites 61
  Hosea the Prophet 66
  Jehoiakim 68
  Jews in First-Century Rome 71
  Jezebel Unveiled 75
  Joab 78
  Joel 80
  Jonah's Historical Setting 83
  Joseph the Carpenter 87
  Joshua 89
  Just Who Was Belshazzar? 91
  The Kinsman Redeemer 94
  The Life of Jeroboam II 96
  Machaerus, Herod, and John
    the Baptist 99
  Malachi's Situation 102
  Mothers' Role in the First Century . . . 104
  Nahum's Historical Setting 107
  Nebuchadnezzar 111
  Nero 115
  Obadiah 119
  Of Marrying Age 122
  Older Adults in First-Century
    Culture 124
  Paul, the Letter Writer 127
  Pharaoh's Army 130
  Philistines 136
  Pilate's Role in Jesus's Death 139

  The Political Climate of Micah 142
  Prophet, Priest, King 145
  The Rich and the Poor in the First
    Century 147
  Robbers 149
  The Role of a Roman Governor 151
  Roles and Responsibilities of
    Persian Queens 154
  Roman Citizenship 156
  Servants in the House Of Pharaoh 159
  Slavery in the Ancient World 163
  Solomon in All His Splendor 165
  Solomon's Foreign Wives and
    Their Gods 167
  Spies in the Land 171
  Tiglath-Pileser III 174
  To Live Like A Jew 179
  Who Was Artaxerxes? 182
  Who Were the Canaanites? 186
  Who Were Oracles? 191
  Who Were the Samaritans? 194
  Wise Men from the East 197
  The Woman Huldah 199
  A Woman's Status 201
  Xerxes I 203
  Zechariah 206
  Zedekiah 208

Places 211
  Abel-Beth-Maacah 212
  Abraham's Travels 217
  Achaia 221
  Ancient Lebanon 225
  Ancient Tyre 229
  Antioch of Syria 234
  The Arabah 237
  Assyria in the Eighth Century 241
  Battle of Carchemish 244
  Caesarea 248
  Cana of Galilee 252
  Capernaum in Jesus's Day 255
  Cappadocia in the First Century 258
  Cedars of Lebanon 262
  Colossae in the First Century 266
  Corinth 268
  David's Jerusalem 271
  Eden 276
  Edom 278
  The Egypt Joseph Knew 281
  Egypt's Influence on the Divided
    Kingdom 286

En-Gedi 289
Ephesus 292
Excavating Gath. 295
The Fall of Jerusalem. 298
First-Century Athens. 302
First-Century Crete 306
First-Century Roads and Travel 308
First-Century Thessalonica 312
Galatia 315
Gethsemane. 317
Gezer. 320
Greek and Roman Temples
    of the First Century 323
Hades 326
Hebron 329
Herod's Temple. 332
The Island of Malta. 336
Jericho in Jesus's Day. 339
Jericho 342
Jerusalem before the Return 346
Jerusalem Gates/Gates and
    Gatekeepers 349
Jezreel. 358
The Kidron Valley 361
Lachish. 364
The Lycus Valley 368
Megiddo 371
Moab 374
Moriah 376
Mount Nebo. 379
Nazareth in the First Century 383
Patmos 386
Philippi. 388
The Promised Land. 392
The Rise of Macedonia 399
The Role of Geography in
    the Warfare of Judges 403
The Roman Forum 406
Rome. 410
The Route of the Exodus 414
Samaria 419
Susa in the Days of Queen Esther. . . . 424
The Temples at Corinth. 430
Ur 432
Valleys and Pastures 437
Waterfalls and Wadis. 442
Zerubbabel's Temple 445
Zion as a Place and Symbol. 449
Zoar 452

Artifacts 455
Agriculture and Farming in
    Ancient Israel. 456
Ancient Altars. 459
Ancient Threshing Floors 463

Ancient Marriage Contracts 465
Ashteroth 469
Banking in the First Century 472
Boundary Markers 475
Bread Making in the Ancient
    World 478
Building Temples in the Ancient
    Near East 481
Chariots. 484
Cisterns in the Ancient
    Near East 487
Clean And Unclean. 493
Coins Used in Banking 496
Crowns Fit for a King. 497
Deeds And Seals in Jeremiah. 499
Earthenware Vessels. 502
Egyptian Cursive. 508
Egyptian Mummification 509
Establishing Weights and
    Measures in Ancient Israel 512
First-Century Armor 520
First-Century Burial. 522
First-Century Dining Practices. 525
Foot Washing in Ancient
    Practice. 527
A "Fortified" City 529
Gezer Calendar. 533
The Gods of Thessalonica 534
The Golden Calves at Dan
    and Bethel 537
The Goliath Inscription 541
Horses in Ancient Warfare 543
Houses in Jesus's Day. 547
How Iron Changed Warfare 550
Idols in Production and Rituals 555
In the City Gate. 558
Incense in Hebrew Worship. 562
Isthmian Games. 564
Lions as Old Testament Imagery 567
Literacy in the Ancient
    Near East 570
Livestock as Wealth in
    the Old Testament Era 574
Meat Sacrificed to Idols 579
The Moabite Stone 581
Music in David's Time 585
". . . And Not a Drop to Drink". 588
Oils, Perfumes, and Cosmetics of the
    Ancient Near East 592
Papyrus 595
Passover in Jesus's Day. 597
The Practice of Roman Crucifixion. . 600
Precious Metals 604
Prisons of the First Century 608
Reaching the Heavens. 611

Roman Agriculture 616
Roman Triumphal Procession 618
Sabbath Law 623
Ships and Shipping in the New
    Testament World 624
Sorcery, Witchcraft, and Divination.. 627
Sound the Shofar! 630
Spices and Perfumes 632

The Tabernacle 635
Ten Words and Ancient Near
    Eastern Laws 638
Wealth, Trade, Money, and Coinage
    in the Biblical World 642
Wearing Purple 647
What Kind of Tambourine? 650
With Harp and Lyre 651

CONTRIBUTORS

Adkisson, Randall L. Healthy Christian Ministries.

Anderson, Jeff S. Wayland Baptist University.

Andrew, Scott A. Nashville, TN.

Andrews, Stephen J. Midwestern Baptist Theological Seminary.

Arbino, Gary P. Gateway Seminary.

Bergen, Martha S. Hannibal-LaGrange University.

Bergen, Robert D. Hannibal-LaGrange University.

Betts, T. J. The Southern Baptist Theological Seminary.

Beyer, Bryan E. Columbia International University.

Branch, Alan. Midwestern Baptist Theological Seminary.

Browning Jr., Daniel C. William Carey University.

Booth, Steve. Canadian Southern Baptist Seminary.

Booth, Susan. Canadian Southern Baptist Seminary.

Brooks, James A. Bethel Theological Seminary.

Boyd, Timothy N. Kansas-Nebraska Convention of Southern Baptists.

Buescher, Alan Ray. Nashville, TN.

Butler, Trent C. Gallatin, TN.

Byargeon, Rick W. Temple Baptist Church, Ruston, LA.

Caldwell, Daniel P. William Carey University.

Cantrell, Deborah. Houston, TX

Cathey, Joseph R. Dallas Baptist University.

Champy III, Harry D. North Georgia Christian School.

Clendenen, E. Ray. Holman Bible Publishers.

Cole, R. Dennis. New Orleans Baptist Theological Seminary.

Cook III, William F. The Southern Baptist Theological Seminary.

Cox, Ken. New Boston, TX

Crockett Jr., Bennie R. William Carey University.

Davis, Conn. Southern Baptist Believers Church, South Coffeyville, Oklahoma.

Draper, Charles W. Boyce College.

Drinkard Jr., Joel F. Campbellsville University.

Dunn, Mark R. First Baptist Church, Duncanville, TX

Dunston, Robert C. University of the Cumberlands.

Faber, Timothy T. Liberty University.

Fowler, R. D. Bethel Baptist Church, Lincoln, NE.

Garrett, Duane A. The Southern Baptist Theological Seminary.

Goodman, Thomas H. Hillcrest Baptist Church, Austin, TX.

Gregg, D. Larry. Covecraft Consultants.

Gritz, Sharon H. Fort Worth, TX

Hall, Kevin. Oklahoma Baptist University.

Hardin, Gary. Centre, Alabam.

Harris, John L. East Texas Baptist University.

Hays, J. Daniel. Ouachita Baptist University.

Howell Jr., G. B. LifeWay Christian Resources.

Hyatt Jr., Leon. Pineville, LA

Hummel, Scott. William Carey University.

Jenkins, David L. Gilmer, TX

Jones, Robert E. Euclid Avenue Baptist Church, Bristol, VA.

Jones, Roberta Lou. Mid-Continent University.

Kimmitt, Francis X. Bryan College.

Knight, George W. Greenville Presbyterian Theological Seminary.

Knowles, Julie Nall. The Baptist College of Florida.

Kullman, Paul E. College Station, TX

Laird, Dorman. William Carey University.

Lane, Harry A. West Side Baptist Church, Greenwood, SC.

Langston, Scott.

Lanier, David E. Southeastern Baptist Theological Seminary.

Lee, Jerry W.

Lemke, Steve W. New Orleans Baptist Theological Seminary.

Lloyd, R. Raymond. First Baptist Church, Starkville, MS.

Lombard, Becky. Truett McConnell University.

Longino, Byron. New Orleans Baptist Theological Seminary.

Lucas Jr., Roy E. Clear Breek Baptist Bible College.

Mariottini, Claude F. Northern Baptist Theological Seminary.

Matthews, E. LeBron. Eastern Heights Baptist Church, Columbus, GA.

McClain, T. Van. Mid-America Baptist Theological Seminary.

McCoy, Glenn. Eastern New Mexico University.

McWilliams, Warren. Oklahoma Baptist University.

Meier, Janice. Nashville, TN.

Miller, Stephen R. Mid-America Baptist Theological Seminary.

Mitchell, Eric A. Southwestern Baptist Theological Seminary.

Moore, R. Kelvin. Union University.

Moseley, Allan. Southeastern Baptist Theological Seminary.

Mosley, Harold R. New Orleans Baptist Theological Seminary.

Newell, James O. The Baptist College of Florida.

Ortiz, Steven M. Southwestern Baptist Theological Seminary.

Peacock, Kevin C. Canadian Southern Baptist Seminary.

Poulton, Gary M., Virginia Intermont College.

Pouncey, George T. First Baptist Church, Mobile, AL.

Rathel, Mark A. The Baptist College of Florida.

Ray Jr., Charles A. New Orleans Baptist Theological Seminary.

Register, M. Dean. Crosspoint Church, Hattiesburg, MS.

Richards, E. Randolph. Palm Beach Atlantic University.

Roark, C. Mack. Oklahoma Baptist University.

Roberts, Sharon. Nashville, TN.

Robinson, Dale "Geno." First Baptist Church of Fair Oaks, Sacramento, California.

Rodriquez, Seth M. Colorado Christian University.

Shaddix, George H. Dunn's Creek Baptist Church, Echola, AL.

Severance, W. Murray. Nashville, TN.

Simmons, Bob. New Orleans Baptist Theological Seminary.

Smith Jr., Argile A. Parkway Baptist Church, Biloxi, MS.

Stevens, Gerald L. New Orleans Baptist Theological Seminary.

Stewart, Don H. New Orleans Baptist Theological Seminary.

Stewart, Mona. William Carey School of Nursing.

Street, Robert A. Campbellsville University.

Swanson, Philip J. Colts Neck Baptist Church, Colts Neck, NJ.

Tate, Marvin E. The Southern Baptist Theological Seminary.

Taylor, Cecil R. University of Mobile.

Terry, John Mark. The Southern Baptist Theological Seminary.

Tolar, William B. Southwestern Baptist Theological Seminary.

Trammell, Timothy. Dallas Baptist University.

Traylor, John. First Baptist Church, Monroe, LA.

Traylor, Lynn O. Liberty Association, Glasgow, KY.

VanHorn, W. Wayne. Mississippi College.

Wallace, David M. Dallas Baptist University.

Weathers, Robert A. First Baptist Church, Shallotte, NC.

Winslow, Blakeley. North American Mission Board.

Wood, Darryl. First Baptist Church, Vincent, AL.

Wood, Fred M. Preach-Teach Ministries.

PEOPLE

AGRIPPA II: LAST OF THE HERODIANS

BY TIMOTHY N. BOYD

Overview of the eastern side of the Banias palace complex. When Agrippa rebuilt Banias (Caesarea Philippi) in honor of Nero, he renamed it "Neronias."

Herod Agrippa II (also known by his Roman name, Julius Marcus Agrippa) is the last of the family of Herod the Great that readers encounter in the pages of the New Testament. He was born in AD 27 in Rome, the son of Herod Agrippa I and great grandson of Herod the Great. His father had a rather checkered career. At one point, he was completely bankrupt; at another point, he was ruler over a kingdom as large as that of Herod the Great. Because of his father's changing situation, Agrippa was shuttled around as a child. He visited the land of Israel for the first time when he was about five years old because his father was fleeing creditors.

When his father's fortunes were finally restored, Agrippa returned to Rome at the age of fourteen to be educated in the royal palace. This allowed him access to the entire Roman ruling family. His father died approximately two years later in AD 44 when Agrippa was about seventeen. The Roman emperor Claudius had grown to like Agrippa and was inclined to give him his father's territory. However, members of the court persuaded Claudius that Agrippa was too young. Because the territory was large and volatile, even an experienced administrator would have been challenged. Therefore, Claudius placed the territory under the authority of Roman governors.

In AD 48, Agrippa's uncle, also a Herod, died. He had ruled over the independent city of Chalcis from AD 41 to 48. After Herod of Chalcis died, the emperor decided to give Agrippa this much more manageable position. In his new position, Agrippa also gained control over the temple in Jerusalem. This gave him the power to depose and nominate the high priest. This authority brought Agrippa into conflict with the religious leaders of the Jews. The Jews felt that Agrippa abused this power by appointing men with no real consideration of the qualifications of the office. For this reason, throughout Agrippa's reign, he and the Jewish leaders were in constant conflict.

In AD 53, Claudius gave Agrippa the territory ruled by his father's uncle, Philip, in exchange for the city of Chalcis. This territory included Abilene (or Abila), Trachonitis, and Acra. When Emperor Nero came to power, he added the city of Tiberias and parts of Perea. Agrippa retained his control over the temple and the high priesthood.

Agrippa established residences in both Jerusalem and Caesarea Philippi. These two cities also held the residence of the Roman governors of Judea. Strong cooperation existed between Agrippa and these governors. The Romans consulted Agrippa on religious matters in Judea because of his knowledge of the Jewish faith.[1]

The way the emperors treated Agrippa shows the friendship that existed between them. Prior to Agrippa, other members of the Herodian family had strong ties to the Roman throne. Agrippa, however, maintained closer ties with the Roman emperors than had the previous Herods. His friendship with the throne extended through multiple emperors, and he was always in good favor with them, reigning longer than any other Herod.

As with most of the other Herodians, Agrippa was a builder. Under his direction, his palace in Jerusalem was extended. Part of this extension was a watchtower built high enough to allow Agrippa to peer into the temple area and observe what was happening. This offended the priests, and they extended the height of a temple wall to block his view. Both Agrippa and Festus, the Roman governor, were displeased with this, and Festus ordered the wall lowered. The priests, however, sent petitioners to Rome to seek an audience with Nero. Through the influence of the emperor's wife, they were granted the right to retain the higher wall.[2]

Even though he did not have a positive relationship with the Jewish religious leaders, Agrippa did fund and direct a remodeling of the temple. He also was known as an advocate for the Jewish religion. For example, the Roman procurator Fadus had taken control over the garments of the high priest. He wanted to keep the garments in the fortress Antonia under the control of the Roman army to demonstrate Roman domination over the Jews. Agrippa persuaded Claudius, the emperor at that time, to allow the Jews to retain control over the garments.[3]

In his private life, Agrippa scandalized the Jewish community as well as other groups by his supposed incestuous relationship with his sister, Bernice. This relationship began when she came to live with Agrippa after the death of her second husband, Herod of Chalcis. The relationship created so much gossip that Agrippa betrothed her to Polemo, the king of Cilicia. Polemo was so enamored with her that he agreed to her request that he be circumcised. This marriage, however, did not last, and she soon returned to Agrippa. Her relationship with Agrippa was finally disrupted when she began a long-term affair with Titus, the future emperor.[4]

Referring to Agrippa II, bronze inscription in Greek reads "King Agrippa Nero"; dated AD 67/68.

Even though Agrippa had been a friend to the Jews, he was firmly committed to the Romans. When the Jews revolted against Rome in AD 66, Agrippa tried to convince the Jews not to revolt. In a speech to the Jewish leaders, Agrippa reminded the leaders of how they could not successfully resist when General Pompey had brought a small Roman army into the region. Agrippa asked the Jews how they hoped to defeat an even more powerful Roman presence; the idea of revolt would lead to defeat and ruin for the nation. The Romans would kill all the people or take them into slavery. The Jews refused to listen to Agrippa and pursued their revolt.[5]

Agrippa and his sister, Bernice, fled to Galilee and allied themselves with the Romans. Agrippa furnished two thousand soldiers to Vespasian, the general who was sent to put down the revolt. Agrippa personally participated in the battle for Gamala, a town near Capernaum. In that battle, he was wounded by a sling stone. Agrippa later entertained the Roman commanders and troops at his palace in Caesarea Philippi after they had defeated the rebels in that region.[6]

After the final defeat of the Jews and the destruction of Jerusalem, the Roman government gave Agrippa territories in Syria to rule for his consistent loyalty to Rome. He continued to rule for at least twenty-five more years. When he died, Agrippa left no heirs. With his death, the line of the Herodian rulers ended.[7]

NOTES

1   See Harold W. Hoehner, "Herod" in *ISBE* (1982), 2:688–98.

2   Josephus, *Jewish Antiquities* 20.8.11.

3   Josephus, *Jewish Antiquities* 20.1–2.

4   Josephus, *Jewish Antiquities* 20.7.3; Richard Gottheil and Heinrich Bloch, "Berenice" in *JE* (1906), www.jewishencyclopedia.com/articles/3050-berenice.

5   Josephus, *Jewish War* 2.16.3–4.

6   Josephus, *Jewish War* 3.4.2; 4.1.3; M. Brann, "Agrippa II" in *JE* (1906), www.jewishencyclopedia.com/articles/913-agrippa-ii.

7   Hoehner, "Herod," 698; Josephus, *The Life* 65.364–67.

AMOS: HIS LIFE AND CALL

BY SCOTT LANGSTON

Base of the altar established by Jeroboam I at Dan.

Amos 1:1 places Amos in the early- to mid-eighth century BC. A more precise date for the beginning of Amos's ministry would be possible if the date of the earthquake mentioned in 1:1 could be ascertained. It must have been severe because the verse refers to it simply as "the earthquake." Evidence of an earthquake dated to the mid-eighth century has been found, according to some archaeologists, at the city of Hazor. On the basis of this and other evidence, some scholars date the beginning of Amos's ministry to about 760 BC.[1] Others prefer a slightly later date, but Amos probably began his work sometime between 760 and 750. Israel and Judah had yet to experience Assyria's renewed power and wrath. Times were peaceful, and many people prospered.

Many of Amos's messages concentrated on the relationship between prosperity and religion. The religion of the day in essence supported the oppression of people. The worship centers were filled with people bringing their sacrifices, but they felt no remorse as they commonly engaged in unethical business practices, perversion of justice, and oppression of the people. The religious leadership did not denounce these actions and, therefore, lent their approval to this kind of religion. The people and the religious leadership failed to connect their actions in the worship service with their everyday actions. They believed that God only wanted ritual acts of worship and that the peace and prosperity of the times signaled God's approval of this religion. The book of Amos denounces and warns against religious leadership that concerns itself only with matters of worship

Aramaic reinterment funerary inscription of King Uzziah: "To here were brought the bones of Uzziah, King of Judah. Do not open."

or doctrine and neglects the just treatment of all people. To Amos, true religion expressed itself in social justice and did not limit itself to ritual acts and doctrine.

Amos's willingness to denounce Israel's religious and political leadership indicates that he possessed courage, integrity, and commitment to God. Israel's leaders had great power, but Amos did not allow himself to be intimidated by them. His integrity helped him not to modify his message to conform to that typically advocated by the religious leaders. This kind of courage and integrity stemmed from his commitment to God.

According to Amos 1:1 and 7:14, he was a shepherd. Scholars, however, disagree over whether he was a poor shepherd who watched others' flocks or a wealthy owner of herds. The words used to describe Amos as a shepherd occur only a few times in the Old Testament, making it difficult to know their exact meaning. One word is used in 2 Kings 3:4 to describe Mesha, king of Moab. This usage suggests it refers to a wealthy owner of herds rather than a simple shepherd, thus indicating that Amos owned herds rather than watched them. He also is described in Amos 7:14 as taking care of sycamore figs. While the poor often ate these figs, they also were commonly fed to cattle. Amos, therefore, may have owned sycamore orchards from which he fed his herds. Amos may have been an influential and somewhat wealthy individual.[2]

Amos also described himself in 7:14 as one who was not part of the religious leadership. Scholars debate whether Amos's words should be understood as "I am not a prophet" or "I was not a prophet." The first rendering suggests Amos never claimed to be a professional prophet; the second indicates that he originally was not one but now claimed authority as one. What is clear, however, is that while Amos was engaged in his original occupation, God chose him to deliver his message. In other words, Amos was a layperson. As one who had no formal religious training, he challenged the priests and prophets. As one from Judah (Tekoa was located near Bethlehem), he addressed his messages to Israel. As one who was wealthy, he confronted the rich and powerful on behalf of the oppressed. Courage, integrity, and commitment to God seem to be apt descriptions of Amos.

NOTES

1   Philip J. King, *Amos, Hosea, Micah: An Archaeological Commentary* (Philadelphia: Westminster, 1988), 21, 38; Bruce H. Willoughby, "Amos, Book of," *ABD*, 1:203–4; James Limburg, *Hosea–Micah*, Interpretation: A Bible Commentary (IBC) (Atlanta: John Knox, 1988), 84.
2   Willoughby, "Amos."

WHO WERE THE ARAMEANS?

BY JOEL F. DRINKARD JR.

Ruins at Tadmor (known in English as Palmyra); located in the central Syrian desert, Tadmor was an important stop for travelers and caravans along the route from Mesopotamia westward. Tiglath-pileser I defeated the Arameans at Tadmor.

Basalt statue of an Aramean king. Dates from the late Hittite period: ninth century BC.

First, *where* were the Arameans? They were in Syria and Mesopotamia—both in many English translations and in history. So, *who* were the Arameans? The Arameans were the neighbors of Israel to the north and east, primarily east of the Jordan River and the Rift Valley as far as the Middle Euphrates and its tributaries.

The Arameans were Semitic tribes who were closely related to the Israelites. The Aramaic language the Arameans spoke was a Semitic language closely related to Hebrew. Abraham was living in Aram when God called him to go to Canaan (Gen. 11:31–12:1). Abraham's brother, Nahor, Isaac's wife Rebekah, and Jacob's wives Leah and Rachel all lived in Aram.

The Arameans occupied much of the territory that linked trade and commerce between Egypt and Assyria-Babylon. They lived north of Canaan-Israel and east of Phoenicia. The primary god of the Arameans was Hadad, a storm god. The Arameans eventually became strong enough that they controlled much of the region of eastern Syria and Assyria. Partly because of this expansion and partly because their language was alphabetic (unlike the cuneiform-syllabic languages of Assyria and Babylon), Aramaic became a common language of trade and commerce as well as diplomacy during the Assyrian and Babylonian empires of the late eighth to sixth centuries BC. Aramaic then became the lingua franca for almost all the Near East during the Persian and Hellenistic periods.[1] Aramaic and Greek were the two primary languages of the New Testament era throughout the Near East.

Bedouin tent and herd near Sheikh Mizken (translated "leader of the poor people") in Syria. Some Arameans were rural tent dwellers; others lived in cities.

The earliest specific mention of the Arameans was in Assyrian texts dated to the time of Tiglath-pileser I (reigned 1115–1077 BC). He fought against the Arameans and defeated them from Tadmor (Palmyra) in modern Syria as far as Babylonia.[2] By this time, the Arameans were spread from central Syria eastward across the Euphrates River at least as far as the Babylonian territory. The Assyrian texts describe the Arameans both as pastoral tribal groups and also as ones who dwelled in towns or villages.

The Arameans mentioned in 2 Kings 5 were those who lived west of the Euphrates in what is modern Syria. They never formed a unified nation. Instead they had a series of independent city-states, including Aram-Damascus. David occupied Aram-Damascus (2 Sm 8:6), and it remained under Israel's control during his reign. Rezon recaptured Damascus from Solomon.

Aramean debt contract established before four witnesses. The contract states a man borrowed twenty-seven silver shekels from Bait' el-Yada', leaving him a slave as deposit; dates to about 570 BC, the thirty-fourth year of Nebuchadnezzar's reign; from Aleppo.

Ben-hadad II (who is probably also named Hadadezer) along with Israel's king Ahab fought against Assyria's king Shalmaneser III at the battle of Qarqar in 853 BC. Ben-hadad II had 1,200 chariots, twelve hundred cavalry, and 20,000 soldiers in the battle; Ahab had 2,000 chariots and 10,000 soldiers.[3] As prophesied by both Elijah and Elisha, Hazael assassinated Ben-hadad in 842 BC and became king (1 Kgs. 19:15; 2 Kgs. 8:13). Hazael is most likely the Aramean king in the Tel Dan stele. In the stele's inscription, the king claims to have killed both the kings of Israel and Judah, Joram and Ahaziah.[4] During Hazael's reign, Aram-Damascus reached its greatest extent east of the Jordan and subjugated Israel and Judah (2 Kgs. 12–13). Tiglath-pileser III (reigned 744–727 BC) conquered the Arameans of Damascus in 732 BC, and the Arameans ceased to be a political force in Syria.

NOTES

1   Benjamin Mazar, "The Aramean Empire and Its Relations with Israel," *BA* 25.4 (1962): 111.

2   James B. Prichard, ed., *ANET*, 3rd ed. with sup., 275.

3   Pritchard, *ANET*, 278–79.

4   William M. Schniedewind, "Tel Dan Stela: New Light on Aramaic and Jehu's Revolt," *BASOR* 302 (1996): 75–79; Matthew J. Suriano, "The Apology of Hazael: A Literary and Historical Analysis of the Tel Dan Inscription," *JNES* 66.3 (2007): 163–76.

THE ARCHAEOLOGY OF DAVID AND SOLOMON

BY STEVEN M. ORTIZ

Solomonic gate and casemate walls at Tel Hazor.

Does the archaeological data have anything to say about the development of a kingdom during the reigns of David and Solomon? In other words, do archaeologists find evidence for a centralized authority during the tenth century BC?

Four areas of archaeological data provide evidence for David: settlement data, monumental architecture, Jerusalem and the temple, and inscriptions.

Shifts in settlement between the eleventh and tenth centuries BC are dramatic. Remains at more than three hundred small villages and towns found throughout the hill country of Samaria and Judah illustrate evidence of a tribal or chiefdom social structure. During the tenth century, the picture changes; no longer do we have hundreds of small villages, but we start to see a process of urbanization, city planning, and centralized authority. Archaeologists have associated this type of settlement pattern to a centralized authority—such as a king, who would control the region from a capital. A king set up centers, building towns and networks to unify his kingdom. While these settlements do not prove David existed, they do suggest evidence of major changes in the social fabric of society, and these major changes suggest a central authority figure such as a king.

In addition, archaeologists can look at the individual cities to determine evidence of a shift from tribes to a state. Archaeologists and historians commonly identify an abundance of monumental building activity with a state. In the tenth century BC and following, many cities underwent drastic change. Builders constructed major fortifications such as city walls, ramparts, and multiple-entry city gates. Well-planned cities with sewage systems, water storage works, organized streets, and public areas became common. Government and public buildings such as large pillared storehouses, stables, and palaces made their appearances. One of the classic case studies of the archaeology of David and Solomon includes the six-chambered gates found at Hazor, Megiddo, and Gezer. The biblical text in 1 Kings 9:15 summarizes Solomon's activities and records that he constructed major fortifications at Hazor, Megiddo, and Gezer. This has become a classic case study in biblical archaeology of connecting a biblical text with the stones on the ground, as the similarity between these gate complexes evidences a relationship. Further, protoaeolic capitals dating from the tenth century BC have been found in the archaeological record from the north down to Judah. These large rectangular capitals are well-carved stones used for palatial edifices, something that would not be found in simple villages.

Naturally when we think of the archaeology of David and Solomon, we need to address the question of Jerusalem and the temple. Unfortunately archaeologists working in Jerusalem have not found much archaeological evidence for David. Realistically, we should expect not to find much! Jerusalem is a living city, having been continually occupied through most of its history. Today not much area is available to the spade of the archaeologist. Most excavations are chance occurrences as a parking lot gets repaved or a sewer is fixed. Jerusalem sat on a hill; the city was frequently destroyed, rebuilt, and repaired. This means that archaeological remains from the tenth century would have been destroyed throughout that history. In spite of these difficulties, archaeologists have found public structures that date to the tenth century such as the Stepped-Stone Structure, as well as a recently discovered public structure popularly reported as possibly being King David's palace.

Looking for the temple Solomon built would be foolish. It was surely dismantled in the Babylonian destruction, and any evidence would have been removed during the rebuilding by Nehemiah and especially by Herod the Great.

All the archaeological data coalesced illustrates that the social revolution that occurred during the tenth century can only be attributed to a centralized authority such as a king. Archaeologists have felt safe in assuming that while we do not have the name David or Solomon associated with any of these activities, they are the likely candidates.

The lack of any name association changed, however, with the discovery of the "house of David" inscription found at Tel Dan. The Tel Dan inscription is a stela commemorating victories by an Aramean king bragging that he smote the "house of David." Now we have archaeological evidence for the name David.

ARMOR-BEARERS

BY E. LEBRON MATTHEWS

Relief from Nineveh's South-West Palace; heavily armed Assyrian archers. The front one was beardless, possibly a eunuch. Each was accompanied by a soldier whose duty was to hold the tail shield in position and guard against any enemies who came too close.

The Hebrew phrase rendered *armor-bearer* literally means "the one carrying his equipment." The word for *equipment* designated a wide variety of items, including containers, tools, weapons, musical instruments, and even jewelry. It occurs about 320 times in the Old Testament and is rendered into English according to the context.[1] The translation "armor-bearer" is derived from a soldier's equipment. The primary task assigned to these soldiers seems to have been carrying the king's or commander's armor, shield, extra weapons, and baggage. However, Goliath was assigned a shield bearer (1 Sam. 17:7). Thus, extraordinary warriors could receive similar assistance.

One of the armor-bearer's duties was positioning a shield to protect his assigned superior. This allowed elite warriors such as Goliath to use both hands with long-range weapons such as javelins or arrows. As combat turned into hand-to-hand fighting, the warrior could exchange these weapons for the shield and sword. The armor-bearer then took the bow and unexpended projectiles. On the battlefield, kings and other army commanders faced the same risks as common soldiers. Consequently the armor-bearer enabled the commander to be ready to defend himself if necesary and yet move freely between units under his command. At times armor-bearers killed wounded enemy soldiers left on the battlefield.[2]

Living four centuries in Egypt without question influenced the military Israel developed during and after the exodus. The Egyptian army began to employ armor during that period, primarily on the army's ranking officers.[3] Private soldiers still dressed in short linen kilts and carried an elongated shield crafted from wood and leather.[4] Egyptian chariot archers wore a mail coat made of 450 bronze scales stitched together in overlapping rows.[5]

Jonathan's armor-bearer was an experienced professional soldier. The Hebrew word for "attendant" in 1 Samuel 14:6 commonly refers to adolescent boys. However, the term had a specific military connotation. It denoted experienced warriors as opposed to militia.[6] This suggests that armor-bearers had proven their ability in combat. The commander entrusted his life to these attendants. In the brutal warfare of the ancient world, an army commander's death often also meant the subsequent extermination of his army and even entire villages of his people. Being an armor-bearer, therefore, was a crucial responsibility.

When Saul became king, Israel did not have a professional army. It relied on mustering the military-age men during a crisis. In Saul's initial campaigns, certain soldiers emerged as being dependable and capable. So the king selected three thousand of these to serve permanently. He organized this force into two units. Two thousand men served directly under him; the rest were under the command of his eldest son, Jonathan. This force became the nucleus of a standing army. Their task was to defend the kingdom until the tribal contingents could be mobilized.

Jonathan and his armor-bearer unexpectedly attacked a Philistine outpost and killed twenty men. Panic gripped the entire Philistine force, and Israel won an important victory. The incident demonstrates the extreme loyalty and bravery of the armor-bearer. When Jonathan proposed that the two men—by themselves—attack a much larger body of Philistines, the armor-bearer readily agreed to go. Most soldiers would have likely considered this a suicide mission with no possibility for success. Jonathan's armor-bearer, though, never hesitated.

David became Saul's "armor-bearer" (1 Sam. 16:21). His responsibilities seem limited to playing the harp. So the term may have a more restrictive application in this case. Nevertheless, it retains three significant attributes of the armor-bearer. First, David was entrusted with the well-being of the king and, by extension, the nation. Second, he had proven experience at the task assigned to him. And third, the position created a close, personal relationship with his superior.

NOTES

1. K.-M. Beyse, "כְּלִי" (*keli*; container, tool, weapon) in *Theological Dictionary of the Old Testament* (*TDOT*), ed. G. Johannes Botterweck and Helmer Ringgren, trans. John T. Willis et al., vol. 7 (Grand Rapids: Eerdmans, 1995), 169–75.

2. Daniel C. Fredericks, "Arms and Armor" in *HIBD*, 116; William White Jr., "Armor-bearer" in *ZPEB*, 1:321.

3. Barbara Mertz, *Red Land, Black Land: Daily Life in Ancient Egypt*, rev. ed. (New York: Dodd, Mead, 1978), 142–43.

4. *What Life Was Like on the Banks of the Nile: Egypt 3050–30 BC* (Alexandria, VA: Time-Life Books, 1996), 124.

5. *What Life Was Like*, 125.

6. H. F. Fuhs, "נַעַר, naar; הַנַּעַר, naarah; נְעוּרִים neurim, נְעֻרוֹת neurot, נֹעַר noar" in *TDOT*, vol. 4 (1998), 482.

BABYLONIAN AND PERSIAN KINGS

BY DANIEL P. CALDWELL

Tomb of Artaxerxes I, who died in 424 BC.

Kingdoms rise and kingdoms fall. With the rise of each new kingdom, changes take place that affect not only the kingdom but also the surrounding territories. These changes can be positive or negative. The rise of the Neo-Babylonian Empire (625–539 BC) and the Persian Empire (539–331 BC) had a tremendous impact on the kingdom of Judah in both positive and negative ways.

Babylon didn't exist long after conquering Judah. Following two short and unstable reigns, Nabonidus was placed on the throne. Though in some ways he was an able leader, the kingdom was weak and conflict was rampant. Making matters worse, Nabonidus brought to Babylon several pagan gods from surrounding cities. Instead of honoring the Babylonian god, Marduk, he gave special devotion to the moon-god, Sin, at the centers of worship at Haran, Ur, and Tema (or Teima). As a result of his religious focus, he alienated the priesthood, the military leaders, and the people of the kingdom. His reign marked the end of the Neo-Babylonian Empire.

Black marble record of Marduk-apla-iddina II, known in the Bible as Merodach-baladan

JUDAH AND THE PERSIAN EMPIRE

While the Babylonian Empire had a negative impact on the Judean people, the Persian Empire would impact them in a positive manner. When Cyrus the Great, ruler of Persia, entered the territory of Babylonia, he had little difficulty defeating the people in 539 BC. The prophet Isaiah two hundred years earlier had prophesied that the great city of Babylon would be overthrown the same way God overthrew Sodom and Gomorrah (Isa. 13:17–22).

Because of the tremendous responsibilities the new empire placed on him, Cyrus initially delegated the rule of Babylon to Darius. Scholars differ on the exact role of Darius. Since his name doesn't appear anywhere but in the book of Daniel, Darius may have been a lesser leader under Cyrus.[1] When Darius was over the kingdom, Daniel was placed in the lions' den (Dan. 6:1–28) and also received the prophecy of the seventy weeks (9:1–20).

Persian horse and rider from the late Persian period.

Cyrus demonstrated unprecedented toleration toward the captives in Babylon. In the first year of his rule, Cyrus decreed that the Jews could return to the Judean territory. His decree also included the opportunity to rebuild the temple. Cyrus graciously returned many of the temple items that were taken when Jerusalem had been destroyed (Ezra 1:7–11).

Many of the Hebrews had become so successful in Babylon that they did not desire to return to Judah. Perhaps they followed Jeremiah's encouragement for them to build homes and to carry on with their lives (Jer. 29:4–10). Daniel remained in Babylon with the exiles who chose to stay behind. However, a large group did return to begin the task of reconstruction.

In the years following the Hebrews' return from exile in 539 BC, the Persian Empire generally maintained peace throughout the ancient Near East. For almost 200 years, the Persians reigned without any significant challenge.

Cyrus died in 530 BC and was followed by his son, Cambyses, who conquered Egypt in 525. His continued success drove him deep into the Ethiopian territory. Yet Cambyses was unsuccessful in subduing Ethiopia. On his return journey to Persia, Cambyses may have committed suicide in 522.

When Darius I ("the Great") succeeded Cambyses, he faced pockets of rebellion and disharmony in the recently conquered territories. Judah was no exception. The Israelites faced opposition to their rebuilding efforts. During Darius's reign, Haggai and Zechariah encouraged the people to complete the rebuilding of the temple. In 516–515 BC, the temple was completed.

Darius was succeeded by Xerxes (486–464 BC), who was the King Ahasuerus of the book of Esther. He received a letter from unidentified inhabitants of Israel stating that Jerusalem was being rebuilt (Ezra 4:6). Xerxes suppressed a revolt in Egypt and abolished the kingdom of Babylon. Xerxes was murdered in 465 and succeeded by Artaxerxes I (465–424 BC).

Artaxerxes I faced no political revolt but was a weak ruler. Under his reign, Ezra obtained the needed treasure for the temple of God in Jerusalem (Ezra 7:11–26). In the twentieth year of Artaxerxes I's reign, Nehemiah, the king's cupbearer, was sent to Judah and appointed as governor over the region (Neh 1:1–2:11; 5:14).

Artaxerxes I died in 424 BC and was followed by his son, Xerxes II. Not yet two months into his rule, Xerxes II was murdered by his half brother. Following his death, the Persian Empire entered into a period of continuous rebellions. When Artaxerxes II became ruler, his younger brother rebelled against him. The rebellion was put down but the damage lingered.

Artaxerxes II was succeeded by his son Artaxerxes III. This spirited but cruel ruler was murdered in 338 BC. The last three kings to rule the Persian Empire were either murdered or killed in battle. The Persian Empire, once splendid and powerful, was waning in its ability to dominate the surrounding nations. This opened the door for a new world power. In its weakened state, Alexander the Great entered into the territory in 334. This sounded the death knell. In less than three years, the Persian Empire fell. A new empire arose as the Greeks began a long period of domination.

Panels at Persepolis in Iran showing homage brought to King Darius (522–486 BC).

FALLEN EMPIRES

Both the Neo-Babylonian and Persian Empires were dominating forces. Individuals and nations marveled and feared the empires' power. Each kingdom would attempt to leave its mark on the successive generations. Yet both empires met the same fate; each rose and ultimately fell.

History has witnessed many great empires rise, dominate for a time, and eventually fall. Earthly kingdoms come with no guarantees. This makes the words of Daniel 2:44 ring truer: "In the days of those kings, the God of the heavens will set up a kingdom that will never be destroyed, and this kingdom will not be left to another people. It will crush all these kingdoms and bring them to an end, but will itself endure forever."

NOTES

1   Edward J. Young, *The Prophecy of Daniel* (Grand Rapids: Eerdmans, 1980), 299–300.

CAESAR AUGUSTUS

BY GERALD L. STEVENS

Altar of Peace dedicated by the Senate to honor Augustus. Built on Rome's Campus Martius between 13 and 9 BC, this monument commemorates Augustus's victories in Spain and Gaul, resulting in a sustained era of peace for the Roman Empire. Reliefs of three sides show the emperor, senators, and their families in procession to the altar's dedication.

Caesar Augustus: his mother was Julius Caesar's niece; his grandmother, who raised him, was Julius Caesar's sister. Although born a plebian, he gained patrician status by Julius Caesar's adoption in early 44 BC, just before Caesar's murder by senatorial conspirators. He was destined to turn his adoptive family's name into a powerful dynastic institution with implications that would have ripple effects for millennia. His given name was Octavian/Octavius. His granted name was Augustus. He was the first and greatest emperor of the Roman Empire, as well as its supreme architect.

CONQUEST AND CONFLICT

Rome's rapid Mediterranean conquest in the second century before Christ brought increasing power and wealth to Romans back in Italy. Aristocratic families garnished huge supplies of slaves to operate their landed estates. Equestrians took advantage of newly opened trade routes for even more lucrative commercial enterprises.

But Rome's internal class conflicts stifled territorial expansion. Powerful aristocratic families based on kinship were pitted against a newer equestrian class based on wealth. The aristocrats had their power base in the Senate. The businessmen had their power base in their money and connections.[1]

Class conflict became class warfare with competing armies.[2] Each involving a coalition of three powerful leaders, two triumvirate experiments were desperate moves to end the incessant fighting. Each attempt at power distribution was doomed. The First Triumvirate (60–53 BC) set up among three generals—Pompey, Crassus, and (Julius) Caesar—fell apart, and Caesar gained sole control of Rome as dictator. Republican senators fearing Caesar's monarchial aspirations formed a conspiracy and murdered him in 44 BC. Out of the political chaos following this assassination came a Second Triumvirate (43–36 BC) among Lepidus, Antony, and Octavian.[3] This attempt also fell apart, producing the famous showdown between Antony's forces in the East and Octavian's forces in the West. Antony lost the decisive naval battle of Actium in 31 BC, committed suicide, and left Octavian sole ruler of all Roman territories. After centuries of conflict, Rome finally had peace.

The veiled bust represents Caesar Augustus at a mature age as Pontifex Maximus.

These years of class warfare and desperate triumvirate experiments simply meant the old political system known as the Roman Republic was falling apart. Anarchy loomed on Rome's horizon. Octavian's victory at Actium was only the beginning of a greater war to stabilize and reconstruct Roman government. This reconstruction had to keep at bay the lurking tensions and power struggles of Roman classes and their institutions.

FROM REPUBLIC TO EMPIRE

Of all the leaders born of Roman blood, history has declared no one more suited for this monumental task than Octavian. He was politically astute, militarily successful, financially wealthy, and an artful negotiator. He brought a calculated public humility to the task of abetting senatorial suspicions of aspirations to kingship. He gained public admiration by his absence of pretense and emphasis on traditional Roman morals and values. He commanded his armies' allegiance with good pay, generous retirement, and strong leadership. Octavian skillfully dodged all the phobias real or imagined genetic to the Roman political psyche, whether tyrannical monarchy, oppressive oligarchy, or the self-destructive class conflicts of the waning Republican years.

Octavian created a *princeps* system ("first man"; "principle man"). This system depended not on a specific public office but on the consolidation of authority into one person through accumulation of titles and responsibilities. Some titles were simply symbolic, but others held significant religious, political, or military connotations. One of these titles, *augustus* ("highly honored"; "most revered"), became the name by which Octavian would be known to history.[4] Another important title was imperator, supreme commander of all Roman legions.

In 27 BC, Octavian began reorganizing the Roman government. His greatest contributions were political and military. He devised a provincial system administrating territories that were conquered, bequeathed, or annexed. The system worked successfully for centuries. The genius of the design was a simple division into two basic types of provinces. The first type of Roman province was senatorial. Senatorial provinces were the stable, older, prosperous territories that were politically more reliable and had traditional civil administration. Senatorial provinces were delegated to the control of the Roman Senate. The apex of a senator's career was for him to be named by the emperor and formally ratified by the Senate, as proconsul (governor) of one of these senatorial provinces. Paul met the proconsul Sergius Paulus on Cyprus on his first missionary journey (Acts 13:7) and appeared before Gallio, the proconsul of Achaia, in Corinth on his second (18:12).

Besides Cyprus and Achaia (Greece), other New Testament examples of senatorial provinces are Asia (see Ephesus) and Macedonia (see Philippi, Thessalonica).

The other type of Roman province was imperial. Imperial provinces were unstable, newer territories prone to insurrection or violence. Such provinces required constant military supervision and were under the direct control of the emperor as imperator, commander of the armies. Thus these provinces had military governments and permanently stationed Roman legions under the command of a legate, a military officer who answered directly to the emperor. Subdistricts within imperial provinces would be delegated to local governors. Governors responsible for tax collection were called procurators.

Procurators were military officers drawn from equestrian ranks. In the New Testament, we meet three governors: Pontius Pilate (AD 26–36), Marcus Antonius Felix (AD 52–58), and Porcius Festus (AD 58–62). Since the territory of Judea was part of the Syrian province, Judean governors were answerable to the legate stationed in Syria. Luke mentioned Quirinius as the legate of Syria when Jesus was born (Luke 2:2).

Octavian also reorganized the Roman army. He divided troops into two main categories, legions and auxiliaries. Roman legions had 5,000 to 6,000 professional soldiers who served for a lifetime. Because Judea was always prone to disturbance and instability, several legions were always stationed in the region. The premier boots-on-the-ground officer, loved and respected for leadership and standing shoulder to shoulder in the heat of battle, was the centurion, the officer over a century (a hundred) men.

Auxiliaries were local recruits from the provinces. Logically, recruits could not serve in their own country. Service usually was for twenty years. Non-Romans desired military service because highly valued Roman citizenship came with honorable discharge. Octavian's reorganized Roman military established itself as the supreme fighting force in the ancient world. Their strict disciplinary codes and brilliant engineering feats drove them to overcome even the most daunting of enemy defenses. One of these extraordinary feats was

The Roman Empire in the Age of Augustus.

building a great siege ramp to scale Masada, where Jewish Zealots who had escaped Jerusalem's final hours held out for three years at the end of the First Jewish War. Remains of this Roman ramp survive to this day.

CONTRIBUTIONS TO CHRISTIANITY

Augustus had a tremendous impact on the world of Jesus, the apostles, and later Christian history. His contributions include the following:

Governmental stability—the end of political chaos. Stability facilitated political and military consolidation of power, contributing to the rapid expansion of the empire. A traveler dealt with the same government even in far-flung regions; this included the same laws, officials, currency, and regulations.

Pax Romana—the "peace of Rome." Centuries of conflict were ended. A time of peace and prosperity followed. Travel and communication became easier and safer. Missionaries could travel, safe from foreign armies and conflicts. In the East, Syria and Galatia no longer had to face the feared Parthian threat, paving the way for Paul's first missionary journey. His second missionary journey was made more feasible because the barbarian tribes of Illyria no longer menaced Macedonia and Achaia. The Roman poet Virgil hailed Augustus as savior of the world because of this peace.[5]

Roman roads—built to move troops. Roman engineers built military roads still standing today as testimony to their extraordinary skills. Along these same roads commercial and private traffic moved swiftly and easily. Communication became regular and much more dependable. Traveling evangelists moved down the same roads as Roman legions. Missionary pastors could send letters to newly established congregations. Paul traveled the Via Egnatia while in Macedonia moving from Philippi through Amphipolis and Apollonia on to Thessalonica (see Acts 16–17).

Religious toleration—a general Roman piety. Traditional Roman values encouraged by Augustus included piety toward all gods. The Roman Pantheon ("all gods") in the heart of the city expressed this traditional piety. A new sect could develop within an established religion, such as Judaism, without arousing Roman suspicion. Thus Gallio immediately dismissed as irrelevant the Jewish charges trumped up against Paul by synagogue leaders in Corinth (Acts 18:16).

NOTES

[1] Both of these wealthy and powerful classes also had to manage a third class, the huge mass of the underprivileged and poor, ready to riot at the first sign of food shortages.

[2] On behalf of the businessmen's party, Pompey engaged his armies in an eastern campaign that brought him to the doorstep of the Jerusalem temple in 63 BC. From that point on, Judea was under the shadow of Rome.

[3] During this Second Triumvirate, the Roman Senate declared Herod king of Judea in 40 BC.

[4] The Romans renamed the eighth month of the year in Augustus's honor because so many important events of his career happened in that month. Thus two months in our calendar bear the names of Roman rulers: July for Julius Caesar and August for Augustus.

[5] Vergil, *Eclogae* 4.4–52.

THE CHALDEANS

BY CHARLES W. DRAPER

Foundation deposit left by Nabopolassar, the last Chaldean king (625–605 BC) in the temple of Shamash the sun god in ancient Sippar, about thirty-five miles north of Babylon.

Though mention of the Chaldeans in the Old Testament is limited, their historical significance was substantial over a long period of ancient history. The term *Chaldeans* was not always applied with consistency in ancient records. Sometimes it referred to tribes of western Semites known collectively as Chaldeans and other times to peoples in the locale who were not Chaldeans ethnically. In the Hellenistic era, the term referred often to astrologers from Babylonia.[1]

HOME OF THE CHALDEANS

Chaldea, the homeland of the Chaldeans, was in southern Babylonia just northwest of the Persian Gulf. The land was primarily marshes and coastal plains. The area was once under control of the Sumerian Kingdom and is associated with Ur, the home city of Abraham, referred to in Genesis 11:31 as "Ur of the Chaldeans." As early as the ninth century BC, the archives of Assyria's King Shalmaneser II refer to the area and its people. The term *Chaldeans* referred to a number of tribes that migrated into this region. Although history does not indicate their locale prior to this migration or the exact time of their entry into the region, it does teach that they settled along the Tigris and Euphrates Rivers and became townspeople and farmers.[2] This era of migration involved many other tribal groups and confederations that settled in various places throughout the Fertile Crescent.

Babylon was a city-state in southern Mesopotamia in Old Testament times. Babylon dominated the ancient Near Eastern political scene at several points between 3000 and 539 BC. The city was located about fifty miles south of modern Baghdad, Iraq. "Babylon may have been an important cultural center during the early period of the Sumerian city-states (before 2000 BC), but the corresponding archaeological levels of the site are below the present water table and remain unexplored."[3]

CHALDEANS AND ANCIENT HISTORY

Shortly after 2000 BC, about the time of Abraham, Babylon's history became available for modern study. Amorite kings, such as Hammurabi (ca. 1792–1750 BC), brought the city to international prominence and ultimately built an impressive empire by conquering other nations, establishing national treaties, and imposing a vassal status on conquered peoples. Because of its expanding empire, Babylon became the political seat for southern Mesopotamia.

The Hittites conquered Babylon about 1595 BC but soon withdrew, leaving a political vacuum. History offers little information about the period that followed. It teaches, though, that the Kassite tribe seized Babylon's throne and held it for more than four centuries. The long Kassite Dynasty was relatively peaceful and helped Babylon's culture reach new heights of international prestige. Seeking some relief, though, from Assyria's growing power and influence, around 1350 BC, Babylon's kings began to work with Egypt. An Elamite invasion brought an end to the Kassite Dynasty about 1160 BC.

As the Elamites withdrew, Babylonian princes came to power and founded Babylon's Fourth Dynasty. During this era, Nebuchadnezzar I (ca. 1124–1103 BC) brought political victory to Babylon by invading the Elamites, recapturing the Marduk statue the Edomites had taken from the Kassites, and returning the statue to Babylon. Afterward, though, Babylon became anemic and remained so for almost two centuries. Several factors afflicted Babylon during this time such as floods, famine, widespread settlement of nomadic tribes, and the arrival of the Chaldeans in the south.

Lyre decoration from Ur. Panel of shell and lapis lazuli representing a banquet scene.

A number of times Chaldean tribal leaders ruled Babylonia. While Babylon was autonomous, rule changed hands among several Semitic tribal peoples. Later, Babylon often came under Assyrian control. The Assyrians repeatedly gained and lost control of the region. Assyrian kings ruled Babylon directly through their own families or as a vassal kingdom with a local titular head subservient to the Assyrians. During much of the seventh and sixth centuries BC, the Chaldeans competed with the Assyrians for control of northern Babylonia, sometimes prevailing.[4] But the cycle continued as Assyrian fortunes improved and declined repeatedly.

Assyria's greatest time of weakness occurred during the impressive expansion of Israel under Jeroboam II (793–753 BC) and a similar period of Judah's prosperity under King Uzziah (792–740 BC). Jeroboam II, encouraged by professional court prophets, mistakenly believed God was pleased with his syncretistic and pagan worship practices. In reality, the idolatrous period sealed the fate of both Israel and Judah. Because Hoshea, king of Israel, failed to pay tribute to Assyria, Shalmaneser V (727–722 BC) besieged Samaria for three years (2 Kgs. 17:3–5). The city finally fell to Shalmaneser in 722 BC (17:6; 18:9–12), and the northern kingdom of Israel passed off the scene permanently. But Judah survived for another 135 years before the new world power, Babylon, lay her waste and took her survivors into exile.

Ironically, the Assyrian Empire's success led to its own collapse. Having maintained a substantial empire for centuries, Assyria reached its maximum size in the middle of the seventh century BC. The entire Fertile Crescent was under Assyrian domination, from Egypt and the shores of the Mediterranean in the west to the Persian Gulf in the east and almost to the coast of the Black Sea and the Caspian Sea in the north.

Chaldean power and influence reached its height during the era known as the Neo-Babylonian Empire (ca. 609–539 BC). This empire was instrumental in the downfall of Assyria. The brief era of Babylon's international power was centuries in the making. Babylon had proven troublesome to the Assyrians over a long period, often in conjunction with Elam, a kingdom bordering Babylonia on the east. Elam, though often attacked by Assyria, continued to support and encourage Chaldean resistance to Assyria.

COLLAPSING KINGDOMS

Even after the fall of Samaria, Judah continued to presume on the Lord's pleasure. Its kings were unmindful of impending doom, despite the faithful ministry of the prophets sent to each generation. Ahaz (735–715 BC) did not test Assyrian resolve, remaining compliant. Hezekiah, Ahaz's son (715–687 BC), instituted substantial religious reforms but unwisely rebelled against Assyria. During his reign, an emissary of Merodach-baladan visited Hezekiah, who naively revealed the wealth of the temple to him, leading to the ultimate devastation of Jerusalem by the Babylonians (2 Kgs. 20:12–18).

Manasseh, Judah's most wicked and longest-reigning king (687–642 BC), sacrificed his sons in a pagan ritual (2 Chr. 33:6). Then Josiah (640–609 BC) reinstituted the observance of Passover and sought to restore faithfulness and integrity to the religious life of God's people. Believing the collapse of Assyria offered an opportunity, Josiah tried to block the army of Pharaoh Neco II in their belated support of the Assyrians. Tragically, Josiah died in battle (2 Kgs. 23) and the decline of Judah accelerated.

Babylon installed Zedekiah, a puppet king, to follow two weak kings: Jehoiakim and Jehoiachin. Remarkably, Zedekiah also decided to rebel against Babylonian rule. Finally, after twenty years of headaches, Babylon's King Nebuchadnezzar resolved the question of Judah decisively by destroying Jerusalem in 586 BC, relocating many survivors to Babylon.

Gold dagger from Ur, about 2500 BC.

CHALDEAN VICTORY

Though they were latecomers to the region, the Chaldeans' success ultimately resulted in the term *Chaldean* becoming virtually synonymous with the term *Babylonian*. Chaldean ascendancy was short-lived. Yet the Chaldeans served as God's instrument in fulfilling his promise to the Israelites through Moses: abandoning covenantal obligations would result in both loss of the land and the people being scattered to the four winds. Second Kings 24–25 documents the tragedy that Habakkuk had vividly described in his prophecy (Hab. 1:5–11). Though shaken to his core by what the Lord revealed to him, Habakkuk clung to hope, as God's promise of judgment was tempered by his grace.

NOTES

[1] Alfred J. Hoerth et al., *Peoples of the Old Testament World* (Grand Rapids: Baker, 1994), 57–58.

[2] James Orr, ed., *The International Standard Bible Encyclopedia* (Peabody, MA: Hendrickson, 1956), 1:589–90.

[3] Daniel C. Browning Jr. and Randall Breland, "Babylon," *HIBD*, rev. ed. (2015), 160.

[4] Hoerth et al., *Peoples,* 57.

CYRUS THE GREAT

BY W. WAYNE VANHORN

Tomb of Cyrus the Great, located near Shiraz, Iran. It is about forty-five feet by forty feet at its base and thirty-six feet high.

When Alexander the Great found the tomb of Persian King Cyrus II, known as Cyrus the Great, in ancient Pasargadae, an inscription was supposedly on the tomb that has since disappeared, although the tomb remains. It is reported to have said, "O man, I am Cyrus son of Cambyses, who founded the empire of Persia and ruled over Asia. Do not grudge me my monument."[1]

RISING TO POWER

Cyrus's meteoric rise to power began near the site where his tomb now stands. With his defeat of Astyages, king of the Medes, in 559 BC at Pasargadae, Cyrus became the leader of both the Mede and Persian kingdoms. Then in the winter of 546 BC, his additional victory over Croesus, king of Lydia (560–546 BC), strengthened his control, swelled his armies, and presented Cyrus as a legitimate rival to the dominant world power of the day, Babylon.

Three years before Cyrus's victory over Astyages at Pasargadae, Nebuchadnezzar, the great king of Babylon, had died. Following his death in 562 BC, Babylon was ruled by a quick succession of incompetent leaders before Nabonidus ascended to the throne in 556 BC. Nabonidus brought a measure of stability to Babylon, but his ineffectual policies and practices spelled the certain doom of the Babylonian Empire at precisely the same time Cyrus was on the rise. On October 29, 539 BC, Cyrus entered the city of Babylon unopposed. The great Babylonian Empire that had conquered the world, destroyed Jerusalem, devastated the temple, and deported the Jews was now itself the victim of a conquering king. With the acquisition of Babylon, Cyrus became the undisputed king of the earth.[2]

RECORDING HISTORY

The current phenomenon of "spin doctors" seeking to gain popular consent for their political candidate's view is hardly new. Cyrus published many propaganda pieces to put a positive spin on his accomplishments and to solidify his rule over conquered peoples. One such propaganda piece is a nine-inch-long, baked clay cylinder discovered in 1879, known as the Cyrus Cylinder. On it, Cyrus recounted his conquest of the city of Babylon. Rather than writing of military prowess, the overwhelming might of his armies, or the superiority of his battle strategies, Cyrus depicted himself as a liberating, benevolent hero to the people of Babylon. He accredited his success to Marduk, a chief god of the Babylonians. He even boasted that Bel and Nebo, also Babylonian gods, loved his rule.

Nabonidus had taken a ten-year leave from Babylon and relocated to the oasis of Tema in the Arabian Desert, leaving his son, Belshazzar, in charge of the capital city. Nabonidus had also forsaken the traditional gods of Babylon, including Marduk, Bel, and Nebo. He worshipped a moon-god called Sin. The priests of Marduk in Babylon detested this religious move and thus ensured they would throw their support behind Cyrus, viewing him as an agent of their great god, Marduk. Cyrus seized the opportunity to propagandize his victory, couching it in terms of Marduk's will.

AFFECTING GOD'S PEOPLE

The Hebrews knew that Yahweh, not Marduk, was the one true God and Lord of history. Yahweh, not Marduk, empowered Cyrus to overthrow Babylon and become the dominant leader of the world (2 Chr. 36:22–23; Ezra 1:1–4; 5:13–15; 6:3–5). Under Yahweh's direction, Cyrus freed the Hebrews exiled in Babylon, permitting them to return to Judah and to rebuild the temple. The ascendancy of Cyrus was a fulfillment of prophecy uttered by Isaiah almost two centuries earlier (Isa. 44:24–28). Yahweh referred to Cyrus as "my shepherd," calling forth the image of the Hebrews as God's flock. God would tend his sheep through his shepherd Cyrus. The prophecy clearly indicated the Lord would make all these things happen, but he would do so through Cyrus.

In Isaiah 45:1–19, the prophet no doubt astounded his audience by declaring Yahweh's designation of Cyrus as "his anointed." This title is the Hebrew word *mashiyach* and was

The Cyrus Cylinder.

Nabonidus Chronicle describing his withdrawal from Babylon for Tema and also Cyrus's founding of the Achaemenid Empire.

Inscribed brick: "Cyrus king of the world, king of Anshan, son of Cambyses, king of Anshan. The great gods delivered all the lands into my hand, and I made this land to dwell in peace."

never used elsewhere of a non-Hebrew. But the anointing concept referred to God's empowerment of people to serve him as he chose. The term was applied to kings, prophets, and priests. The ultimate application of the title, of course, is to Jesus of Nazareth, the one true Messiah of all humankind.

The name Cyrus appears twenty-three times in the Old Testament. In addition to his name in Isaiah (three times), he appears in Ezra, 2 Chronicles, and Daniel. His activity was also a fulfillment of Yahweh's prophecy to Jeremiah (Jer. 29:10–14) that the Lord would remember his people and bring them home from captivity. The language of Cyrus's decree in the Bible parallels the language of the decree inscribed on the Cyrus Cylinder. These parallels indicate that Cyrus used similar language for all captive peoples, cited the name of their gods, granted captives permission to return to their native lands, and reestablished each group's unique worship forms. None of this diminishes the biblical record that the Lord enabled Cyrus. In Isaiah 45:4, the prophet declared, "I call you [Cyrus] by your name, for the sake of my servant Jacob and Israel my chosen one. I give a name to you, though you do not know me." This last phrase candidly admits that Cyrus himself did not acknowledge the Lord in any way other than in the language of political expediency.

The book of Ezra begins with an expanded form of the decree of Cyrus found in 2 Chronicles 36:22–23. The context of the decree underscored that the Lord had put it on Cyrus's heart to free the captive Jews, send them home, and enable the rebuilding of the temple. The Ezra passage added that Cyrus encouraged those Jews who were not returning to contribute to the financial success of the temple rebuilding project (Ezra 1:4). We learn from Ezra 4:3–5 that all the days of Cyrus the people of the land of Israel frustrated the Jews' attempts to rebuild the temple. References to Cyrus in Ezra 5:13–17 are part of a letter the local governor sent to Cyrus's successor, Darius, to ascertain the validity of the rebuilding project. Darius responded in the affirmative that the temple was indeed to be rebuilt at the decree of Cyrus, adding his own authorization (6:3,14).

Three additional references to Cyrus in the book of Daniel are useful for date referencing but carry no real interpretive significance.[3] The story of how Cyrus advanced the cause of God's people serves as a historical example of the Lord's sovereignty over all nations. The God whom we know through Christ Jesus, the good Shepherd, is truly an awesome God.

NOTES

[1] Arrian, *Anabasis* 6.29.

[2] Michael D. Coogan, ed., *The Oxford History of the Biblical World* (New York: Oxford University Press, 1998), 361–65, 375.

[3] See Daniel 1:21 (depicts Daniel as still serving in Cyrus's first year, 539 BC, which was Cyrus's first year of control over Babylon. This would make Daniel 1:21 consistent with 2 Chronicles 36:22–23 and Ezra 1:1–4 where the reference to Cyrus's first year is to his first year of rule over Babylon, not to his first year as king of the Medio-Persian Empire, twenty years earlier); Daniel 6:28 (a passing reference to Cyrus); and Daniel 10:1 (useful for dating Daniel's vision to about 537 BC).

DAVID AND THE PHILISTINES

BY MARVIN E. TATE

Waterfront at Crete. Known in the Old Testament as Caphtor, Crete was the likely home to the Philistines (Amos 9:7).

PHILISTINES' HISTORY

The Philistines were in the land of Canaan long before David was born. Many today still use their name to refer to David's land, for "Palestine" is derived from "Philistine." We first read about them in the fifth year of Pharaoh Ramesses III (reigned 1184–1153 BC), who repulsed a land and sea invasion of his western borders by the Libyans. The Peleset (Philistines) and Tjekker were among the Libyans' allies.[1] Three years later, Ramesses had to deal with another effort to invade Egypt. This time a mixed group from the north, including the Peleset, took a position at Amor (probably in Syria) after victories in areas that had been part of the Hittite Empire. The invaders came with their military equipment, plus oxcarts loaded with women, children, and goods. They were prepared to occupy and settle in new lands.

The land invaders and sea raiders who attacked Egypt during this period are known as the Sea Peoples. The Sea Peoples were Indo-European groups from the Aegean islands, Cyprus, and Asia Minor. They appeared in the areas of the eastern Mediterranean and Asia Minor during the times of great turmoil and movement that marked the end of the Bronze Age and the beginnings of the Iron Age (1200–1100 BC).

The precise origin of the Philistines, however, eludes our present knowledge.[2] Old Testament references link them with Caphtor (Jer. 47:4; Amos 9:7). Most biblical scholars identify Caphtor with the island of Crete. The Kapturi or Kaptara of cuneiform texts and the Keftiu of Egyptian texts support this view. However, no certain archaeological evidence exists to associate the Philistines with Crete, though pottery and other items do relate them to Cyprus. The Philistine use of iron suggests an association with the Hittites in Asia Minor, as does the Philistine use of a three-man chariot similar to that of the Hittites.[3] The explanation for this uncertainty may lie in the likely possibility that people came to use the term *Caphtor* in the broad sense to refer to the Cretan-Aegean world.[4] Before moving into Crete and other Aegean areas, the Philistines may have lived on mainland Greece and even lands farther away.

In any case, the Philistines were part of the powerful movement of the Sea Peoples toward Egypt and Israel. The major area of their settlement in Israel was the southern coastal plain and adjacent territory, specifically in what came to be known as the five Philistine cities (Gaza, Ashkelon, Ashdod, Gath, and Ekron; see Josh. 13:3; Judg. 3:3). We do not know the circumstances of their settlement in this region. Some Philistines probably were there before the battles of the Sea Peoples with Ramesses III.

The Philistine presence was not confined, however, to five towns on the southern coastal plain. We know they lived in other places as well, such as Megiddo and Beth-shean (see 1 Sam. 31:8,12). The Philistines seem to have formed a horseshoe-shaped ring of towns and dominion around the Israelite tribes settled in the central highlands.[5]

The exact nature of the Philistine establishment in the land of Israel is still historically blurred, but evidence points toward a military aristocracy operating as feudal lords under a declining Egyptian influence.[6] The Philistines seem to have adapted themselves to the long-established Canaanite city-state system. These city-states apparently were organized in an essentially feudal way. The pharaohs of Egypt, sometimes with great force, held overall dominion but usually without a highly efficient administrative system or much direct supervision. The Egyptians depended on native rulers to exercise control over the city-states, allowing the rulers considerable autonomy so long as they performed satisfactorily and paid the necessary tribute. The Egyptian presence helped stabilize the political and economic situation and generally was advantageous to the local Canaanite rulers. These rulers in turn depended on vassals who were given smaller towns and grants of land and who were expected to support the ruler to whom they owed their vassalage. The vassals, of course, exacted payments of various sorts and support from landowners and peasants under them.

The Philistine-Canaanite feudal system probably is reflected in the accounts of David's relationship with the Philistines through Achish, who is called "king of Gath" (1 Sam. 27:2–3). Achish likely was a Canaanite vassal king of the Philistines, who ruled Gath and surrounding towns (such as Ziklag) that were under Philistine vassalage.[7]

PHILISTINES, DAVID, AND ISRAEL

The Old Testament use of "Philistine" is rather broad. Various texts use the term to refer to the Philistines proper, others to similar and associated groups.[8] The Old Testament narratives tell of repeated sharp conflict between the Philistines and the Israelites. The accounts of Samson in Judges 13–16 reflect both the interaction and the conflict between the two groups. According to Judges 14:4, "At that time, the Philistines were ruling Israel."

The Philistines' location in the relatively well-supplied and compact area of the southern coastal plain provided a base that was fairly easily defended. Their presence in one way or another up the coastal areas, through the Esdraelon and Jezreel Valleys, and into the Jordan Valley formed a kind of "horse collar" around the Israelite tribes in the central highlands that cut them off from the tribes in Galilee and at least interfered with relationships with tribes across the Jordan.

The Philistines' technology gave them significant military and economic superiority over the Israelites.[9] The Philistines had acquired skill in ironworking (probably from the Hittites) and used iron weapons and chariots. They also used heavily armed infantry,

Terra-cotta anthropoid coffin lid from Lachish gives evidence that the Philistines continued to use distinctive burial methods that reflected their Anatolian and Aegean heritage.

sometimes in single combat as illustrated in David's killing the well-armed Philistine champion Goliath (1 Sam. 17). In addition to man-to-man combat, the Philistines used mobile strike forces of well-organized raiders to move into Israelite territory (see 1 Sam. 13:17–18; 14:15).[10] We see evidence of the Philistines' economic superiority in the short summary in 1 Samuel 13:19–23, which informs us that there was no ironsmith in the land of Israel. The Israelites had to depend on the Philistines for agricultural implements of various types. We also read of Philistine use of gold in 1 Samuel 6.

The Philistines' economic advantage must have been enhanced by their experience and activity as sea and land traders. Their control of roads probably influenced the Philistine drive against the Israelites. Evidently the Philistines saw the Israelites as a serious threat to trade in the Jordan Valley and the Transjordan.

The Philistine push for control of the land had been so successful that by the time David came to young manhood, Israel was fighting for survival as a people. Gaining the upper hand was essential if Israel was going to retain any significant degree of self-rule and economic well-being. Fortunately for David, he was able to begin his career in the midst of Saul's considerable success. David emerged as a warrior fighting with Saul's forces to break the Philistine grip on the central highlands and to maintain the Israelite positions (1 Sam. 17–18). David's success led to a tragic break of relationship with Saul and to his flight to the Negev, where he began guerrilla operations against both Saul and the Philistines (23:1–13). Eventually, however, he secured a base of operations at Ziklag and a more favorable frame of authority by accepting vassalage to Achish at Gath (21:10–15; 27:1–7).

This arrangement apparently gave David a safer and stronger basis for his activities and permitted him to develop his leadership so that he was ready to rise to power after Saul's death. As a vassal, David raided hostile groups in the Negev and gave presents from the plunder to the elders of Judah who ruled in the area (30:26–31), while his overlord Achish was allowed to believe that he was making himself unacceptable to the Israelites (27:8–12).

The Philistine rulers did not trust David enough to allow him to take a direct part in the final battle with Saul (29:1–11). However, David's move to Hebron and his anointing there as Judah's king almost certainly was carried out with their tacit approval.[11] They may not have trusted David fully, but they must have considered favorably the establishment of one of their vassals in a rival kingship to that of the heirs of Saul's kingdom (Abner and Ish-bosheth, 2 Sam. 2:1–11). They would have viewed this development as giving them access to valuable territory and as stabilizing their southern flank.

When David became the king of "all the tribes of Israel," however, the situation changed, and the Philistines lost no time in going after him (2 Sam. 5:1–5,17–21). They attacked in the Rephaim Valley near Jerusalem in an effort to separate David from the northern tribes. They failed and David defeated them at Baal-perazim. This began a major power shift in Israel's favor. Subsequently David forced the Philistines back inside their traditional territory on the coastal plain (5:22–25) and continued to expand his kingdom until it became a sizable empire. However, he never conquered the Philistine heartland on the coastal plain, and Philistia endured alongside the Israelite states for centuries, until its independent existence was ended by the Babylonians in 604 BC.

David's success appears to have been due, in part at least, to his adoption of some Philistine tactics and policies. He seems to have beaten the Philistines with their own methods of warfare, using tough, professional, and mobile strike forces rather than large unwieldy forces used by the Canaanite city-states and to some extent by Saul. Evidently he reversed the situation at Gath, taking it out of the control of the Philistines (1 Chr. 18:1), and made Achish his vassal (at the beginning of the reign of Solomon, Achish was still king at Gath; 1 Kgs. 2:39–41).

David's use of professional mercenary soldiers, along with elite groups of superior fighters (note "the Thirty" in 2 Sam. 23:18–39), is especially striking. Clearly, he did not depend mainly on the farmer militia from the tribes but on his own troops and commanders (like Benaiah) who owed their positions solely to him. Among these troops were 600 men from Gath, under their commander Ittai (2 Sam. 15:17–22), who supported David during Absalom's revolt. The Cherethites and Pelethites (named with the 600 men from Gath in 15:18) are cited repeatedly in association with David. Their presence was decisive in bringing Solomon to the throne after David finally made up his mind about his successor (2 Sam. 8:18; 20:7,23; 1 Kgs. 1:38–40,44; 1 Chr. 18:17). These two groups may have been Philistines or closely related to them.

NOTES

[1] For the history of this period in Egypt, see R. O. Faulkner, "Egypt: From the Inception of the Nineteenth Dynasty to the Death of Rameses III" in CAH, vol. 2, part 2, 241–51; R. D. Barnett, "The Sea Peoples" in CAH, vol. 2, part 2, 359–78.

[2] For a good review of the theories, see Roland de Vaux, *The Early History of Israel*, trans. David Smith (Philadelphia: Westminster, 1978), 503–10; also Barnett, "Sea Peoples."

[3] See Yigael Yadin, *The Art of Warfare in Biblical Lands* (New York: McGraw-Hill, 1963), 2–250.

[4] Barnett, "Sea Peoples," 375; Frederick W. Bush, "Caphtor" in *ISBE*, vol. 1 (1979), 610–11.

[5] G. Ernst Wright, "Fresh Evidence for the Philistine Story," *BA* 29.3 (1966): 70–78.

[6] Norman K. Gottwald, *The Tribes of Yahweh* (Maryknoll, NY: Orbis, 1979), 410–14.

[7] Argued by Hanna E. Kassis, "Gath and the Structure of the 'Philistine' Society," *JBL* 84 (1965), 259–71, and accepted by Gottwald, *Tribes*, 413.

[8] K. A. Kitchen, "The Philistines" in *Peoples of Old Testament Times*, ed. D. J. Wiseman (Oxford: Clarendon, 1973), 57.

[9] Gottwald, *Tribes*, 414–17.

[10] Gottwald, *Tribes*, 415.

[11] Martin Noth, *The History of Israel*, trans. Stanley Godman (New York: Harper, 1958), 162.

ELIJAH: A MAN OF GOD

BY ROBERT C. DUNSTON

The fifth-century monastery of Saint George, along the northern bank of the Wadi Qelt. Tradition holds that the ravens fed Elijah here.

Elijah came from Tishbe, a village of uncertain location, in the area of Gilead east of the Jordan River. During Elijah's time, Gilead comprised a forested, sparsely settled area of the northern kingdom of Israel. Since "Tishbite" is so similar to the Hebrew word for "settler," Elijah's identification as a Tishbite may describe him more as a settler in Gilead than as an inhabitant of a particular village.[1]

Elijah's ministry occurred during the reigns of Ahab (874–853 BC) and Ahaziah (853–852 BC), both kings of the northern kingdom. A good economy had enabled Omri to build a capital city of Samaria. Omri also created a stable government that allowed him to pass his kingship peacefully to Ahab.[2]

Ahab married Jezebel, a princess from the Phoenician city of Tyre. Ahab and Jezebel's marriage cemented ties between the northern kingdom and Phoenicia, provided expanded opportunities for trade, and created an alliance against the expanding power and influence of Damascus. As Solomon had done before him, Ahab allowed his wife Jezebel to worship her gods; he built a temple in Samaria to Baal and set up an Asherah pole (1 Kgs. 16:31–33).

Baal's followers worshipped him as the storm-god who brought rains, and thus fertility, to the land and as the one who provided for the agricultural needs. Baal worshippers believed that during the annual dry season their deity was trapped in the land of the dead unable to return without help. Baal worship involved fertility rites and ritualistic prostitution as the people sought, through sympathetic magic, to coax Baal's sister and lover Anat to go to the underworld and rescue him. Worshippers wrote stories about the deity that suggested Baal "could go on a journey, fall asleep, or even resort to bloody self-mutilation."[3] Baal prophets sometimes employed mutilation in an effort to get his attention (18:27–28).

In Elijah's initial confrontation with Ahab, Elijah prophesied God would withhold rain and dew for the next several years. God intended the extended drought to underscore Baal's inability to free himself from death and provide for people's needs and to demonstrate the one true God's living reality and power (17:1).

Dated to Iron Age II (1000–800 BC), a small ceramic juglet made of gray-black clay. This piece has a widening neck opening and a handle that attaches at the rim. One of the miracles associated with Elijah involved the Lord's providing an unending supply of oil, which sustained a widow and her son during a severe drought (1 Kgs. 17:9-16).

NOTES

[1] Simon J. DeVries, *1 Kings*, vol. 12 in Word Biblical Commentary (WBC) (Waco, TX: Word Books, 1985), 216.

[2] Paul R. House, *1, 2 Kings*, vol. 8 in NAC, 203, 212, 242.

[3] House, *1, 2 Kings*, 220.

ELISHA: HIS LIFE AND MISSION

BY FRED M. WOOD

Elisha first appeared as the son of an apparently well-to-do farmer (1 Kgs. 19:19–21). His home, Abelmeholah, was in a rich, agricultural district of Manasseh. Being last in a group of twelve men, each following his plow, suggests he was the overseer.

Since the Bible nowhere records the anointing of a prophet with oil in a formal ceremony, we should understand Elijah's casting his mantle upon the younger man as the official act. The mantle was a prophet's distinctive garb. Later, when Elijah was taken into heaven, his mantle fell to Elisha.

When Elijah was about to be taken up in the chariot of fire, fifty men from the school of the prophets followed closely behind but did not cross the Jordan with the two prophets. Who were these younger men, these "sons of the prophets"? Possibly they were associated with a guild or brotherhood of prophets. They apparently lived some type of communal life, although they were not celibate. They looked to Elisha as their possible tutor when Elijah left.

Elisha's prayer to be heir of his teacher's spirit and power (2 Kgs. 2:9) should not be considered a selfish request. True, in Jewish law, the older son was entitled to a double portion of his father's possessions. Elisha, however, meant more than this type of boon. He wanted the strength of Elijah's gentleness, which was probably to a large extent a product of Elijah's Horeb experience. The gift Elisha sought was the spirit of vision and insight.

How does one evaluate a person such as Elisha, especially compared with his mentor, Elijah? Elijah was wilderness oriented, rugged, and austere. Elisha ministered to civilized life; his dress, manners, and appearance resembled other citizens. Elijah

Statue of the Canaanite god Baal. Like his predecessor Elijah, Elisha diligently worked to keep his people faithful to God.

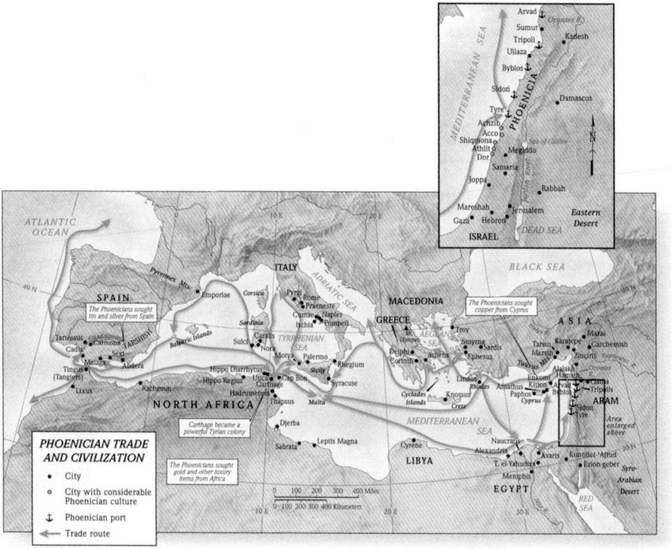

PHOENICIAN TRADE
AND CIVILIZATION
•   City
○   City with considerable
    Phoenician culture
⚓   Phoenician port
←   Trade route

was a prophet of vengeance—sudden, fierce, and overwhelming. Elisha's ministry majored on mercy and restoration. Many of Elijah's miracles were designed to execute wrath. Most of Elisha's miracles brought benefit and healing. Elisha delivered his most powerful sermons through his life of service.

EZEKIEL AND JEREMIAH: A COMPARISON

BY KEVIN C. PEACOCK

Torah scroll from a sixteenth-century-AD Spanish synagogue in the city of Zafed. When God called Ezekiel, he instructed the prophet to eat the scroll, which had writing on both front and back.

Jeremiah was about twenty years Ezekiel's senior. But as contemporaries, each with a life-changing call from God to be a prophet to his people and to the foreign nations, their messages had great harmony. They preached on many of the same subjects, though often with different emphases. They both wrote on individual responsibility (Jer. 31:27–30; Ezek. 18:1–32; 33:7–20), the destruction of the Jerusalem temple (Jer. 7:1–15; 26:1–24; Ezek. 1–24), and a new covenant resulting in a new heart and new spirit (though the term *new covenant* is only in Jeremiah 31:31, and the terms *new heart* and *new spirit* are only in Ezekiel 18:31; 36:26; see Jeremiah 24:7; 31:31–34; 32:38–40; Ezekiel 11:19–20; 36:26–27). These similarities do not mean, however, that God simply called the same type of person to deliver these messages. Each prophet had a unique background, personality, and gifted-ness with which to deliver God's message.

BACKGROUND

Jeremiah's ministry began "in the thirteenth year" of Josiah's reign (627 BC) and extended into the exile to about 580 BC, a ministry of about forty-seven years (Jer. 1:1–3; 40–44).[1] He was "a youth" at the time of his call (1:6), probably about eighteen to twenty years of age.[2] He ministered in and around Jerusalem, while apparently continuing to live in Anathoth, his hometown, located about three miles northeast of Jerusalem (11:21; 12:6; 32:7). He was, therefore, an eyewitness to the fall of Jerusalem.

The Babylonians took Ezekiel from Jerusalem into exile in 597 BC along with Judah's King Jehoiachin and 10,000 captives (2 Kgs. 24:10–14). He began his ministry "in the thir-tieth year," which probably refers to his age, which was when priests normally began their ministry (Ezek. 1:1; see Num. 4:30). His visionary call came in "the fifth year of King Jehoiachin's exile" (Ezek. 1:1–2), which was about 593 BC (assuming a spring new year).[3] So Ezekiel would have been born around 623 BC and taken into captivity at age twenty-five or twenty-six, four or five years before his call from God. In his early years, Ezekiel may have heard Jeremiah's preaching because Jeremiah had caused quite a stir in the city.

The two prophets could have known each other, since they both had priestly back-grounds, though from different families. Jeremiah was "the son of Hilkiah, one of the priests living in Anathoth in the territory of Benjamin" (Jer. 1:1). His priestly lineage probably came from Abiathar, David's priest whom Solomon banished to Anathoth (1 Kgs. 1:7; 2:26–27), thus descended through Eli back to Aaron's son Ithamar.[4] Ezekiel was a priest, son of Buzi (Ezek. 1:3). His familiarity with the Jerusalem temple's layout, correct and aberrant worship forms, Israel's spiritual heritage, and Levitical and priestly issues indicates that even as a young man before the exile, Ezekiel was at least a priest in train-ing, preparing to serve in the Jerusalem temple. Ezekiel's interest in the Zadokite priests (44:15–31) may indicate that his descent was from Zadok back to Aaron's son Eleazar (1 Chr. 6:3–15; 24:3).[5]

Although expecting to be installed as a priest in his thirtieth year, Ezekiel received a call from God to be a prophet. The family life of both prophets became a vital part of their messages. The Lord never allowed Jeremiah to marry (Jer. 16:1–4). His life was to display the loneliness and lack of joy his people would soon experience. Although Ezekiel, on the other hand, was happily married, the death of his beloved wife coincided with the fall of Jerusalem (Ezek. 24:15–27). God did not allow Ezekiel to express his grief publicly, emu-lating the inconsolable sorrow the people would soon experience as their beloved city fell and their loved ones died.

PERSONALITY AND STYLE

Jeremiah's messages of God's judgment filled him with agony and grief (Jer. 8:18–22). A series of prayers known as his "confessions" displays his personal struggles with God about his lot in life and the messages he was to preach.[6]

Ironically, even though almost all of Ezekiel's prophetic oracles are written in first person, seldom do they display his personal thoughts and reactions.[7] For the most part,

Incantation bowl from Nippur, Iraq, with quotations from Ezekiel 21 and Jeremiah 2 in Hebrew. People wrote spells on the inside and outside of such bowls to ward off evil spirits or to imprison those who came near.

he accepted his divine assignments without any protest, even though they took their physical and emotional toll.[8] Unlike Jeremiah, Ezekiel's response was not to complain but instead to see these difficult assignments as God's call to make himself totally available to him, "to place himself and all that he [had and was] at the service of God's cause."[9]

Visions from God were not uncommon for prophets, and Jeremiah had a few (Jer. 1:11–14); Ezekiel's visions were numerous, long, and expanded.[10] Ezekiel did not just see the vision; he became part of it. He personally ate the scroll offered to him (Ezek. 3:2–3); God personally transported Ezekiel from one place to another (3:12–15; 8:3–4; 37:1; 40:1–3); he walked through the old temple (chap. 8) and also the new (chaps. 40–42); he also walked through the valley of dry bones (37:2), and there he delivered God's word (11:4; 37:4,9). His powerful prophecy brought death (11:13) and caused life (37:7–10).

Both prophets accompanied their messages with symbolic actions, but dramatic actions and visual aids were far more frequent in Ezekiel's ministry. He would face the recipients of his message,[11] clap his hands, and stomp his feet to heighten the impact (6:11; 21:14). Other prophets used images and figures of speech; Ezekiel had actual experiences. Jeremiah said of God's words, "Your words were found, and I ate them. Your words became a delight to me and the joy of my heart" (Jer. 15:16), but, for Ezekiel, God's words became a meal (Ezek. 3:2–3). Isaiah pictured God's judgment like a razor that would shave the head, body, and beard of his people (Isa. 7:20), but Ezekiel got a literal haircut (Ezek. 5:1–2).

MINISTRY AND MESSAGE

Jeremiah faced open hostility throughout much of his ministry. Although Ezekiel's audience was stubborn (3:4–11), he did not face hatred and open resistance. The elders of the community consulted with him (8:1; 14:1; 20:1), and the people flocked to hear him after his prophecies about the fall of Jerusalem came true (33:30–33).

Generally speaking, the two major influences on Jeremiah's preaching were the life and ministry of Hosea[12] and the newly discovered law scroll of Deuteronomy.[13] Ezekiel's messages were also infused with two major influences: the messages of Jeremiah and the book of Leviticus. For thirty years, Jeremiah had been preaching in Jerusalem, causing quite a stir, including the first twenty-five years of Ezekiel's life. Many of Jeremiah's prophecies had circulated in writing before and during the exile (Jer. 29:1–20), and communication seemed to have flowed freely, which kept the exiles informed of happenings back in Judah. But Ezekiel was also greatly influenced by his priestly heritage and by the book of Leviticus. He was intensely interested in Levitical and priestly concerns, such as sacrifices, the Israelite worship system, regulations concerning ceremonial purity, and the temple.

Jeremiah denounced the corrupt worship practices and defiled temple and announced God's plan to destroy the temple (7:1–15; 26:1–24). Ezekiel saw God's intention to destroy the corrupted and polluted temple, but, beyond the destruction, Ezekiel envisioned the Jerusalem temple rebuilt and worship restored in purity and holiness (Ezek. 40–48).

NOTES

[1]   Leon J. Wood, *The Prophets of Israel* (Grand Rapids: Baker, 1979), 329–30.

[2]   See Douglas R. Jones, *Jeremiah*, New Century Bible Commentary (Grand Rapids: Eerdmans, 1992), 70.

[3]   Daniel I. Block, *The Book of Ezekiel Chapters 1–24*, NICOT (1997), 83.

[4]   See 1 Samuel 14:3; 22:20; 1 Kings 2:27; 1 Chronicles 24:6. See John Bright, *Jeremiah*, AB, lxxxvii–lxxxviii, for a fuller explanation.

[5]   Block, *Ezekiel 1–24*, 88. See R. Laird Harris, "Zadok, Zadokites" in *HIBD*, 1698–99, for Zadok's lineage.

[6]   Jeremiah 11:18–12:6; 15:10–21; 17:14–18; 18:18–23; 20:7–13,14–18.

[7]   Ezekiel 4:14; 9:8; 11:13; 20:49; 24:20; 37:3. See Block, *Ezekiel 1–24*, 27–30 for a fuller discussion.

[8]   Ezekiel 1:28; 3:14–15; 12:17–20; 21:6; 24:16,27. Ezekiel was struck speechless several times (3:15; 24:25–27; 33:21–22).

[9]   Walther Eichrodt, *Ezekiel: A Commentary*, OTL (1970), 25–26.

[10] Ezekiel 1–3; 8–11; 37; 40–48.

[11] Toward the false prophets (Ezek. 13:17), Jerusalem (21:2), Ammon (25:2), Sidon (28:21), Pharaoh in Egypt (29:2), the mountains of Seir (35:2), and Gog (38:2).

[12] J. A. Thompson, *The Book of Jeremiah*, NICOT (1980), 81–85.

[13] R. K. Harrison, *Jeremiah & Lamentations*, TOTC (1973), 38.

EZRA: SCRIBE AND PRIEST

BY ROBERT C. DUNSTON

Although dating later than Ezra, these split-rib bronze pens were used with carbon ink to write on papyrus, parchment, or wooden leaf tablets. More common would have been pens made of reed, quill, bone, or ivory.

Although a priest, Ezra served as a scribe. Scribes were court officials who held varying levels of authority. Artaxerxes I of Persia appointed Ezra as a scribe and charged him with governing Judah according to God's law (Ezra 7:14,25). Ezra's knowledge of and ability to teach God's law added a dimension to the term *scribe* that became dominant in later Judaism. A Jewish scribe possessed knowledge of God's law and the ability to interpret and apply the law in any situation. Ezra was described as "skilled" (v. 6), a term originally referring to a scribe's ability to write quickly and accurately but later used to refer to a scribe's wisdom and experience. While probably not the first in the long line of Jewish scholars who copied, studied, interpreted, and taught the law, Ezra certainly was one of the greatest Jewish scribes.[1]

EZRA'S TIMES

The Persian king Artaxerxes I sent Ezra to Jerusalem. Artabanus, who likely served as captain of the royal guard, had assassinated Artaxerxes's father, Xerxes I, in August 465 BC and then accused Xerxes's eldest son, Darius, of the murder. Artaxerxes killed Darius,

seized the throne, and enjoyed a long rule
(464–424 BC). In 460 BC, Egypt, aided by
Athens, rebelled against Artaxerxes.
Artaxerxes regained control of Egypt in
454 BC, but he was forced to submit to a
humiliating treaty with the Greeks in
448 BC.[2]

Conditions in Judah remained difficult.
Judah had never recovered from the dec-
imation of its economy and population
resulting from the Babylonian conquest.
Although some Jews had returned from
Babylonian exile and joined the descendants
of those who had never left Judah, the
population in Jerusalem and Judah remained
small (Neh. 11:1–2). Jerusalem's wall was
in disrepair with gaping holes. Although
worship continued in the rebuilt temple,

The pottery inkwell held ink made of one
part gum water to three parts carbon
black. Gum-based inks do better on
papyrus; gallic inks are better for
parchment.

the people were dispirited; faithfulness to God seemed a low priority. For most, making
a living proved difficult. The people needed hope and direction.

With unrest in Egypt, Artaxerxes needed to keep adjoining provinces, such as Judah,
satisfied, loyal, and peaceful. Sending Ezra to Jerusalem to support worship and to ensure
the Jews followed their law worked to Artaxerxes's advantage.[3] In addition, the Jews
needed someone to renew their faith and spirit. God worked through Ezra to extend
Artaxerxes's role and to call God's people to faithful obedience.

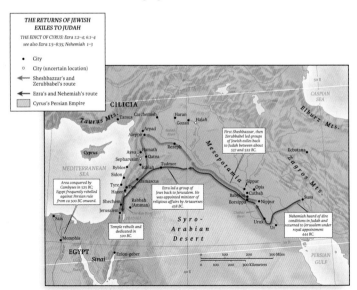

THE RETURNS OF JEWISH EXILES TO JUDAH

THE EDICT OF CYRUS: Ezra 1:2–4; 6:1–4
see also Ezra 1:5–8:35; Nehemiah 1–3

- • City
- ○ City (uncertain location)
- ◀— Sheshbazzar's and Zerubbabel's route
- ◀— Ezra's and Nehemiah's route
- ▢ Cyrus's Persian Empire

CILICIA

Taurus Mts. · Tarsus · Carchemish · Haran · Halah
Arpad · Gozan
Aleppo

Cyprus · Avva · Hamath · Rezeph · Mesopotamia · Ecbatana
Sepharvaim · Qatna
Byblos · Tadmor
Sidon · Riblah · Sippar

MEDITERRANEAN SEA

Area conquered by
Cambyses in 525 BC;
Egypt frequently rebelled
against Persian rule
from ca 500 BC onward.

Tyre · Dan · Damascus · Opis
Hazor · Cuthah · Babylon
Shechem · Rabbah (Amman) · Borsippa · Nippur
Jerusalem

Saïs

Temple rebuilt and
dedicated in
520 BC.

Memphis

EGYPT

Sinai · Ezion-geber

Syro-Arabian Desert

First Sheshbazzar, then
Zerubbabel led groups
of Jewish exiles back
to Judah between about
537 and 522 BC.

Ezra led a group of
Jews back to Jerusalem. He
was appointed minister of
religious affairs by Artaxerxes
458 BC.

Uruk · Ur

Nehemiah heard of dire
conditions in Judah and
returned to Jerusalem under
royal appointment
444 BC.

Susa

CASPIAN SEA

Elburz Mts.

Zagros Mts.

PERSIAN GULF

0   100   200   300 Miles
0 100 200 300 Kilometers

NOTES

[1] Joseph Blenkinsopp, *Ezra-Nehemiah*, Old Testament Library (OTL) (Philadelphia: Westminster, 1988), 136–37; Mervin Breneman, *Ezra, Nehemiah, Esther*, vol. 10 in NAC (1993), 127–28; Robert North, "Ezra" in *ABD*, 726; H. G. M. Williamson, *Ezra, Nehemiah*, vol. 19 in WBC (1985), 92.

[2] Breneman, *Ezra*, 23; G. Byrns Coleman, "Artaxerxes" in *MDB*, 65.

[3] Breneman, *Ezra*, 24; Coleman, "Artaxerxes," 65.

FELIX AND FESTUS: ROMAN GOVERNORS

BY WILLIAM B. TOLAR

Rome ruled the land of ancient Israel from 37 to 4 BC through a client king, Herod the Great. Upon Herod's death in 4 BC, his son Archelaus ruled Judea (and Samaria) for ten years but was removed by Augustus Caesar in AD 6 because of complaints by disgruntled Jewish leaders. Rome then governed Judea from AD 6 to 66 with fourteen "governors" or "procurators" except for a three-year kingly reign (41–44) by one of Herod the Great's grandsons. Antonius Felix and Porcius Festus were numbers ten and eleven in this list and ruled AD 52–60 and 60–62 respectively.[1]

There were two kinds of provinces—imperial and senatorial—and thus, two kinds of procuratorial appointments: by the emperor and by the Senate.[2] The procurator of Judea was administratively under the emperor's "legate" who governed the province of Syria. Procurators appointed by the emperor were regimental commanders and, thus, the highest military tribunal. They exercised power as a superior court because of their military position but could also pass the death sentence on civilians. They could at times intervene in local civilian administrative matters. But the Jews preserved a large measure of autonomy, especially in religious matters.

ANTONIUS FELIX (52–60 AD)

Judea was a highly volatile place in AD 52 when Claudius appointed Felix as the procurator. The emperor had just banished the previous procurator, publicly executed a Roman army commander, and put to death three of the Samaritan leaders who were involved in atrocities against Jewish civilians. Josephus recorded a series of violent events that escalated tensions, ill will, and animosity during the rule of the earlier procurators.

Usually, procurators were drawn from the equestrian class (persons of dignity and high rank), but Felix was a freedman—a freed slave! He was the "first slave in history ever to become the governor of a Roman province."[3] Historians agree that he was appointed originally because of family influences and personal wealth—not because of personal qualifications. Tacitus said of Felix, "With all manner of cruelty and lust he exercised the functions of a prince with the disposition of a slave."[4] Felix was "totally lacking in understanding of or sympathy for the Jews."[5]

According to Josephus, Felix inherited a chaotic situation when he became procurator. He said the land had become filled with "robbers" and "fanatics." Felix was determined to eliminate the terrorism that had plagued Judea for many years, so he bribed informers, used torture, and relentlessly pursued troublemakers. He crucified many of them (including leaders of the Zealots and other religious groups).

The Zealots became more fanatical and desperate. In Jerusalem they organized themselves into a group of assassins called *sicarii*, a name derived from the short, curved daggers they hid under their clothes and with which they killed anyone who sympathized with the Romans. According to Josephus, they committed numerous murders every day in broad daylight, causing everybody to live in terror.

The final event that brought Felix's downfall was his sending Roman troops to put down a serious outbreak of hostilities between Jews and Gentiles in Caesarea. Thousands of Jews were killed; Roman troops, with the consent of Felix, sacked and looted the houses of the wealthiest Jews in the city. Outraged Jewish leaders sent a delegation to Nero who removed Felix from office.

Coin of procurator Antonius Felix.

Coin of procurator Porcius Festus.

PORCIUS FESTUS (60–62 AD)

Nero appointed Porcius Festus to succeed Felix. Unlike Felix, Festus was of a higher social status, an equestrian. We know much less about him than we do Felix because he is mentioned only in Acts and in Josephus—the latter giving him little attention. Most scholars write about Festus in positive tones, stating that he was fair minded, tough, and incorruptible.

Festus inherited problems of many years' standing. He faced a virtually impossible situation. One modern scholar says of Festus, "It appears he was a prudent and honorable man, and in happier circumstances might have proved a successful ruler. But he was charged with an impossible task; after Felix's maladministration the province was a hotbed of bigotry, faction, and intrigue."[6]

Among the many problems Festus inherited upon becoming procurator was the deep, continual, bitter strife between Jews and Gentiles in Caesarea. Eventually blood was shed between the two groups. When Festus arrived in Caesarea, the situation was tense, and the matter was referred to Rome for Nero to decide. The decision did not come until AD 62—long after Paul had been sent to Rome. When Nero decided in favor of the Gentiles, the Jews were infuriated by the decision; bands of assassins spread out once again over the land. More false messiahs arose, and the army had to be called out. Order broke down, and Festus died in office at this critical time. His sudden death in 62 brought renewed vigor to the extremists.

Four years later, in AD 66, the tension between the Jews and Gentiles in Caesarea burst into bloodshed again. This time it turned into a war that spread all over the country, eventually resulting in the destruction of the temple and Jerusalem in AD 70.

NOTES

1   Along with Luke's account in the book of Acts, three important extrabiblical historians provide essential information in our study of Felix and Festus. One is the Jewish historian Josephus (born in Jerusalem ca. AD 38) who wrote *Jewish War* and *Jewish Antiquities*. The other two are Roman historians: Tacitus (ca. AD 55–120) wrote *The Annals* and *The Histories*; Suetonius (ca. AD 69–121) wrote *The Lives of the Twelve Caesars*.

2   "Roman Provinces," *HBH*, 654.

3   William Barclay, *The Acts of the Apostles* (Philadelphia: Westminster, 1976), 167.

4   Tacitus, *Histories* 5.9.

5   John B. Polhill, *Acts* in NAC (1992), 176.

6   G. H. C. MacGregor, "Acts" in *The Interpreter's Bible* (*IB*) (Nashville: Abingdon, 1954), 9:316.

FIRST-CENTURY PRIESTHOOD

BY GLENN MCCOY

Tombs of the Jewish Sanhedrin.

Throughout the Gospels and the book of Acts, the reader frequently encounters individuals called priests, chief priests, and the high priest. Who were these people, and what were their responsibilities in first-century Judaism?

Historically the high priest was one chosen by God for a lifetime of service and to make intercession for the sins of the whole community. His most important responsibility was to enter the most holy place in the temple on the Day of Atonement to offer a sacrifice for his people's sins (Lev. 16:1–34). In addition, he officiated on the Sabbaths, at the feast of the new moon, at the three annual pilgrim festivals (Shelters, Passover, and Pentecost), and at gatherings of the people. Since the office of high priest was hereditary, he was required to maintain a purity of descent.

Several things happened in the first and second centuries BC that compromised the office of the high priest. First, the ruling political figure was also given the title of high priest. This individual frequently acted unethically and even irreligiously. Second, the office was sometimes sold to the highest bidder or given to a person who the appointing political leader thought would further his own cause. For example, Herod the Great (reigned in Judea 37–4 BC) nominated and deposed high priests as he chose. He selected men who would advance his agenda and ignored prior requirements of Jewish law. During the first century AD, the Romans continued the practice of appointing high priests who served their purposes. These actions resulted in unqualified people occupying the office of high priest. It meant the office was neither hereditary nor perpetual. Still the high priest was a powerful person. As president of the Sanhedrin and political representative of the nation of Israel to Rome, the high priest wielded much power.

Chief priest in the broader sense may refer to the chief priest, former chief priests, and members of the aristocratic families who had important positions in the priestly hierarchy.[1] The term is used here in a more limited sense in reference to men holding religious office in the high echelon of temple servants. This list included the captain of the temple, the directors of the weekly course, the directors of the daily course, the temple overseer, and the treasurer.[2]

The captain of the temple was the high priest's right-hand man. He assisted the high priest in the performance of his ceremonial duties, even substituting for him one week before the Day of Atonement. He was a member of the Sanhedrin and also served as chief of police in the temple and had the power to arrest (see Acts 4:1–3; 5:24,26). He was usually next in line for the office of high priest.[3]

Roman period relief of a priest making sacrifice. Bells can be seen around the bottom of the skirt.

The directors of the weekly courses (twenty-four in number) resided wherever they chose and came to the Jerusalem temple for only two weeks of service during the year (in addition to the three pilgrim festivals). The director performed the rites of purification for lepers and women after childbirth (Matt. 8:4; Luke 2:22–24). The directors of the daily courses (some 156 priests were required each week) came to Jerusalem with the same frequency as the directors of the weekly courses. During his day on duty, the director of daily courses had to be present at the offering of sacrifice.

The temple overseer apparently had the power of supervision over the temple (Luke 22:4,52). The treasurers handled the financial affairs of the temple. Lots of money came into the temple coffers in the form of sacrifices and offerings. At the same time, expenses were necessary for the upkeep of the temple, the provision of sacrifices, and the support of the priesthood.

The common priest made up the major part of the priesthood in Jesus's time. There were perhaps more than 7,000 priests (estimates of the number vary) who were divided into twenty-four courses and did service for two weeks (from Sabbath to Sabbath) out of the year (plus major festivals). Each weekly course was divided into four to nine daily courses carrying out their specific responsibilities during the week.

When the priest was on duty, he was extremely busy. There were both public and private sacrifices to offer each day. The public sacrifices seem to have been paid for from temple funds while private sacrifices had to be paid for by the individual. Among the sacrifices the individual could offer were burnt offerings, sin offerings, guilt offerings, and meal offerings. The priests had a choice as to which of these sacrifices they would make. Lots were cast to determine which priest on duty would prepare and offer the daily morning sacrifice (Luke 1:9). This seems to be the ritual Zechariah was performing when the angel appeared announcing that his wife Elizabeth would bear a son (1:13).

When the priest was not on duty, he was free to live where he pleased. Most lived outside Jerusalem. During the remainder of the year, when he did not have temple duty, the priest was trying to make a living. He did receive some support from temple tithes and taxes, but this was not adequate to support an individual, let alone a family. Consequently, the priest had to engage in some sort of trade such as carpentry, masonry, selling merchandise, serving as a scribe, or any number of other professions.

The Levite held a lower rank than the priest and thus could not offer sacrifices. There were some 10,000 Levites (the exact number is uncertain) in the first century. They, like the priests, were divided into twenty-four courses, serving only two weeks of the year. The singers and musicians were the higher order of Levites, furnishing music for temple services and festivals. The temple servants (also Levites) helped with the function and maintenance of the temple. Specific duties included helping the priest with his priestly garments, preparing the Scripture for reading, and cleaning the temple. In addition, the Levites furnished the temple guards. The guards acted as doorkeepers at the temple, patrolled the court of the Gentiles, and closed the doors of the temple when the day was over. The Sanhedrin could call on these guards when needed.[4] Most likely the temple guards were a part of the contingent sent to arrest Jesus on the Mount of Olives.

NOTES

[1]   James A Brooks, *Mark*, NAC (1991), 136.

[2]   Joachim Jeremias, *Jerusalem in the Time of Jesus* (Philadelphia: Fortress, 1969), 160.

[3]   Merrill C. Tenney, ed., *ZPEB* (1980), 4:849.

[4]   Jeremias, *Jerusalem*, 209–10.

FISHERMEN IN THE FIRST CENTURY

BY ARGILE A. SMITH JR.

Located on Mount Nebo in the Church of Saint Lot and Saint Procopius (early Christian martyrs); a mosaic dating to the mid-sixth century AD depicts a man pole fishing.

In Jesus's day, most people living in Israel depended on farming and fishing for food. Fishing thus became an important industry, one that was quite profitable. Fishermen generally made more money than farmers.[1]

While fishing was a good way to make a living, it was not easy. It involved back-breaking work that required fishermen to stay busy for long hours every day. The fishing industry involved a predictable but grueling routine. Fishermen would go out in their boats at night and bring in their catch early in the morning. Then they would separate the fish they caught, salt them down to preserve them, and deliver them to the market. They sold some fish in Jerusalem at the designated entrance to the city that everyone referred to as the Fish Gate.[2]

WHERE DID THEY FISH?

All kinds of fish flourished in the Mediterranean Sea, but the fishermen in Israel did not seem to be drawn there. They gave their attention to the freshwater inland lake commonly known as the Sea of Galilee.

The prominence of the fishing industry was evident in the growth of towns and villages surrounding the Sea of Galilee. Jesus chose Capernaum, a town on the northern shore

Limestone decorative fragment from Egypt, which dates about 2700–2200 BC and shows three flathead mullets.

Bronze harpoons and hooks, Egyptian, dated about 1300 BC. Harpoon use was typically for sport fishing. Single fishermen used rods, lines, and hooks. Those who made their living off of fishing, though, typically used nets.

of the lake, to be the center of his Galilean ministry. Capernaum also happened to be a center of business for the Galilean fishing industry. Fishing influenced the names of towns and villages in the area. For example, not far from Capernaum was the predominantly Gentile seashore town of Bethsaida; its name meant "the fishing place."[3]

Fishermen in Israel favored the Sea of Galilee because they could harvest different kinds of fish there. Three varieties were particularly plentiful: a small fish that resembled a sardine, tilapia (or musht, otherwise known as Saint Peter's fish), and carp. Although fishermen on the Sea of Galilee caught catfish and eels, they normally discarded them because Jewish people did not eat them.[4]

Fishermen focused their work on the Sea of Galilee for another reason. No other significant body of fresh water suitable for fishing existed in Israel. Even the Jordan River held little promise for productive fishing. The Jordan flowed from the Sea of Galilee to the Dead Sea. Fish that made their way from the lake and down the Jordan were not as plentiful or very large. If they got to the mouth of the Dead Sea, they died in the salt water.[5]

WHAT EQUIPMENT DID THEY USE?

The New Testament has an account involving the use of hooks to catch a fish (Matt. 17:27). Hooks were made of bone or iron and attached to a line the fisherman held by hand.[6] However, the vast majority of fishing references in the New Testament involve nets. Fishermen in the first century used three different kinds of nets, each indicated by a different Greek word. Matthew mentions each.

Fishermen sometimes used a simple cast net (Gk. *amphiblēstron*, 4:18), typically round and about thirteen feet in diameter. Fishermen placed heavy objects like stones around the edge so the net would sink quickly. Whether in a boat, on shore, or in shallow water, fishermen would keep this type of net close at hand so they could cast it over a school of fish. Even though this simple net was useful, fishermen could use it only during the day.[7]

Another kind of net was something like a dragnet or a seine (Gk. *sagēnē*, 13:47–48). About sixteen feet high and up to 800 feet long, this net had rocks tied to the bottom and floaters attached to the top. Fishermen in one boat could use it, or they could suspend it between two boats that were guided close to shore. From there they would pull the dragnet onto the shore with ropes. That was why fishermen favored a sandy shore with a gentle slope.

Still another kind of net was a little more complex and resembled a modern-day trammel net (Gk. *diktuon*, 4:20). It consisted of a series of parallel nets fishermen suspended between two boats. Fishermen in a third boat would drive the fish into the nets. This kind of complex net worked particularly well for catching big fish in deep water.

NOTES

[1]   Craig S. Keener, *The IVP Bible Background Commentary: New Testament* (Downers Grove, IL: InterVarsity, 1993), 55.

[2]   Roland K. Harrison, "Fish" in *ISBE* (1989), 2:309.

[3]   Roger Crook, "Galilee, Sea of" in *HIBD*, 618.

[4]   "Fish" in *Eerdmans Bible Dictionary*, ed. Allen C. Myers (Grand Rapids: Eerdmans, 1987), 384; Harrison, "Fish," 309.

[5]   "Fish," in *Eerdmans Bible Dictionary*, 384.

[6]   Roland K. Harrison, "Fishhook" in *ISBE*, 2:309.

[7]   Information on nets in this and the following paragraphs is drawn mainly from "Fishing" in *Eerdmans Bible Dictionary*, 385.

FROM NEBUCHADNEZZAR TO CYRUS II

BY JOSEPH R. CATHEY

The Cyrus Cylinder describes in Babylonian cuneiform script Cyrus II capturing Babylon (in 539 BC), restoring a temple in honor of the Babylonian god Marduk, and encouraging previously captured peoples to return to their homelands so they could worship their gods. Cyrus's decree mirrors the details of Ezra 1:1–11.

Assyria had ruled the ancient Near East for centuries. By 640 BC, this mighty nation-state was at its apex. Thirty years later the great empire of Assyria was no more—collapsing under its own weight of bloated bureaucracy and constant warfare. The heavy demands of paying tribute money, the psychology of terror, and the mass deportations only encouraged other nation-states to revolt at the most opportune time. Assyria's King Ashurbanipal (reigned ca. 668–627 BC) suppressed a rebellion in the ancient city of Arvad (in modern western Syria) as well as submitted Hamath, Phoenicia, and Nariri to his vassalage.[1]

For the next half century, Assyria would effectively lose control of the western province of Judah. During this time period, peoples in the north (Urartu), south (Babylon), and west (Syria) would revolt against Assyria's reign.[2] One could argue that during this time the people of Judah sowed the seeds that led to the nation's downfall.

RISE OF AN EMPIRE

For Judah, the seventh century BC was a tumultuous time in which the nation witnessed great upheavals politically, geographically, and theologically. Perhaps the seminal event that foreshadowed the conquering of Judah occurred in 605 BC. Nebuchadnezzar II, the Neo-Babylonian prince regent and military commander, had broken the Assyrian yoke and effectively conquered the Egyptians at Carchemish. The Babylonians pushed the Egyptians to the south—back to their homeland—and placed the northern territories (such as Syria and the northern Mediterranean coast) under Babylonian hegemony. After his father's death, Nebuchadnezzar II took the throne. During this time of transition and confusion, Egypt as well as Judah took the opportunity to revolt against Babylon.[3]

Brick with a Babylonian inscription that reads: "Cyrus, king of the world, king of Anshan, son of Cambyses, king of Anshan. The great gods delivered all the lands into my hand, and I made this land to dwell in peace."

As early as 601 BC, Nebuchadnezzar had reasserted control over Egypt and effectively pushed the nation back across the Sinai. As the Babylonian king pressed southward, he encountered marked resistance from southern independent city-states. Perhaps the greatest resistance was that of Judah. Nebuchadnezzar promptly set his sights on the errant state. The Babylonians were quick to implement exile as a form of punishment to any wayward nation; Judah would not be spared.[4] At issue in Judah were three disparate political factions vying for kingship. Jeremiah clearly delineates these three factions—one, pro-Egyptian; the second, pro-Babylonian; and the third, for an independent Judah.

REBELLION OF A NATION

Judah's King Jehoiakim (608–598 BC) gave in to the pro-Egyptian party and sought favor and military support from Egypt. Egypt, though, could not save Judah this time. Nebuchadnezzar surrounded Jerusalem and deported the intelligentsia and royalty and took vast treasures (2 Kgs. 24:8–17).

In the interim period from 597 to 587 BC, Babylon experienced a rebellion at home—possibly instigated by their own military officers. Judah took this opportune time to once again revolt against their Babylonian overlords and assert their independence. The nation of Judah once again allied with Egypt via Pharaoh Hophra and stood against the mighty Babylon.

Under Nebuchadnezzar's leadership, the Babylonian army left a path of destruction as it besieged and/or destroyed nearly every fortified city in central Judah before finally razing Jerusalem in 586 BC. The archaeological record confirms both the total destruction and the fact that many of the cities were not rebuilt for several years.[5]

RESTORATION OF A PEOPLE

Under the direction of Cyrus, Gobryas (a Persian general) took Babylon; by the end of October 539 BC, the capital was in Persian hands. While Cyrus ceded the title "king of Babylon" to his son Cambyses II, he took the more traditional Mesopotamian designation "king of the lands" for himself. Cyrus instituted a policy of tolerance toward other religions and issued an edict that released captured peoples, including the Jews (Ezra 1:2–4; 6:3–5).

The Persians also differed from the Assyrians in terms of cultural sensitivities to conquered peoples. While the Assyrians had been interested in integrating conquered peoples into the military machinery of the state, the Persians allowed conquered peoples certain freedoms (worship of their own gods, religious peculiarities, along with cultural

The Audience Palace of Cyrus the Great had these jambs. This one has a figure of a bull-man and a fish-man. These figures may represent Cyrus's religious tolerance.

sensitivities). As long as they continued to offer tribute and supplied what the Persians requested, they could stay in their homelands. If, however, the conquered peoples did not meet the Persians' demands, instead of freedom, they faced deportation to Persia. Deportees were always under strong Persian rule.

Once coming to power, Cyrus allowed the Jews to return to their homeland. His motives may not have been altogether altruistic. He may have wanted the Jews back in their homeland so they could serve as a buffer between Persia and Egypt. In any case, Sheshbazzar the prince of Judah accompanied the first Babylonian exiles back to Judah in 538 BC to begin restoration of the temple.

NOTES

1. A. K. Grayson, *Assyrian Rulers of the Early First Millennium BC (858–745 BC)* (Toronto: University of Toronto Press, 2002), 211.

2. William W. Hallo and William Kelly Simpson, *The Ancient Near East: A History*, 2nd ed. (New York: Harcourt Brace, 1998), 140–41.

3. Marc Van De Mieroop, *A History of the Ancient Near East: ca 3000–323 BC* (Malden, MA: Blackwell, 2007), 276–77.

4. See James D. Purvis and Eric M. Myeres, "Exile and Return: From the Babylonian Destruction to the Reconstruction of the Jewish State," in *Ancient Israel: From Abraham to the Roman Destruction of the Temple*, ed. Hershel Shanks (Washington, DC: Biblical Archaeology Society, 1999), 201–2.

5. John Bright, *A History of Israel*, 4th ed. (Louisville: Westminster John Knox, 2000), 344–45; Dan Bahat, "Jerusalem" in *OEANE*, 226–28.

HAGGAI THE PROPHET AND HIS MINISTRY

BY STEPHEN R. MILLER

Part of the Temple Mount called Zerubbabel's Marking. Change in style of stonework shows Herod's extension on the southwest corner. The rougher stones to the north probably date to Solomon, which Zerubbabel reset after the exile. The lower four courses appear to be undisturbed and may be in their original positions.

MESSAGE	HAGGAI TEXT	DATE
Rebuke and repentance	1:1–15	Sixth month, first day (August 29, 520 BC)
Call to courage	2:1–9	Seventh month, twenty-first day (October 17, 520 BC)
Call to holiness and a reminder of sin's consequences	2:10–19	Ninth month, twenty-fourth day (December 18, 520 BC)
A glorious future for God's people	2:20–23	Ninth month, twenty-fourth day (December 18, 520 BC)

THE PROPHET

Haggai's name means "festal" or "my festival." The significance of the name is not certain. Likely his parents named him Haggai because he was born on Passover, Pentecost, the Festival of Shelters, or another of Israel's great feast days.

This prophet is the only person named Haggai in the Old Testament, but extrabiblical evidence indicates this was a popular Jewish name in the postexilic era. Eleven persons are named Haggai at Elephantine Island (a Jewish colony in Egypt) and four in texts from Babylonia.[1]

Like seven other prophetic books, Haggai provides no information about the prophet's parents or ancestry. Other than his name, we know nothing of his personal life.

Haggai gave no details about his call to ministry, but he referred to himself as a prophet five times (Hag. 1:1,3,12; 2:1,10). Ezra twice called him a "prophet" (Ezra 5:1; 6:14). Haggai affirmed the divine authority of his prophetic messages with phrases such as "the word of the LORD came," "the LORD of Armies says this," and "this is the declaration of the LORD of Armies" at least twenty-five times in his two short chapters. Jews recognized the book's

Ruins at Elephantine Island in the Nile River at Aswan, Egypt. Legal documents found here indicate many Jews settled here, especially in the sixth century BC. They erected a Jewish temple here.

canonicity from the outset; Hebrews also cites the book (Heb. 12:26; cf. Hag. 2:6,21). The Dead Sea Scrolls also contain portions of the book of Haggai.

HIS MINISTRY

According to the biblical record, Haggai was the first prophet to preach in Jerusalem after the Babylonian captivity—the postexilic period. Presumably he returned to Jerusalem from Babylon with Zerubbabel in 538 BC. Haggai carefully dated each of his messages. His first prophecy was "in the second year of King Darius, on the first day of the sixth month" (1:1). "Darius" is the Medo-Persian king Darius I (reigned 522–486 BC). On the Hebrew calendar, "the sixth month" was Elul; this included portions of our August and September. The first day of Elul in 520 BC (Darius's second year) was August 29, about two months before Haggai's contemporary, Zechariah, began his prophetic work (Zech. 1:1–6). Haggai's last message came less than four months after the first. Ezra records the historical background for Haggai's ministry and mentions Haggai and Zechariah by name (Ezra 5:1; 6:14).

Haggai's prophecy consists of an introduction and four brief messages, each beginning with "the word of the LORD came" (1:3; 2:1,10,20).[2] The chart below summarizes these messages with their dates.[3]

Haggai's writing has been labeled "elevated prose."[4] His style was generally simple and direct but effective and powerful. The prophet's use of repetition and other rhetorical devices gives evidence of his literary skill. For example, the threefold exhortation to "be strong" in Haggai 2:4 is stirring.

NOTES

[1] Edwin Yamauchi, "Ezra–Nehemiah" in *The Expositor's Bible Commentary*, ed. Frank E. Gaebelein (Grand Rapids: Zondervan, 1988), 4:635; Richard A. Taylor, "Haggai" in *Haggai, Malachi*, NAC (2004), 43.

[2] For a brief introduction and survey of Haggai, see Stephen R. Miller, *Nahum, Habakkuk, Zephaniah, Haggai, Zechariah, Malachi*, Holman Old Testament Commentary (Nashville: Broadman & Holman, 2004), 114–32.

[3] For these dates, see Joyce G. Baldwin, *Haggai, Zechariah, Malachi*, TOTC (1972), 29.

[4] Taylor, "Haggai," 73.

THE HISTORICAL SETTING OF HABAKKUK

BY J. DANIEL HAYS

Site of ancient Lachish, which was one of the last cities to fall to Nebuchadnezzar and his army. After taking Lachish, the Babylonians continued their military campaign and conquered Jerusalem in 586 BC.

Unlike several of the other Old Testament prophetic books, Habakkuk does not present an opening historical superscription identifying the time (e.g., "in the fifth year of king so-and-so"). As we read through the book, however, we can deduce the setting from statements in the text. Habakkuk lived in the southern kingdom of Judah. His dialogue with God took place just prior to one of the Babylonian invasions of Judah (597 or 586 BC). The prophet Jeremiah also lived and prophesied at this time. The lengthy book of Jeremiah, along with the corresponding chapters in 2 Kings from this same period (2 Kgs. 22–25), painted a clear picture of the tumultuous times in which Habakkuk lived. A series of weak, unfaithful kings, in collusion with corrupt priests and false prophets, had led Judah away from the true God of Abraham and Moses and into idolatry. Not surprisingly, as the people turned away from serving God, they abandoned the moral code embedded in God's law, especially as expressed in Deuteronomy. Further, they allowed serious social and economic injustices to flourish. The dialogue in the book of Habakkuk took place in this context.

THE HITTITES: A HISTORICAL PERSPECTIVE

BY CLAUDE F. MARIOTTINI

Temple gate at Bogazkoy, the lower part of the city complex.

Historical and archaeological evidence indicates at least four distinct ethnic groups were known as Hittites or Hethites.[1] The first were called the Hattians. These people lived in Asia Minor in the third millennium BC. Their capital city was Hattusa, and they spoke a distinctive language, which archaeologists call Hattian or Proto-Hittite. The second group known as Hittites was the Indo-European invaders who settled in Asia Minor about 2000 BC and who conquered and assimilated the Hattians into their own culture. They called their kingdom Hatti and spoke a language called Nesian or Hittite. The third known group of Hittites were those who survived the collapse of the Hittite Empire around 1180 BC. With the dissolution of the empire, some Hittite centers of power survived in the region of northern Syria, particularly at Carchemish, Hamath, and Kue. "Syria during the first half of the first millennium BC was ruled by kings of two ethnic groups, called 'Arameans' and 'Hittites.' To distinguish these kingdoms from the second-millennium Anatolian kingdom most scholars today refer to them as 'Neo-Hittites.'"[2] The fourth ethnic group of people known as Hittites were the people who lived in the land of Canaan. While most English translations do not differentiate them, based on recent scholarship the CSB refers to these "sons of Heth" as Hethites.[3]

Discovered among the remains of royal archives of Boyuk Kale at Bogazkoy; the Treaty of Kadesh (dated 1296 BC) is one of the oldest-known peace treaties between ancient countries. The treaty was an alliance between Hattusilis, king of the Hittites, and Egypt's Ramesses II.

IN ANATOLIA

Until the end of the nineteenth century, history was relatively silent about the Anatolian Hittites. The oldest-known references to the Hittites were in Egyptian documents. One document refers to the battle of Kadesh on the Orontes between Ramesses II, a pharaoh of the Nineteenth Dynasty of Egypt, and Muwattalis, king of the Hittites.[4] Another reference to the Hittites appears in the Amarna letters. A Hittite king sent this particular letter to Pharaoh Akhenaten on the occasion of Akhenaten's inauguration as the new king of Egypt. The letter has been dated around 1380 BC.[5]

At the beginning of the twentieth century AD, archaeologists began excavating at the ancient Anatolian village of Hattusa, modern Bogazkoy, Turkey. During excavations, archaeologists discovered thousands of cuneiform tablets written in an unknown language. When the language was deciphered, scholars concluded that the Hittite language was not similar to the spoken languages of the ancient Near East. They concluded instead that the Hittite language had the characteristics of an Indo-European language, meaning those spoken in Europe and the areas in south and southwest Asia into which European peoples migrated and settled.

The Hittites of Anatolia probably came from the Caucasus region, located between the Black and Caspian Seas, at the beginning of the third millennium BC. After arriving, they mixed with the ancient Hattic inhabitants of Anatolia and eventually established an empire that included Anatolia, northern Mesopotamia, and Lebanon.

Several events contributed to bring the demise of the Hittite kingdom in Anatolia. The most important was the appearance of invaders, often identified with the Sea Peoples, about 1200 BC. Hittite documents speak of a naval battle between the Hittites and the Sea Peoples and the burning of Hattusa, the capital of the Hittite Empire. In addition, a severe drought produced famine throughout the kingdom, forcing the Hittite king to ask Egypt for help.

IN CANAAN

With the end of the Hittite Empire in Anatolia, a portion of the population moved into northern Syria, where they continued and preserved Hittite culture. Archaeologists call this group Neo-Hittites. The north Syria Hittites lived in several small city-states, which the Assyrians conquered and incorporated into their vast empire during the ninth and eighth centuries BC. According to 1 Kings 10:29, Solomon exported horses and chariots to the "kings of the Hittites." These Hittite kings were the Neo-Hittite rulers of Carchemish, Hamath, and Kue (Cilicia).[6]

When Joshua was preparing to enter the land of Canaan after Moses's death, the Lord promised Joshua that Israel's territory would include all the land of the Hittites (Josh. 1:4). Assyrian documents mention this land north of Canaan, referring to it as Hatti land, the land of the Hittites.

Scholars disagree about the identity of the Hittites/Hethites within Canaan mentioned in the Old Testament. Some scholars believe these people belonged to the group of Hittites from the Anatolian regions. Others see them as native Canaanites, with no connection to the Anatolian Hittites. Those who hold to this second view point to the fact that all those in Canaan mentioned in the Old Testament have Semitic names.[7]

The Table of Nations in Genesis 10 lists Noah's grandson Canaan as the father of Heth, the person many consider to be the ancestor of Canaan's Hethites. The Old Testament indicates that the Hethites lived as far south as Hebron (Gen. 23:1–3) and Beer-sheba (26:23–25,33–34). The biblical text shows that the patriarchs and later Israelites had many contacts with the Hethites. After Sarah died, Abraham bought the Cave of Machpelah from the Hethites to bury his wife (23:3); the Hebrew literally reads "sons of Heth." The cave Abraham bought was located in Hebron, a place also known as Kiriath-arba (23:2), which is in southern Judah. Numbers 13:29, however, indicates the Hethites also lived in the hill country of central Canaan. Esau, Isaac's son, married two Hethite women (Gen. 26:34; Ezek. 16:3). Solomon, on the other hand, married Anatolian or Syrian Hittite women (1 Kgs. 11:1).

Pair of Hittite deities, silver, dated about 1400–1200 BC. These figures combine Hittite-style features (large head and ears) with Syrian elements (headdress and posture); from Anatolia.

Terra-cotta vase fragment decorated with an image of a deer; from Alishar, which was part of the Hittite Empire; dated 1600–1400 BC.

CULTURAL INFLUENCE

Although scholars have disagreed about the extent of legal, cultural, and religious influence the Hittites had on ancient Israel, they generally agree that the Old Testament does reflect one area of Hittite culture: the form of the covenant.

The Hittite Empire from the Late Bronze Age II and III (ca 1400–1200 BC) provides extensive materials that aid us in the study of the covenant traditions of Israel. The most important covenants were international treaties that regulated relationships between two distinct social or political units.

The form of the covenant between God and Israel has many parallels with Hittite treaties. These include (1) a preamble of the covenant in which the Great King identifies himself, (2) a historical prologue in which the Great King tells what he has done, (3) the covenantal stipulations in which the nation binds itself by accepting the covenant's

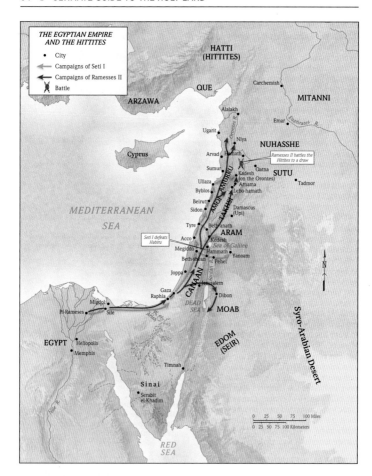

THE EGYPTIAN EMPIRE
AND THE HITTITES
- • City
- Campaigns of Seti I
- Campaigns of Ramesses II
- Battle

HATTI
(HITTITES)

QUE

ARZAWA

Carchemish

MITANNI

Alalakh

Ugarit

Niya

Emar

Euphrates R.

NUHASSHE

Cyprus

Arvad Hamath

Ramesses II battles the
Hittites to a draw

Sumur

Kadesh
(on the Orontes)

Qatna

SUTU

Ullaza

Amama

Tadmor

Byblos

Lebo-hamath

MEDITERRANEAN
SEA

Beirut

Sidon

Damascus
(Upi)

Tyre

Beth-anath

ARAM

Acco

Kedesh

Seti I defeats
Habiru

Megiddo

Sea of Galilee

Hammath

Beth-shean

Yanoam

Pehel

Joppa

N

Jerusalem

Gaza

Dibon

Raphia

CANAAN

MOAB

DEAD
SEA

Migdol

Pi-Rameses

Sile

EGYPT

Heliopolis

EDOM
(SEIR)

Syro-Arabian Desert

Memphis

Timnah

Sinai

Serabit
el-Khadim

0 25 50 75 100 Miles
0 25 50 75 100 Kilometers

RED
SEA

demands, (4) the preservation of the covenant, (5) the public reading of the covenant, (6) the list of witnesses, and (7) the covenantal blessings and curses.

CONCLUSION

The Hittites established a great empire in the second millennium BC in Anatolia. Documents and monuments they left behind reveal that their empire extended as far as Mesopotamia, and yet people knew little of their history and culture until a century ago. The Hethites were among the Canaanites with whom the patriarchs interacted for good and bad. In many ways, the Hittites and Hethites as a people remain enigmatic. Because they are not a single group, some issues regarding their exact identity and origins remain mysteries.

Despite these uncertainties, one unquestionable fact remains: these people influenced the history and culture of Israel in many ways.

NOTES

[1] H. A. Hoffner, "The Hittites and the Hurrians," *People of Old Testament Times*, ed. D. J. Wiseman (Oxford: Clarendon, 1973), 197.

[2] Hoffner, "Hittites," 199.

[3] Bryant G. Wood, "Hittites and Hethites: A Proposed Solution to an Etymological Conundrum," *Journal of the Evangelical Theological Society (JETS)*, 54.2 (June 2011), 239–50.

[4] John Bright, *A History of Israel* (Louisville: Westminster John Knox, 2000), 113.

[5] Aharon Kempinski, "Hittites in the Bible: What Does Archaeology Say?" *BAR* 5.5 (1979): 23–24.

[6] Kenneth A. Kitchen, "Hittites" in *NIDBA*, 241.

[7] Hoffner, "Hittites and Hurrians," 214.

HOSEA THE PROPHET

BY LEON HYATT

Reconstructed Canaanite high place and altar established by Jeroboam I (930–909 BC) at Tel Dan in northern Israel.

Hosea was one of four writing prophets who lived and preached during the eighth century BC. Isaiah and Micah served God in Judah, while Amos and Hosea ministered in Israel. The only information we have about Hosea's life is what is in his book. Concerning his background, Hosea revealed only his father's name, which was Beeri. Concerning his experiences in life, he told only of his marriage. He told that story, not for its own sake, but as an illustration of God's feelings toward Israel.

The first message God gave Hosea was a command to marry, but the kind of woman God told him to marry likely seemed startling and puzzling. Jehovah told Hosea to take to himself "a woman of promiscuity, and have children of promiscuity" (Hos. 1:2). Hosea obeyed God and married a woman named Gomer, daughter of Diblaim. The description of the children God told Hosea to take was exactly the same as the description of the woman, literally "a woman of fornication and children of fornication."

The meaning of these strange instructions has had various interpretations. Some suggest the woman and the marriage were only symbolic. This view seeks to relieve the shame of a prophet's marrying a fallen woman. Turning the story into a symbol does not relieve the moral dilemma, and it ignores the fact that Hosea told the story as a real experience. Others suggest that Gomer was stained by immorality, perhaps even prostitution, before Hosea married her. This view conflicts with God's holiness and the moral standards he expects of his servants. Still others suggest that God described the woman not in terms of what she already was but in terms of what she was going to become. This explanation relieves the moral dilemma somewhat, but it does not deal with the fact that the children were described with the same words as the woman. The words should have the same meaning in each case. Nothing in the story suggests that the children were guilty of adultery or prostitution. A fourth suggestion is that "of promiscuity" described the society and atmosphere in which everyone in Israel lived at that time. The reason God gave for his instruction to Hosea supports this view. God told Hosea to take the woman and the children "for the land is committing blatant acts of promiscuity by abandoning the LORD" (1:2). This view also explains best how both the woman and her children could be described with the same words, "of promiscuity."

The description certainly fits the times in which Hosea lived. The whole land was unfaithful to its God. Hosea may have wondered if any woman and children could live in and come out of such a corrupt society and devote themselves to the sacrificial life need-ed in a preacher's family. God told Hosea to go ahead and marry. He intended to use the marriage for his own purposes.

In time, Gomer clearly fell into the corruptions of the times and became unfaithful to Hosea. The first hint is in 1:3, which says Gomer bore Hosea a son, while verses 6 and 8 say only that Gomer gave birth to a daughter and then to a second son. The text makes no definite statement that the daughter and the second son were Hosea's. Hosea 2:2–13 begins by seeming to describe Hosea's anguish because his wife had become a prostitute open-ly. However, starting with verse 6, the wording describes not Hosea's anguish but God's anguish over Israel's unfaithfulness to him. In chapter 3, Hosea said God told him to go love an adulteress. In response, Hosea bought a woman out of slavery for the price of the least valuable of slaves. The chapter implies she had fallen into degradation and slavery because of her sins. Hosea took her into his home and proposed that both of them live without physical intimacy with each other or with others for many days. Apparently, his purpose was to give them time to adjust to each other and see if they wanted to try their marriage again. Some hold that this woman is someone other than Gomer. This explana-tion is unnatural and strained. What prophet would take a woman to live with him who was not his wife? We do not need to soften the full impact of Hosea's experience with Gomer. His experience powerfully shows the amazing love and forgiveness of a man truly in love. It also shows how this woman had to learn how to love her husband enough to be faithful to him.

JEHOIAKIM: RACING TOWARD DISASTER

BY LEON HYATT JR.

Carchemish rises on the horizon, just left of center; this city was under Hittite and then Neo-Assyrian rule. Nebuchadnezzar overthrew Carchemish in 605 BC and made it part of the Babylonian Empire. After Carchemish fell, Nebuchadnezzar's father Nabopolassar died, an event that brought Nebuchadnezzar back to Babylon to rule.

The story of Daniel begins "in the third year of the reign of King Jehoiakim of Judah" (Dan. 1:1). When Jehoiakim came to the throne of Judah, the Assyrian Empire was embroiled in its final desperate struggles with the rising power of Babylon. Jehoiakim's own nation of Judah was in its death throes because of its rebellions against God. Jehoiakim's reign (608–598 BC) only made matters worse.

ASCENSION TO THE THRONE

Jehoiakim's father was the good king Josiah (640–609 BC), but Josiah made a serious mistake when he attempted to prevent Egypt's Pharaoh Neco (Jer. 46:2) from taking his army past Judah. Neco's purpose was to assist the Assyrians against the armies of Babylon's King Nabopolassar. Josiah personally led his army against Neco at Megiddo and was killed, so the people of Judah chose Josiah's son Jehoahaz to succeed him (2 Kgs. 23:29–30; 2 Chr. 35:20–25). Before facing the Babylonians, Pharaoh Neco sent for Jehoahaz and deposed him. He later took him to Egypt as a prisoner, where he died (2 Kgs. 23:33–34; 2 Chr. 36:14).

Neco replaced Jehoahaz with another of Josiah's sons, twenty-five-year-old Eliakim, renamed Jehoiakim, who ruled for eleven years (2 Kgs. 23:36; 2 Chr. 36:5). Neco also made

Judah pay an enormous amount of tribute (2 Kgs. 23:34–35; 2 Chr. 36:3), forcing Jehoiakim to begin his reign under heavy oppression and a crushing financial burden.

SOCIAL AND POLITICAL CONDITIONS

Domestically the nation of Judah was in serious disarray because of its peoples' deeply ingrained rebellion against God. Josiah had made a determined effort to call the people of Judah back to God (2 Kgs. 22:1–23:25), but his efforts failed. The priests and the people responded only with passive submission (23:3,9), and God promised to destroy them (vv. 26–27). Jehoiakim added to God's wrath by joining the people in their rebellion.

Internationally Judah was faced with oppression from every aggressive nation in the ancient Near East. After placing Jehoiakim under his authority, Neco battled with Babylon's armies for three years. Then Babylon's King Nabopolassar sent his son Nebuchadnezzar with a massive army to attack the Egyptians at Carchemish, where Nebuchadnezzar won a resounding victory.

Nebuchadnezzar chased the bedraggled Egyptian army all the way back to Egypt. As Nebuchadnezzar passed through Judah, he placed Jehoiakim under his control. Judah then became a nation subject to Babylon instead of Egypt (2 Kgs. 24:1). At that time, Nebuchadnezzar made captives of some of the most promising young men from Judah's leading families and sent them to Babylon so his wise men could train them. His plan was to use these captives later to control the Israelite people. Among the young men were Daniel, Hananiah, Mishael, and Azariah—whose names the Babylonians changed to Belteshazzar, Shadrach, Meshach, and Abednego (Dan. 1:17).

While in Egypt, Nebuchadnezzar received word that his father had died, and he hastened home to be installed as king of the Neo-Babylonian Empire. He ruled as an absolute monarch from 605 to 562 BC, though with a divinely orchestrated interlude to humble his pride (4:1–37).

Jehoiakim was consistent. No matter whether Egypt or Assyria or Babylon was in ascendancy, he managed to be oppressed by each one.

JEHOIAKIM'S FOOLISH POLICIES

King Jehoiakim could not have been more wrong in the way he dealt with his problems. To pay the tribute money Neco demanded of him, he placed a heavy property tax on all of his people (2 Kgs. 23:35). At the same time, he came under heavy attack from Jeremiah for building an elaborate palace and failing to pay wages to those who worked to build it (Jer. 22:13–17).

Wanting to free himself of Nebuchadnezzar's heavy oppression, Jehoiakim decided to take advantage of a time when Nebuchadnezzar was occupied with other problems, so he rebelled against him. Nebuchadnezzar's response was to encourage Chaldean, Syrian, Moabite, and Ammonite raiders to attack Judah (2 Kgs. 24:12). Those nations, also under oppression by Nebuchadnezzar, could have joined with Jehoiakim to seek better conditions for all of them; but Jehoiakim's misjudgment caused them all to turn against him. Judah was left standing alone, surrounded by enemy nations.

Jehoiakim dealt with prophetic criticism by persecuting the prophets. Jeremiah preached during Jehoiakim's entire reign and directed many of his sermons toward the king. Jehoiakim rejected Jeremiah's every warning. When Jeremiah had his scribe Baruch read the entire scroll of his sermons in the temple, Baruch was brought before Judah's officials in the king's palace to read the scroll to them. The officials in turn took the scroll to the king and read it to him. Each time a few columns were read to the king, Jehoiakim cut them off from the scroll and threw them into the fire. He continued until nothing was left. Jeremiah was able to reproduce the whole scroll, however, and add much more besides (Jer. 36:1–32). Because of Jehoiakim's rebellions, Jeremiah prophesied that the people would not mourn the king's death and his body would be cast into an open field like a donkey's corpse (22:18–19; 36:30).

Probably because of a second rebellion, Nebuchadnezzar finally placed Jehoiakim in shackles to take him to Babylon as a prisoner (2 Chr. 36:6). Neither Scripture nor Babylonian records tell how Jehoiakim actually died or how Jeremiah's prophecy about the abandonment and exposure of Jehoiakim's body was fulfilled, but they must have been painful and humiliating.

Eleven years and three months after Jehoiakim's captivity, Nebuchadnezzar overran Judah, killed many of its people, and took most of the remainder into captivity (2 Kgs. 24:8,18–25:21). Jehoiakim bore his share of the blame for that awful disaster.

JEWS IN
FIRST-CENTURY ROME

BY WILLIAM B. TOLAR

Senate building in the Roman Forum.

When his life was in serious danger in Egypt, Julius Caesar was rescued by a Jewish mercenary army. The Romans had earlier chosen an Idumean named Antipater (the father of Herod the Great) to be a military adviser to Jewish national leaders. Antipater led the army that rescued Caesar. As a result, Caesar rewarded the Jews for their help by granting special privileges and rights both on taxation and in their religious practices. He also appointed Antipater to be governor over the Jews but, of course, under Roman authority.

Antipater (and his son Herod) thus made some powerful and influential friends in Rome. Jewish merchants would now be far more welcome in Rome, and their business opportunities increased tremendously. Jewish families could move to the great city and live there with the approval of those who followed Julius Caesar's powerful leadership. Even after Caesar's assassination in 44 BC, his supporters and successors Mark Antony and Octavian (later designated as Augustus Caesar) led the Roman Senate in 40 BC to declare Herod to be "king of the Jews" under Roman rule. The special tax and religious privileges Julius Caesar had granted continued. The roads and sea-lanes continued to be wide open for the expansions of a Jewish presence in Rome. Monotheistic Jews did not have to worship Rome's national gods and goddesses.

So by the time Jesus was born (during the reign of Augustus, the grandnephew of Julius Caesar), the Jewish people had enjoyed special privileges under the sovereignty of Rome for nearly forty years. Herod the Great (reigned 37–4 BC) was a brilliant businessman and one of history's greatest builders. He led an incredible surge of business activity that brought Roman businessmen, architects, and engineers into the country to help build cities such as Caesarea Maritima. Commerce between this great seaport and Rome was daily and direct. Jewish merchants and their families had direct access to the capital city. Their number probably surged in the years immediately preceding

House of Augustus at Palatine Hill in Rome.

the birth of Christ while Herod and his family members exercised influence with Rome's leaders.

In the latter part of the first century BC and in the first half of the first century AD, Jews in Rome seem to have lived and worshipped generally as they did in other cities of the world at that time. They lived together in close proximity because of racial and religious differences with most of Rome's inhabitants. The daily life of devout Jews centered on family life, work, and local synagogue activities. Their monotheism separated them from their polytheistic pagan neighbors, so they probably spent their time mostly with other Jews, except for business activities. Other racial and religious enclaves were present in Rome, so the Jews were not the only ones who lived segregated lives among their own kind in the big city.

Coin of Caesar Augustus.

Jewish people, however, had to be especially careful in Rome, which was relatively tolerant of foreign religions if those religions were not politically active and did not advocate rebellion against Rome and its national religions. Polytheists could worship Rome's gods, but Jews would not; so they had to be extra careful to show they were loyal, honest, hardworking, and nonthreatening to Rome's customs and manners.

The Romans tolerated most all religious groups on principle as potential invokers of all gods' divine graces upon the state and society. However, only the Jews were excused from supporting the imperial cult because of the special favors Julius Caesar and his successors granted. These special privileges, and the rigorous and aggressive defense of them by the Jews, caused many Romans to have contempt for them. Jews would not worship the deified emperors or serve in the military legions of Rome, but the Jewish community was not numerous enough to prove a real danger. In Rome itself, the regulations governing the Jews were somewhat stricter than they were in other parts of the empire, and on several occasions the Jews were exiled from the city. In general, however, they were not molested. The privileges granted to the monotheistic Jews, in spite of their refusal to worship the emperors, were possible only because their religion was limited to a single small race.

If a non-Roman religion did not proselytize Roman citizens away from their national religion, refuse obedience to the state by refusing to pay taxes, threaten public morality, or create public strife, then Rome was typically tolerant of it. Officials could be indifferent to various religions when tolerance served their purposes, and they could be incredibly brutal when it did not.

Jews and proselytes from Rome were in Jerusalem at Pentecost when Peter preached his sermon about Christ (Acts 2:10–11). In all probability, some converted Jews went back to Rome and started the first Christian church in the capital city. The date would have been about AD 28 to 30.

On his second missionary journey, Paul met a Jewish couple named Aquila and Priscilla in Corinth "who had recently come from Italy . . . because Claudius had ordered all the Jews to leave Rome" (Acts 18:2). After many years of tolerance by former emperors of non-Roman religions in Rome, Claudius during his reign (AD 41–54) issued an edict (ca. AD 49) banishing the Jews from Rome. According to the Roman historian Suetonius, Claudius did this because "the Jews constantly made disturbances at the instigation of Chrestus."[2] Many scholars believe this was a confused or misspelled reference to "Christus," the Latin spelling for Christ. Unbelieving Jews in Rome had apparently reacted violently to Christian preaching that Jesus was the Christ, as we find them doing in Acts in response to Paul's preaching. The emperor's decree meant many Jews and Jewish Christians were expelled from their homes. Thus the church in Rome was comprised mostly of Gentile Christians until Jews were permitted to return after Claudius's reign.

NOTES

[1]   Josephus, *Jewish War* 1.10.3.
[2]   Suetonius, *Claudius* 25.4.

JEZEBEL UNVEILED

BY JULIE NALL KNOWLES

Looking toward the Mediterranean Sea, Roman columns sit on ancient foundations at Tyre, Jezebel's hometown.

The writer of 2 Kings (9:37) so hated Ahab's foreign wife that he cleverly punctuated the Hebrew *yzbl* so her name would be pronounced like their word "dung-heap" (a crude epithet): *'i-zebul* ("Where is the prince [Baal]?") became *'i-zebel* ("Where is the dung?").

Jezebel married Ahab to seal a diplomatic union between the monarch of Israel and her father Ithobaal (biblical Ethbaal), who in 887 BC usurped the throne of Tyre, the island city known as a fortress.

Two years later, a commander named Omri seized control of Israel. For Omri's new city on the hill of Samaria, Ithobaal probably garnered more trade than Hiram, the Tyrian king who helped build Solomon's temple. Meanwhile, brutal Ashurnasirpal II ruled expanding Assyria, and Israel became a buffer between the eastern threat and the sea. To secure their alliance, Ithobaal either suggested to Omri that his daughter marry Israel's crown prince or negotiated directly with Ahab after he became king.

In that day, princesses were moved like pawns in a political game. Conquerors demanded families as tribute (1 Kgs. 20:3)—one king of Tyre took "his daughters, his nieces, and his son across the channel to the Assyrian king."[1] Monarchs gave their daughters to officers (1 Kgs. 4:11,15) or friendly rulers (2 Sam. 3:3; 1 Kgs. 3:1; 11:1). Diplomatic wives functioned as envoys of their parents' states—royal harems competed for markets to exchange goods and services from their homeland.[2]

Prosperous and powerful, Tyre stood on a resplendent island "perfect in beauty" (Ezek. 27:3) with a magnificent temple to the rain god Baal. "There I saw it," wrote Herodotus.

"There were two pillars, one of refined gold, one of emerald, a great pillar that shone in the night-time."[3] Tyrian engineers may have copied these columns as Jachin and Boaz for the temple in Jerusalem (2 Chr. 3:17); similar pillars may have been erected for Baal's temple that Ahab built in Samaria (1 Kgs. 16:32). According to Josephus, Ithobaal was a priest of the fertility goddess Astarte (Ashtoreth),[4] so Ahab provided for that worship as well (16:33).

A daughter of both a priest and a king would extend substantial foreign influence. Heathen personnel at Jezebel's table (1 Kgs. 18:19) conceivably came with her. All of them were prepared to proselytize Israel. Tyre sold many luxuries—purple dye, wares in precious metal, carvings of ivory, even exotic monkeys (1 Kgs. 10:22). As her homeland's agent, Jezebel may have decorated Israel's palace in such Phoenician-style ivories that it was labeled Ahab's "ivory house."

Ahab seems to have fallen for her completely. "That her looks may not have been Semitic is more than likely."[5] With common cosmetics—cochineal rouge accenting lips and cheeks (Song 4:3), galena making eyes appear larger (Jer. 4:30; Ezek. 23:40), henna on nails and flowers in her hair[6]—Jezebel must have created a considerable stir. Though Ahab had a harem (1 Kgs. 20:3–7), another woman is never named. Besides, Jezebel was educated and efficient.

While temple prostitution honored Astarte, Baalism supported human offerings (Jer. 19:5; 32:35); Yahwism forbade both practices. Surely someone protested the deaths at Jericho. Jezebel may have countered by eliminating many Yahwist prophets (1 Kgs. 18:4,13), or she may have created places for her court mouthpieces.

As the Chronicler retold Jezebel's story, he identified Israel's apostasy with sexual promiscuity. Jezebel advanced temple prostitution that bewitched many Israelites, much as she had charmed Ahab.

Monumental stairs located at the top of ancient Samaria, a city whose name was later changed to Sebaste. The steps, which may be located near the site of Ahab's palace, were actually part of a temple built during the reign of Septimus Severus (AD 193–211). Samaria served as capital of the northern kingdom of Israel.

In her closing performance, Jezebel played neither whore nor witch, but a queen. Israel's *gebirah* (queen mother) could have rallied popular support by a royal appearance. Accordingly, Jezebel applied cosmetics—emphasized eyes with bluish-gray paint called *puk*[7]— and arranged her hair, covering it with a fine fabric "wrapped turban style."[8] Like a regent, she placed herself at a window of her palace in Jezreel. When her son's murderer Jehu arrived, Jezebel taunted Jehu by calling him "Zimri," another assassin who had a short reign. At Jehu's command, Jezebel was hurled down from the window to the pavement. Her blood splattered as he drove over her lifeless body (2 Kgs. 9:30–33).

NOTES

[1] Richard S. Hanson, *Tyrian Influence in the Upper Galilee* (Cambridge, MA: ASOR, 1980), 10.

[2] Victor H. Matthews and Don C. Benjamin, *Social World of Ancient Israel, 1250–587 BCE* (Peabody, MA: Hendrickson, 1993), 165.

[3] Herodotus, *Histories* 2.44.

[4] Josephus, *Against Apion* 1.18.

[5] Norah Lofts, *Women in the Old Testament: Twenty Psychological Portraits* (New York: Macmillan, 1949), 143.

[6] Edith Deen, *The Bible's Legacy for Womanhood* (New York: Doubleday, 1969), 128–29.

[7] Victor H. Matthews, *Manners and Customs in the Bible*, rev. ed. (Peabody, MA: Hendrickson, 1991), 122.

[8] Deen, *Bible's Legacy*, 129.

JOAB: A MAN AFTER HIS OWN HEART

BY T. VAN MCCLAIN

The forest of Ephraim where Joab disobeyed King David's command to spare Absalom's life.

Scripture describes David as a man after God's own heart (1 Sam. 13:14). Joab could aptly be described as a man who was after *his* own heart.

Joab was the son of David's sister Zeruiah. Her three exceptional sons were Abishai, Joab, and Asahel. Abner, an enemy general, reluctantly killed Asahel in self-defense (2 Sam. 2:19–23). Abner later came over to David's side, but Joab murdered him treacherously. David clearly disavowed some of Joab's actions, but he did not deal with Joab for his crimes.

Joab became commander of David's army due to his bravery in the capture of the city of Jerusalem. Joab proved himself a proficient warrior and commander in a battle against Ammonite and Aramean forces (10:6–14). When King David fell into sin with Bathsheba, Joab assisted the king in his murderous plot to end the life of Uriah the Hittite. Second Samuel 12:26–31 describes Joab's conquering Rabbah, the capital city of the Ammonites; apparently he wanted to honor King David by allowing him the privilege of leading the army into the city. Was this an act of respect to David? Actually, his actions could have been a way of both showing respect and protecting his position.

David's son Absalom killed his brother Amnon in revenge for raping his sister; then he fled the country. Joab was instrumental in reconciling Absalom with his father, David. However, Absalom then attempted to usurp the throne. In a later battle, Joab put Absalom to death, running spears through his heart while Absalom hung by his hair in a tree—

although David had clearly indicated he did not want Absalom to die. David mourned for Absalom, but Joab convinced him to refrain from mourning. In a bid to gain the confidence of those who had followed Absalom and Amasa, David offered Amasa command of the army in place of Joab. Amasa accepted the offer, and in jealousy, Joab would later murder Amasa.

Joab did show some wisdom in advising King David not to take a census, but Joab was overruled, and the census was taken (chap. 24). As a consequence of David's sin, a great pestilence came upon Israel.

Joab did show loyalty to David at times and offered sound advice, but Joab was a man who followed his own heart and did not seek after God's heart. As a result, he received his just reward (1 Kgs. 2:34).

Part of the underground water tunnel that leads from inside the city of Jerusalem to an outside water source. At the end of the tunnel is a forty-three-and-one-half-foot shaft that drops down to the Gihon Spring. The tunnel system provided the people of Jerusalem access to water, even when the city was under attack from outsiders.

JOEL: THE MAN AND HIS MINISTRY

BY ALLAN MOSELEY

Ostracon found at the seventh-century-AD monastery of Epiphanius near Luxor, Egypt. It contains a text from the book of Joel.

Nothing is known about the prophet Joel outside his book. The Old Testament mentions several other men named Joel, but none of those could be the prophet. Joel's father, Pethuel (1:1), is also unknown. Perhaps Joel did not provide more information about himself because he was well known to his contemporaries and further introduction was not needed. The book reveals nothing about Joel's hometown and occupation. Since Joel seems to have had sympathies with the temple and priesthood (1:9,13,16; 2:14,17), some have suggested that he was a priest or a temple prophet. This, however, is speculation; any Israelite faithful to the Lord would have thought often of temple worship. Others have speculated that Joel's frequent references to Jerusalem (2:1,15,23,32; 3:1,6,17,20) indicate that he must have lived in or near Jerusalem. This too is not known; all orthodox Israelites viewed Jerusalem as central to the Lord's activity and plan.

What then can we know about Joel? First, he knew the Lord's law. In 2:13, he quoted Exodus 34:6. He declared that the locust plague in his day was the Lord's judgment. Joel likely knew that the law stated that one of the Lord's judgments for Israel's sin would be a locust plague. According to Deuteronomy 28:38, one result of Israel's sin would be that the people would "sow much seed in the field but harvest little, because locusts will devour it."

Second, Joel believed the Lord rules over everything. The Lord's management of the locust plague proved that he rules over nature. The swarm of locusts was "his army" and "his camp" (2:11). The Lord called them "my great army that I sent against you" (2:25). Joel also believed that the Lord rules over nations and their histories. Specifically, the book of Joel mentions the Phoenicians (Tyre and Sidon, in 3:4), the Philistines (v. 4), the Greeks (v. 6), the Sabeans (v. 8) who dominated the trade routes in Arabia, the Egyptians (v. 19), and the Edomites (v. 19). Joel heard God summon these nations and all others to hear the pronouncement of his judgment on them (2:2,11,12). He, the Lord, would determine their futures, as he determines the entire course of human history.

Third, Joel cared deeply about the spiritual condition of the people of Israel. He passionately called them to mourn over their sin and its results, and he implored them to repent (2:12–14). Superficial repentance, or the observance of repentance rituals, would not suffice. The mere tearing of clothes as a sign of repentance was insufficient. Joel saw that the Lord required the people to tear their hearts with mourning over sin, turn from their sin, and return to the Lord (vv. 12–13). Joel urgently called all the people to gather together to seek the Lord (vv. 15–17).

Fourth, Joel cared about the Lord's glory, or his reputation. He urged the people to pray for the Lord to spare them so that other peoples would not question the Lord's presence or power (v. 17). Israel's glory was not what motivated Joel; it was the Lord's glory. Joel wanted the Lord's glory to be manifested so that people would know him. He saw that a purpose of the Lord's activity in history was to show himself so people would know him (2:26–27; 3:17).

Fifth, Joel evidently knew the preaching of other prophets. The words Joel used often reflect intimate awareness of other prophets' messages. The best-known example is Joel's reference to the "day of the Lord" (1:15; 2:1,11,31; 3:14). Other prophets used the same phrase to refer to the Lord's coming judgment (Isa. 13:6,9; Jer. 46:10; Ezek. 30:3; Amos 5:18; Obad. 15; Zeph. 1:14). Unless Joel coined the phrase, he had likely heard it from other prophets, and he used it in the same way. When Joel called the nations to a confrontation with the Lord's judgment, he invited them to beat their plowshares into swords and their pruning hooks into spears (3:10). Both Isaiah and Micah used those same words (Isa. 2:4; Mic. 4:3), but Joel used them in reverse. Joel's reference to the Lord's roaring from Zion (3:16) is also in Amos 1:2. The image of a fountain flowing from the temple (Joel 3:18) is in Ezekiel's vision of a future temple (Ezek. 47:1). Clearly Joel knew what other prophets had preached. Though the Lord inspired him uniquely to write a distinct message through his own personality, Joel's use of common prophetic language indicates he highly valued the work of other biblical prophets.

Plaque from Fosse temple at Lachish depicting a woman looking out of a balustraded window, a popular Phoenician theme, possibly connected with the goddess Astarte and ritual prostitution.

Sixth, God gave Joel visions of the future. Some prophecies seem to refer to the near future (2:18–27), some to the more distant future (3:1–8), and some to the far distant future (2:28–32; 3:9–21). Some of Joel's prophecies predict judgment, and some predict blessing. In the short term, God would restore what had been lost in the locust plague (2:19–27). Joel 3:1–8 seems to refer to a time further in the future when God would judge Israel's enemies. Still further in the future, God promised he would pour out his Spirit "on all humanity" (2:28–29). The apostle Peter quoted that prophecy when he preached on the day of Pentecost after Jesus's ascension, so those words of Joel refer to the church age in which we live. Two of Joel's prophecies seem to reach into a time yet to come. Joel described ominous cosmic events (2:30–32) that resemble the apocalyptic images in the book of Revelation. And in 3:9–21, Joel prophesied that one day God will judge all nations and restore all creation. At some point in the future, God will gather the nations to hear his judgments against them and to see the exaltation of God's people and God's city Jerusalem (3:16,17,21).

JONAH'S HISTORICAL SETTING

BY JOHN L. HARRIS

Portion of an epic poem about the military exploits of the Assyrian King Tukulti-Ninurta I, dated about 1230–1210 BC.

God spoke to Jonah in the first half of the eighth century when Jeroboam II (793–753 BC) ruled Israel and the Assyrian Empire was experiencing a period of decline. The Assyrian weakness allowed Jeroboam II to regain large amounts of territory that had previously been lost (2 Kgs. 14:25).

NINEVEH AND THE ASSYRIAN EMPIRE

Ancient Nineveh was located in Mesopotamia on the Tigris River. It was one of the oldest and most important cities in ancient Assyria. In the third millennium BC, Nineveh was part of the Akkadian Empire and served as a major religious and cultural center. During this time, the temple of Ishtar was built. The city did not become prominent, however, until about 1500 BC, when the Assyrian kings constructed several new palaces and renovated the temple of Ishtar. Late in the eighth century, Assyria's King Sennacherib (704–681 BC) made Nineveh the capital city.

For most of the ninth century, Assyria experienced one of the golden ages of its history. However, in 827 BC, a major rebellion broke out because King Shalmaneser III (858–824 BC) was unable to contain the power of the provincial governors who usurped his authority. Although the rebels were defeated in 820, the years of internal strife had

Black limestone obelisk of Assyrian King Shalmaneser III (858–824 BC). Erected in the center of Nimrud, it depicts his military campaigns and tribute received.

weakened the nation and marked the beginning of a century of internal discord and significant deterioration for Assyria.[1]

When Adad-nirari III (810–783 BC) succeeded to Assyria's throne, he inherited a weak and declining kingdom. Then matters only worsened, for after Adad-nirari III died, a series of weak kings followed: Shalmaneser IV (782–773 BC), Ashur-dan III (772–755 BC), and Ashur-nirari V (754–745 BC). This time period was the weakest period of the Neo-Assyrian Empire. Less powerful, the Assyrian kings decreased their foreign campaigns and had to deal with internal rebellions in the cities of Ashur, Arrapkha, and Calah.

In addition to the political and militaristic struggles during this period, the Assyrians experienced several natural phenomena, including a famine, a total solar eclipse, and an earthquake, all of which many Assyrians attributed to divine anger.[2] According to the Assyrian Eponym Chronicle, during the reign of Ashur-dan III, the nation's woes were exacerbated by a famine that occurred in 765 BC and either returned in 759 or continued for the entire seven-year period.[3] On June 15, 763 BC, Assyria experienced a total eclipse, an event the people would have considered an ominous sign. Even though it would not have directly damaged the empire, an eclipse certainly would have created considerable anxiety and trepidation. Being a rarity, the eclipse gave rise to prophetic utterances regarding public disasters. Predictions included statements such as "a deity will strike the king and fire consume the land" and "the city-walls will be destroyed."[4] Another natural omen, an earthquake (Amos 1:1), occurred during the reign of Jeroboam II. In the Assyrian texts, an earthquake was taken as a menacing sign for both king and nation.

NINEVEH AND THE BOOK OF JONAH

During the eighth century, an Assyrian king, nobles, and the general public would have given a visiting prophet respect and proper consideration. According to the Mari texts, men from one city-state would commonly enter another for political, medical, and religious purposes; prophets were often included among the delegations sent from one country to another to negotiate terms of treaties.[5] The use of the phrase "king of Nineveh," instead of "king of Assyria," and the mention of the "nobles" (Jonah 3:6–7) have caused some confusion. The Hebrew Bible commonly designates a king by only one city within the region he ruled. Perhaps the closest parallel to the "king of Nineveh" is in 1 Kings 21:1, where Ahab is called "King Ahab of Samaria" in contrast to the "king of Israel."[6]

Clearly a king could be associated either with the capital or a main city within the empire. In light of the weakness of the Assyrian monarchy and the power of the provincial governors, the mentioning of the "nobles" probably indicates that the position of the Assyrian king was so unstable that any action or proclamation required the approval of the provincial governors.[7]

Clearly, life was difficult for the Ninevites at the time of Jonah's visit. With all the political struggles and natural calamities still fresh on their minds, the Ninevites might have had a sense of urgency and possibly were sensitive to signs and omens. The Assyrian belief system that maintained the existence of a link between celestial and terrestrial events no doubt lay at the foundation for accepting Jonah's presence and preaching as a divine warning.[8] Assyrian tradition dictated that when an eclipse did happen, the king would declare a solemn fast and hand his position of authority over to a substitute monarch until the anticipated danger to the throne due to divine anger passed.[9] According to Jonah 3:5–9, after hearing Jonah's message, the people of Nineveh proclaimed a fast and adorned themselves with sackcloth, and the "king of Nineveh" stepped down from his throne, took off his robe, put on sackcloth, and sat in ashes. These actions were in keeping with the designated proceedings described in ancient texts that detail an Assyrian king's actions during a solar eclipse. So although the Assyrian cuneiform records make no reference to the Ninevites' penitence, it is plausible for the type of contrition to avert divine wrath described in the book of Jonah to have taken place.

When Jonah visited Nineveh, the Assyrian Empire was in the midst of political turmoil and constant religious paganism. God decided that annihilation was the best course of action and sent his prophet to communicate this message. The Ninevites,

Terra-cotta model of sheep's lung used to teach divination.

Votive image of Assyrian goddess of war and fertility, Ishtar.

however, did the unexpected; they turned from their evil ways. Unlike the nation of Israel, they considered God's message and did what was required to avert destruction. Ironically it was the Assyrians, the people who did what God's own people would not do, who were responsible for the total destruction of Israel. The readers of the book of Jonah could hardly have failed to notice the paradox.

NOTES

1   A. Kirk Grayson, "Assyria: Ashur-dan II to Ashur-Nirari V (934–745 BC)" in *The Prehistory of the Balkans; and the Middle East and the Aegean World, Tenth to Eighth Centuries BC*, CAH (1982), 268–69; T. Desmond Alexander, "Jonah" in vol. 23a TOTC (Downers Grove, IL: InterVarsity, 1988), 77–78.

2   D. J. Wiseman, "Jonah's Nineveh," *Tyndale Bulletin* (*TynBul*) 30 (1979): 47.

3   Billy K. Smith and Frank S. Page, *Amos, Obadiah, Jonah*, NAC (1995), 204–5; Alexander, "Jonah," 80.

4   Wiseman, "Jonah's Nineveh," 45–46.

⁵   Wiseman, "Jonah's Nineveh," 42–43.

⁶   Edward J. Young, *An Introduction to the Old Testament* (Grand Rapids: Eerdmans, 1964), 263. Designating a king by only one city he ruled was not uncommon. See Douglas Stuart, *Hosea-Jonah*, WBC (1987), 441.

⁷   Smith and Page, *Amos, Obadiah, Jonah*, 205; P. J. N. Lawrence, "Assyrian Nobles and the Book of Jonah," *TynBul* 37 (1986): 131.

⁸   A. Kirk Grayson, "Mesopotamia" in *ABD*, 4:754.

⁹   Wiseman, "Jonah's Nineveh," 47.

JOSEPH THE CARPENTER

BY GLENN MCCOY

Carpenters used axes and adzes for cutting, trimming, and smoothing timber. In the absence of specialized tools for shaping and planing, the adze was in constant use both in simple carpentry and in exact joinery. Different sized adzes were used for light and heavy work.

The Scriptures refer to both Joseph (Matt. 13:55) and Jesus (Mark 6:3) as carpenters. In Bible times, sons customarily learned trades from their fathers. Perhaps Joseph learned this trade from his father and in turn passed it on to Jesus. Most likely, Joseph and Jesus worked side by side at a carpenter's shop in Nazareth. A. T. Robertson suggested that the description of Joseph as the carpenter in Matthew 13:55 indicates he was "the leading, or even for a time the only carpenter in Nazareth till Jesus took the place of Joseph as the carpenter."[1]

The Greek term for "carpenter" (*tektōn*) originally applied to a worker in wood or builder with wood. Later the term referred to any artisan or craftsman who worked in metal, stone, or wood.[2] In all likelihood, the carpenter did not limit his work to woodworking but did metalworking and masonry when the job required these skills.

The carpenter's skills were needed to build any and all kinds of structures. Certainly in the first century, these objects would have included yokes, plows, threshing boards, benches, beds, boxes, coffins, boats, and houses.[3] Some more enterprising carpenters may have helped in building local synagogues or even larger structures such as markets, food shops, theaters, or aqueducts.

Most carpenters likely spent a majority of their time building and repairing houses. A majority of houses in Israel were built of stone. Still, the upper story, roof, and doors were made of wood. Larger homes even had wooden floors and wall panels. "Roofs were constructed by laying timber beams from wall to wall and filling the gaps with matting that was plastered down with mud."[4] Trees were cut down and squared up for the beams. Wooden beams were held together by nails or wooden/metal pegs, or beams were cut so they would fit together naturally by themselves.[5]

In Joseph's day, enough timber grew in the region to meet local building demands. The carpenter could choose from cypress or cedar trees in the northern part of the country, sycamore (a fig-like tree), acacia, oak, and ash. Most of these trees did not grow tall enough

Iron nails, Roman Era.

Heavily used metalworker's hammerhead; first–second centuries AD.

and straight enough to provide long timbers. Hence, David and Solomon, in an earlier day, imported cypress and cedar from Lebanon when they built their palaces and the temple (2 Sam. 5:11; 1 Kgs. 5:8).

The ancient carpenter had essentially the same basic tools used by today's carpenters, though the ancient tools were crude and simple. Tools the first-century carpenter used include the adze (an ax-like tool used to shape wood), a mallet (an oversized hammer, usually made of wood), a hammer (normally made of stone), and an ax (made of iron and bound to a shaft with a cord). Other tools at a carpenter's disposal included handsaws (made of metal blades with teeth that cut into the wood), a larger saw for bigger timbers or trees, a bow drill used to bore holes in wood, chisels of various sizes, awls (pointed for boring wood), wood planes, spokeshaves, and files.

NOTES

1. Archibald Thomas Robertson, *Word Pictures in the New Testament* (Nashville: Broadman, 1930), 1:111.
2. Robertson, *Word Pictures*, 306.
3. C. U. Wolf, "Carpenter" in IDB, 1:539.
4. Ralph Gower, *The New Manners and Customs of Bible Times* (Chicago: Moody, 1987), 153.
5. Gower, *New Manners*.

JOSHUA: LEADER OF THE CONQUEST

BY BRYAN E. BEYER

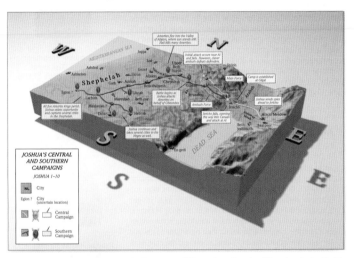

Amorites flee into the Valley of Aijalon, where sun stands still. Hail kills many Amorites.

Initial attack occurs near Ai and fails. However, clever ambush defeats defenders.

Camp is established at Gilgal

Joshua sends spies ahead to Jericho

Main Force

Battle begins as Joshua attacks Ai on behalf of Gibeonites.

Ambush Force

Jericho falls, opening the way into Canaan and attack at Ai

All five Amorite kings perish. Joshua seizes opportunity and captures several cities in the Shephelah.

Joshua continues and takes several cities in the Negev as well.

MEDITERRANEAN SEA

Joppa
Lod
Upper Beth-horon
Gezer
Lower Beth-horon
Ashdod
Ashkelon
Shephelah
Gath
Ekron
Chephirah
Ai
Gibeon
Dilshah
Mizpah
Jerusalem
Azekah
Beth-shemesh
Lachish
Libnah
Gath
Eglon ?
Mareshah
Beth-zur
Hebron
Ai
Gilgal
Jericho
Makkedah ?
Debir
Acacia Meadow
Baal-peor
Beth-jeshimoth
En-gedi
DEAD SEA

JOSHUA'S CENTRAL AND SOUTHERN CAMPAIGNS

JOSHUA 1–10

City	
Eglon ?	City (uncertain location)
	Central Campaign
	Southern Campaign

Bronze arrowhead; from Tel Dan; Late Bronze Age (1550–1200 BC).

Chisel ax-head.

Hittite sickle sword.

Joshua son of Nun played a significant role in God's purpose for Israel. Under his leadership, the Israelites conquered Canaan and divided it among the tribes. Joshua's name means "Yahweh has saved" or "Yahweh is salvation." His name is thus related to the names Isaiah and Hosea, and the name Joshua was Jesus's Hebrew name as well.

Joshua's work essentially involved two purposes: conquer the land of Canaan, and allot it to Israel's tribes. The conquest of Canaan included three major campaigns: a central campaign, a southern campaign, and a northern campaign.[1] These campaigns lasted approximately five to six years altogether; as they concluded, Israel had achieved effective control of Canaan, though some groups of people remained in the land.[2]

After the battle of Jericho, Joshua achieved control of the central plateau without a fight by making a treaty with the deceitful Gibeonites. In doing so, he cut the land in half, isolating northern and southern Canaan. A southern coalition of kings recognized the threat Joshua posed, but Joshua and his army routed the coalition and then extended the battle southward, conquering the major cities and towns. To the north, Jabin king of Hazor assembled another coalition of kings to face Joshua. God again gave Joshua success as Israel's army defeated the coalition and then pressed the battle throughout the northern territory's cities and towns. Israel thus achieved effective control of the promised land.

The Lord gave Joshua many strengths. First, he was a good leader; the people saw God's hand on him and followed him. Second, he was a good general; he remembered the land well from when he surveyed it as one of Israel's twelve spies, and he used his knowledge of the land to help Israel achieve victory. Third, he was a man of faith; he persevered for forty-five years as he awaited the fulfillment of God's promise.[3] He also expressed his faith publicly on many occasions and led the Israelites in renewing their faith pledge to God.

Bronze quiver fragment from Urartu. The relief illustrates the Tree of Life flanked by priests.

NOTES

[1] Bill T. Arnold and Bryan E. Beyer, *Encountering the Old Testament: A Christian Survey*, 2nd ed. (Grand Rapids: Baker Academic, 2008), 172–76.

[2] Donald H. Madvig, "Joshua" in *The Expositor's Bible Commentary*, ed. Frank E. Gaebelein, vol. 3 (Grand Rapids: Zondervan, 1992), 311.

[3] "The time periods referred to in vv. 7 and 10 give us an insight into the period of time covered by most of the Book of Joshua. Israel was sentenced to forty years of wandering in the wilderness after the spies came back with their report (Num 14:33-34). Verse 10 shows that forty-five years had elapsed since the time of this sentence, so the conquest to date had occupied some five years." David M. Howard Jr., *Joshua*, vol. 5 in NAC (1998), 329.

Bronze Hittite helmet from Urartu.

JUST WHO WAS BELSHAZZAR?

BY ROBERT C. DUNSTON

Ruins of a castle at Haran; Roman period; later occupied as a Crusader castle in the Byzantine Era. Haran had been the chief home of the moon-god Sin, whose temple was rebuilt by several kings, among them Ashurbanipal and Nabonidus.

Daniel 5:1–31 records events that occurred at and just after the great feast Belshazzar hosted for a thousand of his nobles. During the meal, they drank their wine from the gold vessels that Babylon's King Nebuchadnezzar had taken from the Jerusalem temple. As they drank and celebrated, they praised their gods and, in the process, desecrated the holy vessels the Hebrews consecrated for the worship of God.

Suddenly a finger appeared in the air and began to write on the plaster wall of the king's palace. Belshazzar was terrified and offered wealth and position to anyone who could interpret the words. The queen informed them that Daniel could interpret the meaning. When he arrived, he refused the wealth and position but gave Belshazzar a lesson in God's previous dealings with Nebuchadnezzar. Whereas Nebuchadnezzar had eventually repented, Belshazzar had continued to sin. Daniel then read the inscription— *Mene, Mene, Tekel,* and *Parsin*—and explained that it meant Belshazzar's days, as well as those of Babylon's kingdom, were numbered. After awarding Daniel what he had promised, Belshazzar was killed that same night.

Only the book of Daniel mentions Belshazzar. Chapter 5 refers to him as "king" and indicates that Nebuchadnezzar was his "predecessor" (lit "father"; vv. 2,11,13,18). Until the latter part of the nineteenth century, Bible students knew little about Belshazzar. Since that time, a variety of sources have been discovered that provide additional information about him.[1]

Nabonidus, who ruled Babylonia from 555 to 539 BC, was Belshazzar's biological father rather than Nebuchadnezzar; and Nabonidus was not a biological descendant of Nebuchadnezzar. Some Bible students believe that following Nebuchadnezzar's death, Nabonidus inherited his harem, perhaps married one of his wives, and adopted one of Nebuchadnezzar's sons as his own in an effort to solidify his hold on the empire.

A simpler explanation is more likely. The word *father* in Semitic languages can refer to a biological father, grandfather, ancestor, or a king's predecessor. *Son* can refer to a biological son, grandson, descendant, or king's successor. As Stephen Miller points out, on the Assyrian black obelisk of Shalmaneser III, "Jehu is called the 'son of Omri,' although Jehu was not a descendant of Omri. He was of another lineage altogether."[2]

Terra-cotta cylinder describing work on the temple of the moon-god Sin at Ur by Nabonidus (555–539 BC). The cylinder also includes Nabonidus's prayer for himself and his son Belshazzar.

Rather than Marduk the high god in Babylon, Nabonidus worshipped the moon-god Sin, like his mother, who was high priestess of the moon-god in Haran.[3] The priests of Marduk wielded great power economically and spiritually, and Nabonidus and others resented them. To break the priests' power, Nabonidus encouraged the people to worship Sin rather than Marduk and revived many long-abandoned rites that honored Sin. His actions infuriated the priests of Marduk and sparked an uprising among the people. In response, Nabonidus moved his residence from Babylon to Teima, an oasis southeast of Edom in the Arabian desert.[4] Worship of Sin was prominent in Teima, and Nabonidus probably felt far more comfortable there.

During Nabonidus's long absences from Babylon, his son Belshazzar ruled in his place. The name *Belshazzar* means "Bel protect the king." Bel served as another name for Marduk. Thus Belshazzar's name linked him to the worship of Marduk and would have made him far more acceptable to the citizens of Babylon than his father.

Although Belshazzar performed the basic duties of king, he was never officially crowned king and never had the authority to participate as king in the Akitu festival. This celebration of the Babylonian new year was the most important festival of the year and was considered necessary to secure Marduk's blessing on the kingdom. Nabonidus's absence required the cancellation of the ceremonies, which no doubt angered the people.[5]

After being gone for about ten years, Nabonidus returned to Babylon. As he did, Cyrus of Persia moved his army closer to the city. Nabonidus fled Babylon but was later taken prisoner. The city of Babylon fell to the Persians in 539 BC. Some Bible scholars suggest Belshazzar knew Babylon would soon fall to the Persian army and decided to hold a banquet anyway, enjoying his last days as king even as the city was on the verge of defeat. Others suggest that Daniel 5:1–31 does not hint at the imminent fall of Babylon. The fact that Belshazzar is terrified by the ominous sign of the finger writing on the wall indicates he had no reason at that time to fear an invasion. In addition, his promoting Daniel to third highest in the empire suggests Belshazzar expected to rule for a long time to come and expected Daniel to hold his new office for many years. The threatening words seem to have been not so much a judgment on Babylon but a judgment on Belshazzar for his disregard for God and the holy objects used in his worship.[6]

Daniel 5:30 states that Belshazzar was killed on the same night the finger wrote on the wall. Some believe he was killed as part of a coup rather than as a result of an invading army. After his death, the Persians conquered Babylon and created their own great empire. "Darius" (5:31) might have been a throne name for Cyrus the Great or for Cambyses, the son of Cyrus, who for part of his life had the title "king of Babylon."

NOTES

[1]   Stephen R. Miller, *Daniel*, NAC (1994), 147.
[2]   Miller, *Daniel*, 149.
[3]   D. Winton Thomas, *Documents from Old Testament Times* (New York: Harper & Row, 1958), 89.
[4]   John Bright, *A History of Israel*, 4th ed. (Louisville: Westminster John Knox, 2000), 353.
[5]   John J. Collins, "Belshazzar" in *Harper's Bible Dictionary*, ed. Paul J. Achtemeier (San Francisco: Harper & Row, 1985), 102.
[6]   John E. Goldingay, *Daniel*, vol. 30 in WBC (1987), 107–8.

THE KINSMAN REDEEMER: HIS RIGHTS AND RESPONSIBILITIES

BY ROBERT A. STREET

Field of Boaz, near Bethlehem.

English Bibles often translate the Hebrew noun *go'el* as "kinsman" ("family redeemer" in Ruth 2:20; 3:9,12; 4:1,14). The word is based on the verb *ga'al* and describes a person who has a familial responsibility. This kinsman's obligation was to protect the family's and clan's interests.[1] Three specific areas of human responsibility are apparent from the use of *go'el* in the Old Testament, those related to property, descendants, and justice. The fourth use of *go'el* is with reference to God as the Redeemer.[2]

PROPERTY

Redemption of property is an important part of Hebrew Law as depicted in stipulations related to the Jubilee Year and to animal sacrifice. The Hebrews were not to sell permanently their family or tribal land (Lev. 25:23). The basic concept of the Jubilee Year was the "general return of lands and real property to the original owners or their heirs."[3] Rather than simply focusing on the Jubilee Year, an examination of the kinsman's role proves enlightening. If a brother (family member) sold property, the kinsman was to redeem it (v. 25). If the brother was too poor to care for himself, the kinsman was to "support him" (vv. 35–36). When the brother sold himself into slavery to a foreigner, he was to be redeemed by his brother, his uncle, his cousin, a near kinsman, or he could even redeem himself by paying the redemption price (vv. 47–55).

DESCENDANTS

The story of Ruth describes something akin to levirate marriage (see Deut. 25:5–10), which emphasized the perpetuation of a bloodline. In this type of marriage, the brother of a deceased man was to marry the widow to perpetuate his brother's name. Though levirate marriage[4] might not properly be part of the kinsman redeemer obligation,[5] it is clearly connected with the Ruth and Boaz narrative.

Boaz was a relative (2:1; Hb. *moda*) of Ruth through her marriage to one of Elimelech's sons. Boaz did not become the *go'el*, the kinsman redeemer, until the end of the story, when he accepted responsibility not only for redeeming the land but also for redeeming Ruth. This marriage was in accord with the concept of levirate marriage, where a kinsman would marry a widow of a relative to ensure the continuance of the relative's name (bloodline) in Israel.

JUSTICE

Limiting the role of the kinsman redeemer to the picture presented in the book of Ruth misses many details about his responsibilities. The most unusual kinsman obligation is related to justice. In Numbers 35:19, the *go'el* is "the avenger of blood" (*go'el ha-dam*). The book of Numbers clearly describes a situation in which a relative is killed and the kinsman's resultant duty is to see that justice was carried out.

NOTES

[1] Jan de Waard and Eugene A. Nida, *A Translator's Handbook on the Book of Ruth* (London: United Bible Societies, 1973), 43.

[2] "[*ga'al*]" (redeem) in *A Concise Hebrew and Aramaic Lexicon of the Old Testament*, ed. William L. Holladay (Grand Rapids: Eerdmans, 1971), 52.

[3] Roland de Vaux, *Ancient Israel* (Grand Rapids: Eerdmans, 1997), 175.

[4] Solomon Schechter and Joseph Jacobs, "Levirate Marriage" in *JE*, www.jewishencyclopedia.com/articles/9859-levirate-marriage.

[5] R. Laird Harris, "[*ga'al*]" (redeem) in *TWOT*, 1:144–45.

THE LIFE OF JEROBOAM II

BY CLAUDE F. MARIOTTINI

An aerial view of modern Damascus.

Jeroboam II carried on Joash's policies of aggressive expansion of Israel's borders. He was able to contain Syrian invasion by conquering their capital, Damascus. The restoration of the borders of Israel, "from Lebo-hamath as far as the Sea of the Arabah" (2 Kgs. 14:25), was a return to the ideal boundaries of Israel that existed in the days of Solomon (1 Kgs. 8:65).¹ Jeroboam's conquests were made possible because of Assyria's weakness and its involvement with military campaigns elsewhere in its empire. With the absence of Assyria in Israel, the door was wide open for Jeroboam to step in and restore Israel's boundaries to the ideal borders of the Solomonic era.

The recovery of territory that Israel had lost brought a great flow of wealth back into the northern kingdom. With the increase of territory came the increase of revenue brought in by trade and taxation. Israel controlled many of the important trade routes and as such was receiving the tolls of the caravans that used those routes. The standard of living in Israel improved. The economic prosperity was good; John Bright said that no living Israelite could remember better times.²

According to Amos, people were able to build better houses, "houses of cut stone" (Amos 5:11). The rich people had summer and winter houses. The description Amos provided of a banquet scene within one of these palatial abodes clearly describes the prosperous life of many Israelites in the eighth century BC.

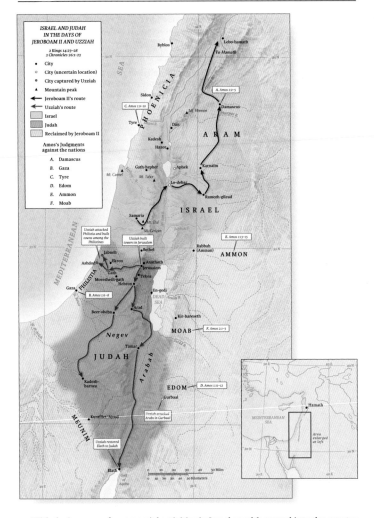

ISRAEL AND JUDAH
IN THE DAYS OF
JEROBOAM II AND UZZIAH

2 Kings 14:23–28
2 Chronicles 26:1–23

- City
○ City (uncertain location)
● City captured by Uzziah
▲ Mountain peak
← Jeroboam II's route
← Uzziah's route
Israel
Judah
Reclaimed by Jeroboam II

Amos's Judgments
against the nations

A. Damascus
B. Gaza
C. Tyre
D. Edom
E. Ammon
F. Moab

With the increase of commercial activities in Israel, wealth poured into the country. Great fortunes were quickly made, the arts flourished, and the cities began to grow in number and size. Beneath all this glamour and wealth there was a disastrous by-product caused by increased economic prosperity: the gap between the rich and poor became more pronounced. The wealthier classes imported new comforts and enjoyed undreamed-of luxuries. The poor profited little from the new commercial relations, for they had no capital to invest. The prophet Amos's message is addressed to a group "who are steadily driving the landed peasantry away from their earlier solid independence into the condition of serfs. The small farmer no longer owned his own land; he was a tenant of an urban class to whom he must pay a rental for the use of the land, a rental that was often the lion's share of the grain which the land produced."[3]

The presentation by the writer of 2 Kings of the religious life during Jeroboam's reign was not positive. Spiritually, Israel was in a deep depression. Over the years, Israel had been slipping away from God, and under Jeroboam's leadership, the spiritual decay of the nation was at an all-time high. Under Jeroboam, the nation of Israel was militarily strong but spiritually weak.

NOTES

[1]   Yohanan Aharoni and Michael Avi-Yonah, *The Macmillan Bible Atlas* (New York: Macmillan, 1968), 89.

[2]   John Bright, *A History of Israel* (Philadelphia: Westminster, 1983), 259.

[3]   James L. Mays, *Amos* (Philadelphia: Westminster, 1969), 94.

MACHAERUS, HEROD, AND JOHN THE BAPTIST

BY DAVID E. LANIER

Herod built his fortress palace at Machaerus, overlooking the Dead Sea (in background). Covering 43,000 square feet, the palace sat atop the hill to the left and was detailed with colonnades, courtyards, and mosaics.

The name Machaerus ("black fortress," today preserved in the locally used name *Mukawir*) does not appear in Scripture. Alexander Jannaeus, the Maccabean king (103–76 BC), originally built the fortress, which was destroyed by Roman forces in 57 BC. It lay in waste until Herod the Great, a friend of the Romans, rebuilt and fortified the site. Machaerus stood at the southern frontier of the region of Perea and was Herod's first line of defense against attacks from Arabia. The fortress overlooked the gorge of Callirrhoe, east of the Dead Sea. Standing 3,860 feet above the Dead Sea and 2,546 feet above the Mediterranean, the site was extremely defensible. At a mere eighteen miles southeast of the mouth of the Jordan, it was accessible to Herod and his friends.[1] When Herod died (4 BC), his son Herod Antipas inherited the fortress. The ancient Jewish historian Josephus identifies Machaerus as the place where Herod had John the Baptist brought in order to behead him.[2]

At the death of Herod Agrippa I in AD 44, the fortress reverted to Roman control until the First Jewish Revolt in AD 66. The Romans abandoned it to the rebels, who held out until AD 72, when Rome's General Lucilius Bassus besieged and destroyed it. Josephus describes the site at the time of its siege and destruction by the Tenth Legion: "The nature of the place was very capable of affording the surest hopes of safety to those that possessed it, as well as delay and fear to those that should attack it."[3]

According to Josephus, even inside the walls was a rocky hill that was so high it could be taken only with the utmost difficulty. The fortress was surrounded with ditches that were frighteningly deep and could not be filled with dirt. The western valley extended to the Dead Sea. Machaerus occupied the commanding position on the other side of this natural defile. On the east, the valley was about 150 feet deep and extended to the foot of a mountain. To the north were defensive valleys also, not as deep but still impracticable to cross.[4]

Josephus relates that when Herod the Great rebuilt the site, he surrounded a large area with walls and towers. He constructed a city for the convenience of the defenders, with a road that led to the top of the highest mountain. He added a second defensive wall around the top of the mountain with towers at the corners, about 240 feet high. In the middle of that enclosed area stood a magnificent palace. The site had many reservoirs for the collection of water to enable the fortress to withstand a protracted siege, and the citadel was stocked with large quantities of darts and instruments of war.[5] In addition to the military strength of the site, the springs at Callirrhoe were known for their medicinal properties. Hot and cold mineral springs were considered beneficial for strengthening the nerves, and a plant called rue grew there in abundance, thought to counteract the negative effects of demons.[6]

Archaeological excavations have confirmed many of Josephus's descriptions of both the upper and the lower cities, including protective walls and towers at the base of Machaerus and at the rim of the citadel at the top.[7]

Reconstructed Roman ballista. Each legion of the Roman army was equipped with ten ballistae, used to propel stone missiles into enemy territory. The ballista could hurl stones weighing up to fifty pounds over 1,000 feet, which were extremely effective in breaking through stone fortification walls.

Caesarea Maritima

Mediterranean Sea

Jordan River

Jericho

Jerusalem

Herodium

Machaerus

Masada

HEROD'S FORTRESS PALACES

NOTES

¹ Merrill Unger, "Machae'rus" in *The New Unger's Bible Dictionary*, ed. R. K. Harrison, rev. ed. (Chicago: Moody, 1988), 796.

² Josephus, *Jewish Antiquities* 18.5.2. See Matthew 4:12; 14:6–12; Mark 6:16–29; Luke 3:19–20.

³ Josephus, *Jewish War* 7.6.1.

⁴ Josephus, *Jewish War* 7.6.1.

⁵ Josephus, *Jewish War* 7.6.2. This may have been the site of Antipas's birthday banquet (Mark 6). Or it may have been held in Galilee, as many nobles from that area were invited. If that were the case, it would have taken some time to retrieve John's head and bring it back. Either way, the head would have been

delivered after the banquet had ended. If the nobles were enjoying an extended stay at the palace, it would have taken little time (see Mark 6). See Harold W. Hoehner, *Herod Antipas* (Cambridge: Cambridge University Press, 1972), 146–49.

[6] Josephus, *Jewish War* 7.6.3.

[7] Stanislao Loffreda, "Machaerus" in *ABD*, 4:457; Josephus, *Jewish War* 7.6.2. Shimon Gibson, *The Cave of John the Baptist* (New York: Doubleday, 2004), 246.

MALACHI'S SITUATION

BY E. RAY CLENDENEN

Wilderness beside the Jordan River at Bethany, where, according to tradition, John baptized Jesus.

Four-horned altar from Megiddo, circa 975–925 BC.

God's people had returned to their homeland of Judah, which, after the Persian conquest of Babylon, was a Persian province. The date of Malachi's prophetic activity is disputed. But the view is virtually unanimous that it occurred during the reigns of the Persian Kings Darius I (521–486 BC), Xerxes I (486–465 BC), or Artaxerxes I (465–424 BC). The people had rebuilt the temple (515 BC) and reestablished worship. But the excitement and enthusiasm engendered by the prophets Haggai and Zechariah had waned. As Malachi addressed God's people, he faced cynicism, hypocrisy, and spiritual apathy. Times were hard. He also faced a failure of leadership.

With three interrelated addresses, Malachi confronted three problems. First, the priests no longer served God wholeheartedly or the people conscientiously. They were insulting God with indifferent and careless worship and had contributed to Judah's indifference toward God (Mal. 1:2–2:9).

Second, blaming their economic and social troubles on the Lord's supposed unfaithfulness, the people were living selfish lives. Watching

Akkadian seal depicting offerings being brought to a goddess, circa 2350–2200 BC.

Egyptian funerary statue showing a calf being sacrificed, circa 2477 BC.

out only for themselves, they gave little more than a nod to their responsibilities to God or to one another (2:10–3:6).

Third, the people also had a self-protective sense of ownership of their personal property. This caused them not only to bring God their worst animals as sacrifices but also to refuse to pay the tithes, which would have supported the temple personnel and the landless poor (3:7–4:6). Priests and people were interested only in self and in "what's in it for me?"

To address the situation, the prophet Malachi weaves together vivid portrayals of the people's sinful attitudes and behaviors, instruction about what must be done, and motivation in both positive and negative terms. For example, speaking through the prophet, the Lord begins by directing Judah's attention to his past demonstrations of loyal love and contrasts his treatment of them with his judgment on Edom. The book concludes with the Lord's threat if they fail to respond properly: "Otherwise, I will come and strike the land with a curse" (4:6).

A MOTHER'S ROLE IN THE FIRST CENTURY

BY SHARON H. GRITZ

Arab woman blows air into a sealed goatskin, which contains milk. She will seal the opening; afterward she and her family will take turns rocking the filled skin on the frame in order to make butter.

Motherhood represented an important role for first-century Jewish women. This responsibility began for many as early as age sixteen, if not younger. Bearing a child ensured the continuity of the family name, thus fulfilling a vital function in the family. In a broader sense, providing children meant the stability and growth of the Jewish people or nation. Consequently, the Jews valued mothers and viewed children as a blessing, a gift and reward from the Lord (Ps. 127:3–5).

GIVING BIRTH AND INFANT CARE

Most women gave birth at home with the help of a midwife. A woman's mother and perhaps other female family members would have aided as well. Even if they offered no medical help, these family figures provided emotional support. Childbirth in the first-century Greco-Roman world was risky. Medical knowledge and practices were limited, vague, or wrong. Consequently infant mortality was high. Some estimate that 30 percent of babies did not survive their first year.[1] Mothers also died giving birth. These deaths occurred across all socioeconomic levels.

Red-polished ware figurine of a woman carrying a baby on a hooped cradleboard; dated to the Middle Bronze Age, 2200–1550 BC; Cypriot.

Immediately after birth, the midwife or another female assistant washed the baby and rubbed the infant's skin with salt (Ezek. 16:4; the purpose of the salt is unclear). Both boys and girls received this treatment.[2] After this, babies were swaddled by being wrapped with a square of fabric and tied with strips or bands of cloth. Believing it kept the baby's limbs straight, mothers would swaddle their infants for several months; swaddling also kept the children warm. Salting the infant's skin and wrapping the baby in swaddling clothes was part of the midwife's care. Mary likely had none of the customary female support system when she gave birth far from home. Supporting this possibility is Luke's indication that Mary herself wrapped Jesus and placed him in the manger.

Mothers breastfed their infants for two to three years. Jewish law even required women to do this for twenty-four months.[3] Certain rituals or cultural practices accompanied the child's birth, including naming the infant. Both fathers and mothers could name the newborn, whether it was a girl or boy. They often used family names or names with special meaning. Circumcision initiated male babies into Jewish society; this took place eight days after birth. Mothers also observed the rite of purification following childbirth.

EDUCATING CHILDREN

Mothers served as the main parental influence on all their children until their sons reached the age of five to seven. From their mothers, boys and girls learned many basics of their Jewish faith—hearing the stories of Israel's heroes, being instructed in morals, memorizing certain passages of the law.

While his son was still young, the father assumed responsibility for his education by teaching him a trade, usually his own vocation, such as carpentry, metalworking, or fishing. Fathers also taught their sons religious laws and life duties. Mothers continued the training of their daughters by instructing them in all the domestic skills expected of women. Additionally, girls had to learn the law's regulations concerning purity issues and the responsibilities of women. A girl remained under her mother's influence until she married.

DAILY TASKS

Mothers (and wives) worked hard to maintain their households and meet their families' needs. Each helped to hold together and preserve the all-important family unit. Their activities demanded time-consuming manual labor. A woman's tasks included cooking and cleaning. Beyond this, she had to perform those duties that related to her husband, duties that included washing her husband's face, hands, and feet. Women could delegate many of their domestic chores to any bond servants or hired help if they had them.[4]

Food preparation consumed much of a mother's day. She sifted grain to remove any impurities and would then grind the grain into flour for baking bread. Preparing food also included gardening and butchering. The mother often milked the family's goat. Some even worked in the fields. Some women made trips to the local market for food and supplies, although some scholars suggest only the men could perform this domestic chore since society did not expect women to visit a public area where nonfamily men might be present.[5]

Mothers were responsible for making and keeping clean the family's clothing. This included spinning the thread, weaving the fabric, sewing, mending, and washing. Women made the trip to the local well many times a day, especially in the morning and evening, to secure fresh water to meet the family's daily needs. Women also kept the small lamps burning in the house by filling them with oil. Mothers or young daughters also gathered small twigs to provide fuel for fire in clay ovens. Mothers kept their homes clean, often assigning floor sweeping to a young daughter. They also met the needs of any guests or visitors to the home.

NOTES

[1] Carolyn Osiek and Margaret Y. MacDonald with Janet H. Tulloch, *A Woman's Place: House Churches in Earliest Christianity* (Minneapolis: Fortress, 2006), 65.

[2] Larry G. Herr, "Salt" in *ISBE* (1988), 4:286.

[3] Leonie J. Archer, *Her Price Is beyond Rubies: The Jewish Woman in Graeco-Roman Palestine* (Sheffield: Sheffield Academic, 1990), 227.

[4] Ben Witherington III, *Women in the Ministry of Jesus* (Cambridge: Cambridge University Press, 1984), 4.

[5] Archer, *Her Price*, 227.

NAHUM'S HISTORICAL SETTING

BY ROBERT A. STREET

Ancient site of Nineveh, first excavated in the mid-1800s by the Englishman A. H. Layard. He unearthed Sennacherib's palace, and later excavations unearthed massive palaces belonging to Ashurbanipal and Esar-haddon.

Unlike most of the prophetic books, Nahum does not mention any king of any country to help identify his historical context. Nahum says only that he was an Elkoshite. Even the location of Elkosh is uncertain.[1]

Nahum's message is identified in Hebrew in 1:1 as *massa' Nineveh*, variously translated as "the pronouncement concerning Nineveh" (CSB), "an oracle concerning Nineveh" (ESV), "the burden of Nineveh" (KJV), among others. The reference to Nineveh is an excellent place to begin as we set Nahum in history. Nineveh, however, had a long history (see Gen. 10:11). Nahum also refers to the fall of the Egyptian city of No-Amon, also known as Thebes (Nah. 3:8).

Using this historical background, dating the book is not extremely difficult. The fall of Nineveh sets the latest date for the book, its *terminus ad quem*, which was 612 BC. The earliest date for the book, its *terminus a quo*, is the fall of Thebes to Ashurbanipal in 663 BC. Thus, the historical setting is between 663 and 612 BC. Gordon Johnston believes that Nahum can be dated after Ashurbanipal's last campaign in the west in 640 BC when he reasserted sovereignty over Judah and other Syro-Palestinian vassals, since 1:12,15 says that Assyria would not invade Judah again.[2]

ASSYRIAN DOMINANCE

The historical setting and background for Nahum was one of Assyrian (Ninevite) oppression, which actually began in the eighth century with Tiglath-pileser III (reigned 744–727 BC), who captured and controlled the Fertile Crescent from the Persian Gulf to Gaza. He actually aided Ahaz (735–715 BC) in defending Judah against the Syro-Ephraimitic alliance. A later Assyrian monarch, Esar-haddon (681–669 BC), invaded and conquered Upper Egypt in 671 BC. A few-years later, Assyria's King Ashurbanipal (668–627 BC), son of Esar-haddon, destroyed Thebes in 663 BC. After conquering Thebes, Ashurbanipal, who was "the last strong king of Assyria,"[3] placed Psammetichus I (Psamtik) on the throne of Egypt. This was the same Psamtik who revolted against Assyrian control and gained independence in 654 BC. Perhaps the rebellion at home made it impossible for Ashurbanipal to deal harshly with Psammetichus. Shamash-shum-ukin, who was Ashurbanipal's brother and the king of Babylon (a subkingdom of Assyria at this time), formed an alliance with Elam and Arabia that sought to overthrow Ashurbanipal. The alliance did not accomplish its goal, even though it continued to fight until about 648 BC and the death of Shamash-shum-ukin.

When the eight-year-old Josiah (2 Kgs. 22:1) became Judah's king in 640 BC, Ashurbanipal had subdued the entire ancient Near East. During the latter years of Ashurbanipal's reign, the Assyrian Empire suffered from decay. Ashurbanipal became more interested in art and scholarship than in running his empire.

At Ashurbanipal's death in 627 BC, his son Ashur-etel-ilani (627–623 BC) ascended the throne. Coinciding with Ashurbanipal's death were rebellions by both the Babylonians under Nabopolassar in 626 BC and the Judean vassals. Furthermore, the Median Empire began its rise, as did the threat of the Scythians, from the area now known as the Steppes of Russia. All of these forces were more than the Assyrian Empire could bear. The Assyrian monarch Sin-shar-ishkun (reigned 623–612 BC) lost two chief Assyrian cities, Ashur in 614 and Nineveh in 612 BC.

Jezreel Valley as seen from Megiddo, where armies of Pharaoh Neco II defeated King Josiah and his soldiers at the Battle of Megiddo in 609 BC.

This conflict impacted tiny Judah. Going back to 722 BC and the destruction of Samaria, Judah was really all that was left of the once proud Hebrew nation. The Judean kingdom existed mainly as a vassal state under Assyria's control until the death of Ashurbanipal.

KINGS OF JUDAH

A cursory examination of three kings of Judah during the years between the fall of Thebes and the fall of Nineveh can help us better understand Nahum's historical setting. The Judean monarch at the fall of Thebes was Manasseh, who was an idolatrous and evil ruler. He "shed so much innocent blood that he filled Jerusalem with it from one end to another" (2 Kgs. 21:16). Second Chronicles adds that Manasseh repented in his later years, although 2 Kings does not mention this. Amon, Manasseh's

Clay tablet, the Annals of Tiglath-pileser III (ruled 744–727 BC), recording details of building operations and military campaigns of Tiglath-pileser III. It mentions the kings of Ammon, Ashkelon, Edom, Gaza, Judah, Moab, and Tyre.

son, reigned only two years before his servants assassinated him (2 Kgs. 21:19–23). Following Amon's assassination, his eight-year-old son Josiah became king.

Josiah asserted political independence while the rebellion was taking place in the other countries following Ashurbanipal's death. Josiah's assertion of political and religious freedom was spurred on when workers discovered the book of law (probably parts of Deuteronomy) in 622 BC while rebuilding the temple.

ASSYRIA'S DEMISE

The death throes of Assyria occurred under Ashur-uballit II. After Nineveh fell to the Medes and Babylonians in 612 BC, Assyria's King Ashur-uballit II retreated to Haran. The resistance continued; in 610, the Babylonians captured Haran. In 609 BC, Pharaoh Neco II marched to join forces with the Assyrians. At Megiddo, King Josiah met the Egyptian monarch, who was on his way to Haran. In the ensuing battle, Josiah died; his forces were defeated (2 Chr. 35:20–24). Josiah seems to have been supporting the rebels against Assyria. Jehoahaz, Josiah's son, was Judah's next king.

Jehoahaz served only three months before Neco replaced him with Jehoiakim (Eliakim), another of Josiah's sons. Neco took Jehoahaz captive to Riblah in Hamath and demanded tribute money, which Jehoiakim paid. Jehoahaz was later sent from Riblah to Egypt, where he died.

After Megiddo, Neco continued to Haran to help the Assyrians as they fought the Babylonians. His help, though, was of no avail; the Babylonians were victorious. Undeterred, Neco continued his campaigning on behalf of Assyria. In 605 BC, Neco and the Egyptians, along with the remnants of Assyria's army, suffered a crushing defeat at Carchemish at the hands of the Babylonians. With Assyria's defeat and Babylon's victory at Carchemish, Judah became subject (vassal) to Babylon's King Nebuchadnezzar.

The historical period of Nahum was evil both inside and outside of Judah. Not only did the Assyrians worship a multitude of gods, but also the people of Judah did not remain faithful to the Lord. Nahum offered hope to Judah and Jerusalem that the oppression would end and God would comfort his people. The enemy, symbolized by the city of Nineveh, would be utterly and totally destroyed. It was.

NOTES

1. According to Pseudo-Epiphanius, the location was in southwest Judah near Begabar, modern Beit Jibrin. Jerome placed Elkosh at Hilkesi of Galilee (modern El-Kauzeh). The city of Capernaum ("village of Nahum") has been proposed but is unlikely. A location on the Tigris River at Alkush (Al-Qush, Alqosh) opposite of Nineveh was proposed in the sixteenth century. The tomb of Nahum is said to be at Alkush.

2. G. H. Johnston, "Nahum's Rhetorical Allusions to the Neo-Assyrian Lion Motif," *BSac* 158 (2001): 302.

3. Burlan A. Sizemore Jr., *The Centuries of Decline* (Nashville: Convention Press, 1970), 73.

NEBUCHADNEZZAR: KING OF BABYLON

BY CLAUDE F. MARIOTTINI

Full scale model of Ishtar Gate of Babylon at Berlin State Museum.

Nebuchadnezzar II, the Neo-Babylonian Empire's second king, was the most famous king of the Chaldeans, a people whom Jeremiah called "an established nation, an ancient nation" (Jer. 5:15). As king, Nebuchadnezzar brought fame and prosperity to the empire. Of all the foreign kings the Old Testament mentions, this Nebuchadnezzar is the most prominent and the one with whom Bible students are most familiar. Nebuchadnezzar reigned from 605 to 562 BC.

THE KINGSHIP OF NEBUCHADNEZZAR

Nebuchadnezzar had a reputation as a great builder. He boasted in "Babylon the Great that I have built to be a royal residence by my vast power and for my majestic glory" (Dan. 4:30). The city spanned the Euphrates River by means of a 1,200-foot bridge (the longest in the ancient world). There were eight gates, each named for a god, the most prominent being the Ishtar Gate, opening onto the "Processional Way" that led through the city. The Ishtar Gate was attached to his palace, whose outer walls were made of baked brick, and each brick was stamped with Nebuchadnezzar's name. Also there was the so-called Hanging Gardens, which he built for his wife, Amytis, the daughter of the king of Media. The most prominent building was the stepped tower or ziggurat called Etemenanki, which was 300 feet on each side and perhaps 300 feet high and is often called the tower of Babel. Near it was Esagila, the temple of Marduk, their chief god, but cuneiform documents speak of more than fifty temples and chapels in the city, and more than 6,000 figurines were found there (see Jer. 50:38).[1]

According to Babylonian texts, Nebuchadnezzar received praise as a lawgiver, a judge, and a king who was devoted to justice and who opposed injustice and corruption. His motivation for fairness was to please his god, Marduk, and to thus enjoy a long life: "O Marduk, my lord, do remember my deeds favorably as good [deeds], may (these) my good deeds be always before your mind (so that) my walking in Esagila and Ezida—which I love—may last to old age."[2]

Nebuchadnezzar's name appears in two different forms in the Hebrew Bible, which could be rendered Nebuchadnezzar (fifty-eight times) and Nebuchadrezzar (thirty-four times), although most English translations render them both Nebuchadnezzar for consistency (contrast KJV, NRSV, JPS). Since Babylonian documents use *Nabu-kudurri-utsur,*

Lion relief from the throne room of Nebuchadnezzar's palace in Babylon.

meaning "Nabu has protected the son who will inherit,"[3] Nebuchadrezzar was probably closer to the original form.

Nebuchadnezzar's father, Nabopolassar, led a Chaldean revolt against the Assyrians and in 626 BC founded the Neo-Babylonian Empire. After establishing an alliance with the Medes, he and his allies took Nineveh, the Assyrian capital, then proceeded to defeat the Assyrian army at Haran and finally the Assyrian in 605 BC. They were then confronted by the Egyptian army led by Pharaoh Neco, which had been detained by King Josiah of Judah, who had been defeated and killed at Megiddo (2 Kgs. 23:29; 2 Chr. 35:20–24).

Nabopolassar, unable to fight because of an illness that eventually killed him, sent his oldest son, Nebuchadnezzar, to confront the Egyptians. Nebuchadnezzar soundly defeated Neco at Carchemish and subjugated Sidon, Tyre, Philistia, and other countries in Syro-Palestine (see Jer. 46:2; 47:2–7). At this time, Nebuchadnezzar learned of his father's death and returned to Babylon, where he was crowned king of Babylon in 605 BC.

NEBUCHADNEZZAR IN THE BOOK OF KINGS

The Old Testament presents more than one view of Nebuchadnezzar. The book of Kings presents him as Jerusalem's conqueror. After his victory against Egypt at Carchemish, Nebuchadnezzar made Jehoiakim his vassal-king of Judah. Jehoiakim submitted to Nebuchadnezzar for three years (604–601 BC). In 601, Egypt and Babylon met again with heavy losses on both sides. Nebuchadnezzar returned home to reorganize his army, and Jehoiakim, counting on Egyptian help, revolted against the Babylonians (2 Kgs. 24:1).

Nebuchadnezzar did not campaign against Israel from 600 to 598 BC, but he sent mercenary soldiers to fight against Jehoiakim (2 Kgs. 24:2–3). Then in 598 BC, Babylon advanced against Judah. Egypt promised to help Jehoiakim, but Egypt's military help did not materialize (v. 7). Jehoiakim died sometime in 598 BC, although the circumstances are unclear,[4] and his son, Jehoiachin, was made the new king of Judah (597 BC). Three months later, Nebuchadnezzar took Jerusalem and deported to Babylon Jehoiachin the king of Judah, his mother, the royal family, the palace officials, the army officers, fighting men, craftsmen, and smiths. He also took all the

Royal building inscription cylinder of Nebuchadnezzar from Lugal-Marada temple at ancient Marad.

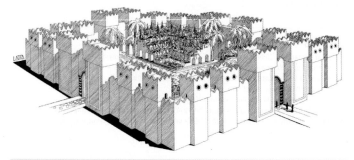

Reconstruction of Nebuchadnezzar's hanging gardens in Babylon, built for his wife Amytis.

men of substance and those who were capable of war. According to 2 Kings 24:12–16, 10,000 people were taken into exile. Nebuchadnezzar also took all the temple and palace treasures and broke all the golden vessels used in temple worship. Jehoiachin remained a prisoner in Babylon for thirty-seven years, until Evil-merodach, Nebuchadnezzar's son, freed him (2 Kgs. 25:27–30; Jer. 52:31–34).

In 596 BC, Nebuchadnezzar placed Zedekiah on Judah's throne as the new king, but Zedekiah rebelled in his ninth year. In 588 BC, Nebuchadnezzar came back to Jerusalem and once again besieged the city. Archaeology has confirmed that many of Judah's fortified cities were destroyed at that time.[5] In March 586 BC, Babylon conquered Jerusalem and burned the temple as well as the great houses of the city. At this time, a second deportation took place; only the poorest were left behind.

NEBUCHADNEZZAR IN THE BOOK OF JEREMIAH

The book of Jeremiah offers an expanded interpretation that affirms the sovereignty of God and his guidance in Judah's destruction. Jeremiah proclaimed that God would "hand ... over" Judah and their treasures to the king of Babylon, who would "plunder them, seize them, and carry them off to Babylon," along with Pashhur, the temple official who had the prophet beaten (Jer. 20:4–6). Then when Nebuchadnezzar had Jerusalem under siege, Zedekiah sent Pashhur to ask Jeremiah to beg God for help. But the Lord answered that he himself would fight against the people of Jerusalem "with an outstretched hand and a strong arm, with anger, rage, and intense wrath," with "the sword, famine, and plague." Only those who surrendered would live (21:4–10). God had already handed over Jehoiachin (called Coniah) to be carried away by Nebuchadnezzar (22:24–30; 24:1), all because the people refused to listen to God's prophet who had been begging them to repent since Josiah's thirteenth year (25:3–7). Ever since 605 BC, Jeremiah had been warning Judah that "my [God's] servant Nebuchadnezzar" was coming, who would "completely destroy them and make them an example of horror and scorn, and ruins forever" (25:1–9).

God calls Nebuchadnezzar his "servant" three times in Jeremiah (25:9; 27:6; 43:10). Old Testament writers generally used the title "servant of Yahweh" to designate persons who had a special relationship with God and who were obedient to God's will in the life of his people. Jeremiah uses it to indicate Nebuchadnezzar was the one God appointed to have dominion over the nations and to act as the instrument of God's justice. Therefore, rebellion against Nebuchadnezzar was rebellion against God. The Lord commanded Jeremiah to write his oracles on a scroll as a warning to Judah (36:1–4). According to Jeremiah, Nebuchadnezzar's conquest and subjugation of the nations would happen with God's approval (27:6–7).

NOTES

[1]   Edwin Yamauchi, "Nebuchadnezzar," in *NIDBA*, 333; Daniel C. Browning Jr. and Randall Breland, "Babylon," in *HIBD* rev. ed. (2015), 160–64; H. W. F. Saggs, "Babylon," in *Archaeology and Old Testament Study*, ed. D. W. Thomas (Oxford: Oxford University Press, 1967), 44.

[2]   James B. Pritchard, ed., *ANET*, 307.

[3]   Ludwig Koehler and Walter Baumgartner, *HALOT* (2000), 660.

[4]   Eugene H. Merrill, *Kingdom of Priests: A History of Old Testament Israel* (Grand Rapids: Baker, 1987), 451.

[5]   Kathleen M. Kenyon, *Archaeology in the Holy Land* (Nashville: Thomas Nelson, 1960), 304–5.

NERO: RULER OF ROME

BY CHARLES A. RAY JR.

Bronze statuette likely made in Gaul showing Nero in imperial dress.

Bronze statuette likely made in Gaul showing Nero in imperial dress.

Nero was born in AD 37 as Lucius Domitius Ahenobarbus. His father's family could trace an unbroken line of nobility back more than 200 years. His grandfather on his mother's side was the popular Roman General Germanicus, a descendant of the great Emperor Augustus. Nobility, however, does not guarantee civility. Michael Grant begins his biography of Nero saying, "Nero was born of murderous parents, and brought up in a murderous atmosphere. And he too was murderous. But only when frightened, though unfortunately he got frightened easily."[1]

ASCENT TO POWER

Nero's uncle Gauis Caligula became emperor the year Nero was born. Two years later, Nero's mother, Agrippina, was accused of plotting to kill her brother, Caligula, and was banished from Rome. Nero was placed in the care of his father's sister. Nero's fortunes turned the following year (AD 41), when Caligula was murdered by his own palace guards. Caligula's uncle Claudius was selected as the next emperor, and he allowed his niece, Agrippina, to return from exile.

Upon her return to Rome, Agrippina immediately remarried, this time to a wealthy orator, who died suddenly three years later. In AD 48, Claudius's wife was forced to commit suicide for her alleged involvement in a plot to assassinate Claudius; by the following year, Agrippina was the new wife of the emperor.

Claudius had one son, Britannicus, by his former wife, but Agrippina set out to undermine his claim to the throne. In her first year of marriage to Claudius, she arranged the engagement of Nero to Claudius's daughter Octavia, and the following year she convinced Claudius to adopt her son. At this time Nero's name was changed to Nero Claudius Drusus Germanicus.

That same year, Agrippina secured the Roman senator, orator, and philosopher Seneca as Nero's personal tutor. Seneca had been exiled to the island of Corsica in AD 41 under the influence of Claudius's first wife, and Agrippina was instrumental in securing his return to Rome. Nero's career accelerated rapidly, soon eclipsing the younger Britannicus. Nero's name appeared first on official inscriptions; his image, not that of Britannicus, appeared on coins; and he was allowed to march in parades at the head of the emperor's palace guard, the praetorian guard.[2]

In February AD 54, Britannicus turned thirteen, the age at which Claudius had allowed Nero to become a legal adult. Claudius gave some indication of giving a similar status to Britannicus, a situation that would have threatened Nero's claim to the throne. Claudius made a new will, but he died in October without having taken any steps to strengthen Britannicus's position. With the aid of Burrus, the commander of the praetorian guard, Agrippina had Nero declared emperor and Claudius's revised will suppressed. Burrus owed his appointment as commander to the political maneuvering of Agrippina, and rumors circulated that she was responsible for Claudius's death, probably through poisoning.

GOLDEN YEARS

Agrippina had assumed significantly more political clout under Claudius than was customary for the wife of an emperor. Nero was not yet seventeen when he ascended to the throne (reigned AD 54–68), and for at least the first year of his reign, Agrippina exercised even more power. Her portrait appeared on coins with Nero's, hers occupying the more prominent place. Rumors circulated in the first century that Agrippina controlled Nero in part through an incestuous relationship with him.[3]

Soon, however, the relationship between Nero and his mother deteriorated. She threatened to champion Britannicus over Nero, and early in AD 55 Nero enlisted help in having Britannicus poisoned. He then forced Agrippina to move out of the palace to another residence across town. Working together, Burrus and Seneca used Nero's poor relationship with his mother to channel his energies, at least partially, to the task of governing the empire. The result was a period early in Nero's reign of almost five years during which Rome experienced stability.

Nero appears to have been influenced by Seneca's concepts of generosity and leniency. On one occasion, he attempted to eliminate all forms of indirect taxation from the empire. The move proved to be economically impractical but increased Nero's popularity among the people. Nero was reported to have taken his judicial duties seriously, studying written briefs overnight before making decisions. He appears to have worked hard at removing some of the abuses common among previous emperors. Paul wrote his letter to the church at Rome sometime during this period of Nero's reign, most likely during the mid-to-late 50s.

YEARS OF GROWING TYRANNY

Nero had shown an early interest in the performing arts and athletic competition. Most Roman nobility believed strongly in the superiority of the Roman practical arts of war and government. While the pursuit of the arts for relaxation and diversion was encouraged, serious pursuit of the arts was left for slaves and other foreigners.

Nero did not share this opinion and had worked privately to excel in music, oratory, and art. His mother had always discouraged these pursuits, and Burrus and Seneca were able to limit Nero's performances to private audiences. A series of events beginning in AD 59 changed things.

Nero became less tolerant of his mother's attempts to control him and finally resolved to have her murdered. Following a bungled attempt to have her drowned in a collapsible boat, Nero had her killed on charges of plotting to assassinate him. In contrast to Agrippina's domineering control, the counsel of Burrus and Seneca must have seemed mild. Without that contrast, the two men had less success controlling Nero's wilder side.

In the following years, Nero became more determined to fulfill his interests, which included singing, acting, chariot racing, and pursuing sexual exploits. When Burrus died in AD 62, Nero replaced him with Tigellinus, who encouraged Nero's licentious self-absorption. Without the aid of Burrus, Seneca asked Nero if he could retire from government. Although Nero refused his request, Seneca became less involved in governmental affairs. That same year, Nero divorced his wife, Octavia, and married Poppaea, who was the wife of a friend and pregnant with Nero's child. Two years later, Nero began to make public appearances on the stage and in athletic events, much to the dismay of the Roman Senate and other nobility.

Nero also was active in remodeling and enlarging his own palace. Eventually his rather large palace became the entrance hall into an immensely larger palace known as the Golden House. Depending on which estimate one accepts, the Golden House and surrounding gardens covered between 125 and 370 acres.[4] The notorious fire of July AD 64 caused destruction, which made possible this massive construction project.

The origin of the fire is unknowable, though several aspects of the situation led to finger pointing in Nero's

Bust of Emperor Gaius Caligula (AD 37–41).

direction. Reports circulated that during the fire gangs of men were seen throwing torches into buildings and threatening anyone who tried to extinguish the flames. After burning for six days, the fire appeared to be stamped out only to reignite on the property of Tigellinus, the new commander of the emperor's palace guard.

Nero's own attitude toward the fire seemed suspect as well. Inspired by the sight of the city burning, he sang in its entirety his original composition, *Fall of Troy*, while he played his lyre. The ancient sources differ as to where the performance took place, either on the roof of his palace or in his private theater.[5] The public outrage was intense and was not abated by the emperor's acts of benevolence. Needing a scapegoat, Nero blamed the fire on the Christians in the city and began an intense time of persecution. Paul and Peter were probably martyred in the aftermath of this event.

The following year, a conspiracy against the emperor erupted. Nero brutally suppressed it. As discontent continued to grow in Rome, Nero went to Greece, where he spent a year competing in various athletic games and other events. To no one's surprise, Nero won every event he entered, even the ten-horse chariot race in which he fell from his chariot and was unable to complete the race.

Nero finally returned to Rome in January 68 to at least three separate uprisings. His feeble attempts at restoring order failed miserably. When the Senate voted to condemn Nero to death by flogging, his palace guard deserted him. On June 9, 68, Nero committed suicide. His famous statement, "What an artist dies with me," was uttered as he gave directions on how to decorate his tomb.[6]

NOTES

1 Michael Grant, *Nero* (New York: Dorset, 1970), 13.
2 Grant, *Nero*, 26.
3 Grant, *Nero*, 32.
4 Grant, *Nero*, 140.
5 Grant, *Nero*, 126.
6 Miriam T. Griffin, *Nero: The End of a Dynasty* (New Haven, CT: Yale University Press, 1985), 182.

OBADIAH: THE MAN AND HIS MESSAGE

BY KEVIN C. PEACOCK

Ruins of Triple Arched Gate at Petra.

About the only thing we know for certain about Obadiah the prophet is that he was a prophet. His name was a common one that means "servant of the LORD." (At least twelve people in the Old Testament had the name.) Obadiah, however, could have been his title rather than his name. Scholars date Obadiah anywhere from the ninth century to the fifth century BC,[1] but the most traditional dating of Obadiah's prophecy would be during the exile, shortly after the fall of Jerusalem in 586 BC. He spoke of the attack on Jerusalem in the past (Obad. 11); but Edom's fall (ca. 533 BC) was still in the future, making Obadiah likely a contemporary with Jeremiah and Ezekiel.[2]

Foreigners (i.e., the Babylonians) invaded Jerusalem and divided the spoils of the city (v. 11). The Edomites, distant relatives and near neighbors to the Judeans, could have assisted Judah; instead, they sided with the invaders, gloated over Jerusalem's fall, and took advantage of their brothers' plight (vv. 10–14). They then fled to their mountain fortresses, feeling smugly secure after their mistreatment of God's chosen people (vv. 3–4). Obadiah's message was directed against such wickedness and pride. Their actions proved the Edomites to be God's enemies, and they would soon face his justice. The Lord's purpose for his people was not finished, and God's reign would become universal and eternal.

Israel's contentious history with the Edomites originated with Jacob and Esau (or Edom; see Gen. 25:30). Settled in Seir on the southeastern edge of the Dead Sea (Gen. 36:1–9),

Sheep near the Wadi Hasa (Brook Zered), the border between Edom and Moab.

The Rock of Edom in the Wilderness of Zin.

the Edomites denied the Israelites passage through their territory after the exodus, threatening them with force (Num. 20:14–21; 21:4). Centuries of struggle between the two peoples followed (see 1 Sam. 14:47–48; 2 Sam. 8:13–14; 1 Kgs. 9:26–28; 11:14–22; 2 Kgs. 8:20–22; 14:7; 2 Chr. 21:8–10; 25:11–12; 28:17). When the Babylonians destroyed Jerusalem in 586 BC, the Edomites sided with the attackers to take advantage of Israel's plight (Ps. 137:7; Ezek. 25:12–14; 35:10–11). Later, a strong Arab presence appeared in Edomite territory during the Persian Empire (late sixth to fourth centuries BC; see Neh. 2:19; 4:7; 6:1). "By late in the fourth century BC, the Arab kingdom of Nabatea was centered around Petra [the Edomite capital]. Pressure from the Nabateans displaced many Edomites into the Negev of Judah. This region then came to be called 'Idumea,' preserving [a form of] the ancient name of Edom."[3]

NOTES

[1] See J. LeCureux, "Obadiah, Book of" in *Dictionary of the Old Testament Prophets*, ed. Mark J. Boda and J. Gordon McConville (Downers Grove, IL: IVP Academic, 2012), 570, for the proposed dating options.

[2] See John Barton, *Joel and Obadiah*, OTL (2001), 120–21, for details and comparisons.

[3] See 1 Maccabees 4:29; Raymond B. Dillard and Tremper Longman III, *An Introduction to the Old Testament* (Grand Rapids: Zondervan, 1995), 387–88.

OF MARRYING AGE

BY ROBERTA JONES

A mosaic of the wedding festival of Ariadne and Dionysus found at Philippopolis. The mosaic is Roman and dates to the first century AD.

Jewish parents often arranged a betrothal for their son or daughter. In the betrothal period, which was a legal and binding engagement, the man and woman lived separately. They waited until after marriage for intimate relations. Yet, as with a legal husband and wife, only death or divorce broke a betrothal. During their betrothal, Joseph discovered Mary's pregnancy. Even though disappointed, Joseph chose kindness. He planned to spare Mary any public humiliation (Matt. 1:18–20). Joseph seemingly considered his predicament in light of Old Testament Scriptures. Deuteronomy 22:20–21 suggested stoning women guilty of adultery; however, another choice allowed the man to write a divorce certificate if he found his wife to be "displeasing" (Deut. 24:1).

Marriage customs in other countries influenced Israel. Two factors in Greece contributed to a higher ratio of men to women. Many women died in childbirth. Further, Grecian parents often abandoned baby girls. This female shortage likely encouraged men to marry increasingly younger wives. Sadly, Grecian cemetery inscriptions indicate many extremely young girls died in childbirth. If women survived childbirth, they expected to live about thirty-seven years.[1]

Rome ruled Israel at the time of Jesus's birth. Emperor Caesar Augustus strongly favored marriage. Ten-year-old girls could be engaged and marry two years later. Upper-class women, however, usually waited until their late teens to marry. They would not tarry too long, for twenty-year-old unmarried women might be penalized. Roman men usually married in their twenties or possibly older. A male who married younger was to show

physical signs of maturity or be age fourteen before he wed.[2]

Jewish brides between ages thirteen
and sixteen were especially common. But
unlike other cultures, some women married past twenty. Many Jewish men married at eighteen to twenty. By the second
century AD, many rabbis declared that
men who were still unmarried at the age
of twenty or older were sinning against
God. Jewish culture urged early marriage
for two reasons. First, an early marriage
would likely produce offspring to continue the family name. Second, matrimony was considered a means by which
young men could control their sexual
passions.[3]

Although we cannot verify the ages at
which Mary and Joseph married, Israelite
customs suggest they were young. Consider,
also, Jesus had at least six younger half-sib-
lings (Mark 6:3).

Josephus, a Jewish historian writing in
the first century AD, explained typical
customs of those times. As a betrothed
couple, both Mary and Joseph likely expected that Joseph would oversee their family.
For, Josephus declared, a woman was
"inferior to her husband in all things." He
also warned abusive husbands and encouraged obedient, dutiful wives.[4] Josephus
suggested a woman could be stoned if
convicted of not preserving her virginity.
Men should marry, "at the age fit for it,
virgins that are free, and born of good
parents."[5]

Marriage scene etched in gold glass,
likely from Rome, inscribed "Live in
God." Dated to the fourth–fifth centuries
AD.

Terra-cotta lekythos (oil flask) dated to
about 550–530 BC from Attica, Greece.
The best man rides with the wedding
couple in a cart that is being drawn by
two donkeys.

NOTES

1. C. C. Kroeger, "Women in Greco-Roman World
and Judaism" in *Dictionary of New Testament
Background*, ed. Craig A. Evans and Stanley E.
Porter (Downers Grove, IL: InterVarsity, 2000),
1278.
2. C. S. Keener, "Marriage" in *Dictionary of New
Testament Background*, 683–84.
3. Keener, "Marriage," 684.
4. Josephus, *Against Apion* 2.25.
5. Josephus, *Jewish Antiquities* 4.8.23.

OLDER ADULTS IN FIRST-CENTURY CULTURE

BY DORMAN LAIRD

GRECO-ROMAN ATTITUDES AND ACTIONS

In the Greco-Roman world of the first century, family members (typically children and grandchildren) were to provide complete and essential care for older relatives. Doing so

Relief depicting Roman men carrying a sick or injured man. Basil, the bishop of Caesarea, founded a hospital in Cappadocia around AD 370. The facility, which came to be called "Basileias," took care of the poor, orphans, the elderly, lepers, the sick, and the infirm.

was a sacred duty. Failure to do so could result in penalties and fines and in Athens even the restriction of a person's citizenship rights.[1] Among the Romans, children likewise had the legal responsibility of taking care of their aged parents.[2] However, because of the high rate of infant and child mortality, life expectancy was only between twenty and thirty years. Only about 6 to 8 percent of the empire's population lived to be more than sixty years old.[3]

The Romans expected adults who reached a senior age to remain useful in the society as long as they were in control of their faculties.[4] The oldest living male of a household (the *paterfamilias*) had total rights over his natural descendants (male and female), his wife, his adopted sons, and even the children of his sons in the male line of his descendants. That is, the oldest living male ancestor "controlled his descendants . . . their persons and 'their' property—in law they had no possessions of their own. He held everything."[5] He was responsible for representing the family before the gods, for approving descendants' marriages, and even for deciding whether a newborn was legitimate and therefore worth keeping. In principle, the rule of the *paterfamilias* continued over his descendants regardless of how old they were. A mature man or even an old man could still be regarded legally as the child of his living father and subject to his authority.[6] Only when the paterfamilias died did the members of his household become legally independent.[7]

Figurine from Tanagra (north of Athens, Greece) depicts an elderly man; dated to early Hellenistic Era (332–152 BC).

Cultural records from the era reveal that Romans held ambivalent attitudes toward older individuals. Some art pieces and dramatic presentations disdainfully depicted the elderly as toothless and wrinkled men and women. In contrast, some images respectfully reveal older couples as being supportive and loving of each other in their old age. Additionally, the Romans typically respected and appreciated older senators for their wisdom. As a show of that respect, the law would allow aging senators to be excused from attending all the sessions of the Senate if they so chose. Also, men older than fifty-five could be excused from some public duties.[8]

CHRISTIAN ATTITUDES AND ACTIONS

The differences between Christian attitudes and those of Greeks and Romans toward the aged and the poor were stark. Believers were motivated to care for people out of Christian love because all individuals have inherent value as image bearers of God.[9] Believers' conviction in personal and corporate benevolence led Christians to offer care during times of an epidemic outbreak, something that had been unheard of for a religious group in the classical world.[10]

During the first two centuries, especially in times of epidemics, the systematic care that believers gave to those who were sick—whether Christian or pagan—seemingly had a powerful effect on public attitudes about Christianity. For instance, "during the plague of Cyprian [AD 250], Christian churches, even though they were undergoing their first large-scale persecution, devised in several cities a program for the systematic care of the sick. . . . Their activity contrasted with that of the pagans, who deserted the sick or threw the bodies of the dead out into the streets."[11]

The compassion shown to the aged and the indigent who received nursing care from Christians was met with gratitude by pagans, resulting in many conversions to Christianity.[12] Strong evidence indicates that the model of care the church practiced ultimately led to the creation of what some believe to be the earliest hospital open to the public, the Basileias, completed about AD 372. At the time of the construction of the Basileias, a social conscience about the institutional care of the aged had clearly developed. Along with the provision of separate areas for the poor, the homeless, orphans, lepers, and the sick, the facility also included a section for older patients.[13]

NOTES

1. "Greece" in *The Ancient World*, vol. 1 of *The Greenwood Encyclopedia of Daily Life*, ed. Gregory S. Aldrete (Westport, CT: Greenwood, 2004), 1:25–26.
2. Martin Goodman, *The Roman World 44 BC–AD 180*, 2nd ed. (London: Routledge, 2012), 196.
3. Goodman, *Roman World*, 196.
4. Goodman, *Roman World*, 196–97.
5. Francis Lyall, *Slaves, Citizens, Sons: Legal Metaphors in the Epistles* (Grand Rapids: Zondervan, 1984), 120.
6. Lyall, *Slaves, Citizens, Sons*, 120–21.
7. Karl-J. Holkeskamp, "Under Roman Roofs: Family, House, and Household," in *The Cambridge Companion to the Roman Republic*, ed. Harriet I. Flower (New York: Cambridge University Press, 2004), 122–23.
8. Goodman, *The Roman World*, 196.
9. Gary B. Ferngren, *Medicine & Health Care in Early Christianity* (Baltimore: Johns Hopkins University Press, 2009), 117–18.
10. Ferngren, *Medicine & Health Care*, 117–18.
11. Ferngren, *Medicine & Health Care*, 118.
12. Ferngren, *Medicine & Health Care*, 121.
13. Ferngren, *Medicine & Health Care*, 124–25.

PAUL, THE LETTER WRITER

BY E. RANDOLPH RICHARDS

Two leaves from a set of hinged writing boards inscribed with astrological omens. Fragments of the original wax showing part of the cuneiform text still survive. Very few such boards, which once were plentiful, have been recovered. These were intended for Sargon's (721–705 BC) palace at Khorsabad.

In the first century, most writers used black ink, which was made from lampblack or ground charcoal. This ink was cheap and easy to make but not waterproof. Although someone could wash a document off and reuse it, writing could also be lost accidentally if the letter became wet. For the protection of the documents, people often kept valuable scrolls in waxed leather cases. Ancient writers also had a cheap source of pens. Most used a small reed cut about eight to ten inches long, much like our fountain pen today.

Ancients wrote on a variety of materials. For sending a quick note, they often wrote on shards of broken pots. Such notes were called ostraca. For quick notes or receipts to

From the Roman Era, stili used to write on wax-surfaced wooden writing tablets.

Scribes commonly used erasers made of sandstone. The erasers shown are from Tell Defenneh (Tahpanhes, Egypt).

be given to another, people also commonly wrote on the back of an old document. For a temporary note, ancient writers often used wooden tablets, which were thin sheets of wood with a recessed middle. The recessed middle could be written on directly with ink or more commonly was filled with a thin layer of wax. The raised rim protected the wax when the tablets were stacked. The wax was easily smoothed and reused.

Nevertheless, for dispatched letters during the time of Paul, the two major options for "paper" were parchment and papyrus. Parchment sheets were made from the hide of a calf, goat, or sheep. These sheets (if properly done) were tough but light and flexible. The sheets were sewn together to make a longer strip that was rolled up—what is today commonly called a scroll. Parchment was tough and long-lasting, but it was probably more expensive and more difficult to write on than papyrus. Letter writers in Paul's day probably preferred papyrus.

Papyrus reeds grew in abundance along the banks of the Nile. Reeds were more than five feet tall. The reed is about as thick as a man's wrist. To make papyrus paper, the reeds were cut into sections and sliced lengthwise in thin, tape-like strips. These strips were laid side by side on a pattern board. Another layer of strips was placed on top of these at a right angle. The dried sheet was then smoothed and trimmed to a standard size.

Papyrus was not normally sold in individual sheets. Like parchment, sheets were pasted together to make a scroll. When a secretary finished a letter, he cut off the excess papyrus to be saved for another patron. If the letter was longer than he anticipated, he could glue on additional sheets. Rolls of either parchment or papyrus could be made any length, but a roll of twenty sheets (ca. twelve feet) seems to have been the standard in the time of Paul. Theoretically, scrolls could be continuously lengthened, but ancients had discovered that scrolls of more than thirty feet became too cumbersome to handle.

Today, paper and pen are so inexpensive as to be negligible. In antiquity, this was not so. The entire process of writing his letter to the Romans probably cost Paul (in today's dollars) more than $2,000.[1] This did not include the cost of paying someone to carry it to Rome. About two-thirds of the cost was materials. The remaining one-third was labor, the expense of a secretary.

Many students of the New Testament are surprised to learn Paul used a secretary. The evidence in his letters is clear. In one letter, we even know that secretary's name: Tertius (Rom. 16:22). Ancients rarely wrote in the letter, "I am using a secretary," because the practice was expected. Etiquette, however, required the writer to finish the letter's final comments in his own handwriting, much as we sign a letter. In an original ancient letter, you can see the shift in handwriting at the end. Writers also commonly made a comment, such as "I am writing this in my own hand."[2] Paul often made such a comment (see 1 Cor. 16:21; Gal. 6:11; Col. 4:18; 2 Thess. 3:17).

NOTES

[1] I outline how I arrived at this figure in E. Randolph Richards, *Paul and First-Century Letter Writing* (Downers Grove, IL: InterVarsity, 2004), 165–69.

[2] For a full explanation with examples, see E. Randolph Richards, *The Secretary in the Letters of Paul* (Tübingen: Mohr Siebeck, 1991), 68–90.

PHARAOH'S ARMY

BY DUANE A. GARRETT

The Jezreel Valley as seen from atop Megiddo. Controlling Megiddo meant being able to guard the route where the International Coastal Highway entered the valley. The north-south highway linked Egypt to Syria.

Egypt's golden age of imperial and military glory was the period known as the New Kingdom (Eighteenth, Nineteenth, and Twentieth Dynasties; 1550–1069 BC). Egypt waged war to the west (Libya), to the south (Nubia), and to the north (the Mitanni Empire of Syria during the Eighteenth Dynasty and the Hittite Empire of Anatolia during the Nineteenth Dynasty). During the Twentieth Dynasty, as Egyptian power waned, Egypt repelled an invasion of "Sea Peoples" from across the Mediterranean Sea. The New Kingdom was also the period in which the exodus occurred.

The Egyptian military machine developed during the wars against the Hyksos, foreigners who dominated northern Egypt 1786–1550 BC. The Egyptians who drove out the Hyksos established the Eighteenth Dynasty and the New Kingdom Era. After expelling the Hyksos, the new Egyptian army did not lay down its arms and go back to the plow. They were a thoroughly militarized society, and they had come to believe that an aggressive foreign policy was the best defense against future humiliation at the hands of foreigners.

SOURCES OF INFORMATION

A primary source of information is the accounts of military successes left by Thutmose III (Eighteenth Dynasty; reigned 1479–1425 BC), Ramesses II (Nineteenth Dynasty; reigned 1279–1213), and Ramesses III (Twentieth Dynasty; reigned 1184–1153 BC). These inscriptions and the accompanying artwork tell us a great deal about Egyptian weapons, tactics, and standard procedures.

Thutmose III left behind accounts of his many campaigns into the land of promise. His most daring exploit was the conquest of the Canaanite city of Megiddo, which had revolted against Egyptian domination with the encouragement of the Syrian city of Kadesh. Thutmose, approaching Megiddo from the southwest, took his army through the narrow Aruna Pass rather than swing around the hills that stood between him and the city. This maneuver forced him to string out his forces, and it could have led to catastrophic defeat. But his enemies were not expecting him to take the narrow pass and made no effort to block it. He surprised them by emerging from the pass and arraying his army for battle before the city gates. Perhaps parts of the Syrian and Canaanite armies were away defending other approaches and did not make it back to the city in time to participate in the battle. At any rate, the forces that did confront Thutmose were defeated outside the gates and had to be hauled up the walls into the city by the inhabitants. Eventually, Megiddo capitulated. In a later campaign, Thutmose carried boats on oxcarts from Byblos to the Euphrates River. Able to move troops up and down the upper part of the river, where it bisected the Mitanni Kingdom, he was able to campaign in the western half of Mitanni and wage war in Syria and Canaan while blocking Mitanni support from coming across the river.

The most famous battle of ancient Egyptian history is that between Ramesses II and his Hittite counterpart, Muwatallis II, at Kadesh on the Orontes River in Syria in about 1274 BC. Driving his army into Syria for an encounter with the Hittites, Ramesses foolishly believed a report from two captured men that the Hittites were still far away. (They were in fact concealed behind the city of Kadesh.) The Egyptian army was attacked while its leading units, including the pharaoh, were making camp; the rest of the Egyptian army was still on the march. Pharaoh's forces in the vanguard managed to hold off the enemy

Recorded on the interior walls of the first hall of the Ramesses II temple at Abu Simbel, Egypt, the massive Egyptian army maneuvers their horses and chariots in preparation for invading Kadesh.

until the remainder of his army arrived, and disaster was averted. The battle ended as something of a Hittite victory. (Ramesses failed to take Kadesh, and Egyptian power was confined to the area of Canaan, having been driven from Syria.) Even so, the pharaoh claimed to have won a great victory through his personal prowess in battle.

Ramesses III, in the eighth year of his reign, had his greatest victory in a battle fought on the northern frontier of Egypt itself. He repulsed the Sea Peoples, who had attacked Egypt with a combined sea and land invasion. He thus saved Egypt from foreign domination. This great victory included a rare example of a sea battle fought by the ancient Egyptians. They used boats as rapid transports for their troops, but these were mostly river craft used on the Nile for the rapid deployment of forces. But Ramesses had to fight ship-to-ship battles against the Sea Peoples.

Other sources offer information about Egyptian warfare. Horemheb, the last pharaoh of the Eighteenth Dynasty, issued a decree that tells us something about Egyptian military administration. Also, officers in the Egyptian army sometimes had their tombs inscribed with accounts of their bravery in battle. Finally, Egyptian artwork and artifacts, principally from tombs, gives us a better understanding of Egypt's military. Several chariots, for example, were found in tombs.

ORGANIZATION

The pharaoh was the supreme commander of the armed forces and, if he was a vigorous ruler, would personally lead his army into battle. The vizier (the pharaoh's highest-ranking administrator) was in effect his chief of staff, and he might command the army in the field as the pharaoh's representative. Officers were chiefly drawn from the aristocracy; the lowest-ranking officer, perhaps analogous to a lieutenant, was a commander of fifty.

Egypt's military exploits were not limited to land battles. Egyptian seagoing ship (model) of the Old Kingdom (2500 BC); reconstructed according to a relief found in the pyramid of Pharaoh Sahu-Re at Abusir, one of the oldest reliefs showing details of a seagoing ship.

Common soldiers were conscripted from the peasant classes (about one man in ten might serve time in the army). Foreigners might also serve in Egypt's army. The army of Ramesses II was organized into four divisions of 5,000 men. Each division was named for a god (Ptah, Re, Seth, and Amun), and a fifth division was under the pharaoh's direct command.[1] Divisions were subdivided into smaller units, down to the fifty-man platoon. Chariots were organized into squadrons of twenty-five.

WEAPONRY

Prior to the New Kingdom, Egyptian foot soldiers were all light infantry, having no armor except for rawhide shields and using short spears as their offensive weapons. Archers had simple, primitive longbows. By the time of the New Kingdom, leather body armor (with some metal attached); helmets; and short, bronze, scimitar-like swords were in use. The archers, now armed with more powerful composite bows, were a military force to be reckoned with. Still, they were not heavy infantry such as would later be part of the Greek phalanx or the Roman legion. The Egyptian army was a rapid strike force that relied on its chariots and archers.

The Egyptian war chariot first came into use during the New Kingdom; other great powers, such as the Hittite Empire, also employed massed chariots at this time. The

Relief from the funerary temple of Hatshepsut at Thebes. The image depicts two sailors in the royal Egyptian navy. The first sailor is equipped with a battle-ax and a fan-shaped military standard. The second is also armed with the same type of battle-ax.

two-horse war chariot had two wheels and a crew of two: a driver and a shield bearer. The driver approached the enemy and then fired arrows; he might use a javelin or sword at closer quarters. The chariot was of light wickerwork and designed for speed; it was not armored. The massed chariot attack was meant to terrify the lightly armed foot soldiers who opposed it. Centuries later, when infantry was more heavily armored and was disciplined to hold its ranks, the chariot became obsolete.

Egyptians did not use a cavalry but employed mounted troops as scouts. Exodus 14:5 suggests such scouts were shadowing the Israelites as they departed. The Bible also indicates that Egyptian infantry set out with the chariot corps in pursuit of the Hebrews (v. 6), but no infantry appear to have been present when the chariots were destroyed at the sea (v. 23). Perhaps they were trailing behind the mounted forces and only arrived after the debacle.

TACTICS

The Egyptian military typically arrayed themselves for battle as a main body with a wing on each side. Such maneuvering, however, would not have been employed while pursuing a large body of refugees, as the Israelites were.

The New Kingdom Egyptians' preferred tactic apparently was to make a rapid strike with their chariot forces. They never developed the slow and methodical art of siege warfare, and evidence from the battles at Megiddo and Kadesh suggests they could be bold to the point of recklessness. This is consonant with what we see in Exodus 14, where they rush into the sea without pausing to ask whether this was a sound idea. Under normal circumstances, the Israelites would have been no match for the Egyptian chariots. Being untrained peasants who only days before had been working as slaves, the Hebrews would have scattered like fallen leaves in a storm before a properly executed Egyptian attack.

VALOR AND MORALE

The Egyptians highly valued personal courage. A soldier who showed valor in battle would be awarded the "golden flies," a military decoration analogous to modern medals for bravery. More than that, he would receive wealth and slaves as his share of the booty. A certain Ahmose son of Abana, on the wall of a rock-cut tomb, left an account of his deeds of valor and of the honors he received while under the service of early Eighteenth Dynasty pharaohs. Another soldier, named Amenemhab, told of his many battles while campaigning with Thutmose III, and he especially made a point of describing how often he was in hand-to-hand combat.[2]

Egyptian commanders also bolstered the morale of their men by speaking of how their gods fought for them. They might call upon Montu, the Egyptian war god, but during the New Kingdom they extolled the all-conquering power of Amun.

Most importantly, the pharaohs of the New Kingdom personally boosted their troops' and the nation's morale by assuming the role of military hero. Thutmose III, in the Megiddo narrative, is bold and resolute where his general staff is timid and conventional. Ramesses II, in the account of his action at Kadesh, is positively Herculean, single-handedly slaying the enemy hordes while his confused soldiers seek to recover and reorganize themselves. The iconography of the time, portraying the pharaoh as a gigantic figure striding in to vanquish Lilliputian enemies, is the ultimate piece of morale-building propaganda: Egypt is invincible because the pharaoh is invincible.[3]

Relief at Medinet Habu depicts the army of Ramesses III as they prepare for battle with the Sea Peoples.

EGYPTIAN ÉLAN AT THE RED SEA

From the above discussion, one may suggest that a central feature of the New Kingdom Egyptian army, and especially of its chariot corps, was the high value it placed upon élan. This was a particular kind of courage that enabled someone to charge headlong into the thick of battle. It was also a tactic designed to force the outcome of battle by overwhelming the enemy with the sheer audacity of one's attack. Alexander the Great and Napoleon, both great captains, employed this strategy. It was more than a tactic; it was for certain armies their central creed. The New Kingdom Egyptian army belonged in this class. The officially cultivated faith in Amun and his pharaoh, the examples set by Thutmose III at Megiddo and by Ramesses II at Kadesh, the recognition Egyptians gave to the valor of individual soldiers, and the nature of the war chariot as a weapon of shock attack all suggest that devotion to élan was central to Egypt's military culture. But as a military philosophy, élan had a major drawback, as the Romans under Caesar demonstrated when they were attacked by Gallic warriors rushing madly upon them, screaming and swinging their broadswords. When the legions held their lines in the face of these onslaughts, the élan of the Gauls was quickly transformed into terror and chaotic flight, and Caesar rapidly conquered all of Gaul. Therefore, the Bible credibly describes both the Egyptians' furious rush into the sea and their subsequent panic when they realized God was fighting for Israel (Exod. 14:25).

NOTES

[1] The figure of 5,000 men per division is based on a comment in Papyrus Anastasi I, but whether that represents the standard size for an Egyptian division at the time is open to question. It may have been smaller. See Anthony J. Spalinger, *War in Ancient Egypt: The New Kingdom* (Oxford: Blackwell, 2005), 149–50.

[2] For the inscriptions of Ahmose son of Abana and of Amenemhab, see James Henry Breasted, *Ancient Records of Egypt*, vol. 2 (Chicago: University of Chicago Press, 1906), 3–18, 227–34.

[3] For descriptions of the Egyptian military, see esp. Spalinger; also Rosalie David, *Handbook to Life in Ancient Egypt* (New York: Facts on File, 1998), 225–54.

THE PHILISTINES

BY CLAUDE F. MARIOTTINI

Ruins of a collapsed tower at Ashkelon.

A few years after the Israelites conquered their land, a group of people invaded Canaan and settled along the coastal plain between Joppa and the desert area south of Gaza. These people became known as the Philistines. They became the rulers of five cities—Gaza, Ashdod, Ashkelon, Ekron, and Gath—known collectively as the Philistine pentapolis.

EARLY HISTORY

The words *Philistines* and *Philistia* appear more than 250 times in the Old Testament. Archaeological evidence and what the Bible says about the culture and social organization of the Philistines provide evidence of their foreign origin. Archaeologists believe the Philistines came from the eastern Mediterranean area, but their original homeland and migration route are unclear. The Philistines came to Canaan with the migration of the Sea Peoples. According to Amos 9:7 and Jeremiah 47:4, the Philistines came from Caphtor, that is, Crete. Some of the Philistines may have come from Asia Minor. If this is true, their civilization had a large Carian (from southwest Anatolia) element. The Cherethites and the Pelethites of 2 Samuel 8:18 were mercenaries who served as David's bodyguards. Scholars believe the Cherethites were Cretan mercenaries and that the Pelethites referred to the Philistines.

The Philistines appear in Egyptian documents as the Pelasata. In one of these documents dated to the reign of Ramesses III (ca 1183–1152 BC), Ramesses mentioned a naval battle that took place at the mouth of the Nile in which the Egyptians fought a coalition of Sea Peoples. Among the Sea Peoples who invaded Egypt, Ramesses III mentions the Shakarusha, the Pelasata, the Danuna, and others.[1]

In describing his struggle against the Sea Peoples, Ramesses said the Sea Peoples came from isles in the midst of the sea and that they advanced against Egypt, relying on their iron weapons. Images on the walls of Ramesses's temple at Medinet Habu depict the Philistines as armed with swords and round shields. A few soldiers wore what looked like laminated corselets. The Philistine soldiers' headgear was topped with feathers.[2]

In his account of the battle, Ramesses declared he was victorious in his struggle against the invaders and took many prisoners. Although Ramesses claimed victory over the Sea Peoples, the attack weakened Egypt. Unable to defeat the invaders completely, Ramesses had to make an alliance with the Philistines.

Ramesses allowed the Philistines to settle in the eastern Mediterranean coast. He made them his vassals and employed many of the conquered soldiers as mercenaries and placed them in the garrisons on the borders of the empire. The Philistine territory went from the northwestern Negev north to the city of Ekron and from the Mediterranean Sea to the western slopes of Judah.[3] As the Philistines began settling into Canaan, they were still under Egyptian control. After Ramesses's death, Egypt's power in Canaan waned and Ramesses's successors were unable to regain control of Canaan. Exploiting Egypt's political weakness, the Philistines eventually gained their independence. From the end of the twelfth and through the eleventh centuries, the Philistines expanded their presence in Canaan and consolidated their power by assimilating the culture and language of Canaan's indigenous people.[4]

Ruins at Gaza.

Silver coin from Aradus (on the Phoenician coast) depicting the Philistine god Dagon and a ship.

IN SCRIPTURE

The Philistines appear in the Bible as Israel's enemy. During the period of the judges, the Philistines were already a menace to the Israelites. In the days of Shamgar, who was one of Israel's minor judges, the Israelites were already fighting the Philistines. Shamgar delivered Israel by killing 600 Philistines with a cattle prod (Judg. 3:31). Samson judged Israel for twenty years at the time the Philistines were expanding their power in Canaan, but he was unable to defeat them (15:20). The Philistines defeated the Israelites and captured the ark of the covenant at Ebenezer and took it to Ashdod, where the temple of Dagon, the primary Philistine god, was located (1 Sam. 5:1–2). After this battle, the Philistines extended their presence in Canaan, moving into the central mountain range.

After Samson died, the Danites, under pressure from the Philistines, had to migrate from the territory Joshua had allotted to them. One of the cities allotted to the tribe of Dan was Ekron (Josh. 19:43), a city that eventually became one of the five cities in the Philistine pentapolis (13:3). The Danites moved from the Shephelah to the northernmost part of Canaan where they conquered Laish, a Canaanite city, and renamed it Dan (18:27–29).

Anthropoid coffin from ancient Gaza, thirteenth century BC.

The book of 1 Samuel indicates the Philistines increased the number of settlements they controlled. They influenced and controlled the northern Negev and were present in much of the territory that belonged to the tribes of Simeon, Judah, and Dan (prior to the Danites' relocation). Israel established the monarchy in order to deal with the threat the Philistines posed as they expanded into the central mountain range. Years later in a battle on Mount Gilboa, the Philistines defeated Israel's army and killed Israel's King Saul and his sons Jonathan, Abinadab, and Malchishua (1 Sam. 31:2). The Philistines desecrated Saul's body by cutting off his head and hanging his body on the walls of Beth-shean (vv. 9–10).

PHILISTINES IN ZEPHANIAH

Zephaniah used the seventh-century political situation and couched his words in the language of the conquest of Canaan. He saw Judah's enemies as Canaanites. Philistia was to receive the same fate as the Canaanites and lose its inhabitation by conquest and complete annihilation. The Philistines were in the land God promised to Israel, but they did not belong there; so, like the Canaanites of old, the Philistines would be eradicated. The Philistine cities would be depleted of their residents, and Judean shepherds would live there instead (Zeph. 2:6–7). Zephaniah's words found fulfillment when the Babylonians invaded Canaan.[5] In 604 BC, Nebuchadnezzar conquered the four Philistine cities and deported their kings to Babylon. As Zephaniah had predicted, the conquest of the four Philistine cities was the end of Philistia as a political entity.

NOTES

1. John Bright, *A History of Israel* (Philadelphia: Westminster, 1981), 174.
2. R. K. Harrison, "Philistines" in *NIDBA*, 362–63.
3. G. Ernest Wright, "Fresh Evidence for the Philistine Story," *BA* 29 (September 1966): 69–86.
4. Bright, *History of Israel*, 176.
5. Kenneth A. Kitchen, "The Philistines" in *People of Old Testament Times*, ed. D. J. Wiseman (Oxford: Clarendon, 1973), 67.

PILATE'S ROLE IN JESUS'S DEATH

BY THOMAS H. GOODMAN

The "Ecce Homo" arch spans the Via Dolorosa in Jerusalem. It marks the traditional spot where Pilate presented Jesus to the crowds and said, "Here is the man!" (Ecce homo in Latin; John 19:5).

Pilate's encounter with Jewish leadership at Jesus's trial was not the Roman governor's first experience navigating the complexities of Judean politics. Extrabiblical references to Pilate reveal a leader who became vulnerable to the emperor's criticism as Pilate proved himself increasingly incapable of providing regional stability. This vulnerability was a factor in how he handled Jesus's trial. Pilate should have upheld Roman justice and released Jesus. In the end, however, Pilate did what was best for Pilate.

In Jesus's day, Judea was under the governance of Roman procurators, a role in which Pilate served from AD 26 to 36. A procurator was a governor whom the emperor appointed directly; he was to manage the military, financial, and judicial operations of strategically sensitive regions of the Roman Empire.[1] The Roman government established a procurator's residence at the harbor city of Caesarea Maritima, located on the Mediterranean coast.

FIVE INCIDENTS

Five incidents reported in biblical and extrabiblical sources set the context for the accounts of Pilate's involvement with Jesus's crucifixion.[2] The first incident took place immediately after his being appointed governor. The Jewish historian Josephus reports that Pilate's soldiers posted standards bearing the emperor's image within sight of the temple in Jerusalem. Regarding the act as idolatrous, the Jews demanded the standards be removed. When Pilate threatened them with execution, the protestors bared their necks in defiant willingness to die rather than back down. Pilate was the one to back down. He removed the standards to Caesarea Maritima.

In the second incident, Pilate killed some Galileans who were offering sacrifices (Luke 13:1). We have no explanation about what provoked the killing, but the incident illustrates the occasionally tumultuous relationship between Pilate and his subjects.

Third, Pilate used money from the temple treasury to construct an aqueduct. The Jews objected to what they regarded as sacrilege of the temple offerings, and Pilate had the protestors beaten into subjection.

Fourth, according to the Jewish philosopher Philo, Pilate had votive shields hung in Herod's Jerusalem palace. Some believe the shields bore the name of the emperor as a deity. Regardless, the Jews found the shields to be offensive and appealed directly to Tiberius Caesar when Pilate refused to respond to their objections. Tiberius ordered that Pilate remove the shields to Caesarea Maritima and reprimanded his procurator for the unnecessary controversy.

Fifth, Josephus reports that Pilate ordered the execution of a number of Samaritan villagers who had followed a rebellious leader to Mount Gerizim. Hearing of this, Tiberius recalled Pilate to Rome in AD 36 and replaced him with Marcellus.

These five incidents provide a helpful context for understanding Pilate's role in Jesus's death. Three leadership patterns that Pilate displayed in these historical records also show up in the records of Jesus's trial: general incompetence, vacillation, and vulnerability to imperial criticism.

THREE LEADERSHIP PATTERNS

First, Pilate was out of his depth trying to introduce Roman rule into the politically volatile province of Judea. He "displayed a general lack of sensitivity, tact, and knowledge" with the strange subjects he ruled.[3] In Jesus's trial, Pilate sought to maintain standards of Roman jurisprudence, yet he could not understand why his efforts to release the innocent man ended up raising the threat of revolt in Jerusalem. After his attempt to shift the decision to Herod (Luke 23:5–15), to satisfy the bloodlust by a flogging (Luke 23:16), and then to offer the crowd Jesus for Barabbas (Matt. 27:15–21), he still faced an unruly mob. Unable to uphold Roman judicial standards and maintain order at the same time, he yielded to the easiest course to stability and gave Jesus up.

Second, Pilate tended toward vacillation. He posted the military standards and later the votive shields in an apparent declaration of his intent to exert Roman rule, only to waver

The harbor at Caesarea Maritima. Herod the Great acquired this region from Augustus Caesar in 30 BC and constructed a massive harbor and accompanying modern city, replete with opulent Hellenistic architecture. In AD 6, Caesarea became the capital of the province of Judea and the official home for those serving as governors.

quickly when things got complicated. This vacillating too showed up in Jesus's trial. Seven times in John 18:28–19:16, Pilate alternately went out to speak with the crowd and went in to speak with Jesus. That physical back-and-forth parallels what must have been his mental back-and-forth. On the one hand, after investigating Jesus, he knew that to kill him would be an abdication of the justice he was responsible to uphold. On the other hand, he knew that to release Jesus would so upset the turbulent crowd that the region could erupt in revolt.

Third, the extrabiblical and biblical sources display a procurator who was vulnerable to the waning favor of the emperor. In the incident with the votive shields, Philo reports that when the Jews complained to Tiberius, the emperor wrote Pilate, "reproaching and reviling him in the most bitter manner for his act of unprecedented audacity and wickedness, and commanding him immediately to take down the shields." In Jesus's trial, the Jewish leadership played on this vulnerability, saying, "If you release this man, you are not Caesar's friend" (John 19:12). After receiving previous imperial reprimands, Pilate had no motivation for defending Jesus if doing so meant losing the peace—and his job. Pilate's motivation for his decision was simple: he wanted "to satisfy the crowd" (Mark 15:15).

NOTES

[1]   David S. Dockery, ed., *Holman Bible Handbook* (Nashville: Holman, 1992), 628.

[2]   The ancient Jewish writers Josephus and Philo are the sources for the extrabiblical stories about Pilate. The first account is found in Josephus, *Jewish Antiquities* 18.3.1, and Josephus, *Jewish War* 2.9.2–4. The third appears in Josephus, *Jewish Antiquities* 18.3.2. The fourth in Philo, *On the Embassy to Gaius* 38.299–305. The fifth, Josephus, *Jewish Antiquities* 18.4.1–2.

[3]   Brian C. McGing, "Pontius Pilate and the Sources," *Catholic Biblical Quarterly (CBQ)* 53.3 (1991): 438.

THE POLITICAL CLIMATE FOR MICAH

BY R. KELVIN MOORE

Underground water system at Hazor built in the ninth century BC and in use until the Assyrians conquered Hazor in 732 BC.

Micah dated his ministry during the reigns of Kings Jotham, Ahaz, and Hezekiah (Mic. 1:1), who ruled from about 740 to 686 BC. Between 740 and 700 BC, the Assyrians (mentioned in 5:6; 7:12) invaded Israel repeatedly. Much of Micah's ministry dates before the destruction of Samaria (1:6) or 722 BC. Isaiah and Micah, contemporaries, both preached to the southern kingdom of Judah.

The rise and fall of the Assyrian Empire played a major role in Judah's economic prosperity and political stability in the eighth century BC. The death of King Shalmaneser III in 824 BC led to a period of decline for Assyria that lasted almost one hundred years. Judah benefited from the decline economically and politically. But the political climate changed during the reign of the Assyrian King Tiglath-pileser III (745–727 BC, called Pul in 2 Kgs. 15:19), whose military and administrative policies led to the rise and dominance of the Assyrian Empire.[1] Tiglath-pileser had conquered all of northern Syria by 740 BC. His policies of aggression threatened other nations, including Judah and Israel.

Judah's political health in the time of Isaiah and Micah can be summarized in one word: crisis. Within an approximate thirty-five-year period, Isaiah and Micah ministered during three national crises, any of which could have led to Judah's destruction. Scholars refer to these as the Syro-Ephraimitic crisis (734 BC), when Israel and Judah lost their independence; the Ashdod Rebellion (711 BC), when Hezekiah was forced to pay Assyria

Relief from Nimrud showing women prisoners leading camels captured by Tiglath-pileser III (744–727 BC).

a heavy fine; and the Sennacherib crisis (701 BC), resulting in deliverance but another heavy fine.

The Syro-Ephraimitic crisis[2] (Isa. 7:1ff) began as Israel's King Pekah and Syria's King Rezin recognized the danger posed by the rise of Assyria. Pekah and Rezin formed a military alliance against Assyria. Pekah and Rezin knew if they could coax Judah's King Ahaz to join the alliance, they would strengthen their armies. King Ahaz, though, refused to join. Pekah and Rezin invaded Judah. Simplicity marked Pekah and Rezin's plan: they intended to dethrone Ahaz and place a puppet king on the throne. Isaiah encouraged Ahaz to trust the Lord. Ahaz's response must have disappointed Isaiah and Micah. Instead of trusting God for protection, Ahaz requested assistance from Assyria! Tiglath-pileser III eagerly assisted Ahaz, but the aid did not come cheaply. To pay tribute, Ahaz depleted his treasuries and stripped the temple (2 Kgs. 16:5–9,17–20). Additionally, Judah became an Assyrian vassal (2 Chr. 28:20–21).

Taylor Prism, a terracotta foundation document describing Sennacherib's campaigns, including his siege of Jerusalem in 701 BC.

Encouraged by the surging Egyptian Empire, several nations that had become vassals of Assyria organized a rebellion against Assyria's King Sargon II (722–705 BC). Bible scholars refer to this as the Ashdod Rebellion because the inhabitants of Ashdod spearheaded the insurrection. Sargon II, at the pinnacle of power, reacted with swift and lethal force that shattered the rebels. Little doubt exists that without another intervention of the Lord, had Judah chosen to participate in the Ashdod Rebellion, the nation would have suffered the same disastrous fate.

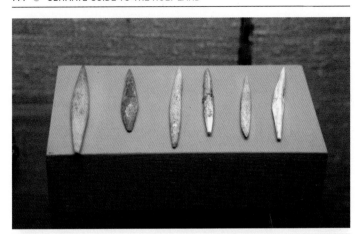

Bone arrowheads used at Lachish during Sennacherib's siege when iron became scarce.

In 704 BC, Sennacherib succeeded Sargon II. Evidently Judah's King Hezekiah believed that a new king on the Assyrian throne offered the best opportunity for rebellion. In what has become known as the Sennacherib crisis, Hezekiah led Judah to rebel against Assyria (2 Kgs. 18:13–19:37; Isa. 36:1–37:38). Sennacherib marched toward Judah. Isaiah encouraged Hezekiah that, because the Assyrians had taunted God, Sennacherib would never capture Jerusalem (37:5–7). As Isaiah prophesied, 185,000 Assyrian soldiers perished in a single night. Sennacherib retreated. Although Sennacherib reigned for an additional twenty years, he never returned to Jerusalem.

Considering the political stability and economic prosperity of the latter half of the eighth century BC, one might expect spiritual conditions resembling a revival. Nothing could be further from the truth. Judah was in a state of spiritual decay. Worship was ritualistic, devoid of repentance and genuineness. The Hebrews severed their Sabbath worship from their weekly living. In essence, many of the Hebrews said, "I have sacrificed on the Sabbath and can live any way I choose during the week." The Hebrews evidently were "long on religion and short on morality."[3] Micah prophesied the destruction of Judah: "Zion will be plowed like a field, Jerusalem will become ruins, and the temple's mountain will be a high thicket" (Mic. 3:12). With such religious insensitivity, little wonder that Judah, a little more than a hundred years after the prophets Isaiah and Micah, experienced God's displeasure. The Babylonians destroyed much of Judah and Jerusalem in 586 BC.

NOTES

1   Daniel C. Browning Jr. and Brian Stachowski, "Assyria" in HIBD, rev. ed. (2015), 138–39.

2   Scholars so name this crisis because of Isaiah 7:2: "And it was told the house of David [nation of Judah], saying, Syria is confederate with Ephraim" (KJV). "Syro" symbolized Syria and "Ephraim" symbolized Israel. Thus "Syro-Ephraimitic" symbolizes the combined forces of Syria and Israel.

3   Alec Motyer, *Isaiah: An Introduction and Commentary* (Downers Grove, IL: InterVarsity, 1999), 45. Motyer wrote that we can "pray on Sunday and prey on our neighbours for the rest of the week," 46.

PROPHET, PRIEST, AND KING

BY W. WAYNE VANHORN

Fig tree in modern Anathoth, hometown of Jeremiah, about three miles northeast of Jerusalem.

During the historical period covered by 1 and 2 Kings, approximately 970–586 BC, the prophets, priests, and kings led their covenant people at various times and in different ways. Of these three groups, the kings assumed the greatest leadership role due to the coercive nature of political power when aligned with military force, not to mention the people's voluntary submission in asking for a king. The priests performed religious duties related to the temple or other shrines. The individual prophets were active in inverse proportion to the righteous actions of the kings. When the kings sinned against the Lord by violating his covenant instruction, the prophets appeared to confront the kings and to pronounce judgment if repentance did not ensue.[1]

THE PROPHETS

During this period, Israel witnessed three types of prophets: the individual prophets, who confronted the sins of kings and people; the institutional prophets, who basically served as yes-men for the kings; and the prophetic guilds, called twelve times in 1 and 2 Kings "the sons of the prophets" (2 Kgs. 2:5). A group of "the sons of the prophets" resided at Bethel and another at Jericho (vv. 3,5). The latter group had at least fifty men (v. 7). Some of "the sons of the prophets" were married (4:1). We know little else of these groups except their submission to the preeminence of Elisha.

In Jordan, this area west of Ajloun is called Mar Elias, which is Arabic for Saint Elijah. Tradition has long associated this area with Tishbe, hometown of Elijah.

Noteworthy individual prophets featured in 1 and 2 Kings include Ahijah, Jehu, Elijah, Elisha, Micaiah, and Isaiah. By far the most important prophets of 1 and 2 Kings were Elijah and Elisha, whose stories dominate from 1 Kings 17 through 2 Kings 13. God commissioned these individual prophets to denounce the sins of the kings and their people and to warn them of the grave consequences for their covenant violations as stipulated in the Law.

THE PRIESTS

The priesthood originally held an important place in the covenant community. The priests were responsible for maintaining the religious shrines, whether the tabernacle in the wilderness or the temple in Jerusalem.[2] The priests also had to educate the covenant people in the instruction Moses received on Mount Sinai (called the Torah). Historically however, the priesthood became an establishment answerable to the king.

THE KINGS

The most significant theological truth about the period of the kings is that only nine of the forty-one kings "did what was right in the LORD's sight" (1 Kgs. 15:5). The most notable example of these good kings was David. He became the proverbial measuring stick by which all other kings were assessed. When the Lord informed Jeroboam he would be king of Israel, Ahijah the prophet commended him to do what was right "as my servant David did" (11:38).

NOTES

1 See Paul R. House, *1, 2 Kings*, vol. 8 in NAC.
2 R. Laird Harris, "Priests" in *HIBD*, 1328.

THE RICH AND THE POOR IN THE FIRST CENTURY: A CONTRAST

BY MONA STEWART

Overview of ruins at Hamat Gader (meaning "Hot Springs of Gadara"), southeast of the Sea of Galilee on the Yarmuk River. Jews drawn to the area for the springs' medicinal benefits built a synagogue, the floors of which were carpeted with decorative mosaics. One of the mosaics asks God's blessings on a group of wealthy contributors "whose acts of charity are constant everywhere and who have given here five coins of gold. May the King of the Universe bestow the blessing upon their work. Amen. Amen. Selah."

Greek ostracon (piece of broken pottery with writing) reads, "Give to Tatris in Mesore for her wage one artabas (of wheat)." An artabas is approximately ten gallons.

In the first century, the orphan and the widow were in the lowest economic class and most in need of aid. The rich and powerful took advantage of those who had no social or economic status. The court system often defrauded the poor. To be poor implied the person was both impoverished and wrongly oppressed.[1]

"In the first Christian century, one out of three persons in Italy and one out of five elsewhere was a slave."[2] Yet not all slaves fit in the same category as the poor. Roman masters provided their household slaves with food, clothing, and shelter. Some even provided them with an education. Most of the free poor, however, existed with meager sustenance and often struggled to find even the barest of essentials.

Often the poor were tenant farmers indebted to absentee rich landowners. Crop failure meant losing everything. Their meager homes, food, and clothing indicated an impoverished lifestyle. The basic diet was bread (made of barley), wine, and olive oil, supplemented with porridge and fish. Providing their families a mere existence was a daily chore.

In contrast, the rich enjoyed large dwellings, excessive and expensive clothing, and the finest food available. They enjoyed three meals daily while the poor were fortunate to have one. The evening meal often consisted of multiple courses. Jewelry was plentiful and ostentatious; both males and females wore rings on many fingers.

Large bathhouses could accommodate thousands at a time. Hot and cold baths were available after which slaves provided massages. Gymnasiums were often located close to the baths and provided another luxury exclusively for the rich. Brothels were plentiful and frequented by the affluent males.

Music, large libraries, and theaters helped fill part of the leisure time of the wealthy. Ruins of theaters built into the side of a hill or mountain stand all over Europe, Asia Minor, and Israel today testifying to the opulent lifestyle. These structures could seat many thousands and had excellent acoustics. The sections down front were reserved for the wealthy while the upper sections were for the common people. This was important because people often used theaters to promote and spread political propaganda. Excavations of towns and villages have yielded large marketplaces with stalls for various crafts—stalls owned predominantly by the rich.

The children and often the slaves of the wealthy received an education. An educated slave would later become the teacher for the next generation of children. "The poor had neither the time, the money, nor the need for an education."[3]

Funerals for the rich and powerful were grand and opulent affairs. Paid musicians and mourners accompanied the family and friends to the burial site. The tombs of the wealthy were elaborate. While alive, the rich would have great monuments built to honor them after death. The funerals of the poor were simple affairs usually held outside the towns and villages.

NOTES

[1]　Gary V. Smith, "Poor, Orphan, Widow" in *HIBD*, 1311.

[2]　James A. Brooks, "Slave, Servant" in *HIBD*, 1511.

[3]　John McRay "Rome and the Roman Empire" in *HolBD*, 1212.

ROBBERS

BY TIMOTHY TRAMMELL

Close-up of Herod the Great's tomb, which was discovered in 2007 on the side of the Herodium, which is eight miles south of Jerusalem. During Herod the Great's reign, both theft and the number of bandit groups increased.

The Greek word for *robber* primarily describes the armed bands of brigands who were intentionally brutal in carrying out their activities. These were marauders who usually operated outdoors, attacking caravans and individual travelers. Jesus set the scene of his parable of the good Samaritan east of Jerusalem in the rugged Judean hills. The robbers, usually in sizable bands, would often use such terrain as their hunting ground. Consequently the wise traveler would seek safety in numbers, especially if he was carrying goods or valuables, for the violent nature of these bands was well known.

Another aspect of these robber bands is also significant. The Jewish people were under the domination of the Roman Empire in the first century. Both the Roman overlords and the Jewish landowning elite exploited the peasants. Economic crises caused by famine, high taxation, and social injustice fostered the development of groups seeking to right these wrongs.[1] When foreign conquest was accompanied by the exactions of an unsympathetic ruling class, the rural people saw the bandits as their protectors.

To be more specific, the regressive policies of Herod the Great contributed to the rise of such groups. Although his reign brought an end to much of the political turmoil, his ambitious building projects, with Rome's excessive taxation, made the people's poverty more severe. Payments to the Romans were a continuing burden, as were tithes for the priesthood and the temple in Jerusalem. Josephus records that upon Herod's death, the Jewish aristocracy pleaded with Caesar for a change from "kingly government." They told

Dated to Egypt's Nineteenth-Twentieth Dynasties (1295-1069 BC); a limestone ostracon from Thebes inscribed with a letter. In it, the writer denies stealing precious objects that had belonged to the pharaoh and begs to be released from the imposed penalty of forced labor.

of the multitudes that had perished during his reign, of the estates he had stolen, and that he had "filled the nation with the utmost degree of poverty."[2] The nobility suffered at the hands of Herod—and the poor even more so. Such injustice had forced some people to look to robber bands for redress.

The first half of the first century was marked by famine, inflation, high taxation, and theft of the people's land. Consequently banditry escalated to epidemic proportions. This growth had its beginning in approximately AD 6 with the activities of Judas of Galilee. In discussing the various parties in Judaism, Josephus recorded that Judas founded "the fourth sect of Jewish philosophy"; also known as the "Fourth Philosophy,"[3] this was foundational to what followed, namely the Jewish rebellion or revolt against Rome.

The Jewish rebellion brought with it an explosion of banditry. Many of these bands operated for only a brief time, for banditry was a lonely profession, away from family and society at large. In addition, most procurators made an intense effort to capture and punish these lawbreakers.

NOTES

[1]   Richard A. Horsley and John S. Hanson, *Bandits, Prophets, and Messiahs* (San Francisco: Harper & Row, 1985), 49–50.

[2]   Josephus, *Jewish Antiquities* 17.11.2.

[3]   Josephus, *Jewish Antiquities* 18.1.6.

THE ROLE OF A ROMAN GOVERNOR

BY TIMOTHY TRAMMELL

Roman soldier figurine from the Greco-Roman period. Roman governors had both civil and military forces at their disposal.

Roman coin honoring Caesar Augustus.

When Jesus was born in Bethlehem, the Roman Empire had undisputed control of the Mediterranean world. The Roman governor was a crucial element in Rome's ability to control its provinces efficiently.

THE GOVERNOR AND THE PROVINCES

The Latin word *provincia* is a military expression indicating a particular region that was a general's responsibility. By the close of the First Punic War (241 BC), the Romans had conquered Sicily, which became Rome's first province. By the first Christian century, however, the empire consisted of more than thirty provinces. At first the provinces were ill defined geographically, but by the New Testament era they had come to have rather clearly defined boundaries.

Rome had two types of provinces, senatorial and imperial, designations Augustus Caesar introduced. A senatorial province was more peaceful, did not have legions stationed within its borders, and was governed by a proconsul—which the Senate appointed. The Greek term in the New Testament for a proconsul is *anthupatos*. Luke employed this designation for Sergius Paulus, governor of Cyprus (Acts 13:7), and Gallio, governor of Achaia (18:12). The town clerk of Ephesus used this noun when he quelled the riot during Paul's ministry there (19:38).

An imperial province was under the direct jurisdiction of the emperor and typically had a significant military force stationed within its borders. Technically the emperor himself would be the governor of such a province, but he delegated his authority to a personally appointed legate. Such a governor's official title was a *legatus propraetore Augusti*, "imperial legate of praetorian rank," or a *legatus Caesaris*, "legate of Caesar."[1] He would command the legion in addition to his other duties.

Occasionally the emperor had smaller provinces—yet nonetheless difficult ones—under his control. A procurator, sometimes called a prefect, governed such a province. Judea was one of these. The Synoptic Gospels use the Greek word *hegemon*, "governor," to designate Pontius Pilate as procurator of Judea.

THE GOVERNOR'S RESPONSIBILITIES

Although the primary task of the Roman governor was to maintain the peace, his powers were normally exercised in three areas—military, administrative, and judicial.

Military—The governor commanded the military forces in his province. In some provinces that was his sole responsibility. Controlling bands of robbers and conquered peoples was a necessary function, but how much attention this task required varied from place to place.

Administrative—The amount of time invested in administrative duties also varied in different provinces, with the personality of the governor serving as the determining factor. As one writer phrased it, "Its quantity depended on his view as to how far self-government was a symptom of health or of disease."[2] When Rome saw fit, they entrusted petty sovereigns with the day-to-day affairs of the region.

An important member of the governor's staff, a financial official called a *quaestor,* functioned as a sort of second in command. On behalf of the governor, he received credit or money from Rome for meeting the expenses of the province and supervised the collection of taxes. Since keeping records of financial matters was his responsibility, he gave an accounting annually in both his and the governor's name.

Judicial—In time of peace, most of the governors focused most of their energies on jurisdiction, both civil and criminal. The governor had access to a corpus called the Twelve Tables, a significant segment of Roman law that detailed all-important or disputed points and contained private, public, and criminal statutes.[3]

The governor could be as harsh and arbitrary in dealing with the ordinary person as he desired, just so he did not take money or property for himself. He consulted with a group of advisers before taking harsh action, but their counsel did not bind him.

Following a publicized schedule, the governor visited the cities in the province and held court in each one. Although he had the authority to hear any case, routine cases normally fell to the local judicial processes. The governor might choose to send major litigation—especially those involving treason and revolt—to Rome for trial. The governor had the sole right to inflict the death penalty, so he tried capital cases.

NOTES

[1]   William Smith, *Smith's Bible Dictionary* (Old Tappan, NJ: Revell, 1967), 579.

[2]   A. H. J. Greenidge, *Roman Public Life* (New York: Cooper Square, 1970), 324.

[3]   Greenidge, *Roman Public Life*, 105. See the extensive discussion of forensic topics on 325–30.

ROLES AND RESPONSIBILITIES OF PERSIAN QUEENS

BY MONA STEWART

Relief at Persepolis depicting the king, likely Darius the Great, seated on his throne. Dressed in full regalia, the king would have been receiving visiting dignitaries.

Kings had absolute power and their word was law. Queens had a major role and were second in rank only to the king. Kings often sought their wisdom in decision making. Polygamy was common; kings had large harems. Persian lineage was a requirement to become a Persian queen. Esther could not have become a queen had Mordecai not told her to keep her Jewish roots secret. Children born to concubines could not inherit the throne. Marriages often took place among relatives, even between brother and sister. Persians did not consider this improper or immoral but a way to keep the bloodline pure.

Many queens were indeed evil. The first Greek historian to write about Persia, Herodotus, relates how queens often killed anyone who might have stood in their way—including royal children. He further reported that the ancient Persians had no temples or gods other than nature. They worshipped the sun, moon, sky, earth, fire, wind, and water.[1] The story was told that when Xerxes's wife Amestris reached old age, she buried alive fourteen sons of notable Persians as a thank offering to the god of the nether world.[2]

Queens were secluded from the public and were often unaware of the world outside the palace. They lived in luxury, employed many maids and servants, and had their own royal guards. The queen's wardrobe consisted of royal robes and a crown.

Persians honored and revered women. Queens as well as noble women led military armies, owned land, and received equal pay for equal work. Many Persian women were both beautiful and strong. Queens were allowed to oversee property and supervise large workforces. They practiced hospitality by hosting banquets for the noble women. Their influence was felt throughout the empire. When Xerxes was informed that a woman named Artemisia, commander of a ship, had destroyed an enemy ship, he remarked, "My men have become women, and my women men."[3]

Museums house ancient objects that would have been common in the royal households of Persia, items such as rugs, jewelry, pottery, textiles, art, and golden dinnerware. Further, they display women's hairpieces and makeup, including eyeliners and red dye used for rouge and lip color. Archaeologists have also excavated intricately designed perfume bottles. Doubtless each of these items would have been familiar to Queen Esther.

NOTES

[1]   Herodotus, *Histories* 1.131.
[2]   Herodotus, *Histories* 7.114.
[3]   Herodotus, *Histories* 8.88.

ROMAN CITIZENSHIP: PRIVILEGES AND EXPECTATIONS

BY SHARON H. GRITZ

Toga-clad figure shows a man in the formal dress of the Romans in the first–second centuries AD. The toga, a large trapezoid cloth, typically wool, that wrapped around the whole person, was for citizens; they wore them over a tunica. Slaves typically wore only a tunica.

The Philippians lived in a city that was officially named both a Roman colony and an Italian city (*ius Italicum*).[1] These distinctions raised the status of this urban center and gave it a Roman flavor despite its being in a Greek province hundreds of miles from Rome. Paul reminded the Philippians that their citizenship was in heaven (Phil. 1:27; 3:20). Why did Paul choose the concept of citizenship in writing to the Philippians? What significance did Roman citizenship have in the first-century world?

BECOMING A ROMAN CITIZEN

An individual could become a Roman citizen in several ways. A child born to Roman citizens became one automatically. Initially, only freeborn natives of the city of Rome could be citizens. As the empire expanded beyond Italy, others who were not Roman by birth received this honor. A slave whose Roman-citizen owner awarded him his freedom (manumission) gained citizenship status. Rome also granted this honor to people who performed some valuable service benefiting Roman interests.[2] For example, Rome granted citizenship to auxiliary soldiers who served in the Roman army for twenty-five years. Groups of people were declared citizens all at once through the colonization of their town or its promotion to Latin rights.

The ancient historian Dio Cassius (ca. AD 150–235) stated that citizenship could be purchased, especially during the reign of Claudius (AD 41–54), who continued the practice begun under Caesar Augustus.[3] Actually, persons could not purchase citizenship, but they could pay bribes to lesser officials to add their names to a list of

Emperor Trajan (ruled AD 98–117) issued this bronze military diploma to Reburrus, a Spanish junior officer in the First Pannonian Cavalry regiment. It granted him citizenship and the right to marry; dated AD 103.

candidates for citizenship. Evidently, the tribune Claudius Lysias obtained his citizenship in this way (Acts 22:28).

ADVANTAGES AND RESPONSIBILITIES OF CITIZENSHIP

Being a citizen of Rome made a person a member of the ruling power. Wherever they traveled throughout the empire, citizens were allowed all the rights and privileges of Roman law. Citizenship shaped every area of life. Citizens received better treatment than noncitizens in family matters, such as getting married, having children, and making wills, and in business concerns, such as holding property and making contracts.

Citizens had advantages in legal concerns involving courts, custody, and punishments. For instance, citizens accused of any crime had the right to a fair and public trial. They also could appeal to Rome. This exempted a person from having to leave final control of his case in the hands of local authorities. Paul claimed this right when he appealed to Caesar while stating his case before Festus, the local Roman governor (25:10–12).

Authorities could not use shameful forms of punishment against Roman citizens. This included scourging and death by crucifixion. The Philippian magistrates became alarmed when they learned that Paul and Silas were Roman citizens after they had publicly beaten and thrown into prison without a trial (16:22–39). Rome did punish some cities for such crimes; the most serious penalty was causing them to lose their Roman rights.[4] The early traditions regarding the deaths of Paul and Peter reflect their different citizenship status. Paul, the Roman citizen, was said to have been beheaded. The law considered such a quick death to be merciful and thus proper for a citizen of Rome. In contrast, Peter, the noncitizen, was reportedly crucified upside down.[5]

Generally, authorities used torture when questioning slaves and noncitizens who had been accused of committing some crime; Roman citizens could not receive such treatment. Only the imperial court in Rome could impose the death penalty on a citizen.

Citizens were responsible for all the civic duties Roman law imposed. During the Roman Republic (509–27 BC), citizens had to serve in the army. With the beginning of the Principate or early part of the empire, though, "the onerous military duty of Roman citizens was greatly lessened by the general shift to a volunteer, professional army."[6]

Citizens enjoyed the right to vote, although they had to be in Rome to exercise this privilege. Some individuals, however, were given citizenship status without voting rights. Under the Principate, the right to vote was an illusion, not a reality.

PROVING CITIZENSHIP

Proving citizenship in one's hometown was easy because this was part of the public records. Citizen parents had to register their legitimately born child within thirty days of birth. The difficulty of proving citizenship arose when one traveled. Roman citizens could have private copies made of a document, called a *testatio*, confirming their status. Such a testimony consisted of a diptych, two wooden tablets connected with a cord or hinges. The writing was engraved on the interior sides, covered with a bright wax. Seven witnesses had to attest to this certificate of citizenship.[7] Perhaps a citizen who took trips frequently would, by habit, carry such a document with him. Retired auxiliary soldiers received a document in bronze that held up better for travel. In time, Roman law considered making a false claim of citizenship to be a capital offense. The guilty party could be prosecuted and even receive the death penalty.[8]

PHILIPPI AND CITIZENSHIP

After winning the battle of Philippi in 42 BC, Mark Antony and Octavian (later known as Caesar Augustus) made the city a Roman colony. This provided its residents with Roman citizenship. The two victors settled many army veterans in the city. When Octavian overcame Antony in 31 BC, he reestablished Philippi as a Roman colony and settled some of the defeated soldiers there. Octavian also gave the city the status of *ius Italicum*. This gave the colonists the same rights and privileges those who lived in Italy possessed and secured their loyalty to Rome. As a Roman colony, Philippi possessed the right of self-government under Roman laws and freedom from direct taxation of the city's citizens and lands.

Paul knew that the church at Philippi understood the implications of being a colony of Rome. No doubt the Philippians prized their Roman citizenship. The apostle reminded the church that they represented a colony of heaven in Philippi.[9] He wanted them to remain loyal to the Lord Jesus Christ and conduct themselves in Philippi as worthy citizens of their heavenly home.

NOTES

1. Richard R. Melick Jr., *Philippians, Colossians, Philemon*, NAC (1991), 24; Ralph Martin, *Philippians*, Tyndale New Testament Commentaries (TNTC) (Grand Rapids: Eerdmans, 1987), 18.
2. Everett Ferguson, *Backgrounds of Early Christianity*, 3rd ed. (Grand Rapids: Eerdmans, 2003), 62–63.
3. Dio Cassius, *History* 60.17.4–6.
4. Francis Lyall, "Roman Law in the Writings of Paul—Aliens and Citizens," *Evangelical Quarterly* (*EvQ*) 48.1 (1976): 10.
5. Ferguson, *Backgrounds of Early Christianity*, 63.
6. Mary T. Boatwright, Daniel J. Gargola, and Richard J. A. Talbert, *The Romans: From Village to Empire* (New York: Oxford University Press, 2004), 421.
7. Eckhard J. Schnabel, *Paul and the Early Church*, vol. 2 in *Early Christian Mission* (Downers Grove, IL: InterVarsity, 2004), 1156; F. F. Bruce, *Paul: Apostle of the Heart Set Free* (Grand Rapids: Eerdmans, 1977), 39.
8. Brian M. Rapske, "Citizenship, Roman" in *DNTB*, 216.
9. Gordon D. Fee, *Paul's Letter to the Philippians* (Grand Rapids: Eerdmans, 1995), 162.

SERVANTS IN THE HOUSE OF PHARAOH

BY LEON HYATT JR.

Egyptian model of a labor scene, painted wood; dated about 2000–1900 BC. The feet of the worker and hoofs of the oxen are driven in the ground; the scene takes place immediately after the withdrawal of floodwaters.

While Joseph was still a slave, the providence of God enabled him to have close contact with three high officers in Pharaoh's court: Potiphar, captain of Pharaoh's guard (Gen. 39:1–6a); Pharaoh's chief baker; and Pharaoh's chief cupbearer (40:1–23). The captain of the guard was the head of a highly influential unit of the army, the royal bodyguard. "An oriental monarch's bodyguard consisted of picked men attached to his person and ready to fulfill his pleasure in important and confidential concerns."[1]

Egyptologist Peter Brand wrote, "The royal bakeries were a large institution that baked bread, the staple of the Egyptian diet, in large quantities not just for the king and royal family but for all the people who lived and worked on the royal estate."[2] The chief baker presided over the whole operation, which probably included preparing not just baked goods but every dish for meals.[3]

The name of the cupbearer's position originated in his responsibility to be sure no contamination entered the pharaoh's drink or food; however, the position was of such high trust and responsibility that cupbearers typically became powerful advisers of the pharaoh.[4] The chief cupbearer would have been the leader of all those who served in that highly respected position.

Portions of a Stele of the Vizier Naferrenpet, who served during Egypt's Nineteenth Dynasty. This fragment depicts Naferrenpet (left) offering to Ptah of the Valley of the Queens and another deity. Naferrenpet, vizier during the last decade of the reign of Ramesses II, wears the long, high-waisted kilt characteristic of his office, and his head is shaved in the priestly manner.

Double ink jars from Egypt's Nineteenth Dynasty, dated about 1280 BC. The inscription indicates the jars belonged to Vizier Paser, called the "Mayor of Thebes" during the reigns of pharaohs Seti I and Ramesses II.

Though a pharaoh was an absolute ruler, with total authority over every aspect of the nation and with power of life and death over everyone in the nation, of necessity he had to rule through various administrators. A vast array of assistants, servants, and slaves assisted each major administrator.

VIZIER

Pharaoh delegated to this officer the power to run the government. The vizier freed the pharaoh to spend the major part of his time performing rituals that were supposed to preserve order and harmony in the nation. This included receiving foreign emissaries; deciding the most important court cases; appointing officials; and overseeing the construction of temples, monuments, dams, mausoleums, and other great architectural projects.[5]

Joseph most likely was appointed by Pharaoh to the position of vizier. Pharaoh said that in all the land only he would be greater than Joseph (Gen. 41:40), and Joseph's brothers called him "the lord of the country" (42:30,33).[6] His power extended over the entire nation, north and south (41:41–45,55–56). As vizier, Joseph had power to imprison (42:14–20), to determine sentences, and to condemn to slavery (v. 17). Because of the severe drought in Joseph's time, he had to give primary attention to feeding the people.

HIGH PRIESTS

Egyptians considered the pharaoh to be a god; they believed the god Amun-Re united with the pharaoh's father as he conceived the future ruler. As such, the pharaoh was the supreme mediator between the gods and the people and the authority through whom every religious ceremony in the whole land was conducted. In actual practice, the pharaoh was represented by a complicated priestly system that acted in his behalf. The Egyptians believed in many gods and goddesses, some say as many as 2,000; major temples and religious centers were developed for only a relatively small number of the gods. Each major city had its favorite god and temple; a high priest presided over each one.[7] The local high priest in turn supervised a host of lesser priests.[8]

The priests primarily offered sacrifices, conducted religious ceremonies, led religious festivals, practiced fortune-telling and magic, interpreted dreams, and presided over the elaborate rituals and embalmings that accompanied an Egyptian's death and burial. The priesthoods of each different god, however, taught different myths and practiced different rituals that often contradicted one another. The Egyptians were not bothered. They accepted all the different views of the gods and practiced the one or ones that most appealed to them.

Since the high priests were supposed to be acting for the pharaoh, they had tremendous influence on the pharaoh, especially the high priest of the god of the capital city. The pharaoh in turn had great power over the priests because he provided a salary for each one (47:22). Pharaoh exercised his power over a high priest when he gave the daughter of the high priest of On to Joseph to be his wife (41:45).

GENERAL OF THE ARMY

The pharaoh also was the leader of Egypt's army. Many of the pharaohs planned battle strategies and led armies into battle. Nevertheless, every pharaoh had to have a lead general and a large command structure to train, organize, and deploy the soldiers of his large armies. In Egypt, the army also served as the police for the nation.[9] The lead general often had great influence on the pharaoh, and some were held in great respect and personal affection by their pharaohs.

SCRIBES

Though scattered through all of the government departments and other institutions of the nation, another position of high honor and power that was subject to the pharaoh was the scribe, who was highly trained in complicated hieroglyphic writing and without whom Egypt's advanced civilization could not function.[10] The much-treasured legacy of these scribes is the written record they left in tombs, pyramids, and temples, and on objects and scrolls. Without their work, much of what we know about ancient Egypt and its history would have been lost.

Though assisted by officers of high rank and great power and by a great host of lesser officials, the pharaoh of Egypt had absolute authority over appointment, punishment or reward, and removal from office. He actually held in his hands the life and death of everyone. The highest officers and their least assistants were pharaoh's servants and had one concern: pleasing pharaoh. Thus all of Egypt was ultimately the domain of one man.

Limestone wall fragment depicting offering bearers; from Sakkara, Egypt; dated about 2400–2250 BC. The men on the middle register carry birds and ale; in the top row, a priest named Irtyenankh carries a haunch of beef. He is followed by a man who has plucked a sacrificial bird from a cage.

Padiouiset, an Egyptian priest, offers incense to the sun-god. Dated about 900 BC.

NOTES

[1] Thomas Nicol and Edgar W. Conrad, "Guard" in *ISBE*, 2:578.

[2] Peter James Brand, professor of Egyptology at the University of Memphis, in personal correspondence with Leon Hyatt Jr., August 21, 2013.

[3] Roland K. Harrison, "Baker" in *ISBE*, 1:404. Two examples of kings of other nations who furnished huge amounts of food for their courts daily: Solomon (1 Kgs. 4:22–23) and Evil-merodach of Babylon (2 Kgs. 25:29–30).

[4] Benjamin Reno Downer and Roland K. Harrison, "Cupbearer" in *ISBE*, 1:837.

[5] White, *Ancient Egypt* (New York: Crowell, 1953), 47–50.

[6] Kenneth A. Kitchen, "Joseph" in *ISBE*, 2:1128.

[7] Kenneth A. Kitchen, *The Third Intermediate Period in Egypt* (Warminster, England: Aris & Phillips, 1986), 3–6.

[8] White, *Ancient Egypt*, 20–46; Jon Manchip White, *Everyday Life in Ancient Egypt* (New York: Dorset, 1963), 128–42.

[9] Cyril Aldred, *The Egyptians*, rev. ed. (London: Thames & Hudson, 1987), 188–92.

[10] White, *Everyday Life in Ancient Egypt*, 151–52.

SLAVERY IN THE ANCIENT WORLD[1]

BY JAMES A. BROOKS

At Souk Ahras, Algeria, North Africa, view of the slave market (circular area) in the ruins of ancient Thagaste.

Slavery was prevalent and widely accepted in the ancient world. The economy of Egypt, Greece, and Rome was based on slave labor. In the first Christian century, one out of three persons in Italy and one out of five elsewhere was a slave. Huge gangs toiled in the fields and mines and on building projects. Many were domestic and civil servants. Some were temple slaves and others were craftsmen. Some were forced to become gladiators. Some were highly intelligent and held responsible positions. Legally, a slave had no rights, but, except for the gangs, most were treated humanely and were better off than many free persons. Domestics were considered part of the family, and some were greatly loved by their masters. Canaan, Aram, Assyria, Babylonia, and Persia had fewer slaves because it proved less expensive to hire free persons. Still, the institution of slavery was unquestioned. The Stoics insisted that slaves were humans and should be treated accordingly. Israel's law protected slaves in various ways.

A person could become a slave as a result of capture in war, default on a debt, inability to support and "voluntarily" selling oneself, being sold as a child by destitute parents, birth to slave parents, conviction of a crime, or kidnapping and piracy. Slavery cut across races and nationalities.

Manumission or freeing of slaves was possible and common in Roman times. Masters in their wills often freed their slaves, and sometimes they did so during their lifetimes. Industrious slaves could make and save money and purchase their own freedom. By the

Dated from the first century BC, inscribed relief stele commemorating the freeing of a female slave by her mistress.

first Christian century, a large class of freedmen had developed. There was even a Synagogue of the Freedmen in Jerusalem (Acts 6:9).

NOTES

[1] Excerpted from the *Holman Illustrated Bible Dictionary*, rev. and expanded ed. (Nashville: Holman, 2015).

SOLOMON IN ALL HIS SPLENDOR

BY E. LEBRON MATTHEWS

In the steps Solomon took to secure his throne, he demonstrated wisdom and leadership.

In the ancient world, bloody purges were common aftermaths of a new king's coronation. To consolidate power, a new monarch frequently eliminated potential rivals, including members of the royal family. After David's death, Solomon also eliminated potential troublemakers. But unlike many kings of his time, Solomon's order to put Adonijah to death was neither vindictive nor unwarranted. It followed clear evidence that his half brother still entertained hope of becoming king. The deaths of Joab and Shimei reflected Solomon's willingness to listen to the advice of others. His father had instructed him to execute both men.

Solomon cemented an alliance with Egypt by marrying Pharaoh's daughter. The union may have seemed impressive; historically Egypt had been the world's great superpower. But Egypt now existed in name only. During the Twenty-first Dynasty, Egypt was in reality a group of independent states held together by trade and title.[1]

The true significance of Solomon's marriage to an Egyptian princess was the

Tyre, a Phoenician coastal city and home to a major seaport, was vitally involved with Israel in international commerce. King Hiram of Tyre formed a mutually beneficial trade alliance with both David and Solomon. Shown, a Phoenician jug found at Tyre.

political recognition it provided. The loose confederation of Israelite tribes that David had forged into a tenuous kingdom had become a political state equal to its neighbors, including mythical Egypt. The importance of this cannot be overstated. Only a generation earlier, the stability of Israel was threatened. A victorious Philistine coalition had defeated Israel's army and occupied considerable territory west of the Jordan River. Under Solomon, the entire region between the Sinai Peninsula in the south and Syria in the north and between the Mediterranean Sea to the west and the Arabian Desert to the east was under Israel's control. The marriage to an Egyptian princess signified international respect for Solomon's power and prestige.

In ancient Israel, people commonly identified themselves by their tribal affiliation. Solomon reorganized his kingdom into political units called districts rather than maintaining the old tribal confederation. While the move was politically expedient, it ultimately weakened the unity of the nation by removing the tribal identity of its citizens. As a result, unrest in the tribes increased. The scars of his father's civil wars did not heal. But initially the reorganization likely produced a jubilant atmosphere of fresh hope that is common to political change and innovation. Its bureaucracy established the image of a strong and efficient administration.

Solomon aggressively pursued public works projects such as construction of his palace and Yahweh's temple. The infrastructure of Israel improved. Public buildings provided an object of national pride. The temple would serve as the heart of Israel's religion for centuries.

Solomon established further foreign political alliances, especially with Hiram of Tyre. These alliances resulted in peaceful relations with Israel's neighbors. Peace benefited both the economy and the society. Furthermore, the Phoenicians were seafaring traders who provided access to a larger world market.[2] Archaeological evidence suggests that Phoenician merchants set up business throughout Israel. They were joined by merchants from Arabia who brought spices, incense, and gold overland.[3] However, Israel's role in international trade at this time seems mainly to have been in importation, as little evidence exists that they shipped large quantities of materials outside the kingdom.

The early years of the reign of Solomon were known as Israel's Golden Age. It was a time of peace and prosperity. Cultural achievements expanded. The king gained a reputation for his proverbs. In part this was due to his patronage of wisdom literature and his establishment of schools to educate Israel's adolescent boys. Formal education and literary progress produced works such as those recorded in the biblical books of Proverbs and Song of Songs. Solomon in all his splendor was a ruler worthy of allegiance.

NOTES

[1] George Steindorff and Keith C. Seele, *When Egypt Ruled the East*, rev. ed. (Chicago, University of Chicago Press, 1957), 270, 275; John A. Wilson, *The Culture of Ancient Egypt* (Chicago: University of Chicago Press, 1951), 289–92, 320.

[2] Glenn E. Markoe, *The Phoenicians, Peoples of the Past* (Berkeley: University of California Press, 2000), 33–35, 94, 129; D. R. Ap-Thomas, "The Phoenicians," *Peoples of Old Testament Times* (Oxford: Oxford University Press, 1973), 273–81.

[3] B. S. J. Isserlin, *The Israelites* (London: Thames & Hudson, 1998), 185–87.

SOLOMON'S FOREIGN WIVES AND THEIR GODS

BY ALAN BRANCH

Winged lion on the side of the throne of Ashtoreth in the temple of Echmoun. This temple complex was for worship of Echmoun, the Phoenician god of healing. Temple dates to the seventh century BC.

The most obvious indicator of Solomon's unfaithfulness to God is his unparalleled participation in polygamy. For Solomon, polygamy was initially a form of political expediency and a method for forging alliances with surrounding nations. While other Old Testament men engaged in polygamy, Solomon's excessive wealth and political power allowed him to entertain an unrestrained appetite for more women, a lack of discipline that corresponded to his ill-advised foray into supporting paganism.

Solomon imported the worship of foreign gods into Jerusalem and established places for pagan worship on the Mount of Olives (1 Kgs. 11:7). In so doing, he engaged in religious syncretism, an attempt to reconcile the contradictory beliefs between monotheistic Yahwism and the polytheistic teachings of surrounding nations. The writer of Kings listed four pagan gods that Solomon's foreign wives enticed the aging king to worship—Ashtoreth, Milcom, Chemosh, and Molech (vv. 1–13).

Stele of the Moabite warrior god, likely Kamosh (spelled "Chemosh" in the Old Testament), brandishing a weapon. Although the lack of provenance information makes dating imprecise, the style indicates 1200–800 BC. The clothing and hair reflect an Egyptian influence.

ASHTORETH

The Old Testament is unequivocally opposed to goddess worship and uses several terms to critique the practice of worshipping ancient goddesses. Because these terms look and sound familiar, they can be somewhat confusing. First Kings 11:5 says, "Solomon followed Ashtoreth, the goddess of the Sidonians." Ashtoreth can be easily confused with either the terms *Asherah* or *Asherim* mentioned elsewhere in Scripture. In Canaanite mythology, the highest deities were El and his wife, Asherah. The Hebrew word *Asherim* is the plural form of Asherah and refers to various symbols of the goddess Asherah. Among the seventy children of El and Asherah were the god Baal and the goddess Ashtoreth, both of whom were the focus of popular devotion. People commonly considered Ashtoreth to be the wife of Baal and identified her with a widely popular goddess in the ancient Near East known by either of the names Ashtart (Phoenician) or Astarte (Greek). In the ancient Near East, the goddess people knew by the names Ashtoreth, Ashtart, or Astarte was associated with love and war. The Hebrew word *Ashtoreth* is actually a way of showing contempt and condemnation for worship of this goddess since "Ashtoreth" is formed by taking the consonants for Ashtart and combining them with the vowels from the Hebrew word for shame, *bosheth*.[1]

Understanding the goddess worship condemned in Scripture is also confusing because some cultures blended the goddesses Asherah and Ashtoreth into one. Devotees of Canaanite religion in different places and different periods felt free to arrange the pantheon according to their own preferences.[2] The late Old Testament scholar William F. Albright summarized the complexity of the relationship between these goddesses: "The goddesses Ashtaroth [Ashtoreth] and Asherah seem to interchange repeatedly in the

Hebrew Bible, where both are mentioned with Baal."[3] Due to this interplay between the goddesses Asherah and Ashtoreth, the reference to "Ashtoreth, the goddess of the Sidonians" in 1 Kings 11 may be either a way of saying this was the goddess Ashtoreth from the Canaanite pantheon or, more broadly, a generic way of saying Solomon initiated officially sanctioned Canaanite goddess worship.

People almost always associated goddess worship, whether under the name Asherah or Ashtoreth, with fertility cults. Deuteronomy 23:17 warns, "No Israelite woman is to be a cult prostitute, and no Israelite man is to be a cult prostitute." Ritual prostitution was part of the entire complex of beliefs associated with veneration of the male god Baal and his various goddess consorts. Evidently the goddess worship Solomon sanctioned entailed this sort of prostitution several centuries later. Second Kings 23:7 says that Josiah "tore down the houses of the male cult prostitutes that were in the LORD's temple, in which the women were weaving tapestries for Asherah."

MILCOM

The Old Testament teaches that Milcom was the Ammonites' patron deity. The name "Milcom" was a deliberate Hebrew scribal misvocalization of the god's name,[4] a pronunciation the Hebrew scribes apparently created to slander the Ammonites' national deity. Some modern translations consider the name "Milcom" to be an allusion to the god Molech. For example, the NIV translates "Milcom" as "Molek" in 1 Kings 11:5. The CSB translates "Molech" in 1 Kings 11:7 as "Milcom." These different translations reflect ongoing debate concerning the possibility that Milcom and Molech are different names for the same god, with Milcom being the Ammonite version of Molech worship. Supporting this view is the fact that both the names "Milcom" and "Molech" come from the Hebrew word *melek*, which means "king."[5] The account of Josiah's reforms in 2 Kings 23:10–14 seems to differentiate between Molech and Milcom as separate entities. With this in mind, 1 Kings 11:5 may be a reference to veneration of Milcom as king of the gods within the Ammonite pantheon.[6]

At Hazor, under the modern shelter is the high place or altar area, erected during Solomon's time. Such structures gave evidence of syncretistic worship practices.

CHEMOSH

Chemosh was the Moabites' patron deity. The Old Testament calls the Moabites the "people of Chemosh" (Num. 21:29; Jer. 48:46). Additionally, the inscription on the Moabite Stone mentions Moab's King Mesha attributing his victory over Israel to Chemosh.[7] Although the specifics of Chemosh worship are somewhat obscure, evidence indicates the Moabites especially venerated Chemosh as a war god. In fact, the Moabite Stone "is most emphatic on [Chemosh's] intervention and specific guidance in times of war."[8]

MOLECH

First Kings 11:7 says that Solomon built a place of worship for "Molech the abomination of the people of Ammon" (NKJV). As mentioned above, the CSB translates "Molech" as "Milcom" here, though the CSB translator's footnote indicates the word is literally "Molech." We can easily imagine the Ammonites incorporating Molech worship into their polytheistic pantheon, adding the worship of Molech to their practice of venerating their primary god, Milcom. Their being two separate deities helps us understand Josiah destroying places of worship dedicated to both Milcom and Molech. Thus 1 Kings 11 may in fact be differentiating between two separate gods, Molech and Milcom.

Scholars have debated about the specific god or practices condemned under the title "Molech" in the Old Testament. A vocal minority insists that references to "Molech" in the Old Testament are not references to a particular god but to the practice of child sacrifice.[9] The majority opinion, though, explains Molech as an underworld deity who was appeased or worshipped through human sacrifice, particularly the sacrifice of children.[10] Ancient worshippers closely related Molech to a cult of the dead. Leviticus 18:21 specifically condemned worshipping him: "You are not to make any of your children pass through the fire to Molech" (CSB footnote).

NOTES

[1] Scott Langston, "Ashtaroth" in *HIBD*, 127.

[2] Bryce N. Sandlin, "Ashtaroth," *BI* 15.4 (Summer 1989): 19.

[3] William Foxwell Albright, *Archaeology and the Religion of Israel*, 5th ed. (Louisville: Westminster John Knox, 1968), 74.

[4] Richard D. Patterson and Hermann J. Austel, *1, 2 Kings*, vol. 4 in The Expositor's Bible Commentary (Grand Rapids: Zondervan, 1988), 245.

[5] E. Ray Clendenen, "Religious Background of the Old Testament," in *Foundations for Biblical Interpretation*, ed. David S. Dockery, Kenneth A. Mathews, and Robert B. Sloan (Nashville: Broadman & Holman, 1994), 298.

[6] See "Milcom" in *HIBD*, 1124.

[7] "The Moabite Stone" in *The Ancient Near East*, ed. James B. Pritchard (Princeton: Princeton University Press, 1955), 1:209–10.

[8] Gerald L. Mattingly, "Chemosh" in *ABD*, 1:897.

[9] For example, Stephen J. Andrews, "Molech" in *Mercer Dictionary of the Bible* (*MDB*), ed. Watson E. Mills (Macon, GA: Mercer University Press, 1990), 580–81.

[10] See Richard S. Hess, *Israelite Religions: An Archaeological and Biblical Survey* (Grand Rapids: Baker Academic, 2007), 101–2.

SPIES IN THE LAND

BY JOHN L. HARRIS

Modern Shechem taken from the top of Mount Gerizim.

With the Israelites encamped in the desert of Paran at the southern border of Canaan, God directed Moses to select twelve men, one from each tribe, "to scout" (Hb. *tur*) the land (Num. 13:2).

JOURNEY OF THE SPIES

As directed, the spies left the wilderness of Paran and entered the Negev, traveling through the Wilderness of Zin, probably late in July. These dry and barren areas south of Canaan are bordered by the Wadi Arabah on the east, the Sinai on the south and west, and extend from around Gaza to the western shore of the Dead Sea. In these regions, water is constantly in short supply; the Wilderness of Zin receives fewer than two inches of annual precipitation, and the Negev receives only eight to twelve inches of rain a year.[1] The Negev soil is fine and windblown, and the sparse rain does not absorb but quickly runs off into the wadis. This entire region has an adverse environment for sustaining human life and is mostly unsuitable for cultivation. As the spies journeyed, they would have endured a hot and dry climate. Canaan has only two defined seasons: a hot and dry period (summer) running from mid-June to mid-September and a warm and wet period (winter) running from October to mid-April.

In contrast to the surrounding area of the Negev, the hill country's climate is much more favorable, and the area receives abundant rain. The central mountain range and the highlands of Judah receive between twenty and forty inches of annual rainfall, allowing for the collection of water in numerous springs and a greening of the land.[2] The hill country contains rich, red, moisture-absorbing soil and is covered with considerable forests.[3] Referring to this region and its produce, the spies proclaimed the land flowed with "milk and honey" (Num. 13:27).

The spies would have found travel along the central mountain range extremely difficult due to the limestone boulders and occasional cliffs that stood as natural impediments. As the twelve continued northward, they would have followed the ridges and probably would have taken the interregional road known as the Ridge Route or Route of the Patriarchs that ran along the north-south watershed ridge between Hebron and Shechem. Along this route, the spies would have passed the cities of Hormah, Arad, Hebron, Jerusalem, Jericho, Ramah, Gibeon, Bethel, Shiloh, Shechem, Beth-shean, Hazor, Laish (Dan), and Rehob near Lebo-hamath ("the entrance of Hamath").[4] The reference to Lebo-hamath, a city on the east bank of the Orontes River located on one of the main trade routes in the northernmost boundary of Canaan, emphasizes that the scouting mission covered the entire land, a distance of about 250 miles, one way.

The only city singled out for comment was Hebron (meaning "confederacy"), a well-fortified and large town in the hill country of Judah, lying 3,000 feet above sea level and twenty miles south of Jerusalem. The fertile land made Hebron a favorable place for farmers and merchants to buy and sell wheat, barley, olives, grapes, pomegranates, and other produce.[5]

The spies were likely intimidated when they saw the fortified cities of the hill country encircled by ramparts that reached "to the heavens" (Deut. 1:28; see 3:5) and protected by gates and towers. Not every city in Canaan, however, was fortified and protected by walls. Evidence points to the existence of many open villages in the various regions of Canaan; during this time period, the two forms of settlements, walled and open, coexisted.

Given the search area Moses designated, the spies would have encountered a land that in some areas was densely occupied and in others sparsely inhabited. The Jezreel and Jordan Valleys were densely populated, as were most northern hill regions, but the southern part of upper Galilee and nearly all of lower Galilee were sparsely inhabited.[6]

View of the Canaanite city and its protective wall at Arad.

RETURN AND REPORT OF THE SPIES

After traveling for forty days, the spies returned to Kadesh and informed the people about their findings. The report began positively, but it quickly turned negative. The spies testified that the people who lived in the land were powerful and the cities were large and fortified. Specifically, the spies mentioned the descendants of Anak, the Amalekites, the Hethites, the Jebusites, the Amorites, the Canaanites, and the Nephilim.[7] The sons of Anak were notoriously large warriors who lived in the western region of Canaan in the cities of Gaza, Gath, and Ashdod (Josh. 11:21–22). The Amalekites were a nomadic people who lived in the deserts of the southern Negev. The Hethites lived in the Hebron region. The Jebusites lived in and around Jebus (i.e., Jerusalem). The Amorites lived in the hill county, and the Canaanites lived in the lowlands along the seacoast. Some scholars believe that mentioning the Nephilim may have been an exaggeration for rhetorical effect; they were a legendary people thought to be semidivine (Gen. 6:1–4).[8]

NOTES

1   Carl G. Rasmussen, *Zondervan NIV Atlas of the Bible* (Grand Rapids: Zondervan, 1989), 49, 50.

2   Rasmussen, *NIV Atlas*, 18–19.

3   Yohanan Aharoni, *The Archaeology of the Land of Israel* (Philadelphia: Westminster, 1978), 4–5.

4   Thomas Brisco, *Holman Bible Atlas* (Nashville: Broadman & Holman, 1998), 70; Barry J. Beizel, *The Moody Atlas of Bible Lands* (Chicago: Moody, 1985), 93.

5   Rasmussen, *NIV Atlas*, 42.

6   Amihai Mazar, *Archaeology of the Land of the Bible: 10,000–586 B.C.E.* (New York: Doubleday, 1990), 239; Aharoni, *Archaeology*, 158; Rasmussen, *NIV Atlas*, 34.

7   Timothy R. Ashley, *The Book of Numbers* (Grand Rapids: Eerdmans, 1993), 239. Ashley states, "Amalek was the offspring of Eliphaz son of Esau by the concubine Timna (Gen 36:12)." The Amalekites were constant enemies of Israel.

8   R. K. Harrison, *Numbers: An Exegetical Commentary* (Grand Rapids: Baker, 1992), 209; Ashley, *Numbers*, 243.

TIGLATH-PILESER III: REBUILDER OF ASSYRIA

BY STEPHEN J. ANDREWS

Basalt relief orthostats from a doorway portraying the classes of the Assyrian army. This Neo-Assyrian piece is from the period of Tiglath-pileser III.

Ancient Assyrian records confirm that actually three kings with this name existed: Tiglath-pileser I (ca 1116–1076 BC), Tiglath-pileser II (ca 940 BC), and Tiglath-pileser III (745–727 BC). Some historians attribute the founding of the Neo-Assyrian Empire to Tiglath-pileser III.[1] He played a significant role in the last fateful days of the kingdom of Israel.

USURPER TO THE THRONE

History says nothing about the birth and upbringing of Tiglath-pileser III. Assyrian records state that a rebellion occurred in the capital city of Calah (modern Nimrud, Iraq) two months before Tiglath-pileser became king. Two Assyrian documents give conflicting accounts of the identity of his father. Tiglath-pileser may have been of royal birth and possibly a high-ranking official or military officer. Most scholars believe he was not in the direct royal line but actually a usurper who took advantage of a political crisis to stage a coup d'état for the Assyrian throne.[2]

Tiglath-pileser's name in Akkadian, Tukulti-apil-Esharra, means "my trust [is] in the heir of [the temple of] Esharra."[3] Since Esharra was the temple dedicated to the god Ashur, the "heir" in the name is the god Ninurta, the firstborn son of Ashur. Thus Tiglath-pileser's name essentially means "my trust is in the god Ninurta." The Bible calls him Tiglath-pileser (2 Kgs. 15:29; 16:7,10), Tiglath-pilneser (1 Chr. 5:6,26; 2 Chr. 28:20 NASB), and Pul (2 Kgs. 15:19; 1 Chr. 5:26). Pul is a shortened form of *apil*, the Akkadian word for "son" or "heir." A number of Aramaic sources also referred to Tiglath-pileser.[4]

MIGHTY WARRIOR

Tiglath-pileser came to power at a time when Assyrian power had greatly diminished. He faced powerful enemies on the north, south, and east. He reorganized the army and carried out administrative reforms aimed at strengthening his own royal authority and reducing the power of the Assyrian aristocracy.[5]

Like previous kings, Tiglath-pileser led yearly campaigns in an effort to reestablish the Assyrian Empire. He proved to be a formidable general who, in the eighteen years of his reign, effectively changed the balance of power in the ancient Near East. The inscriptions Tiglath-pileser left at Calah and other places attest to his many victories.[6] He routed the army of Urartu, the powerful nation on his north, and defeated Babylonia on the south. Tiglath-pileser also campaigned along the Tigris River and Zagros Mountains to the east and the Mediterranean Sea on the west. He defeated the northern states of Syria and marched on Aram-Damascus, Transjordan, and northern Israel. He placed a gold statue of himself in Gaza and set up a commemorative stele as far south as the "Brook of Egypt."[7]

An Assyrian inscription in basalt dating from the eighth century BC. Found at Tavle village in Turkey.

EMPIRE BUILDER

Assyrian kings had often raided and plundered neighboring states. Some had occasionally reached as far as the Mediterranean. But none had taken an active hand in annexing or incorporating any of the territories west of the Euphrates into the Assyrian Empire. Tiglath-pileser III dramatically changed this pattern.

Tiglath-pileser III conquered Babylonia and established himself as its king. He defeated the states of northern Syria and annexed them into his empire, including the territories of Aram-Damascus, Transjordan, and northern Israel. Tyre, Sidon, Samaria, Judah, and the rest of the smaller kingdoms and city-states became vassals and were obliged to provide tribute. Under Tiglath-pileser's policy of annexation, Assyria gained a reputation as the arrogant remover of boundaries (Isa. 10:12–13).

Although he was not the first Assyrian king to do so, Tiglath-pileser III was the first Neo-Assyrian king to practice mass deportation on a grand scale.[8] Entire villages and districts such as the Galilee district were depopulated.[9] Tiglath-pileser carried out unprecedented "two-way" deportations by resettling hundreds of thousands in distant regions (1 Chr. 5:6,26) and then replacing them by force with persons from still other regions. Assyrian bas-reliefs show parents carrying possessions on their shoulders and grasping their children by the hand. Men are shown walking in long files with their wives following in carts or riding on horses or donkeys.[10] Supposedly, Assyrian deportation suppressed national political loyalties, repopulated abandoned regions, developed agriculture and economic growth, and supplied troops and laborers.[11] Royal governors received instructions to provide the deportees with food and protection. They were not slaves; they paid taxes; they were given civil rights; and some even rose to important posts in the government.[12] Although Tiglath-pileser counted them as the people of Assyria[13] and treated them

Hittite basalt double-lion column base from Tainat dated to the second half of the eighth century BC. The piece has the Assyrian lion-type of the Tiglath period and was incorporated as a Hittite architectural motif.

Royal servant of Tiglath-pileser III.

as his own citizens, these actions did not lessen the pain and suffering of forced deportations.

Since Tiglath-pileser's main interest was rebuilding the Assyrian Empire, he spent little time on building projects. At Calah he did erect a new palace at the edge of the Tigris River. Imported woods and precious metals decorated the palace. Huge stone slabs lined the palace walls. These slabs contained incised cuneiform, bas-reliefs, and depictions of Tiglath-pileser's victories and conquests.[14]

POLITICAL RELATIONS

Like other Assyrian kings before him, Tiglath-pileser III turned his eyes toward the Mediterranean coast fairly early in his reign. There he encountered the kings of Israel and Judah. The Bible records various details of the ensuing conflicts. Unfortunately, the fragmented inscriptions of Tiglath-pileser III provide only a partial picture of his encounters with the people and leaders of Israel and Judah.

Uzziah?—Two texts of Tiglath-pileser III mention an Azriyau whom the Assyrians defeated in 738 BC. Unfortunately, the name of Azriyau's country is broken off. Several scholars have suggested that this Azriyau is none other than Uzziah of Judah (also known as Azariah). But the Bible does not confirm this fact, and the issue must remain unsettled.[15]

Menahem—The Annals of Tiglath-pileser mention tribute money Menahem of Samaria paid in 738 BC.[16] This may refer to the payment mentioned in 2 Kings 15:19. Possibly, as a usurper to the throne of Israel, Menahem had to pay the heavy fine and then likely continued to provide a regular yearly tribute as referred to in the Annals.

Pekah—Two years into the reign of Pekahiah the son of Menahem, Pekah the son of Remaliah, another usurper, assassinated Pekahiah and seized the throne. According to 2 Kings 15:29, Tiglath-pileser campaigned against the confederacy led by Rezin of Damascus and Pekah of Israel and took the cities of Ijon, Abel-beth-maacah, Janoah, Kedesh, and Hazor. He also took Gilead, Galilee, and the land of Naphtali. In the aftermath, Tiglath-pileser deported the Israelites to Assyria and annexed most of the country.

According to 2 Kings 15:30, Hoshea son of Elah assassinated Pekah and assumed the throne. One of the summary inscriptions of Tiglath-pileser III also confirms the removal of Pekah from the throne of Israel during the campaign of 733–732 BC. In the inscription, Tiglath-pileser claimed that he directly installed Hoshea as king of Israel.[17]

Hoshea—One other possible synchronism between Hoshea and Tiglath-pileser may exist. Another summary inscription of Tiglath-pileser III contains language suggesting that Hoshea, or one of his representatives, made a trip to Sarrabani in Mesopotamia in 731 BC to pay tribute and do obeisance. The Bible does not record this trip. Was it possible that Hoshea's control over the state of Samaria was so unstable that such a trip was necessary? Or was Hoshea perceived as less than loyal to the Assyrian crown? Nine years later, just prior to the beginning of the siege of Samaria, Shalmaneser V arrested Hoshea for treason (2 Kgs. 17:4).[18]

Ahaz—According to 2 Kings 16:5–9, Pekah of Israel and Rezin of Aram-Damascus attacked Ahaz, king of Judah. Their combined forces laid siege to Jerusalem and threatened to replace Ahaz on the throne with a usurper, the son of Tabeel (Isa. 7:1–6).

Ahaz responded by seeking help from Tiglath-pileser III. What happened next seems to have been a fairly standard pattern for Assyrian diplomacy and expansion. Ahaz sent a pledge of fidelity, a grievance, a distressed call for help, and a bribe (2 Kgs. 16:7–8). Tiglath-pileser III responded by attacking Damascus, deporting its inhabitants, and executing Rezin (v. 9).

The bribe worked. Ahaz, however, got more than he bargained for. Tiglath-pileser came to his aid, but he also subjugated Ahaz as a vassal. One of the summary inscriptions of Tiglath-pileser lists Ahaz among the many tribute-bearing kings from Syro-Palestine.[19] The payment of tribute listed in the inscription is not necessarily the same as the bribe Ahaz sent (see 2 Kgs. 16:8). The Assyrians expected regular tribute from their vassals, and Ahaz would be treated no differently.

NOTES

[1] George Roux, *Ancient Iraq*, 3rd ed. (New York: Penguin Books, 1992), 305.

[2] See the summary in A. K. Grayson, "Assyria: Tiglath-Pileser III to Sargon II (744–705 BC)" in Cambridge Ancient History (CAH), ed. J. Boardman et al., 2nd ed., vol. 3, part 2 (Cambridge: Cambridge University Press, 1991), 73–74.

[3] Knut L. Tallqvist, *Assyrian Personal Names* (Hildesheim: Georg Olms Verlagsbuchhhandlung, 1966), 233–34.

[4] Ludwig Koehler and Walter Baumgartner, *The Hebrew and Aramaic Lexicon of the Old Testament* (*HALOT*), trans. M. E. J. Richardson, study ed. (Leiden: Brill, 2001), 1687.

[5] Roux, *Ancient Iraq*, 305–6, 347–48.

[6] See H. Tadmor, *The Inscriptions of Tiglath-Pileser III King of Assyria* (Jerusalem: Israel Academy of Sciences and Humanities, 1994). Excerpts from the inscriptions are in J. B. Pritchard, *ANET*, 282–84.

[7] Tadmor, *Inscriptions*, 9.

[8] Bustenay Oded, *Mass Deportation and Deportees in the Neo-Assyrian Empire* (Wiesbaden: Dr. Ludwig Reichert Verlag, 1979), 21.

[9] Zvi Gal, "Israel in Exile: Deserted Galilee Testifies to Assyrian Conquest of the Northern Kingdom," *BAR* 24.3 (1998): 48–53. See K. L. Younger Jr., "The Deportation of the Israelites," *JBL* 117 (1998): 201–27.

[10] Oded, *Mass Deportation*, plates I–VI.

[11] Oded, *Mass Deportation*, 41–74.

[12] Roux, *Ancient Iraq*, 307–8; Oded, *Mass Deportation*, 87–89.

[13] Oded, *Mass Deportation*, 82, 87, 89.

[14] Grayson, "Assyria," 83–84.

[15] Tadmor, *Inscriptions*, 273–76. See H. Tadmor, "Azriyau of Yaudi" in *Scripta Hierosolymitana*, ed. Chaim Rabin, vol. 8 (Jerusalem: Magnes, 1961), 232–71.

[16] Pritchard, *ANET*, 283.

[17] Pritchard, *ANET*, 284; Tadmor, *Inscriptions*, 277.

[8] Tadmor, *Inscriptions*, 189, 278.

[19] Tadmor, *Inscriptions*, 171, 277.

TO LIVE LIKE A JEW

BY DALE "GENO" ROBINSON

Found at Timrat, a village just west of Nazareth, a stone carved with the Hebrew word "Sabbath." Measuring almost eight by twenty-four inches, the carving indicated to Jews the farthest limit they could travel from their village on the Sabbath. This is the only Sabbath boundary marker ever discovered written in Hebrew. It is located just under a mile between Tel Shimron and Mahalul, two Jewish villages from the Roman Era.

This Torah scroll dates from the sixteenth century AD. It was used in the Spanish Jewish synagogue in the city of Zafed (upper Galilee). Part of the scroll was damaged in an earthquake in 1837. The scroll was then placed in a genizah, a repository for old, damaged, worn, or defective scrolls. The scroll is mounted on wooden rollers, that, though not originally belonging to this scroll, are of approximately the same age.

First-century Jews enjoyed a favored status in the Roman Empire. Julius Caesar granted it to them in 48 BC when the Jewish king, John Hyrcanus, sent reinforcements to assist Caesar in his Egyptian military campaign. As a reward, Caesar exempted Jews from imperial requirements contrary to their faith.[1] This special status proved to be a constant irritant to their Gentile neighbors. It allowed the Jews to refrain from participating in Greco-Roman civic responsibilities and ceremonies.

Jewish monotheism repelled and attracted disillusioned idolaters. Circumcision offended the widely held ideal view of the human body. Jewish lifestyles went against common customs. Yet Jews proudly held to those practices as markers of their faith. The Gentiles considered Jewish practices an affront to society; Jews saw them as obedience to God's commands. The most prominent of these practices were circumcision of male children, the Sabbath day of rest, and food restrictions.

CIRCUMCISION

Ancient Egypt, Ethiopia, Edom, and Moab circumcised their male children as a rite of passage to manhood. The Jews practiced circumcision as a mark of their covenant with God. Hebrew boys were circumcised eight days after birth as a sign of their entrance into that covenant (Gen. 17:9–14). It was the universally required element of Jewish faith, practice, and cultural distinctiveness. It was the sign of their uniqueness.

After 334 BC, the Jews' Greek conquerors attempted to impose Hellenistic cultural values and practices on them. Some Jews resorted to a painful and often unsuccessful plastic surgery called epispasm to "reverse" their circumcision.[2] This was an affront to a pious practicing Jew. Jewish ethics and morality attracted many thoughtful Gentiles. Though many Gentiles were God-fearing, few converted. The strict life rules were difficult to accept. Circumcision was a barrier to male converts. Jews, however, never abandoned it.

THE SABBATH

Only the Jews observed a weekly day of rest. God commanded them (Exod. 20:8–11) to honor the Sabbath or seventh day as a special and holy day with rest and worship. From sunset on Friday to the appearance of three stars on Saturday night, the Jews honored *Shabbat*. Their Gentile neighbors, not seeing its value, criticized them. They saw Jewish Sabbath observance as a sign of slothfulness.

Sabbath was a joyful celebration filled with rest, feasts, and joy. It was also dangerous. During wartime, Jews often refused to fight on the Sabbath to their detriment. When the Romans besieged Jerusalem in 63 BC, the Jews continued temple worship and Sabbath observance. The Romans capitalized on this perceived "weakness" and used siege machines on the Sabbath. Jerusalem fell soon afterward.[3]

FOOD LAWS

The Jews were also unique because of their diet. God had declared some foods clean and others unclean for them. Thus Jews found ways to observe their food restrictions and separate themselves from "unclean" Gentiles. If a Jewish businessman ate with a Gentile friend, he brought his own food. Most Gentiles saw these food rules as disruptive to their concept of a unified culture and state. The Jews saw "keeping kosher" as a means of cultural unity, both the source and occasion of purity before God.

FAITH IN JESUS, NOT WORKS OF THE LAW

Sadly, many Jews paid so much attention to these outward signs of their religion that they believed such practices commended them to God. Moreover, some insisted that Gentiles who believed in Jesus as the Messiah also had to keep these "works of the law" to truly be part of the people of God. But Paul would have none of this. The only way to be justified before God, receive the Spirit, and be true children of Abraham is through faith in Jesus Christ (Gal. 3:1–29).

Buff flint knife dated 7500–4000 BC. Joshua had the Israelite men circumcised with flint knives at Gibeath-haaraloth (Josh. 5:2-3).

NOTES

1   Eduard Lohse, *The New Testament Environment*, trans. John E. Steely (Nashville: Abingdon, 1976), 36.

2   Joel B. Green and Lee Martin McDonald, eds., *The World of the New Testament: Cultural, Social, and Historical Contexts* (Grand Rapids: Baker Academic, 2013), 313; Robert G. Hall, "Epispasm: Circumcision in Reverse," *BRev* (1992): 52–57.

3   Josephus, *Jewish War* 1.7.3–4.

WHO WAS ARTAXERXES?

BY T. VAN MCCLAIN

From the palace at Susa, relief of a bodyguard of the Persian King Artaxerxes II; dated 404 to 358 BC.

In one of the most famous battles of ancient history, Xerxes defeated the Spartans of Greece at the battle of Thermopylae in 480 BC. This Xerxes was likely the king of Persia who was the husband of the biblical Esther. Xerxes had another wife named Amestris. Queen Amestris was probably the same as Vashti in the book of Esther, since the word *Vashti* can mean "the best" or "the beloved."[1] The third son of Xerxes and Amestris was named Artaxerxes I Longimanus.

Artaxerxes I Longimanus was the king of Persia from 465 to 424 BC. *Artaxerxes* means "kingdom of righteousness" or "kingdom of justice," and *Longimanus* means "longhanded."[2] The Greek scholar Plutarch said Artaxerxes's right hand was longer than his left. Plutarch also claimed that Artaxerxes was "preeminent among the kings of Persia for gentleness and magnanimity."[3] Artaxerxes's character contrasts with that of his parents—whose reputations for immorality and brutality long outlived them. Artaxerxes is important to Bible students because of his connection to Ezra and Nehemiah. He permitted Ezra to leave Persia and visit Jerusalem in 458 BC, and he authorized his cupbearer Nehemiah for a mission to Jerusalem in 445 BC.[4]

THE RISE OF ARTAXERXES I

Artaxerxes may have shown kindness to Ezra and Nehemiah, but his reign began in intrigue and assassination. The historical sources relate that a powerful royal official named Artabanus had King Xerxes killed in his bedchamber and blamed it on Darius, the eldest son of Xerxes. After some months, the eighteen-year-old Artaxerxes then killed Darius. Eventually Artaxerxes determined that Artabanus was behind the assassination plot and put him to death also. Artaxerxes would later defeat another older brother, Hystaspes, in battle. Hystaspes was a satrap or governor in Bactria who rebelled against his brother's rule.[5]

THE REIGN OF ARTAXERXES I

With a young king on the throne and his army occupied or having been weakened with threats to the kingdom by Hystaspes, 461–460 BC seemed a propitious time to the Egyptians

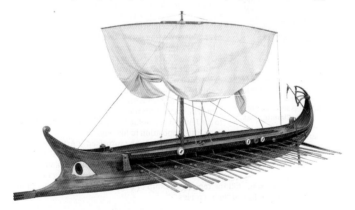

Model of a trireme galley ship. The Greeks used this type of warship against the Persians in the battle of Salamis. Artaxerxes's father, Xerxes, was defeated in that battle. After the battle, Xerxes (probably Ahasuerus in Scripture) went home and married Esther.

Silver bowl; fifth century BC. The cuneiform inscription refers to three Persian kings mentioned in the Bible: "Artaxerxes, the great king, king of kings, king of countries, son of Xerxes the king, of Xerxes, son of Darius the king, the Achaemenian, in whose house this drinking cup was made."

Alabaster vase that honors King Xerxes I; dated 485 to 465 BC. Inscription says: "Xerxes, the Great King." The inscription is in Egyptian, Old Persian, Elamite, and Neo-Babylonian languages and written in hieroglyphics and cuneiform.

to rebel against Persian rule. The Persians would suffer reversals at the beginning of the war; completely subduing Egyptian forces would take about ten years—with Athens and its navy as an ally to the Egyptians in the rebellion.

The accusations of the foes of the Jews, as described in Ezra 4:7–23, would have been of particular concern to the Persian monarch given the fact that Persian forces would have to travel through Israel to quell the rebellion in Egypt. People accused the Jews of being rebellious and evil; they further claimed that tax revenue would suffer if the Jews completed their rebuilding of the city of Jerusalem and its walls. Artaxerxes then stopped the rebuilding of the city.

Eventually Artaxerxes allowed the Jews under Ezra to return to Israel with the king's blessing. Perhaps the king realized that any kindness he showed to Israel would result in a loyal buffer state between his forces and the rebellious Egyptians.[6] Of course, the real reason the king looked favorably on Ezra and his mission to Israel was because God's hand was on Ezra (Ezra 7:6).

The Persian general Megabyzus, who had ended the rebellion of Egypt, was satrap of Syria for a time but eventually rebelled against Artaxerxes. He was finally reconciled to the Persian monarch. Later, though, Artaxerxes sent Megabyzus into exile for shooting a lion before the king could do so while the two were on a hunting expedition. After some time in exile, he would again be restored to favor.[7]

By the time Artaxerxes granted Nehemiah the liberty to return to Israel in 445 BC, the Egyptian revolt and the subsequent rebellion of Megabyzus would have long been over. Moreover, the war between Persia and the Greek city-states apparently came to a halt or truce about 449 BC with the Peace of Callias.[8]

In about 425–424 BC, Artaxerxes died of natural causes—which was a rarity among Persian kings.[9] The relative stability and peacefulness Artaxerxes exhibited in his reign are in accord with what the Scriptures say about him. If he was as generous to his other subjects as he was to the Jews, then one should not be surprised that he had such little opposition to his reign.

One should also not be surprised at Artaxerxes's generosity as he encouraged Ezra and Nehemiah with protection and financial support. Both biblical and extrabiblical sources indicate Persian kings were tolerant of other religions, "actively supported the temple-worship of the gods of their subjects, [and] contributed to the building of their temples."[10]

NOTES

[1] G. H. Wilson, "Vashti" in *ISBE*, vol. 4 (1988), 966.

[2] "Artaxerxes" in *HIBD*, 120.

[3] Plutarch, *Artaxerxes* 1.

[4] This writer presupposes the traditional date of the arrival of Ezra and Nehemiah in Israel. See Eugene H. Merrill, *Kingdom of Priests: A History of Old Testament Israel*, 2nd ed. (Grand Rapids: Baker Academic, 2008), 514–18.

[5] Edwin M. Yamauchi, *Persia and the Bible* (Grand Rapids: Baker, 1990), 248.

[6] Yamauchi, *Persia*, 250, n. 39.

[7] Yamauchi, *Persia*, 250.

[8] Yamauchi, *Persia*, 252.

[9] Yamauchi, *Persia*, 278.

[10] G. B. Gray and M. Cary, "The Reign of Darius" in *The Persian Empire and the West*, vol. 4 in CAH, 187.

WHO WERE THE CANAANITES?

BY TRENT C. BUTLER

Standing stones (Hb. *masseboth*); these mark the likely site of Canaanite worship in Megiddo.

In the narrowest sense of the word, *Canaanite* originally referred to the people living on the northwestern Mediterranean seacoast of Phoenicia (Num. 13:29). Centuries later the Phoenicians came to refer to themselves as Canaanites. In a wider meaning of the term, *Canaanites* referred to the persons living in the valleys and hills throughout Canaan (Num. 14:25,45; Deut. 11:30). They were one of several ethnic groups Israel confronted in the land (Josh. 3:10; 9:1; 11:3). Apparently, Canaan proper stopped at the Jordan River. Gilead and other lands east of the Jordan River were not part of Canaan (Josh. 22:9–10,32).

God's purpose in the exodus was to take his people back to the land of promise (Exod. 3:8), famed for its fruitfulness (v. 17), so they would obey him and let him be their God (Lev. 18:3; 25:38). God's promise and its fulfillment became a central part of Israel's worship (Ps. 105:11; cf. Acts 13:19).

As they prepared to enter the land of Canaan, Israel had one God-given goal—to exterminate the Canaanites (Deut. 20:17). But the Israelites succumbed to the false belief that because the Canaanites dwelt in the land long before the Israelites, they must have known the secrets to its fertility and blessing—worshipping the high god Baal, the master of storms and fertility. If military success with Yahweh was good, they reasoned, then adding some agricultural and fertility success with Canaan's gods could only make things better (3:6–7). Such constant temptation lasted into the postexilic period with Ezra (Ezra 9:1).

ANCIENT NEAR EASTERN TEXTS

Texts from the ancient Near East give us additional information about Canaanites and Baal. Canaan appears in texts from Mari, Alalakh, Ugarit, and Amarna and in the Egyptian Merneptah stele. These affirm that the geographical and ethnic names were known long before Joshua.

Mention of Baal goes back to Egyptian execration texts from about 1800 BC and back to texts from the Syrian city of Ebla after 1500 BC. Most information comes from the texts found at Ugarit on the Syrian coast of the Mediterranean Sea. These texts and artistic renderings closely associated Baal with thunder and lightning and with battle against Yam, the god of the sea. Baal's partner was the goddess Anath. She joined him in battle against Mot, the god of the dead. Defeat of Yam brought Baal the title "King of the Gods." Baal's entrance into Mot's underworld brought temporary death for Baal and for the crops of Canaan until Anath rescued Baal, restoring fertility.

Astarte is another, infrequently mentioned consort of Baal in the Ugaritic materials. In the Bible, she appears often in the forms of Asherah, Ashtoreth, or the plural form Ashtaroth.

Canaanite worshippers believed the local king represented the major god. Sacrifices formed the central worship rites as well as serving as the means of expiating sins and provided opportunities for social gatherings. Annual agricultural festivals included sacred meals and renewal of religious and political commitments.

Sarcophagus fragment depicting a Phoenician shepherd (fifth–fourth centuries BC).

Scene of Amenhotep II and his Asiatic campaign. A stele describing this campaign by Amenhotep II has the earliest Egyptian text mentioning the Canaanites.

Politically Egypt controlled Canaan and took advantage of its geographical location to control international trade routes. The Amarna letters indicate that local city-state kings or governors paid homage and taxes to the Egyptian pharaoh and fought among themselves for local control. From 3500 to about 2000 BC, about twenty city-states dominated, but most had populations of fewer than 2,000. Megiddo, Laish (or Dan), and Ai were the largest cities in this period. Around 2300 BC, Egypt's Old Kingdom collapsed. So did Canaan's cities, so that only a very small population remained.

The Middle Bronze Age (2000–1550 BC) brought trade growth to Phoenicia and population growth in Canaanite cities. Canaanite population thus reached about 140,000. The majority of the population were farmers living outside the major cities, providing food for each family and for the king and his elite administrators. Foreign trading brought in specialty items, including fine garments and pottery and metal goods. Hazor was the dominant city with a population possibly reaching 20,000. The hill country remained basically unpopulated. New siege weapons, chariots, and composite bows helped advance military technology and forced cities to build massive defensive walls. Just before 1550 BC, various armies and causes destroyed most of these cities.

The Late Bronze Age (1550–1200 BC) is the apparent time of the exodus and conquest of Canaan. The region became a battlefield among the Hittites to the north, the Hurrian Mitanni to the northeast, and the Egyptians to the south. Canaanites suffered as they paid taxes, were forced to join enemy military ranks, and even became slaves, particularly to the Egyptians. From about 1425 to 1350 BC, Egypt had peace from its wars but continued to tax and enslave the people of Canaan, cutting its population in half to about 70,000. Shortly after 1300, Pharaoh Ramesses II suffered defeat by the Hittites at Kadesh and turned his ire again against the Canaanites.[1]

After 1300 BC, Egyptian control tightened with more troops and more Egyptian outposts in Canaan and more taxes for the Canaanites. The hill country and the area east of the Jordan had few settlements or people.

Egyptian rule brought the Canaanites poverty and hardship. Only the Egyptian-selected rulers in the twenty or so city-states had any luxuries. People not belonging to the ruling elite in Canaan had few choices. The few talented people became artisans, creating items demanded by the elite. Otherwise, a Canaanite became a farmer on land he did not own, paying much of his crop to the aristocratic or royal property owner or became a nomadic shepherd following sheep and goats to pasture lands, occasionally settling down near or in a village.

The opening years of the Iron Age (1200–1000 BC) changed the situation. Egypt withdrew. The Hittite Empire collapsed. The highland or hill country population increased radically, growing, for example, from five sites in the tribe of Ephraim to 115 sites.[2] Canaanites (and Israelites) gained freedom to govern themselves. Droughts and famines set people on the move, looking for better living conditions. Included were the Sea Peoples coming from Sicily, Cyprus, and Crete. One group of Sea Peoples settled on the southern Mediterranean coast. They became the Philistines, the major challengers of ancient Israel.

ARCHAEOLOGICAL EXCAVATIONS

Archaeological excavations show much about Canaanite daily life. One result surprises: "The strong continuance of Late Bronze Age material culture into Iron Age I can support Israel's presence in the land prior to 1200 and their acceptance of much of the material culture.… The proposition that certain traits distinguish Israelite from Canaanite settlements is highly questionable."[3] Thus daily life remained much the same for Canaanites and Israelites, even down to the way they built four-room houses and made collar-rimmed jars. Archaeologists cannot distinguish between Israelite settlements and Canaanite ones.

Israel's major distinction lay in its official religion. Yet its insistence on a centralized worship and its refusal to use material images of God leave little behind for archaeologists to find. Similarly, stories such as those of Rahab (Josh. 2) and the Gibeonites (Josh. 9) present only two of what probably were many cases of foreigners joining with Israel and bringing with them "Canaanite" artistry and skills.[4]

Excavations have shown that Canaanite religion was dynamic and varied in nature, with different types of worship structures from rural high places to urban temples to funeral sites where the Canaanites worshipped their ancestors. Standing stones or *masseboth* played an important role in many worship sites as did Egyptian obelisks. Archaeologists found that large Canaanite cities had multiple temples, and certain sites served as regional worship centers with professional staffs. The temple courtyard led to the most holy place and had altars for burnt offerings. The courtyard often had workshops for temple metalworkers and potters who produced sacred objects for use in worship. These included ceramic vessels, small statues—especially of female figurines used in fertility and funeral practices—bronze cymbals, small stone statues of gods and goddesses, clay masks, and various types of jewelry and ornaments.[5]

What became of the Canaanites? History offers no solid details. Evidently they were not destroyed in war or taken captive. Many Bible scholars believe instead they eventually were assimilated into other people groups in the area. Although they ceased to exist as a separate people, their influences on religion and culture continued throughout the Old Testament era.

Palace ruins at Ebla (later known as Tel Mardikh). Ebla was the dynastic capital of the region. Excavations at Ebla uncovered thousands of cuneiform tablets dating to the Middle Bronze Age (ca 2000 BC). Several refer to names of cities and persons mentioned in the Bible. Further, many of the texts offer information about worship practices and beliefs related to the Canaanite god Baal. The name *Ebla* means "white rock"—likely a reference to the limestone on which the city was built.

NOTES

[1] Information and population figures cited above, from K. L. Noll, *Canaan and Israel in Antiquity: An Introduction* (London: Sheffield Academic, 2001), 83–116.

[2] Israel Finkelstein, *The Archaeology of the Israelite Settlement* (Jerusalem: Israel Exploration Society, 1988), 186. "An influx of settlers overran the region" (187).

[3] Alfred J. Hoerth, *Archaeology and the Old Testament* (Grand Rapids: Baker Academic, 1998), 216.

[4] See Richard S. Hess, "Early Israel in Canaan: A Survey of Recent Evidence and Interpretation" in *Israel's Past in Recent Research: Essays on Israelite Historiography*, ed. V. Philips Long. Sources for Biblical and Theological Studies 7 (Winona Lake, IN: Eisenbrauns, 1999), 498–512; originally published in *PEQ* 125 (1993), 125–42.

[5] Beth Alpert Nakhai, "Canaanite Religion" in *Near Eastern Archaeology: A Reader*, ed. Suzanne Richard (Winona Lake, IN: Eisenbrauns, 2003), 343–48.

WHAT WERE ORACLES?

BY BENNIE R. CROCKETT JR.

A relief in the east pediment of the Siphnian Treasury at Delphi depicts Apollo (left) and Heracles (right) disputing over a tripod. The central figure, thought to be Hermes, tries to separate the two deities. According to tradition, Apollo uttered his oracles while sitting on this tripod. Heracles was enraged because other gods had denied him the ability to pronounce oracles. Thus, he was attempting to take the tripod from Apollo.

Within their polytheistic cultures, the Greeks and Romans believed that oracles functioned on behalf of their gods. Three basic meanings of *oracle* were prominent in Greek and Roman culture. First, the word referred to the place where a priest or priestess spoke on behalf of a god. Second, the word could refer to the priest or priestess who spoke. Third, the word could refer to the content of divine words spoken.

ORACLE AS A PLACE

Dedicated to Zeus, the oldest and principal oracle from Greece was the city of Dodona in Epirus, northwestern Greece. At this site, ancient travelers worshipped Gaia, mother earth, also known as Diona, the wife of Zeus. The ancients believed these two pagan gods lived in the branches of the oak tree where the priests on the site interpreted Zeus's oracles through the rustling of the oak leaves.[1] In the fourth century BC, worshippers built a temple to Zeus in Epirus,[2] and Octavian (later named Caesar Augustus) enlarged the temple in 31 BC for Apollo.[3]

The most famous oracle in the ancient world was at Delphi in central Greece near Mount Parnassus, north of the Corinth Gulf. All other sacred shrines eventually were secondary to Delphi, and people from the world over consulted the oracle at Delphi.

Possibly the most famous person to interact with the Delphi oracle was Socrates, Plato's mentor. Socrates's friend Chaerephon told him that the oracle declared Socrates to be the world's wisest person. As a result, Socrates moved throughout Athens trying to find a wiser person than himself.[4] Socrates also began to popularize the saying "know yourself," which was inscribed on the wall at Delphi's entrance.[5] Plato later referred to the Delphi oracle as establishing festivals and settling civil law issues.[6]

ORACLE AS A PAGAN GOD OR GODDESS

The ancient Greeks dedicated Delphi to the Greek god Phoebus Apollo. Apollo was the Greek and Roman god of the sun, prophecy, music, poetry, and healing; the name Phoebus described his radiant image. Often Apollo appeared as a beautiful figure playing a golden lyre or as a master archer shooting his bow. By the decree of Zeus, Apollo always told the truth.

Apollo's spokeswoman bore the name Pythia, priestess of the Greek goddess Gaia. In Greek mythology, Pythia was named for Python, the dragon snake that Apollo had slain.[7] At Delphi, Pythia inhaled the underground, sweet-smelling vapors and spoke inspired words from Apollo to Apollo's petitioners (usually for a fee). Usually people came asking for a prophecy related to a spouse or children. Because Pythia spoke (often incorrectly) under the hallucinogenic influence of the vapors, her priest would translate her words into poetic verses and give them to the inquirer.

During the first century AD, Plutarch functioned as a priest in the Delphi shrine, but he recounted the decline of the Delphi oracle.[8] Plutarch blamed demons for the oracles' decline. Undoubtedly, however, the fact that Pythia failed to predict the Greek military victory over the Persians and her willingness to take bribes also contributed to her decline.[9]

Despite the decline of the Delphi oracle, other oracular cults became popular. Asclepius— son of Apollo and Greek god of medicine and healing—spawned an oracular religion in Asia Minor. The cult associated Asclepius with his father, Apollo. A temple of Asclepius was at Pergamum. People came to the site for healings and received the priests' oracular interpretations of dreams or visions of Asclepius. The Asclepius cult was so widespread that by AD 300, more than 400 sanctuaries dedicated to Asclepius existed throughout the Roman Empire.[10]

ORACLE AS DIVINE WORDS

In the first century, many Christians also were familiar with the Sibylline oracles. These oracles (possibly forgeries) were texts based on practices from a variety of cultures and contained oracles from Sibyl, one of Apollo's prophetic priestesses dating back as early as the sixth century BC. Topics covered in the oracles included the prediction of various worldwide catastrophes and, in later times, even some Christian events.[11]

Because of the prominence of Greek and Roman influences on first-century culture, early believers would have thus been familiar with oracles and the worship practices associated with them. In contrast to Greek and Roman polytheism, however, early Christians understood oracles as referring to the words of the one true God. The New Testament

Six restored columns stand at the northeast end of the temple of Apollo at Delphi, situated on Mount Parnassus.

uses the Greek term *logion* (sometimes translated as "oracle") four times to refer to God's self-revelation in words (Acts 7:38; Rom. 3:2; Heb. 5:12; 1 Pet. 4:11).

The contrast of "oracle" in Greek and Roman religions and in early Christianity is dramatic. Rather than consulting rustling oak leaves, idols, or hallucinatory priests who could be bribed, the early Christians rested upon the foundation of the one true God who spoke ultimately and definitively in his Son (Heb. 1:1–2).

NOTES

[1] Homer, *Odyssey* 14.327.

[2] Walter Burkert, *Greek Religion*, trans. John Raffan (Cambridge, MA: Harvard University Press, 1985), 114.

[3] Suetonius, *Lives of the Caesars* 27.

[4] Plato, *Apology* 21–22.

[5] Plato, *Charmides* 164d–65a.

[6] Plato, *Laws* 8.828; 9.856; 11.913–14.

[7] Thelma Sargent, *The Homeric Hymns: A Verse Translation* (New York: Norton, 1973), 24–25.

[8] Plutarch, *The Obsolescence of Oracles in Moralia* 415A; 417E–F.

[9] Burkert, *Greek Religion*, 116.

[10] Luther H. Martin, *Hellenistic Religions: An Introduction* (New York: Oxford University Press, 1987), 50.

[11] See J. J. Collins, "Sibylline Oracles," in *Apocalyptic Literature and Testaments*, vol. 1 of *The Old Testament Pseudepigrapha* (*OTP*), ed. James H. Charlesworth (New York: Doubleday, 1983), 317–25.

WHO WERE THE SAMARITANS?

BY ROBERT A. WEATHERS

Ruins at Aphek. Located on the Via Maris between Caesarea Maritima and Jerusalem, Aphek (later called "Antipatris") was on the Yarkon River and served as a southern border city for the region of Samaria.

Jacob's well at Sychar—between Mounts Ebal and Gerizim. Measurements in the 1930s indicated the well is about 135 feet deep.

At the time of Jesus, the Samaritans "were regarded by the Jews as despised half-breeds."¹ The Samaritans likewise detested the Jews. Their mutual contempt arose from a long and checkered history.

In 922 BC, King Solomon died, and his son Rehoboam inherited the throne (1 Kgs. 12). Rehoboam was a foolish leader who listened to unwise advisers and initiated a series of events that so angered the people that the kingdom disintegrated. The ten northern tribes rebelled and formed their own kingdom. The capital of the northern kingdom of Israel became its best-known city, Samaria.

City gate on top of Mount Gerizim.

Samaria's location made it vulnerable to hostile nations. In 722 BC, the Assyrians swept in, conquered Samaria, carrying leaders and prime citizens into exile. Then, to weaken the morale of the citizens and prevent a future uprising, the Assyrians carted non-Israelite people into Samaria and interspersed them among the remaining Israelites. Over time, these groups intermarried, creating a mixed race known as the Samaritans, impure in the minds of their Judean neighbors.[2]

In addition to the intense racial prejudice, a religious dispute that left enduring scars aggravated the animosity between the Jews and Samaritans. In the sixth century BC, the Jews in the southern kingdom suffered their own exile at the hands of the Babylonians, who invaded Judah and destroyed the temple in Jerusalem (2 Kgs. 25). In turn, the Persians conquered the Babylonians and (in 538 BC) allowed the Jews to return to their homeland. When they arrived, the Samaritans offered to help them rebuild the temple. The Jews rebuffed their despised neighbors. Snubbed, the Samaritans applied their energy to hindering the Jews' efforts to build (Ezra 4–5; Neh. 2–4). An action that further deepened the chasm between the two peoples, the Jews, under the leadership of Ezra, enacted strict segregation policies against anyone of mixed backgrounds, including Samaritans.[3]

The Samaritans eventually built their own temple on Mount Gerizim, and they accepted only the Torah as Scripture. Clearly, when Jesus arrived on the scene, the hostility between Samaritans and Jews was deeply ingrained in their cultures.[4]

NOTES

[1] Gerald L. Borchert, *John 1–11*, NAC (1996), 199.

[2] Borchert, *John 1–11*, 200; Robert H. Stein, *Luke*, NAC (1992), 318; Thomas D. Lea and David Alan Black, *The New Testament: Its Background and Message*, 2nd ed. (Nashville: B&H Academic, 2003), 87.

[3] Borchert, *John 1–11*, 200.

[4] Stein, *Luke*, 318.

WISE MEN FROM THE EAST

BY E. RAY CLENDENEN

Having had a dream that disturbed him, Babylon's King Nebuchadnezzar summoned his wise men. Six different terms are used for these servants of the king in the book of Daniel. They are collectively referred to as "wise men" (Hb. *chakkim*) in 2:12–14,18,24,48; 4:6,18; 5:7–8. But they are called Chaldeans (*kasdim*) in 2:4–5,10. And in 4:9, the general term "magicians" (*chartom*) is used. On the other hand, sometimes they are referred to as comprising two or more presumably specialized groups: "magicians and mediums ['*ashaph*]" in 1:20; "wise men and mediums" in 5:15; "magician, medium, [and] Chaldean" in 2:10; "mediums, Chaldeans, and diviners [*gazerin*]" in 5:7; "magicians, mediums, sorcerers [*mekashephim*], and Chaldeans" in 2:2; "wise man, medium, magician, [and] diviner" in 2:27; and "magicians, mediums, Chaldeans, and diviners" in 4:7 and 5:11. It is difficult to know what to make of this terminology. Clearly "wise men" is the most common general designation, although others are also used.

Perhaps only an insider was equipped to distinguish the various types of "wise men." That term itself described someone who was skillful in technical work, wise in administration, and had considerable expertise in certain intellectual disciplines. The disciplines of these various functionaries probably overlapped. The ability to interpret dreams was evidently shared by several, although the term for "medium" (*chartom*) was derived from an Akkadian word that referred to an interpreter of dreams. Perhaps the factor that unified all these disciplines was the ability to foresee the future by the observation of various signs or omens, including dreams, astronomic phenomena, animal behavior, and the entrails of sacrificial animals. This was called divination.

Practitioners of these arts were used to advise the king on the timing of certain ventures based on such signs. However, casting spells, exorcism, and communication with the dead were also supposedly their forte. Although often said to practice astrology, the ancient Babylonians only observed correlations between certain astronomic phenomena and certain earthly events. The zodiac and the use of horoscopes first appeared in the Hellenistic period. The term for "magicians" is also applied to the Egyptian magicians in Genesis 41:8,24 and Exodus 7–9. Magic was "the exploitation of miraculous or occult powers by carefully specified methods."[1] In ancient Babylon, it was mainly used for deliverance from affliction such as illness or demon possession and could therefore involve exorcism through the use of rites and spells.[2]

Although Daniel is called "chief governor over all the wise men of Babylon" (Dan. 2:48), "head of the magicians" (4:9), and "chief of the magicians, mediums, Chaldeans, and diviners" (5:11), this does not mean Daniel dabbled in the occult or attempted to read the future via the stars. As Stephen Miller explains,

Although Daniel and his friends "entered the king's service" [1:19 NIV], we can rest assured that they did not engage in occult practices. These young men who risked their positions and probably their lives to please God in the matter of the king's food certainly would not have become involved in paganism and witchcraft. Moses grew up in Pharaoh's court and was taught the wisdom of the Egyptians (cf. Exod. 2:10; Acts 7:22), but he recorded the regulations condemning the magic arts (Lev. 19:26,31; 20:6,27; Deut. 18:10–11).[3]

NOTES

[1]   Kenneth A. Kitchen, "Magic and Sorcery: Egyptian and Assyro-Babylonian" in *The Illustrated Bible Dictionary,* ed. J. D. Douglas and N. Hillyer (Leicester: Inter-Varsity, 1980), 2:934.

[2]   Kitchen, "Magic and Sorcery."

[3]   Stephen R. Miller, *Daniel,* NAC (1994), 73.

THE WOMAN HULDAH, DRAWN FROM "PROPHETESSES IN ANCIENT ISRAEL"

BY SHARON ROBERTS

Model of Herod's Temple in Jerusalem as it appeared in Jesus's day. At the bottom left of the picture is a porch with steps and two sets of double doors known as the Huldah Gates.

In ancient Israel, a wife addressed her husband as *baal* (master) or *adon* (lord) (e.g., Gen. 18:12; Judg. 19:26; Amos 4:1). This form of address was comparable to that used by a slave to his master. The wife held the status of a minor and, according to the Decalogue (Exod. 20:17; Deut. 5:21), was listed as one of her husband's possessions. She could not inherit from her husband, nor could a daughter from her father unless there were no male heirs. For a woman's vow to be valid, it had to be witnessed and accepted by a male relative (Num. 30). Whereas the husband could repudiate the wife, she could not initiate divorce. Also, the heavy household duties fell to her: tending flocks, cooking meals, spinning cloth, working the fields.

Despite these conditions, Israelite women were granted a certain level of consideration. They fared better than their counterparts in Assyria, who were treated as beasts of burden, but their lot was slightly worse than that of Babylonian and Egyptian women. Whereas an Israelite could sell his daughters and his slaves, he could not sell his wife. He could divorce her, but the letter of repudiation restored her freedom. The wife also retained part ownership of the *mohar* (money paid by the fiancé to the bride's father) and the dowry received from her parents. A woman's work in the household earned respect from the other family members. This respect increased with the birth of the first child, especially if the child was a boy. Children were expected to obey and revere their mother.

Sometimes, in unusual circumstances, women became influential in religious and political life. Biblical writers referred to Miriam, Deborah, Huldah, and Noadiah, each of whom fulfilled the prophetic role in ancient Israel. The only prophetess to be mentioned during the period of the monarchy was Huldah (2 Kgs. 22:14–20; 2 Chr. 34:22–28). Josiah, after discovering the book of the law in the temple, sent his advisers to her. Their inquiries were met with an immediate answer: the nation would be judged for its disobedience of God. The fulfillment of this prophecy was postponed, however, due to the nationwide revival initiated by Josiah.

As the wife of Shallum, the king's wardrobe keeper, Huldah was automatically placed in close proximity to the king. His high opinion of her is evidenced by his immediate response. She was a contemporary of Jeremiah, and the two may even have been related. Huldah headed an academy in Jerusalem (2 Kgs. 22:14) and, according to the Talmud (Middot 1:3), the temple's Huldah Gate formerly led to the schoolhouse.

A WOMAN'S STATUS

BY MARTHA S. BERGEN

Dated to about 500 BC, a terra-cotta figurine from central Greece depicts a woman seated in front of an oven.

IN ISRAELITE CULTURE

Within ancient Hebrew society, Torah laws were binding for both men and women. Women, just as men, were obligated to follow the Ten Commandments and other moral laws, along with laws governing civil and ceremonial matters. Yet laws differed in relation to the sexes. For example, laws regarding the priesthood, circumcision, and appearance before the Lord three times a year applied only to males. Old Testament laws maintained a distinction between the roles men and women played in Hebrew society. Thus all Old Testament laws directed exclusively toward women dealt with the unique concerns associated with their bodies, such as purification after menstruating (Lev. 15:19; 2 Sam. 11:2–4). To the Jews, the symbolic significance of washing resembled holiness; thus a clean body reflected a clean soul. Though early Jewish literature gave no explicit details on ritual washings related to the menstrual cycle, it assumed a natural connection.[1]

Jewish laws were implemented during Moses's time, but generally they were still applicable to Jews approximately 1,400 years later as evidenced in the New Testament. Israelite law, for example, required a woman to present a purification offering to the priest to become ceremonially clean after childbirth. We know that Mary, Jesus's mother, observed this Levitical law. Because she was unable to afford the accompanying sacrificial lamb, she offered the substitute pair of turtledoves or young pigeons (Lev. 12; Luke 2:22–24).

SOCIAL AND FINANCIAL OPPORTUNITIES

The center of social opportunities for first-century women of both Judaism and Christianity was the home (e.g., Titus 2:4–5). Among a woman's greatest privileges and influence is that of shaping her children for God. A woman in the first century had authority over her children. She nurtured and taught them in the early years of life when foundational values were established. She partnered with her husband to raise them in the Lord's instruction.

Various New Testament passages give evidence of acceptable public social contact between the genders within certain settings. For example, Martha welcomed Jesus to her home in Bethany where she prepared him a meal (Luke 10:38,40). Her role of extending hospitality to guests in her home was normative of Jewish women in this time period.

Terra-cotta figurine of a woman in Greek dress carrying a pitcher; from the Shrine of Demeter at Kourion on Cyprus.

Some social contacts would have been inappropriate for Jewish women; reactions of the Pharisees and teachers of the law confirm this. Mary, a woman with a past, publicly anointed Jesus's feet (Luke 7:37–39). Any woman who touched a man in public almost certainly would have dishonored herself and the man. The woman with the blood issue touched Jesus's garment (Matt. 9:20), thereby making him ceremonially unclean according to Levitical law (Lev. 15:25).

Women were economically dependent upon their husbands or male family members. They did not hold jobs during the first century. However, upper-class women had at least partial control of the family's wealth. The Scriptures speak of such women who supported Jesus and his disciples, namely Joanna, Susanna, and others (Luke 8:3). Lydia, the first known European convert to Christianity, was a seller of purple—perhaps reflective of freedoms people had in areas that were under Roman control but were also outside ancient Israel (Acts 16:14). Purple cloth was an expensive commodity, suggesting Lydia was wealthy. Priscilla and her husband, Aquila, helped Paul in his missionary endeavors (Acts 18:18; Rom. 16:3), hosted a house church (1 Cor. 16:19), and instructed Apollos (Acts 18:26). Priscilla also assisted Aquila in his tent-making activities (18:2–3).

NON-JEWISH WOMEN

During the New Testament era and for hundreds of years prior to that time, Roman women could own property, appear in court, and compose a will. Among the most significant tasks for a woman was making clothes, especially in larger households. Spinning wool showed a family was self-sufficient. Although some wealthy women had their slaves spin wool for the family, many did it themselves.[2] Women were primarily involved with family concerns and rearing children. Other tasks included assisting with the family business, field labor, or midwifery. Educational opportunities were available for wealthy women.[3]

NOTES

[1] "Baths, Bathing" in *JE* (1906), http://www.jewishencyclopedia.com/articles/2661-baths-bathing.

[2] Mary Ann Bevis, *The Lost Coin: Parables of Women, Work, and Wisdom* (New York: Sheffield, 2002), 139.

[3] Lynn H. Cohick, *Women in the World of the Earliest Christians: Illuminating Ancient Ways of Life* (Grand Rapids: Baker Academic, 2009), 225.

XERXES I: HIS LIFE AND TIMES

BY JOSEPH R. CATHEY

A scroll in a silver case; the text is the story of Esther. The piece, which dates to the nineteenth century, would be used in the Jewish celebration of Purim.

Xerxes, known in the book of Esther as Ahasuerus, was one of the last great Achaemenid (Persian) kings. He was the son of Darius I and grandson of Cyrus the Great, under whose power the Achaemenids expanded their geopolitical hegemony up to the city-states of Greece. Xerxes was born around 518 BC to Darius and his queen Atossa. The majority of biblical references to Xerxes are in the book of Esther; the others are in Ezra 4:6 and Daniel 9:1. The events recorded in Esther most likely took place between the completion of the rebuilt temple under Haggai and the return of the exiles under Ezra (515–458 BC).[1]

HIS FATHER'S BATTLE

The battle that was to define Xerxes was not one he began but one he fought against the Greeks to avenge his father's defeat. The Persians had added vast territories under King Darius I's rule. After brutally suppressing opponents at home, Darius turned his attention to a convincing show of strength in the ancient Near East. In the east, he subjugated northwest India; in the west, he pacified various Aegean islands. However, this pacification of the Greek border took four long, bloody years and ended with the Greeks defeating Persia at Marathon in 490 BC.[2] Afterward, Darius's anger "against the Athenians . . . waxed still fiercer, and he became more than ever eager to lead an army against Greece."[3] Darius died, however, before he could mount an offensive against the Greeks.

Shortly before Darius's death, a revolt broke out in Egypt. Darius sent Xerxes to quell the disturbance in 485 BC. In a year's time, Xerxes had laid siege to Egypt, confiscated temple items, and imposed harsh new taxes. Quickly he besieged Babylon and devastated the temple of Marduk. Once these two nations were pacified, Xerxes set his sights on the rebellious Greek city-states.

HIS BATTLE

To preserve the memory of his father, Xerxes determined to completely conquer the Greeks. The plan Xerxes unfolded to the Persian military aristocracy was nothing short of total war. Ancient historians list forty-six nations that supplied men for combat when Persia invaded Greece.[4] Xerxes's naval forces were not as vast as the land contingent but were nonetheless quite impressive. The Persian monarch reportedly put to sea no fewer than 1,200 manned ships from various nations. At the time of his campaign, Xerxes fielded the largest land and naval contingent in the ancient world.

Xerxes left his capital city likely around April 481 BC; he assembled his full land contingent in the fall of that same year at Critalla, about 400 miles east of Sardis. After wintering in Sardis, Xerxes set his sights on what he believed to be the weakest link in his campaign—Hellespont. Under Xerxes's command, the Persian army did what everybody believed to be impossible; they bridged the strait at Hellespont and crossed from the city of Abydos on the southeastern side to the town of Sestos on the opposite side.[5] Once across the strait, Xerxes's army marched to Thermopylae, which was a Greek term meaning "the Hot Gates."

Thermopylae was located in a narrow pass between the mountains of central Greece and an adjacent gulf inlet. The Spartans fought valiantly. Opposing Xerxes, Leonidas, king of the city-state of Sparta, "made his gallant stand on a hill" overlooking the pass.[6] Fighting beside Leonidas were 300 Spartan soldiers (his select royal guard) and about 7,000 hoplite soldiers from surrounding Greek city-states. They killed wave after wave of Persian soldiers in the pass. This small contingent of dedicated Greek warriors killed 20,000 Persian soldiers and Xerxes's two half brothers. After two days of fighting, a Greek traitor came to Xerxes and told him of a path that bypassed the Hot Gates. Some of Xerxes's soldiers followed the path and came secretly behind the Greek army, trapping them from the front and the rear. All but one of the 300 Spartans died at Thermopylae.

After Thermopylae, the Greeks, emboldened, rallied under the leadership of Themistocles, a Greek navy strategist, by engaging the Persian navy at the Straits of Salamis. Employing unconventional tactics, the Greek navy scored a decisive victory against the much larger Persian navy. Xerxes's battles against the Greeks at Thermopylae and the island of Salamis were perhaps *the* two pivotal battles in the west.

The defeat at Salamis caused a demoralized Xerxes to retreat back across the strait at Hellespont and leave his general behind to continue the battle. Seeking repose, Xerxes returned to his winter home at Susa.

HIS STORY—AND ESTHER

How does Xerxes fit with details in the book of Esther? Chronologically Xerxes may have planned and presented his battle plans to the Persian military aristocracy during the 180 days that he showed off his wealth, as described in Esther 1. The battles at Thermopylae and Salamis likely occurred between the events of Esther 1 and 2. The search for a replacement queen (2:1–4) also could have occurred after Xerxes's defeat at Salamis and his subsequent retreat to Susa. Finally, Xerxes's "large tax . . . may readily have followed the exhaustion of the royal treasury by [his] disastrous expedition into Greece" (10:1).[7]

The book of Esther's characterization of Xerxes is similar to what the ancient historians said. Esther characterizes Xerxes as "a bumbling, inept figure who becomes an object of mocking."[8] This type of characterization is the same as Herodotus describing the monarch's petulant flight after his loss at Salamis. Esther's vivid description of Xerxes as dependent upon his advisers (1:12–14) is consistent with the monarch's delegation of power to his generals after his defeat in Greece. Aeschylus, the Greek playwright of Athens, portrays the end of Xerxes as inextricably bound to prideful ambition. "The Greek playwright's critique of the megalomaniacal ego of the Persian kings resonates with a similar evaluation of the Persian monarchy found in the book of Esther."[9] In the end, twenty years after ascending the throne, Xerxes was assassinated by Artabanus—the captain of his bodyguard.

A calcite jar dated 486 to 465 BC. The jar is inscribed "Xerxes, Great King of Persia" in Old Persian, Elamite, Babylonian, and Egyptian scripts. This was Xerxes's gift to Artemisia, queen of Caria, who provided ships and helped in the fight when Xerxes was preparing for and carrying out his invasion of Greece in 480 BC.

NOTES

1   See Mervin Breneman, *Ezra, Nehemiah, Esther*, vol. 10 in NAC (1993), 278.

2   Edwin M. Yamauchi, "Persians" in *Peoples of the Old Testament World*, ed. Alfred Hoerth, Gerald L. Mattingly, and Edwin M. Yamauchi (Grand Rapids: Baker, 1997), 114–15.

3   Herodotus, *Histories* 7.1.

4   Herodotus, *Histories* 9.27.

5   F. Maurice, "The Size of the Army of Xerxes in the Invasion of Greece 480 BC," *Journal of Hellenic Studies* (*JHS*) 50 (1930): 211; N. G. L. Hammond and L. J. Roseman, "The Construction of Xerxes' Bridge over the Hellespont," *JHS* 116 (1996): 88–107.

6   Edwin M. Yamauchi, *Persia and the Bible* (Grand Rapids: Baker, 1990), 204–5.

7   "Xerxes" in *Cyclopedia of Biblical, Theological, and Ecclesiastical Literature*, ed. John McClintock and James Strong, vol. 2 (New York: Harper, 1887), 1001.

8   See Karen H. Jobes, "Esther 1: Book of" in *Dictionary of the Old Testament: Wisdom, Poetry & Writings*, ed. Tremper Longman III and Peter Enns (Downers Grove, IL: IVP Academic, 2008), 163.

9   Karen H. Jobes, "Esther 2: Extrabiblical Background" in *Dictionary of the Old Testament: Wisdom, Poetry & Writings*, ed. Tremper Longman III and Peter Enns (Downers Grove, IL: IVP Academic, 2008), 171–72.

ZECHARIAH: TEMPLE BUILDER

BY MARTHA S. BERGEN

The Church of Saint Peter in Gallicantu, which serves as the traditional site where Peter denied knowing Jesus. Zechariah foretold that the Messiah would be abandoned: "Strike the shepherd, and the sheep will be scattered" (Zech. 13:7).

As seen in the article found in Haggai, "The Temple-Building Prophets," God used Zechariah and Haggai to motivate the postexilic people of Judah to finish rebuilding the temple destroyed by the Babylonian King Nebuchadnezzar in 586 BC. Under the leadership of Jerusalem's governor, Zerubbabel, the temple was completed in 516 BC.

Zechariah's name, which in Hebrew is *Zechar-Yah*, means "Yahweh remembers/remembered." The verb *zachar* means to "remember." Yahweh (God's personal name) was fully aware of Israel's circumstances. He knew the nation's past and future. The temple's current condition did not escape his knowledge. Furthermore, he was concerned about its disrepair. Just as the first temple's success was linked to the Lord's concern for Israel, so would be the success of this second temple.

Zechariah was born in Babylonia and came to Judah under Zerubbabel's leadership. His prophetic role began in 520 BC, two years into the reign of Persia's King Darius and approximately eighteen years after the first group of Jews returned from Babylonian exile. The book of Zechariah opens with reference to the prophet's call from God and cites his genealogical association (Zech. 1:1). His grandfather Iddo is mentioned not only here but also in Nehemiah 12:4,16 as being among the Levitical priests who returned with Zerubbabel. Nehemiah's list gives evidence of Zechariah's priestly heritage. According to verse 16, Zechariah was the head of his priestly family.

The prophetic content of Zechariah was conveyed especially through a series of eight night visions (see chaps. 1–6), intended to incite the Jews by rebuking them for not already having completed the temple. Appropriately, one vision emphasized the high priest and the role he played in Israel's restoration process (see chap. 3). The night visions were also a means of assuring God's people that he would help them because the temple was part of his plan for their new beginning after the exile experience. In essence, God's message through Zechariah was a call for Israel to return to him, a call for repentance and a new start.[1] "So tell the people, 'This is what the LORD of Armies says: Return to me—this is the declaration of the LORD of Armies—and I will return to you, says the LORD of Armies'" (Zech. 1:3). Completing the temple structure would be a way for the Israelites to demonstrate their loyal obedience to the Lord. God in turn stood ever ready to show his love and faithfulness to Israel.

Silver coins from the first century AD. Found in Jericho, they are the type Judas would have received.

Zechariah also laced his prophecies with messianic predictions. Evangelical scholars have suggested that the whole of Christ's life and work is predicted within this book, from Christ's coming to earth in lowliness (3:8) to his ultimate rule beyond time into eternity (14:9). Other key messianic elements are Zechariah's prophecies of Christ's triumphal entry into Jerusalem (9:9), his betrayal for thirty pieces of silver (11:12–13), the scattering of his disciples when he was arrested (13:7), and his crucifixion (12:10–14).[2]

NOTES

[1] Bill T. Arnold and Bryan E. Beyer, *Encountering the Old Testament* (Grand Rapids: Baker, 1999), 466.

[2] Kenneth L. Barker and Larry L. Walker, "Introduction: Zechariah" in *The NIV Study Bible* (Grand Rapids: Zondervan, 1995), 1399.

ZEDEKIAH: JUDAH'S LAST KING

BY RICK W. BYARGEON

Cistern at Lachish. Jeremiah was thrown into a cistern, and Zedekiah ordered his release (38:1-13).

The demise of the Davidic kingdom happened during Zedekiah's reign. From start to finish, he reigned under the heavy hand of Babylonian domination. The power that placed him on the throne eventually took away his kingship, his family, and his life. Zedekiah appears as a weak and indecisive leader. He simply did not have the leadership and spiritual qualities to help Judah survive.

THE RISE OF AN INEFFECTUAL LEADER

Zedekiah was not chosen by the people of Judah but by Nebuchadnezzar. According to 2 Kings 24:17–18, Nebuchadnezzar placed Zedekiah on the throne of Judah in 596 BC because of his loyalty to Babylon.

The Babylonians reappeared in Israel in December 598 BC, to punish Jerusalem. King Jehoiakim died before Jerusalem fell, and Jehoiachin, his eighteen-year-old son, ascended to the throne only to surrender the city to Babylon on March 16, 597 BC.[1] The Babylonians deported Jehoiachin, along with the upper crust of Judean society, to Babylon. This crushing blow set the stage for Zedekiah's rise to power.

According to 2 Kings 24:17, "The king of Babylon made Mattaniah, Jehoiachin's uncle, king in his place and changed his name to Zedekiah." Though Zedekiah was part of the Davidic royal family, the people evidently did not accept him as king. Hananiah's false prophecy undoubtedly reflects a hope in Jehoiachin's return (Jer. 28:4). Other texts also support the notion that Zedekiah did not have full support of his people. For example, Ezekiel dated his prophetic visions on the basis of "King Jehoiachin's exile" (Ezek. 1:2).

ZEDEKIAH'S STORMY REIGN

If Zedekiah lacked the full support of his people, then his decisions and the tumultuous times between 597 and 586 BC did nothing to enhance his credibility. Within three years of taking the reins of government (ca. 594 BC), Zedekiah, at the urging of Egypt—along with Edom, Moab, Ammon, Tyre, and Sidon—gathered to plot a rebellion against Babylon. The plot failed perhaps due in part to Jeremiah, who picketed the event and proclaimed its folly (Jer. 27:1–11). Soon after this foiled plan, Zedekiah traveled to Babylon and swore renewed allegiance to the Babylonian king (29:3; 51:59).

Zedekiah's renewed allegiance did not last. Eventually he led Judah into open revolt against Babylon about 590–588 BC (cf. 2 Kgs. 24:20; 2 Chr. 36:13). Three factors may have contributed to Zedekiah's decision. First, Nebuchadnezzar had been absent from Syria-Palestine since 594 BC. Second, the Egyptian Pharaoh Psammetichus II had defeated Nubia to his south and toured Syria-Palestine as a way of flexing his military might.[2] Perhaps these two factors led Zedekiah to trust in Egypt's power (Ezek. 17:15) and to doubt Babylon's resolve. Finally, a segment of Zedekiah's court, as well as some prophets, claimed that rebellion was God's will (Jer. 28–29). The anti-Babylonian group maintained that God would not allow his city to fall into Babylonian hands (5:12; 14:13).

Jeremiah, however, consistently maintained that God's will was for Judah to submit to the Babylonians. This viewpoint, as you might imagine, was not popular. Jeremiah's fellow citizens considered him a traitor (37:11–21). Large blocks of Jeremiah's prophecy recount the rejection of God's perspective by both priests and prophets (chaps. 26–29) and the royal court (chaps. 34–36). Jeremiah's consistent call to submit to Babylon garnered the prophet multiple arrests and death threats (37:15; 38:1–16).

Zedekiah's failure to listen to Jeremiah eventually led to Jerusalem's destruction. The Babylonians reacted to Zedekiah's revolt by laying siege to the city of Jerusalem for about two years (588–586 BC). Help from Egypt never materialized. Neither did help from God. Numerous times Zedekiah attempted to bargain with God to spare the city. Three times Zedekiah sought a reprieve from God through Jeremiah (37:3,17; 38:14), but to no avail. The answer was the same each time. The city will fall. Possibly even the slave release in Jeremiah 34 was linked to a hope that obeying the law in Exodus 21:2 would cause God to protect the city. Unfortunately, the obedience of the slave owners lasted only a short time. When the siege lifted momentarily, the slave owners reneged on their promises. This led to a stinging pronouncement of judgment: "You have not obeyed me by proclaiming freedom, each for his fellow Hebrew and for his neighbor. I hereby proclaim freedom for you—this is the Lord's declaration—to the sword, to plague, and to famine!" (Jer. 34:17).[3]

Urartian Bronze Age chain. Zedekiah was led off in chains (39:7).

THE END OF ZEDEKIAH'S REIGN

God's prediction proved true. Jeremiah 52:1–7 tells us that the city finally ran out of food and out of time. The Babylonian army tore down the walls, destroyed the temple, and set fire to the city. Many of the citizens began the long march as captives to Babylon (vv. 28–30). Only the poorest people remained in the land (39:9–10). Zedekiah attempted to escape, but the Babylonians captured him at Jericho. He appeared before Nebuchadnezzar at Riblah and watched his sons die before his eyes. It was the last thing Zedekiah saw. The Babylonians blinded him and led him away in chains to prison where he later died (52:9–11).

NOTES

[1] This date is based on correlating our Julian calendar with the Babylonian Chronicle, a source for Nabopolassar and Nebuchadnezzar's activities in the land of Israel. See James B. Pritchard, ed., *ANET*, 564; John Bright, *A History of Israel*, 4th ed. (Louisville: Westminster John Knox, 2000), 327.

[2] J. Maxwell Miller and John H. Hayes, *A History of Ancient Israel and Judah* (Philadelphia: Westminster, 1986), 412–13. Daniel I. Block, *The Book of Ezekiel: Chapters 1–24*, NICOT (Grand Rapids: Eerdmans, 1997), 544: "A papyrus from El Hibeh refers to a visit by the pharaoh to Syria-Palestine in his fourth year, ostensibly as a religious pilgrimage to Byblos. But such royal visits usually also have political undertones, especially since these states had revolted against Babylon as recently as three years previously."

[3] William S. LaSor, David A. Hubbard, and Frederic William Bush, *Old Testament Survey: The Message, Form, and Background of the Old Testament*, 2nd ed. (Grand Rapids: Eerdmans, 1996), 346.

PLACES

ABEL-BETH-MAACAH: ITS HISTORY AND SIGNIFICANCE

BY ERIC A. MITCHELL

Abel-beth-maacah (Tell Abil el-Qameh).

Excavated buildings dated to the late eleventh–early tenth centuries BC; between the upper and lower mounds, on the east side of the tel.

Cooking installation excavated at Abel-beth-maacah; shown are two silos, each measuring more than five feet in diameter. Archaeologists excavated from them ash, bones, and pottery. The indentation in the front left was likely a cooking pit. Ceramic ovens would have been located on the raised platform in the back left corner of this same room. The installation dates to the Middle Bronze Age II (1950–1550 BC), the time of the patriarchs.

Several towns in ancient Israel have the name of Abel (meaning "meadow") accompanied by a modifier indicating a distinction about the location. Those in the Old Testament are Abel-mizraim, "meadow/mourning of Egypt," located at Atad on the eastern side of the Jordan River and north of the Dead Sea, which was where the Egyptians traveled with Joseph to mourn Jacob's death (Gen. 50:11); Abel-shittim, "the Acacia Meadow" located across the Jordan River from Jericho (Num. 33:49); Abel-keramim, "meadow/plain of vineyards," in the Transjordan near Amman (Judg. 11:33); and Abel-meholah, "meadow of the dance," which was likely located in the Jordan Valley south of Beth-shean (1 Kgs. 19:16).

Abel-beth-maacah (also called Abel of Beth-maacah) means "meadow of the house of Maacah," perhaps designating the town as the Abel that lies in the ancient region of the Aramean tribe of Maacah.[1] This twenty-five-acre site is located four and a half miles west of Tel Dan, a mile south of the modern Israeli border with Lebanon; and is twenty-one miles east of Tyre and forty-three miles southwest of Damascus. By the end of the judges period, this was an Aramean border region with Phoenicians to the west and north and Israelites to the south.[2]

During the Late Iron I period (1200–1100 BC), the Aramean clan of Maacah controlled the kingdom of Geshur. This territory was just north of Israel and south of Mount Hermon from the Transjordan across the Golan Heights into the Jordan Valley north of the Sea of Galilee.[3]

RESOURCES

Abel-beth-maacah had all four basic resources required for a good city location in ancient times: (1) for protection, an elevated location with sloping sides, (2) water, (3) agricultural fields, and (4) a nearby route for income-producing trade. Nestled next to the Lebanon range on its west, which separates Israel and Jordan, the site is on a plateau 1,400 feet above sea level and overlooks the Huleh Valley to the south. Archaeologist William Dever described the site as sitting on a "grassy knoll above the falls at the headwaters of one of the sources of the Jordan."[3] The ancient city's tel rises an imposing forty-nine feet above the surrounding fields.

As seen from Abel-beth-maacah, mountains of Lebanon rise in the distance.

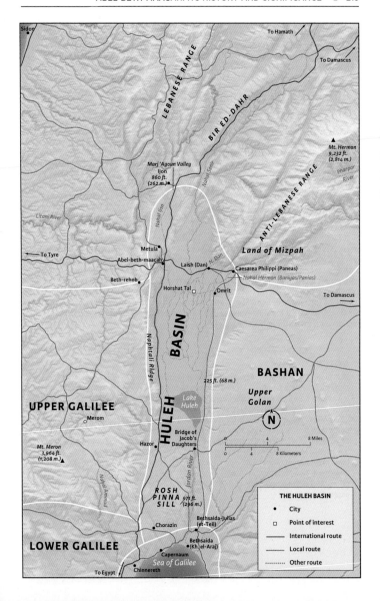

THE HULEH BASIN

- • City
- □ Point of interest
- —— International route
- —— Local route
- ········ Other route

Abel-beth-maacah strategically controlled a significant ancient crossing point for two major routes: first, a trade route from Mesopotamia to Egypt through Lebanon's Beqa'a Valley to its north, and second, an east-west route from Damascus and the Transjordan across the Golan Heights (just south of Mount Hermon) to Abel-beth-maacah and then north and west to Tyre or Sidon. The surrounding agricultural fields were a rich resource. The fields to its north and east rise in elevation toward the north.[4]

ARCHAEOLOGICAL EXCAVATIONS

Only recently have the first-ever excavations occurred at Abel-beth-maacah, which is known locally as Tell Abil el-Qameh. Naama Yahalom-Mack and Nava Panitz-Cohen of Jerusalem's Hebrew University are jointly leading the excavations with Robert Mullins of Azusa Pacific University. The excavations have taken place from 2013 to 2017.[5]

The surveys have revealed many ancient sites within three miles of Abil el-Qameh, which indicates a regional habitation from the Early Bronze to Ottoman periods. The site itself is an oval, stretching north to south with a three-acre upper tel on the northern end that is another thirty-two feet higher than the southern (lower) tel. Current excavations have revealed occupation on the lower tel in the Middle Bronze (2400–1500 BC), Late Bronze (1500–1200), and Iron Age I (1200–1000) after which the lower city was abandoned. The upper acropolis of the city continued in use, however, from Iron Age II to the Hellenistic period (1000–ca 334 BC).[6]

A Benjaminite, named Sheba the son of Bichri, blew a trumpet and called all Israel to reject David's rule. David immediately gave orders to find or capture Sheba and quell the revolt. Sheba had run to the most distant city in Israelite territory from Jerusalem—Abel-beth-maacah. Joab and his men cast a siege ramp against the city to attack it, but a wise woman declared that Abel was known as a place of wisdom. She called her city "a mother in Israel" (a city with "daughter" villages; 2 Sam. 20:18–19). The woman convinced the people of the city to behead Sheba and throw his head over the wall to Joab. Politically for David, having a loyal Aramean city kill the rebellious Benjaminite was better than David's own men killing him.

NOTES

[1] W. G. Dever, "Abel-Beth-Ma'acah: Northern Gateway of Ancient Israel" in *The Archaeology of Jordan and Other Studies*, ed. L. T. Geraty and L. G. Herr (Berrien Springs, MI: Andrews University Press, 1986), 208–10.

[2] Nava Panitz-Cohen, Robert A. Mullins, and Ruham Bonfil, "Northern Exposure: Launching Excavations at Tell Abil el-Qameh (Abel Beth Maacah)," *Strata: Bulletin of the Anglo-Israel Archaeological Society* 31 (2013): 27–28. Tel Abel Beth Maacah Excavations, abel-beth-maacah.org/index.php/about.

[3] Dever, "Abel-Beth-Ma'acah," 214. Nava Panitz-Cohen, R. A. Mullins, and R. Bonfil, "Second Preliminary Report of the Excavations at Tell Abil el-Qameh (Abel Beth Maacah)," *Strata* 33 (2015): 55–56. Cf. B. Mazar, "Geshur and Maacah," *JBL* 80 (March 1961): 16–28.

[4] Dever, "Abel-Beth-Ma'acah," 210.

[5] Dever, "Abel-Beth-Ma'acah," 210–11, 217.

[6] Dever, "Abel-Beth-Ma'acah," 216; cf. Tel Abel Beth Maacah Excavations, abel-beth-maacah.org/index.php/staff/core-staff.

ABRAHAM'S TRAVELS

BY ALAN RAY BUESCHER

Interior of a Bedouin tent. Continuing still today, Bedouin have a long-established tradition of extending hospitality to travelers and visitors.

Archaeologists care little for wandering nomads; they leave little or no material evidence of their lives for future generations to discover. So likewise with Abraham, who built no cities or buildings and left no potsherds, tools, or jewelry in garbage dumps or tombs (at least that anyone has discovered). The concept of Abraham as a nomad or seminomad, however, may not survive the test of scriptural scrutiny. Old Testament scholar D. J. Wiseman described Abraham's lifestyle more akin to pastoral nomadism as described in the Mari texts, in which seasonal farming accompanied the herding of flocks and cattle close to towns and cities.[1]

Abraham's time in the land of promise significantly illustrates his lifestyle: he spent most of those one hundred years settled in Hebron or in the Negev (in Gerar and Beersheba), although he apparently lived in tents rather than permanent structures (e.g., Gen. 13:18; 18:1). In the Negev, the area around Beer-sheba provides the only land available for farming without water irrigation, but agriculture did not rank as the primary means of earning a living. The numerous ancient remains discovered at sites in the Negev reveal their main function as caravan stations for trade merchants traveling to and from Egypt.

Perhaps Abraham participated in this trade, which could account partially for his wealth accumulation. He had flocks, cattle, and camels; he also possessed flour for baking (18:6–8), either from farming or via trade with sedentary farmers in nearby settlements. He possessed much silver and gold (13:2), which he earned or inherited from his time spent in Haran.

Additionally, he may have accumulated some wealth in Egypt and Canaan through market transactions.

Israeli archaeologist Amihai Mazar believes the archaeological discoveries of the Middle Bronze II (MBII) period provide similarities with the patriarchal record in the Bible that cannot be ignored. The Canaanite culture became established primarily along the northern coastal plain and eastward through the valleys of Jezreel and Beth-shean during MBIIA. These Canaanites likely came from the coastal plain around Tyre and also from Aram (modern Syria). Egyptian documents from Byblos as well as documents from Mari during MBIIA contain West Semitic (Amorite) names among the population of Aram and Canaan. One of the Mari texts contains the earliest record of the designation "Canaanite" as one of the population groups of the area. Furthermore, West Semitic or Amorite names correspond closely to Canaanite names.[3]

This Amorite population continued to migrate east into Babylon during MBIIB–C (ca. 1800/1750–1550 BC), spreading its culture throughout the northern portion of the Fertile Crescent. During this time, foreign rulers known as the Hyksos came to power in Egypt. These outsiders were none other than Canaanites. Thus a West-Semitic/Amorite/Canaanite culture extended from Egypt, northward along the coastal plain of the promised land, across the Jezreel Valley, and north along the Fertile Crescent to Babylon. This Canaanite influence that began in MBIIA likely could have made a Semitic language the common language of the day for international trade purposes, and it could explain how Abraham communicated with the Egyptians and Abimelech in the Negev. Akkadian, a Semitic language, became the universal language of scribes, priests, and the legal community throughout the ancient Near East by MBIIB–C and likely began its dominance in MBIIA.

Ruins of the palace at Mari in modern Syria. Mari was the capital city of the Amorites from about 2000 to 1750 BC. The palace covered more than six acres and had more than three hundred rooms. One of the most remarkable finds at Mari was the 15,000-plus texts that detailed everyday life in Mari before its fall. Many of the names on the texts are the same as some from the Old Testament, including Noah, Abram, Laban, Jacob, Benjamin, and Levi.

Camels grazing in the Judean wilderness.

Ruins of Beer-sheba in southern Israel; farmland is in the distance.

NOTES

[1]   D. J. Wiseman, "Abraham Reassessed," in *Essays of the Patriarchal Narratives*, ed. A. R. Millard and D. J. Wiseman (Winona Lake, IN: Eisenbrauns, 1983), 145.

[2]   A. Reifenberg, *The Struggle between the Desert and the Sown: Rise and Fall of Agriculture in the Levant* (Jerusalem: Publishing Department of the Jewish Agency, 1955), 19.

[3]   Amihai Mazar, *Archaeology of the Land of the Bible, 10,000–568 BCE* (New York: Doubleday, 1990), 174–89.

ACHAIA

BY DAVID M. WALLACE

Ruins at Cenchreae, which was the port city for ancient Corinth. The city, which had at one time been bustling with commerce and activity, was hit with catastrophic earthquakes in AD 365 and 375. Some rebuilding occurred beginning around AD 400, but by the sixth century the city was virtually abandoned.

LOCATION AND GEOGRAPHY[1]

Achaia in the New Testament refers to a geographic area in the southern portion of Greece, which included the cities of Athens, Corinth, and Sparta, as well as the Cyclades Islands—a group of more than 200 islands southeast of the mainland. Bounded by the Adriatic Sea on the west and the Aegean Sea to the east, with the Gulf of Corinth largely splitting it in half, Achaia is about the size of Maine.

The region has only two discernible seasons. Winter lasts October to April and is usually mild; it sees about forty inches of rain and some snow. Summer, which lasts May to September, is hot and dry, yet many areas get relief because of coastal breezes.

Mountains cover approximately three-fourths of the land, leaving only a quarter of the land available for farming. Although the mountains of Achaia are not unusually high, they are numerous. Mountain ranges and ridges crisscross the region, creating numerous ravines and valleys. Rain and melting snow produce many streams and even some large rivers in the mountains during the rainy winter season. During New Testament times, the resulting floods in the valleys below kept farmers from tilling the land. The rapidly flowing water was typically muddy, rendering it unusable to humans. Erosion was a problem; silt would fill the harbors.

In general, travel in the region was difficult. Snow often covered the mountain passes in winter. Crossing the swollen rivers was hazardous and, at times, impossible. Silt-filled

View of the sea at Delos, which the Greeks considered to be the religious heart of the Cyclades Islands. Greek mythology claimed that both Apollo and his sister Artemis were born at Delos.

harbors could halt boat and ship travel. Constructing bridges was impractical because of the sheer number of ravines, valleys, and rivers. Many travelers thus waited until the summertime and would use the then-dry riverbeds as roadways.

Although Achaia was dominated by mountains, it was mostly surrounded by water. No one in Achaia was ever more than forty miles from the sea. Many inlets and harbors dot the coastline. Although Achaia was primarily a rural and agricultural region, Achaians were also active seafaring people.

RESOURCES IN ACHAIA

The resources of Achaia varied greatly. Timber was in short supply. Most resources were agricultural. The region around the city of Argos produced a significant citrus crop. By terracing the hillsides, the people of Achaia were able to grow grapevines and olive trees. Because of the stony terrain, growing wheat was impossible, so the people imported it. Farmers instead raised barley and millet. Pastures, which would not support cattle, were better suited to raising sheep and goats. The area around Laconia produced copper and iron. Workers mined silver and lead from the region of Attica, on the peninsula southeast of Athens. Corinth and Athens produced potters' clay in abundance. These two cities became quite famous for their ceramics. White marble was quarried on the Cyclades Islands.

A plateau at the foot of the mountains near the region of Elis, on the Adriatic Sea to the west, had perhaps the best pastureland in the region. Elis was good for raising horses and cattle and for growing flax.

Corinth saw much activity from the shipping trade. Because the city was only one and a half miles from the Isthmus of Corinth, and because traveling around the southern tip of

Achaia at Cape Malea was long and dangerous, travelers and merchants customarily pulled cargo and smaller ships across the narrow, four-mile-wide Isthmus of Corinth on a tramway from Cenchreae to Lechaeum, the western harbor of Corinth, saving about 150 miles in travel distance.

NOTES

[1] Information in this article comes primarily from Charles F. Pfeiffer and Howard F. Vos, "Greece," in *Wycliffe Historical Geography of Bible Lands* (Chicago: Moody, 1967), 407–16.

ANCIENT LEBANON

BY JOHN TRAYLOR

Entryway into the Baalbek Temple, which is in the Beqaa Valley of Lebanon. During the Roman period, the city became an important center for the worship of Jupiter, Mercury, and Venus.

Like Solomon before him (1 Kgs. 5:6), Zerubbabel arranged for cedarwood to be imported from Lebanon for the construction of the temple (Ezra 3:7). Lebanon is on the eastern end of the Mediterranean Sea immediately west of Syria and north of modern Israel. The land is rectangular in shape and divides itself into four sections running parallel to the coast. From west to east, the sections are the Coastal Plain, the Lebanon Mountains, the Valley of Lebanon, and the Anti-Lebanon Mountains.

Generally speaking, the southern border of Lebanon in the Old Testament era would have run from Mount Carmel on the coast across to Mount Hermon on the southern tip of the Anti-Lebanon Mountains. The northern border would have extended above Arvad on the coast over to the Euphrates River. The Coastal Plain is narrow, never more than about four miles wide with mountain spurs at times pushing into the sea.

PEOPLE AND NAME

The name *Lebanon* comes from a Hebrew verb meaning "be white," probably because of its snow-covered mountain peaks (Jer. 18:14).[1] The ancient Lebanese were Canaanites. Sidon, who established the city of Sidon, was Canaan's firstborn (Gen. 10:15,19). Canaan was called "the land of merchants" (Ezek. 17:4).

The Greeks spoke of Lebanon's Coastal Plain as "Phoenicia" (Acts 11:19) and its inhabitants as "Phoenicians." The Greek term for *Phoenicia* marks the coastal area as a land of dates or palm trees. The Greek term *phoinix* means "date palm" or "red-purple."[2] The Phoenicians were called "purple people" because they extracted and exported purple dye from the murex snail that inhabited the sea's coastal waters. Scholars debate whether the Phoenicians developed the alphabet called by their name, but they certainly distributed the alphabet through trade activities with the world of their day.

Found at Tyre and dated to the first century BC, a two-handled cup with a grapevine design. This piece of lead-glazed earthenware was made from a mold.

Rock strip marking the site of the ancient port of Sidon.

MAJOR CITIES

Major Lebanese cities mentioned in the Bible in order of appearance are Sidon, Hamath, Tyre, Zarephath, Arvad, and Gebal (Gen. 10:19; Num. 13:21; Josh. 19:29; 1 Kgs. 17:9; Ezek. 27:8,9). All of these cities were on the Coastal Plain except Hamath, which was in the northern interior on the Orontes River. Hamath was both a city and a regional area (Num. 13:21). Some take Baal-gad (Josh. 13:5) to be Baalbek, which was a key center of pagan worship in the Valley of Lebanon.[3] As seen in the cases of Hiram king of Tyre, Toi king of Hamath, and Ethbaal king of the Sidonians, these cities were city-states (2 Sam. 5:11; 8:9; 1 Kgs. 16:31).

Gebal is on the northwest Phoenician coast and was occupied as far back as about 5000 BC.[4] Its inhabitants were called Gebalites (Josh. 13:5). Like Tyre and Sidon, Gebal was a thriving maritime center. The Greek name for Gebal was "Byblos," their name for *book*, because the Gebalites exported the Egyptian papyrus plant, which people used for making books. Ultimately *Byblos* came to mean "Bible," a term for many papyrus books.

CROSSROADS OF INVADING ARMIES

Lebanon was at the crossroads of the ancient world and was the corridor through which world armies marched to and from battles. To celebrate their victories, some kings erected monuments at Dog River Pass, which cuts through the Coastal Plain to the sea about seven miles north of Beirut. Egypt's Ramesses II began the practice around 1240 BC, when he erected a monument on the south face of the pass to celebrate his victory over the Hittites at the battle of Kadesh. In the decade of 680–670 BC, Assyria's King Esarhaddon overran Sidon and Tyre and conquered Egypt. He positioned a monument depicting himself next to that of Ramesses II, apparently to show Assyria as being superior to Egypt. In addition to devastating Tyre, Babylon's King Nebuchadnezzar crushed the Egyptians and the Assyrians at the battle of Carchemish (605 BC). He erected his monument on the north face of the pass. Cyrus king of Persia conquered Babylon but erected no monument.

Housing area at Tyre containing ruins from many time periods, from the Iron Age through the Byzantine Empire.

Site of the citadel at Hamath. Located between the modern Syrian cities of Homs and Aleppo on the Orontes River, Hamath shows evidence of occupation to the Neolithic Age. At times, Hamath served as the northern boundary of ancient Israel. The Hebrew word *hamath* means "fortress."

RELIGION

As in the case of other Canaanites, the worship of Baal and his female consort, Asherah, dominated the religion of ancient Lebanon. People believed Baal to be the god of fertility. Worshippers along with the priests and priestesses would engage in so-called sacred prostitution to encourage the gods to mate in heaven to produce fertility on earth among human, animal, and vegetable life (Hos. 4:13). Worship could involve child sacrifice (Jer. 19:5). Baalism multiplied in the northern kingdom when Israel's King Ahab married Jezebel the daughter of Ethbaal, king of the Sidonians (1 Kgs. 16:31). Jezebel attempted to make Baalism the religion of Israel.

NOTES

1. William Sanford LaSor, "Lebanon" in *ISBE* vol. 3 (1986), 98.
2. Mario Liverani, "Phoenicia" in *ISBE*, 3:853.
3. "Baal-gad" in *HolBD*, 139.
4. Adrianus Van Selms, "Gebal" in *ISBE*, vol. 2 (1982), 420.

ANCIENT TYRE

BY PHILLIP J. SWANSON

Main arch in Roman-era Tyre.

A FAVORABLE LOCATION

Tyre (*Tsor* in the Phoenician language) means "rock" and aptly names and describes the ancient city. Tyre was situated on a rocky island about one-half mile off the eastern coast of the Mediterranean Sea. It owed its long history, in part, to its location and the fortifications various kings erected on the island. The expanse of water between Tyre and the mainland afforded the city a measure of security. Although the straits between Tyre and the coast did not span a great distance, any attacker would have to be proficient on the seas. The construction of a wall encircling the island, estimated to have been 150 feet high in some places, added to the city's security.[1] The city boasted two harbors, the earliest being a natural cove toward the northern end of the island, called the Sidonian port. This port provided adequate protection to Tyre's growing fleet. King Ithobaal I (887–856 BC) later built another harbor at the southern end of the island, referred to as the Egyptian port.[2]

As secure as Tyre may have been, living on an island has its disadvantages. All necessities not already on the island had to be brought in by boat. Tyre lacked sufficient drinkable water and food, as well as building supplies. To acquire these resources, they depended on a supply from the mainland. The town of Ushur, part of Tyre, on the mainland, probably provided that service to the island inhabitants.[3]

AN ENTERPRISING CITY

As with many ancient cities and towns, knowledge of Tyre's origin and earliest inhabitants has faded with time. Its emergence as a significant force in the ancient Near East appears to have begun in the tenth century with the ascension of King Hiram (970–936 BC) to the throne. For two centuries before that time, Tyre's sister city, Sidon, was the dominant force. Hiram enlarged the island by joining it with a second island.[4] He also rebuilt and reestablished worship at the temples of Melkart and Ashtart.[5] This same King Hiram assisted Kings David and Solomon with the building of David's palace and Solomon's temple. In fact, during Israel's golden age, treaties were in force between the two nations.

Roman columns in ancient Tyre.

Block with inscription mentioning "Tyrdos."

Although ties existed between Tyre and Israel, when King Ahab married Jezebel, the daughter of the king of the Sidon—which was under Tyrian dominance—he further cemented the relationship between the two nations.

Tyre's prosperity, especially during Hiram's time, was proverbial. During this time, Tyre became one of the most significant city-states in the known world. Industry flourished. Fishing was primary to the economy. Going beyond the simple catching of fish for sustenance, the Tyrians developed fisheries as large industrial plants.[6] Additionally, Tyre gained a reputation for its highly effective red dye.[7] Expanding its economic base even further, Tyre developed artists and craftsmen. Hiram's association with the construction of David's palace and the Jerusalem temple is well known and well documented in 2 Samuel 5:11 and 1 Kings 5:18, respectively. Second Chronicles 2:13–14 reports the skill and activity of Huramabi, a Tyrian who worked on the temple. The text describes him as one who was proficient with all kinds of metals, wood, stone, yarns, and linen.

Tyre's greatest importance centered on its capacity for seamanship and overseas trade. Ezekiel 27 provides a list of the cargo Tyre's sailors carried: lumber, linen, various metals, ivory, emeralds, wines, wool, and many other commodities. Tyrian ships carried goods to every part of the known world.[8] Isaiah 23:3 proclaims that Tyre "was the merchant among the nations." Beginning with King Hiram, Tyre was not content to simply exist as merchants and seamen in their travels to foreign ports. From the tenth to ninth centuries BC, Tyre engaged in colonizing efforts around their world—efforts that possibly reached as far as Spain.[9] The most important of these colonies were Carthage and Utica in northern Africa.

A PENDING JUDGMENT

The picture that emerges of Tyre is of a city of great importance to its neighbors around the world. So what caused Israel's prophets such dismay that profound judgment against Tyre was the only answer?[10]

Most likely, the cause was not related to any single factor. The alliance made between Ahab and his Phoenician wife, Jezebel, introduced idolatry into the land, but that was a common enough occurrence throughout Israel's history.

Ezekiel reported that Tyre took advantage of Israel's misfortune (especially Jerusalem) when it found itself decimated by the Babylonians (Ezek. 26:2–7). Quite possibly, even more disgusting to the prophet, the ruler of Tyre proclaimed himself to be a god (28:2–5). In the mind of the prophet, these two events would be more than sufficient to warrant God's judgment. Amos explained the matter further by saying that Tyre turned its back on the treaty between Israel and Tyre, a "treaty of brotherhood" (Amos 1:9). Tyre had sold the inhabitants of Jerusalem into slavery to the Edomites.

Judgment was going to come to Tyre according to the testimony of the prophets. The only question was *when*.

A DISASTROUS END

For all its economic prosperity, Tyre's history was going to change for the worse with the rise of the Assyrian Empire. Through the ninth and eighth centuries BC, Assyria forced Tyre to pay tribute to them and also attacked Tyre on several occasions.[11] Although the Assyrian kings did subjugate Tyre, their actions did not approach the devastation the prophets pronounced.

The city did not fare any better under the Babylonians. Babylon's King Nebuchadnezzar attacked Tyre in 585 BC and laid siege to the city for thirteen years. Tyre finally relented and became a Babylonian province.[12] Nonetheless, the city-state remained intact.

The lot fell to Alexander the Great (332 BC) to carry out the sentence of the prophets. As he moved against Tyre, the city dug in once again to withstand the onslaught of another enemy. They held out for seven months, to no avail. As one historian put it, Tyre was "obliterated."[13]

NOTES

[1] Glenn E. Markoe, *Phoenicia* (Berkeley: University of California Press, 2000), 197.

[2] Markoe, *Phoenicia*, 198.

[3] LaMoine F. DeVries, *Cities of the Biblical World* (Peabody, MA: Hendrickson, 1997), 78–79.

[4] Michael Grant, *The Ancient Mediterranean* (New York: Meridian Pocket, 1969), 121–22.

[5] Avraham Negev, ed., *The Archaeological Encyclopedia of the Holy Land*, rev. ed. (Nashville: Thomas Nelson, 1986), 388.

[6] Markoe, *Phoenicia*, 197.

[7] Grant, *Ancient Mediterranean*, 122.

[8] Negev, *Archaeological Encyclopedia*, 387.

[9] Negev, *Archaeological Encyclopedia*, 388.

[10] See Isaiah 23; Jeremiah 25; Ezekiel 26–28; Joel 3; Amos 1 and Zechariah 9.

[11] DeVries, *Cities*, 81.

[12] DeVries, *Cities*.

[13] Grant, *Ancient Mediterranean*, 213.

ANTIOCH OF SYRIA

BY ROBERT E. JONES

Dating to the third century BC, a colossal Charonian carving in the mountainside overlooking Antioch. Ancient records indicate the figure was carved in an attempt to save the city below from a plague afflicting persons in the area.

ANTIOCH'S PRE-CHRISTIAN HISTORY

Around 300 BC, Seleucus I (Nicator) founded Antioch as his capital city, one of sixteen cities Seleucus named in honor of his father Antiochus. Seleucus located the city on the bank of the Orontes River about fifteen miles from the Mediterranean Sea, giving the city access to a nearby port. Following Seleucus's death, successive kings enlarged and fortified the city. In 83 BC, the city fell into the control of Armenia for nineteen years.

Then in 64 BC, the Roman general Pompey defeated Syria, and Antioch came under the control of the Roman Empire, becoming both the capital and the military center of the Roman province of Syria. During the Roman period, Antioch grew and became increasingly impressive. Officials improved the roads leading to the city and further developed the nearby seaport. As a result, communication with the entire Mediterranean world became more rapid and secure. These improvements later would prove helpful for the spreading of the gospel westward in the Roman world.

Antioch became a prosperous city during the Roman period, in part from its political position but also because of commerce. Examples of goods one could purchase in Antioch were fine leather, shoes, perfume, spices, textiles, and jewelry, as well as locally produced gold and silver products. Also Antioch had schools of rhetoric and teachers of Greek wisdom that attracted students from across the Mediterranean world. All of these combined factors have led some historians to consider Antioch the third-greatest city in the Roman world behind only Rome and Alexandria.

Tetradrachma of Seleucus I (Nicator), who founded Antioch as his capital.

Prosperity, luxury, and ease led to an emphasis on "luxurious immorality."[1] The pleasure garden of Daphne, about five miles out of Antioch, became a virtual "hotbed of every

Antakya today (ancient Antioch of Syria) is part of the Republic of Turkey, although Syrian maps still show it as part of Syria.

kind of vice and depravity"[2] that made the city infamous. In the pleasure garden, which was about ten miles in circumference, stood the temple of Daphne, amidst a beautiful grove of laurels, old cypresses, and flowing, gushing waters. Nightly the temple prostitutes would practice sensual rights in the name of religion. These activities led to the so-called Daphnic morals, a phrase that referred to immoral living.[3]

In 20 BC, Augustus established local games that later came to be known as the Olympic Games of Antioch and one of the most famous festivals in the Roman world. Every four years during July and August, people traveled to Antioch from all over the Greco-Roman world to attend these games, which included boxing, wrestling, chariot racing, and other forms of competition. The games ceased briefly from AD 41 to 54, but later Claudius reinstated them.

ANTIOCH IN THE FIRST CENTURY

From its beginning, Antioch had a mixed population that eventually numbered approximately 500,000 people by the first century AD and possibly double that number by the third century. By the beginning of the Christian era, about 25,000 Jews may have lived in Antioch. Such a large and influential Jewish community would have offered a fertile field for Christian teaching. In addition Antioch was also a cosmopolitan city where many Greek-thinking Gentiles lived. In a sense, then, Antioch was a place where two worlds, those of the Jews and the Greeks, came together. In such a setting as this, Christianity flourished.

Acts 11:19 records the scattering of believers from Jerusalem because of persecution surrounding Stephen's death. Some believers made their way north to Antioch, initially preaching the gospel to Jews only. Once in Antioch, these Christian missionaries apparently discovered they did not have to fear attacks from the Jews as they had in Jerusalem. One reason may have been the cosmopolitan atmosphere in Antioch that allowed for both classical and Asian cults. Therefore, new religions were no novelty in Antioch. A second reason may have been that the Jews successfully attracted a large number of Gentiles to their synagogues, and many of these Gentiles actually became proselytes to Judaism. This group of Gentiles may have been a target for the Christian preachers. In addition, according to Acts 11:21, many Gentiles, probably from the God fearers who had been attracted to the Jewish synagogues, became believers; thus the composition of the church in Antioch would have been largely Gentile. We might say, then, that Antioch became a cradle of Gentile Christianity and the Christian missionary effort.

We could hardly overstate the importance Antioch had in the early history of Christianity. "Antioch of Syria was second only to Jerusalem as a center of early Christianity. Antioch was a commercial center in the Roman Empire. It was a citadel of the Greco-Roman culture, and it became the primary home of Christianity when it moved beyond its Jewish beginnings to the Gentile world."[4]

Due to Antioch's strong economy, the Antioch believers were able to provide the financial resources necessary for the growth of the missionary enterprise. Moreover, Antioch's geographical location served well for the city to be a focal point for the expansion of Christianity toward the west. Indeed, from this city Paul and Barnabas, and later Silas, left for their missionary journeys. To the Antioch church they would return from time to time to report on their successes.

NOTES

[1]   William Barclay, *The Acts of the Apostles* (Philadelphia: Westminster, 1976), 89.
[2]   Charles F. Pfeiffer and Howard F. Vos, *The Wycliffe Historical Geography of Bible Lands* (Chicago: Moody, 1967), 247.
[3]   William Ewing and Howard F. Vos, "Daphne" in *ISBE* (1979), 1:866.
[4]   LaMoine F. DeVries, *Cities of the Biblical World* (Peabody, MA: Hendrickson, 1997), 345.

THE ARABAH

BY DAVID M. WALLACE

Peering through "Solomon's Pillars" for an overview of Timnah, an ancient Egyptian mining village in the Arabah.

The historic land of Israel has many diverse physical features. Travelers heading east from the Mediterranean Sea will encounter the coastal plains, the Shephelah region, the Judean hill country, the Jordan Valley, and the eastern plateau.

These five areas run north and south. The two geographical areas that cut across the land westward are the plain of Esdraelon in the north from the Jordan Valley to the Mediterranean at Mount Carmel and the Negev, from the land south of the Dead Sea west to the River of Egypt. This small region of the world has perhaps more changes in landscape than any other. The region called the Arabah was a significant area in the history of ancient Israel.

The longest and deepest natural depression on earth, known as the Rift Valley, extends from northern Syria to eastern Africa and is one of the most important features in Israel's geography. This natural depression includes the area known as the Arabah.

Arabah is the word used in the Bible to describe all or part of the Great Rift Valley in Israel. It ran from the Sea of Galilee in the north, through the Jordan Valley southward to the Dead Sea, and continued all the way south to the Gulf of Aqaba. In the Bible, the Arabah most commonly refers to the region south of the Dead Sea to Ezion-geber. This was the land of part of Israel's wanderings in the wilderness.

Arabah is a noun and place-name that is variously translated in the Bible as "dry," "infertile," "burnt-up," "desert," "wilderness," "valley," and "plain." The place is a wasteland and one of the most desolate and forbidding areas on earth. The root meaning of the word is uncertain, but it most assuredly referred to an arid region.

The Arabah proper begins just south of the Dead Sea and near the Scorpions' Ascent, running through Wadi el-Arabah and terminating at the Gulf of Aqaba. Just south of the Dead Sea the terrain is about 1,300 feet below sea level; it gradually ascends to about 720 feet above sea level before descending to sea level at the gulf, a distance of some 110 miles. Most of the land surrounding the depression of the Arabah is above sea level.

The climate is characterized by hot summers and relatively mild winters. During the summer months of June through September, the daytime temperatures can exceed 120°F

Pharaoh's Island at the north end of the Gulf of Aqaba near Taba and Elath.

Shepherd with sheep along the Desert Highway between Amman (Rabbah) and Aqaba near Al Qatraneh.

(49°C). The average daily temperatures during the winter months of November through March are about 60°F (15.5°C).

Rainfall is sparse, occurring usually in the winter months, with a total annual accumulation of one-half to two inches. After rare thunderstorms, the ground may briefly be covered with grass and flowers, but they will soon die because of the hot sun and dry climate. Due to the lack of precipitation, plants are generally limited to sagebrush, camel thorns, and acacia. However, the areas with more water produce spina-christi trees, which are shaped like umbrellas. Underground water from the highlands on each side makes this desert growth possible. Because the eastern side is higher than the western, it receives more rain. Therefore more erosion comes from the east, created by streams slowly moving dirt, gravel, and sand into the plain.

Just south of the Dead Sea is a wide, barren salt and mudflat area that was once underwater. Here the Arabah is 1,275 feet below sea level. It is surrounded by low cliffs. At the base of these cliffs are a few springs that provide some water and produce a fair amount of desert vegetation.

South of the salt and mudflats lies Sela (Petra), rising to 300 feet above sea level. Sela was an Edomite fortress during the Israelite wanderings. Beyond Sela, the valley widens to as much as twenty-five miles before narrowing again as it slopes downward to the Gulf of Aqaba at Ezion-geber. The entire area has very little vegetation except for occasional oases.

The southern section of the Arabah narrows to only six miles, with steep cliffs on each side. To the east lie the granite mountains of Midian, and to the west is Nubian sandstone terrain.

Another characteristic of the southern Arabah is the distinctive, broad, dried-out mud-flats. These mudflats were created by sediment washing into the valley from streams and rain. But because of so little water and drainage, the sediment does not reach the Gulf of Aqaba. This process forms mudflats that are extremely slippery after rain.

An important north-south route, known as the King's Highway, existed in the Arabah during biblical times. The road was controlled by the Edomites and Amorites when the Israelites asked permission to travel it (Num. 20:17).

Along this route were economically important copper mines. Copper ore appears in the sandstone of the southern Arabah, and mining occurred at Punon, Irnahash, and Timnah. Punon is probably the site where Moses raised the bronze serpent (Num. 21:4–9; 33:42–43). Timnah, once called Solomon's mines, was mined by the Egyptians, possibly year-round. Copper and iron were mined at these locations. The Israelites would have avoided the mines when they were fortified by garrisons.

Other important mining and smelting areas were Khirbet en-Nahas, seventeen miles south of the Dead Sea, and Meneiyyeh, twenty-two miles north of the Gulf of Aqaba. Archaeology makes clear that this area of the Holy Land was one "whose rocks are iron and from whose hills you will mine copper" (Deut. 8:9).

The Hebrews lived in and crossed the Arabah while wandering in the wilderness on their way from Egypt to the promised land. Deuteronomy 2:8 tells us that they traveled down the Arabah from Kadesh-barnea to Ezion-geber. They claimed this land (Josh. 1–12) and the eastern side of the Jordan River as well (Deut. 3:1–20). Then they turned north and traveled through Wadi Yitm to go around the territories of Edom and Moab.

The Arabah lies primarily in the territory of Old Testament Edom. The Edomites based their economy on agriculture and commerce more than on the copper mines of the region. Agriculture was possible in the northeast portion of their territory. Their prosperity depended largely on caravans traveling from India to the Mediterranean Sea over their roads. When Edom controlled the trade routes, their economy was strong; otherwise they lived in decline. A strong army was essential to a healthy economy.

Numbers 20:14–21 tells the story of the Edomites refusing to allow Moses and the Israelites to pass through their territory on the King's Highway. Moses was trying to reach the land east of the Jordan River so they could begin their conquest of the promised land. And because of the threat the Edomite army presented, Israel did not challenge their position. (See also God's directions not to challenge Edom in Deut. 2:4–8.) The passage indicates the Arabah had fields, vineyards, and wells from which to drink. Moses and his people were forced to travel northeast around Edom and take a more indirect route to the land "across the Jordan in the wilderness, in the Arabah" (1:1).

The Israelites endured many difficulties during their wanderings in the wilderness of the Arabah. They traveled with donkeys. Camels are never mentioned. After many years in the desert, Israel's wanderings were extended because of the long, forced detour around Edomite and Moabite land in the Arabah. The most suitable land for living was already claimed by the Amalekites in the south and the Edomites and Moabites in northern Arabah.[1]

The land was hot, dry, dusty, and windy. This trip to the promised land was not for the faint of heart. It was a hostile environment at best.

The principal roads in the Arabah provided easier travel and the benefit of finding people with whom to trade for needed goods. However, the Israelites were not always welcome guests (Num. 20:14–21).

Finding water was always a challenge. Besides the occasional oasis, water resources included subterranean reservoirs that could be tapped from the surface and natural open pools along wadis where rainwater collected.

Other challenges included the land's being generally unsuitable for farming. The Israelites used cliffs to provide shelter from wind and storms. Goats were essential to their survival. Goats can live many days without water and show no ill effects. This freed the Israelites to travel long distances without a water source.

NOTES

[1] John Bright, *A History of Israel*, 2nd ed. (Philadelphia: Westminster, 1972), 128.

ASSYRIA IN THE EIGHTH CENTURY

BY DANIEL C. BROWNING JR.

Scene on the black obelisk of Shalmaneser III depicting Shalmaneser accepting tribute from Israel's King Jehu. This is the only discovered image of a Hebrew king.

Assyria, which first emerged as an important power in northern Mesopotamia during the time of Abraham, Isaac, and Jacob, waxed and waned for centuries until Israel's divided monarchy period (late ninth–seventh centuries BC). This era of Assyria's renewed dominance, known as the Neo-Assyrian Empire, is well known from cuneiform documents, bas-reliefs (sculptured panels) from Assyrian royal palaces, and other archaeological evidence.

Almost annually, the Assyrian king gathered his troops and set out in predatory campaigns. He invaded smaller nations and gave them an ultimatum demanding "presents" and allegiance. From these now-subservient nations, the Assyrian king demanded annual tribute payments—typically gold, silver, or other products of value. Those who resisted were subjected to violent military action. The Assyrian army dominated in the field because of its cavalry; thus, many foes took refuge within fortified citadels. The Assyrians, however, having become experts at siege warfare, invariably breached the walls and took resistant cities. Survivors of the assault were subjected to extreme cruelties. Rulers' heads were severed and set on pikes. Supporters of the resistant ruler were flayed alive or impaled, while prisoners were hauled away as slaves.

Artists duly recorded all these actions. Assyrian rulers, beginning with Ashurnasirpal II (883–859 BC), built huge palaces decorated throughout with bas-reliefs showing these atrocities. Back in the conquered area, the Assyrian king would set up a puppet ruler and impose heavy tribute on the already-devastated nation. Those delivering tribute to the royal palace passed through halls and rooms decorated with the macabre scenes as reminders of what awaited those who would resist or rebel.

After the reign of Assyrian king Shalmaneser III (858–824 BC), Assyria entered an eighty-year decline. The eighth century BC began with brighter prospects for the Hebrew kingdoms.

Basalt statue of King Shalmaneser III (858–824 BC).

Indeed, the first half of the century saw a period of peace and growth unknown since the united monarchy. Prosperity did not equal righteousness, however. Israel in particular was consumed with social, economic, and religious decay. By midcentury, judgment was due, and the golden age ended suddenly at the hands of Assyrian resurgence.

Assyrian power restarted with Tiglath-pileser III's accession to the throne in 745 BC. He reestablished Assyria's aggressive expansionist ways, reorganized the government, and transformed the nation into a true empire. He reformed the military, making it even more fearsome; his policy of mass deportation meant tens of thousands of persons were forcibly displaced from conquered nations. Tiglath-pileser revived the practice of building palaces decorated with depictions of Assyrian aggression, now including pitiful scenes of refugees marching in long files to relocation.[1] Tiglath-pileser soon turned his attention to Syria. By 738 BC, several panic-stricken states became vassals, including Aram-Damascus under King Rezin and Israel under King

Assyrian relief of Assyrians' siege of Lachish; two Hebrew captives led away (right); two others being flayed alive (left).

Menahem. Second Kings 15:19–20, which refers to Tiglath-pileser by his Babylonian throne name, Pul, details Menahem extracting silver from the rich and giving it to the Assyrian king "so that Pul would support him to strengthen his grasp on the kingdom" (15:19). Thus the Assyrian Empire entered the biblical record. The financial burden of tribute payments and the terrifying prospects resulting from withholding it made national policy of dealing with Assyria the number-one issue for kings of Israel and Judah, as the frequent turnover of subsequent monarchs testifies.

Hosea speaks of Ephraim/Israel going "up to Assyria" (Hos. 8:9; see 5:13; 7:11; 12:1). These are apparent references to kings who paid tribute and entered Assyrian vassalage as a survival strategy. Hosea knew, though, that Assyria was not Israel's salvation (14:3) but, rather, its destruction (9:3; 10:6; 11:5). God would send Assyria, the invading nation, as "fire on their cities," which would "consume their citadels" (8:14). Tiglath-pileser fulfilled these images (2 Kgs. 15:29) in 733 BC; his successors destroyed the northern nation forever (17:5–6) in 722 BC. Those who survived were going into exile, where they would "eat unclean food in Assyria" (Hos. 9:3). Concerning his people, the Lord proclaimed, "Assyria will be his king, because they refused to repent" (11:5).

NOTES

1   Georges Roux, *Ancient Iraq*, 3rd ed. (London: Penguin Books, 1992), 305–8.

BATTLE OF CARCHEMISH

BY KEVIN C. PEACOCK

Step pyramid and temple at Saqqara, Egypt.

Carchemish is not mentioned in Ezekiel (but see 2 Chr. 35:20; Isa. 10:9; Jer. 46:2). Nevertheless, chapters 29–32 speak of divine judgment on Egypt and its pharaoh. The battle of Carchemish played a crucial role in that judgment, after which the nation was no longer a power to be reckoned with. Ezekiel's judgment was ultimately fulfilled when the Persian king Cambyses conquered it in 525 BC.

Our knowledge of the ancient Near East is due in large part to cuneiform texts from Assyria and Babylonia. Many of these are chronographic texts that comprise seventeen king lists and twenty-five chronicles. The chronicles offer a yearly (with gaps) account of the king's military actions and other significant events. Chronicles 1–13b are known as the Babylonian Chronicle Series, which covers the period from Nabopolassar's founding of the Babylonian/Chaldean Empire in 626 BC to the Seleucid Empire in the third century BC.[1] Though often referred to as the Babylonian Chronicle, as if it were a unified text, it is actually a collection of tablets from many places, which mostly ended up in the British Museum in London. They are sometimes referred to not as a text but as a genre.[2]

Chronicle 5 covers the early years of Nebuchadnezzar II, from 604 to 595 BC, which includes his capture of Jerusalem in 597. It also describes Pharaoh Neco II's campaign to support the Assyrians at Haran in northern Syria in 610 or 609 BC. The Egyptians retreated from the Babylonians under King Nabonidus (625–605 BC), however, to Judah, where Neco II deposed King Jehoahaz II and installed Jehoiakim as king in 609 BC. Babylon campaigned in the north until they encountered the Assyrians at Carchemish, about fifty miles west of Haran. The Babylonian army under the command of crown-prince Nebuchadnezzar was victorious and drove the Egyptians southwest about 150 miles and defeated them again at Hamath. "The battle of Carchemish ... was, for the kingdom of Judah, one of the most consequential battles in ancient times."[3]

THE IMPORTANCE OF CARCHEMISH

Carchemish/Karkemish (modern-day Jerablus) held a strategic location on a major bend of the Euphrates River. Just west of the river, the city of Carchemish controlled an important river crossing in northern Syria. Controlling Carchemish meant controlling the international east-west trade route. The Babylonians desired to control Carchemish, the Phoenician coast, and the territory inland because

Babylonian Chronicle for 605–595 BC.

most Babylonian trade was with the west, and much wealth lay in Syria-Palestine. Carchemish was Babylon's gateway to the Mediterranean, and they could ill afford to have the Egyptians block it. Egypt controlled the Way of the Sea (Via Maris, see Isa. 9:1; Matt. 4:15) through central Syria as far as Carchemish. The Via Maris was the major trade route that followed the Mediterranean coast and linked Egypt with Mesopotamia.

The Neo-Babylonian Empire's brief history thus was marked with numerous campaigns into "the land of Hatti" (i.e., Syria-Palestine), campaigns vital for securing a lifeline of prosperity.[4] With the Medes being gone and the collapse of the Assyrian Empire, the main struggle for the control of Syria-Palestine in the last few years of the seventh century BC was between Egypt and Babylon. Carchemish was the key.

THE BATTLE OF CARCHEMISH

The Egyptians put up a strong resistance at Carchemish against the Babylonians, but in June–July 605 BC they finally withdrew, fleeing for their lives.[5] The Babylonian Chronicle, referring to Nebuchadnezzar, reports,

He defeated them (smashing) them out of existence. As for the remnant of the Egyptian army which had escaped from the defeat so (hastily) that no weapon had touched them, the Babylonian army overtook and defeated them in the district of Hamath, so that not a single man [escaped] to his own country. At that time Nebuchadrezzar conquered the whole of the land of Ha[math].[6]

Nebuchadnezzar likely pursued the fleeing Egyptian forces down the Mediterranean coast (see Jer. 46:2–12). The city of Riblah in southern Syria became the main Babylonian garrison center in southern Syria. Immediately after hearing of his father's death in Babylon, Nebuchadnezzar hurried home to secure his throne.[7]

Nebuchadnezzar then marched back to Hatti-land, secured his dominance there, and "took the heavy tribute of Hatti-land back to Babylon." He exerted control over Judah probably at this time. Daniel 1:1 states, "In the third year of the reign of King Jehoiakim of Judah, King Nebuchadnezzar of Babylon came to Jerusalem and laid siege to it." Then he took some of the temple vessels to Babylon (v. 2).[8] The Hebrew term translated "laid siege" may simply mean "showed hostility" or "treated as an enemy" and not an actual siege.[9] Nebuchadnezzar bound Jehoiakim in chains "to take him to Babylon" (2 Chr. 36:6) but could simply have been exerting dominance. This probably happened late in 605 BC.[10] The "heavy tribute of Hatti-land" thus included temple articles (v. 7) and Daniel and his three friends, who were taken into exile (Dan. 1:1–7).[11] For four successive years, Nebuchadnezzar campaigned in Hatti, securing his control over Syria-Palestine (Jer. 47:4–5; Hab. 1–2).

THE SIGNIFICANCE OF THE BATTLE

Biblical reflection on the battle of Carchemish and its immediate aftermath reveals several emphases:

God's Final Judgment on Assyria—For all practical purposes, the Assyrian Empire ceased to exist in 609 BC at the battle of Haran when its last king disappeared from history. But a few Assyrians probably joined the Egyptian forces at Carchemish. Nebuchadnezzar was the ax, but Yahweh's hand wielded it. Yahweh had promised that Assyria would be defeated (Isa. 10:5–34; 14:24–27; 31:8–9; Zeph. 2:13; Zech. 10:11; see Nahum), and Ezekiel used Assyria's defeat as a warning for Egypt (Ezek. 31:2–18).

Judah's New Boss—Immediately after Carchemish, Jeremiah began prophesying of Babylon's seventy-year rule over Judah and the entire land (Jer. 25:1–14; 29:10; 36:1–3). If Judah would voluntarily submit to Babylon, then destruction might not come (21:8–9; 38:2–3). Jeremiah sent his message on a scroll to Jehoiakim (36:1–19), but Jehoiakim refused to heed Jeremiah's warning and chose instead to rebel (v. 29).

Punishment for Egypt—Carchemish was a humiliating loss for the Egyptian army (Jer. 46:2–26), which fled slithering like a serpent seeking refuge (v. 22). "The king of Egypt did not march out of his land again, for the king of Babylon took everything that had belonged to the king of Egypt, from the Brook of Egypt to the Euphrates River" (2 Kgs. 24:7). Egypt's pride and aggression against its neighbors brought Yahweh's judgment (Jer. 46:7–8,26). The Egyptians trusted their own might, their own king, and their own gods (v. 25); therefore, Yahweh punished them, thrust them down, and put them to shame (vv. 15,21,24).

Judgment for God's People—Shortly after the battle of Carchemish, Nebuchadnezzar approached Jerusalem, and "the Lord handed King Jehoiakim of Judah over to him, along with some of the vessels from the house of God" (Dan. 1:2a). God caused Nebuchadnezzar's dominance over Judah. Why? Because King Jehoiakim "did what was evil in the sight of the LORD his God" (2 Chr. 36:5b; cf. 2 Kgs. 23:36–24:4). The subsequent exile was God's judgment on his people's sin (Dan. 9:5–14; cf. Deut. 28:32–64; 1 Kgs. 8:33–34,46–51). Because Israel refused to heed Yahweh's repeated warnings through his prophets (Dan. 9:6), the people suffered the consequences for their sin.

NOTES

[1] See D. B. Weisberg, "Non-Israelite Written Sources: Babylonian" in *Dictionary of the Old Testament Historical Books*, ed. Bill T. Arnold and H. G. M. Williamson (Downers Grove, IL: IVP Academic, 2005), 731–33.

[2] British Museum tablet 21901, lines 38–50, in D. J. Wiseman, *Chronicles of Chaldean Kings (626–556 BC) in the British Museum* (London: Trustees of the British Museum, 1956), 58–61. See also D. J. Wiseman, "Historical Records of Assyria and Babylonia" in *Documents from Old Testament Times*, ed. D. Winton Thomas (New York: Harper & Row, 1961), 77–79, from which the translation of the tablet here is taken.

[3] LeMoine F. DeVries, *Cities of the Biblical World* (Peabody, MA: Hendrickson, 1997), 53.

[4] Georges Roux, *Ancient Iraq* (New York: Penguin Books, 1977), 343.

[5] D. J. Wiseman, *Nebuchadrezzar and Babylon*, The Schweich Lectures of the British Academy (Oxford: Oxford University Press, 1985), 16. Excavations of the town and citadel in 1912–14 reveal that the city was burned about this time. The site is on the Turkish-Syrian border and is covered by a Turkish military base. Access is greatly restricted, and future excavations are highly unlikely.

[6] Wiseman earlier translated the final phrase "the whole of the land of Hatti," meaning Syria-Palestine. In 1985, he retranslated the phrase "the whole region of Hamath," referring to northern Syria. See Wiseman, *Nebuchadrezzar and Babylon*, 17.

[7] Wiseman, *Nebuchadrezzar and Babylon*, 17–18.

[8] On the chronological discrepancy between Daniel 1:1 and Jeremiah 25:1, see Tremper Longman III, *Daniel*, NIV Application Commentary (Grand Rapids: Zondervan, 1999), 43–44.

⁹ See Deuteronomy 20:12; 2 Kings 16:5; 24:10–11; Song of Songs 8:9. See Wiseman, *Nebuchadrezzar and Babylon*, 23. The Babylonian Chronicle mentions no siege of Jerusalem at this time.

¹⁰ Wiseman, *Nebuchadrezzar and Babylon*, 23. See Jack Finegan, *Handbook of Biblical Chronology*, rev. ed. (Peabody, MA: Hendrickson, 1998), 254. The text does not state that Jehoiakim was actually taken into exile; it could mean that he was threatened with the possibility.

¹¹ Ezekiel was probably taken into exile with King Jehoiachin and a group of 10,000 captives in the so-called "first deportation" in 597 BC. See Christopher J. H. Wright, *The Message of Ezekiel* (Downers Grove, IL: InterVarsity, 2001), 19–20.

CAESAREA: HEROD'S PORT CITY

BY TIMOTHY TRAMMELL

An aqueduct carried water into Caesarea Maritima from Mount Carmel, which was nearly ten miles away.

Surrounded by the sea, this rock-cut, freshwater swimming pool at Herod's Palace in Caesarea Maritima was seemingly built in defiance of nature. The entire pool complex (including dining halls, baths, and porticos) measured about 200 by 360 feet.

From an insignificant Phoenician fishing village to a major Mediterranean port and the capital of a Roman province is quite a transformation, but that is the story of Caesarea. This dramatic metamorphosis took place because of the vision and vanity of Herod the Great, ruler of the Jewish people from 37 BC to his death in 4 BC. Herod is remembered for his monumental building projects, and none was more impressive and remarkable than Caesarea Maritima, "Caesarea-on-the-Sea."

CAESAREA BEFORE HEROD

Called Straton or Strato's Tower, the original fishing village apparently had been built in the fourth century BC by Strato I, king of Sidon. Located on the coastal plain, it was a minor settlement on the caravan route between Tyre and Egypt. Pompey, the Roman military leader, claimed the village for Rome in 63 BC and elevated its status to that of autonomous city. Under Roman rule, Caesarea first became a part of Syria. Later Mark Antony gave it to Cleopatra of Egypt. Finally Augustus Caesar ceded the city to Herod, who named it after his patron.

CAESAREA UNDER HEROD

In 40 BC, the Roman rulers Antony and Octavian (Augustus Caesar) bestowed on Herod the title "king of the Jews." When the Roman senate confirmed the title, Herod sailed from Italy. With the help of Rome, he raised an army and in 37 BC conquered Jerusalem. He began a decade-long consolidation of his power and then initiated his building projects about 25 BC. Herod first began translating his architectural visions into stone in Jerusalem, erecting a theater with an amphitheater nearby, following these projects with a gigantic royal palace.

But Herod's dream was to construct a completely new city on the Mediterranean coast where no city had previously stood. This would be an international city that would rival the opulence and magnificence of the capital of the empire, with port facilities that would outstrip the size and significance of Alexandria, Egypt. He stipulated that the city would be laid out on the Roman grid plan, with a forum, baths, temples, tenements inside the walls, and villas outside.[1]

But why this location? Why not at Joppa, the city that had for centuries served Israel as a port? Herod's reasons were both political and religious. Joppa was Jewish and national, while Caesarea was cosmopolitan and Roman.[2] Building temples in Judea where Greek gods and Roman emperors were to be worshipped would have been unthinkable. So Herod, always the cunning diplomat, chose Caesarea and explained to Jewish religious leaders that he was merely seeking to please Caesar and the Romans, not at all following his own inclinations.[3]

Josephus recorded that Herod built the city of "white stone" and of "materials from other places, and at very great expense."[4] The stone was chiefly limestone and was likely quarried in the mountains approximately ten miles away across the plain of Sharon. These local materials were supplemented by marble and statuary brought from Rome.

The Temple—A central feature of the city was a temple dedicated to Augustus Caesar, Herod's patron. Built on an elevated platform and noted for its beauty and grand proportions, the temple was visible to sailors from a great distance. Two statues, "the one of Rome, the other of Caesar,"[5] adorned the temple.

The Amphitheater—South of the city and built on a promontory that jutted into the Mediterranean, the amphitheater was situated so that those seated in it had a magnificent view of the sea. This structure was discovered in 1961. During the excavation, the workmen found an important dedication tablet. The inscription on the tablet mentioned Tiberius Caesar and Pontius Pilate. "This is the first archaeological evidence of the famed procurator of Judaea under whose rule . . . Jesus' crucifixion took place."[6]

The Hippodrome—In the eastern section of the city, Herod built a hippodrome, called by the Romans a circus—measuring 1,056 by 264 feet and seating 20,000 spectators. A square granite pillar stood in the center, with three conical blocks erected nearby. Highly polished,

Ruins show Herod spared no expense in building his palace at Caesarea Maritima. He used only imported materials and covered many of the walls with marble.

these three blocks reflected sunlight and thus excited the horses during the races. The Romans called the pillars Taraxippos, meaning "horse-frightener."[7]

The Aqueduct—Determined to build a world-class city, Herod made sure Caesarea had an abundance of fountains, reflecting pools, and public baths. The challenge with this ambitious plan, though, was the lack of clean and drinkable water. To resolve this issue, Herod had workers construct an aqueduct to bring water from the closest springs, which were "nine miles distant, in the foothills of Mount Carmel. To reach them, thousands of laborers armed with picks, hammers, and chisels tunneled more than four miles through rock."[8] Archaeological remains visible to this day give evidence of this extraordinary accomplishment.

The Harbor—As impressive as his other structures were in Caesarea, Herod put his most vigorous efforts and innovative planning into the harbor. The sandy, unstable coastline lacked coastal islands or bays that could be incorporated into a harbor. So Herod had to design and construct a totally artificial harbor. "To bar undertrenching of breakwaters by currents and heavy seas, [Herod's workmen] first laid a foundation of rubble on the ocean floor wider than the breakwater that would rest on it."[9] Then using enormous stone blocks, the workmen built a breakwater 200 feet wide in twenty fathoms of water. The southern breakwater stretched west from the coastline, then turned north—about 600 yards in total length. The northern breakwater extended 300 yards due west from the shore, leaving an entrance from the north for ships. Archaeological evidence seems to indicate that on either side of the harbor's entrance were three huge statues that helped guide the ships. Along the landward side of the harbor was the quay where workers unloaded the cargo and stored the goods in nearby vaults.

This massive harbor project challenged the creativeness of Rome's most skilled engineers. Hydraulic concrete that hardens underwater was used extensively. An ingenious sluice system periodically flushed the harbor to reduce silting. The finished harbor encompassed approximately 200,000 square yards. Indeed, as the largest anchorage constructed to that time, the harbor of Caesarea "could be called the world's first modern harbor."[10] Although these harbor structures have fallen prey to twenty centuries of waves and to a sinking coastline, the shadowy underwater remains can still be seen quite clearly from the air.

CAESAREA IN THE NEW TESTAMENT

Herod the Great died in 4 BC. With his death, his son Archelaus became ruler of Judea and Samaria, bringing Caesarea under his control. But even the Romans could not condone Archelaus's viciousness, so they exiled him to Gaul in AD 6, and Caesarea became the capital of the Roman province of Judea. This set the stage for a number of events recorded in the New Testament.

NOTES

1. Robert L. Hohlfelder, "Caesarea Maritima," *National Geographic* 171.2 (1987): 270.

2. George Adam Smith, *The Historical Geography of the Holy Land* (New York: A. C. Armstrong, 1895), 139.

3. Josephus, *Jewish Antiquities* 15.9.5.

4. Josephus, *Jewish Antiquities* 15.9.6.

5. Josephus, *Jewish Antiquities* 15.9.6.

6. Zev Vilnay, *The Guide to Israel*, 22nd rev. ed. (Jerusalem: Daf-Chen, 1982), 368.

7. Vilnay, *Guide*, 369.

8. Hohlfelder, "Caesarea Maritima," 270–71.

9. Hohlfelder, "Caesarea Maritima," 275.

10. Hohlfelder, "Caesarea Maritima," 271–77.

CANA OF GALILEE

BY ROY E. LUCAS JR.

Cana of Galilee, locally called "Kafr Kenna," is located about four miles northeast of Nazareth. Two churches, one Roman Catholic and the other one Greek, claim to preserve ruins related to Jesus's miracle at Cana. This is a popular destination for visitors. Others believe, though, Jesus's first miracle was in a different location—a small and barren hill called "Khirbet Kana," which is about eight miles north of Nazareth.

THE LOCATION OF CANA

Bible scholars have located three sites in Galilee that are possible locations for the ancient city of Cana: Kafr Kenna, Kerem al-Ras, and Khirbet Qana. One other site, though less viable as a candidate for ancient Cana and much to the north, is Qana of Lebanon.

The traditional site, Kafr Kenna ("village/city of Cana"), shown to visitors since the Middle Ages, lies about four miles northeast of Nazareth on the road to Tiberias. At Kafr Kenna, a Roman Catholic church and a Greek Orthodox church each assert that they preserve the traditions related to the miracle of water turned to wine. The lack of archaeological evidence from the Roman period, however, has caused some to doubt Kafr Kenna is the site of the biblical Cana.[1] Additionally, the Semitic name should have come across in Greek as *Qana*, not *Kanna*—with only one "n" and not two.

In recent years, the Israeli Antiquities Authority sponsored excavations on the edge of Kafr Kenna. The locally used name of this site is Kerem al-Ras. Excavators located a large Jewish village dating to the time of Jesus. Unlike the excavations at Khirbet Qana, those at Kerem al-Ras revealed several large stone pots.[2]

Some scholars believe Qana of Lebanon meets the requirements of the Cana mentioned in John's Gospel. Lebanese archaeologist Youssef Hourani has excavated several items there including six stone wine pots. His proposed site is southeast of the city of Tyre and fifteen miles west of the Israeli border.[3]

Khirbet Qana (also spelled Khirbet Kana; "ruins of Cana") holds the position of being the site archaeologists favor most strongly. Recent excavations unearthed various kinds of artifacts from the first century AD, including fragments of small stone pots.[4] (The stone water pots mentioned in John 2:6, though, would have held about twenty to thirty gallons each.)

Khirbet Qana is about eight miles north of Nazareth. Several roads led down the northern side of Nazareth into the Beth Netofa Valley where the city of Sepphoris was located. A road went north and then east down the Beth Netofa Valley before coming to the Wadi Arbel pass, which led down into the area north of the Sea of Galilee to Capernaum. The trip covered twelve miles from Cana to the Sea of Galilee, and it would take about six hours to walk.[5]

This site fits the geographical location more than Kafr Kenna. Khirbet Qana "overlooks a marshy plain featuring plenty of reeds. To date, that site has not been excavated, but cisterns and the remains of buildings are visible, and nearby tombs are cut into the rocks. Some first-century coins also have been found on the site."[6]

LOCAL LIVELIHOOD

The region where Cana was located contained small villages (like Capernaum) with populations varying from 100 to 400 residents. Larger towns (Bethsaida) had populations of 2,000 to 3,000. Yet even larger, Tiberias and Sepphoris had populations that grew to about 8,000 to 12,000.[7] In general, Galileans had the opportunity to be involved in light industry and agricultural activities.

The Beth Netofa Valley below Cana had fertile soil. When adequate rains fell in winter, the valley produced abundant crops. In first-century Israel, the most important crops were wheat, olives, and grapes—with grapes yielding the most profit. The local farmer tried to grow more produce than his family could consume, and the surplus, if any, he sold.[8]

Alongside the agricultural endeavors, a citizen of Cana could serve the community in a number of ways. He might be a leather worker, shoemaker, ditch digger, carpenter,

In the Asochis Valley; the otherwise nondescript hill in the middle of the image is thought to be the actual site of Cana of Galilee.

blacksmith, baker, or even a quarry worker. In the first century AD, every town had a local store; some towns had more than one. Normally residents could buy everyday necessities like eggs, fruits, and vegetables. Some stores specialized, offering perfumes and breads; others employed blacksmiths and dyers. Perhaps most surprising is the fact that some stores even served as local restaurants.[9]

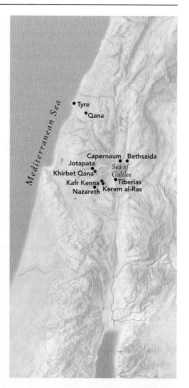

NOTES

[1] John McRay, "Cana of Galilee" in *Archaeology and the New Testament* (Grand Rapids: Baker, 1991), 173–74; Jonathan L. Reed, *The HarperCollins Visual Guide to the New Testament: What Archaeology Reveals about the First Christians* (New York: HarperCollins, 2007), 5.

[2] Reed, *HarperCollins Visual Guide*, 5.

[3] Rima Salameh, "Lebanese Town Says It's Wine Miracle Site," *Free Lance-Star* (Fredericksburg, VA), February 12, 1994.

[4] Reed, *HarperCollins Visual Guide*, 5.

[5] Anson F. Rainey and R. Steven Notley, *The Sacred Bridge: Carta's Atlas of the Biblical World* (Jerusalem: Carta, 2006), 352.

[6] Andreas J. Kostenberger, *John* (Grand Rapids: Baker, 2004), 92.

[7] Reed, *HarperCollins Visual Guide*, 66–67.

[8] Ze'ev Safrai, *The Economy of Roman Palestine* (New York: Routledge, 1994), 72–73, 126.

[9] Safrai, 121, 126.

CAPERNAUM IN JESUS'S DAY

BY DAVID M. WALLACE

Interior of the rebuilt synagogue at Capernaum; worshippers would sit on the benches along the wall. Although the visible structure dates from the fourth century AD, the foundation below was part of the synagogue that existed in Jesus's day.

GEOGRAPHY

Located in Lower Galilee along the Sea of Galilee, Capernaum stretched west to east along the lakefront. The lake was on the southern edge of the city, and mountains rose steeply to the north. Lower Galilee was a beautiful, fruitful, fertile region dominated by the Sea of Galilee.

Lying at the northern end of the Jordan Rift Valley, the Sea of Galilee is a freshwater lake at 696 feet below sea level with a depth of about 150 feet. The Jordan River, which enters the lake just to the east within walking distance of Capernaum, is the primary water source for the Sea of Galilee. The lake is heart shaped, about thirteen miles long and eight miles wide at most. Because of the steep surrounding hills, sudden storms sometimes occur. The hills and mountains surrounding the lake rise from 1,500 to more than 3,000 feet above sea level. Snow-capped Mount Hermon overlooks the region.

Summers are hot and humid, and winters are warm and wet. The rainy season is between October and the end of April. Rainfall is sufficient for farming, and permanent streams flow through the area. The year-round warm weather encourages growth wherever there is water. A flood plain, ideal for growing crops, lies along the north end of the lake near Capernaum, where the locals grow many foods mentioned in the Bible.

LOCAL RESOURCES

Located on the international trade route from Egypt to Syria and beyond, Capernaum saw caravans from around the world pass by, since it was one of the major cities of Galilee in Jesus's time. While much of Galilee was covered with forests in Jesus's day, lower Galilee was also blessed with fertile soil, plenty of rain, and a near-tropical climate, excellent for agriculture. Farmers terraced the hills and used the fertile valley for growing their crops, such as olives, figs, date palms, citrus fruit,[1] walnut trees, grapes, wheat, and even wild-flowers.[2] Black basalt stones found near the water and in the surrounding fields were typically used for buildings.

The fish in the Sea of Galilee were the staple of the local economy. Today the lake holds about forty species of fish.[3] Fishing boats departed Capernaum before dawn and returned at dusk.[4] Fishermen used hooks and lines, spears, and nets.[5] Businesses made and repaired these tools, and some built and repaired fishing boats. Located at the water's edge was a jetty for boats. The local fish was both salted and pickled to store for later use or to export to other towns. Much of this work appears to have been done at nearby Magdala, about two miles away. A first-century AD fishing boat was discovered in 1986 at nearby Kibbutz Ginosar. It is now on display at the Yigal Allon Museum at the kibbutz.[6] Jesus and his disciples may have used boats similar to the one discovered.

Model of an ancient boat at Nof Ginosar on the Sea of Galilee. Often called the "Jesus boat," the ancient vessel was discovered stuck in the mud when the sea receded during an unusually dry season.

Church built over the ruins of what is believed to be the home of Simon Peter at Capernaum. Archaeological evidence indicates early believers met for worship on the site. Inside the modern church, the floor is made of thick glass, which allows visitors to look into the structure below. Ruins of basalt-stone houses are in the foreground.

Others in Capernaum earned their living by transporting the local produce and fish to other markets. Basalt implements, such as grain grinders and olive presses, may have been made at Capernaum.[7] Common glass and ceramic ware were also produced there for local use. Market days were probably held in tents or booths near the shoreline.[8] Aramaic and Hebrew, as well as Greek and Latin, were the languages of Capernaum.[9]

SIZE AND POPULATION

The Bible mentions Capernaum sixteen times, all in the Gospels. The city appears to have been founded after Old Testament times. Capernaum was small and had no defensive walls or civic buildings.[10] The synagogue may have been the only public building. Some believe the population was as few as 600 to 1,500.[11] Others estimate it between 5,000 and 6,500.[12]

The Romans assigned a government and military presence in Capernaum. This included a garrison, commanded by a centurion who had built the Jewish synagogue (Luke 7:1–10). The Romans also collected taxes there. Capernaum is where Matthew, a tax collector, worked when Jesus called him to be his disciple (Matt. 9:9).

Archaeology indicates the population of Capernaum was lower-class. Exploration has unveiled no large houses or other finds that would indicate wealth, such as imported or decorative objects. The almost entirely Jewish population made their living from farming and fishing. Any extra income had to go to the tax collectors.[13]

Visitors today will see remains of a limestone synagogue built some 100 to 400 years after Jesus lived in Capernaum. But black basalt walls, four feet thick, have been discovered under all four corners of the synagogue. Many believe these walls are the remains of the synagogue in which Jesus preached. Visitors today will also see the remains of what many believe was the house of Simon Peter, where Jesus may have lived and performed miracles (8:14–17).

NOTES

1 LeMoine F. DeVries, *Cities of the Biblical World* (Peabody, MA: Hendrickson, 1997), 269.

2 Harry Thomas Frank, *Discovering the Biblical World* (New York: Harper & Row, 1975), 20.

3 William H. Stephens, "The Sea of Galilee" in *Where Jesus Walked*, ed. William H. Stephens (Nashville: Broadman, 1981), 73.

4 Frank, *Discovering the Biblical World*, 206.

5 Phillip J. Swanson, "Occupations and Professions in the Bible" in *HolBD*, 1038.

6 DeVries, *Cities of the Biblical World*, 269.

7 Henry H. Halley, *Halley's Bible Handbook* (Grand Rapids: Zondervan, 2007), 568.

8 Jonathan L. Reed, *Archaeology and the Galilean Jesus* (Harrisburg, PA: Trinity Press, 2000), 155.

9 J. E. Sanderson, "Capernaum" in *Major Cities of the Biblical World*, ed. R. K. Harrison (Nashville: Thomas Nelson, 1985), 77.

10 Reed, *Archaeology*, 153–54.

11 Reed, *Archaeology*, 152.

12 Sanderson, "Capernaum," 75.

13 Reed, *Archaeology*, 164–65.

CAPPADOCIA IN THE FIRST CENTURY

BY ALAN RAY BUESCHER

Urgup, about twelve miles east of Nevsehir, is one of the most important centers in Cappadocia. The erosion by water and wind produced these formations, called the "Fairy Chimneys."

According to 1 Maccabees 15, by at least 139 BC, Jews inhabited Cappadocia, which was part of the Roman Empire at this point. Quite likely, the first Christians in Cappadocia came from such Jewish communities. Though the growth of Christianity was apparently slow there, near the end of the fourth century the Cappadocian fathers—Basil of Caesarea, Gregory of Nyssa, and Gregory of Nazianzus—directed the growth of the church in central and eastern Asia Minor through their writings and ministry. All three of these men helped define the orthodox doctrine of the Trinity at the Council of Constantinople in AD 381.[1] The influence of early Christians in Cappadocia would give direction to Christians and Christian theology through the centuries.

GEOGRAPHY, CLIMATE, AND PEOPLE

The geography and climate of Cappadocia, located in the highlands of central-eastern Asia Minor, may partially explain the slow growth of Christianity in this region. To the south, the Taurus Mountains hampered easy access to the region of Cilicia on the northeastern Mediterranean coast. Traveling west toward Galatia, the elevated steppe seemed never-ending. The regions most accessible to Cappadocia existed to the north (Pontus and northeastern Galatia) and east (Armenia).[2]

Brutal Cappadocian winters entertained blizzards—sometimes making roads impassable until spring. Heavy snows could confine people inside their homes for as long as two months. When the snows melted and farming season had begun, swarms of beetles always posed a potential threat to grain crops.[3]

Perhaps their harsh environment and living conditions contributed to their character and reputation. An early adage remarked, "A venomous viper bit a Cappadocian ... the viper died."[4] No one had many kind words to say about Cappadocians. Worthless, deceitful, selfish, brutish—these describe how many viewed them.[5]

As a result of its geography and climate, throughout ancient history, Cappadocia remained on the outskirts of great civilizations and cultures that thrived along the Mediterranean coast and lowlands. Greek culture and Roman rule struggled to influence this rugged region, and Christianity was no exception.

ROMAN RULE

Cappadocia, while not lacking in natural resources, became significant to the Romans not only as another source of income to fuel its expansion, but also as a frontier border from which to defend its empire from outside attack and to protect its interests in the Near East.

Archelaus, appointed by Marcus Antonius as the last king of Cappadocia before Cappadocia became a Roman province, ruled from 36 BC until his death in AD 17. Archelaus understood and sought political alliances. However, approximately three years before his death, the authorities summoned Archelaus to Rome, charging him with treason. The results of this trial remain unknown. Upon Archelaus's death, the Romans immediately incorporated Cappadocia into their empire as a province—with little objection from the Cappadocians. Their agreeing was perhaps largely aided by a reduction in taxes.[6]

Roman procurators of equestrian rank replaced the Cappadocian monarchy from AD 17 until 72. Cappadocia, with only two significant cities (Tyana and Mazaca) at the time of its

At Zelve, volcanic rocks and cones provided comfortable dwelling places for the area's inhabitants. Zelve remains one of the best-preserved examples of a cave-dweller community.

Coin dating AD 81–96 from Caesarea, Cappadocia; reverse has an image of a club.

incorporation into the Roman Empire, posed a unique situation for Rome. Without municipal governments in place, the procurators did little to alter the existing feudal internal organization.

Roman rule provided a catalyst for more urban development, but the growth of cities was slow. The lower classes lived in feudal villages, and many of the Cappadocians in Rome came from the large slave population in Cappadocia.[7] Mazaca served as the capital city for the Cappadocian kings through the reign of Archelaus in AD 17. Archelaus renamed the city Caesarea in honor of Emperor Caesar Augustus. Located on a plateau on the north side of the 1,300-foot, volcanic, snow-capped Mount Argaeus, Caesarea developed into the leading Roman city of the region. Not until the fourth century AD, however, did it boast several schools, gymnasiums, and temples to the Greek gods Zeus, Apollo, and Fortune.[8]

Although Rome had lowered taxes on the feudal lords, much revenue flowed to the Roman emperor from the lands previously owned by Archelaus. Mines yielded translucent marble, crystal alabaster, onyx, silver, lead, and iron. Varieties of domesticated animals flourished in Cappadocia: sheep, goats, cattle, pigs, mules, camels, and horses. However, most of the revenues generated from the land came from the minerals and precious stones.[9]

Despite the land's rich resources, most of Cappadocia remained backward and impoverished. Many people lived in caves carved in the soft volcanic rock formations, often sharing their homes with their animals. The land yielded enough grain for export, but most of the wine and olive oil that locals consumed was imported.[10]

WAR AND PEACE

The Euphrates River provided the region's eastern border, dividing the Roman Empire to the west from Rome's primary adversary to the east, the Parthians, whose empire encompassed a large part of present-day Iran. The country of Armenia, on the east bank of the Euphrates, also provided an additional buffer from the Parthians, making the politics of Armenia of great interest to the Romans and Parthians alike as they vied for control in the Near East.[11]

Peace prevailed between the Roman province of Cappadocia and the Parthians for sixteen years after the Roman procurator took office in AD 17. However, when Armenia's King Artaxias died in AD 34, a hostile three-year struggle began between Rome and the Parthians to determine the next ruler of Armenia. Rome never actually sent forces against the Parthians; rather Pharasamanes, the king of Iberia, took the lead in skirmishes against the Parthians. Rome had chosen Pharasamanes's brother, Mithridates, as their candidate for king of Armenia. History is silent about how this war affected Cappadocia, but the settlement reached between Rome and the Parthians in AD 37 established Mithridates as the new ruler of Armenia.[12]

The greatest struggle for Armenia arose in the reign of Nero, with Cappadocia becoming a strategic military outpost for Rome during the Parthian and Armenian War, which waged from the mid-50s to 66. Rome recruited throughout Cappadocia and Galatia to fill its legions, which normally were composed of Roman citizens. As a result, some Cappadocians gained Roman citizenship through enrolling in the legion. The wives and children of these military recruits also gained citizenship upon their husbands'/fathers' return to civilian life. Rome and Parthia reached a peace settlement in AD 66, and Rome withdrew its legions from Cappadocia.[13]

CHRISTIAN GROWTH

Acts 2:9 indicates that Parthians (Jews or proselytes) witnessed the miracle of Pentecost together with residents of Cappadocia. Cappadocia proved to be a great laboratory for witnessing the efficacy of the gospel of Jesus Christ to penetrate hearts conditioned to resist change by a harsh and relatively isolated environment. The Jewish Diaspora had planted Jewish communities in Cappadocia, and this provided the basis for the expansion of the gospel in the Roman Empire. Perhaps that first seed of God's grace germinated in a Cappadocian heart in Jerusalem on Pentecost and transplanted itself to a people of volcanic crags and feudal lords. The seed grew slowly, with its flowers blossoming and fruit ripening in the fourth century through the ministry and writings of the Cappadocian fathers.

NOTES

[1] Raymond Van Dam, *Becoming Christian: The Conversion of Roman Cappadocia* (Philadelphia: University of Pennsylvania Press, 2003), 1–2.

[2] Raymond Van Dam, *Kingdom of Snow: Roman Rule and Greek Culture in Cappadocia* (Philadelphia: University of Pennsylvania Press, 2002), 13.

[3] Van Dam, *Kingdom of Snow*, 13–15.

[4] Van Dam, *Kingdom of Snow*, 13.

[5] Van Dam, *Kingdom of Snow*, 1.

[6] William Emmett Gwatkin Jr., "Cappadocia as a Roman Procuratorial Province," *University of Missouri Studies* 5.4 (October 1930): 5–16, 19; William Emmett Gwatkin Jr., "Cappadocia" in *ABD*, 1:870–72.

[7] Gwatkin, "Cappadocia as a Roman Procuratorial Province," 17–19; Van Dam, *Kingdom of Snow*, 24–25.

[8] Jack Finegan, *The Archeology of the New Testament: The Mediterranean World of the Early Christian Apostles* (Boulder, CO: Westview, 1981), 83; Van Dam, *Kingdom of Snow*, 15.

[9] Gwatkin, "Cappadocia as a Roman Procuratorial Province," 19; Van Dam, *Kingdom of Snow*, 15.

[10] Van Dam, *Kingdom of Snow*, 15–16.

[11] Jesse Curtis Pope, "Parthians" in *EDB*, 1010.

[12] Gwatkin, "Cappadocia as a Roman Procuratorial Province," 30.

[13] Gwatkin, "Cappadocia as a Roman Procuratorial Province," 44–45, 55.

CEDARS OF LEBANON

BY W. MURRAY SEVERANCE

Hiram's monument near Tyre; he was the Phoenician king who supplied cedar to Solomon.

The large cedar of Lebanon was dangerously near extinction; attempts have been made to save the tree.

One of the few clusters of cedars of Lebanon gives but a glimpse of what the forests may have been.

Cedar was a highly prized wood even before the pyramids of Egypt were built. Today only patches remain of the once formidable forests in Lebanon. At one time, Israel contained vast forests but never to be compared with Phoenicia.

King Solomon contracted with Hiram, king of Tyre, to provide beams and paneling for building the temple. From the Lebanon mountains, timbers were pushed down to the seacoast of Tyre and Sidon along an artificial path, called a *vovtou*, made of rounded trunks. Once at the seacoast, the timbers were tied together into large rafts and floated the one hundred miles in the Mediterranean Sea to Joppa; at other times, to Egypt and other ports. From Joppa they were dragged with infinite care thirty-five miles up steep and rocky roads to Jerusalem.

Why was cedar such a valuable commodity? The cedar chest of today demonstrates its value; closets in larger homes often are paneled in cedar for the same reasons. Other than the rich reddish-brown color, the most noticeable aspect of cedar is its aroma. The odor is not offensive to humans, but insects resist it. The smell may remain in clothes for a period of time, but that fact is a small inconvenience when compared to losing the garments to moths.

Most conifers, cedars included, prefer moist habitats in hilly or mountainous areas. The Lebanon and Anti-Lebanon mountains provide an ideal locale. They stretch for about a hundred miles just inland and parallel to the Mediterranean Sea where they catch the moisture-laden clouds from the sea. The average height of these mountains is 6,000 to 7,000 feet, but several peaks tower to more than 10,000 feet. In Solomon's time, the upper slopes were covered with those marvelous trees.

Some of the trees grow to heights of 120 feet, but most are sixty to eighty feet in height. The girth of some trees is thirty to forty feet. Like those other ancient olive trees in the garden of Gethsemane, some cedars of Lebanon are thought to be about 2,000 years old. Their branches spread out, as witnessed in Numbers 24:6; Psalm 92:12; and Hosea 14:5. These horizontal branches begin some ten feet above the ground and grow outward for a consid-

Joppa, where cedars of Lebanon were unloaded to be transported to Jerusalem.

erable distance, sometimes wider than the height of the tree. Numerous branchlets give cedars their distinctive tiered appearance. Old trees are gnarled and majestic, a truly awe-inspiring sight.

The cedars of Lebanon not only furnished timbers and paneling for building purposes, but they also furnished a symbol of strength, splendor, longevity, and glory. Ezekiel compared the king of Assyria to a great cedar of Lebanon (Ezek. 31). The Shulammite compared her lover to the cedars of Lebanon, calling him "majestic" (Song 5:15).

COLOSSAE IN THE FIRST CENTURY

BY ROBERT A. WEATHERS

Tell Colossae near the modern town of Honaz, Turkey. Nothing more than a small hill, the site of Colossae has never been excavated.

Although the exact time of its founding is shrouded in uncertainty, Colossae emerged as early as 485 BC as a city rooted in the former Phrygian Empire. In 480 BC, Herodotus, a Greek historian, called it a "great city of Phrygia."[1] Another historian, Xenophon, wrote that it was a "large and prosperous city."[2]

This greatness was largely a result of the city's position in the Lycus Valley of Asia Minor, a lush area fed by the Lycus River. The city benefited from travelers who would usually come to Colossae first as they entered the valley on the way to Ephesus, about one hundred miles to the west. In addition, the popular city of Hierapolis was just thirteen miles away, and Laodicea was even closer, a mere twelve miles away (see Col. 4:15–16). After enjoying a brief stay in Colossae, then Laodicea, a visitor could journey to Ephesus and then to Rome, roughly an 1,100-mile trip.[3]

In its early history, the area accumulated great wealth. The river provided fertile pastures for grazing and fields for growing produce, so Colossae enjoyed a thriving sheep and cattle industry. Additionally, the city had grown rich from growing and selling figs and olives. Colossae also shared with Laodicea an abundance of chalk deposits, left by the flowing river, which provided merchants with ample resources for dying cloth. As a result, Colossae was famous for its wool manufacturing, especially for its production of a fine, reddish-purple cloth called colossinus.[4]

Colossae began a slow decline when the Roman Empire chose to shift the route through the valley. Asia became a Roman province in 190 BC, and the Romans decided that the best place for a capital city for this district was Laodicea. Therefore, they rerouted the road system to make Laodicea the most important junction in the region. Prosperity was literally diverted from the smaller city of Colossae. The decline of the city was slow but assured. Writing about twenty years prior to Paul, a Greek geographer named Strabo noted that the receding city had become a "small town."[5] In Paul's day, Colossae "had declined in political and financial importance," making it perhaps "the least important city to which Paul ever wrote."[6]

Even so, despite Colossae's political and economic weaknesses, the city was layered with a mixed and colorful population. Phrygian descendants still lived there, and the Roman military and political presence was dominant. Commerce had brought in various ethnic groups and religions. Included in these groups would have been a large population of Greek-speaking Jews. Many of these Jews descended from families imported into the Lycus Valley by the Seleucid King Antiochus the Great (223–187 BC).

In AD 60, a devastating earthquake struck the valley. Hierapolis and Laodicea were heavily damaged but managed to recover and remained strong for years. Already weakened from shifting politics and economic blows, Colossae never fully recovered. Most inhabitants moved to nearby stronger cities. In its latter history, Colossae was pummeled by invading armies, until finally, in the twelfth century, "the church was destroyed by the Turks and the city disappeared."[7] Ancient Colossae has never been fully excavated.

A cornice stone at Colossae.

NOTES

[1] Richard R. Melick Jr., *Philippians, Colossians, Philemon*, NAC (1991), 162; See Herodotus, *Persian Wars* 7.30.

[2] Gene Lacoste Munn, "Introduction to Colossians," *Southwestern Journal of Theology* (*SwJT*) 16.1 (1973): 9; Xenophon, *Anabasis* 1.2.6.

[3] Edgar J. Banks, "Colossae" in *ISBE* (1979), 1:732; Melick, *Philippians, Colossians, Philemon*, 162.

[4] Scott Nash, "Colossae" in *EDB*, 269–70; Melick, *Philippians, Colossians, Philemon*, 163; Banks, "Colossae," 732; Munn, "Introduction," 10.

[5] Melick, *Philippians, Colossians, Philemon*, 163; see J. B. Lightfoot, *Saint Paul's Epistles to the Colossians and to Philemon*, rev. ed. (Grand Rapids: Zondervan, 1879), 16.

[6] Munn, "Introduction," 10.

[7] Banks, "Colossae," 732; see Melick, *Philippians, Colossians, Philemon*, 162–63.

CORINTH: A ROMAN GREEK CITY

BY BOB SIMMONS

Canal across the isthmus from Corinth to Cenchreae. The canal was first attempted by Nero but was not completed until 1893. The canal is three and a half miles long, seventy-five feet wide at the top, and sixty-five feet at the bottom.

GEOGRAPHY AND HISTORY

Corinth was located on the Peloponnesus, that southern part of Greece connected to the mainland by an isthmus. The Isthmus of Corinth was ten miles long and four miles wide. It was so prominent that the famed Isthmian games were named after it. Its name came to describe every such piece of land—a narrow stretch connecting two larger land areas. In Paul's day, a strong wall six miles in circumference surrounded Corinth. Each end stopped at the base of the rock-mountain called the Acrocorinth, which was 1,886 feet high. This long wall and this high rocklike mountain together surrounded the city and provided it with needed protection.[1]

Corinth had both enjoyed and endured a surprising past. For centuries, it was one of the richest and most important Grecian cities. But in 146 BC, the Roman leader Mummius invaded and decimated Corinth, killed its men, and enslaved its women and children.[2] The city remained devastated until 44 BC when Julius Caesar led Rome to rebuild it. Its new population consisted mostly of freedmen.[3]

Once rebuilt, Corinth used its advantageous geographical position to achieve a strong financial status. Workers dragged small ships both ways across its narrow isthmus on a cleverly constructed road to opposite harbors four miles away. The eastern harbor was Cenchreae; Schoenus and Lechaeum (or Lechaion) were on the west.[4] Larger ships had to have their cargos carried across the isthmus to other large ships waiting on the opposite side. This process allowed ships going to or from the Aegean Sea to avoid the 200-mile, dangerous fourteen-day journey around the stormy southern tip of the Peloponnesus. Spending money in Corinth's shops and then taking the city's produce aboard, these sailors made the city famous again—and wealthy. Corinth had quite a reputation for its ceramics

Facing south, the Lechaion Road in Corinth was lined with shops on the right, temples, baths, and fountains on the left. The Acrocorinth (or "upper Corinth") rises almost 1,900 feet in the background.

and its works in bronze.[5] It was never an agricultural power and never needed to be. Corinth eventually became the leading city of the new senatorial province created there.[6]

POPULATION

Population changes took place during the time of Roman control. Rome sent people from numerous countries into the Corinthian area. Many new settlers were former slaves or discharged Roman soldiers, some indeed from Greece. Rome had brought still others to Corinth from Asia, Syria, Judea, Egypt, and other regions.[7] These strangers came to Corinth bringing their own customs, languages, and religious superstitions. Longtime residents of the Achaian region, many Jews probably had chosen to remain in Corinth when possible or to return there when they could.

This "invasion" of foreigners eventually changed or diluted some of Corinth's Greek religious ways and views. Newcomers gave some of the deities their own temples. They even worshiped the Egyptian Isis and Serapis there. Gradually, gods and goddesses new to the Corinthians became prominent. By Paul's day, the formerly strong Greek city gradually had become far less decidedly Greek. Likewise, Corinth's Roman population had lost many of its distinctive Roman ways. The Rome-owned Greek city had changed drastically over the years.[8]

NOTES

1   R. E. Glaze, "Corinth" in *HolBD*, 299.
2   Glaze, "Corinth," 299.
3   W. J. Woodhouse, "Corinth" in *Encyclopedia Biblia* (London: Adam & Charles Black, 1899), 898.
4   J. E. Harvey, "Corinth" in *International Bible Encyclopedia* (Chicago: Howard Severance, n.d.), 710.
5   J. Murphy-O'Conner, "Corinth" in *ABD*, 1:1136.
6   Murphy-O'Conner, "Corinth," 1138.
7   J. H. Harrop, "Corinth" in *New Bible Dictionary* (London: Inter-Varsity, 1982), 1136.
8   Murphy-O'Conner, "Corinth," 1138.

DAVID'S JERUSALEM

BY GARY P. ARBINO

Remains of the Stepped-Stone Structure.

In a brilliant strategic move, David decided to capture a Canaanite stronghold in Judah's hill country for his capital. The city was known as Jebus in the time of David (Judg. 19:10–11; 1 Chr. 11:4–5), but also as *Urusalim* in the Amarna letters of the fourteenth century BC.

A FORTIFIED CITY

The Canaanite city encompassed the twelve-acre spur of hill south of what became the Temple Mount. The hill was bounded on the west by "the valley" (later known as the Tyropoeon) and on the east by the Kidron Valley. The hill extends about 2,000 feet and slopes down toward the south. The two valleys join at the southern tip of what would later become the city of David. As Psalm 125:2 poetically notes, the city is situated on the lowest of the local hills.

From the taunts recorded in 2 Samuel 5:6 and 1 Chronicles 11:5, the Jebusite inhabitants felt secure in their stronghold, called in Hebrew the *Metsudat Tsion* or "stronghold of Zion" (2 Sam. 5:7). This stronghold was probably located at the northern end of the town near its highest and most vulnerable point.

On the eastern slope of the hill, archaeologists have uncovered a massive architectural feature known as the Stepped-Stone Structure. This terraced mantle of stone courses laid over a substructure of terraces, rib walls, and fill extends down the slope at least 120 feet from the crest of the hill. Its full extent has not yet been determined. From its size and position, this is often considered to be the supporting foundation for the *Metsudat Tsion*, reused by David after his capture of the city.

In addition to the fortress on the north, fortification walls surrounded Jebus. Archaeologists have uncovered little if any of the western wall system from the tenth century. Possibly a structure exposed in the nineteenth century could be a western gate from this period. On the east side of the city, it seems that a Middle Bronze Age (2200–1550 BC) wall continued to be used throughout the Late Bronze and Iron Ages (1550–586 BC). This wall,

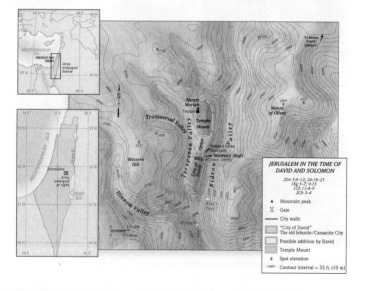

JERUSALEM IN THE TIME OF DAVID AND SOLOMON

2Sm 5:6–12; 24:18–25
1Kg 5–7; 9:15
1Ch 11:4–9
2Ch 3–4

▲ Mountain peak

Ⅱ Gate

▪▪▪▪▪ City walls

☐ "City of David"
The old Jebusite/Canaanite City

☐ Possible addition by David

☐ Temple Mount

x Spot elevation

⌐2480 Contour interval = 33 ft. (10 m)

measuring some eight feet thick, was located halfway up the east slope at the top of a steep rock outcrop. Near the northern extent of this wall, below the Stepped-Stone Structure, famed archaeologist Kathleen Kenyon excavated what appears to be a gate in the wall.

STRATEGIC LOCATION

After reigning for more than seven years in his own tribal territory at Hebron, David needed to expand his influence (2 Sam. 5:1–5). Jebus was centrally located between his tribe, Judah, and the rest of the tribes. Although assigned to the Benjaminites (the tribe of David's former rival, Saul), no tribe had yet possessed it. Located on the border between Judah and Benjamin (Josh. 15:8), the city was attacked years earlier by the Judahites (v. 63; Judg. 1:8) who could not hold the city, and so it was given to the Benjaminites (Josh. 18:28) who also could not keep it (Judg. 1:21). The city remained a Jebusite enclave until the time of David, thus making it a perfect centralized capital city, one he could make his own city.

WATER FOR THE CITY

So David and his mighty men, his personal army, besieged Jebus. The biblical text notes that Joab became the commander of David's army when he took charge of the attack of Jebus. He accomplished this by going through the *tsinnor*, often translated as "water shaft" (1 Chr. 11:6; 2 Sam. 5:8). Most biblical scholars assume this means he climbed up a shaft in the water system near the Gihon Spring on the east slope of the city, entered the city, and let the Israelite army into the city. This spring, named for its intermittent "gushing" (*Gihon* is derived from a Hebrew root meaning "to gush"), is the only perennial water supply in the city of David.

Recently archaeologists have discovered two massive fortification towers and a deep pool at the spring and dated them to the Middle Bronze Age (2200–1550 BC).[1] These are outside of the Middle Bronze Age walls but seem to have been connected to the walls and

A segment of the city wall in Jerusalem dating to the First Temple period (1000–586 BC). This section of the wall, which protected the north side of Jerusalem, is almost twenty-three feet wide and more than 200 feet long.

possibly accessed by Kenyon's gate. Archaeologists have agreed that these walls were still in use during the days of the Jebusites and David. Certainly the spring was still used. A tunnel provided additional, more secure access to the spring. Commonly referred to as Warren's Shaft, this tunnel, carved from the soft limestone, crossed under the city walls and gave hidden access to the spring pool. Until recently, the tunnel appeared to end in a forty-foot natural vertical shaft where people would lower jugs to get water. This shaft was long thought to have been Joab's *tsinnor*. Recent excavations, however, indicate the vertical section was not exposed during the time of David and Joab; rather the tunnel connected to a cave whose mouth opened at the pool. So we do not know what exactly Joab's *tsinnor* was, but it does seem to have something to do with a water channel.

DAVID'S CAPITAL

Regardless of the precise method, David had taken the city with his army and so in effect it was his spoil of war, his personal stronghold. Thus David had shrewdly created a fortified capital city that was not the possession of any tribe yet was centrally located.

According to 2 Samuel 5:9 and 1 Chronicles 11:8, David and Joab immediately began improvements to the city. Although Joab could be credited with restoring the city to life (an allusion to residential restoration?), David would receive credit for building the northern end of town, the fortress and palace areas, including the area "from the *millo*."

The term *millo* seems to mean an in-filled area, and many take this to mean a terrace system (1 Chr. 11:8). If this is the case, then the *millo* may refer to the terrace and fills used to extend the city northward toward the Temple Mount. Since David actually purchased the Temple Mount and placed the ark shrine there (2 Sam. 6; 24; 1 Chr. 21–22), we could reasonably conclude that he would begin filling in the space between the city of David and the Temple Mount. David's placement of the ark in the city of David was an important step in the creation of this as his capital city. Clearly David showed his loyalty to God in this act. On another level, we see his vision and political and religious acumen as he solidified for himself and the people his role as God's chosen and then solidified Jerusalem for Israel's capital (2 Sam. 6).

In 2 Samuel 5:11, we read that David also built a palace for himself. According to verse 17, David had to go down to reach the *Metsudat Tsion*. If this fortress sat atop the Stepped-Stone Structure, then we would need to look upslope to the north to find the palace. Recently renowned archaeologist Eilat Mazar has uncovered monumental architecture in this area that she dates to the early Iron Age II (1000–900 BC), the time of David. Given its six-to-eight-foot-wide walls, Mazar calls her find the "Large-Stone Structure." Mazar connects her finds to a short section of casemate wall (a typically Israelite wall style) uncovered nearby by Kenyon as well as some ashlar blocks (large, square-cut stones) and a proto-Aeolic column capital (decorative architectural remains, often found associated with Iron Age royal buildings) discovered downslope. Evaluating her findings, Mazar cautiously argued that her structure comprises the foundations of David's royal palace.[2]

The palace would have been an imposing building at the highest part of town. It would have served as the reception hall for emissaries to the young kingdom (2 Sam. 8:9–10) and housed the royal family (5:13–16). From there, David's wife Michal could look down on the procession bringing the ark into town (6:16), and David could look down on his city across the rooftops and see Bathsheba bathing (11:2). In his palace, David could even keep an eye on his last remaining potential rival from Saul's house (2 Sam. 9).

David's rebuilding of the Jebusite city also included residential areas. Recent excavations have uncovered houses inside the city wall on the east slope. These houses are constructed into the mantle of the Stepped-Stone Structure. Some archaeologists date these houses to the time of David.[3] These domestic units are solidly built and are located just below the stronghold and the palace area. These may have been the houses of David's officials and elite soldiers (8:15–18; see 1 Chr. 11:10–47). Just below the Middle Bronze Age (2200–1550 BC) wall on the east slope, the Israeli archaeologist Yigal Shiloh excavated another residential neighborhood. This domestic area, outside the city walls, was unprotected and poorly constructed, with some evidence of household religious activity.[4] The difference between houses inside and outside the walls may illustrate some social stratification in David's Jerusalem. The Bible also records that the nobility owned estates outside the city walls (2 Sam. 14:30–31).

David's Jerusalem was his stronghold, a city small in size but complete with royal and administrative architecture, fortifications, a complex water supply, socially diverse domestic areas, and nearby agricultural lands.

NOTES

[1]   Ronny Reich and Eli Shukron, "Light at the End of the Tunnel: Warren's Shaft Theory of David's Conquest Shattered," *BAR* 25.1 (1999): 22–33, 72.

[2]   Eilat Mazar, "Did I Find King David's Palace?" *BAR* 32.1 (2006): 16–27, 70.

[3]   Jane Cahill, "Jerusalem in David and Solomon's Time: It Really Was a Major City in the Tenth Century BCE," *BAR* 30.6 (2004): 26–27.

[4]   D. T. Ariel and A. De Groot, "The Iron Age Extramural Occupation at the City of David and Additional Observations on the Siloam Channel," in *Excavations at the City of David*, vol. 5, ed. D. T. Ariel, Qedem 40 (Jerusalem: Hebrew University, 2000), 155–69.

EDEN: ALL WE KNOW

BY KEVIN HALL

Tigris River at Diyarbakir, in eastern Turkey.

With the discovery of ancient Near Eastern libraries that contained ancient Akkadian and Sumerian texts, it became common to associate the biblical name "Eden" with the Akkadian term *edinu* (Sumerian, *eden*), meaning "plain, steppe."[1] This explanation of the name made sense to those who thought it likely that Eden was in or around the broad plains of "the land between the rivers," Mesopotamia. More recently, however, Aramaic and Ugaritic studies have yielded evidence associating the name with the idea of a "garden of abundance."[2] This explanation comports well with the basic meaning of the Hebrew term *'eden*, "luxury, delight."

In this context of a region named Eden ("luxury, delight") with a well-watered garden, we can instructively consider ancient Near Eastern parallels. Ancient Near Eastern monarchs such as Assyria's King Sennacherib lavished their capitals with parks and gardens irrigated by springs outside of the city. So if the Bible intends for us to imagine a spring pouring forth from Eden to irrigate a garden or park, then the biblical text describes "a situation that was well known in the ancient world: a sacred spot featuring a spring with an adjoining, well-watered park, stocked with specimens of trees and animals."[3]

The scriptural account of Eden's location is more interested in asserting the "cultural and political centrality" of Eden within the ancient Near Eastern world than with providing a road map for pinpointing Eden's location.[4]

NOTES

[1] Howard N. Wallace, "Eden, Garden of" in *The Anchor Bible Dictionary* (*ABD*), ed. David Noel Freedman (New York: Doubleday, 1992), 2:281–83.

[2] J. H. Walton, "Eden, Garden of" in *Dictionary of the Old Testament: Pentateuch* (Downers Grove, IL: InterVarsity, 2003), 202–7.

[3] Walton, "Eden," 204.

[4] Walton, "Eden."

EDOM: ITS LAND AND PEOPLE

BY GEORGE H. SHADDIX

This narrow and natural crag called the Siq is the only access route to the ancient Nabatean city of Petra.

The nation of Edom originated with Esau, the older son of Isaac and Rebekah (Gen. 25:21–24). Esau and Jacob were twins, but Esau was the firstborn. These two brothers grew into men with different interests. Jacob enjoyed staying around the house. Esau, who had a ruddy and rough appearance, enjoyed the outdoors. Genesis 25:25 describes Esau at his birth: "The first one came out red-looking, covered with hair like a fur coat, and they named him Esau." As these twin boys grew up, Esau became a skilled hunter (v. 27). These two, Esau and Jacob, struggled with each other even before birth (v. 22), and this struggle extended beyond the two individuals to the two nations, Edom and Israel, that would be their descendants.

Two major events marked Esau's life. First, he sold his birthright to Jacob for some red stew (vv. 29–34); according to verse 30, "That is why he was also named Edom," which is related to the verb *ādam,* meaning "be red," as well as the noun *dām,* meaning "blood." Second, Jacob, with the help of his mother, Rebekah, got the blessing of his father, Isaac. This blessing usually went to the firstborn. Once Isaac had given Jacob Esau's birthright, though, he could not take it back and give it to Esau. These events set the stage for long-standing hostility between these twins and their descendants.

In marrying two Hittite women (26:35), Esau disregarded God's covenant with his father, Isaac, and his grandfather, Abraham. Later he married the daughter of Ishmael, who was Abraham's son by Sarah's handmaid. Again, these factors built tension between Esau and his parents, Esau and his brother, and ultimately the nations of Israel and Edom.

THE LAND

Esau settled in the mountain region south and east of the Dead Sea, where red sandstone is prevalent. This area extended south to Elath and Ezion-geber on the north shore of the Gulf of Aqaba (Deut. 2:8).[1] Moab's southern border was the northern border of Edom. Sometimes Edom was called Seir (see Gen. 32:3).

This mountainous area is forty miles wide and one hundred miles long. The sides of the area "rise steeply from the valley."[2] The northern part of the plateau forms a spacious grazing ground. Mountains in the north rise 1,500 to 2,000 feet; some in the south reach 2,600 feet. Many areas are inaccessible peaks and gorges. These features help us understand why Genesis 36:8 says that Esau lived in the mountains of Seir. In the days of Obadiah, the capital of Edom was Sela, which means "rock." It is usually identified with the Nabatean rock-city known as Petra.

ITS PEOPLE

The descendants of Esau conquered the Horites who lived in this area before them (cf. Gen. 14:6; Deut. 2:22). After leaving Egypt, the Israelites approached Edom. Moses sent messengers to ask the king of Edom for permission to go through their land (Num. 20:14–21). Moses sent the messengers from Kadesh telling them to refer to the Israelites as "your brother Israel" (v. 14). No doubt this was an effort to encourage the Edomites to be generous and allow them to go through the land. The animosity between Jacob and Esau evidently continued; the Edomites would not allow the Israelites to go through their land.

This refusal was in spite of Moses's promises that they would go along the King's Highway and not through the fields or vineyards, nor would they drink water from a well in the land. The king's response was, "You will not travel through our land, or we will come out and confront you with the sword" (v. 18). To be sure that Israel did not come through their land, the Edomites came against them with a large army. The Israelites turned away and did not attempt to go through the land of Edom.

DISPOSSESSED AND DESTROYED

Balaam, in his final oracle (Num. 23–24), declared, "Edom will become a possession; Seir will become a possession of its enemies, but Israel will be triumphant" (24:18). When Saul was king of Israel, "he fought against all his enemies in every direction," including Moab, the Ammonites, Edom, Zobah, and the Philistines. "Wherever he turned, he caused havoc" (1 Sam. 14:47).

Then when David became king, he struck down 18,000 Edomites and put garrisons of soldiers throughout Edom. The Edomites became subjects of David (2 Sam. 8:13–14). Solomon assembled a fleet of ships at Ezion-geber on the Red Sea in the land of Edom—an indicator that Edom was under Solomon's rule. These ships sailed to Ophir and brought back to Solomon 420 talents of gold (sixteen tons; see 1 Kgs. 9:26–28). During the reign of Judah's King Jehoram (850–843 BC), Edom revolted and appointed its own king (2 Kgs. 8:20).

Edom is mentioned many times in the Prophets and is "noted in the Bible for its pride, treachery, greed, and violence" (see 2 Chr. 20:10–11; 25:14,20; Jer. 49:16; Amos 1:9,11; Obad. 3). Its treatment of the people of Israel when the Babylonians invaded is a particular sore spot (see Ps. 137:7; Ezek. 25:12; 35:15; 36:5; Joel 3:19; Obad. 10–14). God's judgment on Edom is declared several times (see Isa. 34:5–17; Jer. 49:7–22; Lam. 4:21; Ezek. 25:12–14; 35:1–15; Amos 1:11–12; Obad.).[3] Devastation probably came in the sixth century. Kyle McCarter concluded his discussion of the dating of the destruction of Edom, "The precise date of the final expulsion of the Edomites is undetermined, but is placed late in the sixth century by general agreement. The archaeological evidence, still regrettably meager, shows the last part of that century to have been a period of general collapse in Edomite culture."[4]

NOTES

[1] Burton MacDonald, "Archaeology of Edom," *Anchor Yale Bible Dictionary,* 2:295.

[2] W. Ewing, "Edom; Edomites" in *ISBE* (1952), 2:899.

[3] E. Ray Clendenen, "Malachi," in *Haggai, Malachi,* NAC (2004), 250–51.

[4] P. Kyle McCarter Jr., "Obadiah 7 and the Fall of Edom," *BASOR* 221 (1976): 89.

THE EGYPT JOSEPH KNEW

BY STEPHEN R. MILLER

Temple of Isis façade on the island of Philae, at Aswan. Isis was one of the great mother goddesses, the protector of the living and the dead.

According to the early chronology, Jacob entered Egypt about 1876 BC. Since Joseph preceded his father by approximately twenty-five years (Gen. 37:2; 41:46), he arrived about 1900 BC during the reign of Amenemhet II (1929–1895 BC), third pharaoh of Egypt's stable Twelfth Dynasty. Evidence suggests an increase of Asiatics during Amenemhet's time, apparently brought in as household servants. However, Egyptian records indicate that sometimes Asiatics (like Joseph) attained important government posts. Joseph lived for 110 years (50:22), dying about 1805 BC during the reign of Amenemhet III (1842–1797 BC). Amenemhet III's reign marked the zenith of economic prosperity in the Middle Kingdom. Perhaps this is partially due to Joseph's administrative skills and the acquisition of land for the pharaohs during the years of famine (47:20). Statues and other likenesses of these pharaohs have survived, providing a remarkable glimpse into the faces of people Joseph knew.[1]

EGYPT IN JOSEPH'S TIME

Joseph's Egypt was a fascinating place. The capital of the empire was in the north—near Memphis, about thirty miles south of modern Cairo. The great Nile (the longest river in the world) was abuzz with activity. Large temples and statues were visible throughout the land. The three huge pyramids of Giza and the Sphinx had already weathered the desert

Granite figure of Amenemhet III, who ruled in the Twelfth Dynasty, is shown in the classic pose of a Middle Kingdom official. The dates of his reign (1855–1808 BC) fit the time frame of Joseph's living in Egypt.

sands for more than half a millennium. The Great Pyramid of Khufu rose about 481 feet high, and each of its four sides stretched about 756 feet. This one pyramid contains 2.3 million stone blocks, averaging at least two and a half tons each. Originally covered with gleaming white limestone, the Giza pyramids must have been quite a spectacle. The Greeks designated the Great Pyramid one of the seven Wonders of the Ancient World, and it is the only one that remains.[2]

Religion was a crucial part of Egyptian life. The Egyptians worshipped a myriad of deities. Seven hundred and sixty-five gods decorate the walls of the vestibule leading into the tomb of Thutmose III (1504–1450 BC).[3] Amun (Amun-Re) was hailed as the king of Egypt's gods. Osiris was vital because he was the god of vegetation and the afterlife. The life-giving Nile River was even thought to be Osiris's bloodstream,[4] ironic in light of the first exodus plague—when the river turned to blood (Exod. 7:14–25). Other noteworthy gods were Nut (sky goddess), Isis (goddess of mothers and love), Hathor (goddess of love, joy, and sky; portrayed with horns, with cow's ears, or as a cow), Thoth (moon-god and god of writing, sometimes depicted as a baboon!), and various sun-gods—Re (or Ra), Aten, and Atum. Egyptians worshipped the pharaohs as the embodiment of the god Horus (represented by a falcon), doubtless the motivation for hauling the millions of tons of stone to build the pharaohs' pyramid tombs.

Drawing on the interior of the tomb of Khnemhotep II at Beni Hasan has what appears to be Hebrew-dressed people on the upper left corner.

Figurine of a man plowing; from the Middle Kingdom (2055–1650 BC).

The Egyptians believed in life after death. If they passed Osiris's examination, they entered a beautiful paradise called the Field of Reeds. If not, their hearts were devoured by the hideous monster Ammit. But those in the Field of Reeds still were not safe. If all earthly memory of a person was lost, the deceased could suffer the Second Death, a permanent annihilation of the spirit. Preservation of the body by mummification and likenesses (tomb paintings, statues) of the deceased were, therefore, necessary to maintain their memory and, in turn, their eternal life. No wonder the pharaohs filled the land with images of themselves: their eternal life depended on it!

During Joseph's day, Egypt led the world culturally. In fact, the twentieth and early nineteenth centuries BC have been designated the apex of Egyptian literature and craftsmanship. Reading and writing were the most important subjects in the schools, and the scribe (the most desired profession in Egypt) spent years mastering the 700 signs of Egyptian hieroglyphics. Two great literary works were composed in the Twelfth Dynasty, "The Instructions of Amenemhet" and "The Story of Sinuhe." Jewelry recovered from Middle Kingdom tombs exhibits superb craftsmanship, and tomb paintings show musicians with instruments (e.g., zither, lute, drum, harp, and flute).

Isis wearing a heavy collar with hawk's head terminals and on her head a modius, a symbol of fertility, is surmounted by cow's horns.

EVERYDAY LIFE IN JOSEPH'S EGYPT

The vast majority of Egypt's population (perhaps 1.5 million in Joseph's time) lived on the narrow strip of productive land along the Nile. Principal cereal crops were wheat and barley. Rainfall was sparse, and farmers depended on the Nile's inundations to water the land. If the Nile rose too little, famines such as that in Joseph's time could result. Early Egyptian records mention such famines, one lasting seven years.[5] In addition to agricultural activities, scenes on tomb walls depict fishing, hunting, bread making, and brick making, as well as potters, carpenters, decorators, goldsmiths, and sculptors.

Most clothing was made of linen. Men usually were depicted wearing skirtlike garments of varying lengths, and women, ankle-length gowns held up by shoulder straps. Both men and women applied cosmetics heavily, and women were frequently buried with their mirrors. Short hair was the rule, but both sexes often wore wigs. Men were typically clean shaven (Gen. 41:14), though images of the pharaohs often depicted them with fake beards. Originally, the Sphinx had a beard.

Mummies from ancient Egypt indicate the average height of women was about five feet, and men, about five feet, five inches. Of course, there were exceptions. Amenhotep II (who may have been the pharaoh of the exodus) was six feet in height, and Senusret III stood six feet six inches tall.[6] Analysis of mummies also reveals that Egyptians suffered from arthritis, tuberculosis, gout, gallstones, tooth decay, and parasites.

Egyptian pottery "soul house," with a portico, two rooms, ventilators on the roof, and stairs to the terrace. Such models were placed on graves. Visitors would place food for the dead in the courtyard. The model also shows the essentials of a town or country house, including an area for food preparation outside, plenty of shade and ventilation, and extra living space on the roof. Dated to the Twelfth Dynasty, about 1990–1800 BC, the time of Joseph.

The Egyptian diet included bread (mainly from barley), grapes, dates, figs, olives, cabbage, cheese, goat meat, pork, various fowl, and fish. Barley beer and wine (grape, date, or palm) were popular drinks. Sugar cane was introduced later, but the rich could afford honey.

Monogamy was the norm, though nobles and pharaohs could have many wives and a large harem. Ramesses II had eight principal wives and fathered more than a hundred children. Love poems suggest people pursued marriages for love, and tomb paintings often portray a husband and wife in loving embrace. Unlike Potiphar's wife (Gen. 39:7–19),[7] marriage partners were expected to be faithful. This is underscored by the penalty for adultery: burning or stoning.[8] Egyptian children played games and had toys and dolls. Family pets included dogs and cats.

Following Egyptian custom, both Jacob and Joseph were embalmed or mummified (50:2,26). In Jacob's case, the entire process for mummification and mourning took seventy days (50:3), a number cited in at least five Egyptian texts and by Herodotus. Joseph died at the age of 110, which was apparently considered the ideal life span, for this same age is mentioned in at least twenty-seven Egyptian texts.[9]

NOTES

[1] According to the late chronology, Joseph lived in Egypt during the latter part of the weak and obscure Thirteenth Dynasty (1782–1650 BC) and in the first part of the Fifteenth Dynasty–Hyksos (1663–1555 BC). Records of the kings of this period are meager. For further study, see Peter A. Clayton, *Chronicle of the Pharaohs: The Reign-by-Reign Record of the Rulers and Dynasties of Ancient Egypt* (London: Thames & Hudson, 1994), 90–4; and Daniel C. Browning Jr. and E. Ray Clendenen, "Hyksos," in *HIBD*, 796–98.

[2] Clayton, *Chronicle,* 47; Lorna Oakes and Lucia Gahlin, *Ancient Egypt* (London: Amness, 2003), 66; and http://www.book-of-thoth.com/article_submit/history/alternative-history/the-keys-locks-and-doors-of-thegreat-pyramid.html.

[3] Alberto Siliotti, *Guide to the Valley of the Kings* (New York: Barnes & Noble, 1996), 30.

[4] John J. Davis, *Moses and the Gods of Egypt: Studies in the Book of Exodus* (Grand Rapids: Baker, 1971), 94.

[5] John A. Wilson, trans., "The Tradition of Seven Lean Years in Egypt" and "The Prophecy of Neferti," in *ANET,* 31–2, 444–46.

[6] Davis, *Moses and the Gods,* 105; Clayton, *Chronicle,* 84.

[7] "The Story of Two Brothers" (ca. 1225 BC) tells of an adulteress turning on a young man who spurned her (*ANET,* 23–5). The fictional tale no doubt reflects reality.

[8] Joyce Tyldesley, *Judgement of the Pharaoh: Crime and Punishment in Ancient Egypt* (London: Weidenfeld & Nicolson, 2000), 66; A. Rosalie David, *The Egyptian Kingdoms* (New York: Elsevier Phaidon, 1975), 109.

[9] John J. Davis, *Paradise to Prison: Studies in Genesis* (Grand Rapids: Baker, 1975), 304. For an example written in the Middle Kingdom period, see "The Instruction of the Vizier Ptah-Hotep," *ANET,* 414.

EGYPT'S INFLUENCE ON THE DIVIDED KINGDOM

BY KEN COX

At the Karnak Temple in Egypt; interior of the Bubastite portal. The inscriptions brag of Shishak's military campaigns against Israel and Judah, during which he claims to have destroyed 156 towns and villages.

Nile River crossing to Beni Hasan. Vegetation forms a ribbon of green on either side of the river.

The Serapeum at Saqqara was the burial place for sacred bulls, which the ancient Egyptians worshipped as the incarnations of Ptah, their god of creation. After the division of the kingdom, King Jeroboam brought calf worship in Israel.

Egypt exerted no significant religious influence on Israel and Judah through its complex array of gods and idols.[1] Yet, after being harbored in Egypt, Jeroboam instituted calf worship in Israel (1 Kgs. 12:28–29). However, the more prominent apostasy through Baal and Ashtoreth worship Israel borrowed from Canaanite neighbors.[2]

One of Egypt's exports during the divided kingdom period was papyrus writing material. Using papyrus grown along the Nile, the Egyptians processed, layered, and stuck the plant stems together to form scrolls. These scrolls were common both as writing material in ancient Egypt and for production of biblical scrolls in Canaan. Baruch, the scribe, used papyrus scrolls to record the prophecies of Jeremiah. Israel duplicated this technology by planting papyrus in Galilee for parchment production.[3]

Jacob's descendants in the promised land were sandwiched between the military and commercial powers of Assyria, Babylon, and Aram to the north and Egypt to the south. The narrow land bridge of Canaan connected the nations that often moved through their borders.[4] Egypt's primary influences on the divided kingdom were as a threatening military power or an unreliable ally.[5]

God's Word prohibited the tribes of Israel from relying on Egypt for military support. Deuteronomy 17:14–20 describes the character of Israel's future kings. The Lord forbade the kings to return to Egypt to acquire horses. Scriptures had portrayed Egypt as a place of darkness and bondage. God's power of salvation had lovingly delivered his people from the stranglehold of Egyptian power. God's people, therefore, were not to return to Egypt after the exodus. They were to trust in God, not political allies, for their security.

King Solomon broke this commandment. Israel's alliance with Egypt, though, was short-lived. Pharaoh Shishak antagonized Solomon during the final years of Solomon's reign by granting refuge to Jeroboam.[6] After Solomon's death, Jeroboam likely requested permission to return to Canaan where he incited a rebellion against the newly enthroned King Rehoboam.

Pharaoh Shishak's enmity was not limited to harboring Jeroboam. After Israel divided, in the fifth year of Rehoboam's reign, Shishak attacked Jerusalem and carried off the treasures of the temple (1 Kgs. 14:25–26). This Egyptian victory is recorded on the walls of the temple in Karnak.[7] Shishak took the gold shields Solomon had made for his personal guard.

When Pharaoh Neco's forces killed Judah's King Josiah, Pharaoh was leading his Egyptian army north, toward Damascus, to aid his allies in Assyria. Babylon was rising as a world power after the fall of Nineveh in 612 BC. Babylon's King Nebuchadnezzar defeated Pharaoh Neco at Carchemish in 605 BC.[8]

After Egypt's defeat at Carchemish, Jerusalem was in a tug-of-war between Babylon and Egypt. Pharaoh Hophra wanted to reestablish domination of Judah and attempted to halt Babylon's final siege of Jerusalem.[9] Hophra's intervention in Judah was unsuccessful, and in 586 BC the Babylonians devastated Jerusalem.

NOTES

[1]   Daniel C. Browning Jr. and Kirk Kilpatrick, "Egypt" in *HIBD*, 469.

[2]   "Gods, False" in *Unger's Bible Dictionary*, ed. Merrill F. Unger (Chicago: Moody, 1966), 412–13.

[3]   "Papyrus" in *Unger's*, 823.

[4]   J. McKee Adams, *Biblical Backgrounds*, rev. Joseph A. Callaway (Nashville: Broadman, 1965), 25.

[5]   Roland de Vaux, *Ancient Israel* (Grand Rapids: Eerdmans, 1997), 248.

[6]   John D. Currid, *Ancient Egypt and the Old Testament* (Grand Rapids: Baker, 1997), 179.

[7]   Currid, *Ancient Egypt*, 180.

[8]   Richard D. Patterson and Hermann J. Austel, "1, 2 Kings" in *1, 2 Kings, 1, 2 Chronicles, Ezra, Nehemiah, Esther, Job*, vol. 4 in The Expositor's Bible Commentary, ed. Frank E. Gaebelein (Grand Rapids: Zondervan, 1988), 289.

[9]   Ralph H. Alexander, "Ezekiel" in *Isaiah, Jeremiah, Lamentations, Ezekiel*, vol. 6 in Expositor's (1986), 888.

EN-GEDI: HISTORY AND ARCHAEOLOGY

BY JOEL F. DRINKARD JR.

A view of the mountains of En-gedi with caves that could provide hiding places for fugitives.

En-gedi is an oasis in a barren area of the Judean wilderness. En-gedi lies along the Wadi Ghar, or Nahal Arugot, also probably to be identified as the Valley of Beracah (2 Chr. 20:26). This area is desolate with only a few scrub bushes and wild grasses, apart from wadi beds and around the few springs. The limited rainfall provides sparse grazing for the bedouin flocks today, much as it would have in David's day. The many caves along the hillsides provide shelter from midday heat and nighttime cold. They also are the dens for the wild animals of the region, the bears and lions of David's day. Those same caves could provide a hideout for David and his men fleeing from Saul. David would know the region well; he would know which caves would be least noticeable to Saul's army, which would provide the best view of approaches, and which lay near water sources.

En-gedi is the major spring and oasis along the western shore of the Dead Sea. It lies almost midway down the length of the Dead Sea. The name in Hebrew means "spring of kids," which fits with the description of the nearby hills as "Rocks of the Wild Goats" (1 Sam. 24:2). A short distance from the spring is a beautiful waterfall and pool. The available water creates an oasis of lush vegetation in stark contrast to the desolate hills just a few hundred yards away. The immediate area around the spring and waterfall has been inhabited at least since the Chalcolithic period (4000–3200 BC). The Chalcolithic remains include a well-preserved shrine or sanctuary about ninety-five feet by sixty-two feet. The shrine has a wall enclosing a courtyard with two buildings. The larger building to the north is a broad-room structure about sixty-two feet by twenty-two feet. The other building, also a broad-room structure, is on the east and is about twenty-five feet by sixteen feet. The enclosure wall has two gates, the larger one on the south and the smaller one on the northeast. The courtyard has a circular structure in the center about ten feet in diameter, made of small stones. Its function is unknown. Both buildings and gates had doors; the stone sills and hinge holes are still present.

The main building had a niche in the middle of the back wall surrounded by a low wall and had benches on both sides. Apparently sacrifices were made in this building because the floor had pits on both ends filled with burned bones, horns, pottery, and ashes. The excavators suggested that the enclosure was a cult site, perhaps a central sanctuary.[1] About six miles south of En-gedi, a major find of the Chalcolithic period was made. A cache of more than 400 copper-bronze objects was found in a cave in Nahal Mishmar. The cache included "crowns," wands or standards, maces, and chisels suggesting a cultic function for the objects. In addition to the copper-bronze objects, several hematite and hippopotamus tusk objects were found. The objects show superb artistic and technical workmanship. Since no other major sanctuary from the Chalcolithic period has been found in the surrounding region, it is possible that the Nahal Mishmar copper treasure may have belonged to the En-gedi shrine. Perhaps the priests of this shrine took the cult objects to the cave in Nahal Mishmar for safekeeping when they abandoned the site, hoping to return later and retrieve them. They then may have died or been killed before being able to retrieve the objects, and their secret location remained hidden for more than 5,000 years until 1961 when the cave was explored.[2] If these objects did belong to the En-gedi shrine, that sanctuary would have been the most important one of the Chalcolithic period yet known in Israel. Since the shrine was not destroyed but was abandoned, the remains would have been prominently visible and could have been known by David 3,000 years ago. Perhaps his stronghold at En-gedi was on top of one of the steep hillsides around the sanctuary.

The excavators found no evidence of remains belonging to the time of David at En-gedi. There was a settlement, now called Tel Goren, from the seventh and sixth centuries BC, late in the period of the divided monarchy. This settlement had a number of buildings noted for having large store jars partially sunken into the floors. These buildings were apparently part of an industrial complex that produced perfume and/or medicines. From later periods, Persian through Roman-Byzantine, there is evidence of the cultivation and processing of balsam plants. Belonging to the settlement of the earliest stratum, the seventh century BC, were seals and jar handles bearing Hebrew inscriptions and stone weights with signs indicating one, four, and eight shekels. A royal stamp impression, "of/for the king, [from] Ziph," was found on the handle of a store jar. But there were no Iron I remains that would date to the period of Saul-David-Solomon.

We should not be surprised that archaeologists haven't found a settlement belonging to the time when David fled into this region. He wanted an isolated hiding place, not a built-up community. To hide in a desolate, uninhabited area is much easier. Had there been a settlement, Saul would have known of it. David knew the area; he knew the good hiding places and the sources of water. The many caves in the surrounding hills would provide excellent hiding places.

The Hebrew Bible refers to the strongholds to which David fled throughout the wilderness of Judah. Three times the reference is specifically to "the stronghold" (1 Sam. 22:4,5; 24:22). Some scholars[3] have suggested "the stronghold" was Masada, the mountain fortress about ten miles south of En-gedi, later made famous by Herod's palace and the zealots' stand against the Romans in AD 66–73. The name *Masada* means "stronghold," and the Hebrew word for "stronghold" used in 1 Samuel is closely related to the name *Masada*. Certainly the top of Masada would be almost impregnable. The flat-top hill rises more than a thousand feet from the floor of the Dead Sea Valley, with steep slopes on all sides. Even on the west where Masada has the least rise from the valley below, there is a drop of 300 feet. The top would also provide a perfect view of all approaches and ample opportunity for a small band of men to escape to one side while an army approached from the opposite direction. Presumably the other strongholds in the wilderness of Judah would have given similar opportunity for escape. Indeed the biblical text describes that type of escape from Saul (23:24–26).

The steep wadi slopes from Qumran south to Masada along the western side of the Dead Sea have been explored by Israeli archaeologists since the 1960s. They discovered numerous caves showing habitation from the Chalcolithic period through the Second Jewish Revolt of AD 132–135. Many of the caves were nearly inaccessible. Steep cliffs with almost sheer drops of 600–750 feet were not uncommon. One of the caves in Nahal Mishmar had Iron I shards belonging to the time of Saul, David, and Solomon. The archaeologists concluded that for more than 5,000 years these caves have provided places of refuge in times of danger— exactly the use David made of these caves and strongholds!

NOTES

[1] Benjamin Mazar, "En-Gedi," *NEAEHL*, 2:405.

[2] P. Bar-Adon, "The Nahal Mishmar Caves," *NEAEHL*, 3:822–27.

[3] Yohanan Aharoni, *Land of the Bible,* rev. ed. (Louisville: Westminster John Knox, 1979), 290 and n. 9.

EPHESUS: A HISTORICAL SURVEY

BY RANDALL L. ADKISSON

South Street at Ephesus. Giving evidence of how heavy traffic was in the city's earlier history, chariot ruts in the pavement stones are still visible.

Located at the mouth of the Cayster River, Ephesus served as an important access route for trade into and out of the interior of Asia Minor and its profitable land routes. Both the location and imperial favor the city enjoyed through several different eras propelled Ephesus as a cultural and commercial wonder of the ancient world. Estimates place the population during Paul's time at 250,000 residents.[1]

The history of Ephesus is long and storied. Evidently established as a free Greek colony for the purpose of opening trade routes into the interior, the city dates at least to the mid-eleventh century BC. Ephesus was one of twelve cities comprising the Ionian Confederacy. The port at Ephesus gave merchants access to the coastal road running north through Smyrna to Troas, as well as an interior route to Colossae, Hierapolis, Laodicea, and farther to the Phygian regions. As nearby ports succumbed to erosion and political intrigue, Ephesus flourished in importance and prestige.

One ancient myth records that Amazons, a culture of mighty female warriors, were the earliest builders of the town, establishing a temple where the "mother goddess of the earth was reputedly born."[2] Ephesus's connection to pagan goddess worship prospered under each successive occupation. The Greeks established a strong cult to Artemis. The Romans accepted the association between the city and goddess worship, equating Artemis with their goddess Diana.

From its position as a free city-state, Ephesus fell into subservience, first to King Croesus of Lydia in 560 BC and then to the Persians. By defeating the Persians, Alexander the Great brought the city back into Greek hands and into his empire in 334 BC. At his death, the city's ownership passed to Lysimachus, one of Alexander's generals. Lysimachus lost the region when defeated by Seleucus I in 281 BC. Ninety-one years later, the Seleucid Empire fell to the Romans. In appreciation to King Eumeness II of Pergamum for his assistance against the Seleucids, Ephesus and the surrounding region were ceded to the Pergamum Empire. The city prospered and was peacefully bequeathed to the Romans by Pergamum's last king, Attalus III, in 133 BC.

The grand theater at Ephesus was built in the third century BC. Through the years it was modified until it reached its final form during the reign of the emperor Trajan (AD 98–117). The theater had seating capacity for 24,000.

Relief of the mask of tragedy at the grand theater; Ephesus.

From this period through the New Testament era, Ephesus functioned as a strong and vibrant part of the Roman Empire. As a proconsular seat and the capital of the Roman province of Asia, the city enjoyed influence and standing in the region and beyond. The temple complex was a center of commerce and tourism. The city also served as an ancient banking institution. A city of great prominence, ancient Ephesus reflected its wealth and culture in its buildings and landscape. A traveler entering the first-century city was walking on the streets of the fourth-largest city in the world.[3]

As a central feature of the city, the temple of Artemis was listed as one of the seven wonders of the ancient world and stood four times larger than the Athenian Parthenon. At 420 feet long and 240 feet wide, the temple was as tall as a six-story building, its roof being supported by more than one hundred large columns. The impressive temple reflected and compelled an expansive industry of tourism associated with worship of the goddess. Travelers from across the ancient world swelled the ranks of the inhabitants in Ephesus during April for a festival involving a great procession to the temple, as well as various athletic and musical competitions.

The large population and influx of tourists allowed Ephesus to maintain a huge theater, the ruins of which may still be visited today. Seating approximately 24,000, the theater had sixty-six tiers of seating.[4] From the entrance to the theater, the Arcadian Way, a broad marble paved thoroughfare flanked by ornate columns, buildings, and shops stretched through the city to the port.

Archaeological efforts at Ephesus suggest a city that once swarmed with people and commerce. From the impressive and imposing main thoroughfare—flanked by ancient baths, a smaller theater, government buildings, a music hall, and a multistory library—stretched smaller streets leading to the city's vast area of residences and warehouses. The ruins highlight the ancient city's character. A thriving port city, Ephesus was adorned with both the advantages and vices of its position and commerce.

Ephesus successfully combined the cultures and histories of many different people and periods. The city's original population assumed the flavor of Greek culture and religion. With Roman conquest, the city continued to thrive, synchronizing the various religions and welcoming immigrants from across the region. Records reveal subcultures of Egyptian, Jewish, Greek, and Roman citizenry.

NOTES

[1]   Mitchell G. Reddish, "Ephesus" in *HolBD*, 425.
[2]   Merrill F. Unger, *Archaeology and the New Testament* (Grand Rapids: Zondervan, 1962), 249.
[3]   Reddish, "Ephesus," 425.
[4]   Gerald L. Borchert, "Ephesus" in *ISBE* (1982), 2:116.

EXCAVATING GATH: AN INTERVIEW

WITH DR. AREN MAEIR

Dr. Maeir with the stone horned altar, which was excavated in 2011. It measures about twenty by twenty by forty inches.

Q: What kind of significant finds have you uncovered in these past seasons?

MAEIR: We have many, but I'll mention a couple: (1) The so-called Goliath inscription: a small shard, dated to the tenth or early ninth century BC, in which two names of non-Semitic, Indo-European origin are written, in an archaic alphabetic script. These names (ALWT and WLT) are somewhat similar to what the original name of Goliath was, and serve as a nice indicator that during the Iron Age IIA (more or less the time of King David) there were people at Gath, the home of Goliath according to the Bible, who had names similar to the name Goliath. (2) In the lower city, we discovered a building (probably a temple) in which we found a large stone altar.

Q: Could you please describe this stone altar?

MAEIR: The altar was made of hard limestone. It is the only two-horned altar known in the Levant; others (one or two) have been unearthed at Cyprus. The decorations on the altar are similar to those on other Levantine Iron Age altars.

An aerial view of Tell es-Safi, biblical Gath.

Recent excavations at Gath.

Q: How would you describe the gate?

MAEIR: The gate is located in the middle of the northern side of the lower city, right opposite a water well, which is still in use today; in fact, during the time of the modern Arab village, one of the paths leading up to the village reused the path that ran through the Iron Age gate. It appears that the gate has stone foundations and a brick superstructure.

Q: What do the gate and fortification walls tell us about the ancient city of Gath?

MAEIR: They tell us that Gath was a large, fortified city during the tenth–ninth centuries BC, probably the strongest city-state in the region at the time. This strong Philistine presence probably meant that the Judahite kingdom could not expand into this region until after Gath's destruction by Hazael king of Aram-Damascus in 830 BC.

The top of the massive city wall, indicated by the rough stones, is visible in the archaeological dig squares.

THE FALL OF JERUSALEM

BY BYRON LONGINO

Scene depicting the fall of Lachish; this decorated the walls of Nineveh's Southwest Palace. The scene depicts siege engines ascending a man-made ramp. The battering ram is ramming against the tower at the city gate.

Wall panel showing Sargon II (left) receiving a high official, probably his son and thus the next king of Assyria, Sennacherib.

CONDITIONS BEFORE THE FALL

The Chaldeans were a people group who migrated into southeastern Mesopotamia between 1000 and 900 BC. Over time, they gained control of the region of Babylonia. People began to refer to them both as Chaldeans and Babylonians. The Chaldeans continued to grow in power, so that by the eighth century BC they were the chief rivals of the Assyrians, the then-dominant world power. During Assyria's dominance, the Chaldeans served as allies of Judah against the Assyrians. With the fall of the Assyrians and the rise of the Neo-Babylonian Empire, however, Judah came under the rule of the Chaldeans, becoming a vassal state in 604–603 BC.[1]

When the Babylonians suffered defeat at the Egyptian border in 601 BC, Judah under King Jehoiakim revolted. Judah's independence, though, was short-lived; in 598 the Babylonians under Nebuchadnezzar besieged Jerusalem. The Babylonians deported King Jehoiachin (Jehoiakim's son), the royal family, and 10,000 citizens.

Nebuchadnezzar placed Zedekiah (Jehoiachin's uncle) on the throne of Judah. Expecting Egyptian support, Zedekiah rebelled. Nebuchadnezzar swiftly responded, conquering Judah's fortress cities and besieging Jerusalem. The Babylonians captured Jerusalem in 586 BC, burned the city, and destroyed the temple.

THE BABYLONIAN STRATEGY

The primary means of capturing a city in biblical times was a siege. This involved surrounding the city with an army and cutting the city off from food, water, and other

The Babylonian Chronicles cover the years 605–595 BC. They begin by telling the story of the battle of Carchemish, when Nebuchadnezzar finally routed the Egyptian forces in Syria, and record the extension of Babylonian power to the Mediterranean. They record Ashkelon being captured in 604 and Babylon's first capture of Jerusalem in 598 BC.

resources. If successful, this tactic typically led to the eventual surrender of the city to the attackers.

Armies used various methods to harass a besieged city. They built ramps around the city wall and placed mobile towers against the walls. The towers allowed attackers to shoot at the defenders or send projectiles, including torches, down into the city. Attackers would weaken the city's wall by setting fires at its base and/or digging tunnels under it. Ladders enabled attackers to scale the wall. Further, soldiers used battering rams to break through city gates.[2] Jeremiah records that the Jerusalem inhabitants defended their city in part by tearing down some of their houses in order to construct defenses against the siege works (Jer. 33:4).

Nebuchadnezzar's forces penetrated the city only after they breached a spot in the walls. After breaching a city's wall, the conquering army typically pillaged and burned the city (2 Kgs. 14:12–14; 25:9–11).[3]

CONDITIONS DURING THE FALL

Archaeological excavations in the area of Jerusalem now known as the Jewish Quarter uncovered four ancient latrines. At least one dates to the time of Nebuchadnezzar's destruction of the city in 586 BC. Analysis of the contents reveals that the inhabitants of the city had stopped eating their normal diet and instead were eating backyard plants; in other words, whatever they found growing wild inside the city.

Archaeological excavations have uncovered large stones scattered where the walls once stood and houses that had been reduced to charred ruins. Smashed pottery littered the area. Archaeologists also recovered arrowheads in the houses and at the northern sections of the city fortifications.

CONDITIONS AFTER THE FALL

The Babylonians punished peoples who continued to revolt by exiling them to distant areas of the kingdom. After destroying Jerusalem, Nebuchadnezzar deported a significant number of Judeans to Babylonia (2 Kgs. 25:8–21). This was the third deportation. The first occurred in 605 BC, when Daniel and other nobles from Judah were taken into exile. The second deportation in 597 BC included King Jehoiachin, the royal family, 7,000 warriors, and 1,000 metalsmiths and craftsmen (24:10–16). A fourth deportation occurred in 582 BC (Jer. 52:30).

The Babylonians demolished Jerusalem and other major sites, but they did not totally destroy Judah. The Babylonians allowed some people to remain to work the land (Jer. 52:16). The people who remained worshipped in the temple ruins.

Foundation cylinder with the record of public works of Nebuchadnezzar II; dated 604–562 BC. The cylinder was found in the temple foundations in the ancient Sumerian city of Marad. The inscription mentions walls, water supply, towers, and temples, and contains his prayers for riches and a long reign.

NOTES

1. The paragraphs in this section are based on the article by Tony M. Martin, "Chaldea" in *HIBD*, 276.
2. "Siegeworks" in *HIBD*, 1500.
3. Victor Matthews, *The Cultural World of the Bible: An Illustrated Guide to Manners and Customs*, 4th ed. (Grand Rapids: Baker Academic, 2015), 162.

FIRST-CENTURY ATHENS

BY DAVID M. WALLACE

Parthenon and Acropolis in Athens, Greece.

GEOGRAPHY AND TRADE

Athens is located on the small Attica Peninsula near the eastern edge of Achaia, where the Mediterranean and Aegean Seas meet. The region around Athens is extremely hot and dry in summer, with short rainy seasons in winter. In spite of an average of only sixteen inches of rain annually, this area was rich in olive trees and vineyards. Olive oil and wine were chief exports. Timber was scarce; most resources in Achaia were agricultural.

Athens became famous for manufacturing pottery due to the excellent clay beds nearby. Both silver and lead mines were located at Laurium, on the southern tip of Attica. Nearby Mount Pentelicus provided the famous marble, which artisans throughout Athens and beyond used. Access to water and excellent harbors near Athens and throughout Achaia made exporting products easy.

HISTORY AND CULTURE

According to tradition, Cecrops, who had come to Athens from Egypt about 1556 BC, founded the city. Yet archaeological evidence indicates settlement during the fourth

Tower of the Winds, in the Roman forum in Athens. Built in the first century BC, the originally domed tower was equipped with a bronze weather vane, a water clock, an astronomical clock, and sundials.

millennium BC. The city was built around a steep, easily defended hill known as the Acropolis. Athens grew in ancient times to a population of about 250,000 people.[1]

Athens reached its zenith during the fifth century BC but lost much of its political influence as a result of the Peloponnesian War with the Spartans near the end of that century. After the Romans conquered Greece, they made Athens a Roman territory (146 BC). Rome ruled first-century Athens. "In deference to her glorious past, they granted Athens the status of a free and federated city."[2]

Rome's General Sulla destroyed much of the city in 86 BC after Athens rebelled and allied itself with Mithridates of Pontus. However, when Paul arrived on his way to nearby Corinth, Athens continued to enjoy fame as a center for the arts, architecture, history, culture, philosophy, learning, and sports. The university there was perhaps the most important in the Roman world at that time.[3] Many great classical structures remained standing and intact. Athens was a city of magnificent stone, ivory, and marble buildings that celebrated its history, culture, and the worship of its gods and goddesses. It was still a beautiful city in the first century AD, in spite of some of its former glory having faded.

When Paul visited, a wall encircled Athens, protecting it from any potential siege. Two parallel walls, some 250 feet apart, running from the sea to the city about five miles inland, kept the city connected to the sea.[4]

Near the Ilissus River, outside the city wall, stood the horseshoe-shaped stadium where athletes and spectators honored Athena. Footraces, boxing, javelin, and wrestling were some of the events. The stadium opened to the north; its racetrack was about 200 yards long and thirty-six yards wide.[5]

To find lodging and get oriented to the city, Paul and his traveling companions would have entered Athens through the Dipylon (double) Gate and continued along the Panathenaic Way to the agora or marketplace. The agora was the city's social, commercial, and political center. The city itself was comprised of three areas—the Acropolis, the agora, and the Areopagus.

THE ACROPOLIS

Although the Bible does not say, Paul likely ascended the marble staircase to the top of the Acropolis and toured the buildings, which glorified pagan gods. The Acropolis was a spectacular outcropping of stone rising some 500 feet above the surrounding plain and city. During the golden age of Athens when Pericles reigned (443–429 BC), the Parthenon was built on top of the Acropolis and dedicated to Athena, the goddess of wisdom for whom the city was named. Construction had taken about fifteen years. Other structures on top of the hill included the temple of Wingless Victory (the temple of Athena Nike), the Erechtheum (a temple dedicated to Athena and Poseidon), and the Propylaeum. The temples, shrines, monuments, and public buildings gave Athens its unique character. It was a showplace for art and architecture.

THE AGORA

Below the Acropolis to the north-northwest was the agora. This marketplace or business center was the city's social and political hub. During New Testament days, Athens had both a Greek agora and a newer Roman forum.

"By Paul's time the Greek agora had become more of a museum for monuments recalling Athens's former glory."[6] The new Roman forum had become the modern center of city business and activity. This is probably where Paul talked and debated with philosophers and the religious and civic leaders. While Paul held discussions with the Jews in the local synagogue, he also made direct appeals to the local people in the agora (Acts 17:17).

THE AREOPAGUS

As Paul debated the Epicureans and Stoics, his preaching about Jesus sounded to the Greeks like he was introducing them to a new god. Those who heard Paul sent him,

Close-up of the Propylaeum (Acropolis entrance) shows the building to the north of the Propylaeum (left) and temple of Nike (right). Nike was the goddess of victory.

therefore, to the Areopagus. Both the council and a marble hill immediately northwest of the Acropolis were called the Areopagus. The group was "a civic body responsible for the religious and moral life of Athens. As such it had to approve any new deity."[7] The site was named for Ares, the god of war. The hill was also one of the locations where the city council met and possibly the site where Paul appeared before the council.[8]

NOTES

[1] J. D. Douglas and Merrill C. Tenney, "Athens" in *The New International Dictionary of the Bible* (Grand Rapids: Zondervan, 1987), 108.

[2] Frank Stagg, *The Book of Acts: The Early Struggle for an Unhindered Gospel* (Nashville: Broadman, 1955), 179.

[3] Douglas and Tenney, "Athens," 108.

[4] Arthur A. Rupprecht, "Athens" in *ZPEB*, 403.

[5] Charles F. Pfeiffer, ed., "Athens" in *The Biblical World: A Dictionary of Biblical Archaeology* (Nashville: Broadman, 1976), 118.

[6] Thomas V. Brisco, *Holman Bible Atlas* (Nashville: Broadman & Holman, 1998), 251.

[7] Walter A. Elwell, ed., "Athens" in *Baker Encyclopedia of the Bible* (*BEB*) (Grand Rapids: Baker, 1989), 230.

[8] Merrill F. Unger, *Archaeology and the New Testament* (Grand Rapids: Zondervan, 1964), 237.

FIRST-CENTURY CRETE

BY TIMOTHY T. FABER

Remains of the Church of Saint Titus at Gortyn, Crete; dated to the eighth century AD.

Crete had a reputation, and it was not a good one. In Titus 1:12, Paul quotes the sixth-century BC Greek poet Epimenides: "Cretans are always liars, evil beasts, lazy gluttons." Not only did Paul make use of this quotation, but he went on to say, "This testimony is true" (v. 13).

What caused Epimenides to make such a statement about his fellow Cretans? The people of Crete claimed that the tomb of Zeus, the chief Greek god, was located on their island. Epimenides's sentiment was based in the concept that Zeus, being a god, could not be dead—and those who claimed his tomb was on the island had to be lying. Therefore, all Cretans must be liars. By Paul's time, Epimenides's words had become a popular slogan that highlighted the widespread reputation of Cretans as untruthful.[1]

A people known as Minoans inhabited Crete at least as early as 2800 BC. Rather than being isolationists, the Minoans were a seafaring people that influenced the entire Mediterranean world with a "rich culture" of impressive "architecture, pottery, metalwork and painting."[2] Minoan civilization collapsed about 1400 BC, possibly due to a massive earthquake.

Their history made the Cretans a proud people. Centuries later, as different world powers dominated the region, the Cretans were able to maintain a somewhat separate identity—even from the Greeks, Romans, and others who sought to claim the island as their own. Factions did develop among the Cretans, though, based partly on their affinity with various powers seeking to conquer them and also on both nationality and ethnic origins. The centrally located city of Gortyn is an example of the Cretans' changing affinities and affiliations.

Ruins of the praetorium (governor's residence) at Gortyn, Crete. Gortyn, centrally located on the island, served for a time as the capital of the Roman province of Crete and Cyrene.

Hannibal, born in 247 BC, became a Carthaginian general who led a revolt against Rome—a revolt that became a war. Gortyn temporarily served as a refuge for Hannibal as he was fleeing Rome in 189 BC. Opposition to the Romans unified the Cretans for decades after Hannibal's departure. In fact, they were able to repulse a Roman attempt at conquest in 74 BC.

Just a few years later, though, in 66 BC, the city of Gortyn changed its affiliation and sided with Rome in their eventual conquest of Crete. Rome rewarded this support by making Gortyn the capital of the Roman province of Crete and Cyrene[3]—a province that stretched into North Africa.

The history of Crete during the first and second centuries AD is rather ambiguous. What little exists does not give a definitive snapshot of Christianity on the island. In the city of Gortyn, however, are the remains of the Church of Saint Titus. Tradition claims Titus's ministry was headquartered in Gortyn and that he died there in AD 107.

Mediterranean cultures surrounded and infiltrated Crete, but the Cretan peoples also became an influence upon the entire Mediterranean world. Located in the middle of the Mediterranean Sea, almost equally between Greece, North Africa, and Asia Minor, Crete was a great place for seafaring trade—both legitimate and otherwise. Human trafficking and piracy were a real part of life on Crete. Whether Crete was more the victim or the perpetrator of piracy is unclear; the evidence for both possibilities is staggering.[4]

NOTES

[1] Walter C. Kaiser et al., *Hard Sayings of the Bible* (Downers Grove, IL: InterVarsity, 1996), 675–76.

[2] Avraham Negev, ed., *Archaeological Encyclopedia of the Holy Land* (Jerusalem: G. A. Jerusalem Publishing House, 1972), 82.

[3] Dana Facaros and Michael Pauls, *Crete* (London: Cadogan Guides, 2010), 216–17.

[4] Barry Unsworth, *Crete* (Washington, DC: National Geographic Society, 2004), 27.

FIRST-CENTURY ROADS AND TRAVEL

BY PAUL E. KULLMAN

The Cardo Maximus, a main north/south street at Gerasa (modern Jerash).

Ruins of a Roman aqueduct along the Appian Way, outside of Puteoli.

TRAVEL THROUGHOUT THE EMPIRE

Before Rome built its vast array of roads, travel was a burdensome hardship and often dangerous. Caravans used the roads as established trade routes that brought economic vitality to cities, towns, and villages. The same roads, however, brought travelers many dangers such as bandits and occasional interactions with military troop movements. First-century travelers journeyed primarily by walking, but other modes of travel included wagon, chariot, and donkey. Road construction methods allowed heavy wagons, war chariots, and military siege engines to travel throughout the empire without the burdensome mud they encountered on ordinary dirt pathways. Roman engineering, famous for its architecture, aqueducts, bridges, and road construction, eventually made travel to various locations throughout the empire possible.

The superiorly designed road system allowed governmental patrons the advantage both to defeat nations and to spread Roman influence and culture. A good roadway system also gave Rome the benefit of new business opportunities such as overnight lodging, mercantile shops, and commercial services. Christianity would benefit greatly as believers used this same network to spread the gospel.

TYPES OF ROADS AND STREETS

Several factors affected first-century road design and construction. One was the road's setting, either rural or urban. In urban settings, the Romans followed the Greeks' meticulous city-planning habits, strategically building each city with its center at the agora (marketplace). Jewish cities had the most important places of activity at the city gate and temple (Jerusalem). Walled cities typically had a grid of major streets with alleyways branching off to provide pedestrian access to smaller neighborhoods and shops. In rural settings, being able to move military troops across expansive terrain was the primary reason for constructing good roads. However, once built, the road system benefited civilian traffic and the transportation of commerce.

Another more technical factor was the different approach the Romans and Jews took in rural road construction. Rome used its military soldiers and engineers—and its immense

The oldest and most famous road of the Roman Empire, the Appian Way served as the main route between Rome and Greece. More than 350 miles long, the road was constructed in the fourth century BC by the Roman magistrate (or censor), Appius Claudius Caecus.

vassal labor—for achieving the best-constructed roads. When not actively engaged in military assignments, soldiers provided the important maintenance labor needed. Well-constructed and maintained roads helped troops and governmental couriers to perform business rapidly on behalf of the empire.

The Jewish approach to constructing a roadway system was different. Prior to New Testament times, roads in Israel were ordinary trade routes across nothing more than centuries-old, well-worn paths where people had removed rocks and boulders and had leveled the dirt. Roads the Jews built were less durable; the people lacked the means and methods of both construction and maintenance. Many established roads ran along dry riverbeds or other natural landmarks; these tended to lengthen a journey rather than facilitate travel in a straight line.[1] Roman design changed all of that by the first century AD.

MATERIALS AND CONSTRUCTION

Transportation via good roadways is a high priority for any government, whether local or national. Governments invest large capital to ensure that people can travel quickly and without delay. Proper planning is essential to meet the various geographical challenges across a diverse empire. The Romans did not invent the road design, but they did enhance its constructability from its first use during the Bronze Age. Since the road system ran like arteries throughout the empire, they physically tied hundreds of villages, cities, and provinces together. Therefore, this civil engineering endeavor had to be well designed and built to last.

Romans designed their city-street pattern with one major roadway running north-south and the other east-west. This served as an axis for a grid that allowed street construction to be built in straight lines. Street widths ranged from six and a half feet to twenty-six feet.[2] Workers used the site work method of "cut and fill" to move dirt they excavated from higher ground to fill in the low areas, resulting in straight roads. The Romans' road engineering was successful and durable because of the multilayer system they used. They began with a subbase layer where they first excavated soil and refilled the area with compacted soil and rubble. This supported layers of foundational material. They then set a surface topping of flat stones or bricks in a mixture of lime, sand, pozzalana (volcanic ash where available), and water. These, the basic ingredients in concrete, are still in use throughout the world today. The roads crowned in the center and sloped downward toward the outer edges, which had a continuous curbstone for drainage.

Most first-century roads used milestone markers to measure distance to specific destinations such as from a town to a city. Across Israel, the discovery of about 500 milestone markers bearing ancient inscriptions as early as AD 56 provide tangible evidence that ancient cities and towns were linked together by providing navigational information to the first-century traveler. In AD 69, the Roman Legion X recorded on a milestone marker the construction of a new road from Scythopolis (Beth-shean) to Legio (Megiddo).[3]

Rome took pride in its engineering achievements, and roadways were its crown jewel. Concerning the Jewish roads already in existence, the Romans redeveloped and absorbed them into a capital improvement master plan. They paid for these with vassal contributions, giving further testimony to the Romans' power, influence, and success. Local governmental overseers provided the funds for routine road maintenance once a road was built.

NOTES

[1] Max Schwartz, *The Biblical Engineer: How the Temple in Jerusalem Was Built* (Hoboken, NJ: Ktav, 2002), 48.

[2] J. Julius Scott Jr., *Customs and Controversies: Intertestamental Jewish Backgrounds of the New Testament* (Grand Rapids: Baker, 1995), 240.

[3] David F. Graf, Benjamin Isaac, and Israel Roll, "Roads and Highways (Roman)" in *ABD*, 5:782–87.

FIRST-CENTURY THESSALONICA

BY TIMOTHY TRAMMELL

The White Tower is the most famous tower in Greece and is the symbol of Thessalonica. Built in AD 1500, the tower was part of the city's defense system and served as the city jail.

HISTORY

Prehistoric settlements in the area date to 2300 BC. Thessalonica was at first a small village called Alia, but it was subsequently named Therma because of the thermal springs to the east and south of it. Cassander, one of the four key generals who had served under Alexander the Great, enlarged the city in 315 BC, naming it Thessalonica after his wife, Thessalonike, the half sister of Alexander. He formed the city by forcing twenty-six villages to unite; then he designated it his capital.[1]

In 167 BC, the city came under Roman control when Rome defeated Perseus, king of Macedonia. At that time the kingdom was divided into four districts with Thessalonica as capital of the second district. In 146 BC Macedonia was made a Roman province, and Thessalonica became the provincial capital. As the capital of Macedonia, it was known as "The Metropolis of Macedonia"—literally, the "mother city" of the province.

The economic strength of the city was solidified in 130 BC when Rome constructed a roadway, the Via Egnatia, linking Thessalonica with the Adriatic Sea on the west and Neapolis on the east.[2] The city supported Antony and Octavian (later Augustus Caesar) in their conflict against the Triumvirs (ca. 42 BC) and thus received the status of a free city. As a result, Thessalonica was allowed to administer her own affairs.

However, the city's privileged status was interrupted in AD 15 for a few years. The increasing prosperity of the region caused a protest against what the leadership of the city considered high taxation. This caused Tiberius to change Macedonia from a proconsular province to an imperial province, that is, one under the direct control of Caesar.[3] Yet this ultimately proved to be positive, for this gave the city intimate and immediate access to Rome. Claudius reversed this action in AD 44 by making Macedonia a senatorial province again.[4]

LOCATION

Ancient Thessalonica was located on the eastern coast of the province of Macedonia between the Balkan mountain range and the Greek peninsula. It was near the Axius and

The Odeum, restored, at the Roman forum in Thessalonica. In the background are current excavations at the forum. The fact that Thessalonica has been continually inhabited has made excavation difficult throughout most parts of the city.

the Haliacmon Rivers, both major waterways. Although nearby Pella had been the capital chosen by Philip II, father of Alexander the Great, Cassander selected Thessalonica because of several favorable geographic features. Situated on the Thermaic Gulf, it offered protection from the dangerous southeast winds. In addition, the hills surrounding the city provided shelter from the north winds that blew in from central Europe.[5]

The region surrounding Thessalonica was rich in natural resources. Located on the edge of the great central plain of Macedonia, the area had fertile soil and abundant rainfall. The mountains around the city were covered with timber, providing wood for houses and boats. The mild climate enabled the people to grow grain and fruit but not Mediterranean crops such as dates and olives. Fish filled the nearby lakes and rivers. Mines producing gold, silver, copper, iron, and lead dotted the surrounding area.[6]

In the first century AD, Thessalonica was the main seaport and naval base of Macedonia. The Via Egnatia, Rome's major road to its eastern provinces, ran along the northern outskirts of the city. In addition, the main route from the Danube down to the Aegean Sea passed through Thessalonica, which means the city was situated at the junction of these two important thoroughfares.

RELIGIOUS CLIMATE

In the first century AD, the worship of Dionysus and the mystery god Cabirus was popular in Thessalonica. Devotees of Zeus, Heracles, Apollo, Asclepius, Aphrodite, Demeter, Athene, Serapis, Isis, and the Dioskuri were also part of the religious life of the city.

Further, evidence of Thessalonian involvement with the imperial cult—that is, worship of rulers—is abundant. Even prior to the Roman period, Alexander the Great had been accorded divine honors. These honors came because of supposed revelations received at the oracles at Delphi—oracles that affirmed his divinity. Inscriptions even into the second and third centuries AD ascribe divine status to him and tell of a priesthood that served his cult in Thessalonica. Citizens worshipped Julius Caesar and Augustus Caesar. Titles such as "god" and "son of god" are found on inscriptions and coins from the period.[7]

NOTES

[1] John B. Polhill, *Paul and His Letters* (Nashville: B&H Academic, 1999), 181; Gene L. Green, *The Letters to the Thessalonians*, Pillar New Testament Commentary (Grand Rapids: Eerdmans, 2002), 2.

[2] Jerome Murphy-O'Conner, *Paul: A Critical Life* (Oxford: Oxford University Press, 1997), 114.

[3] Tacitus, *Annals* 1.76.

[4] Dio Cassius, *History* 40.24.1; Suetonius, *Claudius* 25.1.

[5] Green, *Thessalonians*, 2.

[6] Green, *Thessalonians*, 6.

[7] Green, *Thessalonians*, 39–40.

GALATIA: ITS HISTORY

BY DON H. STEWART

The Galatians' ancestral roots trace back to the better-known Celts of France and England. Originally called Keltoi or Galatai by the Greeks or Gauls by the Romans, a group of Celts migrated from central Europe southward and entered Greece and Macedonia around 280 BC. Galatia as a region came into being in 278 BC when 20,000 Celts (three tribes: the Trocmi, the Tectosages, and the Tolistobogii) crossed into Asia Minor and took over the region that is currently centered at modern Ankara (Turkey). From the Greek word *Galatai*, the region itself came to be known as Galatia.[1]

Being powerful warriors, the Gauls came across the Strait of Bosporus from Europe at the invitation of Nicomedes, the king of Bithynia, around 278 BC, to help Nicomedes gain a victory in what had been a long-term civil war in Bithynia (a geographical region located on the north-central coast of Asia Minor). Once that task had been accomplished, the Gauls, who had brought their families with them, settled mainly into the rural areas, reaching as far south as the territories of Phrygia and Pamphylia. They continued to be a distinct ethnic group, identifiably different from the tribes of Asia Minor.[2]

Coin of King Mithridates VI from Pontus (120–63 BC). The consummate enemy of Rome, Mithridates expanded his rule northwest into Bithynia and southeast into Cappadocia.

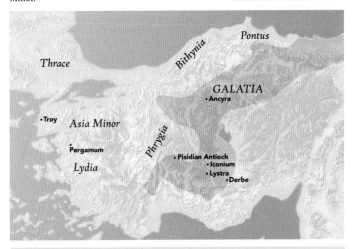

The region of Galatia.

Originally brought to Asia Minor to be mercenaries, the Gauls became instead a "loose cannon," fighting on their own and for their own interests as they began raiding western and north-central Asia Minor. The first check on the Gaulish ambitions came in 275 BC, when the Seleucid king Antiochus I defeated the Gauls and contained them.

By the time of their defeat by Antiochus, the Gauls controlled the northern part of the central plateau of Asia Minor. They and their descendants existed in part by continuing to raid neighboring tribal regions in western and north-central Asia Minor for many years. Finally, in 232 BC, Attalus I, king of Pergamum, was able to defeat the Gauls and restrict the Galatians within the boundaries of their territory. "Their territory was over 200 miles from southwest to northeast, bounded by Lyconia and Pamphylia to the south, by Bithynia, Paphlagonia and Pontus to the north, by Cappadocia to the east and by Phrygia to the west."[3]

Even in defeat, the Galatians retained their independence, keeping their language and Celtic traditions. Ancyra served as their governmental capital. Over the next two centuries, they remained actively involved in the power struggles of the region, finally allying themselves with the Romans against Mithridates VI of Pontus (95–63 BC). In 64 BC, General Pompey rewarded the Galatians for their support by making Galatia a client kingdom of Rome and granting them additional territories.

The last king to rule the entirety of the occupied region of central and northern Asia Minor alone was Amyntas (36–25 BC). At his death, the Romans assumed greater control of the region, reorganizing it into a Roman province. The Romans officially named the region Galatia and expanded the region to the south and east and included the territories of Pisidia, Phrygia, and Pamphylia.

Roman copy of the Greek statue, "The Dying Gaul." Attalus I of Pergamum commissioned the work (230–220 BC) as a recognition of his victory over the Galatians. True to form, the Gallic soldier typically had this style hair, a moustache, and went into battle naked, carrying only a weapon and shield.

NOTES

1   Colin J. Hemer, "Gauls" in *ISBE* (1982), 2:415; G. Walter Hansen, "Galatians, Letter to the" in *Dictionary of Paul and His Letters (DPL)*, ed. Gerald F. Hawthorne and Ralph P. Martin (Downers Grove, IL: InterVarsity, 1993), 323–24; Stephen Mitchell, "Galatia" in *ABD*, 2:870.

2   William M. Ramsay and Colin J. Hemer, "Galatia" in *ISBE*, 2:378.

3   Hansen, "Galatians," 324.

GETHSEMANE

BY DARRYL WOOD

Small chapel located in what is known as the Cave at Gethsemane. Archaeological evidence indicates the cave was used for producing olive oil. The olive presses would have been used in the fall and winter of the year, after the olive harvest. Jesus and his disciples would have been in Jerusalem at Passover, which was in the springtime.

The word *gethsemane* derives from two Hebrew words and translates literally as "press of oils." Production of olive oil was prevalent in ancient Near Eastern cultures. It made sense to place a press or presses at the location where the product was grown. So the Gethsemane of the Gospels seems to have been at a place where people grew olive trees and manufactured olive oil. In the siege of Jerusalem by Titus in AD 70, the Roman army cut down all trees in and around the city; any olive trees in the area during Jesus's time do not remain.

Jesus and the disciples left the Passover supper to go to the Mount of Olives (Matt. 26:30; Mark 14:26; Luke 22:39). Matthew and Mark indicate that they went to a specific place named Gethsemane (Matt. 26:36; Mark 14:32). John specified the location as being "across the Kidron Valley, where there was a garden" (John 18:1). The Kidron Valley runs just to the east of Jerusalem's walls, with the Mount of Olives lying immediately across the valley. The Mount of Olives rises 300 feet higher than the Temple Mount. Quite possibly Gethsemane existed on the slopes of the Kidron Valley, between the valley floor and the peak of the Mount of Olives, facing the Temple Mount.

Identification of the exact place where Jesus crossed the Kidron and his destination on the Mount of Olives eludes Bible scholars. Throughout church history, however, writers have speculated about the specific locale.[1] A large cave on the lower slopes might have been a

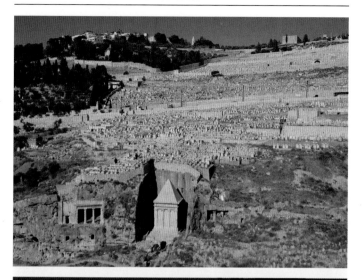

The Tomb of Zechariah (with the pyramid roof) and the Tomb of Absalom (conical roof), both in the Kidron Valley. Although neither is the burial site of its Old Testament namesake, both of the burial monuments would have been in place when Jesus walked through the valley to and from Gethsemane.

quiet place for contemplation if it was indeed there in the first century. Evidence indicates this cave held an oil press for olive production or was a storage cistern. A building now sits over this cave.[2] A more traditional site on the hillside is at a large rock inside the Church of All Nations. Regardless of the exact location, in the first century, olive trees dominated the area and provided a garden-like atmosphere.[3]

NOTES

[1] For an extensive summary of the opinions of ancient writers related to the location of Gethsemane, see Clemens Kopp, *The Holy Places of the Gospels* (New York: Herder & Herder, 1963), 337–50.

[2] Joan E. Taylor, "The Garden of Gethsemane: Not the Place of Jesus' Arrest," BAR 21.4 (1995): 26, 28, 35.

[3] W. Harold Mare, *The Archaeology of the Jerusalem Area* (Grand Rapids: Baker, 1987), 247–48.

GEZER: GATEWAY TO JERUSALEM

STEVEN M. ORTIZ

A boundary stone at Gezer. The inscription reads in Greek, Alkiou, and in Hebrew, Techem Gezer, meaning, "Belonging to Alkios, Boundary of Gezer." This is one of thirteen such boundary stones that have been found at Gezer.

Gezer was an important city in the biblical period. It has become well known in biblical archaeology due to the existence of a major gate system that is similar to gates found at Hazor and Megiddo—archaeological evidence that illuminates a small reference to the building projects of King Solomon. First Kings 9:15 states that after building the temple, his palace, and Jerusalem, Solomon rebuilt "Hazor, Megiddo, and Gezer." Most scholars believe Solomon chose these three important cities because they guarded key regions of the kingdom. The city of Gezer is located on a main juncture of the Via Maris. It guarded the Aijalon Valley and the route from the coast up to Jerusalem and the Judean Hills. Someone wanting to attack Jerusalem first had to take out Gezer, as it served as the last sentinel to protect Jerusalem from the coast.

People recognized Gezer's importance even before Solomon fortified the city. Several Egyptian sources mentioned Gezer as various Egyptian pharaohs conquered the city and bragged about the conquest in campaign reports. The conquest of the city is mentioned in: (1) the annals of Thutmose III (about 1468 BC); (2) the Amarna Letters, which describe it as a vassal city of Egypt during the fourteenth century BC; and (3) the Merneptah Stele, which contains the first mention of Israel outside the Bible.

The biblical city of Gezer is identified as Tell el-Jezer, about halfway between the modern cities of Tel Aviv and Jerusalem. It is a thirty-three-acre mound located in the foothills of Judah. In addition to the historical sources, the site is well known due to several archaeological expeditions. Two major excavations were carried out in 1902–1909 by R. A. S. Macalister and in 1964–1973 by William G. Dever and Joe D. Seger. Smaller excavations were conducted by Alan Rowe (1934) and Dever (1984, 1990).

The mound of Gezer was initially occupied around 3500 BC. The settlement continued to grow until it was a walled city during the Middle Bronze Age (about 2000–1500 BC) when major fortifications (gate, tower, and protective sloping bank or *glacis*) were built and the

Dr. Harold Mosley digging at Gezer. To the right and waist high is a dark horizontal line just below the Solomonic casemate construction, thought to be the burn layer of 1 Kings 9:16–17.

"High Place" was founded. This is typical for all major Canaanite cities during the Patriarchal period. Gezer was a major Canaanite city-state throughout the second millennium BC. The city was destroyed (about 1500 BC) and rebuilt during the Late Bronze Age when it came under Egyptian dominance as evidenced by several palaces and residences.

During the Israelite conquest and settlement, Gezer played an important role as one of the leaders in a coalition against Joshua. Although the king of Gezer organized a large coalition of kings and their cities to go against the Israelites, Joshua defeated the king of Gezer as well as the Canaanite coalition (Josh. 10:33). In spite of the victory by Joshua's forces, Gezer remained in Canaanite hands throughout the period of the Judges (Josh. 16:10; Judg. 1:29) even though it formed the boundary for Ephraim's tribal allotment (Josh. 16:3) and was assigned as a Levitical city (21:21). David fought against the Philistines near Gezer (2 Sam. 5:25; 1 Chr. 20:4). These texts of the early Israelite state formation clearly show that Gezer sat on the border between the tribes up in the hill country and the Philistines on the coast. Archaeological evidence confirms this picture from the biblical text.

Gezer came into Israelite hands by a conquest by the Egyptian pharaoh, who gave it to Solomon as a dowry for his marriage to Pharaoh's daughter (1 Kgs. 9:16). Most scholars associate Siamun as Solomon's Egyptian father-in-law. Archaeology has confirmed that the city was destroyed at this time and immediately upon the destruction is evidence of major construction activity: a four-entryway monumental city gate, a palace, a casemate wall, a water storage system, public buildings, and guardrooms.

Pharaoh Shishak (about 950–925 BC) destroyed the city. Archaeological evidence shows the city was rebuilt and experienced another destruction at the hands of the Assyrians in 733 BC. An inscription and relief of Tiglath-pileser III (eighth c. BC) mentions this Assyrian conquest. The city had minor occupation until the Persian period. Gezer became known as Gazara in the Hellenistic period and became an important city for the Hasmonean rulers. During the New Testament period, the major city moved north across the valley and is probably the Emmaus of the Gospel accounts.

The ancient site of Gezer is so important for biblical history that a major excavation project was initiated in 2006 to investigate the site. Archaeological research continues to illustrate that the events recorded in Scripture are based on actual historical events of the kings of Israel and Judah.

GREEK AND ROMAN TEMPLES OF THE FIRST CENTURY

BY DON H. STEWART

The Parthenon rises in the distance, atop the Acropolis in Athens, which was a prominent city in the Roman province of Achaia.

Interior of the Pantheon in Rome. The structure was originally constructed to honor the seven gods of the seven planets recognized by the state religion of Rome. Although the building has been revised several times through the centuries, it has been in continual use since its construction was completed in AD 125.

When Hellenism was at its height, the concept of inter-action between people and the gods was prevalent among the intellectuals. Greeks thought of the gods as superhu-man, and temple architecture reflected religious systems that encouraged people to negotiate directly with the gods in an effort to buy divine favor. Convenient access to the idols of the gods was important. This was accom-plished by providing open architectural designs for the temples and by erecting multiple temples to the same gods and goddesses. These temples were located in population centers stretched across the empire to provide maximum accessibility.

At times, a single temple would house multiple gods or goddesses. For instance, the Parthenon in Athens housed the idol of Athena and a number of other idols. In Rome, the Pantheon was the temple honoring all gods, although it actually housed statues of the seven "deities the Romans associated with the heavens—including Mars, Mercury, Venus, and Jupiter."[1] A statue of each deity was located in its own large niche along the interior wall of the circular Pantheon.

From Corinth, bust of Zeus, dating from the first century AD.

In the environment of the Greco-Roman world, a bur-geoning number of beautifully appointed temples served as houses of worship for an almost innumerable number of gods and goddesses. At least one such temple was built on the acropolis (the high place) of nearly every major city, as well as many smaller ones. Most communities had a patron god or goddess. The Romans followed the Greeks' lead, extending the Greek passion for building religious temples, and they did so wherever the gods or goddesses had not been honored before.

NOTES

[1]   Jason McManus, ed., *Empires Ascendant: Time Frame 400 BC–AD 200* (Alexandria, VA: Time-Life Books, 1987), 93.

HADES: A FIRST-CENTURY UNDERSTANDING

BY STEVE W. LEMKE

Part of the Ben Hinnom Valley, which is on the southern end of the city of Jerusalem. The valley was the site where people gave their children as burnt offerings to the Canaanite god Molech (2 Chr. 28:3; 33:6).

When Jesus told Simon Peter and his fellow disciples that God would build his church so securely that the gates of Hades would not prevail against it (Matt. 16:18), what exactly did he mean by *Hades*? How did New Testament Christians understand the concept? Is Hades distinguishable from similar concepts such as Sheol, Gehenna, or hell?

THE ABODE OF THE DEAD

More than sixty times, the Old Testament refers to the place of the dead as *Sheol*. This was the shadowy dwelling place of the dead in the underworld, virtually synonymous with the grave or death itself (Gen. 37:35; Ps. 16:10; Prov. 5:5; Isa. 14:9). When scholars translated the Old Testament from Hebrew into Greek in the Septuagint during the intertestamental period, translators rendered the Old Testament Hebrew word *Sheol* with the Greek word *Hades*.[1] Thus when Peter referenced Psalm 16:10 in his Pentecost sermon (Acts 2:27), the text used *Hades* to translate the Hebrew word *Sheol*. When the New Testament uses it this way, *Hades* simply refers to the abode of the dead, following the Old Testament pattern.

In Greek mythology, Hades (also called Pluto) was the brother of Zeus and king of the underworld. Mythology claimed that Hades abducted Persephone, daughter of Zeus, and forced her to live in his underworld realm. This domain over which Hades ruled came to be called by his name or by Tartarus. The New Testament uses both terms but pours new meaning into them.

In Matthew 16:18, the primary sense of the word *Hades* probably refers to death. Death has no power over the church. Jesus told the disciples he would be crucified in Jerusalem and then raised on the third day (Matt. 16:21). When he was resurrected, he became the "firstfruits" of the resurrection; his resurrection paved the way for all believers to be raised to life, for he will abolish death (1 Cor. 15:24–26). Believers may experience death, but death is not their final destination. Death and Hades have no more power over believers than they did over Christ himself. Jesus spoke of giving the church the "keys of the kingdom of heaven" (Matt. 16:19). But Jesus has another set of keys. Because of his victory over death, he has the keys to death and Hades (Rev. 1:18). Jesus has gone to prepare a place for believers—a place in which death, grief, crying, and pain have been abolished (John 14:1–3; Rev. 21:1–4). Many interpreters understand the "gates" or "forces" of Hades in Matthew 16:18 to represent Satan's constant opposition to the church. So Jesus was assuring the disciples that Satan will never overpower the church.

Bronze head of Hades; dated first–second centuries AD. The Greeks believed Hades was grim and merciless but not evil.

HADES AS HELL

Even in the Old Testament, however, Sheol does not always refer to the final resting place for all persons. Although all people go to Sheol, only ungodly or foolish persons remain in Sheol. The Old Testament teaches that God will raise godly and wise persons to a new life with him (Job 19:23–27; Ps. 49:1–19; Isa. 26:4–19; Dan. 12:2–3). Dating to the intertestamental period, noncanonical books portray Hades as the place of torment for the wicked, while the righteous enter paradise (Pss. Sol. 14:1–7; Wis. 2:1; 3:1). These two senses of the word *Sheol* led to a theological disagreement between the Sadducees and Pharisees. Sadducees believed that all the dead continued in Sheol,

Greek mythology taught that Hades ruled the underworld. The priest Hadaios dedicated this votive relief to the god Hades who is depicted climbing into a chariot. The relief was uncovered west of Corinth, in the Derveni region; dated to the second century AD.

whereas Pharisees affirmed that God would resurrect the just to eternal life. Some believed Hades was the lower region of Sheol and paradise was the top level of Sheol.

This distinction between Hades as a hellish place of torment rather than the abode of all the dead emerges more clearly in the New Testament. Several New Testament texts draw a clear distinction between "death" and "Hades" (Rev. 1:18; 20:13–14). Jesus's account of Lazarus and the rich man (Luke 16:19–31) draws one of the clearest distinctions between the two abodes. Jesus described the righteous man Lazarus as being beside Abraham (a Jewish euphemism for being with God in paradise), while the unrighteous rich man was in a fiery torment (vv. 23–25,28). An enormous chasm or gulf separated these two places (vv. 23,26). Jesus painted a similar picture in his depiction of the eternal destiny of the people of Capernaum who were unrepentant even after seeing miracles performed. Jesus said they would not "be exalted to heaven" but would "go down to Hades" (Matt. 11:23–24; Luke 10:15). Again, Hades here is the abode of the unrighteous dead, while the righteous dead are lifted upward. In Revelation 20:13, Hades is essentially a holding place for the unrighteous dead until judgment, after which they will be cast into the lake of fire.

The New Testament often uses words such as *Gehenna* or *Tartarus*, or descriptions such as "the bottomless pit" or "the abyss" to describe hell. Gehenna was originally a valley or ravine just south of the walls of Jerusalem. *Gehenna* is a Greek transliteration of "valley of Hinnom" in Hebrew. In the Hinnom Valley, idolaters burned children as an offering to the heathen god Molech (2 Chr. 28:3; 33:6). By the time of King Josiah's reign, people regarded the Hinnom Valley as a place of abomination (2 Kgs. 23:10–14). In Gehenna, God imposed judgment on idolaters and those who rejected him (Jer. 7:31–34; 32:35). Gehenna thus came to symbolize hell's unending fires where the unclean and ungodly dead are continually tormented.

In the New Testament, *Gehenna* always refers to hell, a place of fiery torment, not simply death (Matt. 5:22, 29–30; Mark 9:43–47; Luke 12:5; Jas. 3:6). Jesus warned that sinful disobedience could lead to a fiery Gehenna (Matt. 5:22,29–30). In Gehenna, both the soul and body are destroyed (Matt. 10:28). James described uncontrolled speech as being set on fire by Gehenna (Jas. 3:6).

Another Greek word used to describe hell is *Tartarus*, a term Greeks used to describe a place of eternal torment. In his second epistle, Peter described Tartarus as a place where rebellious angels were imprisoned pending final judgment (2 Pet. 2:4). Another biblical synonym for Hades is the "abyss." Romans 10:6–7 (citing Deut. 30:12–14) contrasts the ascent into heaven with descending "down into the abyss" of death. In Luke 8:31 and Revelation 9:1–3; 20:1–3, however, the abyss is the abode of demons, similar to Tartarus in 2 Peter 2:4. In Revelation 9:1–11, the abyss is opened, releasing a horde of demons. The "angel of the abyss" named Apollyon (meaning "destruction," Rev. 9:11), also called the beast or antichrist, will be thrown into the lake of fire (19:20). Satan, too, is chained in the abyss for a thousand years (20:1–3), until he also is thrown into the lake of fire (v. 10).

Believers need not fear death or the forces of Satan. Christ has already defeated these threats and has won the victory (Rom. 8:36–39; 1 Cor. 15:55–57; Rev. 1:18).

NOTES

[1]   E. Ray Clendenen, "Hades" in *HIBD*, rev. ed. (2015), 689.

HEBRON

BY JEFF S. ANDERSON

A Herodian building in a remarkable state of preservation, erected by King Herod over the caves of Machpelah at Hebron in Israel. The building was used as a Christian church during the Crusades but was converted to a mosque when Saladin drove out the Crusaders and established the tenets of Islam in the region.

The city of Hebron was founded seven years before Zoan (Num. 13:22), which is the city of Tanis in Egypt. As records give information about the founding of Tanis, we can confidently place the founding of Hebron as a city in 1737 BC. Archaeological evidence, however, indicates that the region has been continually inhabited since approximately 3500–3300 BC.

Located about nineteen miles south of Jerusalem in the southern hill country of Judah, Hebron sits on one of the highest points in the hill country, at an elevation of 3,040 feet above sea level. Hebron's original name was Kiriath-arba (Gen. 23:2; Josh. 20:7), and the original city was in the enviable position of possessing a prolific spring plus extremely fertile soil in the surrounding countryside. For generations, it was an agricultural center of grape and olive oil production.

The archaeological evidence, what little there is of it, generally supports the biblical account. One archaeologist quipped, "Hebron ... is one of the biblically most important and archaeologically most disappointing sites in Palestine."[1] William F. Albright conducted surveys of the region in the 1920s, and an American expedition dug in the 1960s. Work resumed in the 1980s with the Judean Hills Survey Expedition, sponsored by the Israelis. The political situation there has made archaeological work difficult for the past several decades. Al-Khalil, modern-day Hebron, is part of the West Bank, under Palestinian authority.

Interior of the Machpelah in Hebron. Shown are the striped stone-layered cenotaphs, which are not the actual tombs but structures marking the site of the subterranean burial caves. Buried at Machpelah are Abraham and Sarah; Jacob and Leah; and, shown, Rebekah on the left and Isaac on the right. King Herod (37 BC–AD 4) built the structures over the burial caves.

Alabaster bowl from the Middle Bronze Age I (2200–1950 BC), carved in Hebron.

Basically two areas of archaeological importance exist in and around Hebron: the ancient city (Tel Hebron) and the traditional tomb of Abraham on a slope opposite the ancient city (Haram al-Khalil). Regarding the ancient city itself, archaeological evidence supports a major settlement of about six to seven acres in the Judean hills dating to the Middle Bronze Age, the period compatible with Abraham and the other ancestors of Israel.[2] This settlement was surrounded by a wall that is partly visible even today. The site was later abandoned temporarily in the Late Bronze Age (the time of the conquest) but was inhabited once again to an even greater capacity in the Iron Age, the period associated with David. A spring in the city continues to provide cold water year-round, an important commodity in the Judean desert. Today the site of the ancient city overlooks the modern city of Hebron. The Cave of Machpelah (Haram al-Khalil) is also an important archaeological site. For archaeologists its enormous popularity is also its downfall. The problem is that the monumental structure supposedly built by Herod covers the area, and there has been no systematic excavation of remains under the building. Evidence of several shaft tombs exists, but the structures above the surface prohibit excavation.

View of Hebron looking toward the south.

One important find regarding Hebron wasn't found in Hebron itself but on storage jars discovered in and around Jerusalem and Judah.[3] These jars contained seal impressions on their handles. Almost a thousand such impressions are known. These seals are known as *lamelekh* impressions, an expression that means "belonging to the king." One of the jars includes the impression "belonging to the king of Hebron." Because all the *lamelekh* jars were found in the cities involved in the conflict with Sennacherib, scholars generally date the jars to the time of the conflict between Judah and Assyria, around 600 BC. A specific reference like this to a particular city is rare among archaeological finds in Israel.

NOTES

[1] Harry Thomas Frank, *Bible, Archaeology, and Faith* (Nashville: Abingdon, 1971), 127.

[2] Avi Ofer, "Hebron," in *NEAEHL*, 2:608; Amihai Mazar, *Archaeology of the Land of the Bible: 10,000–586 BCE* (New York: Doubleday, 1990), 455–58.

[3] Mazar, *Archaeology*.

HEROD'S TEMPLE

BY TIMOTHY TRAMMELL

Protruding from the southern end of the western side of the Temple Mount are the springer courses of an arch that supported a monumental stairway leading up to the Temple Mount Plaza. The arch, named Robinson's Arch after the American who first identified it, was part of Herod's expansion of the temple.

Men's plaza at the Western Wall in Jerusalem. The exposed rock face here at the prayer plaza rises to a height of about sixty feet; originally, the wall stood almost two-hundred feet tall.

During Jesus's earthly ministry and the first Christian century, the temple in Jerusalem, Herod's temple, was the heart of Jewish worship.

SOLOMON'S TEMPLE

Bible students refer to Herod's temple as the "second temple." The first temple was the magnificent structure Solomon built. The biblical description of Solomon's temple suggests that the inside ceiling was 180 feet long, 90 feet wide, and 50 feet high. The highest point of the structure soared to about 207 feet or approximately ten stories. Nebuchadnezzar and the Babylonians destroyed the temple in 586 BC.

When the Jewish people returned from the Babylonian captivity, Zerubbabel led the people to build a new temple. But those who had seen Solomon's temple considered this structure disappointingly inferior (see Ezra 3:12–13). Zerubbabel's temple was the one Herod the Great determined to rebuild and enlarge. Since Herod was really an Idumean rather than a Jew, he thought doing this would "please the Jews as well as win recognition for himself"— particularly in the eyes of his Roman overlords.[1]

THE TEMPLE PLATFORM

Reconstruction began between 20 and 19 BC, and the majority of the work was completed in eighteen months. But to provide a foundation for the massive structure Herod and his workmen envisioned, an enlarged platform was essential. Laborers built massive retaining walls on the slopes of Mount Moriah to hold the platform in place. The completed structure, with its arches and vaults, was 1,575 feet long and 919 feet wide, yielding almost 1.5 million square feet in area.[2] Portions of these retaining walls are still visible today, especially on the eastern, southern, and western sides. The western exposure is the best known, called the Western Wall. Today this wall is a center of Jewish worship and the site of national celebration.

The huge limestone blocks used to build the structure came from quarries within the city of Jerusalem. The smallest of the quarried and dressed stones, known as ashlars, weigh two to five tons each; many larger ashlars weigh about fifty tons each. The largest ashlar, at forty feet long, ten feet high, and thirteen feet thick, weighs an astonishing four hundred tons.[3] Two Muslim structures occupy the Temple Mount today, the Dome of the Rock and the Al-Aqsa Mosque.

At Herod's temple, one could enter the Court of the Gentiles, the dominant area of the Temple Mount, through eight gates: two on the south, four on the west, one on the north, and one on the east. The court was surrounded on all four sides by columned porticoes. On the south was the Royal Porch, with a total of 162 columns aligned in four rows. The last row was attached to the south wall. Josephus recorded that the thickness of each column was such "that three men might, with their arms extended, fathom it round, and join their hands again."[4] The columns were more than thirty-five feet tall.

On the east, north, and west sides of the court, the porches had two rows of columns. They were roofed, and they opened to the court. The porch along the east was named Solomon's Porch or Colonnade. John recorded that Jesus walked in this area during the Festival of Dedication (John 10:22–23).

The southeast corner of the court was the "pinnacle of the temple" mentioned in Matthew 4:5 in connection with Jesus's temptation. This point overlooked the Kidron Valley some one hundred yards below. Early church history states that James, the half brother of Jesus, was thrown down from this point and killed in AD 66.

THE TEMPLE PROPER

The Greek New Testament has two terms that can be translated as "temple." The first, *hieron*, designates the entire temple complex. The other, *naos*, referred to the temple proper, the sanctuary.[5] The *naos* was set on a small terrace and was surrounded by a stone balustrade that was just over three feet high. On the balustrade was a sign written in both Greek and Latin, which warned non-Jews: "No Gentile may enter within the railing around

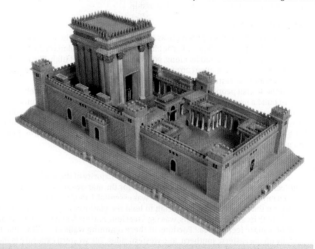

Model of the sanctuary of Herod's temple.

the Sanctuary and within the enclosure. Whosoever should be caught will render himself liable to the death penalty which will inevitably follow."[6]

Within the balustrade were three distinct areas. The first section was called the women's court because women could go no farther. Around it were small storage rooms. Between these rooms were thirteen coffers, each in the form of an inverted trumpet, into which people placed offerings. These offerings covered the expenses of the temple.

The next section was the court of the men of Israel. It was elevated above the court of the women; men entered by ascending fifteen semicircular steps. Access was gained through six gates, three on the north and three on the south, and by an opening, the Nicanor Gate, from the women's court.

Moving into and through the court of the priests, one came to the inner recesses of the sanctuary. This structure measured 172 feet long, broad, and high, and it had two stories. It consisted of a porch, the holy place, and the most holy place.

Twelve steps led up about 10 feet from the court of the priests to the porch, which featured a façade measuring about 172 feet wide and high. Beyond the porch was the holy place, an area that measured 68.8 feet long by 34.4 feet wide, with walls 68.8 feet high. In this room stood the golden lampstand, the table of showbread (Bread of the Presence), and the altar of incense. A thick veil served as the west wall.

Beyond the veil was the most holy place. It measured 34.4 feet square with walls 68.8 feet tall. At the time of the second temple, this area was empty.[7] The high priest entered this sacred area annually on the Day of Atonement to repent, sprinkle sacrificial goat's blood, and obtain forgiveness for his sins and those of the people.

By any standard, Herod's temple was magnificent. One would surmise that this edifice would stand throughout the centuries. Tragically, however, during the Roman invasion in AD 70, the temple was destroyed, as Jesus predicted (Matt. 24:2).

NOTES

[1] Floyd Filson, "The Significance of the Temple in the Ancient Near East. Part 4: Temple, Synagogue and Church," *BA* 7.44 (1944): 79.

[2] Leslie J. Hoppe, "Herod's Quarries," *The Bible Today* (*TBT*) 48.1 (2010): 35.

[3] Simon Goldhill, *The Temple of Jerusalem* (London: Profile Books, 2004), 60–61.

[4] Josephus, *Jewish Antiquities* 15.11.4.

[5] "Temple" in *The New International Dictionary of New Testament Theology* (*NIDNTT*), ed. Colin Brown, 4 vols. (Grand Rapids: Zondervan, 1978), 3:781.

[6] Leen Ritmeyer, *The Quest: Revealing the Temple Mount in Jerusalem* (Jerusalem: Carta Jerusalem and the LAMB Foundation, 2006), 346.

[7] For full details of Herod's temple, see Ritmeyer, *The Quest*.

THE ISLAND OF MALTA

BY GEORGE W. KNIGHT

Aerial view of Malta.

Saint Paul's Bay, Malta.

Malta is the largest of a group of five islands collectively known today as the nation of Malta.[1] It is approximately eighteen miles long and eight miles wide, making an area of about ninety-six square miles. The location is in the Mediterranean Sea sixty miles south of Sicily and about 220 miles north of the Libyan coast in North Africa. On the north and west coasts of the island are located many bays and inlets that provide natural harbors. The largest is near the middle of the island; the one traditionally associated with Paul is about eight miles to the northeast. Malta's history includes cultural elements from Sicily, Italy, Phoenicia, Carthage, and Rome.

The largest influence on first-century Malta began with the coming of the Phoenicians about 1000 BC. They established a settlement on the island as part of the expansion of their trade empire to the west. The abundance of natural harbors and location near their shipping lanes made this an ideal location for protection, rest, and resupply. Their occupation grew, and, in addition to the shipping installations along the coast, a city, Malta, was built near the modern Citta Vecchia. Excavations have shown it to have been a city of importance and wealth. Large Phoenician tombs are found there. By the sixth century BC, Carthage came to power, and that culture also left its mark. But the Roman Empire ultimately shaped the Malta of Paul's day.

The island's history that is reflected in the land of Paul's shipwreck began with Roman control in 218 BC when the island became part of the province of Sicily. Augustus Caesar granted the island nation its own procurator; although civil war crippled the small country during those days, when Paul arrived the island was thriving.

Leading into the first century AD, the island was often visited by pirates who, according to Cicero, spent their winters there.[2] These outlaws were usually controlled by Rome's power, but when Paul landed there, their influences were surely a part of the local inhabitants' culture.

Archaeological excavations on the island have identified early Christian tombs. Additionally an excavation of a Roman villa at "San Pawl Milqi . . . is traditionally the site of

Publius' villa where the shipwrecked St. Paul was received." Also of significance was a Punic sanctuary that fell into disuse toward the end of the first century and later was converted into a Christian church.[3]

NOTES

[1] This discussion relies on the following: A. Claridge, "Melita" in *The Princeton Encyclopedia of Classical Sites*, ed. Richard Stillwell (Princeton, NJ: Princeton University Press, 1976), 568–69; Ernst Haenchen, *The Acts of the Apostles*, trans. Bernard Noble and Gerald Shinn (Philadelphia: Westminster, 1971); Dennis R. Macdonald, "The Shipwrecks of Odysseus and Paul," *NTS* 45 (1999): 88–107; John Polhill, *Acts*, NAC (1992).

[2] Cicero, *Against Verres* 11.4.103–4.

[3] Claridge, "Melita," 569.

JERICHO IN JESUS'S DAY

BY WILLIAM F. COOK III

At Jericho, part of the bath complex at Herod's palace, likely the frigidarium.

Jericho is in the southern Jordan Valley. The city is 740 feet below sea level, the lowest inhabited city in the world. The lowest point on the face of the earth, the Dead Sea (1,300 feet below sea level), is about eight miles south of the city. To the west of Jericho rises Mount Quarantania, the traditional site of Jesus's forty-day fast and temptation. Five miles east is the Jordan River and the traditional site of Jesus's baptism. Qumran, where the Dead Sea Scrolls were discovered, is located about eight miles south of the city on the northwest shore of the Dead Sea. Jerusalem is approximately thirteen miles southwest of Jericho. Old Testament Jericho (Tel es-Sultan) is located two miles north of New Testament Jericho. The Old Testament site was not inhabited in Jesus's day.

Although less than seven inches of rain falls annually, mostly between November and February, Jericho in Jesus's day was an oasis in a barren land. God provided the city with water, good soil, a moderate winter climate, and a strategic location. Springs near the foot of the western hills provide the city its fresh water. The major spring is known as Elijah's fountain. Flowing eastward, the stream waters the heart of the oasis. Water from other nearby springs brought in by an aqueduct enlarged the oasis. The combination of water availability and the rich alluvial soil made Jericho an attractive place for settlement.

These conditions made Jericho suitable for farming. Grapes, pomegranates, wheat, and vegetables thrived here. The area was also famous for its sycamore and balsam trees. The Jewish historian Josephus and the Roman geographer Strabo both commented on Jericho's famous groves.[1] The Jericho balsam was renowned for its medicinal qualities and for its use in perfume. These factors, along with the mild winter climate, made Jericho an attractive location for the winter capital city during the reigns of the Hasmoneans and Herod the Great. That it was culturally and politically aloof from Jerusalem added to its attractiveness.

New Testament Jericho, also called Herodian Jericho, had its beginnings in the period following the Jews' returning from Babylonian exile. When the Ptolemies and Seleucids controlled the Jewish homeland, they considered Jericho to be royal property.[2] This royal setting continued in the first century BC. Excavators have unearthed extensive remains at New Testament Jericho. Today two large mounds distinguish the site. The earliest building project was a Hasmonean complex. The palace covered more than six acres and became the pleasure resort of the reigning kings.[3]

Herod was especially fond of Jericho. The city gave him a place of repose from Jerusalem's demands. He captured Jericho in 37 BC from Antigonus, a Hasmonean descendant. Josephus describes how Herod had his brother-in-law, the high priest Aristobulus, drowned in the swimming pool at the site of the Hasmonean palace.[4]

Herod built extensively at Jericho, transforming the city into something of a garden. Further, he constructed a number of public buildings: an amphitheater, hippodrome, a gymnasium, parks, gardens, pools, villas, a fortress, and most impressive—a large palace complex. His magnificent winter palace was built in three stages and may be considered three separate palaces. Herod's most extensive project was the third palace, which covered more than seven acres. This palace was planned and built following exceptional architectural standards. Because the palace extended to both sides of the Wadi Qelt, its residents could enjoy the seasonal flow of water. Another of Herod's building projects was a complex accommodating horse races, athletics, boxing, theater, and musical shows. It was unique in the entire Greco-Roman world.[5]

Jericho in Jesus's day was probably spread over the irrigated areas of the plain like a garden city; homes were side by side with royal villas. Many members of the Jerusalem aristocracy used the city as a winter resort. Excavations of a nearby cemetery give evidence of extensive habitation in this period.[6]

The area surrounding Jericho is lush with vegetation. The Old Testament referred to Jericho as the City of Palms (Deut. 34:3; Judg. 1:16; 3:13).

Following Herod's death at Jericho in 4 BC, his palaces began to decline. After the removal of Herod the Great's son, Archelaus, Roman prefects ruled Judea (with the exception of AD 41–44). The prefects ruled from Caesarea on the coast rather than Jerusalem and vacationed elsewhere. Although the palaces may not have been as well maintained, the city remained impressive and important. Under Roman rule, Jericho remained an important town for travelers coming from Galilee (around Samaria) and the Transjordan to Jerusalem.

When Jesus entered Jericho, he would have seen a beautiful city, the magnificent hippodrome, a large palace complex, winter villas, large plantations, and a bustling community. The presence of a chief tax collector in Jericho (Zacchaeus) is understandable since the city was on the main road from the Transjordan to Judea. After the Jewish revolts of AD 66–70 and 132–135, Jericho's importance greatly diminished.

NOTES

1   Josephus, *Jewish War* 4.8.3; Strabo, *Geography* 16.41.
2   Gideon Foerster, "Jericho: Hellenistic to Early Arab Periods: History" in *NEAEHL*, 2:681.
3   Ehud Netzer, "Jericho: Exploration since 1973" in *NEAEHL*, 2:683.
4   Josephus, *Jewish Antiquities* 15.3.2–3.
5   Ehud Netzer, "Roman Jericho (Tulul Abu el-ʿAlayiq)" in *ABD*, 3:739.
6   Netzer, "Roman Jericho."

JERICHO:
A STRATEGIC LOCALE

BY DAVID L. JENKINS

The base of a round Neolithic tower dated to about 8000 BC. The tower, which measures about twenty-eight feet in diameter at the base and twenty-five feet tall, has an internal staircase. Especially considering that workers had only stone tools, the tower was a remarkable engineering feat.

The Wadi Qelt, a dry riverbed in New Testament Jericho. The wadi ran through the middle of Herod's winter palace complex.

The word *Jericho* means either "a place of fragrance," maybe referring to the prolific flowers native to the area, or "place of the moon," alluding to this being a site where people worshipped the lunar gods, which they believed controlled the seasons. Jericho has deep roots in the early history of Bible lands and places. Surrounding the ancient city were walls so massive that houses were built upon them (Josh. 2:15). The remains of Old Testament and prehistoric Jericho lie beneath a mound known as Tell es-Sultan. This mound is located on the west side of the Jordan Valley, approximately ten miles north of the Dead Sea and four miles west of the Jordan River.

A spring, 'Ain es-Sultan, provides ample water to the site, producing up to a thousand gallons per minute. The spring hydrates an oasis that stretches from Jericho eastward toward the Jordan. This spring and the area's fertile soil attracted settlers from as early as the Mesolithic Age (10,000–8000 BC). The oldest known building on the site dates to about 9250 BC. Unlike other inhabited places from early in the Neolithic Era (8000–4500 BC), Jericho was a walled site. "By 8000 BC a walled town (the world's earliest) of about 10 acres had been built."[1] The wall, constructed of huge stones, stood more than nineteen feet tall. "A massive round tower within the wall was amazingly well constructed. The tower measured 8.5 m [27.9 ft] in diameter and is preserved to a height of 7.7 m [25.3 ft]; it was built with a solid stone core, and a steep stairway led to its top."[2] Jericho has consequently been called the "Citadel of the Neolithic Age."[3] Archaeologists have thus found at Jericho evidence of prehistoric nomads who were hunter-gatherers; later, those who developed a village on the site; and still later, those who established permanent dwellings, farmed the area, and had domesticated animals. Also emerging durling this era was the expansion of human technology. People moved from developing polished stone implements to making crudely fired ceramic vessels. Jericho is the oldest biblical city to show all of these types of progression.[4]

Archaeological evidence indicates the site was abandoned about 4000 BC but began to repopulate about 700 years later. By the time of Abraham, Isaac, and Jacob, people in Jericho were living civilized lives. Archaeologists have found at Jericho tombs dated to about 1600 BC, wooden furniture, fine pottery, wooden boxes with inlaid decorations, and basketwork.[5] As the Israelites settled into Canaan, Joshua assigned Jericho to the tribe of Benjamin (Josh. 18:21). Even though ancient Jericho was destroyed some time after this, a small settlement remained, assuring the continuity of life in that area.

By the time Jesus encountered Zacchaeus the tax collector there, no doubt Jericho was more than a small, nondescript village. In fact, Herod the Great had fortified the city and built several new palaces there, naming them after his friends. He retired and died in Jericho. Jericho's, and by extension Zacchaeus's, wealth no doubt came in part from taxes on the salt, sulfur, and bitumen (natural products of the Dead Sea) as they passed through the city. Wealth acquired from this trade likely contributed considerably to the city's many building projects. The Synoptic Gospels record Jesus's encounter with beggars in Jericho (Matt. 20:29–34; Mark 10:46–52; Luke 18:35–43). Beggars would have considered such a prosperous city an ideal place to assure an income for themselves.

Another plus for Jericho was the city's location near a major ford in the Jordan River. This made the city a natural gateway from the Transjordan and the plains of Moab to the region that lay westward beyond the Jordan River (Num. 22:1; 26:3; 31:12; 33:48,50; 35:1; Deut. 32:49; Josh. 2:1). Situated on the major east-west trade route, Jericho controlled the traffic flow from the Transjordan area into the central hill country. This included the city of Jerusalem, which was approximately fourteen miles southwest of Jericho. To further enhance the importance of Jericho's geographical significance was its location on an important north-south highway that connected the city to Beth-shean to the north. Consequently for an invading army to possess Jericho carried many benefits, including control of the major entrance to western Canaan from the Transjordan, possession of the water rights and oasis-like garden land east of the city, and control of the mineral traffic in the area of the Dead Sea.

Part of the ruins of Herod's palace at Jericho.

NOTES

[1] Karen Joines and Eric Mitchell, "Jericho" in *HIBD*, 886.

[2] Amihai Mazar, *Archaeology of the Land of the Bible 10,000–586 B.C.E.* (New York: Doubleday, 1992), 41.

[3] LaMoine F. DeVries, *Cities of the Biblical World* (Peabody, MA: Hendrickson, 1997), 189.

[4] Charles F. Pfeiffer, ed., *The Biblical World* (Nashville: Broadman, 1976), 306.

[5] Pat Alexander, ed., *The Lion Encyclopedia of the Bible* (Pleasantville, NY: Reader's Digest, 1987), 264.

JERUSALEM BEFORE THE RETURN

BY JERRY LEE

Looking across the Kidron Valley toward the Temple Mount in Jerusalem. Today the Temple Mount is dominated by the Dome of the Rock, which is the gold-domed building in the foreground.

John Bright estimated Judah's population as possibly 125,000 even after the deportation of exiles in 597 BC. At that time, 10,000 exiles were marched away to Babylon (2 Kgs. 24:14). The population was reduced further by the execution of leading citizens, additional deportations in 586 and 582 BC (Jer. 52:28–30), and flights of groups to the safety of surrounding areas until the number of inhabitants dwindled to "scarcely above 20,000 even after the first exiles had returned" in 536 BC.[1]

A month after Jerusalem's fall, Nebuzaradan began the systematic destruction of Jerusalem. The Babylonians defiled the temple with a pagan feast and then dismantled, looted, and burned it. They systematically destroyed the houses of the city and broke down the walls. No significant ruins of any building dating prior to 586 BC have been discovered by archaeologists. Only floors remain and a portion of the city's wall.

The inhabitants were driven from Jerusalem. All governmental buildings were razed. The Babylonians set up a government at Mizpah, about eight miles north of Jerusalem. Many prominent political and military leaders fled to Egypt for safety. One group of such people forced Jeremiah to accompany them to Egypt.

The Babylonians were thorough in their destruction. They razed all of Judah's fortified cities. Debir, Lachish, Beth-shemesh, and others were destroyed. Some cities were not reoccupied until many years later.[2] The people subsisted among such ashes and destruction.

The kingdom was but a fraction of its former glory. The borders were severely reduced. The northern border was below Bethel, and the southern boundary did not reach Hebron. The vast Negev (south) had been occupied by the Idumeans who pressed northward as far as Hebron. These were former Edomites who had been thrust from their land by increasing hordes of Arabians. On the east, the Jordan River was the boundary; to the west, the mountain area near the Mediterranean was the boundary. Michael Avi-Yonah declared that the reduced kingdom was about twenty-five miles north to south and about thirty-two miles from east to west, making it about 800 square miles. Of that, at least a third would be unproductive desert and mountains.[3]

The Babylonians forced the leading citizens and artisans into exile. The poorer and lower classes of society remained in the land. Peasants were left to cultivate the lands and fields. They had to cultivate the crops to keep from starving to death and to pay tribute imposed by Babylon on Judah. That the people left in the land were poor probably reflected Babylon's policy to stifle nationalism. With a vacuum of leadership, these people who had such limited experience became community leaders.

Many families were disrupted or destroyed. Doubtless many orphaned children wandered aimlessly. Many people suddenly became widows or widowers. Biblical injunctions on choosing a mate were ignored. As the children grew up without religious guidance, and as other people entered the land, they began to intermarry. When Ezra returned, he found intermarriage with pagans to be a major problem. Even the high priest's grandson was married to Sanballat's daughter (Neh. 13:28). Consequently the people even lost the proficiency to speak Hebrew. Instead, they spoke various languages. Ultimately Aramaic from Babylon became a common language. The inhabitants' knowledge of God's Word was limited. They were not even aware of basic standards taught in God's Word.

The northern Negev where it meets the central plains. During the exile, the vast Negev (south) had been occupied by the Idumeans, who pressed northward as far as Hebron.

Economically the people were devastated. They lived, apparently, on limited means. They had no money or inclination to begin building programs to improve their status. In addition, they were impoverished by inflation (Hag. 1:6). What they did earn was like putting something into a purse with holes in it. The inhabitants eked out a living, but they lived in poverty.

Such a devastating defeat by the Babylonians raised serious religious questions about Yahweh's status. The people may have thought that if Yahweh was an all-powerful God, why did he allow his land and people to be devoured by foreigners? Consequently many of the pagan cults began to flourish. Those who lived through the Babylonian holocaust wondered if they should not serve other gods. Like those who forced Jeremiah to flee with them to Egypt, many probably turned to worship the "queen of heaven," Astarte/Artemis, again. Other pagan gods also were worshipped by many. A form of Yahwism remained, but it was diluted and polluted with syncretism as the people worshipped other gods.

Some of the people still adored the Temple Mount and offered some sacrifices on a makeshift altar in the ruins. They even fasted to commemorate the fall and burning of the city and temple. They also remembered Gedaliah's death with a fast. However, little attention was given to the Word of God. No wonder Jeremiah depicted these inhabitants as "bad figs" to be despised (Jer. 24:8).

The good figs were taken away into captivity. In Babylon, they sought to preserve their sacred books that spoke of Yahweh's holiness and unfailing love. They developed worship cells that became the synagogue movement in which God's Word was studied and faith in God was nurtured. They also kept alive the hope that was ultimately fulfilled in their liberation by Cyrus and their freedom to return to the land.

When the exiles returned, they were shocked by the apostasy and lethargy of those who had remained in the land. Nevertheless, those returning began to rally and inspire the many discouraged and despairing inhabitants. Leaders such as Ezra and Nehemiah demanded that God's instructions regarding marriage, tithing, and worship be obeyed. Gradually but surely the people reconsecrated themselves to God's service and began to rebuild. They became the people through whom God would send the Messiah.

NOTES

[1] John Bright, *A History of Israel*, 3rd ed. (Philadelphia: Westminster, 1981), 344.

[2] Bright, *History of Israel*.

[3] Michael Avi-Yonah, *The Holy Land: From the Persia II Period to the Arab Conquests* (Grand Rapids: Baker, 1966), 19.

THE JERUSALEM GATES

BY GARY P. ARBINO

GATES AND GATEKEEPERS

BY SCOTT HUMMEL

A view of the Damascus Gate. This is the most massive and ornate of all the gates in Jerusalem. The road from this gate leads to Shechem and then to Damascus. Recent excavations have uncovered an ancient Roman entrance beneath the gate (Neh. 3:32).

The book of Nehemiah mentions a total of twelve different gates around the city of Jerusalem. Situating these twelve gates physically is difficult.

The first and last gates in Nehemiah's circuit were in the northern wall, probably originally built by Judah's King Manasseh (reigned 696–642 BC; see 2 Chr. 33:14). The Sheep Gate stood just east of the fortress created by the Hananel and Meah/Hundred towers at the northwestern corner of the temple enclosure (Neh 12:39). It probably exited to an animal market. Rebuilt and consecrated by a priestly family (3:1), this gate was perhaps also sacral—bringing in animal sacrifices for the temple. Archaeological evidence for the Sheep Gate might be found in an underground passage, known in later literature as the Tadi Gate.[1] The Gate of the Guard (or Prison Gate) was located between the Sheep Gate and the northeast corner of the wall (v. 39). Functionally, this gate seems to be connected to the court of the

Jerusalem's Zion Gate, so named because it is situated on Mount Zion. Some also call it David's Gate because the traditional tomb of David faces the gate. This gate was constructed in AD 1540.

guard (Jer. 37–39), which was positioned at the southern part of the temple compound. The absence of archaeological evidence makes a precise placement impossible.

Located along the western wall, a short distance south from the Hananel Tower, the Fish Gate was probably so named because the fish markets were outside of it. Zephaniah 1:10–11 indicates that it was a focus of Babylon's attack. Given the number of crews Nehemiah assigned to this area (Neh 3:2–8), destruction here evidently was severe. A short distance south stood the "Old" Gate. Difficult to translate, the gate name could mean that it led into the "old city" or that it led out to the Mishneh. The next gate, the Ephraim Gate, is not mentioned in chapter 3 but is situated by chapter 12. Named for the road that led north to Ephraim, it was probably near the juncture where the Broad Wall enclosing the Mishneh joined the wall surrounding the Solomonic city (3:8; cf. 2 Kgs. 14:13). Associated with this gate was a plaza (Neh 8:16). No archaeological evidence has been found for these three gates.

South of the Ephraim Gate stood the Valley Gate, the main city gate. About 500 yards farther south along a section of wall that sustained only minor damage was the Dung Gate (Hb. *ashpot*, "rubbish"). Although no archaeological evidence has yet been unearthed for the Persian-period Dung Gate, its location somewhere near the southern tip of the city of David is certain (2:13–15; 12:31,37). It had open access to the Hinnom Valley rubbish heaps, hence its name and use. Just to the north and east of the Dung Gate was the Fountain Gate (or Spring Gate). According to Nehemiah (2:14–15; 3:15; 12:37), this gate (not yet found) was associated with a set of stairs, now excavated, that led upslope into the city of David. Archaeologists also excavated a series of water channels connected to these stairs. The channels ran from the Gihon Spring, about 300 yards up the valley. These channels and their overflow drainage probably created a spring or fountain of sorts near the gate, hence its name.

Nehemiah lists twelve work crews along the eastern wall between the Fountain and Water Gates (3:16–26). This large number suggests that these fortifications had suffered extensive

As seen from Gethsemane, the Eastern or Golden Gate, showing the Kidron Valley rising up to the city walls. This gate, on the eastern side of the city, was constructed in the post-Byzantine period. To prevent the Messiah from entering Jerusalem through this gate, the Muslims sealed it during the mid-1500s.

Herod's Gate in Jerusalem received its name from pilgrims visiting the city who (erroneously) thought the entrance led directly to Herod's palace. Though originally L-shaped, the entrance was rebuilt as a projection from the wall. The entrance gives direct entry into the Old City.

Looking through the six-chambered gate at Megiddo. Located on the northern side of the city, the gate overlooks the valley, about 160 feet below.

damage (2:14–15). Archaeologists confirm that the wall line was moved upslope in this area to the crest of the hill during the Persian period. Recent excavations have shown evidence of late Iron Age fortifications around the Gihon Spring, the likely location for the Water Gate.[2] Two towers (3:26–27) protecting the spring and a pool have been discovered. We assume these towers were part of the Water Gate complex, left intact by the Babylonians or repaired by earlier returnees to Jerusalem. This configuration would have left an open space between the Persian walls upslope and the Water Gate in the Kidron Valley. This then was the "square" (Hb. *rehov*, "open space") where Ezra read the Torah during the rededication ceremony (8:1–15).

Lack of archaeological evidence prevents the final two gates on the circuit from being reasonably located. The Horse Gate was in the eastern external wall somewhere near the southern part of the temple complex (Jer. 31:40). Additional internal gates brought the horses from the Horse Gate into the stable areas (2 Kgs. 11:16). Finally, the Muster Gate, also translated as "Inspection" or *Miphqad* (Neh 3:31), was situated in the eastern wall between the Horse Gate and the northeastern corner. The name is difficult to translate and is not used elsewhere. It is possible that it is the same as the Benjamin Gate (Jer. 17:19; 37:13; 38:7; Zech. 14:10) leading north from Jerusalem.

GATEKEEPERS

Because the gate was the most vulnerable part of the wall, the gate had to be well fortified and designed to restrict access. The doors were made of wood and iron nails (1 Chr. 22:3; Neh. 2:8). To reduce the chance of fire, some doors were plated with bronze (Ps. 107:16).[3] Double doors were necessary because the gate had to be wide enough to allow a chariot through. When the doors were closed, they were "barred" from the inside with a wooden,

Jaffa Gate; for centuries this was the only entrance into the city from the west. Its Arabic name means "Gate of Hebron," as the main road to Hebron started at this gate.

The Dung Gate was used for disposal of garbage and refuse. Beyond the gate is the Hinnom Valley and Silwan, where Jerusalem's original inhabitants settled (Neh. 2:13; 3:13; 12:31).

bronze, or iron-plated bar (1 Kgs. 4:13; Nah. 3:13). "Wooden posts braced the doors, and the doors pivoted in stone sockets"[4] (see Judg. 16:2–3).

While some gates had only two chambers, one on each side of the entrance, the classical Israelite gate was either four or six chambered. For example, the Solomonic gates at Megiddo, Hazor, and Gezer were all six-chambered gates (1 Kgs. 9:15).[5] Benches lined the inside of each chamber, which formed a small room where the guards could lodge. Each pair of chambers had its own doors, which attackers had to breach successively.[6] Towers usually flanked each side of the gate, and watchmen stood on the roof of the gate (2 Sam. 18:24).[7] All this made the gate complex a veritable fortress.

For greater security, many of the large cities built an outer gate complex. This could trap invaders between the outer and inner gates. By forcing a sharp right turn, it created indirect

The Lions' Gate is also called Saint Stephen's Gate because Stephen may have been martyred in this region. This is the only gate currently open on the east side of the Old City of Jerusalem. The gate opens to the Kidron Valley, east of Jerusalem.

access to the gate, forced the invaders to expose their right side, which was not protected by their shields, and made it more difficult to set up battering rams and siege towers against the gates (Ezek. 21:22).[8]

The gates were only as secure as the gatekeepers were courageous and trustworthy (1 Chr. 9:22).[9] They served as watchmen and reported news and potential danger (2 Sam. 18:24). They guarded the nearby storehouses, opened and shut the gates each day, kept the city gates shut during the Sabbath, and defended the gates during assault (Neh 7:3; 12:25; 13:19).

The temple gatekeepers not only protected the temple; they "ministered" in the gates and assisted with the sacrifices (2 Chr. 31:2; Neh. 13:22; Ezek. 44:11). They protected the temple treasures and accounted for the temple utensils (1 Chr. 9:17–28). During his reforms, Josiah called upon the gatekeepers to rid the temple of idols (2 Kgs. 23:4).

As far back as the time of the tabernacle, the gatekeepers were a special class of Levites (1 Chr. 9:19). As such, they enjoyed the Levitical privileges such as receiving support from the tithes imposed on Israelites (Neh. 10:39; 12:47; 13:5) and exemption from taxes (Ezra 7:24). The priests and Levites, including the gatekeepers, performed their responsibilities between the ages of thirty and fifty (Num. 4:3). Even in exile away from Jerusalem and the temple, they maintained their identity as gatekeepers from one generation to the next.

The gatekeepers were organized into a hierarchical structure with a chief gatekeeper (1 Chr. 9:17) and a captain in charge of each gate (2 Kgs. 7:17). The divisions of gatekeepers were assigned to specific gates, sometimes by casting lots and sometimes by royal appointment (1 Chr. 26:12–19; 2 Chr. 35:15). The number of gatekeepers is recorded as high as 4,000, but during the time of Nehemiah only 172 served (1 Chr. 23:3; Neh. 11:19). In times of emergency, non-Levitical gatekeepers could be assigned to guard the city gates, as Nehemiah did when threatened by the Samaritans, Arabs, Ammonites, and Ashdodites (Neh. 7:3).

City gates served contrasting purposes, restricting access for military purposes while providing access for commerce and communication. Since everyone entered through the gates, the courtyards and squares adjacent to them were centers for public life and markets.

Parties settled disputes and trials in the city gates (Deut. 21:19; 22:15). For example, Boaz legally redeemed Ruth in the city gate (Ruth 4:1–11). Citizens brought their disputes before the city elders or even the king who administered justice from his throne, which was sometimes in the city gate (2 Sam. 15:2; 1 Kgs. 22:10). Immediately following a verdict, punishment was carried out publicly at the gates (Deut. 17:5; Jer. 20:2). The prophets demanded "justice at the city gate" (Amos 5:15; see Zech. 8:16).[10]

Religious assemblies gathered at the gates and in the courtyards of the gates. When the people gathered to hear Ezra read the law, they gathered in the square before the Water Gate (Neh. 8:3). Later, in observance of the Feast of Shelters (or Tabernacles or Booths), the people made and lived in their shelters "on each of their rooftops and courtyards, the court of the house of God, the square by the Water Gate, and the square by the Ephraim Gate" (v. 16).

NOTES

1   Leen and Kathleen Ritmeyer, *Jerusalem in the Time of Nehemiah* (Jerusalem: Carta, 2005), 25–28.

2   See Ronny Reich and Eli Shukron, "Light at the End of the Tunnel," *BAR* 25.1 (1999), 22–33; Hershel Shanks, "2700-Year-Old Tower Found?" *BAR* 26.5 (2000), 39–41.

3   Philip J. King and Lawrence E. Stager, *Life in Biblical Israel* (Louisville: Westminster John Knox, 2001), 234.

4   King and Stager, *Life*, 236.

5   Alfred J. Hoerth, *Archaeology and the Old Testament* (Grand Rapids: Baker Academic, 1998), 287; King and Stager, *Life*, 236.

6   Hoerth, *Archaeology and the Old Testament*, 286; King and Stager, *Life*, 236.

7   Roland de Vaux, *Ancient Israel* (Grand Rapids: Eerdmans, 1961), 234; Ephraim Stern, *Archaeology of the Land of the Bible: The Assyrian, Babylonian, and Persian Periods (732–332 BCE)*, vol. 2 in ABRL (2001), 466–67.

8   De Vaux, *Ancient Israel*, 234; King and Stager, *Life*, 234.

9   Gary A. Lee, "Gatekeeper" in *ISBE*, vol. 2 (1982), 409.

10 De Vaux, *Ancient Israel*, 152.

JEZREEL: MILITARY HEADQUARTERS OF THE NORTHERN KINGDOM OF ISRAEL

BY DEBORAH O'DANIEL CANTRELL

Omri, Ahab's father, purchased the hill of Samaria and built Israel's capital there. Shown are the ruins of Ahab's palace in Samaria.

Jezreel, a site in northern Israel, is famously known as the hometown of Naboth and his disputed vineyard. Additionally, it was the place where Jehu's chariot horses trampled Jezebel to death when he usurped the throne (1 Kgs. 21:1–16; 2 Kgs. 9:30–37). Even more significant, it was key to ancient Israel's military defense for more than a hundred years.

Samaria was evidently proving to be a difficult capital city to protect and less than satisfactory as a military headquarters. That the enemy could so easily come to the gates of Samaria placed the entire nation in constant risk. The Israelite rulers eventually realized Samaria's vulnerability, both strategically and possibly economically.

Near the close of Ahab's reign, or possibly during that of his son Joram, the Israelite rulers apparently moved their military headquarters from Samaria to Jezreel—about thirty miles north. This command post was less than two hours from Samaria by chariot or on horseback. Located on the Via Maris (Way of the Sea), the great international highway from Assyria to Egypt, and at the narrowest point of the expansive Jezreel Valley, Jezreel was an ideal launching pad for an attack against Israel's enemies to the northeast, whether the Arameans or the Assyrians. Jezreel was also situated at the northern end of the Way of the Patriarchs, the local north-south route from Jezreel via Dothan to Samaria. Thus Jezreel was ideally situated to protect Samaria from invading armies. Economically Jezreel, on the edge of the well-watered fertile Jezreel Valley, could provide grain and pasturage to feed thousands of horses.

The most important component of Israel's army was its horses. A strong chariotry was essential to success; care of the horses was, therefore, a primary concern. During the famine in Samaria, King Ahab personally went in search of pasturage for his army horses and mules. To sustain military horses required three things: water, food (grain and fodder), and training. Jezreel supplied all of these needs.

The walled compound at Jezreel covered some eleven acres. "A rock-cut moat surrounded the enclosure on all sides, except the northeastern, where the wall and ramp extended along the edge of the steep slope of the ridge. . . . The impressive moat is unique in this period, and indicates the particular strength of the fortifications and the importance of the enclosure."[1] Jezreel had a large, smooth, flat surface area, 948 feet long by 515 feet wide, ideal for working on training maneuvers with the horses inside the safety of the walls. Entrance to the compound was via a chambered gate, which allowed the rapid hitching and unhitching of several chariots at once. At the gate, a bridge or drawbridge over the moat allowed access to the city.

Jezreel has its own perennial spring, the spring of Jezreel; nearby is the spring of Harod (Judg. 7:1; 1 Sam. 29:1). These provided adequate water for thousands of horses. And Jezreel, on the edge of the fertile agricultural plain of the Jezreel Valley, never had to worry about the growing or shipping of grain to feed livestock. In fact, archaeologists have excavated more than one hundred rock-cut bottle-shaped pits at Jezreel. Some of these pits were for

Ruins of Tel Jezreel.

water storage, but many were originally silos for grain, wine, and other perishables. Grain could, therefore, easily be stored in sufficient quantities not only to feed the horses year-round but also to be transported to soldiers in distant battlefields. In this way, hundreds or even thousands of horses and warriors could be easily cared for and maintained in and around Jezreel.

Tactically, Jezreel served as a superior lookout site and proved to be an excellent vantage point for detecting incoming horses and chariotry (2 Kgs. 9:17–21). This is still evident today, as ancient Jezreel overlooks the valley and beyond to the mountains over the Jordan. With Jezreel as the military depot for the Israelite army, Samaria, which had vital fighting chariotry units, was well protected. An enemy would first have to conquer Jezreel before it could proceed to the capital.

NOTES

¹ David Ussishkin and John Woodhead, "Jezreel (Yitze'el), Tel" in *NEAEHL*, 5:1838.

THE KIDRON VALLEY

BY JEFF S. ANDERSON

The Stepped Stone Structure is one of the largest Iron Age structures in Israel. Located in the City of David, its exact purpose has been debated; some believe it supported a royal building, maybe David's palace.

View of the Kidron Valley as seen from the north. The cone-topped Tomb of Absalom rises from the valley floor; the Temple Mount is to the right.

Just east of the Old City of Jerusalem lies a deep valley called the Kidron. This important valley runs north to south and separates the ancient city of David and the Temple Mount from the Mount of Olives to the east. The highest point on the Mount of Olives is 2,636 feet above sea level, some 400 feet above the valley floor, which lies below. The ravine of the Kidron is precipitous as it drops 4,000 feet in just twenty miles, where it ultimately empties into the Dead Sea, almost 1,300 feet below sea level. The slope of the Kidron immediately adjacent to the city of David is equally abrupt. Near the bottom of the valley floor lies a perennial spring called the Gihon, which produces up to 400,000 gallons of fresh water a day, enough for a small city like ancient Jerusalem. Two other peaks on the same ridge join the Mount of Olives; the one to the north is Mount Scopus. To the south is the Mount of Corruption, which is, according to tradition, where Solomon abandoned his promise to God and built numerous high places for Chemosh and Molech, gods of the Moabites and the Ammonites (1 Kgs. 11:78).

A PHYSICAL BOUNDARY

Kidron is a place of ambiguity. In the Old Testament, Kidron is a consistent geographical marker of Jerusalem's eastern boundary. The word *Kidron* means "dark" or "unclear." To cross the Kidron was to cross a geographical boundary, to leave the city of David. The expression, "from the Lord's temple to the Kidron Valley" in 2 Kings 23:6 denotes such geographical limitations.

Both slopes of the Kidron Valley were also infamous burial places with a long history of association with ancient tombs, particularly the slope on the eastern side of the ravine. Many tombs from the time of the kings of Judah were excavated there, shortly after the 1967 Six-Day War.[1] Adjacent and among these tombs today is the village of Silwan, with 40,000 Palestinian and 400 Jewish residents.[2] Significant evidence also indicates that in ancient times the slopes were terraced and used partially for agriculture (2 Kgs. 23:4).[3]

A THEOLOGICAL BOUNDARY

The spatial framework of the Kidron denoted a geographical boundary and a theological boundary as well. To cross the Kidron also meant to cross a metaphorical line. Let's take a few examples. Solomon established a vibrant center of foreign cult worship on the eastern slope of the Kidron, associating the site with idolatry and apostasy. The Old Testament conveys the accounts of three good kings, Asa, Hezekiah, and Josiah, who carried the unclean vessels from the temple to the Kidron Valley, a metaphorical boundary line, and burned the pagan altars and Asherah idols there. Josiah unceremoniously cast the dust of these idols on the graves of the common people (1 Kgs. 15:13; 2 Kgs. 23:4–12; 2 Chr. 15:16; 29:16; 30:14). Later in Jewish, Christian, and Muslim tradition, the upper northern end of the Kidron became known as the Valley of Jehoshaphat, the place of the final judgment (Joel 3:12).[4] The intertestamental book of 1 Enoch (26:1–27:5) graphically depicts the Kidron and surrounding area as a cursed valley, a place where the cursed would gather at the last judgment.

The Kidron thus served as a boundary line, across which existed a spiritual wilderness, a burial ground and a dump of illicit cult objects—a literal and metaphorical graveyard. Today more than 150,000 Jewish, Christian, and Muslim graves cover the western slopes of the Mount of Olives, the valley floor, and the slopes of the Kidron all the way up to the eastern wall of the Old City of Jerusalem.

NOTES

[1]   David Ussishkin, *The Village of Silwan: The Necropolis from the Period of the Judean Kingdom* (Jerusalem: Israel Exploration Society, 1993).

[2]   Raphael Greenberg and Yonathan Mizrachi, *From Shiloah to Silwan* (Jerusalem: Keter, 2011), 34.

[3]   Lawrence E. Stager, "The Archaeology of the East Slope of Jerusalem and the Terraces of the Kidron," *JNES* 41.2 (1982): 111–21 (esp. 113).

[4]   John Briggs Curtis, "An Investigation of the Mount of Olives in Judeo-Christian Tradition," *Hebrew Union College Annual (HUCA)* 23 (1957): 137–80.

LACHISH

BY JOEL F. DRINKARD JR.

Two ostraca letters found at Lachish describing the situation just before Nebuchadnezzar's destruction of Jerusalem.

Lachish (Tel Lachish, Tell ed-Duweir) was one of the major cities in Judah, located about thirty miles southwest of Jerusalem in the Shephelah, the foothills of the Judean mountains. Lachish is located along the Via Maris, the primary international roadway leading from Egypt through Canaan/Israel up to Syria and Mesopotamia. At more than thirty acres in size, the site is the largest tell in the region. The tell is surrounded on three sides by the Nahal Lachish, providing significant natural defense. Both its size and location made Lachish the logical choice to guard that portion of the Via Maris as well as access up into Judah. It also served to guard the border between Philistia and Judah.

A GROWING CITY

The Canaanites built the first major city on the site in the Middle Bronze Age (ca. 2000–1550 BC). That Canaanite city had a strong defensive wall, a palace, and a temple/sanctuary. A supportive embankment, known as a *glacis*, surrounded the walls (and largely gave the site the slope it currently has). A rock-hewn *fosse*, which is a ditch or moat used in fortifications, was found on the west side of the tell at the bottom of the glacis. The large palace was probably the ruler's residence. Since most of this palace lies under the Judean palace-fortress, excavations are incomplete. Artifacts dating to the Middle Bronze Age that were found at the site give evidence of a strong Egyptian influence in Lachish during this era. The city was destroyed, however, at the end of the Middle Bronze Age. The Late Bronze city of Lachish may have been the largest in Canaan after Hazor was destroyed in the thirteenth century BC. The presence of buildings on the edge of the mound as well as a temple in the fosse/moat indicate that the Late Bronze city was unfortified.

The Israelites captured and destroyed the Late Bronze city at the time of Joshua (Josh. 10:31–32). It was part of Judah's tribal territory (15:39). According to 2 Chronicles 11:9, Lachish was one of the fortified cities Rehoboam rebuilt. Lachish had on its acropolis a large palace that probably served as the residence of the governor. It was one of the most important fortified cities of Judah during the monarchy, second in size and importance only to Jerusalem itself. The city is mentioned again in connection with the plot against Amaziah, king of Judah, in 2 Kings 14:19 and 2 Chronicles 25:27. Some unnamed people in Jerusalem plotted the assassination of Amaziah. He learned of the plot and fled to Lachish, perhaps because it was such a strongly fortified city. Nevertheless, the ones plotting against him had allies in Lachish, and Amaziah was assassinated there.

Lachish had a striking feature of a double-wall system protecting it. Whereas other fortified cities in Israel and Judah were protected by a single wall system with a glacis or dry moat adding further protection, Lachish had a nineteen-foot-thick inner wall along with a revetment wall about halfway down the slope of the tell.

Amarna letter from Shipti-Ba'al of Lachish to the Egyptian pharaoh.

Partial remains of the palace-fortress atop Lachish, which fell to the Babylonians in 586 BC. King Sennacherib had earlier laid siege to and conquered Lachish in 701 BC. Warning of the coming Assyrian invasion, Micah said the residents of Lachish would need riding steeds to power chariots for a fast getaway (Mic. 1:13).

This second wall prevented erosion. A sloping glacis ran from the inner wall down to the revetment wall. Both wall structures had stone foundations and mud-brick superstructures. In times of enemy attack, defenders could be stationed along both the inner and outer walls. The city also had a double-gate structure. The road to the city followed along the city's outer wall, exposing anyone attacking the city to defenders on the wall. Massive towers protected the outer gate. From the outer gate, persons entering the city came into a courtyard, made a right angle turn and came to the inner gate, a six-chamber gate that was among the largest found in Syria-Palestine (eighty-two feet by eighty-two feet). The reliefs recovered from Sennacherib's throne room that depict the siege of Lachish clearly show the double-wall structure.

The major building complex inside the city itself was the palace-fortress. This structure was built on a raised platform producing a kind of acropolis. A massive wall connected the palace with the city wall. The palace-fortress complex was in effect an inner fortress. The palace-fortress at the time of the Assyrian invasion was approximately 120 feet by 250 feet in size. It included a large courtyard, two building complexes that have been described either as stables or warehouses, and the palace complex proper. Probably the city served as a military and administrative center and perhaps housed a chariot unit at the time. Micah 1:13 refers to the horses and chariots of Lachish, supporting this possibility. As such, both warehouse and stable complexes likely would have been present in the inner structure.

The city played an important role during the Assyrian campaign against Judah in 701 BC. Apparently, in 701 BC Assyria's King Sennacherib set up his headquarters near Lachish. The city became the focal point in a series of reliefs that later decorated Sennacherib's throne room in his capital city of Nineveh. Remains of the massive siege ramp built against the wall have been excavated on the southwest of the mound. The Assyrian ramp was more than 230 feet wide and 165 feet long. This siege ramp reached the outer revetment wall and allowed the Assyrians to bring their battering rams and siege instruments directly against the wall. The archaeological evidence shows that the defenders in the city built a counter ramp inside the wall as the Assyrians built the ramp outside the wall. The counter ramp was actually several yards taller than the main city wall and provided a higher defensive line inside the main city wall. This counter ramp also kept the Assyrians from scaling the wall. Nevertheless, the efforts proved futile, and Lachish fell to Sennacherib's forces. Numerous arrowheads and other weapons and armor were recovered from the ruins surrounding the area of the ramps. Second Kings 18–19 describes the Assyrian invasion of 701 BC. Although Lachish fell to Sennacherib, 2 Kings 19 records that Jerusalem was not taken at that time. Sennacherib's accounts of the campaign also agree that Lachish fell, but Jerusalem was not taken. He reported concerning Hezekiah, "He himself I locked up within Jerusalem, his royal city, like a bird in a cage." The Old Testament records that Hezekiah paid a tribute of thirty talents of gold and 300 talents of silver to Sennacherib (2 Kgs. 18:14). Sennacherib bragged, however, of Hezekiah paying a larger tribute to end the invasion: thirty talents of gold, 800 talents of silver, precious stones, furniture, musicians, concubines, and much more.

POSTINVASION LACHISH

Lachish was rebuilt after it fell to the Assyrians but as a much less well-fortified city. The palace-fortress remained in ruins. Based on the archaeological remains, Lachish never regained the power or wealth it had previously. Nevertheless, it remained a major fortified city of Judah along Judah's southwestern flank.

Slightly more than one hundred years later, Lachish was again the site of a major siege by a Mesopotamian power, this time the Babylonians under Nebuchadnezzar. The prophet Jeremiah recorded an oracle against Zedekiah dated to the last stages of the Babylonian siege against Lachish. Nebuchadnezzar had laid siege against Jerusalem. The Egyptian army approached Jerusalem, hoping to offer the city its aid. Nebuchadnezzar moved his army, which was besieging Jerusalem, to face off the Egyptians—who quickly returned to Egypt. The Babylonians' siege of Jerusalem resumed immediately (Jer. 37:5–11). Jeremiah mentioned that at that time only Lachish and Azekah remained of the fortified cities of Judah (in addition to Jerusalem, see 34:7). An ostracon excavated in the gate area of Lachish gives a poignant glimpse of the final days: "And he knows that concerning the fire signals of Lachish, we are watching them according to all the signs which my lord gave. Indeed, we do not see Azekah." This report sent to Lachish probably from an outpost between Lachish and Azekah may well record the situation just after Jeremiah's oracle. If so, the report indicates that Azekah had fallen, and only Lachish and Jerusalem remained. And within just days or weeks Lachish fell and lastly Jerusalem.

Lachish is mentioned again only in Nehemiah 11:30 as one of the cities of Judah inhabited by those returning from exile in Babylon. It had a palace and a sanctuary, the Solar Shrine, during the Persian period and into the Hellenistic period. The site was abandoned after the Hellenistic period and was never rebuilt.

THE LYCUS VALLEY

BY ROY E. LUCAS JR.

View of the Lycus River Valley from atop Tel Colossae near the modern town of Honaz, Turkey. Mount Cadmus is in the distance.

GEOGRAPHY

The Lycus Valley, which is triangular in shape, is formed by four mountain ranges. The Salbakus and Cadmus ranges run across the southern end of the valley. The Messogis Mountains form the northwestern side of the valley and the Mossyna Mountains, the northeastern side. Two major rivers run through the Lycus Valley—the Lycus River, which empties into the Maeander River.

Colossae, Hierapolis, and Laodicea were the most significant cities in the Lycus Valley. Laodicea and Hierapolis sat on opposite sides of the Lycus River, six miles apart. Colossae sat on both sides of the Lycus River, about ten miles to the southeast of Laodicea. A major trade route from the Aegean Coast to the Euphrates River ran through the valley. A second road followed the path from Pergamum to Sardis, on to Perga, and finally to Attalia.

Earthquakes frequently struck the Lycus Valley. The Greek geographer Strabo (ca. 63 BC–AD 23) described this valley as "good for earth-quakes."[1] Chalk infused the Lycus River and its streams. The chalk from these riverbeds would bury ancient monuments, cover the fertile land, clog the river flow, redirect streams, and destroy crops. Visible from a distance of twenty miles, these deposits glistened in the sun like glaciers.[2]

Volcanic activity in the region produced rich soil. The resultant abundant vegetation was helpful for those raising livestock. Large herds enriched the producers of wool apparel in all three cities. Due to an abundant water supply, Hierapolis developed a strong textile business. The textile producers used chalk from the rivers in their dyes. The madder root along with the calcareous waters produced a fade-resistant dye. Thermal springs near Hierapolis attracted visitors seeking therapeutic treatments.

HISTORY

Cyrus the Great defeated Lydia's King Croesus in 546 BC, placing the Lycus Valley under Persian control. Alexander the Great conquered the valley in 334 BC. Greek rule continued for about 150 years. The Romans, with the assistance of Pergamum's King Eumenes II (reigned 197–159 BC), defeated the Seleucid King Antiochus III in 189 BC at the battle of Magnesia. Afterward, the Lycus Valley became part of the kingdom of Pergamum. The last king of Pergamum, Attilus III (reigned 138–133 BC), bequeathed the kingdom of Pergamum to the Romans in his will in 133 BC. The region was incorporated into the Senatorial Province of Asia and remained under Roman control for hundreds of years.

Colossae stood as the most important town in the valley during the fourth to fifth centuries BC. Like Hierapolis and Laodicea in later history, it supported a strong textile business from fine wool products. During the Roman period, Laodicea and Hierapolis surpassed Colossae in importance; by the ninth century AD, Colossae was a ghost town.

Some scholars believe Hierapolis was founded in the fourth or third century BC. Others claim it began under Eumenes II of Pergamum. Hierapolis's importance peaked in the second and third centuries AD. Rome's Emperor Hadrian (AD 117–138) financially supported major construction projects there, including a theater seating 12,000 to 15,000 people.

Silver tetradrachm of Syria's King Antiochus II, who named the city for his wife Laodice in the third century BC.

Roman ruins at Laodicea, which is about one hundred miles east of Ephesus.

Laodicea sat between two small tributaries that flowed into the Lycus River: The Asopus River ran to the western portion of the city while the Caprus River flowed east of the city. Pliny the Elder (ca AD 23–79) wrote that Laodicea stood on top of an earlier city, Diospolis, later called Rhoas.[3] "Antiochus II, the Seleucid king [reigned 261–246 BC], founded the city during the middle of the third century. . . . He named the city in honor of his wife Laodice."[4]

Earthquakes struck the region and destroyed Colossae, Hierapolis, and Laodicea in both AD 17 and AD 60. The cities rebuilt after both earthquakes.

NOTES

[1] Strabo, *Geography* 12.8.16.

[2] J. B. Lightfoot, *St Paul Epistles to the Colossians and to Philemon* (London: Macmillan, 1880), 3.

[3] Pliny the Elder, *Natural History* 5.39.

[4] Clyde E. Fant and Mitchell G. Reddish, *A Guide to Biblical Sites in Greece and Turkey* (Oxford: Oxford University Press, 2003), 232.

MEGIDDO:
A CRUCIAL LOCALE

BY JEFF S. ANDERSON

Megiddo was a Canaanite stronghold that overlooked the Jezreel Valley and guarded the main pass through the Carmel Mountains.

Megiddo, the crown jewel of biblical archaeology, is one of the most important sites in Israel and, for that matter, the entire ancient Near East. A World Heritage Site, Megiddo stands watch over the expansive Jezreel Valley. Megiddo had it all: a fertile and well-watered plain nearby, a strategic location on the crossroads of two major trade routes between Asia and Egypt (the Via Maris and Jezreel trade routes), and a defensible location. Ancient letters discovered at el-Amarna, Egypt, indicate Megiddo was one of Canaan's most dominant city-states. Biridiya, king of Megiddo, sent these letters to Egyptian Pharaoh Akhenaten in the fourteenth century BC. Megiddo enjoyed robust periods of occupation from 3500 to 500 BC and was inhabited during every era of Israel's history.

A HISTORICAL BATTLEFIELD

Megiddo preserves a long history of being an international battleground with thirty-four recorded battles in that area.[1] Over successive generations Megiddo witnessed many formidable armies, including the Canaanites, Egyptians, Assyrians, Israelites, Philistines, Persians, and Romans. More than 1,000 years after the fall of the Roman Empire, Napoleon fought near the site in 1799. Concerning Megiddo, he is purported to have proclaimed, "There is no place in the whole world more suited for war than this. . . . [It is] the most natural battleground of the whole earth."[2] In the twentieth century, Megiddo witnessed the defeat of the armies of the Turks and Germans during World War I as well as the victory of the Israelis in the 1948 War of Independence. Today the Ramat David Airfield of the Israeli Air Force is fewer than twenty miles from Megiddo.

THE GREAT TEMPLE

Four excavations have revealed more than twenty different occupation layers at Megiddo from 3500 to 500 BC. Since 1994, Tel Aviv University has assumed work at Megiddo as well as several other projects in the Jezreel Valley. Discoveries in 2012 included a hoard of gold and silver jewelry dating from 1100 BC, but the primary focus of the Tel Aviv operation has been to clarify chronology at the site.

Archaeologists continue to make exciting discoveries at Megiddo to this day. One note-worthy recent project has been the excavation of a huge temple (ca. 11,840 square feet) dating to around 3000 BC, centuries before the arrival of the Israelites. This temple is the most monumental single edifice uncovered in the promised land and one of the largest structures of the Near East.[3]

A Canaanite temple, designed by a professional, highly skilled team of architects, was part of a massive temple complex that was reenvisioned and reconstructed many times over many centuries. With walls more than three and a half meters (ca. eleven and a half feet) thick, the floor of the building contains massive basalt slabs weighing more than a ton each. These are in two rows flanking the longitudinal axis of the temple. These basalt slabs were clearly not for roof support but for some unknown and highly sophisticated cultic practic-es. Two rear corridors called favissa were filled with sacrificial bone refuse, mostly young sheep and goats. The site had no evidence of human sacrifice.

Inhabitants of the lower village accessed this hilltop temple from the eastern slope of the mound and the main entry faced a mud-brick and stone altar that stood at the geomet-ric center of the temple.[4] This magnificent shrine was abandoned for a time and later reoc-cupied. Later temples were built one on top of the other, including the shrine that contained the famous Early Bronze Age round altar.

Dated to about 2500 BC, circular Canaanite altar at Megiddo; the altar measures twenty-five feet in diameter and about four and a half feet high. Four steps lead to the top of the altar. The altar was located behind the actual temple.

BIBLICAL REFERENCES

The Bible contains about a dozen references to Megiddo. The first is to a certain "king of Megiddo," who is on a list of vanquished monarchs that Joshua conquered (Josh. 12:21). Megiddo was then allotted to the tribe of Manasseh (17:11). The book of Judges (1:27), however, indicates that the situation was not that simple. Israel was seemingly unable to completely subdue Megiddo after all. Later in the same book, Deborah and Barak overcame Sisera near this site. The Song of Deborah refers to the "Waters of Megiddo" as the place where God delivered Israel (5:19).

During the Israelite monarchy, Solomon made Megiddo a district administrative capital along with two other major fortified sites: Hazor and Gezer. The gate systems at these three sites are nearly identical. The Bible refers to Solomon's robust building activity, which included the addition of palaces, terraces, and city walls (1 Kgs. 9:15). A century later, the Bible records that Jehu killed Israel's King Joram and Judah's King Ahaziah near Megiddo (2 Kgs. 9:27), while the Tel Dan inscription boasts that Syria's King Hazael was the one who murdered these two kings.

An ivory game board with fifty-eight holes; inlaid with gold; from Megiddo.

A few later references to Megiddo may point toward an emerging popularity of the site in apocalyptic thought. Josiah, the last "good" king from the Davidic dynasty, was fatally wounded at Megiddo in battle against Pharaoh Neco (2 Kgs. 23:29; 2 Chr. 35:22–24). Even though a few more kings ruled briefly after Josiah, for all practical purposes the death of Josiah brought an abrupt and tragic end to the monarchy.

MEGIDDO AND ARMAGEDDON

Without a doubt, one of the most popular biblical texts pertaining to Megiddo is Revelation 16:16. Some interpret that this pivotal location will be where the spiritual forces of the heavens and the kings of the earth gather together for the ultimate battle of good versus evil. The New Testament adopts the term *Armageddon*, a corruption of the Hebrew, *Har-Megiddo*, which translates "Mount Megiddo." This reference in Revelation reveals the context of the sixth and seventh bowls of wrath, which predict the fall of Babylon the Great. Whether the reference in Revelation is to a historical battle or the metaphorical demise of evil, Megiddo retains both a lively past and an intriguing future in the Bible's history and theology.

NOTES

[1] Eric H. Cline, *The Battles of Armageddon: Megiddo and the Jezreel Valley from the Bronze Age to the Nuclear Age* (Ann Arbor: University of Michigan Press, 2000), 1.

[2] Cline, *Battles of Armageddon*, 142.

[3] Matthew J. Adams, Israel Finkelstein, and David Ussishkin, "The Great Temple of Early Bronze I Megiddo," *AJA* 118 (April 2014): 285–305.

[4] Matthew J. Adams et al., "The Rise of a Complex Society: New Evidence from Tel Megiddo East in the Late Fourth Millennium," *NEA* 77.1 (2014): 32–43.

MOAB

BY ROBERT D. BERGEN

Mentioned in twenty-two of the thirty-nine Old Testament books, Moab is remembered in accounts of biblical history from the days of Abraham through the time of Nehemiah. It is the subject of prophecies uttered by Moses and seven of Israel's writing prophets and is mentioned in three different psalms. All but a handful of the references portrayed Moab and the Moabites in a negative light, as Israel's troubler.

THE LAND AND CITIES OF MOAB

The region known as Moab during biblical times is located in what is today modern Jordan. We generally think of ancient Moab as the hilly plain directly east of the Dead Sea. The heart of traditional Moabite territory was situated between the Wadi Arnon (modern Wadi el Mujib) in the north (see Judg. 11:18) and the Wadi Zered (modern Wadi el-Hesa) in the south, which descended westward into the Dead Sea. They served as natural barriers and provided a measure of protection and isolation for Moab.

A second region associated with Moabite culture is the territory just north of the Arnon gorge. Though this area was known as the plains of Moab in biblical times (Num. 22:1), it was not always under Moabite control (33:48).

On its western border along the shore of the Dead Sea, the Moabite heartland lies some 1,300 feet below sea level. However, as one moves eastward, the terrain ascends rapidly. A mere ten miles away from the Dead Sea, the elevation is about 3,000 feet above sea level, a net rise of about 4,300 feet.

This great variation in elevation meant that Moab contained several distinct climatic zones. Nearest the Dead Sea is a desert region that receives less than five inches of rain annually. Atop the plateau is a region that normally receives ten to twenty inches of rain per year and is more conducive to farming.[1] Biblical evidence for the relative productivity of Moabite land is seen in Ruth 1:2, which states that the Israelite Elimelech moved his family there to escape a famine.

Archaeological evidence suggests that Moab had established a series of fortresses along its border near the Zered gorge, overlooking the caravan route known as the King's Highway.[2] Other less conspicuous border defenses were discovered in the Arnon gorge. The Bible seldom mentions major cities in Moabite territory. Moses mentioned a city named Ar (Deut. 2:18); David left his family with a Moabite king in Mizpah (1 Sam. 22:3–4); the prophet Amos pronounced judgment on the palaces of Kerioth (Amos 2:2); and Isaiah (Isa. 15:2; 16:7–9) spoke of Dibon, Kir-hareseth, Heshbon, Sibmah, Jazer, and Elealeh.

THE PEOPLE, HISTORY, AND INFLUENCE OF MOAB

Genesis 19:30–37 provides an account of the Moabite nation's origins from the offspring of an incestuous relationship between Lot and his older daughter. The Moabites were thus understood to be a Semitic people group indirectly related to the Israelites. Knowing that Lot and his sons were with Abram in the promised land (chap. 13) and that the Moabite territory eventually came to be located east of the Dead Sea, we can assume that sometime before the days of Moses the descendants of Moab migrated from the western side of the Dead Sea to its eastern highlands. There they displaced the Emim, a people group that had been living there in the days of Abraham (Deut. 2:10–11). However, the Bible lacks further details regarding the early stages of Moabite history; so far archaeological sites in the Near East have failed to uncover any documents that shed light on this period of their history.

By the time of the Israelite wanderings in the desert, Moabite culture had adopted a monarchical form of government, with a king that governed with the support and assistance of clan leaders known as elders (Num. 22:4,7,10). At that time, Moab had a smaller population than the Israelites and evidently lacked sufficient military resources to defend their territory from an Israelite invasion. Consequently, they sought the assistance of a Mesopotamian shaman, Balaam son of Beor, to eliminate Israel by means of powerful curses (vv. 2–11).

Prior to the rise of the Israelite monarchy, the Moabites consolidated their territorial holdings and at times even dominated their neighbors (1 Sam. 12:9). During the days of the judges, Moabite King Eglon forced the Israelites to bring him annual tribute payments for a period of eighteen years (Judg. 3:14). The best-known Moabite king is Mesha, who mounted a revolt against Israel and ruled from Dibon during the mid-ninth century BC. He is known from an inscribed stone found in Dibon in 1868.

On the other hand, many nations, including Israel, sought on occasion to gain control over Moab and its resources. Israelite leaders whom the Bible mentions as winning wars against the Moabites include the judge Ehud (Judg. 3:15–30) and the kings Saul (1 Sam. 14:47), David (2 Sam. 8:2), Jehoram (also known as Joram) of Israel, and

Moabite Stone, discovered at Dibon in 1868, with an inscription by Moab's King Mesha, circa 840 BC.

Jehoshaphat of Judah (2 Kgs. 3:6–27). But Moab's primary troublers were not the Israelites or their southern neighbors the Edomites but, rather, the nations from Mesopotamia—Assyria and Babylon. "The Assyrian texts imply that Moab fell under Assyrian domination during the eighth century BC."[3] Josephus indicated that the Babylonians conquered Moab five years after the destruction of Jerusalem, thus in 581 BC.[4] The Bible mentions no Moabite activities after that time.

Moabite religion exerted an influence—a decidedly negative one—on its neighbors as well. At various points in Israelite history, the Israelites became involved in the worship of at least two different Moabite deities. During the days of Moses, a number of Israelite men took part in religious rites associated with Baal of Peor. As part of their worship of Baal, they participated in sexual rituals (Num. 25:1–8) and ate sacrificial meals presented to the dead (Ps. 106:28). Out of respect for a Moabite wife he had taken into his harem, King Solomon built a high place for Chemosh, the national god of Moab, just east of Jerusalem (1 Kgs. 11:7–8). The Israelites maintained this high place of worship for more than 300 years, up until the time of its desecration by King Josiah in the reforms of 626 BC (2 Kgs. 23:13).

AN ATYPICAL MOABITE

The name *Moab* may have evoked a negative emotional reaction from the ancient Israelites. Ruth presents, however, a totally different image of those who had been the enemies of the people of God. From her lineage came the One who was and is the Redeemer of humankind (Matt. 1:5). Our reaction, rather than fear and dread, is worship and celebration.

NOTES

1 J. H. Paterson, "Palestine" in *ZPEB*, 4:578.

2 R. K. Harrison, "Moab" in ZPEB, 4:262.

4 J. Maxwell Miller, "Moab" in *ABD*, 4:890.

5 Josephus, Jewish *Antiquities* 10.9.7.

MORIAH: ITS BIBLICAL AND HISTORICAL SIGNIFICANCE

BY GARY P. ARBINO

A close-up of the ruins of the Samaritan temple on Mount Gerizim that John Hyrcanus the Hasmonean king destroyed in 128 BC. Mount Gerizim is the place the Samaritans believe Abraham went to offer Isaac.

In Genesis 22:2 God told Abram to go "to the land of The Moriah" to "one of the mountains about which I will tell you."[1] So we turn to our *Holman Bible Atlas*[2] and look in the gazetteer and notice that it has no entry for "the land of The Moriah." In fact, a search of our concordance proves that "the land of The Moriah" is never mentioned again in the Bible. It is also never mentioned in any extrabiblical text. So where, exactly, was this place?

Turning back to Genesis 22, we get some clues. Verse 4 says that on "the third day" of the journey from Beer-sheba in the Negev wilderness, Abram saw his destination. Enough of the day remained to allow him and Isaac to reach the mountain God chose and return to the others who had traveled with them. So, assuming a spry old man and three youth could probably cover anywhere from fifteen to forty-five miles a day, they traveled between forty-five and 115 miles. We are not told which direction.

Verse 2 tells us that "The Moriah" is characterized by mountains. The main ancient Greek version, the *Septuagint*, points to the mountainous nature of the Moriah. Rather than simply transliterating "The Moriah," the Septuagint uses a phrase that in English reads "the lofty land." Thus "The Moriah" may simply have been a popular early name for the range of highlands along the west side of the Jordan Valley.

Unlike our modern English versions, all of the ancient translations of the Bible translate the word *Moriah*. Since Hebrew proper names rarely take definite articles, translators did not use "The Moriah" as a proper name; they therefore thought the term needed to be translated.

One option holds that *Moriah* came from the Hebrew word for "teach" (*yoreh*). Some of the rabbis thus felt the phrase "the land of the teaching" reflected that this was the place from which all teaching went into the world. Interestingly a place-name with "teach" in it is in another important spot in the Abraham narrative. The first time God spoke to Abram in Canaan, he did so at the oaks of "Moreh" (Gen. 12:6).

The Aramaic translations (Targumim) and several rabbinic sources read the original word as deriving from *yera'*, the Hebrew word meaning "fear/worship." They thus translate the phrase as "the land of the worship," a reference to Abraham's sacrifice.

Several ancient Greek versions, the Samaritan Pentateuch, and the Latin Vulgate translate *Moriah* as "vision"; "the land of the vision." This derives from understanding the word as coming from the verb *ra'ah*, meaning "to see." This is also a meaning within chapter 22 itself, as mentioned above in Abraham's naming of the site.

According to verse 14, Abram named the place Yahweh *yir'eh*, meaning "Yahweh is seen" or "Yahweh has provided."[3] The verse makes a reference to a popular saying: "It is said, 'In the mountain of Yahweh it will be seen/provided [*yera'eh*].'" Later generations ("to this day") would connect this particular mountain to "the mountain of Yahweh." In the Old Testament, this is the name applied to Zion (Jerusalem) because of the temple (Ps. 24:3; Isa. 2:3; Zech. 8:3).

While Genesis makes no specific connection, Israelites later connected Moriah with the Temple Mount and Solomon's temple, built around 950 BC and destroyed by the Babylonians in 586 BC.

If Abraham was at the place where Solomon's temple would later be located, he not only saw Jerusalem but would actually have built the altar for sacrificing Isaac either in or near the city. The site of the temple was just north of the Jebusite city (later called "the city of David") on the upper part of the same ridge. The Egyptian Execration texts from the eighteenth–nineteenth centuries BC already referred to the city as Urushalimu. If one assumes that Salem is a shortened name for Jerusalem in the Melchizedek narrative

Two monks overlook the Kidron Valley from the ancient city of David. The background shows that Jerusalem was a city built on and in the hills.

(Gen. 14:18–20), it was evidently a thriving town with a "king." However, Genesis 22 never mentions this city, which is a bit odd if this important story takes place in or near it and Abram knew its king.

In 2 Chronicles 3:1, a verse not paralleled in the earlier book of Kings, the writer joins several lines of detail about the site of the temple, seemingly drawing from Genesis 22; 2 Samuel 24; and 1 Chronicles 21–22. Chronicles indicates that Solomon built the temple on "Mount Moriah" but does not explicitly mention Abraham or the events of Genesis 22. Instead the focus is on *David's* role in the temple. The text refers to Mount Moriah as the place (1) where Yahweh appeared to David—perhaps implying it supersedes Yahweh's appearance to Abraham; (2) which David himself chose—ignoring Abraham; and (3) where, on the threshing floor of Ornan the Jebusite, David built an altar—perhaps to be seen as supplanting Abraham's.

During the Second Temple period (515 BC–AD 70), people promoted the idea that the mountain of Abraham was connected to a single "Mount Moriah." This was the same as the "mountain of Yahweh" (Zion) where David decided to build the temple, where Solomon actually built it, and where Zerubbabel built the second temple. These links are affirmed by other Second Temple period Jewish texts such as the *Jewish Antiquities* by Josephus, *Jubilees*, the *Genesis Apocryphon*, and the Targum of Jonathan.

MOUNT MORIAH TODAY

Today when you visit the site of Mount Moriah (the Temple Mount or Haram es-Sharif), you are standing on the platform King Herod enlarged to forty-five acres, but the building you see is the Dome of the Rock. Caliph Abd-al-Malik built this magnificent golden-domed structure between AD 688 and 691; it remains substantially unaltered to this day. This building was erected on or near the spot of a Roman temple to Jupiter, which itself was built on the remains of Herod's temple. Surrounding this monument (not specifically a "mosque") are numerous other examples of Islamic-period architecture (AD 638–1917), the most notable of which is the Al-Aqsa Mosque (originally built between AD 709 and 715) in the southwest corner of the mount. There are no remains from either the Byzantine Christian period (AD 330–638; they left the mount as an empty holy space) or from the Roman period following the destruction of Herod's temple in AD 70.

Surviving materials from the Second Temple complex (including Herod's rebuild) are largely limited to the enclosure wall that surrounds the platform. A visitor today can take the underground Western Wall Tunnel walk along the wall where remains from Hasmonean (165–63 BC) and Herodian (63 BC–AD 70) architecture are visible. Most notable is the "master course" of huge, beautifully dressed building stones (the largest is forty-one feet long, eleven and a half feet high, and fifteen feet wide, estimated to weigh 600 tons) used by Herod's builders. Along the south wall, you can walk up the wide Herodian temple staircase. The eastern face of the enclosure wall reveals the seams between Herod's additions and the earlier construction. While nothing remains from the first (Solomon's) temple, several later structures on the mount have been traditionally related to Solomon. Centrally, the "Rock" inside the Dome is purportedly the site of Abraham's altar on Moriah, the place of the most holy place for the temple, and the spot from which Muslims believe Muhammad ascended to heaven after his night visit to Jerusalem.

NOTES

1   Author's literal translation.

2   Many of the specific geographic and chronological references in this article are from Thomas Brisco, *Holman Bible Atlas* (Nashville: Holman Reference, 1998).

3   The Hebrew *yir'eh* is usually translated "see" in verses 2 and 14, and "provided" in the context of verse 8—like the English phrase "see to it."

MOUNT NEBO: ITS HISTORY, GEOGRAPHY, ARCHAEOLOGY, AND SIGNIFICANCE

BY T. J. BETTS

Pottery excavated at Mount Nebo.

Mount Nebo as seen from the Jordan River Valley.

In Numbers 23:14, Balak the king took Balaam the seer up to "Lookout Field on top of Pisgah" with the intention of having Balaam look down on the camp of the people of Israel and curse them. Deuteronomy 34:1 recounts how God took Moses up to "Mount Nebo, to the top of Pisgah, which faces Jericho" to show him the land he had promised to Abraham and his descendants.

LOCATION AND GEOGRAPHY

In the dry wilderness region of western Jordan, Mount Nebo extends west from Jordan's central plateau, which in biblical times was called the plains of Moab. Even though erosion has been a constant factor in the region, Mount Nebo still rises to a flat top surrounded on all sides by steep slopes. The word *Pisgah* could be another name for it or may be a reference to a prominent peak on it. The mountain is about six miles northwest of Madaba, which was an important settlement on the border of Moab. Additionally, Mount Nebo is about eleven miles from Heshbon, which was at the border between the tribes of Reuben and Gad as the tribes of Israel settled in the promised land. Mount Nebo is almost seventeen miles southeast of Jericho, the great Canaanite stronghold that protected the approach into the land of Canaan from the east. Mount Nebo is about twelve miles east of the mouth of the Jordan River. It is 2,680 feet above sea level and rises about 4,000 feet above the Dead Sea. (The surface of the Dead Sea is the lowest elevation on earth, historically about 1,300 feet below sea level, although it has receded an additional one hundred-plus feet in the past five decades.) Mount Nebo has two peaks called Siyagha and al-Mukhayyat.[1]

While some have presented other candidates for possible locations of Mount Nebo, three words appear to point to this location as the correct one. First, the word *Neba*, which is the modern word for Nebo, was discovered on one of its ridges. Second, the word *Siaghah* is identical to the Aramaic word *Se'ath*, the word used to translate Nebo in the Targum of Onqelos in Numbers 32:3 where it is called the place of Moses's burial. *Siaghah* is an alternate spelling of the highest summit, Siyagha. Third, the name Tal'at es-Sufa refers to the ascent leading up to the ridge of Mount Nebo from the north. It is related to the Hebrew word *tsuph*, which was part of the Nebo mountain range.[2]

Mount Nebo provides a spectacular view of the region. Beginning the panorama to the north, one may see the eastern side of the highlands of Gilead, which were divided between the tribes of Reuben, Gad, and Manasseh. About fifty miles northwest in Israel, the strategic Beth-shean Valley, which served as an access point from the Jordan River to Israel's inland and the Jezreel Valley, is visible along with the region of ancient Naphtali. To the west, one may view the central mountain range of Judah, including the Mount of Olives; and on the clearest days, one may catch a glimpse of the hills surrounding the eastern side of Jerusalem. To the southwest of Mount Nebo, one can spot Bethlehem and the Herodium, one of Herod the Great's magnificent palatial building projects, which lies about three miles south of Bethlehem. Directly south, one can see the Dead Sea toward ancient Zoar.[3]

East of the mountain range where Mount Nebo is located are rolling hills and then, beyond them, mostly desert. Southeast of Mount Nebo is the heart of Jordan, the Ard As Sawwan Desert. Just north is the Ard As Sawwan Plain, and north of it is the Syrian Desert.

ARCHAEOLOGY AND HISTORY

Excavations at Mount Nebo have uncovered material remains from the biblical era. First, archaeologists have discovered Assyrian-type and Moabite-type pottery in Moabite settlements and tombs. The Judean pottery tradition is also strong, however, pointing to the Judeans who lived in the area as attested in the Old Testament. Second, excavations uncovered Assyrian clay coffins in two of the tombs along with an Assyrian-style cylinder seal.[4] The Assyrian presence in the region is attested in both biblical and extrabiblical texts. At the end of the fourth century AD, a Byzantine church was built on the summit commemorating Moses's encounter with God. In the sixth century, it was enlarged into

Byzantine church atop Mount Nebo.

a basilica full of beautiful mosaics. It was then neglected for many years until the Franciscan Order bought it in 1933. Since then, the Franciscans have excavated and restored much of the church and have also erected other memorials.

One interesting Jewish tradition concerning Mount Nebo comes from the noncanonical book of 2 Maccabees. Numerous caves dot the region, and 2 Maccabees 2:4–8 states that prior to the Babylonian invasion in the sixth century BC, God led Jeremiah to take the tent of the Lord's presence, the altar of incense, and the ark of the covenant to a Mount Nebo. There he discovered a huge cave and hid the sacred pieces. Whether Jeremiah did this or not, this is still part of the story of Mount Nebo.

The mountain likely received its name in honor of the Babylonian god, Nebo or Nabû. Daniel's comrade, Azariah, received the Babylonian name "Abednego" ("servant of Nebo").[5] Given that Assyrians and Babylonians both worshipped this god, the name suggests that the mountain may have been significant to Mesopotamian invaders as they conquered these lands.

NOTES

[1] "Mount Nebo," Tourist Israel: The Guide, 10 May, 2018, www.touristisrael.com/mount-nebo/16954.

[2] Henry A. Harper, *The Bible and Modern Discoveries* (London: A. P. Watt, 1895), 139; W. Ewing, "Nebo, Mount," *ISBE*, ed. James Orr (1939).

[3] "Mount Nebo," Near East Tourist Agency, 10 May 2018, www.netours.com/content/view/257/30.

[4] Elizabeth Bloch-Smith, *Practices and Beliefs about the Dead* (Sheffield: Sheffield Academic, 1992), 196.

[5] Leonard J. Coppes, "§1280 [*něbō*]" (*Nebo*, Nebo) in *TWOT*, 545–46. The letter "g" in "Abednego" is most likely an intentional misspelling of this pagan god's name in the Scriptures.

NAZARETH IN THE FIRST CENTURY

BY ROY E. LUCAS JR.

Mary's Well, located inside the Greek Orthodox Church in Nazareth, was likely the only water source of Nazareth for centuries.

Eliminate Gabriel's announcement to Mary, and Nazareth's visibility wanes. Subtract Nathaniel's comment about nothing good coming from Nazareth, and the city fades. But remove its foremost citizen, Jesus, and Nazareth vanishes.

The Jewish Talmud, which refers to sixty-three Galilean villages, disregards Nazareth, as does the Apocrypha. The first-century Jewish historian Josephus never mentions the town. Archaeological investigation substantiates Nazareth's lack of significance.

LOCATION AND RESOURCES

Nazareth lies in an "elevated and steeped plateau-land"[1] at about 1,150 feet above sea level. It is fifteen miles southwest of the Sea of Galilee and twenty from the Mediterranean. Six miles east of Nazareth runs the Via Maris, the road that connected Egypt and Israel with Damascus.

Nazareth has wet winters. Winter temperatures vacillate between forty and fifty degrees Fahrenheit with occasional freezing temperatures. Annually, Nazareth receives twenty to thirty inches of rain. Dew forms on about 200 nights. Summer temperatures vary between sixty-five and eighty-five degrees. Nazareth's altitude, adequate rainfall, and hilly surroundings on all sides but the south help produce abundant vegetation. Nazareth's single water source, a spring, may have both hindered its growth and served as its social center.

CULTURE

Rome appointed Herod the Great as king of Judea (37–4 BC). Herod Antipas, Herod's youngest son, ruled as tetrarch in Galilee and Perea from 4 BC to AD 39 (Luke 3:1). This means Nazareth was under the rule of Herod Antipas throughout Jesus's earthly ministry.

Galileans were reportedly "generous, impulsive, simple in manners, full of intense nationalism, free, and independent of the traditionalism of Judea,"[2] the region that included Jerusalem. The reason the rabbis in Jerusalem despised the Galileans, "was likely due to the unpolished dialect, lack of culture, and the hamlet-size of the Nazareth community."[3]

Overview of the modern city of Nazareth. The conical structure in the center is the Church of the Annunciation.

Nazareth covered approximately ten acres. Lower population estimates range from 400 to 500 citizens; higher estimates reach 1,600 to 2,000.[4] Nazareth's occupants owned land, were tenant farmers, or provided craft services for those needing their skills. "The remains of olive and wine presses, water cisterns, grinding stones, and other materials found scattered about, all indicate the poor, peasant nature of Nazareth during the time of Jesus."[5] Local artisans made eating and cooking utensils. Regionally grown foods included wheat, barley, beans, peas, lentils, onions, cucumbers, olives, grapes, and figs.

Houses in Nazareth typically had two to four rooms with mud-packed floors. Homes were constructed of native stone. Roofs consisted of mud packed on flat thatch. Larger houses had second stories. Joseph and Jesus were *tektons*—a Greek term that may refer to carpenters or stonemasons.

The number of family members and a household's income dictated house size. Many homes were small and built close together. Three or four of these close-built homes formed an open courtyard; a stone wall encircled and secured the compound. These multihouse units shared a kitchen area with an outside oven, cistern, and millstone. Families often kept animals in a ground-floor room of the house.

The religious background in first-century Nazareth is not easily discerned. Evidently the Roman provincial (Gentile) cultures of nearby Sepphoris and Tiberias had little effect on the surrounding region, including Nazareth, which seems to have had a significant Jewish population. The contents of two rock tombs near Nazareth indicate the presence of a Jewish settlement there during the Roman period. Rabbinic tradition also indicates priests at one time lived in Nazareth. Although no first-century synagogue buildings have been excavated in Nazareth, the New Testament states that one existed (Matt. 13:54; Mark 6:1–2; Luke 4:16).

NOTES

1 Paul Barnett, *Behind the Scenes of the New Testament* (Downers Grove, IL: InterVarsity, 1990), 38.

2 J. Dwight Pentecost, *The Words and Works of Jesus Christ* (Grand Rapids: Zondervan, 1981), 520.

3 Jerry W. Batson and Lucas P. Grimsley, "Nazareth, Nazarene" in the *HIBD*, rev. ed. (2015), 1148.

4 Donald L. Blake Sr., *Jesus, A Visual History: The Dramatic Story of the Messiah in the Holy Land* (Grand Rapids: Zondervan, 2014), 42; Bernard J. Lee, *The Galilean Jewishness of Jesus: Retrieving the Jewish Origins of Christianity* (New York: Paulist, 1988), 65.

5 John C. H. Laughlin, *Fifty Major Cities of the Bible* (New York: Routledge, 2006), 194.

PATMOS

BY GARY HARDIN

Entrance foyer in the Cave of the Apocalypse, on Patmos. According to tradition, John was in this cave when he received his visions.

Patmos, a small rocky island in the Aegean Sea, stretches ten miles long and six miles wide. Its formation resulted from volcanic activity in the Dodecanese, a cluster of islands in the Aegean Sea near Asia Minor. About sixty miles southwest of Ephesus, Patmos provided the last stop on a voyage from Rome to Ephesus. Its crescent shape created a natural harbor for ships.

With its rocky soil and an abundance of flowering plants and shrubs, the island featured low hills, small plateaus, and a large number of coves. Patmos experienced a mostly mild climate. Ancient sources suggest that a large quantity of trees originally covered the island. The trees were cut down, leaving Patmos bare.[1]

The Cariens, ancient inhabitants of Caria in southwest Asia Minor, were likely the original inhabitants of Patmos. The Doriens and Ionians, ancient Greek groups, colonized the island in the eleventh century BC. The island's early inhabitants adored the goddess Diana, considered the patroness of the island. At the time of John's exile, Patmos featured a temple to Diana, who bore a close resemblance to Artemis (Apollo's twin), the goddess whom early Greeks believed protected all living things.

The Romans typically condemned lower-class criminals to work in mines or to die in combat as gladiators. Rome banished some upper-class criminals to a lonely island. The Romans used two groups of Aegean islands—the Cyclades and Sporades—as places of banishment. Emperors Domitian and Diocletian chose Patmos as a place of exile for the better class of offenders. Patmos was a suitable place for exile because it was desolate, barren, sparsely settled, seldom visited, and infested with snakes and scorpions.

Overlooking part of the shoreline at Patmos.

Patmos had no significant historical role until the Christian era. During late Roman and Byzantine times, a religious aura rested on Patmos, due mainly to John's exile. During the Middle Ages, pirates attacked and depopulated Patmos and plundered the island for its resources, including the animals.[2]

Around 1088, a new period began for Patmos, when the Greek monk Christodoulos Latrenos built Saint John's Monastery on the site of an earlier temple to Artemis. This monastery resembled a fortress and became Patmos's most famous landmark. The years that followed brought more change. Patmos saw the development of numerous churches and monasteries and became a place of learning for Greek Orthodox monks, who assembled a notable library on the island. Today the library of Saint John's Monastery contains one of the most important collections of items from Greek monastic history. The collection includes embroidered stoles from the fifteenth to the eighteenth centuries, rare icons, illuminated manuscripts, and church furniture from the seventeenth century. The monastery chapel features art that dates back to the early 1200s.[3]

NOTES

[1] R. C. Stone, "Patmos" in *ZPEB* (1976), 5:619.

[2] "Patmos," accessed October 26, 2003, www.abrock.com/Greece-Turkey/patmos.html.

[3] "Patmos," www.abrock.com.

PHILIPPI: A HISTORICAL AND ARCHAEOLOGICAL STUDY

BY STEVE BOOTH

Roman gate to the city of ancient Neapolis.

In contrast to many biblical sites, visitors to the archaeological site of Philippi today are able to visualize the lay of the land in large part as it looked when Paul first visited the city around AD 49 or 50. From the summit of the naturally fortified hill (acropolis) that was a part of ancient Philippi, a large fertile plain stretches westward. This locale in modern-day Greece was ideal for a settlement dating back to 360 BC, originally called Krenides ("springs"). Its natural advantages included an abundant supply of water, rich agricultural land, and a defensible location.[1] In addition, rich gold and silver deposits were in the surrounding area.

LOCATION, LOCATION, LOCATION

Philip II of Macedon, Alexander the Great's father, recognized the strategic value of this town, took it over in 356 BC, and renamed it after himself. He fortified the acropolis and built a wall around the city, some parts of which still remain. "The wealth [he] received here enabled him to enlarge his army and unify his kingdom."[2] In 168–167 BC, Rome conquered Macedon and eventually made this region a province, dividing it into four administrative districts.[3]

Another factor that raised Philippi to a higher level of importance was the construction of the famous Via Egnatia (Egnatian Way), begun approximately 145 BC and completed around 130 BC. This highway connected Rome to the east and ran through the middle of Philippi, serving as its main street. As a major stopping place, Philippi benefited from the movement of Roman troops back and forth as well as from commerce that developed due to the increased ease of transportation. Just ten miles southeast of Philippi on the Via Egnatia, the port city of Neapolis (modern Kavalla) made interaction with the regions beyond even more accessible.

The event that really put this city on the map of the Roman Empire was the battle of Philippi in 42 BC. Just beyond its western wall, Octavian (later known as Caesar Augustus) and Mark Antony squared off against Brutus and Cassius, who had been instrumental in Julius Caesar's assassination two years earlier. Antony and Octavian were victorious, while Brutus and Cassius both committed suicide on the battlefield. The victors enlarged and further fortified the city, establishing it as a Roman colony and naming it Colonia Victrix Philippensium.[4] They also resettled veterans there, granting them generous sections of farmland.

The alliance between Antony and Octavian broke down, and the score was settled in the battle of Actium in 31 BC. As victor, Octavian settled many of Antony's soldiers in Philippi and renamed this strategic city Colonia Iulia Augusta Philippensis after his daughter Julia (Augusta being added in 27 BC after he received the title from the Senate).[5] The status of colony was the highest privilege granted a Roman city and gave its citizens the same civil rights as if they lived in Italy, including freedom from taxation. The official language was Latin, which is verified by many of the inscriptions from the period, although Greek continued to be the language of the marketplace.[6]

In Paul's day, the city of Philippi was modest in size with a blended population of descendants from the Roman veterans, Greeks that predated the Romans, and native Thracians that predated the Greeks. Also living there were immigrants from Asia Minor that were involved in commerce like Lydia of Thyatira (Acts 16:14) and some Jews.[7] Roman soldiers

Monumental stairway leading to Basilica A in Philippi.

were stationed in Philippi to protect the Via Egnatia. The inhabitants were "proud of their ties with Rome, proud to observe Roman customs and obey Roman laws, [and were] proud to be Roman citizens."[8]

PAUL'S ARRIVAL

With Paul's landing at Neapolis, Christianity advanced from Asia to Europe. Traveling the Via Egnatia to Philippi, Paul would have entered the Neapolis Gate, part of which archaeologists have uncovered. Traveling west, Paul would have soon passed the impressive theater of Philip II on his right. Although later modified and enlarged in the second and third centuries, its basic form would have looked similar to the one still visible today. The same is true of the Roman forum on the city's main street. Various administrative buildings, shops, monuments, and temples bordered this large public square.[9] This is the marketplace where the slave girl's owners dragged Paul and Silas before the magistrates and where they suffered severe beating before being thrown into prison (Acts 16:19–23).

Evidence of the emperors' cult—including public displays honoring Augustus and his adopted sons Gaius and Lucius Caesar—were also in the forum. A few years prior to Paul's arrival, the then-reigning Caesar Claudius (AD 41–54) had already introduced the cult of Livia (wife of Augustus and Claudius's deceased grandmother).[10] The people generally appreciated and revered the Roman rulers for maintaining peace and providing protection, justice, and relief in times of hardship.

A remarkable mix of other pagan worship practices coexisted in first-century Philippi as well. The traditional Greek gods like Zeus, Apollo, Dionysus, and especially Artemis had their place, though sometimes known by their Latin counterparts, including a shrine to Silvanus. Ancient Thracian religions persisted too, for example, Artemis Bendis and devotion to the Hero-Horseman.[11] Sanctuaries to gods from Egypt included those honoring Isis and Serapis as well as the Phrygian Cybele, the great mother-goddess.

NOTES

[1] Holland L. Hendrix, "Philippi" in *ABD*, 5:313–14; Gordon D. Fee, *Paul's Letter to the Philippians* (Grand Rapids: Eerdmans, 1995), 25.

[2] Lee Martin McDonald, "Philippi" in *DNTB*, 787.

[3] Peter T. O'Brien, *The Epistle to the Philippians: A Commentary on the Greek Text* (Grand Rapids: Eerdmans, 1991), 3–4.

[4] F. F. Bruce, *Paul: Apostle of the Heart Set Free* (Grand Rapids: Eerdmans, 1977), 219.

[5] Bruce, *Paul*.

[6] McDonald, "Philippi," 788.

[7] Hendrix, "Philippi," 315.

[8] Gerald F. Hawthorne, *Philippians*, WBC (1983), xxxiii–xxxiv; O'Brien, *Philippians*, 4.

[9] Chaido Koukouli-Chrysantaki and Charalambos Bakirtzis, *Philippi* (Athens: Hellenic Ministry of Culture, 2006), 38–41.

[10] Chaido Koukouli-Chrysantaki, "Colonia Iulia Augusta Philippensis," in *Philippi at the Time of Paul and after His Death*, ed. Charalambos Bakirtzis and Helmut Koester (Harrisburg, PA: Trinity Press, 1998), 16.

[11] Koukouli-Chrysantaki and Bakirtzis, *Philippi*, 25–28.

In the bottom right is the bema (speaker's platform) at Philippi.

Bull head at Philippi draped with garland and accompanied by what may be two priests.

THE PROMISED LAND: A CRUCIAL LOCALE

BY KEN COX

Tyre was important to Israel not only because of its harbor but also because of its craftsmen and nearby cedar forests.

After four decades of living in a barren desert (Deut. 1:3), God's chosen people were to live in a fertile region located on highly traveled international caravan routes.

The land of Canaan was a vital location in the ancient world. It formed a strategic land bridge between Europe and Asia to the north and Africa to the south. Within its narrow boundaries were fertile fields, choice pasturage, strategic heights for cities, and well-established commercial trade routes. Surrounding peoples made this land bridge a crucial part of the ancient world. By planting his people in tiny Canaan, God would reveal his truth to the uttermost parts of the earth.[1]

THE REGION AND RESIDENTS

Canaan is part of the region that touches the eastern coasts of the Mediterranean Sea. North of the Mediterranean is Asia Minor, the current country of Turkey. A mountain chain stretches from west of the Black Sea, continues eastward beyond the Caspian Sea, curves to the southeast, and concludes at the Bay of Bengal, east of India. The range stretches north of Asia Minor and Mesopotamia into Asia. These mountains, the Balkans, Caucasus, Elburz, Hindu Kush, and Himalayan ranges, form a northern boundary and curb winter winds to produce a favorable climate for the area south of the range. The Syro-Arabian Desert constitutes a southern boundary to the region. The area that is between the mountains and the southern deserts and that stretches from the Mediterranean Sea to the Persian Gulf forms the biblical world.[2]

The Arabian and Libyan Deserts prohibit population and travel in the largest land area of the region. These deserts and the Mediterranean Sea squeeze the productive land into an agriculturally productive area called the Fertile Crescent. The Fertile Crescent reaches from the Tigris and Euphrates Rivers of Mesopotamia, arches northwest to Haran, west through

Truly a land flowing with milk and honey, the fertile fields of Canaan were a stark contrast to the desert regions of Egypt. Shown, Kishon River from Mount Carmel.

Dan marks the northern boundary of Canaan. The springs at Dan are one of the three main sources for the Jordan River.

Snow covers the peaks of Mount Hermon most months of the year.

Syria, southwest through Canaan, and concludes in the agriculturally rich delta and valley of the Nile River.

Civilizations formed in the fertile river valleys throughout this region. In Asia Minor, the Halys River was the site of consolidation for Hittite military power.[3] In Mesopotamia, the Euphrates and Tigris Rivers provided irrigation for farming. In Egypt, the annual floods of the Nile made fertile fields along its course and in the delta.

The Medes, a group of nomadic tribes, became a powerful Mesopotamian presence as they built cities and armies. The dynasties of the pharaohs established Egyptian monuments to their world-class power by building pyramids and armies. Between the armies of Asia Minor, Mesopotamia, and Egypt lay the land of Canaan.

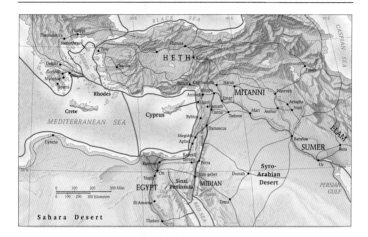

During years of peace, travelers and traders traversed Canaan. Merchants from Mesopotamia traveled to Egypt and vice versa. Grain from Egypt made its way from the ports of Egypt to the maritime cities of Canaan. From there, Phoenician sailors connected Canaan to the rest of the world.

Conflict also came to the region of Canaan as ambitious pharaohs from Egypt and armies from Mesopotamia met to wage war in the valleys of Canaan. The breaks in the mountains on either side of the Jordan became battlefields for legendary conflicts. Sites such as Megiddo came to be known for battles and became symbols for future conflicts. The climactic battle of evil versus righteousness in Revelation 16:16 occurs in Armageddon (Hb. *har*, "hill," plus Megiddo).

Since Canaan was subject to commercial traffic and military encounters, a mixture of peoples ended up living there. The Hethites, Girgashites, Amorites, Canaanites, Perizzites, Hivites, and Jebusites at the time of Joshua's conquest reflect the variety and intermingling of nations after centuries of interchange and conquest.[4] One of the peoples who inhabited part of the region had a long-lasting impact on the land; patriarchal Canaan came to be known as Palestine, a name derived from its Philistine inhabitants.[5]

NATURAL DIVISIONS AND RESOURCES

In addition to being a crossroads for regional powers, Canaan had distinctive qualities within its borders that made it valuable to potential residents. The land promised to Abraham was approximately 150 miles long and seventy miles wide. The eastern and western boundaries of Canaan were the Jordan River and the Mediterranean Sea. Beersheba marked the southern border, and Dan was the northern limit. These borders expanded and decreased by military and commercial acquisitions during Israel's history. For instance, after the conquest of Canaan, Israel inhabited the Transjordan Plateau. Over time, several sites in the plateau were lost and regained by Israel's military forces.

Canaan is divided into four contrasting strips of land running north and south, each with unique, desirable traits. Geographical features form the designations for the different areas.

The Coastal Plain—The westernmost strip of land is the coastal plain, which begins at Gaza and continues north to Tyre. This coastal region possesses fertile farmland and is irrigated by springs and seasonal rainfall.[6] Located in the southernmost region of the coastal plain was the plain of Philistia, which was the stronghold of Israel's perennial enemy, the Philistines. The Philistines recognized the assets of the land and chose it as a home when they migrated from the island of Caphtor (Crete, Amos 9:7). The productive farmland contributed to the Philistines' wealth and political power. A major trade route, the Way of the Sea (*Via Maris*), connecting Egypt to Damascus, passed through the Philistine cities of the southwest plain.[7]

Moving north, the fertile plain of Sharon is the next division of the coastal plain. This area runs north from Joppa to Mount Carmel. This entire region was once covered by extensive forests.

Yet farther to the north, the verdant plains of Acco and Esdraelon complete the coastal region. From Tyre to the north, the coastland had natural ports that were manned mostly by Phoenician sailors. The best known of these ports were at Tyre and Sidon.[8]

The Central Hill Country—Moving eastward from the Mediterranean, the central hill country is the second strip of land. A ridge of mountains beginning in the north in Lebanon continues south to Beer-sheba. The mountains cause abrupt climatic changes and provide strategic locations for cities. The western side of the mountain ridge receives seasonal precipitation from atmospheric moisture from the Mediterranean. The resulting fertile hills of Judea are called the Shephelah. These hills ascend to the heights of Hebron and Jerusalem and provide defensible positions for its residents. The hills north of Jerusalem in Samaria are lower in altitude and create openness and accessibility. In peacetime, this convenience encouraged travel and trade. In times of war, however, the lower altitudes made the capital cities difficult to defend. North of Samaria is upper and lower Galilee. This country is suitable for vineyards and provides excellent pasturage for flocks.

On the eastern slopes of the mountains are the wilderness regions of Judea. Since the mountain heights block rainfall in this region, the limited vegetation can sustain only sparse flocks. The arid conditions provide natural defenses against aggressor armies. Near Jerusalem this rugged terrain slopes steeply downward to the Jordan River.

The Jordan River Valley—The third strip of land is the Jordan (or Rift) Valley. This valley is part of a geological rift that begins in Asia Minor and extends south to Victoria Falls in Zambia, Africa.[9] Abundant springs flow from Mount Hermon to form tributaries that empty into the Sea of Galilee, which is nearly 700 feet below sea level. The land around the Sea of Galilee is fertile. The Jordan River flows south for about sixty-five miles through dense vegetation and arid wilderness to the lowest body of water on earth, the Dead Sea, about 1,300 feet below sea level. Evaporation is the only outlet for all the water draining into the Dead Sea from the Jordan River. This stagnation prevents aquatic life but produces abundant minerals. The water and minerals supplied by the springs, river, and lakes create high demand for this part of Canaan.

The Transjordan Plateau—Yet farther east from the Mediterranean Sea is the fourth strip of land, the Transjordan Plateau. The land rises from the Jordan River Valley and reaches the plateau that extends eastward approximately thirty miles to the Arabian Desert. The fertile land of Bashan and Gilead in the north contrast with the arid heights of Moab and Edom on the southeastern shore of the Dead Sea.[10] Before flowing into the Jordan, rivers irrigate and divide the northern and central Transjordan Plateau. The flocks Israel captured as they began their conquest of Canaan reflect the value of this highly productive region north of the Dead Sea.

Another major trade route of Canaan was located in this strip of land. The King's Highway ran from the Gulf of Aqaba east of the Jordan to Damascus.[11] Caravans traveling to and from Arabia used this highway.

NOTES

[1] J. McKee Adams, *Biblical Backgrounds*, rev. Joseph A. Callaway (Nashville: Broadman, 1965), 25.

[2] William Sanford LaSor, David Allan Hubbard, and Frederic William Bush, *Old Testament Survey: The Message, Form, and Background of the Old Testament* (Grand Rapids: Eerdmans, 1996), 619.

[3]   George L. Kelm, "Hittites and Hivites" in *HolBD*, 655.

[4]   Adams, *Biblical Backgrounds*, 25.

[5]   Merrill F. Unger, "Palestine" in *The New Unger's Bible Dictionary*, ed. R. K. Harrison (Chicago: Moody, 1988), 953.

[6]   Timothy Trammel, "Palestine" in *HolBD*, 1063.

[7]   LaSor, Hubbard, and Bush, *Old Testament Survey*, 622.

[8]   LaSor, Hubbard, and Bush, *Old Testament Survey*.

[9]   LaSor, Hubbard, and Bush, *Old Testament Survey*, 626.

[10] Trammel, "Palestine," 1064–68.

[11] "Kings Highway" in *HolBD*, 847–48.

THE RISE OF MACEDONIA

BY MARK R. DUNN

The Macedonian Empire, Europe's first world superpower, shaped world history in a way that not only dominated life during the New Testament era but still resonates in our world today. Macedonia burst upon the consciousness of the world through the exploits of its favorite son, Alexander the Great (356–323 BC). Three hundred and fifty years after Macedonia exposed the world to Greek culture, the world of the New Testament era was still gripped by Greek influence. Hellenistic Greek dominated as the international common language of the eastern Mediterranean provinces. The New Testament authors, desiring the widest exposure for the good news, wrote in Greek. Hence, Macedonia indirectly influenced the language of the sacred texts that have proclaimed the message of Jesus Christ across the ages.

What led to the Macedonians' rise to supremacy in both Greece and the world? Their struggle for national unity eventually led to world dominance and achievements that changed the course of history. For hundreds of years before its meteoric rise to fame, Macedonia was an isolated region on the northern periphery of the Greek world. Saturated with rugged

House A at Pella. The house dates from the fifth-fourth centuries BC. Pella was the hometown of Alexander the Great and was the capital of one of the Macedonian districts.

Philip of Macedon gold coin.

mountains and timberland to the north and west and watered by numerous rivers winding through the coastal plains to the south and east, Macedonia was untamed and undeveloped. Its northern limits stretched into the Balkan regions, at times reaching to the banks of the Danube. Mount Olympus sat on its southeastern coastal border. Macedonia also faced challenges from her neighbors, bounded by Thrace on the east, Illyria to the northwest, Epirus to the southwest, and Thessaly to the south.[1]

Originally populated by non-Greeks, Macedonia in its early history saw many people seeking to obtain control of the region. Sensing the instability, the Dorian-speaking Greeks moved in the twelfth century BC into south-central Macedonia and eventually dominated the region. The Argead Dynasty emerged and ruled Macedonia from the ninth century BC until the death of its last king, Alexander IV, in 309 BC.[2]

The Argeads first ruled from the city of Aegae and later from Pella.[3] By the fifth century BC, the mixed population of Macedonia had adopted the Greek language. Because Athens dominated the coastal regions, Macedonian rulers focused on extending their power over the highlands and plains—a lofty goal rarely accomplished.[4]

Macedonia had abundant natural resources in timber, livestock, grain, and minerals, which Greece and other peoples desired. Eventually Macedonia became the foremost supplier of such items to the Greeks. The abundant resources attracted Greek expansionist schemes. Macedonian leaders responded resolutely and led Macedonia to dominate Greece by the mid-fourth century BC.

The beginning of the fifth century BC witnessed the arrival of the armies of Persia to campaign against the Greeks. Unable to resist the Persian might, the Macedonians avoided conflict by supplying the Persians with timber for shipbuilding. However, Alexander I, king of Macedonia during the period of the Persian occupation, also secretly provided aid to the Greeks in their fight against the Persians. An admirer of Greek culture, Alexander I sought to bring Greek influence to Macedonia. The efforts of Alexander I and his successors to import Greek culture led to the Hellenization of Macedonia.[5]

The Persian invasion gave the Macedonians the opportunity to observe both Persian tactics and the Greeks' response. In spite of their long history of fighting among themselves, they were forced to unite against the threat of a superior common enemy. The strength and success of the Greeks against the Persians and the future possibilities for a united Greece did not go unnoticed by the Macedonians.

When the Persian War ended in 448 BC, the Greek city-states resumed their previous rivalries and often ranged into Macedonia.[6] The Argead struggle to consolidate Macedonian holdings now faced an added challenge. Nevertheless, the Macedonians made progress in the coastal plains. Having gained strength, the Macedonians established Pella as their new capital city in about 410 BC.[7] Pella came to be the birthplace of Macedonia's most famous rulers: Philip II and his son Alexander the Great.

In 365 BC, Perdiccas III ascended the Macedonian throne. By now, gold had been discovered in eastern Macedonia and was exported through the port city of Amphipolis. Athens desired control of Amphipolis and forced Perdiccas to conquer it in their behalf. With Athenian aid, he did so but kept the city for himself. Instantly wealthy with Macedonian gold, he hired an army and set about consolidating the holdings of the Macedonian crown.[8] This stroke of leadership set the stage for Macedonia to gain Greek and world dominance.

In 360 BC, Perdiccas died, and his brother Philip II seized the throne. Philip first focused on securing Macedonia. In 356 BC, he captured Macedonia's gold mines and named the adjacent city for himself: Philippi. Then Philip moved southward. Successful in his expansion efforts, by 338 BC Philip had gained control of Greece. A year later, as he mobilized his army to invade Asia Minor, Philip was assassinated.

The road to Macedonian greatness had many difficult steps, but the last one was the most challenging. Alexander seamlessly continued his father's plans. Philip had trained Alexander for the throne, securing the famous Macedonian philosopher Aristotle as his tutor. Aristotle cultivated in Alexander a love for Greek culture and possibly the sense that Alexander was destined for greatness and that he was the one who would bring about a world dominated by Greek culture.[9]

Alexander ably served as Macedonia's regent during Philip's Greek campaigns. He was also a spirited warrior; at the battle of Chaeronea, he led the decisive cavalry charge that brought victory over Athens and Thebes and completed Philip's bid to control Greece. Then at age twenty, Alexander III became Macedonia's king and heir of his father's expansionist vision. With inspired leadership, he quickly subdued uprisings that had sprung up in Greece after Philip's death. Alexander first secured Macedonia, pressing its northern frontier to the Danube. He then turned south. Thebes revolted, and Alexander responded by razing Thebes and enslaving its inhabitants. Athens and the rest of Greece readily acceded to Alexander.[10]

With lightning speed that staggered his opponents, Alexander accomplished in less than two years what more than 500 years of Greek strife had not: the unification of Greece under a visionary leader. Now Alexander pursued his father's dream of liberating Greek lands in Asia Minor. His vigorous leadership yielded unimagined results by conquering the fragile Persian Empire with all its old-world holdings, including Egypt and Babylon.

While in Egypt, Alexander established on the Nile Delta a city in his own name. Alexandria would become a leading city of learning. The city library actively collected world literature. Jews living in Alexandria secured copies of the Hebrew Scriptures and began translating them into Greek. The Greek Old Testament, called the Septuagint, was influential even in Israel and became the "Bible" of the early church while the New Testament books were being produced and collected. The Septuagint also influenced translations of the Hebrew Scriptures into European languages such as Latin and English. Unforeseen by the Macedonians, their indirect influence on propagating the Bible was enormous.

Greek culture (Hellenism) breathed fresh air into the old world. Hellenism emphasized varied pursuits such as commerce, communication, construction, travel, education, the sciences, sports, the arts, and philosophy. These elements were then drawn into cultural civic centers served by democratic governments. Above all, Hellenism encouraged freedom and the love of life.[11] Macedonian military prowess cleared the way for Greek culture to liberate the dispirited masses. The response was so positive that Greek culture was popular for centuries after Macedonia's demise and well beyond the New Testament era. Macedonia's lasting legacy was not merely in its astounding military gains but in the cultural changes it unleashed.

In twelve short years, Alexander conquered the eastern world; and just as quickly he was gone, dead in Babylon in 323 BC at age thirty-three. His generals reverted to the old Greek legacy, splitting the Macedonian Empire into four sections to be used as bases to campaign for the whole. Two divisions of the Macedonian Empire directly influenced the Holy Land. Seleucus seized Babylon, Mesopotamia, Persia, and India and established his government in Syria, Israel's old nemesis. Ptolemy grabbed the Holy Land, Egypt, and parts of Asia Minor. Naturally the two regimes fought over the promised land, and Jewish residents suffered. One hundred and twenty-five years of relatively peaceful Ptolemaic rule were followed by thirty much harsher years under the Seleucids, culminating in terror under the rule of Antiochus IV. To strengthen their hold on the Holy Land, the Seleucid regime forced Hellenism upon the Jews, aspects of which conflicted with Jewish religious practice.[12]

Macedonia's glory did not last long. Having lost its king and empire, Macedonia struggled to control its Greek holdings. Finally, in confident control of its coast, Macedonia founded the harbor city of Thessalonica in 315 BC. By the New Testament era, Thessalonica would be Macedonia's leading city.

Macedonia's power and influence steadily waned. In 215 BC, the first of three wars with Rome began. In 146 BC, the Romans annexed Macedonia as a senatorial province, implying military occupation was unnecessary. Soon afterward, the Roman governor in Macedonia ordered construction of the Egnatian Way, a Roman highway. The road connected Thrace and Macedonia with the Adriatic coast and to Rome. A century later, Mark Antony and Octavian marched east along the Egnatian Way to Philippi to battle Julius Caesar's assassins. A century later, Paul traveled west along the Egnatian Way preaching the gospel in Macedonia, visiting Neapolis (now Kavala), Philippi, Amphipolis, Apollonia, Thessalonica, and Berea (see Acts 16–17).

NOTES

[1]   While the exact borders are uncertain, what was once ancient Macedonia probably lies within the boundaries of southeastern Albania, Macedonia, and northern Greece. See Helmut Koester, "Macedonia," in *HIBD*, 1063.

[2]   F. F. Bruce, "Macedonia" in *ABD*, 4:454; James F. Strange, "Macedonia" in *ISBE* (1986), 3:206.

[3]   Aegae is located near modern Vergina, roughly forty-eight miles southwest of Thessaloniki. Even after Pella became the Macedonian capital, the Macedonians continued to bury all their kings at Aegae except for Alexander the Great. See Strange, "Macedonia," 206.

[4]   "Macedonia" in *Encyclopedia Britannica* (Chicago: Encyclopedia Britannica, 2005), 7:620.

[5]   Strange, "Macedonia," 206; Duane F. Watson, "Greece and Macedon" in *Dictionary of New Testament Background* (*DNTB*), ed. Craig A. Evans and Stanley E. Porter (Downers Grove, IL: InterVarsity, 2000), 424–25.

[6]   See "Historical Review of Macedonia," www.macedonia.com/english/history/review/ www.macedonia.com.

[7]   Jona Lendering, "Macedonia 4," *Livius*, www.livius.org/articles/place/macedonia/macedonia-4.

[8]   Lendering, "Macedonia 4."

[9]   Timothy Boatswain and Colin Nicolson, *A Traveller's History of Greece*, 3rd ed. (New York: Interlink, 2001), 84.

[10] R. D. Milns, "Alexander the Great" in *ABD*, 1:146.

[11] "Hellenism" in *The Columbia Encyclopedia*, 6th ed., www.bartleby.com.

[12] Arthur A. Rupprecht, "Macedonia" in *ZPEB*, 4:24.

THE ROLE OF GEOGRAPHY IN THE WARFARE OF THE JUDGES

BY ERIC A. MITCHELL

Kishon River Valley; Sisera gathered his soldiers and 900 iron chariots to the Kishon River as he prepared to fight Deborah and Barak.

Geography can help determine military strategy. Armies choose a battleground (if possible) to highlight their strengths as well as their enemy's weaknesses. Typically, each side wants the high ground because of its good defensive capabilities. In the Elah Valley battle (where David faced Goliath), the Philistines had the high ground on the hill to the south at Socoh while the Israelites had the high ground on the ridge to the north at a small walled town (likely Shaaraim, Hb. for "two gates"; 1 Sam. 17:52).[1] Saul's choice of encampment north of the Philistines rather than east of them precluded any Philistine advance or retreat. The Philistines were checkmated; if they moved east into the Judean hills or if they returned westward to home, Israel would attack them from the rear—thus Goliath's forty-day challenge (17:16).

Although geography and weather were crucial to victory, they were not the key factors in determining the outcome of Israel's battles. This was evident when Ben-hadad, king of

Aram-Damascus, lost a battle against Israel's King Ahab in the mountainous countryside surrounding Samaria (1 Kgs. 20). In consoling the Aramean king, Ben-hadad's advisers commented, "The LORD is a god of the mountains" (v. 28). To counter this wrong view of God, the Lord again brought Israel victory when the Arameans attacked them on the plain. Jonathan's attack on the Philistine garrison is another example of an Israelite victory despite the geography of the battlefield (1 Sam. 14). In that instance, the Philistines had the high ground. Jonathan literally had to climb a cliff followed by his armor-bearer to reach the Philistines watching from above; however, God used Jonathan to rout the Philistines.

In the battle of Deborah and Barak versus the Canaanites (led by Sisera) in Judges 4–5, geography and weather combine in a unique way. When Israel cried out to God for deliverance from Canaan's king Jabin, his commander Sisera plus his army of troops and chariots were stationed in the valley just east of Megiddo. Deborah the prophetess was judging Israel in the central hill country just north of Jerusalem; Barak was in his hometown of Kedesh in Naphtali, overlooking the southwestern shore of the Sea of Galilee.

God planned the battle. He chose the commander, the troops, the gathering and campsite, the enemy, the battlefield terrain, the plan of attack, the timing, and—as we will see—the weather.

The effect of Sisera's 900 iron chariots upon Israel's ranks would have been similar to 900 armed and armored Humvees attacking two light infantry divisions today. The chariot in ancient times was not large, usually only about five feet from wheel to wheel and was pulled by one or two horses. They typically carried two warriors, a driver and an archer, both of whom would have a sword. The chariot would also carry javelins for them to throw at the enemy. A chariot charge could have a devastating effect on an infantry, scattering them in the field. Using chariots, soldiers would often dart in, fire arrows point-blank at frontline troops, and then quickly get out of range. Since chariots needed smooth ground, the steep slopes of Mount Tabor (a rounded cone-shaped mountain rising out of the eastern valley of Megiddo) were a good collection point for the nearby tribal warriors and yet safe from chariotry.[2]

With Barak and his 10,000 troops stationed on the slopes of Tabor, God drew the Canaanite chariots and army out across the floodplain of the little Kishon River. The Canaanite chariots would have had to move directly eastward from Megiddo crossing the Kishon and its feeder streams to approach the Israelites at Mount Tabor. Normally the Kishon is not much larger than what we would call a small creek. The Kishon winds its way through the flat valley of Megiddo from southeast to northwest. The valley has only a small exit to the northwest between the slopes of the Carmel mountain range on the southwest and a ridge to the northwest that separated the valley from the coast. Because of this poor drainage,

Barak stationed his troops on the slopes of Mount Tabor when facing the Canaanites. Mount Tabor rises to about 1,843 feet above sea level.

rain would cause the Kishon to overflow its banks, and much of the valley became a swamp. The Canaanites marched out toward Tabor, but when they were in the valley, God sent a surprise attack—a thunderstorm.[3] The Canaanites' heavy iron chariot wheels sank into the soft muddy ground. At that moment, the Canaanites saw the disaster, and they turned to flee (5:22). At the same time, Deborah ordered Barak to attack. The Israelite warriors charged downslope into the bogged-down chariots—a direct reversal of fortunes for the Canaanites. Barak caught the Canaanites in mud that not long before had been solid ground. It was a slaughter.

We would expect that at the moment of attack Barak and his men pulled out their weapons and charged, but the men of Naphtali and Zebulun who rushed down the slopes of Tabor had no spears or shields (see 5:8). This could mean they fought with swords only. First Chronicles 12:33–34 indicates, however, that a Naphtali warrior's normal weaponry was spear and shield and that Zebulun fought with all sorts of weapons. The lack of weapons likely means these men had no regular weapons but had resorted to whatever was available (Judg. 3:31—Shamgar delivered Israel with a cattle prod; Judg. 15—Samson defeated the Philistines with the jawbone of a donkey). Perhaps the Canaanites had banned the Israelites from owning weapons or blacksmithing. A similar situation existed at the end of the period of the judges and beginning of the monarchy, when Saul and Jonathan were the only Israelites with swords when they fought the Philistines (1 Sam. 13:19–22). In that instance, the Philistines were regulating the blacksmith trade so Israel could not make or sharpen their own weapons or tools. Perhaps the men of Naphtali and Zebulun were using farm implements such as "plows, mattocks, axes, and sickles" (1 Sam. 13:20). In any case, even though the Canaanites' weaponry overmatched their own, the Israelite forces attacked, pursued, and annihilated the Canaanite army to the last man.

NOTES

[1] This city with two gates was recently discovered by Israeli archaeologist Yosef Garfinkel, Khirbet Qeiyafa Archaeological Project, http://qeiyafa.huji.ac.il.

[2] Thomas Brisco, *Holman Bible Atlas* (Nashville: B&H, 1998), 148.

[3] Deborah mentions the rain in several ways in her song about the battle in Judges 5. In verse 4: "The earth trembled"—thunder; "The skies poured"—rain; "The clouds poured"—heavy rain. In verse 20: "The stars fought from the heavens"—divine intervention, perhaps again rain. In verse 21: "The river Kishon swept them away"—flooding.

THE ROMAN FORUM

BY SCOTT HUMMEL

Temple of the Vestal Virgins in the Roman Forum.

At the heart of the city of Rome was the Forum with its monuments, government buildings, and ancient temples. The Roman Forum was in a valley that ran among the hills on which Rome was built. The Forum was more than 600 yards long, 250 yards wide, and ran in a northwest-southeast direction. The Via Sacra, the oldest and most famous street in Rome, ran down the spine of the Forum.

According to tradition, when Rome was founded in 753 BC, the area of the Forum stood outside the small community built on the Palatine hill. Only after the marshy valley was drained could the area be incorporated into the city.[1] The transformed valley became Rome's marketplace and civic center where leaders conducted the city's most important commercial, legal, political, and religious business.[2]

The political and religious importance of the Forum grew when the Roman kings built there the palace known as the Regia and the temple of Vesta. The round temple of Vesta had a conical roof like an ancient hut with an opening in the center to allow the sacred fire's smoke to exit. The worship of Vesta, the goddess of the sacred fire and guardian of Rome, was performed by the Vestal Virgins who were chosen as young girls to serve for thirty years during which time they were required to maintain their chastity.[3] If they did not, they were buried alive. Because the fire ensured Rome's protection, any Vestal Virgin who let the sacred fire go out was flogged.[4] During their service, they lived next to the temple in the Vestal house under the care of the pontifex maximus or high priest. As the only priestesses in Roman religion and as guardians of the sacred fire, the Vestal Virgins were shown great respect by the public and given privileges no other women enjoyed.[5]

The Republican Period (510–27 BC) witnessed dramatic changes. Many of the shops lining the Forum were forced out to make room for several temples and basilicas, and the Comitium or assembly area became the Forum's focal point. The Basilica Aemilia was a large rectangular hall, lined with columns and ending with a large semicircular recess.[6] The hall housed court proceedings and other governmental functions. The basilica was beautifully decorated and considered one of the most beautiful buildings in the world.[7]

Overview of the Roman Forum. Pictured left is the columned porch of the temple of Saturn. The three white columns in the distance are from the temple of Castor. To its left is the temple of Antonius and Faustina. On the horizon is the Roman Colosseum.

Roman temples were usually rectangular and built on a high platform. The front steps led through a columned porch to the main room where the statue of the god stood. Religious ceremonies were conducted outside at the altar instead of inside, which was the home of the god.[8] The temple of Saturn also served as the state treasury and housed the standards of the Legions and the decrees of the Senate. Sacred treasures were held in its underground chamber. The Romans worshipped Saturn as a god-king who ruled over a golden age of prosperity, peace, and equality.[9]

With the rise of the republic, the Regia became the official headquarters of the Pontifex Maximus, who carried out the sacred duties of the state and cared for the Vestal Virgins.[10] The Comitium was an open area where assemblies gathered. It became the epicenter of the government because it included the Rostra or speakers' platform and the Curia or Senate House. Some of the most famous speeches in Roman history were delivered from the Rostra, such as those given by Cicero and Mark Antony. It was a large platform adorned with the beaks (rostra) of ships captured from the naval battle of Antium in 338 BC.[11] The Senate deliberated in the Curia, which held 300 senators on three tiers of steps.[12]

The fall of the Roman Republic and the rise of the Roman Empire were reflected in Julius Caesar's massive renovation of the Forum. Augustus completed Caesar's reconstructions and added the temple of Divus Julius where Caesar's body had been cremated in the Forum.[13] The buildings of the Forum demonstrated the subordination of the Senate and the elevation of the emperors to the status of gods. The emperors themselves were now worshipped in the Forum. Emperors further diminished the political importance of the Forum by building several other forums known as the Imperial Fora. They also assumed the office of the Pontifex Maximus (who had traditionally lived in the Forum), but they built their palaces elsewhere.

By the time Paul arrived in Rome (ca. AD 60), the Forum was less the seat of power and more a seat of monuments, temples, and triumphal arches. A massive fire ravaged most of Rome in AD 64 and destroyed many of the Forum's buildings. Nero blamed the Christians for the fire and martyred many of them, possibly including Paul.

The Forum had recovered from previous fires and earthquakes. It fell into permanent decline, however, with the transfer of the imperial residence to Constantinople and with subsequent invasions. When Constantine established Christianity as the official religion of the empire, the temples fell into ruin or were converted into churches. The Forum's state of ruin became so complete that for centuries it was known only as Campo Vaccino, "the cow field."[14]

NOTES

[1] The Romans built the Cloaca Maxima to drain the valley. At first it was an open canal, but circa 200 BC it was arched over. Luca Mozzati, *Rome*, trans. Felicity Lutz and Susan White (Milan: Mondadovi Electa, 2003), 15; see Ernest Nash, *Pictorial Dictionary of Ancient Rome* (London: Zwemmer, 1961), 1:442.

[2] D. B. Saddington, "Rome," in *Major Cities of the Biblical World*, ed. R. K. Harrison (Nashville: Thomas Nelson, 1985), 210.

[3] Stewart Perowne, *Roman Mythology* (London: Paul Hamlyn, 1969), 32; Samuel Ball Platner, *A Topographical Dictionary of Ancient Rome* (London: Oxford University Press, 1929), 557.

[4] See Herbert Rose, "Vesta, Vestals" in *The Oxford Classical Dictionary* (Oxford: Clarendon, 1970), 1116; and Perowne, *Roman Mythology*, 32.

[5] Perowne, *Roman Mythology*, 32.

[6] Platner, *Topographical Dictionary*, 71. This basilica floor plan was later adopted by many churches.

[7] Mozzati, *Rome*, 15; Platner, *Topographical Dictionary*, 74.

[8] Saddington, "Rome," 215.

[9] H. J. Rose, *Religion in Greece and Rome* (New York: Harper, 1959), 225; John Ferguson, *The Religions of the Roman Empire* (Ithaca, NY: Cornell University Press, 1970), 215; H. H. Scullard, *Festivals and Ceremonies of the Roman Republic* (Ithaca, NY: Cornell University Press, 1981), 206.

10 Saddington, "Rome," 211, 218.

11 Ian Richmond and Donald Strong, "Rostra" in *Oxford Classical Dictionary*, 937; Nash, *Pictorial Dictionary*, 2:272.

12 Mozzati, *Rome*, 15.

13 Richard Stillwell, ed., *The Princeton Encyclopedia of Classical Sites* (Princeton, NJ: Princeton University Press, 1976), 764.

14 Nash, *Pictorial Dictionary*, 1:446.

ROME: THE GROWTH OF THE ETERNAL CITY

BY MARTHA S. BERGEN

Ruins of the amphitheater that stood on the outskirts of Carthage in North Africa, which was part of the Roman Empire. The amphitheater was often the scene of violent and bloody entertainment—combat to the death between armed men, between men and animals, or fighting between animals.

The city of Rome, nicknamed the Eternal City, stands as one of the most influential cities in the course of human history. Some of the most famous personalities, architectural features, and events in all of Western culture came under the influence of ancient Rome. Julius Caesar, Augustus, Nero, the Colosseum, the Forum, gladiator fights, and Christian martyrdoms are all inseparably linked to this city. Rome's rule shaped the destinies of nations and individuals as well as the course of Christendom. In light of Rome's wide-ranging significance, knowing something of its history and development is helpful.

THE BIRTH OF ROME

An ancient myth credits the founding of Rome in 753 BC to Romulus and Remus, descendants of the Trojan hero Aeneas. According to the story, these two individuals were ini-

Terra-cotta figurine of a gladiator from the first century AD.

tially nursed on the banks of the Tiber River by a she-wolf and then raised by a shepherd. Romulus later executed his brother for breaking one of the city's laws. Named for its first king, the city was called Roma.

Archaeological studies suggest that the earliest period of the region's history can be traced to the second millennium BC, when the Italian Peninsula attracted Indo-European tribes seeking a new home. Settlers were drawn to the region in part by the warm and hospitable climate. Located in the Mediterranean basin, the central region of the Italian Peninsula received abundant sunshine and favorable amounts of rain. They were also drawn by the region's geographical advantages—fertile soil, defensible hills, and the presence of the Tiberis (modern English, "Tiber") River, the third-longest river in the Italian Peninsula. The location that became Rome was considered especially desirable because it provided the best place to cross the Tiber River. Thus the site was a natural crossroads for people and goods traveling any direction throughout the Italian Peninsula.

The Umbrians, Sabines, and Samnites (or Oscans) in the area north of the Tiber River, and Latins to the south, moved into the region and displaced central Italy's original inhabitants.[1] Also immigrating into this region late in the eighth century BC were non-Indo-European tribes from Asia

According to writers of the time, the opening celebration at the Roman Colosseum lasted one hundred days; 9,000 wild beasts were slaughtered, and 2,000 gladiators fought and died. The facility was designed so the 50,000 spectators could evacuate in five minutes.

Minor known as the Etruscans. They were more culturally advanced than the Indo-European settlers and thus dominated central Italy during its earliest phase of development.[2]

The Latins receive credit for establishing a settlement on Palatine Hill close to the mouth of the Tiber River, about twenty miles from the Tyrrhenian Sea. Though precise details are lost in antiquity, historians have shown that the Latins established a series of additional settlements on the hilltops in the area of Palatine Hill. To protect themselves from the Etruscans, the Latins also established a fortress known as Roma on a nearby island in the Tiber River.[3] These separate settlements would later unite to form a single entity known as Rome. Because of their favorable location, the island fortress and the nearby hilltop villages became an important center for trade, even containing some paved roads. For a number of years, Latin kings ruled the region.

The Etruscans apparently conquered the city in the sixth century BC, resulting in the last three kings of Rome being from that civilization.[4] During the Etruscan period, Rome had many major construction projects, including the building of the great temple of Jupiter on Capitoline Hill and a temple dedicated to the goddess Diana on the Aventine Hill.[5]

Somewhere between 510 and 506 BC, an alliance of Latin settlements fought against and defeated the Etruscans.[6] Abolishing the monarchy, they established the Roman Republic. In the new system, government consisted of magistrates, called consuls, who were elected annually, and a Senate that played an advisory role to the consuls. Members of the Senate had been leading citizens from the aristocratic families in the old republic.

Over the next 200 years, the city of Rome fought an extended series of battles against various invaders and people groups within the Italian Peninsula. Following a war against the Gauls in the early fourth century BC, the Romans constructed a twenty-four-foot-high, twelve-foot-thick wall of volcanic rock around the seven hills of their city—an area of more than 1,000 acres.[7] This helped ensure that Rome would be not only the largest and most favorably situated city in the peninsula but also the best protected. The whole of Italy fell under Rome's control by 275 BC. Over time, the acquisition of provinces outside the Italian Peninsula occurred (i.e., Sicily, Macedonia), leading to an increase in the city's size and wealth.

The port city of Ostia, located downstream from Rome on the coast of the Tyrrhenian Sea at the mouth of the Tiber River, served as Rome's primary commercial port. Founded in the fourth century BC, the city also became the home of Rome's navy. As water traffic increased, Claudius (41–54 AD) built Portus, an artificial harbor about two miles north of Ostia, to handle Rome's growing maritime enterprises.[8]

ROME IN THE NEW TESTAMENT ERA

By the first century AD, Rome had become the most important city in the world. Its empire stretched from Spain to Syria and from Egypt to Germany. The wealth gained from her conquests allowed Rome to become the center of architectural magnificence. It was said of Caesar Augustus (reigned 27 BC–AD 14) that he "found Rome built of brick, and left it a city of marble."[9] Its citizens received their water via the Aqua Claudia, a forty-two-mile-long aqueduct built between AD 38 and 52, that brought water from a source near Subiaco.[10] By the first century AD, Rome had a sophisticated sewer system with several components to it, the largest of which was the Cloaca Maxima. Originally started as a drainage ditch in the sixth century BC, improvements through the centuries meant that by 33 BC the system had become an underground canal with a vaulted roof.[11]

At the beginning of the New Testament era, a series of paved roads, some of which are still used today, linked Rome to other parts of the Italian Peninsula. The most famous of these is the Appian Way, a coastal road leading to Capua, initially constructed in 312 BC. A second major artery was the Via Valeria, a military road built in 306 BC that ran eastward through the Apennine Mountains and connected Rome with the Adriatic region.[12] With these and other lesser roads, Rome had excellent land routes that permitted trade and travel in every direction.

In the first century, Rome had a number of truly remarkable and unique architectural features. The most impressive of these in Paul's day was the Circus Maximus, the greatest chariot racetrack in the empire. Though its first construction probably dates to the sixth century BC, it was modified through the centuries, especially by Julius Caesar (100–44 BC), who enlarged it to accommodate 150,000 thousand spectators and extended the track, making it 1,800 feet long and 600 feet wide. Smaller in scale but more famous was the Colosseum, a massive structure that stood 187 feet high and could hold about 50,000 people. The Colosseum was built between AD 71 and 80, a few years after the apostle Paul's death, and served as the site for gruesome gladiatorial fights that resulted in the slaughter of large numbers of people and exotic animals. Theaters—the largest of which was at Pompey and seated 27,000 spectators—were used to put on plays depicting acts of rape, cannibalism, and murder.[13]

Along with its wealth, impressive architectural features, and immorality, imperial Rome was also a center of urban filth and degradation. By the end of the first century, the city's population was estimated to be more than 1,000,000.[14] Many of these were unemployed or underemployed and had to live in dirty, poorly maintained tenement housing. Because its sewers emptied raw sewage into the Tiber, the river was heavily polluted.

Thus in many ways, Rome in the first century was a city ready for the good news of Jesus Christ.

NOTES

[1]   W. Warde Fowler, *Rome*, rev. M. P. Charlesworth, 2nd ed. (London: Oxford University Press, 1947), 14–15.

[2]   E. M. Blaiklock, "Rome" in *ZPEB*, 5:162.

[3]   Fowler, *Rome*, 18.

[4]   Fowler, *Rome*, 20.

[5]   Christopher Hibbert, *Rome: The Biography of a City* (New York: Norton, 1985), 315–16, 320.

[6]   Michael Grant, *History of Rome* (New York: Scribner's Sons, 1978), 36.

[7]   Grant, *History of Rome*, 54–55.

[8]   Tim Cornell and John Matthews, *Atlas of the Roman World* (New York: Facts on File, 1982), 92.

[9]   Blaiklock, "Rome," 164.

[10] Cornell and Matthews, *Atlas*, 91.

[11] Hibbert, *Rome*, 316.

[12] Cornell and Matthews, *Atlas*, 37.

[13] Hibbert, *Rome*, 45, 49, 50–51.

[14] Cornell and Matthews, *Atlas*, 90.

THE ROUTE OF THE EXODUS: DON'T GO BY THE WAY OF THE PHILISTINES

BY STEPHEN J. ANDREWS

Ayun Musa, which translates to the Springs (or Wells) of Moses.

Vistas of Edomite territory near Petra.

Recent archaeological and geographical research in Egypt and Sinai has begun to offer new insights that help identify some of the major stations along the journey.[1] The starting point of the exodus was Rameses, one of the supply cities the Israelites built for Pharaoh (Exod. 1:11; 12:37; Num. 33:3). Rameses is generally regarded to be the large archaeological complex at Tell el-Dab'a/Qantir.[2]

Succoth (Exod. 12:37), Etham (13:20; Num. 33:6), Pi-hahiroth (Exod. 14:2; Num. 33:7), and Migdol may refer to Egyptian forts or military installations in the Wadi Tumilat area. The Wadi Tumilat extends east from the delta region toward Lake Timsah and was a major transportation corridor in biblical times. The two largest sites in the wadi, Tell er-Rataba and Tell el-Maskhuta, have been identified with Pithom (Exod. 1:11) and Succoth, but it is uncertain which is which.

The exact location where Israel crossed the sea is unknown and still fervently debated.[3] Options for the site range from Lake Sirbonis in the north near the Mediterranean Sea to the northern edge of the Gulf of Suez.[4] Some texts identify the body of water as "the sea" (14:9,16,21; Num. 33:8); others call it *Yam Suph* or "Sea of Reeds," traditionally translated "Red Sea" in English Bibles (Exod. 13:18; 15:4; Num. 33:10).[5] Recent research suggests *Yam Suph* is near modern Lake Ballah in the Gulf of Suez.[6]

ROAD NOT TAKEN

God chose not to lead Israel along the "road to the land of the Philistines" (Exod. 13:17). This was a military transit route extending across north Sinai from the eastern Nile Delta to Gaza. The Egyptians called this road the Way of Horus. Its huge fortified headquarters was located at Tell Hebua (ancient Tjaru). Recent excavations there have revealed a massive fort on a narrow strip of land with water on two sides. This installation was designed to be an "ominous obstacle" to those arriving from the east and those leaving from the west.[7] Up to ten smaller fortified way stations protected the route and facilitated the movement of officials, troops, and merchants into and out of Canaan. Archaeologists

Wadi Gharandel, which may be the location of Elim (Exod. 15:27; 16:1).

have found storage areas for weapons, grain silos, and water reservoirs at most of the stations.[8] Large numbers of troops could easily be billeted along the route. God knew that by going this way the Israelites would lose heart and want to return to Egypt (Exod. 13:17).

THE RED SEA TO MOUNT SINAI

Following the delivery at the Red Sea, Moses led Israel into the Wilderness of Shur, possibly along a southeast direction. Their destination was the mountain (Mount Sinai) where Moses had previously met God (Exod. 3:12). Scholars debate the location of Mount Sinai and the direction taken to arrive there. Three possible major routes (northern, central, or southern), a few alternative routes, and more than a dozen candidates for Mount Sinai have been identified. The southern route along the eastern coast of the Gulf of Suez with Mount Sinai located at Jebel Musa near the lower tip of the Sinai Peninsula has traditionally been regarded as the most probable and continues to fit most of the evidence well.

Numbers 33:8–15 lists a total of eight Israelite encampments on the way to Mount Sinai. Their precise locations are unclear. Marah and Elim were associated with water. Two possible candidates for Marah are Bir el-Mura or `Ayun Musa.

Elim contained an abundance of water, shade, and food with twelve springs and seventy date palms (Exod. 15:27). Wadi Gharandel with its acacia, tamarisk, and palm trees is possibly Elim.[9] From Elim, the Israelites moved to the Wilderness of Sin, one of seven smaller wildernesses or areas that made up the Sinai Peninsula (16:1).[10] Here God provided manna and quail (16:1–14). Upon leaving, the Israelites moved to several unspecified locations (17:1).

Then the Israelites turned east near the Wadi Feiran, a rising passageway through granite terrain, and headed for Rephidim (Exod. 17:1).[11] After leaving Rephidim, Moses and the Israelites traveled through the Watiya Pass in the Wilderness of Sinai and probably encamped in the er-Raha plain "in front of the mountain" of God (19:2).[12] Jebel Musa has long been regarded as the location of Mount Sinai, but other possible candidates, Jebel Serbal, Ras Safsaf, and Jebel Katerin, are also nearby.

MOUNT SINAI TO KADESH

After a year's stay, Israel left Mount Sinai and took one of two possible paths. One option followed the route of the Wadi Nasb, which leads gently down to the western coast of the Gulf of Aqaba near modern Dahab. Traveling north along the coast, they passed a network of oases and arrived at Ezion-geber (modern Eilat). The sites of the oases may be reflected in the twenty encampments in Numbers 33:16–35. The other possible path left Mount Sinai and followed the ridgetops farther inland until the travelers came to Ezion-geber.

From Ezion-geber Moses led Israel in a northwesterly direction through the Wilderness of Paran to Kadesh-barnea in the Wilderness of Zin (Num. 20:1; 33:36). The actual location of Kadesh-barnea has been debated, but the modern consensus places it at either `Ain Qudeirat or `Ain Qadis in the northeastern Sinai Peninsula.[13] Both sites contain an oasis and are less than ten kilometers (six miles) apart. `Ain Qudeirat holds an advantage because it is located at the intersection of two major ancient roads, the route from Edom to Egypt and the road from the Red Sea to the Negev and north to Canaan. This fact may help explain the decision of the Israelites to invade Canaan by way of Arad, since Arad lay north of Kadesh-barnea on this road (Num. 14:39–45; Deut. 1:41–46).[14] From here the twelve spies were sent out (Num. 13).

KADESH TO MOAB

When Moses and the Israelites departed from Kadesh through the Wilderness of Zin, the king of Edom denied them passage through the mountains of Edom at Punon to connect with the King's Highway (Num. 20:14–17). They were required to turn south and follow the "way of the Red Sea" through the Arabah to Ezion-geber again (Deut. 2:1). From there, they moved northeast again along the fringes of the desert, bypassing Edomite and Moabite military outposts on the "road to the Wilderness of Moab" (v. 8). After they reached the Pisgah highlands, they requested permission to pass through the land of Sihon, king of the Amorites. Sihon attacked and was defeated (Num. 21:18b–30). Then Israel was able to complete its exodus and move on to the plains of Moab to begin the conquest of the promised land.

Landforms on the west coast of the Sinai.

NOTES

1   James K. Hoffmeier, *Ancient Israel in Sinai: The Evidence for the Authenticity of the Wilderness Tradition* (Oxford: Oxford University Press, 2005), 89–90. The locations for the sites in this article are based primarily on information in Barry J. Beitzel, *The Moody Atlas of the Bible* (Chicago: Moody, 2009) and Thomas V. Brisco, *Holman Bible Atlas* (Nashville: Broadman & Holman, 1998).

2   Hoffmeier, *Ancient Israel*, 53–58.

3   Hoffmeier, *Ancient Israel*, 75–109. See also Ralph L. Smith, "Red Sea" in *HIBD*, 1369–70.

4   Smith, "Red Sea," 1370.

5   Hoffmeier, *Ancient Israel*, 81–85.

6   Hoffmeier, *Ancient Israel*, 88.

7   Hoffmeier, *Ancient Israel*, 65, 93.

8   Gregory D. Mumford, "Forts, Pharonic Egypt" in *The Encyclopedia of Ancient History*, ed. Roger S. Bagnall et al. (Oxford: Blackwell, 2013), 2729.

9   Hoffmeier, *Ancient Israel*, 162–63.

10 The seven are: Shur, Etham, Sin, Sinai, Paran, Zin, and Kadesh.

11 The campsites beside the Red Sea, Dophkah, and Alush (Num. 33:11–14), are not mentioned in the Exodus account. The locations of these sites are uncertain. See Hoffmeier, *Ancient Israel*, 165–71.

12 Beitzel, *Moody Atlas*, 113.

13 Hoffmeier, *Ancient Israel*, 123–24; See also Joel F. Drinkard Jr., "Kadesh" in *HIBD*, 974–75.

14 Drinkard, "Kadesh," 974.

SAMARIA: ITS RISE AND FALL

BY GARY P. ARBINO

Countryside as seen from Ahab's capital city of Samaria.

First Kings 16 tells of King Omri founding Samaria, the new capital city of the northern kingdom of Israel. Recent analysis of data from excavations in the twentieth century has illustrated a complex early occupational history for the site.[1] Examining the archaeology and the biblical text together indicates that the site was occupied in Iron Age I (1200–1000 BC), abandoned, and then transferred to Shemer as a family estate.

The site, itself imposing, was an excellent military and commercial choice for a capital. The hill of Samaria rises to about 1,400 feet above sea level and dominates the surrounding countryside, including important trade routes, which it overlooks. Valleys surround it on three sides, making it defensible. Strategically located within the heart of the northern kingdom, Samaria controlled Israel. The one thing the site lacked was a good water supply; a stone water system was created to solve this deficiency.

Most of the excavations focusing on the Iron Age II (1000–800 BC) have centered on the acropolis, only a small portion of the city.[2] Here archaeologists have uncovered a citadel measuring about 200 by 100 yards. The citadel is an enclosure surrounded by a casemate (double) wall system. The casemate fortifications are impressive; the masonry bears a marked similarity to the highly skilled Phoenician craftsmanship from the era. Inside the citadel were a palace, storerooms, public buildings, and courtyards with rectangular pools (see 1 Kgs. 22:38). The citadel was decorated in the high style befitting an international capital. Hundreds of beautiful Syrian-style ivory fragments, depicting both local and Egyptian motifs and accented with gold foil, were found both at Samaria and at the Assyrian cities of Arslan Tash and Nimrud, where they were probably taken as spoils when Samaria was captured late in the eighth century. First Kings 22:39 and Amos 6:4 mention this lavish decoration, which had become a symbol of the nobility's utter lack of compassion for and abuse of the poor. While international connections and commerce do not necessitate religious infidelity, at Samaria they were part of the overall situation that the biblical writers chastised. Even the dishes were opulent. A beautiful and delicate high-quality red-burnished pottery is known as "Samaria ware" because archaeologists first found it in this city. Although they later found this same pottery in other cities, the finest pieces were in ancient Samaria.

The grandness of the place was, sadly, paralleled by a decline in absolute allegiance to Yahweh. Interestingly, the biblical text never says Omri participated in the worship of Baal specifically, something stated for most all later members of the dynasty (1 Kgs. 16:31; 22:53); yet his policies and treaties clearly paved the way for this to become a "legal" religion in Israel. Omri's son Ahab built a Baal temple in Samaria for his new Phoenician queen, Jezebel, who became the local patron of the religion (16:32).

Excavators recovered some sixty-three potsherds with writing on them (known as *ostraca*) from the citadel of Samaria. These record shipments of oil and wine and seem to be tax receipts. As evidenced by the types of names found on these documents, they also clearly reflect the syncretistic nature of the population of Samaria during Iron Age II: the names honored both Yahweh and Baal.

From ancient Hadatu (now Arslan Tash, Syria). After conquering Hadatu, Assyria established a new palace there and decorated the palace's Phoenician and Aramean furniture with ivories.

Phoenician ivory from Nimrud depicts two seated figures; ninth–eighth centuries BC.

Dated to the eighth century BC, one of the decorative ivories found at Samaria. The figure represented a palm tree.

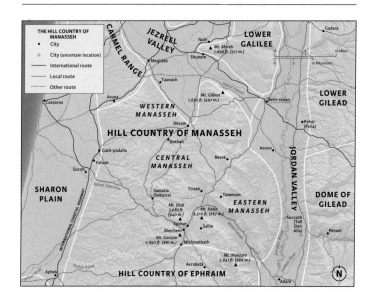

Iron Age Acropolis of Samaria

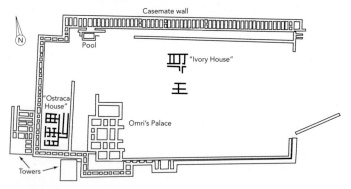

Archaeology shows that following his purge and removal of the Omride rulers, King Jehu also worked on building Samaria. He continued the cosmopolitan quality of the capital. Samaria reached its zenith during Jeroboam II's long and powerful reign (782–753 BC).

Over the course of more than a decade, Assyria chipped away at the northern kingdom, finally capturing the capital. Comparisons of the Assyrian documents and archaeological

Fortifications at Samaria.

evidence with the biblical record have resulted in ongoing debates in the academic community about the details of Assyria taking Samaria.³ What is now clear is that Samaria was not destroyed but by 720 BC was in Assyrian hands. Much of Samaria's population, especially the nobility and a contingent of the Israelite chariot corps, had been deported to other parts of the empire. In their place new peoples were moved in. The new inhabitants of Samaria worshipped both Yahweh and the gods of their homelands. The mixing of Israelite bloodlines formed the basis for the tension between those of the north, later known as Samaritans, and those from Judah, later known as Jews. This complex situation comes to full flower by the time of Jesus and is reflected in the New Testament.

NOTES

1   Ron Tappy, "Samaria" in *OEANE*, 4:463–67; Nahman Avigad, "Samaria (City)" in *NEAEHL*, 4:1300–1310.

2   See Avigad, "Samaria"; James D. Purvis, "Samaria (City)" in *ABD*, 5:914–21.

3   Ron E. Tappy, "The Final Years of Israelite Samaria: Toward a Dialogue between Texts and Archaeology," in *"Up to the Gates of Ekron": Essays on the Archaeology and History of the Eastern Mediterranean in Honor of Seymour Gitin*, ed. Sidnie White Crawford (Jerusalem: W. F. Albright Institute of Archaeological Research and Israel Exploration Society, 2007), 258–79.

SUSA IN THE DAYS OF QUEEN ESTHER

BY DANIEL C. BROWNING JR.

A glazed brick frieze representing the Persian Royal Guard, from the palace of Darius at Susa; dated to the sixth century BC.

The tomb of Cyrus the Great, which bore the following inscription: "Mortal! I am Cyrus, son of Cambyses, who founded the Persian Empire, and was Lord of Asia. Grudge me not, then, my monument."

In the middle of the sixth century BC, the Persian Empire overtook the Neo-Babylonian Empire. Shortly after coming to power, Cyrus the Great formed the Persian Empire by uniting the kingdoms of the Medes and the Persians. Cyrus took Babylon in 539 BC and in the following year issued an edict allowing the Jews to return to Jerusalem and rebuild their temple (Ezra 1:1–4).

While many Jews returned to their homeland, many did not, and so a diaspora (meaning "scattered") community of Jews continued in the area around Babylon. These Jews, now free, began to conduct commerce and settle in other cities, including those in Persia to the east of Babylonia. Primary among the Persian cities was Susa, where the story of Esther occurred in the fifth century BC.

ARCHAEOLOGY AND HISTORY

Susa (Hb. *Shushan*) is identified with the town of Shush, a collection of mounds on a natural extension of Mesopotamia into southwest Persia, modern Iran. This region, ancient Susiana, was sometimes under the control of the dominant state of southern Mesopotamia, sometimes independent, and sometimes part of the large Persian states. Susa was usually its capital.

After the British made a brief investigation of the area in 1851, the French excavated Susa almost continuously from 1884 until the Iranian revolution halted all foreign activity in 1979. Excavations revealed that Susa was occupied without major interruption from about 4200 BC until the Mongol invasions of the thirteenth century AD.[1]

Early occupation at Susa paralleled the development of civilization in neighboring Mesopotamia. Susa, sharing the Uruk culture of southern Mesopotamia in the mid-fourth millennium BC, developed sculpture, wheel-turned pottery, and an accounting convention using tokens enclosed in a clay envelope—an important step in the development of cuneiform writing. Breaking from Mesopotamia after 3200 BC, Susa produced its own still-undeciphered abstract symbols called Proto-Elamite. By 2800 BC, Susa was back in the Mesopotamian sphere as an essentially Sumerian city-state. Sargon the Great controlled Susa as part of his Semitic Empire from 2350 BC. When that empire failed early in the twenty-second century, though, the city became part of the Elamite kingdom of Awan, only to be

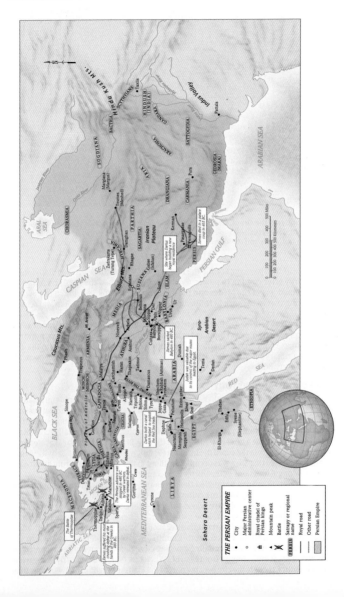

THE PERSIAN EMPIRE

• City
○ Major Persian administrative center
⚜ Royal citadel of Persian kings
▲ Mountain peak
⚔ Battle
PERSIS Satrapy or regional name

—— Royal road
—— Other road
Persian Empire

reconquered by Shulgi, a powerful Sumerian king of Ur. About 2000 BC, Elamite and Susianan invaders destroyed Ur and its empire.[2] As the Elamite civilization took shape, Susa was integrated as a major center, so that the first ruler of the Sukkalmah Dynasty (ca. 1970–1500 BC) called himself "King of Anshan and of Susa."[3]

Elam reached its cultural and political peak in the Middle Elamite period (ca. 1500–1100 BC), and Susiana became increasingly Elamite in language and religion. A new capital replaced Susa around 1500 BC, but Susa regained its prominence about 1200 BC under the Shutrukid kings. This dynasty conquered Babylon, from which they looted several iconic monuments of Mesopotamia, including the Naram-Sin stele and the stele of Hammurabi, containing his famous law code.[4] A French archaeological team discovered these iconic Mesopotamian monuments on the Susa Acropolis about 1900, near the lavishly rebuilt temple of Susa's chief god, Inshushinak.[5] This brief Shutrukid Empire collapsed about 1100 BC, and all of Elam entered a dark age with almost no written records until late in the eighth century BC.

When Elam reemerged into the light of history in 743 BC, Susa was one of three capitals of the later Neo-Elamite kings who found themselves in a struggle against Assyria, the prevailing Mesopotamian power. The Elamites were often allied with Babylon in the latter's frequent attempts to rebel from Assyrian domination. For example, Elam supported the Chaldean Merodach-baladan (Isa. 39:1) in his bids for Babylonian freedom against the Assyrian Kings Sargon II and Sennacherib. The last great Assyrian king, Ashurbanipal, effectively destroyed Elamite power and pillaged Susa in 646 BC. Ezra 4:9–10 reports that "Osnapper"—apparently Ashurbanipal—deported Elamites of Susa and settled them in the region of Samaria. Meanwhile, the plateau of Persia was consumed by the

Elamite inscription from Susa details Shilhak-Inshushinak conquering lower Babylonia. Shilhak-Inshushinak, king of Anshan and Susa (ca. 1150–1120 BC), built many monuments honoring the god of Susa.

Dating to 1250 BC, the Chogha Zanbil Ziggurat near Susa was built under the orders of Elam's King Untash-Gal for the worship of Inshushinak, the Elamite god of the afterlife.

growing Median and Persian kingdoms, and a modest Elamite kingdom was reestablished around 625 BC at Susa.

In a vision dated to about 552 BC, Daniel saw himself at Susa, at the Ulai Canal (Dan. 8:1–2,16). The vision began with a two-horned ram that surely represented the Persian Empire (also called the Achaemenid Empire). The Persian Empire was created with Cyrus the Great uniting the Medes and the Persians in 550 BC. Cyrus took Susa in 539 BC, just before his capture of Babylon that made the Persians masters of the Near East. This was the Cyrus who ended the exile of the Jews with his edict in 538 BC (Ezra 1:2–4).

IN ESTHER'S DAY

Cyrus and his son Cambyses II may have used Susa some during their reigns, but the vast majority of the Persian remains on the site date to the reigns of Darius I the Great (522–486 BC) or Artaxerxes II (404–359 BC).[6] Darius made Susa his main capital. This and the great Royal Road that built connecting Susa with Sardis brought many important foreign visitors to the city. Herodotus relates that when the cities of Ionia, Greece, rebelled against Darius and sought help from Sparta, they indicated on a map "Susa where lives the great king, and there are the storehouses of his wealth; take that city, and then you need not fear to challenge Zeus for riches."[7] The Greek geographer Strabo concurred, saying the Persians "adorned the palace at Susa more than any other."[8]

The site of ancient Susa is spread over four distinct mounds, called by the French the Acropolis, Apadana, Ville Royal, and Ville des Artisans. The Acropolis, as the name suggests, is the tallest, with stratified archaeological remains eighty-five feet deep. The earliest occupation and most of the Elamite and earlier finds were discovered there, including the Hammurabi Code stele and other looted Mesopotamian treasures.[9] North of the Acropolis, Darius I created the Apadana mound (and effectively reshaped the whole city) by constructing a huge thirty-two-acre gravel platform on which he built a palace. The palace consisted of residential quarters in the south with an official government center and audience hall—an apadana—to the north.[10]

Archaeologists discovered a foundation inscription written in three languages in which Darius I described building the palace by using materials and workmen from throughout his vast empire. This impressive complex is the setting for the story of Esther during the reign of Darius's successor, Xerxes I (referred to by his Hebrew name Ahasuerus in the Bible). After his ill-fated military campaign against Greece (highlighted by the battle of Thermopylae, the sack of Athens, and culminating in defeats at Salamis and Plataeai, 480–479 BC), Xerxes retired to Susa.

A monumental gateway discovered in the 1970s east of the palace complex contains inscriptions of Xerxes, attributing its construction to Darius. The inscription implies Xerxes continued to use the complex. As the gateway is the only known access to the palace, it is tempting to associate it with the "King's Gate" where Esther's kinsman Mordecai sat (Esth. 2:19,21; 5:9,13; 6:10). The residential quarters would correspond to the "palace" in the story (5:1). Within outer walls, this structure had a series of inner courtyards aligned east to west. The first of these served as an entrance courtyard and may be the "outer court of the palace" of Esther 6:4. The third courtyard gives access to what appear to be the royal apartments and may thus be the "inner courtyard" where a nervous Esther made her uninvited approach to the king (4:11; 5:1).[11]

The audience hall was hypostyle—filled with six rows of six columns each. More columns filled three porticos on the west, north, and east sides. The columns themselves featured fluted shafts on square bases, topped with capitals in the form of two bull torsos facing in opposite directions. They rose sixty-five feet, an achievement unparalleled in the ancient world. The entire palace, residence, and apadana were decorated exclusively with glazed brickwork depicting mythical animals and figures of the immortals, the elite guard troops of the king.[12]

The royal parts of the city, consisting of the Acropolis, Apadana, and Ville Royal mounds, were enclosed in an impressive city wall. A canal diverted from the Chaour River on the west ran along the north and east sides of the royal enclosure, separating it from the unfortified lower city to the east, represented by the fourth mound, the Ville des Artisans. These distinct parts of the city may be reflected in the text of Esther, where "the fortress of Susa" (9:6,11,12) can refer to the royal walled section, while "Susa" without further qualification (vv. 13–15) may indicate the lower city.[13]

LATER SUSA

Susa's importance as a capital ended with the conquests of Alexander the Great, although the city continued to exist and prosper under Hellenistic, Parthian, Sassanian, and Islamic rule. It was finally abandoned in the thirteenth century AD. Nevertheless, Susa has been and remains a site of pilgrimage for Jews, Christians, Muslims, and Mandeans who venerate a medieval structure now enclosed in a mosque as the tomb of the prophet Daniel. While the Tomb of Daniel has been known from at least the seventh century AD,[14] Susa has no shrine that is associated with Queen Esther.

NOTES

1 Holly Pittman, "Susa," in *OEANE*, 5:106–7.
2 Pierre de Miroschedji, "Susa" in *ABD*, 6:243.
3 François Vallat, "Elam (Place)" in *ABD*, 2:424–25.
4 Pittman, "Susa," 109.
5 Miroschedji, "Susa," 243.
6 Pittman, "Susa," 109.
7 Herodotus, *Histories* 5.49.
8 Strabo, *Geography* 15.3.
9 Edwin M. Yamauchi, *Persia and the Bible* (Grand Rapids: Baker, 1990), 282–85.
10 Pittman, "Susa," 109.
11 Miroschedji, "Susa," 244.
12 Roman Ghirshman, *Persia: From the Origins to Alexander the Great*, trans. Stuart Gilbert and James Emmons (London: Thames & Hudson, 1964), 138–42.
13 Miroschedji, "Susa," 244.
14 Sylvia A. Matheson, *Persia: An Archaeological Guide* (Park Ridge, NJ: Noyes, 1973), 150.

THE TEMPLES AT CORINTH

BY MARK A. RATHEL

In the distance are the seven standing columns of the temple of Apollo, one of the most prominent landmarks of Corinth. The columns rise about twenty-four feet high and are about six feet in diameter. In the foreground are the ruins of the western shops.

If Paul entered the city of Corinth on the main road from the north (the graveled Lechaion Road), he would have encountered the temple of Asclepius, the god of healing. Asclepius's origin is unknown. Later Greek religions regarded him as the son of Apollos and the recipient of training in the healing arts by the Centaur Chiron. Inside the temple was a pit for nonpoisonous snakes. Asclepius's symbol, a snake wound around a staff, has been used in modern times as a symbol for the medical profession. The temple of Asclepius functioned like a sanatorium with a dormitory in which patients slept, a well for purification, and a facility for the regimentation of diet and exercise. Often the one looking for healing made a votive terra-cotta offering of the diseased body part. At the Asclepius temple in Corinth, archaeologists have discovered replicas of hands, feet, eyes, and other body parts. The temple also contained three large dining rooms for hosting ritual feasts in the god's honor.

Continuing from the north entrance to the center of the city, Paul would have encountered the impressive edifice of the temple of Apollo. The temple originally contained thirty-eight large columns; the seven surviving columns measure twenty-four feet in height by six feet in diameter. Apollo was associated with music, archery, prophecy, flocks, herds, law, and civilization.

Farther south, Paul would have passed through a Roman arch and entered the Corinthian marketplace. In this business-government district, Paul would have viewed temples dedicated to major and minor pagan deities. The Romans built the majority of the temples in the marketplace during the reigns of the emperors Augustus, Tiberius, and Claudius; thus the temples would have been of recent origin in Paul's day. In the marketplace, Paul would have seen temples to Poseidon, Heracles, Hermes, Aphrodite, and Athena.

The marketplace at Corinth also contained a temple of Octavia, the sister of the first Roman emperor, Augustus. Corinth, like most cities in the empire, contained in the center of town various temples that honored the emperor or his family. The first emperor and his sister were thought to be descendants of Venus, the Roman goddess equivalent to Aphrodite.

From the marketplace, Paul could have followed a winding trail leading up the Acrocorinth, the 1,886-foot-high mountain that formed the base of old Corinth. If Paul continued his journey south toward the Acrocorinth, he passed ten more temples, including temples to Isis, Demeter, and another to Aphrodite.

Isis was the Egyptian goddess of the sea, fertility, agriculture, and the afterlife. Devotees of Isis proclaimed her to be the ruler over all things. The rituals involved a celebration of the resurrection of Isis's husband, Osiris, from death. The immoralities of the rituals of Isis shocked the tolerant Romans who attempted to suppress the religion.[1]

Archaeologists discovered a temple to Demeter, the goddess of grain, on top of the Acrocorinth. Originally the temple contained fifty dining halls. The myth of Demeter explained the agricultural cycle, a type of annual rebirth, in ancient Greek religion. The agricultural religions invariably involved sexual activity.

Corinth gained fame because of its temples of Aphrodite, the goddess of love, beauty, and fertility. The Greeks associated Aphrodite with the Canaanite fertility goddess Astarte, the female consort of Baal, the worship of whom Old Testament prophets such as Elijah strongly condemned.

Head of a cult statue of Isis. The surface of the face is polished; the hair is colored and may have been gilded. Dated after AD 138; from Thessalonica.

Bust of Aphrodite. Her temple was on the Acrocorinth and overlooked the city.

NOTES

[1]   Everett Ferguson, *Backgrounds of Early Christianity*, 2nd ed. (Grand Rapids: Eerdmans, 1992), 252.

UR: THE "CAPITAL OF THE WORLD"

BY SCOTT HUMMEL

Local Arab tradition holds that Abraham was not from Ur of ancient Mesopotamia but from Sanliurfa, which was just north of Haran. Shown is the Shrine of Abraham at Sanliurfa.

Aerial views of the Euphrates River. Abram followed the river when he headed north out of Ur.

Abram, who would later be known as Abraham, set out from Ur with his entire family.[1] Abram's family was wealthy and included hundreds of servants. Abram headed north along the Euphrates for about a thousand miles until he reached the city of Haran in northern Mesopotamia. Abram's father, Terah, and brother, Nahor, decided to settle in Haran, but Abram obediently answered God's call to leave his country and family to continue to the promised land (Gen. 11:31).

The Sumerian civilization at Ur was already ancient by the time of Abram. In fact, the first great civilization in the world was drawing to a close as Abram made his great journey to Canaan.[2] Ur was established about 5000–4000 BC and grew into one of the most important and leading Sumerian cities. Sumer was composed of several, often competing, city-states in southern Mesopotamia. The Sumerians were incredibly inventive and industrious; they invented the wheel, irrigated the desert, built walled cities, and were probably the first to invent writing. Their sixty-based counting system survives today in the measurements of time with sixty minutes in an hour and in the measurements of degrees in a circle.

Ur was an impressive city for its time, rising sixty feet above the plain and covering about 150 acres. In ancient times, the Euphrates River actually flowed through the city of Ur, and the shoreline of the Persian Gulf came farther north than it does today, much closer to the city. Ur was surrounded by massive walls, which were more than seventy-five feet thick at the base and extended about two miles in circumference. Within the walls stood hundreds of homes, reflecting all levels of society from mansions to hovels. The typical homes were two-storied, brick with wood framing, and included a central open courtyard. Thousands of recovered business documents testify to the dynamic economy and far-reaching trade of Ur.

Archaeologist C. L. Woolley's discovery of royal tombs at Ur in the 1920s further demonstrated the wealth, artistic quality, and religious beliefs of the city around 2500 BC, over 500 years before Abram's birth.[3] While southern Mesopotamia lacked natural resources, political power and trade along the Euphrates River and the Persian Gulf generated the wealth found in the tombs. Extensive irrigation supported flocks and fields of crops, producing a surplus economy. As a result, the royal tombs have produced some of the richest finds in the history of archaeology and demonstrate a remarkably high level of craftsmanship, especially with metalworking. Even though human sacrifice was extremely rare in Mesopotamia, some of the tombs contain the remains of numerous servants who had been ritually killed so they could serve the king in the afterlife.

After centuries of Sumerian domination and prosperity, the Akkadians rose to power about 2350 BC in central Mesopotamia. The Akkadian Empire lasted for nearly 150 years. The Akkadian king Sargon the Great established the world's first empire by controlling all of Mesopotamia from Ur on the Persian Gulf to the Mediterranean Sea. Even though he controlled Sumerian cities politically and militarily, Sargon and later Akkadian kings adopted much of Sumerian culture and religion. Sargon placed Enheduanna, his daughter, as the high priestess of Nanna, the moon god and patron deity of Ur. This established a tradition that lasted nearly 2,000 years.

The whole region fell into a dark age for nearly a century when the Akkadians fell to the Gutian tribes from the east. At the end of this Gutian period, Ur-Nammu, founder of the Third Dynasty of Ur, came to power and restored Sumerian glory and culture. An able general and administrator, Ur-Nammu conquered most of Mesopotamia and then established one of the most prosperous periods in Sumerian history. He expanded international trade, rebuilt temples, repaired irrigation canals, and built numerous ziggurats throughout Mesopotamia. Ur-Nammu even wrote the earliest-known law code. His greatest building achievement was the Great Ziggurat in Ur, which was a huge stepped platform originally rising more than seventy feet high and measuring 200 by 170 feet at its base. A temple stood at the top. The Sumerians viewed the ziggurat as a mountain where the god came down to dwell. The zig-

The ziggurat at Ur, discovered by archaeologist Leonard Woolley in the 1920s, measures approximately 200 by 170 feet at the base. Three levels tall, the inner core is mud brick while the outer shell, which is eight feet thick, is baked brick. At the top was a temple to Nanna, the moon god.

This twenty-four-room house at Ur was reconstructed in the 1990s and dubbed "Abraham's House."

gurat was built of a solid core of unbaked bricks surrounded by a skin of baked bricks set with bitumen. The description of the tower of Babylon in the Plain of Shinar (Sumer) in Genesis 11 sounds remarkably similar to the structure of the ziggurat.

Ur's last Sumerian kings tried to hold on to power by slowing the migrations of Amorites into the region and by fortifying Ur, but crop failures, hostility with other Sumerian cities, and the invading Elamites from the east brought the collapse of Ur as a great world power.

Every year for centuries the priests in Ur, recalling the glory days of the past, recited the "Lamentation over the Destruction of Ur," which included these words:

> Ur, my innocent lamb, has been slaughtered. Its good shepherd is gone. . . . Woe!
> The city and temple are destroyed. O, Nanna, the sanctuary of Ur is destroyed, its people dead.[4]

These words of lament were among the thousands of documents archaeologists uncovered in the city of Ur.

The collapse of the Third Dynasty of Ur in 2004 BC struck Sumerian civilization a mortal blow. Only the Sumerian cities of Isin and Larsa lingered a little longer, but the Amorites, a Semitic people, eventually overwhelmed them as well. Sumerian political control was lost forever and the Sumerian language ceased to be used. Various Amorite dynasties gained control of all the Mesopotamian cities. The most famous of these Amorite kings was Hammurabi of Babylon. During this time of transition and migrations, Abram left Ur for the promised land.

UR'S RELIGIOUS IMPORTANCE

In the centuries that followed, the city of Ur remained an important religious and economic center, but its political power was lost. Many nations would later rule over Ur, but each recognized the religious importance of Ur as the center of worship of the moon god, known as Nanna or Sin. When the Persian king Cyrus the Great conquered Babylon in 539

BC, he boasted that "Sin the Nannar [the Semitic and Sumerian names of Ur's chief deity, the moon god] . . . of heaven and earth, with his favorable omen delivered into my hands the four quarters of the world. I returned the gods to their shrines."[5]

This boast was discovered in excavations at Ur and echoes Cyrus's edict to the Jewish exiles in Ezra 1:2: "The LORD, the God of the heavens, has given me all the kingdoms of the earth and has appointed me to build him a house at Jerusalem in Judah."

The Sumerians worshipped hundreds of gods, but each city had a chief deity that represented the city in the divine council. The ancient literature describes the gods behaving much like emotional, petty, political people with great powers. The moon god, Nanna, had power over the night and monthly cycles and was able to see into the dark future.[6] The people of Ur understood it to be their duty to serve and feed the gods through sacrifices and to avoid angering the often abusive gods. They hoped their service resulted in prosperity and the beneficial power of the gods. Since Abram's father worshipped many gods (Josh. 24:2), he likely worshipped Nanna, who was also the patron deity of the city of Haran where his family settled after leaving Ur.[7] Abram's spiritual journey from idolatry to the worship of the one true God was a much greater journey than the physical journey from Ur to the promised land.

Although Ur began small, it grew to a magnificent city. However, after the collapse of the Third Dynasty of Ur, the city never rebounded to its former glory. Instead, for generations the city continued to exist as a mere shell of its former self. After about 4,500 years of occupation, however, Ur finally did die a quick death—when the Euphrates River changed its course. Without access to the river and with the coast ever farther away, Ur was abandoned and its ruins covered in sand. The great and glorious Sumerian city that seemingly had once been "capital of the world" was no more.

NOTES

[1] Biblical scholars contest the location of Abram's Ur. Ancient documents mention several cities by the name of Ur or something similar such as Ure, Uri, and Ura. According to Islamic tradition, Urfa, which is only about twenty miles from Haran, is Abram's Ur. See Cyrus H. Gordon, "Recovering Canaan and Ancient Israel," in *Civilizations of the Ancient Near East (CANE)*, ed. Jack M. Sasson (Peabody, MA: Hendrickson, 1995, 2006), 3–4:2784. However, Alan R. Millard, "Where Was Abraham's Ur? The Case for the Babylonian City," *Biblical Archaeological Review (BAR)* 27.3 (2001): 52–53, 57), and H. W. F. Saggs, "Ur of the Chaldees: A Problem of Identification," *Iraq* 22 (1960): 200–9, both effectively argued for identifying Abram's Ur with Tell el-Muqayyar in southern Mesopotamia.

[2] For good summaries of Sumerian civilization and history, see William W. Hallo and William Kelly Simpson, *The Ancient Near East: A History*, 2nd ed. (Fort Worth, TX: Harcourt Brace, 1998); Harriet Crawford, *Sumer and the Sumerians* (Cambridge: Cambridge University Press, 1991); and Samuel Noel Kramer, *The Sumerians: Their History, Culture, and Character* (Chicago: University of Chicago Press, 1963).

[3] Woolley discovered more than 1,800 tombs, sixteen of which stood out for their wealth and royalty. These tombs date from 2600 to 2400 BC. Cf. C. L. Woolley, *Ur of the Chaldees: A Record of Seven Years of Excavation* (New York: Norton, 1965), 33–89; and Shirley Glubok, ed., *Discovering the Royal Tombs at Ur* (London: Macmillan, 1969), 8; M. J. Selman, "Ur," in *Major Cities of the Biblical World*, ed. R. K. Harrison (Nashville: Thomas Nelson, 1985), 279.

[4] "Laments for Ur" in Victor H. Matthews and Don C. Benjamin, *Old Testaments Parallels: Laws and Stories from the Ancient Near East*, 2nd ed. (New York: Paulist, 1997), 237.

[5] C. J. Gadd and Leon Legrain, *Ur Excavations, Texts, I: Royal Inscriptions* (London: Trustees of the Two Museums, 1928), 307 (p. 96). See also Selman, "Ur."

[6] Alfred J. Hoerth, *Archeology in the Old Testament* (Grand Rapids: Baker, 1998), 66–67.

[7] William Osborne, "Ur" in *Dictionary of the Old Testament: Pentateuch*, ed. T. Desmond Alexander and David W. Baker (Downers Grove, IL: InterVarsity, 2003), 875.

VALLEYS AND PASTURES: A GEOGRAPHICAL OVERVIEW OF ANCIENT ISRAEL

BY R. DENNIS COLE

Crusader ruins at Acco in northern Israel. During the time of the conquest, Acco was tribal territory allotted to Asher. Yet "Asher failed to drive out the residents of Acco" and some other cities (Judg. 1:31).

Overlooking the Aijalon Valley from the ruins at Gezer. On the right-center of the image are the remains of a Canaanite tower. It joins a wall, under the footbridge; dated to the time of the patriarchs.

The land contained within the classical borders from Dan to Beer-sheba and from the Mediterranean Sea to the Jordan River is a relatively small territory that covers an area of fewer than 7,500 square miles. This land of great theological importance is just a little bigger than the state of New Jersey and much smaller than the great powers that surrounded it. Agriculturally only about 20 percent of Israel is arable land; about half is semiarid to arid.[1] Much of the most-arid land is rocky and hilly. The arable farmlands are located primarily along the coastal plains and the inland valleys—farmlands that were and are some of the most productive in the world. The descriptive phrase of Israel as the "least of the nations" (Deut. 7:7, writer's translation) applied to its population, territory, and military might; Israel's strength, power, and source of blessing was God and his faithful love for his people.

LAND OF CONTRASTS

The territory of ancient Israel was positioned in the southern half of the land bridge that connected Africa and Asia, and between the regions of the ancient empires of Egypt to the southwest, the Hittites to the north, and the Assyrians and Babylonians to the east and northeast. The terrain to ancient Israel ranges from the tree-covered mountainous northern highlands of upper Galilee, Mount Carmel, and the Golan Heights to the barren rocky wilderness areas of the Dead Sea, Negev, and Arabah in the south. Along the Mediterranean coastal plains of Philistia, Sharon, and Acco are rolling sand dunes and lush farmlands occasionally cut by small streams such as the Lachish, Sorek, Yarkon, and Kishon. Most of these streams begin in the mountains of Judah, Samaria, and Galilee, bringing replenishing soils and nutrients to the valleys from the foothills (biblical Shephelah) to the inland coastal plains.

Israel's climate likewise is a study of contrasts from the well-watered regions of the north and west to the parched and rocky desert areas of the Dead Sea and the Negev. With a latitude parallel to the southern USA (Savannah, Georgia = Tel Aviv), the temperatures reflect these variations with summer highs ranging from the upper 80s and low 90s in the coastal north-west around Acco, to the 110 to 120-degree range around the Dead Sea and the southern Negev. Rainfall variations also reflect the changing terrain, with extremely low annual amounts in the lower Negev and Dead Sea regions (less than three inches); the northern areas around Dan and Metulla receive up to forty inches. Most of the rainfall comes from November through April.

At the heart of the land's geological makeup is its limestone core of various hardness levels ranging from the strikingly hard chert and flint to the softer chalky limestone. The cavernous areas in the heart of the Judean, Samarian, and Galilean mountains contain large underground aquifers, which intermittently erupt into springs along the perimeters of the various valleys, even in the more deserted areas of the Dead Sea and Negev. Examples of these springs (names beginning with En- or Ein- both translate as "spring" or "spring of") include such famous regions as En-gedi (where David hid from Saul), to En-harod ("the spring of Harod," where God directed Gideon to choose his army), to Ein-feshkha (near Qumran at the Dead Sea).

LONGITUDINAL ZONES

Israel's geography and its environs divide into six distinctive longitudinal (north-south) zones, with one major diagonal valley, the Jezreel Valley, which separates the Galilee region in the north from the hills of Samaria. First, in the west, is the coastal plain along the Mediterranean Sea. The coastal plain consists of some sand dunes along the shorelines and rich farmlands inland. Elevations extend upward to 300 feet or more. Traditionally this zone has been divided into three major sections: (1) the Acco plain in the north extending from the Lebanon border to the Mount Carmel ridge, which extends almost to the Mediterranean; (2) the Sharon plain, extending from Mount Carmel to the Yarkon

Fields and cropland in northern Israel near Mount Hermon.

River, near modern Tel Aviv; and (3) the Philistine plain, extending from the Yarkon south-ward to the northeast Sinai. The coastal plains' farmlands extend inland as little as two miles near Mount Carmel to as much as thirty miles in the southern Philistine plain. Flowing through these coastal plains are the rivers and streams such as the Sorek, Lachish, and Hadera, which typically have their origins in the hill country.

The second zone is the Shephelah, a term that describes the "foothills" or "lowlands" between the coastal plain and the mountains of Judah. This distinctive geological zone, with elevations reaching a thousand feet, is cut by several valleys. The valleys provided the strategic buffer between the Philistines and the tribes of Judah and Simeon. Cities such as Gezer in the Aijalon Valley, Timnah and Beth-shemesh in the Sorek Valley, Azekah and Shaaraim in the Elah Valley, and Lachish in the Lachish Valley, were often fortified for the protection of Judah's heartland, namely Jerusalem, Hebron, and other major cities.

East of the Shephelah, the third north-south zone is the central hill country, a ridge of mountains extending from north of Beer-sheba, in the south, to Mount Carmel and Mount Gilboa overlooking the Jezreel Valley. Elevations around Hebron and Mounts Ebal and Gerizim reach 3,000 feet or more. North of the Jezreel Valley are the mountains of upper and lower Galilee, with elevations in upper Galilee reaching almost 4,000 feet at Mount Merom. These mountain highlands form the watershed for the "early" (late October–December) and "late" (January–March) rains the Bible describes.

Deep beneath the surface in the honey-combed limestone of the mountains are huge natural aquifers, which erupt into springs along the flanks of the valleys and flow through the Shephelah and into the coastal plains. The rich farmlands of the valleys such as the Sorek functioned as the "breadbasket" for the kingdom of Judah in the Old Testament era. Capital cities such as Jerusalem of Judah and Samaria in the north were located strategically in the central mountains. The pasturage and still waters described in Psalm 23 would be typically located in these hills and the valleys of the Shephelah. Rainfall amounts here were at their peak for growing grasses and other forage plants, and here springs would puddle, providing still waters for the timid sheep.

Looking westward from atop the ruins of Jericho. Beyond the greenery is the Jordan Valley.

East of the peak in the central mountains was the fourth zone, the wilderness of Judah and Samaria. Here the rainfall amounts drop off dramatically as one heads eastward toward the deep geological rift of the Jordan Valley, our fifth longitudinal zone. Average annual rainfall in Jerusalem is around twenty-five inches. Fifteen miles east in Jericho, this drops to about five inches or less. Near the southern end of the Dead Sea, the amount is two inches or less. The arid nature of the wilderness and valley zones decrease as one heads northward up the Jordan Valley from the Dead Sea. The Jordan Valley is part of one of the deepest geological rifts in the earth's surface, reaching 1,380 feet below mean sea level today. Due to heavy use of freshwater irrigation by persons on both sides of the Jordan, the level of the Dead Sea has been dropping steadily, about one hundred feet in the past fifty years.[2] The desert valley south of the Dead Sea, the Arabah, gradually rises to more than one thousand feet above sea level before descending to the Red Sea finger of the Gulf of Aqaba (Eilat). West of the Arabah is the Negev ("southern") region, which extends south of the Beer-sheba Valley and into the Sinai.

East of the Jordan Valley is the sixth zone, the Transjordan (or Eastern) Plateau, with elevations reaching to around 4,000 feet, bounded on the north by Mount Hermon (elev. ca 9,100 feet) and reaching southward through what was ancient Edom. The aquifers of Mount Hermon, which erupt into numerous springs such as those at Caesarea Philippi, Dan, and Ijon, form the upper Jordan River in the Huleh Basin. From Mount Hermon and through the Golan Heights region east of the Huleh Basin are the volcanically enriched soils that provided lush farming opportunities throughout ancient and into modern times. South of the Golan, which is separated from Gilead by the Yarmuk River, are the rich soils and mountain highlands of the ancient territories of the Ammonites and Moabites; to the south are the more desertlike regions of the Edomites.

NOTES

[1] *Israel's Agriculture* (Tel Aviv: Israel Export & International Cooperation Institute, n.d.), 8.

[2] Stephanie Pappas, "Could the Dead Sea Completely Vanish?" *LiveScience*, December 6, 2011, www.livescience.com/17324-dead-sea-completely-vanish.html.

WATERFALLS AND WADIS: WATER IMAGERY IN THE PSALMS

BY R. KELVIN MOORE

The Banias Waterfall and River. This fall is fed by water from the spring near the Cave of Pan. It is a major source for the Jordan River.

The Jabbok River, in the region of Gilead, flows westward into the Jordan River.

God's people needed no one to remind them of their dependence on water. The Hebrews lived in an agrarian society. Two distinct climatic factors characterized the promised land: drought and dryness.¹ The Hebrews lived in a constant threat of drought. Water and the deficiency of water each portrayed dramatic, understandable, and meaningful images for the Hebrews.

Israel received rain in only two periods of the year. The early rains fall in October and November, the latter rains in February and March. During these two rainy seasons, previously dry riverbeds (wadis) could suddenly become swollen in heavy downpours. The potential flood could have been disconcerting. David comforted himself with a reminder that God led him beside quiet waters.

Because rain of any significance rarely fell outside of the two rainy seasons, drought was a dangerous reality in Israel. The writer of Psalm 42:1–2 understood a lack of water: "As a deer longs for flowing streams, so I long for you, God. I thirst for God, the living God." Because they knew about drought, the original hearers of Psalm 42 would have understood the fear and panic the deer experienced. Modern readers can visualize an unfortunate animal, in Psalm 42 a deer, frantically searching for water during a drought. The animal sought water because its life depended on finding it.

The only mention of waterfalls in Scripture is in this same psalm (42:7). Rather than telling of refreshment and enjoyment, the psalmist described raging torrents of despair that had overwhelmed him.

Psalm 98 records another image of water. Maybe during a rainy season the writer observed the Jordan River, white-capped with rushing water. To the psalmist, the crashing waters, rising and falling, may have mimicked hands clapping together.

The Jordan waters rushing would have been a common sight for the psalmist. The Hebrew word for *Jordan* means "the descender," a reflection of the river's significant drop. Beginning at 200 feet above sea level at Mount Hermon, the water drops to more than 1,300 feet below sea level at its terminus, the Dead Sea. For those in the promised land, the Jordan is indeed the descender.

People living in areas of abundant annual rainfall, areas where droughts are rare, may have difficulty appreciating the imagery of water throughout the book of Psalms (and Scripture). But the metaphor created a powerful, unmistakable image for the Old Testament Hebrews.

NOTES

1   "Rain" in *Dictionary of Biblical Imagery*, ed. Leland Ryken, James C. Wilhoit, Tremper Longman III (Downers Grove, IL: InterVarsity, 1998), 694.

ZERUBBABEL'S TEMPLE

BY CONN DAVIS

The pinnacle of the temple at Jerusalem as seen from the southwest across the Kidron Valley. The marked change in the style of stonework along this vertical line clearly shows the smooth, precisely cut stones of Herod's extension to the temple platform on the southwest. The rougher, more pronounced stones along the wall to the north most likely are stones dating to Solomon's time that were reset by Zerubbabel after the Israelites' return from exile. This corner is called Zerubbabel's Marking.

ISRAEL'S FIRST TEMPLE

King Solomon completed the first temple for worship in ancient Israel about 960 BC. He established the temple when the monarchy and the nation were united and mighty. Solomon's construction was remarkable for the thousands of workers involved in seven years of building activity. The temple was not only the national worship center but also served as the most visible symbol of divine blessings upon the government.

The temple remained central to Jewish worship, even into the time of the divided monarchy. Worship in this first temple was inconsistent, though. Some kings refused to reverence the Lord.

This magnificent and luxurious temple existed for nearly four centuries until the Babylonian destruction of 586 BC. Nebuchadnezzar and his army burned this temple to the ground and took all the precious metal vessels and contents to Babylonia.

Forty-seven years later, the Persian Empire replaced Babylonia as the dominant world power in 539 BC. The Persians, much like the Greeks and Romans after them, governed with benevolent style. They instituted progressive reforms such as local provincial rule, paved roads, postal service, and coinage. Cyrus II, the first Persian king, issued a famous proclamation, which was recorded in cuneiform on the Cyrus Cylinder.[1] This edict allowed the return of the Jews from exile to Jerusalem to rebuild their temple (2 Chr. 36:22–23; Ezra 1:1–4). A second proclamation (520 BC), this one by Darius the Great, confirmed and sustained the initial decree of Cyrus. Moreover, Darius commanded Persian political officials in the province to support the rebuilding efforts of the temple (Ezra 6).

ISRAEL'S SECOND TEMPLE

Because of Zerubbabel's leadership role in the reconstruction project (Hag. 1:14), this second house of worship came to be called Zerubbabel's temple. It required four years to complete. The project had the unusual support of the Persian rulers plus two prominent Old Testament prophets, Haggai and Zechariah.

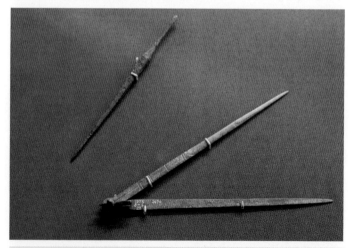

Bronze tools masons and stone carvers used, dating from as far back as the Late Bronze Age. Shown are a stylus for marking the surface and a divider.

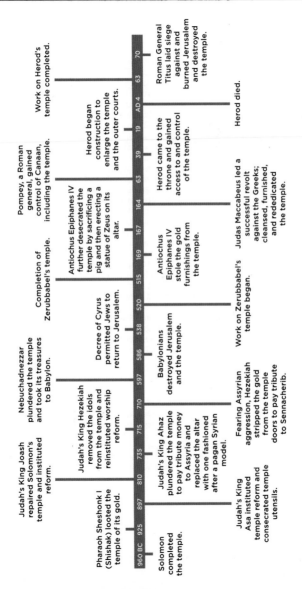

Pharaoh Sheshonk I (Shishak) looted the temple of its gold.

Judah's King Joash repaired Solomon's temple and instituted reform.

Judah's King Hezekiah removed the idols from the temple and reinstituted worship reform.

Nebuchadnezzar plundered the temple and took its treasures to Babylon.

Completion of Zerubbabel's temple.

Antiochus Epiphanes IV further desecrated the temple by sacrificing a pig and then erecting a statue of Zeus on its altar.

Pompey, a Roman general, gained control of Canaan, including the temple.

Work on Herod's temple completed.

Roman General Titus laid siege against and burned Jerusalem and destroyed the temple.

Decree of Cyrus permitted Jews to return to Jerusalem.

Herod began construction to enlarge the temple and the outer courts.

Solomon completed the temple.

Judah's King Asa instituted temple reform and consecrated temple utensils.

Judah's King Ahaz plundered the temple to pay tribute money to Assyria and replaced the altar with one fashioned after a pagan Syrian model.

Fearing Assyrian aggression, Hezekiah stripped the gold from the temple doors to pay tribute to Sennacherib.

Babylonians destroyed Jerusalem and the temple.

Work on Zerubbabel's temple began.

Antiochus Epiphanes IV stole the gold furnishings from the temple.

Judas Maccabeus led a successful revolt against the Greeks; cleansed, furnished, and rededicated the temple.

Herod came to the throne and gained access to and control of the temple.

Herod died.

960 BC 925 897 810 735 715 710 597 586 538 520 515 169 167 164 63 39 19 AD 4 63 70

The return of almost 50,000 Jews (Ezra 2:64–65) marked the first time in recorded history that a conquered people had survived captivity and the loss of their homeland.[2] With unprecedented legal, financial, and moral support from Persian leaders, the Jews began to renew themselves in nation building.

The material wealth and economic prosperity of Solomon's golden age were replaced by severe economic and social conditions after the 586 BC destruction of Jerusalem. This affected the building project. The second temple lacked the impressive quality and grandeur of the first. Nevertheless, masons and carpenters used large cuts of limestone rock and cedar wood to complete their task (6:4). The stonemasons relied on hammers and wooden pegs to break the rocks from quarries. They made individual building stones using picks.[3] When the cut stones and cedar lumber were ready, skilled laborers from the Levites, including the clans of Jeshua, Kadmiel, Judah, and Henadad (3:9), rebuilt the new temple. Using Levites for this task was not without precedent. The Levites had historically been responsible for the operation and maintenance of the temple. From the time of David and Solomon, a large group of Levites had been assigned to temple construction.

Although not as impressive as Solomon's temple, Zerubbabel's temple was not void of splendor. Greek and Roman contacts and references provide historical evidence that the second temple was well constructed and rich in its contents.[4] Cyrus authorized the release of all the gold and silver vessels Nebuchadnezzar had stolen. Thus the returning Jews brought with them to Jerusalem and to the temple more than 5,000 precious metal vessels, including chests, bowls, lampstands, and knives (1:9–11).

Zerubbabel's temple followed the basic rectangular design of Solomon's temple with three areas: the vestibule and entrance, the holy area or sanctuary, and the most holy place where the ark resided. The first and second temples essentially had the same interior dimensions: sixty cubits long by thirty cubits high by twenty cubits wide, approximately one hundred by fifty by thirty-five feet. Without the existence of the ark, the symbol of the dwelling presence of God, worship focus shifted to the large sanctuary area, the holy area, known in Hebrew as the *heikal*.

In 515 BC—seventy years after the destruction of Solomon's temple—the Jews completed in Jerusalem a new temple. The restored nation of Jews had their worship center. Their faith and devotion to the God of their covenant were rekindled. Zerubbabel's temple endured for almost 500 years until Herod the Great rebuilt it as the third temple in 19 BC.

NOTES

1   Jack Finegan, *Light from the Ancient Past: The Archaeological Background of the Hebrew-Christian Religion*, 2nd ed. (Princeton: Princeton University Press, 1959), 218, fig. 86. For a translation of the Cyrus Cylinder text, see *ANET*, 315–16.

2   *A Historical Atlas of the Jewish People*, ed. Eli Barnavi (New York: Alfred Knopf, 1992), 28.

3   *Nelson's New Illustrated Bible Dictionary*, ed. Ronald Youngblood (Nashville: Thomas Nelson, 1995), 921.

4   Roland de Vaux, *Ancient Israel* (New York: McGraw-Hill, 1965), 324–25.

ZION AS A PLACE AND A SYMBOL

BY ROBERT C. DUNSTON

Village of Silwan (ancient Siloam) near the old city of David.

LOCATION AND IMPORTANCE

Between the Kidron Valley and the Tyropoean Valley in Jerusalem lies a plateau shaped like an elongated triangle. The Gihon spring lies on the plateau's eastern side. The plateau's steep slope and the close supply of fresh water provided a good location for a settlement and a fortress. Realizing the good location, the Jebusites constructed on the plateau a fortress they called Zion.[1]

Bible scholars have offered several suggestions for the derivation of the name *Zion*. Some believe the name comes from a Hebrew word meaning "to be dry." Zion would then refer to the relative dryness of the area despite its proximity to the Gihon spring. Others, noting the closeness of the Gihon spring, suggest Zion derives from a Hurrian word meaning "brook" or "river." Still others posit a derivation from an Arabic word meaning "hillcrest" or "ridge." Any of these root words could have provided the name.[2]

The first biblical mention of Zion occurs in 2 Samuel 5:6–9. As David and his private army prepared to attack the Jebusite city of Jerusalem, the inhabitants mocked them, believing their fortress was impregnable. By a clever strategy, David and his troops conquered the city and the stronghold of Zion. The 2 Samuel text seems to use the terms *Jerusalem* and *Zion* interchangeably.[3] David moved into the fortress and strengthened its fortifications. Thereafter, the city was called the city of David.

Bronze coin from Jerusalem, AD 66–70, with Hebrew inscription "to the redemption of Zion."

After capturing Jerusalem, David moved the ark of the covenant into the city (6:17), making Jerusalem his religious and political capital. David's military victories brought neighboring nations under his control. As part of recognizing David's sovereignty over them, he forced the conquered nations to recognize God's sovereignty and bring God tribute (8:1–12). David's rule over all Israel gave credibility to Israel's belief that God ruled all people. Israel's belief and teachings regarding God's sovereignty in turn provided David's empire with legitimacy and made Zion/Jerusalem the seat of David's and God's rule.[4]

Following David's death, his son Solomon extended the city northward and constructed a temple for God and a palace for himself. Solomon brought the ark of the covenant from Zion into the new temple (1 Kgs. 8:1–6) and in a beautiful prayer dedicated the temple to God (vv. 23–53). Although Solomon acknowledged the temple could not contain God, he asked God to be present in the temple, and Zion became known as the place where God dwelled (Isa. 8:18).[5]

Following the building of the temple, Israel's worship centered in Jerusalem. The name *Zion* or *Mount Zion* came to refer to the temple (Ps. 20:2) and to the entire city (2 Kgs. 19:31; Ps. 51:18). Although a specific place, Zion also became a symbol of God's presence and rule.[6] God had chosen Zion (Ps. 132:13) and chosen to dwell there (74:2). From Zion the king ruled (2:6; 110:2) as God's representative—dispensing his justice and righteousness. From Zion God blessed his people (134:3).

SYMBOLIC MEANINGS

As Israel's capital city, Jerusalem came to represent the inhabitants of the city (Isa. 3:8; 51:17) and, by extension, the people of the entire nation. As a synonym for Jerusalem, Zion or "Daughter Zion" also referred to the inhabitants of the capital city (Ps. 147:12; Isa. 52:2) and the nation as a whole (1:27).[7]

Following the division of Israel into the northern kingdom of Israel and the southern kingdom of Judah after Solomon's death, the prophets often spoke of Jerusalem's and Zion's rebellion as representative of the nation's sin. Isaiah said that sin caused both Jerusalem and Judah to stumble (3:8). Micah singled out the inhabitants of Jerusalem as the greatest example of Judah's sin (Mic. 1:5). Amos, another eighth-century prophet, compared the sin of the people of Zion with the sin of the citizens of Samaria (Amos 6:1).

The word *Zion* occurs forty-seven times in Isaiah and nine times in Micah. The only other Old Testament book that uses *Zion* so frequently is Psalms (thirty-eight times). Thus Isaiah and Micah provide excellent examples of Zion as both a place and an important symbol in Judah's theological tradition.

Like other prophets, Isaiah and Micah prophesied God's judgment on Zion and Judah as a result of their sin (Mic. 1:13; 3:9–12). Although Zion would not fall to Assyria (Isa. 10:24–26), the city would eventually experience conquest and destruction. Many nations would come against Zion (29:8). Eventually Babylon would carry some of the people into exile (Mic. 4:10). Conquest would turn Zion into a wilderness resembling plowed fields, ruins, and thickets rather than a once-great city (Isa. 64:10; Mic. 3:12). Zion would be abandoned (Isa. 1:8) and feel abandoned by God (49:14).

Yet God's final word would not be judgment. Despite the destruction, God would preserve a remnant from Zion (Isa. 37:32). God would comfort his people (51:3) and restore them through his justice and righteousness (1:27). He would bring justice and salvation to Zion (46:13) and cleanse and sanctify his city (4:3–6). From Babylon exiles would return with joy (35:10; 51:11) and then God would return to Zion, his dwelling, and once again embrace his people (51:16;

52:8). The inhabitants of Zion would join together praising God's renewed presence with them (12:6).

God's promise to restore his people came true when King Cyrus of Persia conquered Babylon and allowed exiles in Babylon from every nation to return home and rebuild their nations and temples. Many Judean exiles returned to Zion, but the conditions they found hardly matched the prophets' words. The people began to understand that many of the words Isaiah, Micah, and others had spoken regarding Zion's future did not refer to the rebuilding and restoration of an earthly Zion but to the creation of a heavenly Zion.

Someday God would lay a foundation stone in a new Zion (Isa. 28:16) and prepare a new, miraculous birth of his city and people (66:7–11). In the new Zion, mourning and tears would be distant memories, and new life would replace despair (30:19; 61:3). God would reign from Zion (Isa. 24:23; Mic. 4:7–8); Judah's enemies would come to Zion, recognizing the place as God's city and seeking to learn of and follow God (4:2). In this new heavenly Zion, God's kingdom would finally be realized in all its glory and righteousness.

Zion does not figure prominently in the New Testament, although writers connect Jesus to Zion and mention the heavenly Zion. Paul and Peter understood the cornerstone Isaiah had prophesied (Isa. 28:16) to be Jesus (1 Pet. 2:6), who would come from Zion to liberate his people (Rom. 11:26). John and the author of Hebrews pointed toward the heavenly Zion as a place that, although hidden from physical sight, existed and from which God ruled (Heb. 12:22; Rev. 14:1).

As early as the fourth century AD, Christians referred to the southwest hill of Jerusalem as Zion rather than to Zion's original location. It was believed that the house in which the disciples gathered on Pentecost and from which the gospel first began to be preached lay on the southwest hill; this probably provides the best explanation for the transfer of Zion to the new location. For the early Christians, Zion was less a place than a symbol. God had sent his Messiah, Jesus Christ, who was building his kingdom, and would one day consummate the kingdom in a heavenly Zion.[8]

NOTES

[1]   Lamontte M. Luker, "Zion" in *MDB*, 985.

[2]   W. Harold Mare, "Zion" in *ABD*, 6:1096; James Newell, "Zion" in *HIBD*, 1711.

[3]   Georg Fohrer, "Zion and Jerusalem in the OT" in *TDNT abridged ed.* (1985), 295.

[4]   J. J. M. Roberts, "Zion Tradition" in *IDBSup* (1976), 986.

[5]   G. A. Barrois, "Zion" in *IDB*, 4:959; Luker, "Zion," 985.

[6]   Luker, "Zion," 985–86; Mare, "Zion," 1096.

[7]   Elaine R. Follis, "Zion, Daughter of" in *ABD*, 6:1103.

[8]   Barrois, "Zion," 960; Luker, "Zion," 986.

ZOAR

BY HAROLD R. MOSLEY

Date palms growing near the Dead Sea.

Bab Edh Dhra, believed by many archaeologists to be ancient Sodom and/or Gomorrah. The scattered black rocks on the ground are an unusual phenomenon in this area of red sandstone.

Zoar appears alongside Sodom and Gomorrah in the Genesis 19 account of the destruction of those cities. God spared Zoar when he destroyed Sodom and Gomorrah, not because its citizens were more godly but because it was small (*Zoar* means "small") and Lot had entered the city.

Zoar was located near the southeastern shore of the Dead Sea on the River Zered. The Dead Sea is the lowest place on the surface of the earth, 1,292 feet below sea level. The low elevation and the surrounding mountains cause the Dead Sea to get little rainfall—less than four inches annually.

During the middle ages, Zoar prospered because of the abundance of fresh water nearby. It exported dates, sugar, and indigo. At Madaba, Jordan, a sixth-century AD mosaic map of the Middle East shows Zoar surrounded by palm trees. The modern oasis of Jericho in the valley is a reminder of the productivity possible in the area. The ground is fertile. The climate is ideal for growing crops.

Zoar long ago ceased to exist as a town. The reason for its demise is unclear. Perhaps some catastrophe occurred to upset the city. Or perhaps the water supply failed. Zoar ultimately suffered the fate of Sodom and Gomorrah; it passed into extinction. Zoar sits as the forsaken smaller sister of an infamous group of cities so wicked they were destroyed by "burning sulfur" from heaven (v. 24).

ARTIFACTS

AGRICULTURE AND FARMING IN ANCIENT ISRAEL

BY MARK R. DUNN

Arab farmer sowing seed, a task typically done sometime from mid-October to early-December.

Farmer's seed bag from Egypt's New Kingdom (1550–1069 BC).

Three tools used for farming: a pick (top), a hoe or mattock, and a hoe (each from Beth-shemesh; dated 701–586 BC).

Israel had an agriculture-based economy throughout biblical times.[1] Consequently, such references saturate the Bible. An understanding of ancient Israel's agricultural life helps highlight the significance of Jesus's frequent use of agrarian imagery in his teaching.

The geography of the land greatly influenced the development of agriculture.

Israel had flatland along the Mediterranean coast, in the plain of Esdraelon, and in the Jordan plain. Those living there grew grains and various vegetables. The highlands were less productive; farmers first had to clear forests and then build terraces, which held the soil and moisture.

The agricultural calendar opened with the ingathering of olives from August to October, followed by the sowing of grain from October to December. Next came the late sowing of legumes and vegetables from December to February, followed by a month of hoeing weeds. The barley harvest came in March to April. Wheat was harvested in April and May. Grapes were harvested from May to July. Finally, the summer fruit arrived from July to August.[2]

Though common crops included grapes and olives, the following discussion will focus on Israelite grain agriculture. The soil was generally fertile but also famously rocky and at times shallow. Plowing was necessary to break up the ground and loosen stones embedded in the soil, so that water could penetrate and young plants could take root.[3] Israelites used a variety of farm tools, such as plows to prepare the soil. The earliest plows were forked sticks. Centuries later, farmers developed iron-tipped plows that could penetrate the soil about five inches. Harrows broke up clods after plowing. Hoes and mattocks turned up the ground for seeding and weeding.

Farmers commonly sowed grains using the broadcast method,[4] though some used a sack with a hole in it to drop seeds as the plow turned the soil.[5] Workers then used sickles to cut grain. Next the grain had to be winnowed. This required the use of wooden or stone rollers or oxen to break the heads of grain and release the kernels. Workers then used pitchforks, shovels, or fans to toss the grain into the air so the chaff could blow away. Sieves sifted the grain from the remaining unwanted material. Finally, the grain was milled into flour.

NOTES

1   See "Agriculture" in *Nelson's New Illustrated Bible Dictionary*, ed. Ronald F. Youngblood (Nashville: Thomas Nelson, 1995), 27–31.

2   Oded Borowski, "Agriculture" in *EDB*, 28–30.

3   See "Agriculture" in *Nelson's Illustrated Manners and Customs of the Bible*, ed. James I. Packer, Merrill C. Tenney, and White White Jr. (Nashville: Thomas Nelson, 1997).

4   J. L. Kelso and F. N. Hepper, "Agriculture" in *New Bible Dictionary*, ed. D. R. W. Wood, 3rd ed. (Downers Grove, IL: InterVarsity, 1996).

5   Craig S. Keener, *The IVP Bible Background Commentary: New Testament* (Downers Grove, IL: InterVarsity, 1993), 82.

ANCIENT ALTARS

BY GEORGE H. SHADDIX

Monument, likely an altar, in central area of temple of Echmoun outside of Sidon. Echmoun was the Phoenician god of healing. Temple dates to the seventh century BC.

Miniature bronze incense burners, probably for domestic use. From Byblos; first century BC–first century AD.

The simplest altars were constructed of earth built up into a mound. This may have been the type of altar Noah built—and evidently the type Moses later built. Earthen altars were useful, especially for nomadic people. "An earthen altar would not have been very practical for permanently settled people, for the rainy season each year would damage or destroy the altar."[1] Instead, settled people typically used stone to construct altars. These stones were to be natural and not hewn. The stone altar, like the earthen altar, would have no definite shape. The stones would simply be piled on top of one another. Sometimes a single natural rock would serve as an altar (Judg. 6:19–21). So the material the builder used to construct the altar determined its shape.

Scripture appears to make a distinction concerning those who offered sacrifices on each type of altar. Earthen and stone altars were in use before the establishment of the priesthood; therefore, anyone could build an altar wherever they were and could offer a sacrifice (Gen. 8:17–20; 22:9–13). With the establishment of the priesthood, people built more elaborate altars, such as those in the tabernacle and the temple. Only here did the priests offer the sacrifices for the people of God.

Most altars were designed for offering sacrifices; however, some seem to have been built as memorials (Exod. 17:15–16; Josh. 22:26–27).[2]

Altars were not unique to Israel. Other nations also built altars to worship their gods. Archaeologists have uncovered an altar with multiple faces carved into it at Taanach, where Deborah and Barak defeated the Canaanites under Sisera (Judg. 5:19–20).[3] Such adornments were prohibited in Jewish worship. "A striking circular Canaanite altar dating from 2500 BC to 1800 BC was excavated at Megiddo. It was twenty-five feet in diameter and 4 ½ feet high. Four steps led up to the top of the altar."[4] The prohibition in Exodus 20:25–26 against using hewn stone and using steps in conjunction with altars is probably a prohibition against God's people using altars that shared characteristics with the Canaanites' altars.[5] Archaeologists have excavated at Beer-sheba an altar constructed

One of the best examples of a large stone altar is at Megiddo. The temple complex dates from the time of Abraham. The circular altar is about twenty-five feet in diameter and more than four feet tall.

Relief of a Hittite king and queen before the sacred altar. Dates to 1300 BC.

of large hewn stones. This altar has horns on its four corners and dates to the period of the divided kingdom.[6]

The altar was a sacred place in Israel's worship. It represented the presence of God among his people. As offerings were placed on the altar, "the offerings were taken out of man's domain and given to God, and God replied by bestowing blessings (Exod. 20:24). Thus the Covenant itself between God and his people was maintained in force, or re-established, upon the altar of sacrifice."[7]

Because the altar was sacred, nothing was to defile it. If, for some reason, it became defiled, it was to be cleansed as it had been in the days of King Hezekiah (2 Chr. 29:18–19).

NOTES

[1] Joel F. Drinkard Jr., "Altar" in *Holman Bible Dictionary* (*HolBD*), ed. Trent C. Butler (Nashville: Holman, 1991), 38.

[2] Howard Z. Cleveland, "Altar" in *The New International Dictionary of the Bible*, J. D. Douglas, rev. ed., ed. Merrill C. Tenney (Grand Rapids: Zondervan, 1987), 36.

[3] Albert E. Glock, "Taanach" in *The New Encyclopedia of Archaeological Excavations in the Holy Land* (*NEAEHL*), ed. Ephraim Stern (New York: Simon & Schuster, 1993), 4:1431.

[4] Drinkard, "Altar," 38.

[5] H. M. Wiener, W. S. Caldecott, and C. E. Armerding, "Altar" in *The International Standard Bible Encyclopedia* (*ISBE*), ed. Geoffrey W. Bromiley, vol. 1 (Grand Rapids: Eerdmans, 1979), 101–2.

[6] Drinkard, "Altar," 38.

[7] Roland de Vaux, *Ancient Israel: Its Life and Institutions* (Grand Rapids: Eerdmans, 1997), 414.

ANCIENT THRESHING FLOORS

BY PAUL E. KULLMAN

At Samaria, this threshing floor is still used by the locals.

A properly constructed threshing floor requires either a flat rocky area or hard compacted soil with a surface free of loose dust. The preferred site was typically on an elevated area near the edge of town. The winds, which naturally occur on a raised geographical elevation, helped the winnowing operation be productive. Being able to take advantage of the prevailing winds actually determined the threshing floor's exact location. Each threshing floor would be constructed in about a fifty-foot-diameter circle with a "crown" in the center, a raised area that helped shed rainwater.[1] If the crown did not occur naturally, workers would use the abundant stone supply and build up the center of the floor with stone pavers and sand joint filler.

AGRICULTURE

The threshing floor method of harvesting a crop occurred at a common gathering location for the ancient agrarian society. Several farmers, or the whole village, would share a threshing floor. This is one of the earliest forms of a business cooperative, where pieces of the operation provided communal benefit to the local economy. (Similarly, communities often shared winepresses.)

The purpose of a threshing floor is simple. Farmers of the ancient Near East would harvest grain crops, load them into flat carts pulled by draft animals (usually oxen or donkeys), and deliver the grain to a threshing floor. Workers unloaded and sorted the grain for processing. The larger sheaves were spread out uniformly on the ground and crushed by animals treading on them or cart wheels being driven over them (Isa. 28:27–28). Farmers would also use another tool of threshing known as the "threshing sledge."[2] A driver, riding atop a sledge, would direct animals to pull a heavy timber with embedded stones or iron teeth across the harvested grain. Once the harvest was broken up, laborers used the winnowing fork to toss stalks into the wind to separate chaff from the kernels. The kernel, the valuable part of the food product, would fall to the ground, allowing laborers to gather it for storage or market.

The harvest for barley and wheat occurs in the spring and requires many laborers to process. Therefore, the need for an abundance of laborers required families and the community to join together to help bring economic success to a village or small town.[3] After the threshing operation was complete, the threshing floor held an important and valuable commodity, one that the locals had to protect from theft (1 Sam. 23:1).

SYMBOLISM

The Bible uses the term *threshing floor* many times in both a symbolic and literal sense with the agrarian usage being the latter. The threshing floor was frequently a place that symbolized spiritual significance and blessing (Num. 18:27–32; Judg. 6:11–40). For instance, Gideon used the threshing floor as the location for a divine miracle—laying out his fleece. Also, the law speaks of its usage. Concerning the slave who has fulfilled his term of servitude, Deuteronomy 15:14 says, "Give generously to him from your flock, your threshing floor, and your winepress. You are to give him whatever the LORD your God has blessed you with." The threshing floor was the symbolic source of the sacrifice worshippers gave back to the Lord out of thanksgiving for his divine blessings (Num. 15:20; Deut. 16:13). Likewise, the threshing sledge was a symbol of brute force in the judgment of nations or people groups or for victory over Israel's enemies (Isa. 41:15–16; Amos 1:3). The Lord used a harvesting metaphor to speak of judging Babylon, who was "like a threshing floor" at the time of her "harvest." This was a euphemism for his judgment (Jer. 51:33).

John the Baptist used a threshing floor metaphor to describe the coming Messiah and what Jesus would do regarding spiritual judgment (Matt. 3:12). The chaff that separates from the barley and wheat sheaves is deemed useless and destined for the fire, but the valued wheat is gathered and stored in the barn. Sometimes the chaff was gathered and sold as fuel for baking ovens. Likewise, farmers sold the prized wheat kernels to customers for baking bread. This metaphor is a strong visual illustration, as chaff represents the unsaved sent to the fire while the kernels are the saved who are a valuable part of the harvest.

NOTES

[1]   "Threshing Floor" in *Wycliffe Biblical Dictionary*, ed. Charles F. Pfeiffer, Howard F. Vos, and John Rea (Peabody, MA: Hendrickson, 2003), 1701.

[2]   "Threshing Sledge" in *The Baker Illustrated Bible Dictionary*, ed. Tremper Longman III (Grand Rapids: Baker, 2013), 1630.

[3]   F. Nigel Hepper, "Agriculture" in *HolBD*, 24–25.

ANCIENT MARRIAGE CONTRACTS

BY ROBERTA LOU JONES

Ruins of Greco-Roman city on Elephantine Island in the Nile. When the Persians ruled Egypt, beginning in 525 BC, a large camp of mercenaries, including Jewish regiments, settled there. The discovery of the Elephantine Papyri has enabled scholars to reconstruct the life of Jewish inhabitants. Most documents deal with legal aspects of marriage, divorce, commerce, and inheritance.

God planned marriage as a secure relationship between one man and one woman (Matt. 19:5–6). Because of human sin, however, matrimony too often includes fear and insecurity. Biblical examples of imperfect marriages include Leah and Rachel, who shared Jacob (Gen. 29:18–28). Too often, women were merchandise to buy (Exod. 21:7–11) and rewards for military success (Josh. 15:16).

Troubled marriages also highlight secular history. The Lipit-Ishtar Law Code (nineteenth c. BC) instructed a man with children by "a harlot from the public square" to provide her grain, oil, and clothing. With common sense, laws prohibited the harlot and the man's wife from living together. Some relationships suggested mere convenience. An Egyptian queen wrote Hittite royalty, "My husband died . . . send me one of your sons, he might become my husband." Lawmakers tried to improve marriage. Hammurabi ruled Babylon from approximately 1728 to 1686 BC. He observed a gadabout wife who neglected her house and husband. Hammurabi commanded someone to throw the woman in water![1] Sadly, problems between husbands and wives frequently overshadowed love and security.

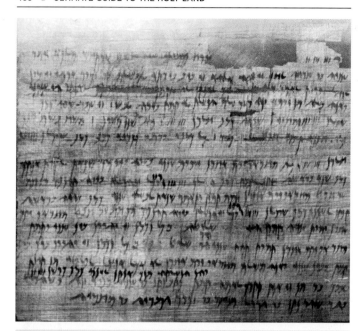

Document, written in Aramaic, recording the marriage of Ananiah ben Azariah and the handmaiden Tamut; ink on papyrus; found at Elephantine in Egypt.

MARRIAGE CONTRACTS

Both verbal and written contracts attempted to stabilize marriages. Although definitions of words varied, many terms and ideas gained wide acceptance in the ancient world.

Bridal Gift—The groom's gift to the bride (Gen. 34:12).

Mohar—The fathers of the couple discussed the possible marriage. The groom gave a "marriage present," a *mohar*, to the bride's father to show his good intentions, to compensate the bride's family, and to strengthen family ties.

Bride Price—Some scholars interpret the *mohar* as a bride price—a purchase of the bride.

Betrothal Period—If the bride's parents agreed, the couple began their betrothal (engagement) period. Society expected the future groom to exercise servant-leadership and to make loving decisions.[2]

Dowry—The bride's father, or family, contributed the dowry—her possessions. The husband managed the dowry for their mutual benefit. A bride with a good dowry represented a financial and social asset.[3] Caleb gave his daughter a field and springs of water (Josh. 15:16–19). Laban offered slaves (Gen. 29:24–29).[4]

Ketubah—By the first century BC, Jewish couples chose a written marriage contract, a *ketubah*. Each groom promised a *mohar* if the couple divorced.

Divorce was marital separation. Men could easily divorce their wives. Some cultures offered women this freedom.[5]

SECULAR MARRIAGES

Babylonian marriage contract between Uballitsu-Gula, son of Nabu-nadin-ahi, and Ina-Esagilbanat, daughter of Sum-ukin; dated 549 BC.

Archaeologists have discovered evidence of marriages in numerous civilizations. History indicates men in Nuzi (2000–1400 BC, Mesopotamia) paid for their brides in livestock, textiles, copper, or silver. Some Nuzi legal contracts allowed delayed payments. Having one wife was the norm—unless the first wife was barren.[6] The Jewish colony of Elephantine (fifth c. BC, Egypt) used papyrus sheets to record marriage contracts. These legal documents mentioned the groom's responsibilities, the bride's dowry, and her personal possessions. Brides listed mirrors, clothing, cosmetic paint, and sandals. The husband agreed to provide the usual food and clothing. In addition, he promised oil for his beloved. (Women in arid Egypt appreciated body oil.)

Slaves also used marriage contracts. Tamut, for instance, mentioned one garment, ointment, a cheap mirror, and possibly sandals in her marriage agreement. Spoken words were also considered binding. The groom told Tamut's owner, "I have come to you to be given in marriage Tamut by name who is your handmaiden. She is my wife, and I her husband from this day and forever."[7]

Zaccur gave his slave Jehoishma a splendid dowry of silver, garments, vessels, and toilet articles. A scribe wrote the contract in the presence of six witnesses.

The fourteenth-century BC world traded horses, exotic animals, chariots, ivory, fancy clothing, precious stones, and gold. In this commercial background, Amenhotep III of Egypt desired another Mitannian princess for his harem. The king of Mitanni demanded a bride price, "without limit, reaching from the earth to the sky." The two rulers exchanged valuable "gifts." Amenhotep sent his ambassador to inspect Princess Taduhepa as a royal Egyptian bridal candidate. The woman passed inspection. So the Mitannian king gave the princess a large dowry, recorded on clay tablets. He begged pagan deities to let the princess be "pleasing to the heart of my brother." Taduhepa and her luxurious items arrived in Egypt where Amenhotep greeted her with great splendor. Thus Mitanni and Egypt arranged a fantastic commercial, political, and romantic venture![8]

BOAZ AND JACOB TAKE WIVES

The marriage of Boaz and Ruth illustrates several Old Testament principles (Ruth 4). At the city gate, Boaz received permission from another kinsman to redeem Naomi's inheritance and to marry Ruth. Witnesses watched and listened. Boaz announced he wanted to raise children to honor Naomi's deceased husband (see Deut. . 25:5–10). The witnesses responded, "May the LORD make the woman . . . like Rachel and Leah, who together built the house of Israel" (Ruth 4:11).

Jacob worked seven years for his uncle Laban, with the verbal agreement to marry beautiful Rachel. Alas, by Laban's trickery, Jacob married the less comely older daughter, Leah. Laban, however, quickly offered Rachel to Jacob as a second wife. Rachel and Leah each received a female slave as partial dowry. Jacob toiled another seven years and eventually paid for two bickering wives. He fathered twelve sons and one daughter by his wives and their servants (Gen. 27–35).

Despite shortcomings, marriage contracts protected people and property.

NOTES

1   "Lipit-Ishtar Law Code," "Suppiluliumas and the Egyptian Queen," and "The Code of Hammurabi" in *ANET*, 1st ed., 159–60, 163, 319, 172, respectively. Hammurabi "reigned 43 years in the first half of the second millennium B.C. His absolute dates are uncertain; his reign began in 1848, 1792, or 1736 B.C." See Gary D. Baldwin and E. Ray Clendenen, "Hammurabi" in *HIBD*, 708.

2   Daniel I. Block, "Marriage and Family in Ancient Israel," in *Marriage and Family in the Biblical World*, ed. Ken M. Campbell (Downers Grove, IL: InterVarsity, 2003), 57–58.

3   Christine Roy Yoder, "The Woman of Substance: A Socioeconomic Reading of Proverbs 31:10-31," *Journal of Biblical Literature (JBL)* 122.3 (2002): 432–35, 444. Yoder views Proverbs 31:10 as a purchase price for a bride, in a culture with marriage being primarily a business transaction.

4   Many terms in marriage contracts varied in meaning. For a discussion of dowry as equivalent to bride-price, see "Dowry" in *HIBD*, 441.

5   John J. Collins, "Marriage, Divorce, and Family in Second Temple Judaism," in *Families in Ancient Israel*, ed. Leo G. Perdue et al. (Louisville: Westminster John Knox, 1997), 113–16.

6   Katarzyna Grosz, "Bridewealth and Dowry in Nuzi," in *Images of Women in Antiquity*, ed. Averil Cameron and Amelie Kuhrt (Detroit: Wayne State University Press, 1983), 199–205.

7   Bezalel Porten, *Archives from Elephantine: The Life of an Ancient Jewish Military Colony* (Berkeley: University of California Press, 1968), 91–92, 206–12, 219–23.

8   George Steindorff and Keith C. Seele (rev. Keith C. Seele), *When Egypt Ruled the East* (Chicago: University of Chicago Press, 1957), 107–9.

ASHTORETH

BY ROBERT A. STREET

This fifteen-ton lion symbolized the Assyrian goddess Ishtar. A pair of these statues guarded her temple at Nimrud. The statue measures eight and one-half feet tall and thirteen feet long.

Terra-cotta stamped relief depicting Ishtar holding her weapon, Eshnunna; from Mesopotamia; dated second millennium BC.

The Canaanites were nature worshippers, and their gods were intricately connected with the region's cycle of nature. With a climate having a wet season and a dry season, half of the year was fertile with prospering crops. The other half was dry and crops perished. The Canaanites assumed that when their gods were unhappy or separated, the land languished and was barren. Believing the gods responded to actions on earth, Canaanite worship searched for ways to entice the gods to be gracious. How could the Canaanites control the gods who brought the prosperity of the crops and the land? By "proper worship," of course. The Hebrews then bought into the Canaanite way of worship centered on a fertility cult.

So who or what were the gods enticing the Hebrews into apostasy and desertion? Judges 2:13 identifies them as Baal and Ashtaroth. "[Ashtaroth] seems to have become a generic term for the female deities of the Canaanites, and when used with Baal, or Baalim, it was the collective term for pagan deities."[1] Baalim and Ashtaroth are plural nouns. As plural nouns, the terms most likely reference a local manifestation of the Canaanite god Baal and the Canaanite goddess Ashtoreth.[2]

Baal is more familiar to readers of the Old Testament. Scripture, however, does little to explain what exactly took place in the Canaanites' nature worship. To ascertain how the Canaanites understood the gods and goddesses influenced the natural world, we must look to parallels from the ancient Near East. The people of Babylon, Assyria, Ugarit, and Egypt practiced nature worship with similar deities.

Baal was the Canaanite fertility god and god of the storm. Hence, they believed he brought the rains to grow crops. The Ugaritic tablets from Ras Shamra, which date about 1400 BC, describe a relationship between Baal and his goddess consort, wife, and sister.

To further complicate matters, Ashtoreth might have gone by several different names.[3] The multiple names might explain why the book of Judges uses the plural forms. A Greek transliteration of her name is Astarte. Though it is not certain, the people of Ras Shamra may have referred to her as Anat. Another possibility is that she was known as Asherah.[4] Her Babylonian and Assyrian counterpart was Ishtar (or Ashtar). Even if not referring to the same deity, the functions were similar. She was the goddess of fertility, the bringer of life, and even the destroyer of death.

The Old Testament provides no physical description of a god or any pagan deities. History teaches, though, that Astarte (Ashtaroth) was symbolized by a wooden pole, a tree, or even a grove of trees. Not surprisingly, the wooden figures representing Astarte have not survived. Stone and terra-cotta Astarte images and symbols from the ancient Near East, though, have survived. In the fourteenth century BC, Ras Shamra portrayed her in clay and terra-cotta figurines, decorative stone friezes, and even ivory carvings. The stele of Ashtoreth from Beth-shean has a depiction of her. Egyptians depicted her counterpart as a nude goddess. While we cannot know for certain that the disloyal Hebrews knew her in these forms, they did worship a goddess like her in the hopes of guaranteeing the land fertility.

Asherah figurine. Mentioned throughout the Old Testament, Asherah was the primary goddess of Syria and Canaan. The people believed she was the wife of the Canaanite god El and also mother to seventy other gods, the most famous being Baal.

WORSHIP PRACTICES

What exactly was the worship activity that took place and made the apostasy so difficult to remove from Israel and Judah? History provides no actual descriptions of what took place. But perhaps no verse gives better hints about Baal and Astarte worship than Amos 2:7: "A man and his father have sexual relations with the same girl, profaning my holy name."

The religion's worship practice included "sacred" prostitution in which the men had intimate relations with

Cultic figurine of Astarte; from Cyprus; dated about 1300 BC.

the priestesses of the goddess, and the women, with the priests of the god. The concept behind such action was one of "sympathetic" magic. The devotees of the cult enacted orgiastic rites in worship. "According to a pattern of sympathetic or imitative magic, whereby the worshiper imitates the actions he desires the gods to perform, male and female worshipers engaged in sacred prostitution, supposing thereby to assure the rhythmic cycle of nature."[5] Their actions were in essence saying, "May Baal, the god of the storm, send the rain to fertilize the earth and cause the crops to flourish." The idea was as the gods saw what was on earth, so it went in heaven and vice versa.

NOTES

[1]   Bryce N. Sandlin, "Ashtaroth" *Biblical Illustrator* (*BI*) 15.4 (Summer 1989): 18.

[2]   Sandlin, "Ashtaroth"; Scott Langston, "Ashtaroth" in *HolBD*, 112–13.

[3]   Jimmy Albright, "Ashtoreth," *BI* 6.1 (Fall 1979): 23–24.

[4]   "§1718 [*ʿashtarot*]" (Ashtaroth) in *TWOT*, 707. See Sandlin, "Ashtaroth," 18–19.

[5]   James King West, *Introduction to the Old Testament*, 2nd ed. (New York: Macmillan, 1981), 216.

BANKING IN THE FIRST CENTURY

BY C. MACK ROARK

Treasury of the Athenians at Delphi. Such treasuries were built in honor of a city's patron god. Athenians visiting Delphi would bring an offering to their treasury in hopes of winning the approval of their favored deity.

From the New Testament itself we learn little about banking in Judea and Galilee. The Greek word translated as "bank" (*trapeza*) occurs fifteen times in the New Testament, but only in one instance does it refer to a place where money was kept and circulated, for the word also means "table" in daily household use. Three times it refers to the money changers' tables (Matt. 21:12; Mark 11:15; John 2:15). Only in Luke 19:23 does it signify a bank,[1] and that would not have been a bank in any modern sense. Under Roman rule in the first century AD, banking was still primitive, in spite of the fact that in various forms banking had been around for centuries.[2]

Banking was the result of a process that began with the barter system, wherein people exchanged goods or services for other goods or services. Although barter continued throughout the ancient world, the development of coinage and the exchange of money for goods and services introduced a new era in commerce. Throughout the Roman world, a unified system of coinage slowly developed.[3] The system was more common in urban areas and less so in the rural villages where Jesus primarily ministered. There bartering

Dated to the fourth century AD, this relief shows a money changer working at his bench, which doubles as his bank.

The banker's ticket, called a tasserae, was adhered to a sealed sack of coins. The mark, which was inscribed with the name of the coin authenticator, or assayer, would serve to verify that the sealed money sack contained genuine coins and an expected amount of money. Bankers exchanged sacks of coins, often without even opening them for verification beyond the banker's mark. This system, which the general population never used, relied on trustworthy slaves for money transport.

remained common practice and, with bartering, the old methods of storing treasures. People of Judea began using coins in the fourth century BC; Roman coins came into use there in the first century BC. Herod the Great, as well as his sons and successors, produced and put into use coins that were serviceable but were in fact of lesser value than imperial coinage.[4] Individuals often carried coins in a purse or pocket.

The minting of coins marked a step forward in commerce but at the same time presented new problems. No one had established a uniform standard for the value of coins, plus numerous nations and city-states were minting their own. Coins could be gold, silver, bronze, or copper; many were stamped with images and icons of the various states.[5] The resulting diversity of coinage gave rise to the money changers, who were in effect small-time bankers. Stationing themselves where traffic passed—at the gates of the city or of the temple—they performed the necessary but often corrupt service of exchanging coins for local use.[6] Their desk was called a *trapeza*, the same word used for a bank in Luke 19:23.

When transactions based on money replaced transactions based on barter, money changers became essential. Also essential, people had to have a repository to hold the cash and provide methods of payment, not unlike today's system of checking accounts and lines of credit.[7]

Banks and banking originated in temples or kingdom treasuries. Especially in Athens, but also throughout the Mediterranean world, temple treasuries were banking facilities.[8] These temple banks were not so much commercial banks designed for actions but deposit banks for the safekeeping of wealth. The assumption that temples were sacred and their contents inviolate was likely behind their use. Also the fact that the temple was a central institution for public life may have been a major reason banks were often attached to them.[9] In addition to temple banks, some cities had royal or state banks, which were tied to the king's treasury. In contrast, private banks served the public.

For the private citizen, perhaps especially in Galilee, banks were not the most important financial institution. The wealthier citizens were more likely to provide loans for the average person than were banks.[10] Even in Rome, where bank accounts had existed for decades, most families relied on a personal strong box, which would contain cash and have a list of due dates for loans and bills.[11] Many people, perhaps most, would have had no need for a bank. Jesus knew his listeners and knew he was addressing people whose meager treasure was not in a bank.

NOTES

1   The parallel text at Matthew 25:27 has "with the bankers" instead of "in the bank."

2   Steven E. Sidebotham, "Trade and Commerce (Roman)," in *ABD*, 6:630.

3   Sidebotham, "Trade," 629.

4   John W. Betlyon, "Coinage" in *ABD*, 1:1085–86.

5   Helmut Koester, *Introduction to the New Testament*, vol. 1, *History, Culture, and Religion of the Hellenistic Age* (Philadelphia: Fortress, 1980), 88.

6   Betlyon, "Coinage," 1086–87.

7   Michael Grant, *From Alexander to Cleopatra* (New York: Scribner's Sons, 1982), 124.

8   Koester, *Introduction*, 90.

9   Grant, *From Alexander to Cleopatra*, 45.

10   Bruce W. Frier, "Interest and Usury in the Greco-Roman Period" in *ABD*, 3:424.

11   Paul Veyne, ed., *A History of Private Life I: From Pagan Rome to Byzantium* (Cambridge, MA: Harvard University Press, 1987), 149.

BOUNDARY MARKERS

BY JOEL F. DRINKARD JR.

A boundary stone at Gezer. As one entered Gezer, the Hebrew inscription read, "Boundary of Gezer." Leaving, the Greek inscription read, "Belonging to Alkios," probably a reference to a landowner in the Roman era.

Boundary markers were common in the ancient Near East. Inscribed stone slabs that stood upright (stelae) marking boundaries are known from Egypt. When Pharaoh Akhenaten (reigned ca 1353–1336 BC) built his new capital city of Akhetaten, he set up boundary stelae marking the boundaries and fields of the city. Fifteen of these stelae have been found. They are inscribed with texts describing the reason the site was chosen, the planning for the city, and the dedication to the god Aten. Boundary stones were also set up along Egypt's border with Nubia to the south.[1] These boundary markers regularly included symbols representing the deities.

In Babylon during the Kassite period (sixteenth–twelfth centuries BC), *kudurru*, which were inscribed stones placed in a temple, recorded land the king granted to vassals. "The size of properties donated to private individuals ranges between 80 and 1,000 hectares (200–2,500 acres), though a surface area of about 250 hectares (625 acres) is most common and appears to have been some kind of standard measure. . . . [The] 250 hectares could provide the nutritional basis for at least two hundred people and hence assure the economic independence and prosperity of a sizable extended family, including service personnel, slaves, and so forth."[2] The *kudurru* stone in the temple was the original document; clay copies were given to the vassal to prove his entitlement to the land grant. In addition to the text describing the land grant, the *kudurru* often bore the symbols of the deities called upon to witness the grant and protect the land.

Kudurru is the Akkadian word for "frontier" or "boundary." Kudurru stones, which were used by the Kassites of ancient Mesopotamia, recorded the granting and transferring of land from the king to one of his subjects. The kudurru stones were inscribed with text that recorded the transfer of property and depictions of gods who were responsible for protecting the agreement.

In 1871, Charles Clermont-Ganneau, a French archaeologist and biblical scholar, was shown stones near Gezer bearing both the Hebrew inscription "the boundary of Gezer" and the Greek inscription *Alkiou*, meaning "belonging to Alkios." Clermont-Ganneau identified the nearby site as ancient Gezer, now a universally accepted identification. Archaeologist R. A. S. Macalister, who had led excavations at the site (1902–1909), published information about six of these boundary markers in his excavation reports on Gezer. A seventh boundary marker was discovered in 1964. These boundary markers all date to the Roman period. Six of the markers bear the same inscription; the seventh has not yet been deciphered. Famed archaeologist G. Ernest Wright proposed that the Greek name indicates the owner of the estate in the Roman era. The town had ceased to exist, but workers for the estate may have lived on the site of the town. The boundary markers indicated the extent of the estate.[3] These are the only inscribed boundary markers known thus far from the land of ancient Israel.

In addition to such inscribed boundary markers, many times a large stone, or even a pile of stones—a cairn—served as a boundary marker. The Old Testament references to boundary markers or landmarks are apparently to this latter type that is not inscribed. The Old Testament contains six references to boundary markers or landmarks. In each instance, the reference deals with the moving of a boundary marker or the encroachment upon the property of others.

In both Egypt and Mesopotamia, inscribed boundary markers included references to the deities to serve as witnesses and protectors of the land. The Old Testament gives no indication that boundary markers had any representation of God. However, in Hebrew understanding, the land ultimately belonged to God. He was the one who gave the land to the Hebrews and oversaw the allotment to the tribes, clans, and families. Since the land belonged to God, the prohibitions in the Old Testament served as God's way of guaranteeing property rights. God protected the property within the boundary markers; no one was to remove or move them.

The boundary marker set the extent of a person's or city's or nation's property. To move the boundary marker, or to remove it, was to jeopardize the individual's or the community's property. And since the land was ultimately God's, to move or remove a boundary marker was an affront to God. Such action amounted to theft of God's property, and God would punish the offender appropriately.

NOTES

1   Randy L. Jordan, "The Stelae of Ancient Egypt," cited August 13, 2007, www.touregypt.net/featurestories/stela.htm.

2   Walter Sommerfeld, "The Kassites of Ancient Mesopotamia: Origins, Politics, and Culture" in *CANE* (2000), 922.

3   H. Darrell Lance, "Gezer in the Land and in History," *BA* 30.2 (May 1967): 34–47 (esp. 47).

BREAD MAKING IN THE ANCIENT WORLD

BY MONA STEWART

Ovens similar to this would have been typical in Old Testament era dwellings or houses. A cooking pot is on top of the oven.

Using a technique that has been in use for centuries, this gentleman is separating wheat on a threshing floor in Gadara, Jordan.

Bread is the oldest of all manufactured foods. It was the basic food in the ancient world and is still the staple in most countries except in East Asia where rice is the staple.

KINDS OF BREAD

Barley meal has husks and is coarser than wheat flour.[1] It is also less appetizing and less expensive. It was the first grain, however, ready for harvest (Exod. 9:31,32). The poor could not afford wheat bread, so barley bread became their staple. The boy in John 6:9 had five barley loaves, which were probably flat disks much like small tortillas. Having barley rather than wheat indicated his family's economic condition. The rich preferred wheat bread.

Bread is as varied as there are countries. The thick, light loaf popular in the West is unfamiliar in the East.[2] Multigrain breads are popular everywhere and often made with as many as nine different grains.

GRINDING THE GRAIN

People used different methods for grinding grain. Women who were either the wives, daughters, or slaves of the wealthy did this work. The poor used hand mills made of two stones. The upper stone was of a lighter material than the lower, which was firmly anchored in the ground. People inserted handles into holes in the upper stone and turned them by hand.[3] Animals turned the larger millstones.

Sowing, gathering, winnowing, grinding, kneading, and cooking were part of daily life in each Old and New Testament home. Community bakeries became available in urban areas where people took the loaves to be baked. Only later did bakeries make bread available for purchase.

BAKING THE BREAD

The earliest breads, which were flat and circular, were cooked on heated stones. Fermenting yeast leavened the dough, causing it to rise. Saving a small part of dough from the previous day also served as a sourdough leavening. The leaven made the texture of the loaf bread much lighter than the previous hard flat cakes.[4]

One of three methods of baking the small, thin cakes was to use a heated stone rather than a permanent oven.[5] Another method of baking was to place the dough in a pan or on a griddle made of clay or iron. This disk-shaped bread looked much like a pancake, about one-half inch thick and up to twelve inches in diameter.[6] Sometimes smaller disks were perforated or carried on a stick by means of a hole in the middle. The third baking method was in an oven of clay or iron (Lev. 2:4). Those preparing the bread would form their dough into different shapes and sizes.

NOTES

[1] William H. Stephens, *The New Testament World in Pictures* (Nashville: Broadman, 1987), 182–85.

[2] George B. Eager, "Bread" in *ISBE* (1939), 516.

[3] Eager, "Bread," 515; Stephens, *New Testament World*, 182–83.

[4] Arthur B. Fowler, "Bread" in *The Zondervan Pictorial Bible Dictionary*, ed. Merrill C. Tenney (Grand Rapids: Zondervan, 1963), 132.

[5] Victor H. Matthews, *Manners and Customs in the Bible* (Peabody, MA: Hendrickson, 1988), 20.

[6] Matthews, *Manners*.

BUILDING TEMPLES IN THE ANCIENT NEAR EAST

BY JOEL F. DRINKARD JR.

The remains of an Israelite temple at Arad.

A temple was God's house or God's palace. The temple was theologically understood as God's dwelling place on earth. In the case of the Jerusalem temple, the division of the entire structure of the temple grounds into precincts of increasing holiness as one approached the most holy place represented one's coming ever closer to God's presence.

Temples were closely associated with kingship in the Bible and in the ancient Near East. Temples were built by kings, by empire builders. A temple became one of the marks of a successful king, especially one establishing a new dynasty; he built a house/palace for himself and his dynasty, and he built a house/palace for his god. The king would often honor his god for giving him the kingdom by building a temple for that god. Each successive king in a dynasty did not necessarily build a new temple, but many kings would renovate, restore, or make additions to a temple after their ascension to the throne or after some significant event. Just one ancient Near Eastern example will illustrate this point. According to the Mesha stele, King Mesha of Moab built a high place for Kemosh (the Moabite deity; Chemosh, CSB) in Qarho because Kemosh had saved him from all his enemies (lines 3–4). In addition, Mesha later in the stele mentioned building a palace ("king's house," line 23) for himself.

The same pattern of temple building is found in Israel/Judah. While earlier shrines and sanctuaries were certainly built for God prior to the monarchy, only with the rise of David and Solomon was the temple built. David began and Solomon consolidated the kingdom. One mark of their achievement included the building of both a temple and a palace.

Following the division of the kingdom into Israel and Judah after Solomon's death, Jeroboam I of Israel built his own temples at Dan and Bethel, both the sites of earlier shrines (1 Kgs. 12:26–33). Again the rationale was simple; a separate kingdom needed its own temples.

In terms of biblical and archaeological data, the Solomonic temple undoubtedly had Phoenician influence. Along with Israelite workers (many of whom were forced laborers, 1 Kgs. 5:13–17), Solomon also employed Phoenician workers of King Hiram of Tyre (1 Kgs. 5:6). Solomon also employed an Israelite-Phoenician artisan, Hiram of Tyre (not King Hiram of Tyre) whose father was Phoenician and mother was an Israelite, to do *all* the bronze work for the temple (1 Kgs. 7:13–47).

Since the primary workers mentioned for wood and metal were Phoenician, and since most of the decorative features were either carved in wood or cast in metal, it seems obvious that most of the artwork for the temple would have Phoenician influence.

Surely the temple was a magnificent structure, but Solomon's palace was much larger. The entire temple could easily fit in just one part of the palace: the "House of the Forest of Lebanon" was one hundred cubits long, fifty cubits wide, and thirty cubits high (ca. 150 by 75 by 45 feet, 1 Kgs. 7:2). Actually two temples could fit in this one structure side by side and still have almost enough room for two more temples turned sideways behind them. In terms of actual floor space, the temple covered 1,200 square cubits, or about 2,700 square feet; the House of the Forest of Lebanon covered 5,000 square cubits or about

The most holy place in the Israelite temple at Arad. The most holy place here is square, the same as at the temple in Jerusalem.

11,250 square feet. Somewhat like Saint George's Chapel at Windsor Castle, the temple, size-wise, was rather small in the royal palace complex.

The temple was undoubtedly constructed of the fine ashlar masonry associated with monumental architecture during the monarchy. Ashlar masonry is characterized by large stones, finely dressed faces, and at times a decorative boss on the outer face. Although no remains of the Solomonic temple have been found (if they exist, they would likely be found beneath the platform of the Herodian temple, which *also* serves as the platform for Haram es-Sharif, where the Dome of the Rock sits today). Such masonry, apparently belonging to the time of Solomon, has been found in major structures at Megiddo, Hazor, and Gezer, all sites the Bible describes as major cities Solomon built or rebuilt. In addition, fine examples of slightly later, ninth-century ashlar masonry have been found at Samaria and elsewhere, apparently reflecting the building activity of Omri or Ahab.

One area where we might expect native Israelite influence is in the stonework of the temple. The text does specify that the stoneworkers were Israelite (1 Kgs. 5:15–18). And we do find, from a later period, unique to Israelite and Moabite-Ammonite sites, the carved stone capitals variously known as proto-Ionic, proto-Aeolic, or volute capitals. These capitals, which stood on top of pier walls, are carved with large volutes, probably representing palm trees or the Tree of Life. Several of these stone capitals have been found at Megiddo and are attributed to Solomonic construction. Although no such capitals have been found in Jerusalem of the Solomonic period, and only one has been found in Jerusalem, these capitals clearly belong to monumental and/or royal structures. Certainly the temple would have had monumental architecture of this sort along with the ashlar masonry.

The temple building itself was based on a fairly common long-room plan known throughout the ancient Near East. Basically the temple had three parts: the porch, the inner room, also called the nave, and the holy of holies or most holy place. From Middle Bronze and Late Bronze Age temples in Canaan and Syria, we find similar floor plans. Temples at Shechem, Megiddo, Hazor, and farther north at Ebla have related, but clearly not identical, floor plans. The most significant aspect of these temples was a direct access (and direct view) from the outside through the inner room to the niche or most holy place. Most of these temples had an inner room or nave that was longer than wide, called a long-room temple. Several of these temples also had pillars or columns in front, reminding one of the two pillars, Jachin and Boaz.

While these other temples have somewhat similar floor plans, the Solomonic temple had certain distinctive features. Clearly the Solomonic temple was not just a copy of some existing temple. In particular, the most holy place was larger and was described as a perfect cube. For many of the Canaanite and Syrian examples, the most holy place was a small niche in which, apparently, the image of the deity was placed. In the Israelite cult, there was no image of God; the ark of the covenant served as the symbol of God's presence.

The one example of an Israelite temple that has been discovered is the small sanctuary at Arad. Although the inner room was of a broad-room (wider than it is long) plan rather than the long room of the Solomonic temple, the Arad temple does preserve a square-shaped most holy place. It also had two incense altars just outside the most holy place. In addition, two flat stone slabs are outside the nave, probably bases for columns or pillars corresponding to Jachin and Boaz at the Solomonic temple. And in the courtyard beyond the nave, there was an altar of sacrifice made of unhewn stones as prescribed in Exodus 20:25. This sanctuary gives clear evidence of the Israelites' temple-building practices. The excavator attributed the earliest phase of this temple to the time of Solomon, and the latest, when the sanctuary was covered over and made inaccessible in Josiah's reform.

CHARIOTS: THEIR DEVELOPMENT AND USE

BY R. KELVIN MOORE

A stone manger or feeding trough still in place in the enormous stables of King Ahab's (869–850 BC) "city of chariots" at Megiddo in Israel. Some scholars maintain the stables date to Solomon.

From Antioch of Syria, this orthostat shows two warriors in a chariot. Dates from the eighth century BC. One drove the chariot while the other's hands were free for battle.

Archaeological evidence indicates the chariot developed in Mesopotamia before 3000 BC and that the Hyksos introduced chariot warfare into Syria and Egypt between 1800 and 1600 BC.[1] The development of the horse-drawn chariot permitted for the first time large empires, such as the Hittite and Assyrian, to dominate.

CHARIOT STYLE AND DEVELOPMENT

Originally, chariots were probably made of light wicker-work and had a boxlike shape. Commonly, the front was curved, the sides straight, with the back open. Oftentimes woven rope comprised the floor—giving the rider(s) a soft and springy footing. An axle with wooden wheels of four, six, or eight spokes supported the carriage.

The chariot's physical appearance developed across the centuries. Eventually, wicker gave way to wood. First to do so, the Philistines fortified their wooden chariots with metal plates (Josh. 17:16–18). The advancement of "armor plate" made the Philistine chariot significantly stronger than the lighter, unfortified chariot belonging to the Israelites. Normally chariots were low slung, but Sennacherib introduced the high chariot, the wheels of which were easily a man's height.[2]

The Egyptians revolutionized chariotry. "The Egyptian chariot was probably the finest in the world in Joshua's day."[3] Previous chariots were heavy, difficult to maneuver, and pulled by slow-moving donkeys. Because of the scarcity of wood along the Nile River, Egyptians normally constructed chariots of much lighter wicker. Rather than using donkeys to pull chariots, the Egyptians pulled their chariots with horses. Thus, made of light materials and pulled by horses, the Egyptian chariots possessed greater speed than earlier chariots. The Egyptians also improved the chariot's design. Egyptian chariots had a lower body that gave the chariot a lower center of gravity. This design provided greater stability than the often clumsy predecessor. The rider stood directly over the axle in the Egyptian version. Such design distributed the rider's weight away from the horses to the chariot and placed less stress on the horses. Under the able leadership of Egyptian designers, the chariot developed into an effective military tool that opposing forces greatly feared.

Normally two individuals, a driver and a warrior, rode in military chariots. But a third rider manned Hittite chariots. Chariots that developed after Assyrian King Ashurbanipal (668–629 BC) carried four riders at times. Two horses pulled the chariot, but occasionally historical monuments show a third horse. The third horse, not actually yoked to the chariot, was a spare.

While mountainous regions rendered the chariot useless, the chariot was a deadly weapon in flat, open terrain. Long, intimidating knives attached to the chariot's wheels shredded enemy soldiers as the chariot raced across the battlefield.

CHARIOTS IN ISRAEL

In their early history, the Israelites did not commonly use the chariot. When they initiated the conquest, they found it impossible to defeat the Canaanites in the open plains because of the Canaanite use of the chariot. The agrarian Israelites found themselves at a distinct disadvantage. But with God's help, the military genius Joshua managed to defeat Jabin, king of Hazor, and Jabin's allies in spite of Jabin's powerful chariot force. Joshua launched a surprise attack at the "Waters of Merom" (Josh. 11:5). To neutralize Jabin's ominous chariot force, the Israelites hamstrung Jabin's horses, that is, cut the large tendon at the back of the hock.[4]

The chariot of King Tutankhamun was gilded wood, bronze, and ivory.

Because early Israelite chariot usage was rare, the Israelites avoided the great royal highway along the Mediterranean Sea. Instead, they favored the hill country to the east where enemy chariots were less maneuverable and less effective.

During the times of the prophet Samuel and King Saul, the Philistines dominated the Israelites for numerous reasons, chariots being one. The chariot played a key role in the Israelite-Philistine life-and-death struggle,[5] which eventually cost King Saul his life. King David's victories over the Philistines were undoubtedly because he introduced the chariot to the Israelite military.[6] Chariot usage among the Hebrews climaxed with King Ahab, who exceeded both David and Solomon. According to Assyrian records, King Ahab engaged the Assyrians at the battle of Qarqar (853 BC) with 2,000 chariots![7]

With the advent of horseback riding by 1000 BC, chariots were no longer the preferred military implement for soldiers and officers. Mounted cavalry replaced chariots as the military instrument of choice. Yet long after the demise of their usefulness in war, chariots continued to be used for hunting and sport racing.

NOTES

[1] Lai Ling Elizabeth Ngan, "Chariots" in *HolBD*, 245.

[2] J. W. Wevers, "Chariot" in *The Interpreter's Dictionary of the Bible* (*IDB*), ed. George A Buttrick (Nashville: Abingdon, 1962), 1:553.

[3] V. Gilbert Beers, "Canaanite Chariots" in *The Victor Handbook of Bible Knowledge* (Wheaton, IL: Victor Books), 141.

[4] William H. Morton, "Joshua" in *Broadman Bible Commentary*, ed. Clifton J. Allen (Nashville: Broadman, 1970), 2:346.

[5] John Bright, *A History of Israel*, 3rd ed. (Philadelphia: Westminster, 1981), 185.

[6] Wevers, "Chariot," 554.

[7] Ngan, "Chariots," 245.

CISTERNS IN THE ANCIENT NEAR EAST

BY CLAUDE F. MARIOTTINI

Water tunnel leading into the cistern at Megiddo. Ahab built the city's water system, including the tunnel and cistern, in the ninth century BC.

The Struthion Pool was a water source for the Antonia Fortress in Jerusalem. The original pool, which was likely built by Herod the Great, would hold about 8,000,000 gallons of water. In the second century AD, Hadrian turned the pool into a cistern.

Smaller cisterns for private use were usually in one of three typical shapes: bottle, bell, or pear. The length of the neck or shaft leading into the cistern and the size of the cistern itself could vary greatly.

Be'er and *bor* are two similar words the Hebrew Bible uses to refer to water sources. The word *be'er* is generally translated as "well," an underground source of water. *Bor* is generally translated "cistern" or "pit." The Joseph story uses *bor* and translates it "pit" (Gen. 37:20); the same word is translated "cistern" in the story of Saul seeking David (1 Sam. 19:22).

Cisterns were common in the ancient Near East and Israel due to the land's dry condition. Canaan was arid. Because of the hot and dry summers, people living in Canaan needed water sources that could provide for their needs throughout the year, especially during the dry months.

Springs were perennial sources of water during the rainless summers. Water from a spring was called "living water." Springs supplied a constant source of water, but in the dry season they often were not enough to provide for a community's needs. In this case, the basic water source for daily use was a cistern.

When people moved away from springs, they had to provide for their needs away from the water source. People in arid places faced hardships related to the lack of water and the limited number of natural water sources. One way to collect water was by digging cisterns. A cistern was an artificial reservoir used for storing water during the dry season and for supplementing a community's water supply.

Updated, open-air cistern built on the earlier Iron Age cistern site in Amman. David's army defeated the Ammonites at Rabbah, which was later named Philadelphia and then Amman, which is the capital of Jordan.

The rainy season in Canaan was short, lasting from mid-October or early November to the end of April. The fluctuation in precipitation during the rainy season made the development of water collection and storage crucial for the economy of the community, the development of agriculture, feeding the herds and flocks, and private consumption. Cisterns enabled the community to collect rainwater during the rainy season and keep it for the summer months. Cisterns were supplied with water from rooftops and runoff from the hills. People cut channels into the earth to lead street waters into the cisterns.

People dug cisterns mostly out of limestone. Limestone, though, was porous. The water thus seeped slowly through the rocks, and the cistern ran dry. In the thirteenth century BC, the inhabitants of the central hills discovered that plaster was impervious to water, and they began plastering the cisterns.

Some cisterns were pear-shaped with a small opening, which allowed them to be covered. The coverings prevented animals, people, or debris from falling in (Exod. 21:33–34). Other cisterns were bottle shaped with a round bottom. These sometimes served as prisons. Cistern capacity varied depending on the community's need. Thousands of small cisterns have been found throughout Israel. At Qumran, archaeologists found four large, three medium-sized, and four small cisterns.[1]

Using water from runoff required elimination of the impurities, so people put rocks at the bottom of cisterns to catch debris. Also, they drilled holes on one side of the cistern to allow water to go to an adjacent cistern, thus filtering the water as it went from one cistern to another.[2]

CISTERNS IN ISRAEL

At the beginning of the Iron Age (ca. 1200 BC), the people who had arrived in the hill country of Canaan dug cisterns on the hills to preserve water, allowing them to live some

At Gergesa, one of the largest basilicas discovered in Israel. Beneath the courtyard of the church, which dates to the fifth–sixth centuries, is a large cistern with two openings. Shown is the reconstructed basalt opening on the south side of the courtyard.

Large water cistern built by the paranoid King Herod (37–4 BC) to provide an almost endless supply of fresh water for his palace-fortress at Masada.

distance from a spring. This innovation led to the establishment of new settlements away from natural water sources, hence the term "dry farming." The cisterns preserved water during the rainy season so farmers and families could use the water in the dry months.

At the time the Hebrews entered the land of Canaan, three bell-shaped cisterns supplied water to one house compound at Ai. These cisterns were cut into layers of Senonian chalk. The cisterns had small openings, which helped keep out contaminants. The cisterns were closed with a flat, round capstone. A cut along the hill channeled rainwater into the cisterns. These three cisterns were linked together. The water from the first cistern flowed into the second and from the second into the third. The first cistern would collect the sediment so that the water could be filtered into the second and third cisterns.[3]

According to archaeologists, the introduction of cistern technology in the hill country of Canaan allowed people to establish small villages throughout the region. The number and size of the cisterns depended on the number of people in the family or clan and their needs. According to an archaeological report, the number of cisterns in the Negev ran into the thousands. "No Iron II fortress or village could have existed in the Negev without these cisterns of various types, the digging of which is Biblically attested."[4]

THE GOOD WORK OF GOD

When Joseph's brothers threw him into the cistern, it was empty. The empty cistern in the Old Testament carries a negative meaning: in some cases, it was a place of imprisonment (Gen. 37:20–24; Jer. 38:6). The Hebrew word *bor*, rendered as "cistern" in the Joseph story, is translated as "dungeon" or "prison" in Genesis 40:15.

When *bor* is translated as "Pit," the word is associated with death. "Down to the Pit" means "to die" (Ps. 28:1). The same word is associated with the entrance of the dead into Sheol: "But you will be brought down to Sheol into the deepest regions of the Pit" (Isa. 14:15).

Joseph experienced his brothers' betrayal. Because of their actions, he had to suffer. He was put into the *bor*, into the gates of Sheol, by his brothers and by Potiphar. Because God was with Joseph, however, the Lord put the brothers' evil to good use: "You planned evil against me; God planned it for good to bring about the present result—the survival of many people" (Gen. 50:20).

NOTES

1   Patricia Hidiroglou, "Aqueducts, Basins, and Cisterns: The Water Systems at Qumran," *NEA* 63.3 (2000): 139.
2   Victor H. Matthews, *Manners and Customs in the Bible* (Peabody, MA: Hendrickson, 1991), 46.
3   Joseph A. Callaway, "Village Subsistence: Iron Age Ai and Raddana," in *The Answers Lie Below: Essays in Honor of Lawrence Edmund Toombs* (Lanham, MD: University Press of America, 1984), 55.
4   Nelson Glueck, "An Aerial Reconnaissance of the Negev," *BASOR* 155 (1959): 4.

CROWNS FIT FOR A KING

BY ROBERTA LOU JONES

STYLES OF CROWNS

Designers showed great creativity in making crowns for important people. Many ancient crowns resembled caps. Assyrian kings often ruled in embroidered, jewel-studded cloth turbans. Persian royalty wore skullcaps with rosettes and jewels. Egyptian pharaohs frequently added to their crowns images of the highly poisonous cobra. Another type of crown originated from simple cloth or leather headbands. Craftsmen borrowed the headband idea and made crowns of gold, silver, and copper.[1] Monarchs in the biblical world seemed to search constantly for suitable royal headgear to express their power and position.

Queen Puabi (or Shubad) lived in Ur about 2500 BC. Her headband-style crown included gold wreaths with dangling willow and beech leaves. Chains of blue lapis lazuli and orange-red carnelian beads added even more splendor.[2]

WORDS FOR CROWN

Scholars often translate the Hebrew words *kether* and *atarah* as "crown." Both words suggest circular headpieces. Additionally, the Hebrew word *nezer* can be translated "crown" and implies dedication or service to God. *Atarah*, *nezer*, and *kether* can be translated with words synonymous with "crown." For instance, in the CSB, the medallion Moses attached to Aaron's turban was called a "diadem" (*nezer*; Lev. 8:9). In Ezekiel 23:42, common men flattered women by putting "tiaras" (*atarah*) on their heads.

CROWNS IN SURPRISING PLACES

In 1962, archaeologists explored the Nahal Mishmar caves near the Dead Sea. The agile adventurers used ropes and ladders to scale down a high cliff to a cave entrance. The archaeologists discovered grain, leather sandals, woven straw platters, and pottery. They also found a surprising cache of metal objects, including ten copper crowns. The archaeologists called this place Cave of the Treasure. Likely, a fertility cult used the crowns in religious rituals during the Chalcolithic Period (4000–3150 BC).[3]

Hammurabi became king of Babylon sometime between 1848 and 1736 BC. He arranged a rock pillar, about seven feet tall, inscribed with 282 laws. That diorite stele is now known as the Code of Hammurabi. The pillar showed Shamash (the sun-god) and Hammurabi wearing regal clothing and crowns.

Replica of a statue in Diana's temple at Ephesus. Her crown, called a castle crown, is made to resemble the city of Ephesus.

The tomb of Egyptian king Tutankhamun (ca. 1361 BC) contained an ornate wooden chair. This throne shimmered with gold, colored glazes, and precious stones. Two winged serpents, both wearing crowns, formed the arms of Tutankhamun's throne. Each chair leg ended in a carved lion's paw. The front panel of the back of the throne showed the royal couple wearing elaborate crowns. His crown included numerous images of the royal cobra. Surely the spreading snake heads properly terrified the king's enemies.[4]

A silver tetradrachma coin shows a radiant crown, which was a diadem with spikes. This coin, likely showing Antiochus VI (145–142 BC), has six spikes. Other coins show as many as fourteen.

THE CROWN OF PSALM 8

King David meditated on God's great name. Then the former shepherd boy considered the moon and stars. David pondered, "What is a human being that you remember him" (Ps. 8:1–4). The answer: "You made him little less than God and crowned him with glory and honor" (v. 5). The psalmist continued, "You made him ruler over the works of your hands" (v. 6). How are we rulers? Humanity represents God as Ruler over all created things. Therefore, the Creator of the world honors human beings by crowning them as his authorized representatives.

NOTES

1 John Rea, "Crown" in *Wycliffe Bible Dictionary*, ed. Charles F. Pfeiffer, Howard F. Vos, and John Rea (Peabody, MA: Hendrickson, 1998), 405–7.

2 P. R. S. Moorey, *UR "of the Chaldees": A Revised and Updated Edition of Sir Leonard Woolley's Excavations at Ur* (Ithaca, NY: Cornell University Press, 1982), 60–77.

3 *Encyclopedia of Archaeological Excavations in the Holy Land* (*EAEHL*), ed. Michael Avi-Yonah and Ephraim Stern, English ed., vol. 3 (Englewood Cliffs, NJ: Prentice-Hall, 1977), 683–90. See P. Bar-Adon, "Expedition C–The Cave of the Treasure," *IEJ* 12.3–4 (1962): 215–26; Isaac Gilead, "Religio-Magic Behavior in the Chalcolithic Period of Palestine," in *Aharon Kempinski Memorial Volume*, ed. Eliezer D. Oren and Shmuel Ahituv (Israel: Ben-Gurion University of the Negev Press, 2002), 103–22.

4 Howard Carter and A. C. Mace, *The Tomb of Tut-ankh-Amen* (London: Cassell, 1930), 46–47, 118–19, 206–7, plates 2, 24, 62, 63.

DEEDS AND SEALS IN JEREMIAH

BY CONN DAVIS

Iron Age Hebrew seals from the Israel Museum in Jerusalem.

Jeremiah proclaimed and passionately experienced God's message of judgment during the last years of Judah, 627–586 BC. Of all the Old Testament prophets, he uniquely shared his ministry with his secretary-scribe, Baruch. Jeremiah dictated God's message directly to Baruch who wrote it down with ink and scroll (Jer. 36:4,18,32). When time came to purchase a piece of family property, Baruch was there to draw up the deed, making sure it was signed, sealed, and secured. What did this sealed contract look like?

BACKGROUND INFORMATION

Jeremiah 32 is "the clearest description that we have of the way in which transfers of property were handled in pre-Exilic Judah."[1] One of Jeremiah's cousins, Hanamel, offered for sale family land in Anathoth, only three miles north of Jerusalem. At the time, Jeremiah was a prisoner in King Zedekiah's courtyard. The transaction occurred during the perilous time of the Babylonian siege and invasion of Jerusalem in 588–586 BC.

Jeremiah and Hanamel were from a family of priests who resided in Anathoth, which was one of the thirteen cities or areas that Aaron's descendants received in the promised land (Josh. 21:13–19). The basic social units within Israel were the tribe, clan, and family.

Under Levitical law, Jeremiah had a responsibility to redeem the ancestral land for his family and clan. God said in Leviticus 25:23–25, "The land is not to be permanently sold because it is mine, and you are only aliens and temporary residents on my land. You are to allow the redemption of any land you occupy. If your brother becomes destitute and sells part of his property, his nearest relative may come and redeem what his brother has sold" (see Jer. 32:7–8).

In Egypt, the land belonged to the temple or religious establishment and to the pharaoh on behalf of the community. In Mesopotamia, the king, along with families and individuals, owned property.[2] God's ownership of the land of Canaan or the promised land, however, was a theological principle for ancient Israel. God gave instructions to Aaron that his tribe, the Levites, were to have the responsibility to care for and to maintain the tabernacle with its services, sacrifices, and contents. Thus God provided them with their own "holy land" inheritance of one-tenth of the land (Num. 18:20–24).

With the approaching threat of Babylonian domination, Jeremiah purchased the field from his cousin, Hanamel (Jer. 32:9). Then he "recorded it on a scroll, sealed it, called in witnesses, and weighed out the silver on the scales" (v. 10). Finally, in front of witnesses in the prison courtyard, he "took the purchase agreement—the sealed copy with its terms and conditions and the open copy—and gave the purchase agreement to Baruch son of Neriah, son of Mahseiah" (vv. 11–12). But what did the sealing of the purchase agreement involve?

SEALS

As early as the fifth millennium BC, peoples of the ancient Near East used seals to identify ownership of property and to secure documents. Seals were made of metal, shells, bone, stone, or baked clay and were either stamps or cylinders that were rolled.[3] Seals were also used for decoration on food items and pottery.

From 3000 BC on, Egypt and Mesopotamia had highly developed literary cultures that used cylinder seals and stamp seals to secure their legal and social transactions. The seals usually were decorative and had the name or title of officials such as the king or his servants engaged in administrative duties.

By 900 BC, ancient Israel used stamp seals to represent authority and to make legal transactions. One of the earliest examples is when Queen Jezebel used the seal of King Ahab (874–853 BC) to validate her forged letters when she attempted a land-grab of Naboth's vineyard (1 Kgs. 21:7–10).

Archaeologists have discovered hundreds of Israelite stamp seals; most were oval or scarab in shape with a raised surface.[4] One of the oldest stamp seals from Israel's excavations is a jasper seal with a roaring lion found at Megiddo, inscribed "[belonging] to Shema, servant of Jeroboam." It dates from the eighth century BC. Archaeologists found Israelite seals in their original rings; other seals formed part of a necklace. When Pharaoh promoted Joseph to the second-most powerful position in Egypt, he gave Joseph his personal ring and a golden necklace to symbolize his authority. Likely the ring and even the necklace may have contained a seal, the design of which would have been unique to Joseph.

ANCIENT DEEDS

The term *purchase agreement* in Jeremiah 32:11–12 is literally "scroll of purchase." Typically, the Hebrew word *sepher*, "scroll," referred to anything someone would write, whether a book (Deut. 29:21); a letter (Jer. 29:1); or a document (Gen. 5:1; Est 8:5), including legal documents, such as a bill or "divorce certificate" (Deut. 24:1) or a purchase contract, as in Jeremiah 32.

Although Jeremiah 32 speaks of a singular "scroll of purchase," verses 11 and 14 make clear that besides the sealed "original," there was also an open, unsealed copy. When Jeremiah purchased the field at Anathoth, Baruch wrote and recorded the details of the sale on a single sheet of papyrus. Using what is called a "double deed" or "tied deed," Baruch recorded the transaction twice—one copy of the deed on the upper part of the sheet and one copy with the same wording on the lower. The upper copy was rolled up and sealed (usually by sewing) to preserve the original from fraudulent alteration. The lower copy remained open for public inspection.[5]

Remarkably, noted archaeologist Yigael Yadin found intact examples of tied deeds in his 1960–61 excavations in a canyon near the Dead Sea. Yadin and his team excavated caves that contained artifacts (including letters) belonging to Bar Kokhba and some of his followers. Bar Kokhba was the leader of the AD 132–135 Jewish revolt against Rome. Among the letters were tied deeds. The deeds were in two halves, the upper part sealed and the lower open. The writing style on the sealed part of the Bar Kokhba documents was smaller and more decorative than the larger, more block-style writing in the lower part. The deeds had signatures affixed beside the tying strings. This sheds light on why Jeremiah had the deed sealed and then witnessed (v. 10) rather than witnessed and then sealed. Says Yadin, "The use of 'tied deeds' is a very old and known practice of the ancient world; . . . This system was used, of course, for the more important documents."[6] Though Yadin's find dated centuries after Jeremiah's time, this particular method of sealing deeds evidently had not changed for generations.

Archaeology thus sheds light on the Jeremiah account and on our understanding of some types of seals used in preexilic Judah. We are likely familiar with ancient seals and how they secured letters, contracts, and important documents. Not all seals, though, were stamped or rolled through a soft clay or wax. Some, like the deed for the Anathoth field, were evidently sewn and then signed to secure them for a later date. The archaeological find from Bar Kokhba helps us better understand the Jeremiah text and helps us better visualize the use of seals with deeds and other ancient documents.

NOTES

[1] John Bright, *Jeremiah, vol. 21 of Anchor Bible (AB)* (New York: Doubleday, 1964), 239.

[2] Roland de Vaux, *Ancient Israel* (New York: McGraw-Hill, 1961), 164.

[3] Bonnie S. Magness-Gardener, "Seals, Mesopotamian" in *ABD*, 5:1062–63; O. Tufnell, "Seals and Scarabs," *IDB*, 4:254–59.

[4] N. Avigad, "The Contribution of Hebrew Seals to an Understanding of Israelite Religion and Society," in *Ancient Israelite Religion*, ed. Patrick D. Miller Jr. et al. (Philadelphia: Fortress, 1987), 195–208. Avigad counted 328 published Hebrew seals, mostly from the eighth to sixth centuries BC. Many more have been found and published since.

[5] "Examples of such documents in two copies are known from Elephantine in Egypt." Bright, *Jeremiah*, 238.

[6] Yigael Yadin, *Bar-Kokhba* (London: Weidenfeld & Nicolson, 1978), 229.

EARTHENWARE VESSELS: POTTERY AND POTTERY PRODUCTION IN ANCIENT ISRAEL

BY JOEL F. DRINKARD JR.

Pottery from Amarneh in middle Euphrates region, 2650–2000 BC.

Clay may have been first used in mud bricks, as mortar in stone structures, and as a sealant for baskets. The earliest pottery was probably accidentally produced when such clay was burned in a fire. This "accidental" pottery was extremely hard and did not deteriorate in heat, wind, or water. Soon people began deliberately making objects and vessels out of pottery. The first objects were crude and entirely made by hand. The potter's wheel was apparently developed in Egypt during the Old Kingdom (2700–2200 BC). The wheel allowed the production of more symmetrical vessels.

By the time of the Israelite monarchy (1050 BC), the potter's wheel was well developed, and firing was more controlled, producing more consistency in vessels.[1] The ancient Israelite potter began his work by gathering clay. Years of experience would teach him the best sources of clay for his vessels, often from a perennial streambed. After gathering clay, the potter would remove all the large impurities—such as sticks, roots, and stones. Then it was washed to remove smaller impurities and allowed to settle so that heavier

Iron Age pottery from Lachish, dated before tenth–sixth centuries BC.

clays would sink to the bottom of the container, and finer clay would rise to the top. The finest clays could be mixed with more water to form a slurry. This served as a slip to finely decorate a vessel. The clay was now ready to be formed into a vessel. Potters would shape coarser clay into the larger, heavier utilitarian vessels of everyday use, such as store jars or mixing bowls. They would form the finer clay into smaller thin-walled vessels such as small bowls and pitchers.[2]

When he was ready to make his vessel, the potter sat at his wheel (Jer. 18:3), which was actually two wheels. Two large circular stones were connected by a wooden shaft. The potter would kick the lower wheel with his feet, which turned the upper wheel. This left both his hands free to work the vessel. He would place a ball of clay in the center of the upper wheel and then use his hands and tools to form the vessel. Jeremiah 18 describes the prophet's visit to a potter's shop where he watched the potter making a vessel. But the vessel was not what the potter intended. We are not told why the potter was not satisfied. In any case, the potter reworked the clay back into a ball and began to manipulate the clay to make another vessel.

After the vessel was shaped, the potter would add handles, spouts, and other extra features. He then applied slips, burnishing, and painted designs. The vessel would then air dry for several days. After the vessel had dried sufficiently, it was fired in a kiln to create the final pottery piece.

The process of making handmade vessels has changed little since the time of ancient Israel. Today's wheels are powered by electric motors rather than foot power, and the pottery is fired in an electric or gas-powered kiln rather than in a pit or crude kiln using wood or charcoal as in Jeremiah's day. But the forming of handmade

Early pinch-pot chalice from Kerak, circa 2500 BC.

Drinking bowl and supports for firing in kiln, 275–250 BC.

Cornet-shaped vessels from Ghassul in the Jordan Valley, Chalcolithic era, 4500–3150 BC.

vessels remains virtually the same. People in some remote regions continue to use foot-powered wheels still today.

While every potter might have his own distinct forms, the basic design of most pieces was similar: store jars from different potters and regions were similar and are recognizable as store jars but distinct from jugs or cooking pots or chalices. Differences in design and decoration marked regional or ethnic differences. More important, over time the pottery shapes and designs evolved. These changes can be traced from excavations and serve as a means of dating the strata (or levels) of excavations. Although not an exact analogy, we can date US coins relatively by the change of design on the front and back. Of course, our coins also have dates, but some coins so worn that the date is not visible can still be dated just by the design. The quarter with a standing Liberty face is older than a quarter with Washington's face. The Washington quarters had the same reverse, an eagle, until the Bicentennial quarters of 1975–76, which had a colonial drummer. From 1999 to 2008, quarters featured one of the fifty states on the reverse, five being produced each year. These changes allow an easy relative dating of the coins.

More than a hundred years ago, archaeologists working in the Middle East from Egypt through Israel, Jordan, and Syria were able to develop a typology of pottery forms that could provide a relative chronology.[3] Archaeologists found they could use the shape, decoration, and texture of pottery to identify the region where it was produced and its relative age. Since pottery is ubiquitous and nearly indestructible (although what are found today are usually pieces or "potsherds"), pottery is abundant in virtually every site.[4] Also, since pottery is typically discarded when broken, most of the pottery in a specific stratum will belong to the time frame of that stratum. Archaeologists carefully catalog where the sherds are found. Then a pottery specialist can "read" the pottery from a specific stratum to date the site relatively. In my home, we have a few pieces of antique china that belonged to my parents and

Potter's wheel with pair of stones for pivoting. The potter's wheel was apparently developed in Egypt during the Old Kingdom (2700-2160 BC).

grandparents. But all our everyday china dates to the past forty years or so. If our house were destroyed by some catastrophe today and excavated in a hundred years, archaeologists could use the everyday china to date the house to the approximate period of 1970 to the present.

The focal text in Isaiah poses an absurd situation: "How can what is made say about its maker, 'He didn't make me'? How can what is formed say about the one who formed it, 'He doesn't understand what he's doing'?" (Isa. 29:16). The answer to the questions posed is: Impossible! How absurd! Clay vessels cannot claim that the potter did not make them or that he has no sense. Clay vessels do not speak, nor do they have a mind. Again, Isaiah says: "Woe to the one who argues with his Maker—one clay pot among many. Does clay say to the one forming it, 'What are you making?' Or does your work say, 'He has no hands'?" (45:9). Isaiah used similar examples a number of times, usually in satires about idols and their makers (see 2:8,20; 17:8; 31:7; 44:10–19; 46:6; 48:5). The absurdity is that humans make idols of wood, stone, metal, or pottery. The idols cannot speak, hear, or move by themselves—yet the worshippers turn to them for help. How absurd!

Then Isaiah reversed the metaphor and made the point that we are metaphorically all clay vessels made by the master Potter, God himself (Isa. 64:8). The difference in the two metaphors is radical; we do not make gods (idols), but God makes us! Jeremiah used that same metaphor to describe God's dealings with nations and peoples: God is the Potter, the nations are the clay (Jer. 18:6–11). The potter-clay imagery is first found in Genesis 2. The word used to depict God "form[ing]" (Hb. *yatsar*, Gen. 2:7–8,19) his creatures is related to the word used for clay vessels (*yetser*, Isa. 29:16). The word for "potter" (*yotser*) is the participle of the same verb (*yatsar*). The same metaphor continues in the New Testament as Paul refers to humans as clay vessels (2 Cor. 4:7).

NOTES

[1]   Ruth Amiran, *Ancient Pottery of the Holy Land* (Jerusalem: Massada Press, 1969), 192; Nancy L. Lapp, "Pottery Chronology of Palestine" in *ABD*, 5:442.

[2]   Robert H. Johnston, "The Biblical Potter," *BA* 37.4 (1974): 89.

[3]   Amiran, Ancient Pottery, 13; Lapp, 433; Johnston, "Biblical Potter," 86.

[4]   Johnston, "Biblical Potter," 87.

EGYPTIAN CURSIVE, FROM "LITERACY IN THE ANCIENT NEAR EAST"

BY STEPHEN J. ANDREWS

The Egyptians developed two cursive scripts. They used demotic script mainly for business, legal, and literary purposes, and they used hieratic script primarily for religious texts.

The image above, written on linen, is a copy of the Book of the Dead of Padimin, written in hieratic script; from Akhmim, Egypt; dated after 664 BC. The fragment shown at the top is from Medinet Habu at Luxor. The text, written in demotic script, is a receipt for allotments of grain paid to the northern treasury.

EGYPTIAN MUMMIFICATION/ MOURNING THE DECEASED

BY SCOTT LANGSTON AND FRED WOOD

Model burial of the Late Predynastic period. The body, which is not mummified but desiccated by the dry, hot sand that covered it, is placed on its left side in a contracted position.

The belief that each individual possessed a *ka* and a *ba* as aspects of personality compelled Egyptians to preserve the body after death. The *ka* functioned as the "double" of the living person and resided with the individual in the afterlife. The *ba*, often translated as "soul," traveled throughout the underworld but also returned to the deceased each morning. Both of these aspects of a person needed a home for eternity. So it became important to preserve the body as that home. This need, therefore, may have helped produce the development of artificial mummification.[1]

The process as practiced by the ancient Egyptians developed over several centuries. In the early days, called the Old Kingdom (2830–2130 BC), only members of the royalty, especially the king, possessed access to it for their families. By the time of the New Kingdom (1570–1070 BC), the practice extended to almost anyone who desired and could afford it.[2]

Mummification scene in a burial chamber of the catacombs of Kom-El-Shogafa.

A wall painting fragment of mourning women from the tomb of Neb-Amon at Thebes.

The process differed according to one's ability to pay.

First, the embalmers removed all the internal organs except the heart. The Egyptians considered the heart necessary to activity in the afterlife. Knowing the internal organs decomposed first, the embalmers mummified them separately. They placed the internal organs in canopic jars in the tomb at the time of the burial. Believing the heart was the seat of intelligence and emotion, the Egyptians left it in the body. Contending the brain had no significant value, they removed it through the nose and discarded it.

Second, the embalmers packed and covered the body with natron, a salty drying agent. They left the body to dry out for forty to fifty days. By this time, the body's moisture had been absorbed, leaving only the hair, skin, and bones. They then stuffed the body cavity with resin, sawdust, or linen to restore the deceased's form and features.

Third, the embalmers wrapped the body in many layers of linen, inserting good luck or protective charms, known as amulets. Since Egyptians considered the scarab beetle the most important good luck piece, embalmers placed it above the heart. The priests recited prayers or incantations at each stage of the wrapping. This often required as many as fifteen days. The final act consisted of putting the body in a shroud or winding sheet.

The entire mummification process required about seventy days.

Those in charge of placing the mummy in a decorated coffin also placed prepared furniture, carved statues, games, food, and other items to be buried with the mummy. One final ritual remained, called "The Opening of the Mouth." Egyptians believed this ceremony gave the deceased ability to speak again, eat again, and have full use of his body in the "other world." Having completed the work of embalming and the accompanying rituals, the embalmers sealed the sarcophagus and pronounced it ready for burial.

Unless the person was affluent or of great importance, his funeral resembled one of today but in the context of Egyptian culture. For the poor or anyone not of royalty, funeral services involved little pomp or ceremony. The preparers steeped the body for a short time in bitumen or natron or perhaps even rubbed the body with these substances. They placed his few personal ornaments on it and wrapped it in one piece of linen. To aid him in the nether world, his staff and sandals accompanied him. A few amulets to help him meet his foe in the grave completed the package.

Mummy of a priest's wife.

Not so, the burial of the monarch, his family, or an extremely opulent person. When a king died, the country died symbolically, all the country's inhabitants wept and tore their garments. Religious officials closed the temples. The people abstained from sacrifices and celebrated no festivals for seventy-two days. Men and women went about the streets in great crowds, sometimes as many as 200 or 300 with mud on their heads. Knotting their garments below their breasts like girdles, they sang dirges twice daily in praise of the dead. They denied themselves wheat, animal food, wine, and any kind of delicacy or dainty fare.

During this time, no one made use of baths or unguents, nor did anyone recline on couches or enjoy the pleasures of sexual love. The people rather continued to sing dirges and spent the days in grief. Meanwhile those preparing the body assembled the paraphernalia necessary for the funeral and placed it in the coffin.

An open canopic chest revealing alabaster jars sculpted in the likeness of a king.

The Scriptures tell us Joseph instructed the physicians in his service to embalm Jacob's body. This varied from ordinary Hebrew custom, but the faithful son planned to fulfill his father's request to carry the body back for burial in the Cave of Machpelah.

NOTES

1   James E. Harris and Kent R. Weeks, *X-Raying the Pharaohs* (New York: Scribner's Sons, 1973), 76. John Baines and Jaromir Malek, *Atlas of Ancient Egypt* (Oxford: Phaidon, 1984), 226.

2   William J. Murname, "History of Egypt: New Kingdom (DYN. 18–20)," *ABD*, 2:348.

ESTABLISHING WEIGHTS AND MEASURES IN ANCIENT ISRAEL

BY CLAUDE F. MARIOTTINI

Bronze lion weight from Nimrud, dated 726–722 BC. The Akkadian inscription on the top reads "Palace of Shalmaneser King." The piece weighs 2,864 grams—about six pounds.

A study of the system of weights and measures of a nation (or "metrology") provides the foundation for understanding some of the factors that shaped the social and economic development of that nation. The systems of weights, measures of length, and measures of capacity in ancient Israel were related to the ancient metrological systems common in Mesopotamia. The ideal condition for trade and commerce in Israel and among ancient Near Eastern nations required an accurate system of weights and measures.

THE METROLOGY OF ANCIENT ISRAEL

In Israel, the demands of the covenant required an honest use of weights and measures since members of the covenant community were to treat one another with respect. Honesty in merchandising is related to the injunction in the Decalogue that prohibits a person to covet that which belongs to another person.[1] This was the reason the laws of holiness in the book of Leviticus urged the Israelites not to defraud each other: "Do not oppress your neighbor or rob him" (Lev. 19:13).

The metrology of ancient Israel was derived from systems that originated in Mesopotamia, primarily in Babylon. As early as the third millennium BC, the Babylonians had developed an elaborate system of weights and measures based on the sexagesimal system.[2] Today's division of hours into sixty minutes and minutes into sixty seconds is based on the Babylonian sexagesimal system. Because of commerce and trade, the Babylonian system of weights and measures made its way into Syria and Canaan.

Since the ancient patriarchs of Israel came from Mesopotamia, they possibly brought with them the system of weights and measures they previously used there. However, a reconstruction of this system is difficult. What the Bible has to teach about the metrology of ancient Israel must be adduced from archaeology, the biblical texts, and the literature of the ancient Near East.

Although the people of Israel used a system of weights and measures that was derived from Babylon, Israel's system was not the exact equivalent of the Babylonians'. Israel adapted Babylon's systems to meet its social and economic needs. Any attempt at comparing the biblical standards of weights and measures with contemporary standards is difficult if not impossible, since values change with the passage of time, and modern American and British standards are radically different from Mesopotamian and biblical systems.

A collection of stone and clay weights from el-Amarna, in Lower Egypt; dated 1350–1320 BC.

WEIGHTS AND MEASURES IN ISRAEL

The terms Israel used to classify weights and measures came from items in everyday life. They derived measurements of length from the length of the limbs of the human body. The cubit was the distance between the end of one's elbow to the tip of the

Five-shekel weight from Iron Age III (eighth–sixth centuries BC). The stone is inscribed with the Hebrew sign for shekel.

middle finger (about eighteen inches). The span was measured from the tip of the thumb to the tip of the little finger while both are extended (half a cubit). Only once does the Old Testament use the finger as a unit of measurement (Jer. 52:21).

The names the Israelites used for measuring capacities were generally the terms they used for the receptacles that held the provisions. The *omer* (Lev. 27:16), a word derived from the Hebrew term for "donkey," refers to a load the animal would carry. The *kor* (1 Kgs. 4:22) was a container to measure flour, wheat, and barley. The *kor* was also a measurement for oil (5:11). The *letek* is a smaller container, equal to half a homer (Hos. 3:2). The Hebrew term *ephah* (Lev. 5:11) referred originally to a basket but later came to refer to a measure of flour, barley, and other grains. The *seah* was a container the Israelites used to measure grain (1 Sam. 25:18, footnote). The *bath* was used to measure liquids such as oil (Ezek. 45:14), water (1 Kgs. 7:26), and wine (Isa. 5:10).

Precious material and metals were weighed on balances with two scales. The weights were made of hard stones called *eben*, a Hebrew word that means "stone" and "weight." These stones were kept in a bag (Deut. 25:13; Prov. 16:11; Mic. 6:11). The Hebrew word that means "to weigh" is *shaqal*, which is the root for the word *shekel*. Thus, the shekel became the basic unit of weight. The value of the shekel was equivalent to the weight of 180 grains of wheat. Three kinds of shekels were in use in the Old Testament era: the king's shekel or the royal standard (2 Sam. 14:26), the

Two of the handles are stamped with "lamelekh Hebron," meaning this was something from Hebron that belonged to the king (or his administration). The jar dates from the reign of Hezekiah, about 715–686 BC. The stamp (seal) assured an honest measure.

From ancient Ur; a carved stone with a handle; likely a weight; dated to Early Dynastic Age III, 2600–2400 BC.

shekel of the sanctuary (Exod. 30:13), and the common shekel (Josh. 7:21). Genesis 23:16 speaks about the shekel literally "passing to the merchant." Determining the value of this shekel is difficult, however, since many merchants had two kinds of weight, one for buying and one for selling.

Because the shekel was the basic measure of weight, determining its value is important.[3] This unit of weight was common to most societies in Mesopotamia. The book of Ezekiel provides the value of the shekel: "The standard unit for weight will be the silver shekel. One shekel will consist of twenty gerahs, and sixty shekels will be equal to one mina" (Ezek. 45:12 NLT). Another translation better reflects the Hebrew text: "The shekel is to consist of twenty gerahs. Twenty shekels plus twenty-five shekels plus fifteen shekels equal one mina" (NIV). This division of the mina into three different categories may indicate that people used weights of twenty-five, twenty, and fifteen shekels.

In Exodus 38:25–26, we learn that 603,550 bekas comes to one hundred talents and 1,775 shekels (CSB footnote). According to this information, the value of the shekel of the sanctuary was as follows: one talent was worth sixty minas; one mina was worth fifty shekels; and one shekel was worth two bekas. According to the book of Ezekiel, one talent was worth sixty minas; one mina was worth sixty shekels; and one shekel was worth twenty gerahs. Because Ezekiel was writing while in exile in Babylon, the value of the mina (sixty shekels) corresponds to the value of the mina in Babylon during the exile.

LAWS ABOUT WEIGHTS AND MEASURES

Ensuring that systems of weights, measures of length, and measures of capacity were fair required the sanction of authoritative law to make certain the weights and scales people used for buying and selling conformed to a standard set by the community.[4] The law about weights and measures in the book of Deuteronomy was enacted to promote economic honesty in buying and selling. What the law forbade was the practice of employing a double set of stones or weights and different ephahs or dry measures—one used for buying and the other used for selling. Babylonian wisdom literature speaks of merchants who use different sets of weights.[5] Thus the law required that in buying and selling, the people of Israel had to use "a full and honest weight" and accurate ephahs (Deut. 25:13–15). A similar law for just balances, just weights, just ephahs, and just hins is in the section of Leviticus commonly known as the Holiness Code (Lev. 19:35–36).

This tablet lists in succession measures of capacity, weights, and measures of area and of length. It probably served as a textbook in schools for teaching the measures and their units, as well as for the writing of numerals. The numerals were written in fractions, units, tens, and sixties, and multiples of these up to theoretical quantities—the highest being the equivalent of more than 14,000,000 gallons.

Israel's prophets accused the merchants of planning to "reduce the measure while increasing the price and cheat with dishonest scales" (Amos 8:5; see Hos. 12:7; Mic. 6:10–11). Some biblical scholars believe that during his religious and economic reforms at the end of the eighth century BC, King Hezekiah introduced official weights called *lmlk* weights, which helped standardize weights for Judah. The Hebrew word *lmlk* means "belonging to the king." Archaeologists have also uncovered jars, the handles of which bear a *lmlk* stamp. The stamped handles may indicate an attempt to establish uniform volume measurements as well.[6]

NOTES

1   Walter C. Kaiser Jr., *Toward Old Testament Ethics* (Grand Rapids: Zondervan, 1983), 136.
2   M. Pierce Matheney, "Weights and Measures," in *HolBD*, 1403.
3   Roland de Vaux, *Ancient Israel* (Grand Rapids: Eerdmans, 1997), 203.
4   De Vaux, *Ancient Israel*, 195.
5   W. G. Lambert, *Babylonian Wisdom Literature* (Winona Lake, IN: Eisenbrauns, 1996), 133, line 108.
6   John Bright, *A History of Israel* (Philadelphia: Westminster, 1981), 283.

TABLE OF WEIGHTS AND MEASURES
WEIGHTS

BIBLICAL UNIT	LANGUAGE	BIBLICAL MEASURE	U.S. EQUIVALENT
Gerah	Hebrew	1/20 shekel	1/50 ounce
Beka	Hebrew	1/2 shekel or 10 gerahs	1/5 ounce
Pim	Hebrew	2/3 shekel	1/3 ounce
Shekel	Hebrew	2 bekas	2/5 ounce
Litra (pound)	Greco-Roman	30 shekels	12 ounces
Mina	Hebrew/Greek	50 shekels	1 1/4 pounds
Talent	Hebrew/Greek	3,000 shekels or 60 minas	75 pounds/ 88 pounds

Length

BIBLICAL UNIT	LANGUAGE	BIBLICAL MEASURE	U.S. EQUIVALENT
Handbreadth	Hebrew	1/6 cubit or 1/3 span	3 inches
Span	Hebrew	1/2 cubit or 3 handbreadths	9 inches
Cubit/Pechys	Hebrew/Greek	2 spans	18 inches
Fathom	Greco-Roman	4 cubits	2 yards
Kalamos	Greco-Roman	6 cubits	3 yards
Stadion	Greco-Roman	1/8 milion or 400 cubits	1/8 mile
Milion	Greco-Roman	8 stadia	1,620 yards

TABLE OF WEIGHTS AND MEASURES
WEIGHTS

METRIC EQUIVALENT	VARIOUS TRANSLATIONS
.6 gram	gerah; oboli
5.7 grams	beka; half a shekel; quarter ounce; fifty cents
7.6 grams	2/3 of a shekel; quarter
11.5 grams	shekel; piece; dollar; fifty dollars
.4 kilogram	pound; pounds
.6 kilogram	mina; pound
34 kilograms/ 40 kilograms	talent/talents; 100 pounds
8 centimeters	handbreadth; three inches; four inches
23 centimeters	span
.5 meter	cubit/cubits; yard; half a yard; foot
2 meters	fathom; six feet
3 meters	rod; reed; measuring rod
185 meters	miles; furlongs; race
1.5 kilometers	mile

TABLE OF WEIGHTS AND MEASURES WEIGHTS			
BIBLICAL UNIT	**LANGUAGE**	**BIBLICAL MEASURE**	**U.S. EQUIVALENT**
Dry Measure			
Xestes	Greco-Roman	1/2 cab	1 1/6 pints
Cab	Hebrew	1/18 ephah	1 quart
Choinix	Greco-Roman	1/18 ephah	1 quart
Omer	Hebrew	1/10 ephah	2 quarts
Seah/Saton	Hebrew/Greek	1/3 ephah	7 quarts
Modios	Greco-Roman	4 omers	1 peck or 1/4 bushel
Ephah [Bath]	Hebrew	10 omers	3/5 bushel
Lethek	Hebrew	5 ephahs	3 bushels
Kor [Homer]/ Koros	Hebrew/Greek	10 ephahs	6 bushels or 200 quarts
Liquid Measure			
Log	Hebrew	1/72 bath	1/3 quart
Xestes	Greco-Roman	1/8 hin	11/6 pints
Hin	Hebrew	1/6 bath	1 gallon or 4 quarts
Bath/Batos	Hebrew/Greek	1 ephah	6 gallons
Metretes	Greco-Roman	10 hins	10 gallons

TABLE OF WEIGHTS AND MEASURES
WEIGHTS

METRIC EQUIVALENT	VARIOUS TRANSLATIONS
.5 liter	pots; pitchers; kettles; copper pots; copper bowls; vessels of bronze
1 liter	cab; kab
1 liter	measure; quart
2 liters	omer; tenth of a deal; tenth of an ephah; six pints
7.3 liters	measures; pecks; large amounts
9 liters	bushel; bowl; peck
22 liters	bushel; peck; deal; part; measure; six pints; seven pints
110 liters	half homer; half sack
220 liters/ 525 liters	cor; homer; sack; measures; bushels
.3 liter	log; pint; cotulus
.5 liter	pots; pitchers; kettles; copper bowls; vessels of bronze
4 liters	hin; pints
22 liters	gallon(s); barrels; liquid measures
39 liters	firkins; gallons

FIRST-CENTURY ARMOR

BY GREGORY T. POUNCEY

Relief depicting Roman soldiers, first century AD.

Bronze Roman helmet with a peak-like projection at the back of the neck, believed to be Celtic in origin. This type of helmet was popular among the legions. Many of this type have been found at Montefortino in northern Italy.

In Paul's day, the Roman army contained four classes of soldiers.[1] The first class, known as *velites*, included the youngest and poorest of the soldiers. They fought on the front lines and were lightly armored, considering their position on the battlefield. The second class, or *hastati*, fought behind the *velites*. They were the strongest and most heavily armed forces. The *principes* included the most capable soldiers in the prime of their careers. They provided the third line of defense for the army. The final line, the *triarii*, included the oldest soldiers and were considerably smaller in number than the other divisions. They provided a connection to the army's central command.

According to descriptions of the armor of the *hastati*, Paul probably had these soldiers in mind as he referred to a Christian's spiritual armor (Eph. 6:10–20). The Greek historian Polybius described the equipment of the *hastati*.[2] His weapon list included a large shield, a sword hanging on the right side, two spears, a brass helmet, a brass breastplate, and greaves (leg protection below the knees). Soldiers who came from the higher classes had a coat of mail underneath the breastplate.

A soldier wore two belts, the first underneath the armor. This belt gathered the tunic so movement was possible without hindrances from the undergarment.[3] The second belt fit over the outside armor and held the sword. Both belts functioned as a piece of armor that held all the others in place. Polybius described the breastplate as the armor that protected the heart.[4] Some soldiers in that day wore segmented armor, while others wore a one-piece breastplate made of brass.[5]

The Jewish historian Josephus described the soldier's shoes as thickly studded leather-soled shoes.[6] Their main purpose was to create a solid foundation for the soldier so he would not slide when fighting on a hillside. They also provided limited protection from the weather. The shield was wooden and covered with calfskin. It was large, four by two and one-half feet.[7] The shield extinguished burning arrows that embedded themselves between the layers, where the lack of oxygen would snuff out the flames.

The helmet was a large, one-piece bowl with a front guard, cheek pieces, and neck guard.[8] Most helmets contained a feather or crest piece (up to eighteen inches tall) designed to make the soldier appear taller and thus more intimidating. A soldier's sword was double-edged and worn on the outside belt.

Paul envisioned Christians fitting the spiritual armor in place through prayer and then engaging the enemies of God—not in one's own strength but in the power the Lord provides.

A Roman centurion made of basalt, from the early Roman period.

NOTES

[1] H. M. D. Parker, *The Roman Legions* (Oxford: Clarendon, 1928; repr., New York: Barnes & Noble), 14.

[2] Polybius, *The Histories* 6.23.

[3] Peter T. O'Brien, *The Letter to the Ephesians*, Pillar New Testament Commentary (Grand Rapids: Eerdmans, 1999), 473.

[4] Polybius, *The Histories* 6.23.

[5] John Warry, *Warfare in the Classical World* (New York: St. Martin's, 1980), 191.

[6] Josephus, *Jewish War* 6.1.8.

[7] Polybius, *The Histories* 6.23.

[8] Michael P. Speidel, *Riding for Caesar* (Cambridge, MA: Harvard University Press, 1994), 106.

FIRST-CENTURY BURIAL

BY THOMAS H. GOODMAN

Roman burial stones described or depicted the deceased person's past achievements, common elements from his daily life, or anticipated details of the next life. Many (like the one shown) had an epitaph for the deceased. The stones were usually attached to the tomb wall or under the niche that held the person's ash urn.

Funeral practices in the first-century world varied. Romans, Egyptians, Parthians, Jews, and Christians each had their own convictions on what constituted proper handling of a body.

ROMAN

When the dying person took his final breath, his eyes would be closed by a close family member. The others gathered would begin to call out the name of the now-deceased person as a sign of grief. Persons would then wash and anoint the body before dressing it. If available and especially if earned in life, a crown was placed on the deceased person's head. A family member would then place a coin in the person's mouth so the deceased could pay the mythological ferryman Charon to row him across the river Styx to the land of the dead. The body would lie in state for about seven days, with the feet toward the door of the house. Next came the funeral procession and disposal of the body. Financial resources dictated how elaborate these services would be.[1]

The Book of the Dead was a collection of funerary texts used in Egypt for about 1,500 years.

From the early days of Rome's history, both burial and cremation were practiced widely. By the first century AD, cremation had become "almost universal among the Romans."[2] At the end of the funerary procession, the body was placed upon a funeral pyre and burned. Families kept the ash remains in carved chests, ceramic containers, or glass cinerary urns. Some ash containers were kept in homes. Others were placed in columbaria, tombs that allowed many to be interred in a small space.

During Hadrian's reign (AD 117–138), craftsmen began making increasingly decorative sarcophagi.[3] Cremation's popularity decreased as more people used sarcophagi. Often, but not always, after a body had decomposed, family members would gather the bones into smaller boxes called ossuaries (see more detail below). Except for the highest-ranking dignitaries, burials always occurred outside the city.[4]

EGYPTIAN

Though many Romans who occupied their land practiced cremation, Egyptians regarded the practice with "extreme horror, for it deprived the dead man once and for all of any chance of enjoying the offerings made by the living."[5] Many Egyptians continued to practice embalming, in keeping with their ancient conviction that the process of mummification and the rituals associated with it ensured the person's transition to, and full participation in, the next life.[6]

PARTHIAN

The Parthian Empire (238 BC–AD 224) was located mostly in what we know today as Iran (the region of the former Persian Empire). In the first century, the carry-over religion of the region was Zoroastrianism (began ca. 1200 BC). Although burial was the traditional practice of the region, the Zoroastrians practiced neither burial nor cremation, convinced that a dead body would compromise the purity of the elements of earth and fire. Zoroastrians left bodies on an open raised structure called a *dakhma* or "tower of silence," to be eaten by birds. "Outside of some Jews and the Christians, the only people of the ancient world to believe in a resurrection of the flesh were the Zoroastrians."[7]

JEWISH

Burial in caves or rock sepulchers, rather than cremation, was the universal Jewish practice. After a person died, Jews washed the body and then wrapped it with cloth strips rather than repose it within a sarcophagus; they also used heavy spices to help cover the smell of decay. Jews always tried to bury an individual before dark on the day of death.

Accompanied by family members, professional mourners, pipers, and even strangers, pallbearers would carry the coffin or funerary bier to a well-marked grave in a field (see Luke 11:44) or to the burial cave. A large stone covered the cave opening.

Typically, a year after the burial, a family member would visit the burial site to collect the remaining bones and place them in an ossuary (lit "bone box"). Jews may have considered this a joyous occasion that marked the end of the time of mourning.[8] Ossuaries were stacked together in extended family sepulchers.[9] A father's wishes in a rabbinic teaching on mourning illustrate this practice: "My son, bury me at first. . . . In the course of time, collect my bones and put them in an ossuary."[10] Indeed, the Jews regarded such secondary burial among the most important of family duties.

CHRISTIAN

Jewish and Roman Christians followed the body-preparation steps that were common in the day: washing the body, wrapping it in cloth, and covering it in spices. They also continued the Jewish practice of burial (on the day of death) rather than cremation. Why the preference for burial? Writings of the early Christian apologist and theologian Tertullian (ca. 160–225 AD) offer a hint. He wrote of a Christian who intended to join the army, which would, upon a soldier's death, cremate the body. Because of the practice, Tertullian objected, saying: "And shall the Christian be burned according to camp rule, when he was not permitted to burn incense to an idol, when to him Christ remitted the punishment of fire?"[11]

Christians also shared funerary meals by providing food for the family, especially in the case of martyrdom. Afterward, "Christians met on the anniversary of the person's death, not of his birth (death was for the Christians the 'birthday of immortality'); and the meal became a eucharist or love-feast."[12]

NOTES

[1] J. M. C. Toynbee, *Death and Burial in the Roman World* (Ithaca, NY: Cornell University Press, 1971), 43–44.

[2] C. J. Hemer, "Bury, Grave, Tomb" in *NIDNTT*, 264.

[3] Toynbee, *Death and Burial*, 40.

[4] Toynbee, *Death and Burial*, 48.

[5] Arthur Darby Nock, "Cremation and Burial in the Roman Empire," *HTR* 25.4 (1932): 341.

[6] "Funerary Art, Roman Egypt," Louvre, accessed 21 February 2013, www.louvre.fr/en/routes/funerary-art.

[7] Everett Ferguson, *Backgrounds of Early Christianity*, 3rd ed. (Grand Rapids: Eerdmans, 2003), 250.

[8] Ferguson, *Backgrounds*, 246

[9] Craig A. Evans, *Jesus and the Ossuaries: What Jewish Burial Practices Reveal about the Beginning of Christianity* (Waco, TX: Baylor University Press, 2003), 12; see Hemer "Bury, Grave, Tomb," 264.

[10] Evans, *Jesus and the Ossuaries*, 11.

[11] Tertullian, *The Chaplet*, or *De Cornoa* 11 in Ante-Nicene Fathers, ed. Alexander Roberts and James Donaldson, vol. 3 (Peabody, MA: Hendrickson, 1994), 100.

[2] Ferguson, *Backgrounds*, 244.

FIRST-CENTURY DINING PRACTICES

BY MARTHA S. BERGEN

Triclinium with carved couches at Petra.

Several times the Gospels speak of Jesus and others "reclining at table." This was not, however, the usual posture for ordinary day-to-day meals. Families typically sat on the floor or squatted around a rug or low tables on which sat a communal pot of lentil or vegetable stew along with bread. Sometimes, though, seating was available for special ceremonies or events associated with royalty or the wealthy. By the first century AD, some among the Jews had adopted the Roman practice of using the triclinium for meals. The triclinium was an arrangement of tables in a U-shaped format with couches or cushions extending in a perpendicular angle from the outer sides. This left the inner part of the "U" open, which allowed servants easy access for placing or removing food as needed. Guests, along with their host, would recline or lean on their left arm, leaving their right arm free. Thus persons would use the right hand for eating, since the left hand was relegated for unclean tasks. The right hand was the main utensil, although people did use spoons with some foods. People used bread for scooping stew from the communal pot or soaking up gravies, soups, or sauces.[1]

When Jesus directed the disciples to make preparations for the Last Supper, he was perhaps asking them, in part, to find a place with a triclinium. The intimate arrangement of the triclinium setup, along with what Jesus wanted to share with the Twelve, would have made this setting most appropriate, including his act of servanthood in washing the disciples' feet. Furthermore, associated with the triclinium arrangement were cultural dictates for guest placement. Next to the host were the two most-honored guests; the highest-honored was on the host's right, the next, on his left. The mother of James and John, fathered by Zebedee, no doubt had this cultural norm in mind when she asked Jesus that her sons be allowed these privileged positions in his kingdom (Matt. 20:20–21). Scripture lends support that on the night of the Passover meal preceding Jesus's arrest, the apostle John was seated to Jesus's right, while, ironically, Judas was likely the one to his left (John 13:22–27). The fact that Jesus could hand Judas the piece of bread dipped into the dish would necessitate close physical proximity between the two, especially considering their reclining position.

Banqueters shown reclining on draped and cushioned couches. They are accompanied by servants and other attendants; dated to the fourth century BC; from the Nereid Monument at the Arbinas tomb, from Xanthos, Lycia.

NOTES

[1] Ralph Gower, "Food" in *HIBD*, 589–90; Fred H. Wight, *Manners and Customs of Bible Lands* (Chicago: Moody, 1953), 59, 63.

FOOT WASHING IN ANCIENT PRACTICE

BY DON H. STEWART

Gothic-style archway near the Gate of the Chaisa at Jerusalem. It has been filled in for secondary use as a Muslim public basin; the pipe near the ground brings in water for washing feet.

Dated from the eighth–seventh centuries BC; a basin for washing a person's foot. Once the basin was filled with water, a person would rest his or her foot on the raised platform in the center.

By the first century AD, hospitable foot washing for one's guests was a standard cultural practice of Near Eastern peoples. In fact, to fail to offer such a gesture was an insult. Thus, at minimum, hosts provided a bowl of water and a towel by the door for guests to wash their own feet. On occasion, the host would provide one or more household servants to wash and dry the feet of the arriving guests. Sometimes a wife might wash the feet of special guests.

What happened to Jesus when he was a dinner guest at the home of Simon (a Pharisee) highlights the social importance of washing a guest's feet in the first century (Luke 7:36–50). Jesus knew Simon had not followed the common and expected hospitable courtesies of the day. Failing to wash his guest's feet indicated Simon was rejecting Jesus and was trying to publicly humiliate him.[1] Jesus wanted Simon to understand that Jesus recognized that his host had slighted and insulted him.

Paul also addressed the importance of washing someone's feet as an expression of hospitality. Paul addressed how Timothy was to determine which widows qualified for church benevolence. Those who qualified had "brought up children, shown hospitality, washed the saints' feet, helped the afflicted, and devoted herself to every good work" (1 Tim. 5:10).

NOTES

[1] Kenneth E. Bailey, *Jesus through Middle Eastern Eyes: Cultural Studies in the Gospels* (Downers Grove, IL: IVP Academic, 2008), 247.

A "FORTIFIED" CITY

BY R. DENNIS COLE

City gate at Gezer.

Jeremiah's call to prophetic ministry was a call to the daunting task of announcing God's word of judgment to an unrepentant generation. The failed leadership of kings, priests, and prophets in this era had led to the announcement of God's final invoking of the curses of the covenant. Jeremiah announced that these curses would lead to the destruction of Judah and Jerusalem at the hand of Nebuchadnezzar's army. Infuriated at the prophet's words, the people even of his own hometown of Anathoth, just six miles north of Jerusalem, would seek Jeremiah's life (Jer. 11:18–23).

The Lord revealed to Jeremiah that Jerusalem's leaders would oppose him from every side. He was to stand immovably and resolutely like "a fortified city"—against all opposition. The fortifications are portrayed in metaphorical terms, using symbolic language of iron pillars and bronze walls (1:18–19), language not uncommon in the biblical world. For example, in excavating Balawat, archaeologists uncovered an example of Assyrian bronze-reinforced doors.[1] Pharaoh Thutmose III described himself as a rampart of iron, suggesting he was invincible.[2] Likewise, Jeremiah was to brace himself against his adversaries more firmly than the strongest walls of stone and wood. And though kings such as Jehoiakim and Zedekiah would wage war against Jeremiah as if he were a fortified city, placing him in prison and abusing him more than once, God's promised presence would provide the strength to endure the battles. Jeremiah's historical context would have made him thoroughly acquainted with fortified cities.

INTERNATIONAL POLITICS OF REBELLION

The thirteenth year of the reign of Judah's King Josiah, about 626 BC, saw the beginning of the end of the great kingdom of Assyria. The Babylonian insurgents under Nabopolassar threw off the bondage of Assyrian domination. This allowed other kingdoms such as Judah to consider similar tactics to bring relief from the harsh burdens their ruthless captors had imposed on them.

One of the typical responses of rebel states was to fortify strategic cities on the borders of their traditional homeland along with other key cities of the territorial infrastructure. Under Hezekiah, some seventy-five years before Jeremiah's call to ministry (ca. 705 BC), numerous cities on the western and southern borders of Judah were fortified to solidify Judah's defenses against an Assyrian attack. Strategically located cities such as Timnah, Ekron, Libnah, and Lachish saw extensive building projects designed to strengthen walls to prevent the boring and undermining techniques of siege engines. These cities would provide a network of forward battle lines designed to protect Jerusalem against attack.

Similarly, when Zedekiah rebelled against Nebuchadnezzar of Babylon in 589 BC, he reinforced the defenses at Lachish and expanded the fortifications at Beth-shemesh, Hebron, and elsewhere. In the end, these fortifications were no match for the powerful war machines of Assyria and Babylon. The defense of Israel and Judah was ultimately in God himself, as when Jerusalem was delivered from Sennacherib's army in 701 BC (2 Kgs. 19:8–36).

CITY PROTECTION

Fortified cities, whether small such as the four-acre enclosure at Timnah in the Sorek Valley west of Jerusalem or larger cities such as the thirty-one-acre site of Lachish in southwest Judah, were surrounded by stone-based walls with mud-brick superstructure. In some cities such as Lachish, a double wall would serve to defend the city against attack. Massive stone buildups called revetments were added at more vulnerable points such as the city gate.

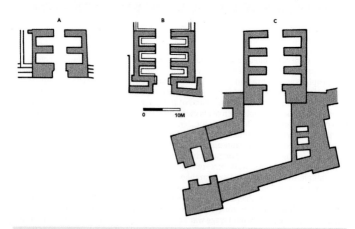

(A) Four-chambered gate at Beer-sheba. (B) Six-chambered gate at Gezer with stone benches for judges. (C) Gate and courtyard at Megiddo.

Ruined wall from ancient Lachish.

Wall and gate architecture went through several stages of development from the Bronze Age to the Iron Age, the latter representing much of Israel's kingdom history. Smaller villages, such as those that provided the early Israelites of the period of the judges their architectural base, were unfortified. These "ring settlements" consisted of small houses strung together in a circular arrangement, with a small opening where the circle overlapped serving as a gate. As Israelite city fortifications emerged during the kingdom period, the outlying villages, where a majority of the population lived, received less attention. Protection for the inhabitants of the villages depended on the fortified cities as a place for retreat during siege or attack.

WALLS

Two basic types of walls were used in the protection of the Israelite town: the solid wall and the casemate. The solid wall consisted of a foundation of cut and uncut stones, first layered into a subterranean trench about eighteen to forty inches in depth. This foundation was then built up to a height of six to ten feet. On the stone, workers would then add layers of large mud bricks until the wall reached a height of roughly ten to fifteen feet or more above the normal ground layer. These walls ranged from six feet in thickness in smaller towns to more than twenty-three feet in places such as Jerusalem.[3] As the wall approached the gate area, they were more heavily fortified by having deeper foundation trenches and larger stones weighing hundreds of pounds—some of which were laid to greater heights.

Casemate wall construction consisted of two parallel walls, each about a yard thick, with a vacant space between them of about six to ten feet. This inner area was subdivided by small lateral perpendicular walls that subdivided the casemate into rooms. People used these rooms for storage or small shops during times of peace and prosperity. In times of war or siege, these compartments could be filled with dirt and stone rubble making a solid wall twelve to twenty feet thick. Casemate walls were more common in the ninth and early eighth centuries BC, but they gave way to the more durable solid walls from the late eighth century (time of Hezekiah) to the end of Judah in 586 BC. Archaeologists have excavated excellent examples of tenth to ninth-century-BC casemate-construction fortifications at Hazor, Megiddo, and Gezer, all key cities in the network of kingdom construction during the reign of Solomon (1 Kgs. 9:15).[4] Occasionally walls were reinforced with long lateral wooden timbers between each of two or three layers of stone, adding further support in case of earthquakes, which were not uncommon in ancient Israel and Judah (Isa. 13:13; Amos 1:1; Zech. 14:5).

GATES

Access points to a city were vital to commerce and religious activity, yet they presented challenges to the city's defensibility. The gate structure was a multistoried building with defensive towers on both sides of the outer section of the entryway. From the days of Solomon to the end of the Israelite kingdom of Judah, the most common gate forms were those with four- or six-chambered gates.[5] Some of the chambers, such as those at Gezer, had stone benches on the perimeter of the room where the local judges sat as they carried out their judicial activities. Many gate areas had accompanying large outer courtyards where people from nearby villages and farmlands would bring their agricultural and manufactured goods for sale to the local public. Others like Beer-sheba contained small inner courtyards.

As the threat of an Assyrian siege loomed greater and greater in the latter part of the eighth century BC, Israelite architects began to construct outer revetment walls for added protection. Rather than have the gate directly accessible by the ramp that common people normally used moving in and out of the city, builders erected L-shaped walls on deep foundations. The new design provided only indirect access to the inner gate building itself. The bulky siege machines were less maneuverable in the close quarters of the indirect gate systems. Even small advanced fortified sites such as Timnah came to use this form of defense bulwark.

NOTES

[1]   Grant Frame, "Balawat" in *OEANE*, 1:268. Balawat was a fortified station on the road from Nineveh to Arrapha (modern Kirkuk, Iraq).

[2]   J. Hoffmeier, "The Gebel Barkal Stela of Thutmose III (2.2B)," in *The Context of Scripture,* ed. William W. Hallo (Leiden: Koninklijke Brill NV, 2003), 2:15. This phraseology is used numerous times by Thutmose III and is also used in other historical and poetic contexts.

[3]   Hezekiah's western wall in the fortification of Jerusalem was about twenty-three feet thick.

[4]   For detailed discussion of city fortifications, see Philip J. King and Larry Stager, *Life in Biblical Israel, Library of Ancient Israel (LAI)* (Louisville: Westminster John Knox, 2001), 231–36; Z. Herzog, "Fortifications (Levant)" in *ABD,* 1:844–52.

[5]   Examples of four-chambered gates are at Beer-sheba, Ashdod, and Mizpah. Archaeologists have uncovered six-chamber gates at Hazor, Megiddo, Gezer, and Lachish.

THE GEZER CALENDAR *FROM* "IT'S ABOUT TIME"

BY WARREN MCWILLIAMS

The Gezer calendar was discovered by R. A. S. Macalister at Tel Gezer (Arabic Tell Jezer) in Palestine. This limestone plaque probably dates from about 925 BC, approximately the time of King Solomon. The calendar may have been a practice exercise for a schoolboy. The seven lines report a twelve-month calendar composed of agricultural activities.[1] It reads as follows:

His two months [mid-September–mid-November]: Ingathering (olives)

His two months [mid-November–mid-January]: Sowing (grain)

His two months [mid-January–mid-March]: Late sowing

His month [mid-March–mid-April]: Chopping flax (or, grass)

His month [mid-April–mid-May]: Barley harvest

His month [mid-May–mid-June]: (Wheat) harvest and measuring (grain)

His two months [mid-June–mid-August]: Vine harvest

His month [mid-August–mid-September]: Summer fruit.

The Gezer calendar.

NOTES

[1] Jack Finegan, *Handbook of Biblical Chronology* (Princeton: Princeton University, 1964), 33; Philip J. King and Lawrence E. Stager, *Life in Biblical Israel* (Louisville: Westminster John Knox, 2001), 87–88.

THE GODS OF THESSALONICA

BY SCOTT HUMMEL

Although predominantly an Egyptian deity, Isis was worshipped throughout the Roman Empire, as evidenced in this temple of Isis at Pompeii.

Thessalonica was located in Macedonia. Even though many Greeks looked down on the Macedonians as semibarbarian, Greek mythology recognized that the Macedonians were related to the Greeks as "cousins."[1] By the time of Alexander the Great, who was himself Macedonian, the Macedonians had largely become "Greek" in culture and religion. The Macedonians told Greek myths and worshipped Greek gods. Mount Olympus itself was located in Macedonia about fifty miles from Thessalonica.

The two main sources of Greek mythology are Homer (who wrote the *Odyssey*) and Hesiod (who wrote *Theogony*).[2] Although many myths dealt with only the gods, the majority of the myths described the interaction between gods and heroes. The myths permeated all of Greek society as expressed through literature, art, drama, temple worship, and stories told to children. Myths helped define social roles and values as well as describe the character of the gods. While the gods were perceived as immortal and powerful, each had its own sphere of influence. One god was not worshipped to the exclusion of the others, because to neglect one god was to neglect that area of reality.[3]

Among the Greek gods were Titans, Olympians, and lesser gods. The Titans were the earliest gods and represented the basic elements of reality. At Mount Olympus, the twelve Olympian gods led by Zeus overthrew the Titans. All the other Olympian gods were either the siblings or children of Zeus. By the time of Paul, many of the Greek gods were equated with Roman gods. For example, the Roman god Jupiter was equated with Zeus.

Countless myths offer details about Zeus and his numerous affairs with goddesses and women. Many of his children, such as Hercules, became the heroes of old. Heroes were greater than normal men but less powerful than the gods. After their deaths, the heroes were worshipped with special honors.[4] Hero worship later paved the way for ruler and emperor worship. Following Alexander the Great, the main Greek and Macedonian kings portrayed themselves as descended from the gods. Some kings were honored as divine after their deaths, but others, such as Antiochus IV, were worshipped as gods, even in life.[5]

Since the Greeks believed the gods took pleasure in the quality of their temples and images, Greek artisans produced some of the best architecture and art in the ancient world. The statue of Zeus at Olympia and the temple of Artemis at Ephesus were among the seven Wonders of the Ancient World.

Worshippers offered prayers, incense, and sacrifices to the gods in the temples. In exchange for sacrifices or offerings, the worshippers hoped to receive a blessing or a divine message (oracle) from the gods. The most famous oracle in Greece was located at the temple of Apollo in Delphi. There the priestess inhaled vapors within the temple. In an ecstatic state, she uttered the message of Apollo, which the priest then interpreted for the worshipper.[6]

One of the primary gods of Thessalonica was Serapis. Adopted into Greek culture, Serapis had been the Egyptian god of the underworld and the Nile River. Devotees understood Serapis to provide fertility and protect seafarers, traits that made Serapis attractive to the culture of Thessalonica.

Not everyone in Greece believed the oracles, priests, or myths. In fact, for centuries a growing number of Greek philosophers grew increasingly skeptical about the existence of the gods. They sought instead more natural explanations of the world, and they grew increasingly embarrassed by the immorality of the gods as expressed in their myths. They also objected to anthropomorphism (gods in human form) and began to argue for a single disembodied mind, force, or principle.[7]

While walking through Thessalonica, Paul would have passed temples to Zeus and Aphrodite. Thessalonians also worshipped the Egyptian god Serapis and his wife Isis as evidenced by the remains of their temples. The two most prominent traditional gods in Thessalonica were Dionysus and Cabirus. Since Dionysus was the god of wine and joy, his celebrations and worship involved intoxication and orgies. Cabirus was a lesser god elsewhere in Macedonia and Greece but was the chief and most popular god in Thessalonica. During the time of Paul, the mystery religion of Cabirus would have been one of the most important cults in the city. Much remains unknown about the religion, but we know Cabirus was worshipped as a fertility god. The cult's mythology held that Cabirus had

At Corinth, mosaic of Dionysus, god of wine; dated first century BC to first century AD.

been martyred by his two brothers and had been buried at Mount Olympus, but he would often return from the dead to aid his followers, especially sailors.[8]

With the rise of Roman control, the Thessalonians embraced worship of the goddess Roma and Caesar Augustus. Paul probably saw the temple of Augustus in Thessalonica, and he certainly would have seen the divinity of Caesar proclaimed on coins minted in Thessalonica. Many of the coins had even replaced the image of Zeus with that of Augustus. Any challenge to emperor worship or promotion of another kingdom or lord threatened retaliation from Rome.[9]

Religion permeated every aspect of life and society in first-century Thessalonica. Festivals, theater, education, war, government, and athletics were all religious events or institutions. Turning from Greek religion meant more than turning from idol worship; it meant turning from one's traditions, community, and family. Although many Greeks saw Christianity as having "turned the world upside down" (Acts 17:6), Paul knew it meant turning the world to the only true and living God.

NOTES

[1] For the relationship between the Macedonians and Greeks, see N. G. L. Hammond, *The Macedonian State: Origins, Institutions, and History* (Oxford: Clarendon, 1989), 12–15.

[2] See Jasper Griffin, "Greek Myth and Hesiod," in *Greece and the Hellenistic World*, ed. John Boardman, Jasper Griffin, and Oswyn Murray (Oxford: Oxford University Press, 1988), 73–82; Simon Price, *Religions of the Ancient Greeks* (Cambridge: Cambridge University Press, 1999), 12–14.

[3] Robert Parker, "Greek Religion" in *Greece and the Hellenistic World*, 248.

[4] Parker, "Greek Religion," 250; Maria Mavromataki, *Greek Mythology and Religion* (Athens, Greece: Haitalis, 1997), 148.

[5] Hammond, *Macedonian State*, 21–22; Peter Green, *Alexander to Actium: The Historical Evolution of the Hellenistic Age* (Los Angeles: University of California Press, 1990), 397–99; Bruce K. Waltke, "Antiochus IV Epiphanes" in *ISBE* (1979), 1:146.

[6] Price, *Religions of the Ancient Greeks*, 37; Mavromataki, *Greek Mythology and Religion*, 145–46.

[7] Antonia Tripolitis, *Religions of the Hellenistic-Roman Age* (Grand Rapids: Eerdmans, 2001), 14–15; Griffin, "Greek Myth and Hesiod," 80; Parker, "Greek Religion," 266.

[8] Michael W. Holmes, *1 and 2 Thessalonians*, NIV Application Commentary (Grand Rapids: Zondervan, 1998), 19; Karl P. Donfried, "The Cults of Thessalonica and the Thessalonian Correspondence," *NTS* 31 (1985): 338–39; Charles A. Wanamaker, *The Epistles to the Thessalonians*, New International Greek Testament Commentary (NIGTC) (Grand Rapids: Eerdmans, 1990), 5, 12.

[9] Wanamaker, *Thessalonians*, 5–6; David W. J. Gill and Conrad Gempf, eds., *The Book of Acts in Its First Century Setting*, vol. 2., The Book of Acts in Its Graeco-Roman Setting (Eugene, OR: Wipf & Stock, 2000), 408, 415; Ben Witherington III, *The Acts of the Apostles: A Socio-Rhetorical Commentary* (Grand Rapids: Eerdmans, 1998), 503.

THE GOLDEN CALVES AT DAN AND BETHEL

BY CONN DAVIS

Part of the Canaanite high place and altar complex at Dan in northern Israel; dated to the thirteenth–twelfth centuries BC.

The predecessor to Jeroboam's two calves was the golden calf in the wilderness that Aaron built after the exodus from Egypt. Aaron and Jeroboam used remarkably similar language after building their golden calves: "Israel, these are/here are your gods, who brought you up from the land of Egypt" (Exod. 32:4,8; 1 Kgs. 12:28).

From Mesopotamia to Egypt to India, residents of the region have historically used the bull/calf image for religious practices. They have understood the calf as a pedestal or base on which their gods rested. The greatest example in the Old Testament was the Canaanite idol Baal, which sometimes existed as a bull. Israel lived in a constant state of spiritual crisis because of their syncretistic worship of Baal while attempting obedience to the Almighty God of their covenant. The classic confrontation between Elijah and the prophets of Baal on Mount Carmel witnessed to this tragic situation.

The Egyptian and Canaanite backgrounds of calf worship are significant, for Israel had extensive interaction with both cultures. The ancient Egyptian capital of Memphis became a religious center for the worship of the Apis bull. This idol represented strength and fertility. Likewise, the Canaanites perceived Baal as a symbol of fertility and strength, and as a storm-god.[1]

Found in Royal Graves at Ur, this gold bull's head is from the sounding box of a harp from the tomb of Queen Pu-abi (formerly read as Sub-ad). The originals were in the Iraq Museum, Baghdad.

A bronze bull found in Antioch of Syria (Antakya, Turkey). Dates possibly from the ninth–eighth centuries BC.

JEROBOAM'S CALVES

Some scholars believe Jeroboam I built his two calves to symbolize the invisible God as either standing or enthroned on the calf.[2] According to this view, the two shrines rivaled the ark of the covenant with its mercy seat on which God resided.

For the calves' placement, Dan and Bethel were strategic geographic locations. Dan was on Israel's extreme northern border; Bethel was on the southern edge, only twelve miles north of Jerusalem. Furthermore, Bethel had a rich spiritual tradition with historic connections to Abraham and Jacob.

ARCHAEOLOGICAL FINDINGS

Archaeologists have found little evidence of Jeroboam's shrine at Bethel. However, the Israeli archaeologist Avraham Biran discovered important remains from Dan. He excavated a limestone block platform or high place that Jeroboam built.[3] The main section of this rectangular-shaped worship area measured about sixty by twenty-five feet.

Biran believed that this sanctuary was the remains of the "shrines on the high places" built with the golden calf (1 Kgs. 12:31). The destruction of Jeroboam's shrine at Dan probably occurred when Ben-hadad of Syria attacked Dan and other towns of northern Israel about 885 BC.

Another Israeli archaeologist, Amihai Mazar, excavated an important related site in the hills of Samaria close to Dothan. He described the find of a circular worship area approximately 5,200 square feet. His most crucial discovery was a unique bronze figurine of a bull, about seven inches in length and five inches in height. He analyzed the metal composition of the small image as being 92 percent copper, 4 percent lead, and 4 percent tin. Moreover, he dated the high place/worship area and the bull figurine to the time of the judges, 1200 BC. Archaeologists refer to this type of bull image as a zebu bull because of a hump on its back and other features. The zebu bull originated in India and spread to the ancient Near East by 3000 BC.[4]

The best biblical descriptions of the construction of idols such as these calves comes from select passages in Isaiah and Jeremiah (Isa. 40:18–20; 44:9–17; 46:6–7; Jer. 10:3–5). The two basic building methods involved the skills of a carpenter and a metalsmith/

THE KINGDOMS OF ISRAEL AND JUDAH
1 KINGS 12

- City
★ Capital city
○ City (uncertain location)
▲ Mountain peak
Israel
Judah
—— International roads
—— Local roads

craftsman. The carpenter took the wood from a cedar or oak tree and carved an image known as a carved or graven image. The metalsmith then covered or lined the wood image with gold. In the second method, a metalsmith formed gold or metal into a mold in a fire and hammered it into final shape—a cast or molten image. Second Kings 17:16 describes the two calves as "cast images."

NOTES

[1] See K. A. Kitchen, "Golden Calf" in *The Illustrated Bible Dictionary* (Wheaton, IL: Tyndale House, 1980), 1:226.

[2] John Bright, *A History of Israel*, 2nd ed. (Philadelphia: Westminster, 1972), 234.

[3] Avraham Biran, "Tel Dan," *BA* 43.3 (Summer 1980): 175.

[4] Amihai Mazar, "The Bull Site," *BASOR* 247 (Summer 1982): 27,29,32–33.

THE GOLIATH INSCRIPTION

BY JOSEPH R. CATHEY

The Philistine city of Gath (Tell es-Safi), located in the Shephelah, was Goliath's hometown.

The Goliath inscription is a small piece of inscribed tenth–ninth-century BC pottery (*ostracon*; plural *ostraca*). What makes the ostracon significant is that it has an inscription of two Philistine names. Both of the names are close etymologically to the biblical *Goliath*. The letters of the inscription were Hebrew while the names were Philistine in origin. Archaeologically speaking, this is a significant find because it is one of the earliest Hebrew inscriptions found in a verifiable archaeological context. The popular press and media quickly labeled it the "Goliath inscription."

Archaeologists found the inscription in the 2005 excavation of the ancient city of Gath (Tell es-Safi). Gath lies in the central section of Israel between Jerusalem and Ashkelon. Principally Gath guarded the main north-south route of the Shephelah, which has foothills that run west from the plain toward Gezer in central Israel. Excavations at Gath began in 1899.

Gath shows significant occupation from the early Chalcolithic period (4500–4000 BC) until the modern period (about 1948). Representative archaeological finds from Gath include marked jar handles (some with stamps), figurines, and shekel weights from the end of the Solomonic era.

Archaeologists find ostraca (inscribed pottery) infrequently in Israel today. Most recovered ostraca contain nothing more than a single word, a few letters, or a single letter. Some

Dating from the tenth to mid-ninth centuries BC, this shard discovered at Tell es-Safi contains the oldest Philistine inscription ever found and mentions two names remarkably similar to the name Goliath.

ostraca have only half of a letter inscribed. What makes this inscription interesting are the names that were inscribed and the place in which it was found. Whoever inscribed the names used Hebrew characters to write out Philistine names.[1] Those who inscribed the ostracon most likely used a sharp pointed instrument. We know from history that the Philistines were actually from the Aegean and thus had Indo-European names. Yet with their migration into Canaan, they slowly began to culturally assimilate the local alphabet (in Hebrew) to express their own unique language. Although the inscription does not actually preserve the name "Goliath," it does preserve names that are similar etymologically.

The biblical significance of this ostracon is twofold. First, we can definitely say that as early as the tenth–ninth centuries BC the early Hebrew script was used in Israel.[2] This script was used by those in the Philistine city of Gath to designate certain individuals. Second, we can infer from this inscription that individuals with names similar to the biblical Goliath were familiar to those at Gath. Consequently, having someone named Goliath to reside at Philistine Gath would not have been uncommon.

NOTES

[1] Aren Maeir, "Gath Inscription Evidences Philistine Assimilation," *BAR* 32.2 (2006): 16.

[2] Frank Moore Cross and Lawrence E. Stager, "Cypro-Minoan Inscriptions Found in Ashkelon," *Israel Exploration Journal (IEJ)* 56.2 (2006): 150–51.

HORSES IN ANCIENT WARFARE

BY DANIEL P. CALDWELL

Reconstruction of the bands from the Balawat Gates of the palace of Shalmaneser III (858–824 BC) outside Nineveh.

Of all the domestic animals, the horse was one of the last to be tamed. This may be due to its size or perhaps its high-strung temperament, which would make it difficult to catch and tame. Nonetheless, the horse has a long and distinguished history. The advent of its use by people changed humankind forever.

EARLY USE AND DOMESTICATION

The people responsible for domesticating the horse were probably nomadic Aryan tribes. The animals grazed about the grasslands bordering the Caspian and Black Seas. The Aryan nomads possibly began as herders of a breed of partially wild but docile reindeer. Out of practical considerations, they later switched to horses. Unlike the reindeer, horses are not migratory animals. The reindeer's movement was dictated by the location of special foods on which they fed.[1]

Initially horses were herded for a variety of uses. Their flesh provided food, and their hides were used to make hut coverings and clothes. Since there were few trees in the grasslands, the manure could be dried to fuel their fires. Eventually the mares were even used to supply their herders with milk. In time, the herders used the less-spirited breeds to transport their personal property. The natural consequence thereafter was for the men to transport themselves by riding the horses, which made the task of herding, hunting, and migrating much simpler. It was only the beginning of people's use of the horse as a domestic animal.

Early horsemen generally rode the horses bareback and without bits (mouthpieces) and reins. Riders guided the horses by applying pressure with their knees and by leaning their bodies in the desired direction. To advance their means of transporting and riding the horse, later generations developed special items (called tack) to better control the animals. These included bridles made of bone and antlers and crude saddles without stirrups. Eventually horses were employed to pull small four-wheeled and two-wheeled carts. These devices served as the forerunners of early forms of military equipment.[2]

Aside from hunting, the single greatest use of the horse in ancient history was for combat. The introduction of the horse into battle changed warfare. It provided a swiftness and strength not seen before. The impact of its use was devastating for any foe.

HORSES AND CHARIOTS IN BATTLE

The horse in war is seen in two different contexts. The first is driven in pairs or in a group of three to four while pulling a chariot. The chariot was the earliest means of transportation in combat. The earliest known chariots date to about 2500 BC. These early chariots were not the advanced two-wheeled devices seen in early art. They were actually four-wheeled carts with wheels made of solid wood. These simple chariots were both heavy and

Terra-cotta model of a mounted warrior with Assyrian shield. Seventh century BC; from Cyprus.

Bronze bit, likely produced by the Medes about 1800 BC.

Basalt relief from Carchemish, dated 950–850 BC.

awkward to drive. Since they had no pivoting front axle, the cart would require a wide, skidding turn. Even though originally a team of oxen, donkeys, or wild asses pulled the chariot, the horse eventually became the animal of choice for speed and strength.

Around 1600 BC, a two-wheeled chariot was developed. This vehicle was lighter than its predecessor and much easier to maneuver. Because of its lighter weight, it also was faster and more versatile on the battlefield. This chariot was pulled by two or sometimes three horses.[3] Two men worked the typical chariot: one would be a bowman to fire at enemy forces, while the other would control the vehicle. Over time, chariots were developed that could carry up to five warriors. Some of these warriors were archers, and the others protected the archers and directed the chariots into battle. The greatest contribution of the horse-drawn chariot was the tactical mobility it provided to the archer. Tightly packed foot soldiers were the formation of choice in early battle. Offering the military commanders both control during the battle and mutual protection, a force of chariots could stand off at long range and rain arrows down on the enemies' heads. Because of the chariots' speed, any attempts for the enemies to attack head-on could be easily evaded. If, on the other hand, the foot soldiers spread out to minimize the damage from the enemy's arrows, they would lose the benefit of strength in numbers, and the charioteers could easily overrun them. The power of the chariot as a device both of transportation and of battle became the central weapon of the peoples of the ancient Near East in the second millennium BC.[4]

HORSES AND THE CAVALRY

The second historical context in which we see horses is in a primitive form of cavalry. From as early as the second and third millennia BC, men rode horses into battle. Some of the earliest groups to fight effectively on horseback were the Hittites, Assyrians, Babylonians, and Hyksos. The latter group may have been responsible for introducing horses to Egypt. Egypt in turn would ultimately introduce the horse to Canaan.

The ancient rider warriors used two common weapons, spears and bows. While both were effective in dealing with the enemy, the more lethal method was the bow. The horse-archers could advance quickly on enemy foot soldiers but keep their distance while shooting the arrow. Many of these riders rode without reins to keep their hands free to shoot their bows. They later developed an attack and retreat method of combat. While maintaining a full gallop, they would ride within range of the enemy, release a volley of arrows, and then retreat. However, the retreat was simply a disguised means of continuing the attack on the unsuspecting enemy. One group of horse-archers, the Parthians, were so skilled that they were able to shoot as skillfully backward in retreat as they did forward in their attack.[5]

Horses ridden or driven in war not only gave a speed and strength advantage to the individual soldier but also served as a mobile command post. A commander of the army would not have this advantage at ground level. The height advantage enabled the rider or driver to view the battle more clearly and effectively lead his army in battle.

HORSES IN SCRIPTURE

Most biblical references to the horse are associated with military use. The most common Hebrew term for *horse* was *sus*. Depending on the context, the term could be interpreted to mean horse in general or a type of war horse.[6] Although the Scriptures offer a few references to horses prior to the monarchy period, the common use of the horse in Israel did not begin until the time of David and Solomon. Solomon was the first to use horses for military purposes in Israel.

The Old Testament portrays horses typically as the property of kings, not the common man. They were used for a variety of purposes. The horse provided an excellent means of transportation (horseback and by chariot) for royalty, aristocrats, and the wealthy. When Joseph interpreted Pharaoh's dream, Pharaoh honored Joseph by allowing him to ride in a chariot drawn by horses (Gen. 41:43).[7]

A few passages mention the use of horses for other tasks. For instance, in the judgment oracle against Jerusalem, Isaiah 28:28 mentions horses being used for threshing grain. Many agree horses were far too valuable to use in such menial work. Thus the passage would be understood in a poetic fashion as Isaiah's attempt to describe the destructive action of an enemy.[8]

The Mosaic law also warned against possessing many horses for excessive pleasure and war (Deut. 17:16), as did Samuel (1 Sam. 8). However, the supremacy of the horse in warfare caused the Israelites to ignore this law. This could be the reason Solomon imported horses from Egypt (2 Chr. 1:16) and had thousands of stalls built to house them (1 Kgs. 4:26; 2 Chr. 9:25). In the Assyrian writings of Sennacherib's conquests, horses are listed among the spoils taken from the defeated nation of Judah.[9]

The domestication of the horse and its eventual use in combat has left a mark on civilization. However, in spite of how majestic and noble the horse is and in spite of how effective it may be in warfare, God reminds us that our ultimate trust is to be in him. The psalms and the prophets warned against trusting in horses rather than the Lord for victory:[10] "Some take pride in chariots, and others in horses, but we take pride in the name of the LORD our God" (Ps. 20:7).

NOTES

1   Elwyn Hartley Edwards, *The Encyclopedia of the Horse* (New York: DK Publishing, 1994), 28–29.

2   C. E. Crawford, "Horses and Horsemanship" in *The New Encyclopedia Britannica* (Chicago: Encyclopedia Britannica, 2002), 20:651.

3   G. R. Taylor, "Technology of War" in *The New Encyclopedia Britannica*, 29:535.

3   Taylor, "Technology of War."

4   Edwards, *Encyclopedia of the Horse*, 35.

5   F. J. Stendebach, "סוס" in *TDOT* (1999), 10:180.

6   For other references to horses being used for means of transportation, see 2 Samuel 15:1; 2 Kings 5:9; 14:20.

7   John N. Oswalt, *The Book of Isaiah Chapters 1–39*, NICOT (1986), 523–24. For other passages supporting this poetic understanding, see Isaiah 17:4–6; 27:12; 41:15–16.

8   James B. Pritchard, ed., *The Ancient Near East: An Anthology of Texts and Pictures* (Princeton: Princeton University Press, 1973), 1:200.

9   See Isaiah 31:1; 36:8–10; Ezekiel 17:15.

HOUSES IN JESUS'S DAY

BY PAUL E. KULLMAN

After the third Jewish revolt against the Romans, known as the Bar Kokhba revolt (AD 132–136), the Jews were not allowed to live in Jerusalem. Many of them thus settled in the region north of the Sea of Galilee. One such community was at Yehudiya, which dates to about AD 200–400. During the Ottoman period, many Arabs, using stones and materials they found on the site, resettled here and built these structures on top of the centuries-old foundations and footprints of the earlier structures. These remains thus give a good impression of what an early Jewish village would have looked like.

DESIGN

Houses in the first century were designed and built with the most simple details. Workers used tools such as the handsaw, adze (stone chisel), bow drill, hammer, and mallet. Many homes today are still built with similar construction methods in rural locations in Third World nations where the poor have few options. First-century house design used the basic square or rectangular shape with a short span across the narrowest width. This span was accomplished using wood beams set upon load-bearing dried mud-brick walls or locally mined and cut stone.

The roof composition was constructed with dried wood poles, thatch, or tiles that spanned perpendicular to the thicker, wood-beam supports. The same wood beams served as lintels above some of the wall features, such as doors. The roof surface was a layered composition of dried, compacted mud covered with brick paver or flat stone, which was typically a durable and impervious surface. Most ancient houses had an outside stairway that led to a flat roof area, which people used for various domestic activities, such as drying fruit or sleeping on hot nights or when the owner needed an outside work space or simply an area of repose. The roof area would sometimes adjoin other houses, depending on the spatial density of the building layout area and whether this was a rural or urban house. This enabled neighbors to share a common wall, which meant less labor and expense than building four walls, as was required in a freestanding house. Interestingly, each Israelite house typically had a parapet to keep a nonowner from falling off and creating a "blood guiltiness" condition (Deut. 22:8). This practical safety feature is still used on modern flat roofs and balconies as required by local building codes.

A prodigious amount of archaeological excavations have exposed many stone-wall foundations. The foundations reveal that most small, common houses were approximately fifteen by fifteen feet, although some may have been about thirty by thirty.[1] The floor plan consisted of two to four rooms with at least one larger area for sleeping and another to accommodate cooking. Some houses had livestock stabling inside the house, for use during the cold winter months. The door would be the only entrance; small windows helped with air circulation or smoke exhaust. The floors were compacted dirt covered with straw or loose gravel. More affluent houses had marble floors or at least a plaster surface.

Most houses were modestly furnished, usually with a table and chairs. People slept on pallets on the floor. Essential supplies included cooking pots, an oven, plates, lamps, and storage jars known as amphora. Of course, the more affluent owners' homes had vases, beds, and furniture for reclining. Excavations reveal that many houses depended on cisterns for water.

TYPES OF HOUSES

In the New Testament era, house construction reflected the owner's financial resources. Small houses were more numerous and built of austere means. Many times, these smaller houses were clustered around a shared courtyard, especially in areas where a city's

Using a method that dates back centuries, this Iraqi stone house has a roof constructed of wooden poles that have been covered over with thatch and compacted mud.

population density restricted expansion. The courtyard served as an entertainment and outdoor cooking center that neighbors shared.

Meanwhile, the wealthy would build large, spacious, and palatial houses that usually occupied the hillside areas of cities. In Jerusalem, the affluent neighborhood was known as the upper city in contrast with the lower city (or the Tyropoeon Valley) separated by the Herodian Wall.[2] These affluent houses would be multilevel structures with large and open spaces, many of which were used for sleeping. The larger homes also had additional living areas designated for entertaining. Some rooms were designated as work areas for the servants, who had their own separate sleeping quarters. Interior finishes include exposed cedar beams from Lebanon and marble from Greece or Italy. The wealthy were not only Jewish aristocracy but also foreign ambassadors and, of course, the Romans—both government and military.

NOTES

[1]   John S. Holladay Jr., "House, Israelite" in *ABD*, 3:314–16.

[2]   Marsha A. Ellis Smith, ed., *Holman Book of Biblical Charts, Maps, and Reconstructions* (Nashville: Broadman & Holman, 1993), 158–59.

HOW IRON CHANGED WARFARE

BY JOSEPH R. CATHEY

A two-man Assyrian chariot, bearing the sacred standards; from the North-West Palace at Nimrud; dated about 865–860 BC.

Metals allowed the introduction of technology that undoubtedly changed the entire landscape of the ancient Near East. The refining of metals and the ability to work with them were at the forefront of human technological development. Nowhere is the refining of metals more pronounced than in the areas of religious iconography, tools, and weapons.

Evidence is prevalent from the Neolithic cultures onward illustrating the rise of humans working various metals. As early as the eighth millennium BC, people worked native copper, bitumen, and obsidian into items such as decorative pins, pendants, and religious iconography.[1] Although copper was the earliest metal to be mined, smelted, and cast—due to its prevalence and ease of working—one should not discount meteoric iron. As early as the second millennium BC, the ancient Near East knew and most likely made use of meteoric iron, "the iron from heaven."[2]

The Scriptures witness iron's dramatic rise from humble beginnings. Genesis 4:22 explains that Tubal-cain worked as a metalworker. Some believe that Tubal-cain's metallurgy included weapons as well as agricultural tools.[3]

The shift from bronze to iron came about for reasons of practicality and utility. Although bronze is much easier to work than iron, the necessary element for bronze, namely tin, is

Arrowheads from Lachish; dated tenth–sixth centuries BC. At the beginning of the Iron Age, iron was scarce and was too valuable to be used for expendable projectile points. Only after the tenth century did it become widespread enough to replace bronze arrowheads with iron ones.

Tools used in metalworking; the long handles and light blades would have made these suitable for forge work.

extremely rare.[4] Due to an abundance of ore and improvements in smelting, iron became the prevailing utilitarian metal from approximately 1200 to 800 BC.[5] In the Late Bronze Age (period of the judges), iron was not as technically advanced as bronze. Bronze is harder than iron, therefore a bronze knife or sword would keep its edge longer and would not bend or break as readily as iron. The key to the later technological breakthrough with iron was the carburization process by which iron becomes steel.[6] Steel is harder and stronger than bronze, and it will keep an edge better. The advent of carburized iron (steel) gave a value to iron that it previously did not have.[7] Once iron (and later steel) weapons became dominant, they remained the choice of armies throughout the ancient Near East, mainly due to the ease of use, maintenance, and the edge-holding ability inherent to this ferric metal.[8]

The Hebrew text of the Old Testament distinguished types of iron as well as bronze. Ezekiel 27:19 mentions the concept of "wrought iron," which was a commodity brought to the wealthy city of Tyre. This phrase is difficult to translate due to its occurring only here in the Hebrew Old Testament. Some biblical scholars have argued that the prophet intended this phrase to mean an approximation of "workable iron" or a "consolidated bloom iron."[9] The prophet Jeremiah likewise knew of hardened iron and contrasted its superiority over bronze (Jer. 15:12).

Archaeology clearly shows that by the twelfth century BC, Israel was making vast use of iron weapons. Surveys from Israelite sites during this era show thirty-seven arrowheads, five knives/blades, five daggers, five spearheads, one spear butt, seven javelin heads, and two lance heads.[10] In contrast, this same survey explored commonly held Philistine sites,[11] which yielded an equally impressive assortment of weapons. As expected, archaeologists uncovered a greater number of Philistines blades—thirteen to the Israelite ten. The infrastructure required for metallurgy was slightly more tilted toward the Philistines' favor than the Israelites. Likewise, the biblical account indicates that the Philistines often fought from the mounted chariot position rather than as dismounted infantry. A cursory examination of the bulk of Israelite weaponry appears to indicate that the Hebrews preferred standoff weapons (metal-tipped arrows, shafts, and lances) that would afford the infantry distance from the chariots.

Iron helmet with bronze inlay around the rim; Assyrian; eighth century BC.

Judges 4 gives an impressive window into the mindset of early Israel and their preference for range weapons. The text illustrates the writer's appreciation of Canaanite warfare, namely the iron chariot (see 1:19). The writer explains that Canaan's King Jabin had used his vast numbers of iron chariots to oppress Israel for more than twenty years. Likewise, the Canaanite commander Sisera used 900 iron chariots in his battle against Israel. Undoubtedly, the iron chariot was a paradigmatic shift in warfare of the ancient Near East.

The archaeological remains of the first millennium BC have yielded impressive finds associated with chariots of the ancient Near East. The shift in mobile warfare platforms was gradual due to the technology associated with making these war machines. Ancient Egyptian and Asiatic imagery highlights the importance of iron char-

Reconstructed copper smelting furnace from Timnah, in southern Israel. The furnace, dating to the twelfth century BC, has a round tuyère (heat-exchange pipe) in the back and a slag pit in the front.

iots as mobile firing platforms as well as for flanking and harassing dismounted infantry. To find chariots equipped with bow cases, quivers of arrows, axes, and even long swords was not uncommon.[12] Details from Egypt's New Kingdom (1550–1070 BC) have provided ample insights into chariot construction. Elements such as a D-shaped floor (for quick mounting and dismounting), hip-high sides (for shield mounting), and ample storage for battle weapons made the iron chariot a highly desirable commodity.[13] Iron Age chariots eventually spread throughout the entire Near East (Hatti, Egypt, Canaan, Assyria, and Babylon).

As this platform grew, the key to effective deployment was reconciling speed and maneuverability with firepower and security. The bite of the iron swords, arrows, javelins, and spears necessitated a triple function within the charioteer corps. Three soldiers were required to effectively fight a concerted battle—a driver, a fighter, and a defender (often depicted as deploying a shield covering the fighter).[14]

Iron and the technology that it brought to the ancient Near East was a double-edged sword. On the one hand, it was a meteoric jump in offensive weapons (sword, arrow, spear, and lance). This advantage was offset, however, by the development and usage of the iron chariot as seen in Judges 1; 4. Truly elements such as geography and maneuverability would hamper the iron chariot in the hill country of Israel. However, once iron weapons became commonplace in the field of martial combat, nations would never again embrace a lesser metal for blood or conquest.

NOTES

[1] See Paul T. Craddock, "Metallurgy: Metallurgy in the Old World" in *The Oxford Companion to Archaeology*, ed. Niel Asher Silberman, 2nd ed. (Oxford: Oxford University Press, 2012), 378.

[2] Thoman Zimmermann, Latif Özen, Yakup Kalayci, and Rukiye Akdogan, "The Metal Tablet from Bogazköy-Hattuša: First Archaeometric Impressions," *Journal of Near Eastern Studies (JNES)* 69.2 (October 2010): 228–29.

[3] See Kenneth A. Matthews, *Genesis 1–11:26*, vol. 1 in NAC (1996), 287. Matthews suggests that Tubal-cain most likely worked meteoric iron.

[4] One distinct impediment was the temperature and equipment necessary to smelt ores. For example, to smelt copper, the temperature has to reach no less than 1,981°F and silver, 1,762°F—versus iron at 2,786°F. Even when iron was smelted, it often had to be worked by hammer (e.g., forging) and then shaped in a much more labor-intensive process.

[5] See J. D. Muhly, "Metals: Artifacts of the Neolithic, Bronze, and Iron Ages" in *The Oxford Encyclopedia of Archaeology in the Near East (OEANE)*, ed. Eric M. Meyers (Oxford: Oxford University Press, 1997), 4:13.

[6] T. Stech-Wheeler et al., "Iron at Taanach and Early Iron Metallurgy in the Eastern Mediterranean," *American Journal of Archaeology (AJA)* 85.3 (1981): 245.

[7] James D. Muhly, "How Iron Technology Changed the Ancient World and Gave the Philistines a Military Edge," *BAR* 8.6 (1982): 43–44.

[8] Allan C. Emery, "Weapons of the Israelite Monarchy: A Catalogue with Its Linguistic and Cross-Culture Implications" (PhD diss., Harvard University, 1999), 135–55; see M. Heltzer, "Akkadian *ktinnu* and Hebrew *kidon*, 'sword,'" *Journal of Cuneiform Studies (JCS)* 41.1 (1989): 67–68.

[9] Dan Levene and Beno Rothenberg, "Early Evidence for Steelmaking in the Judaic Sources," *Jewish Quarterly Review (JQR)* 92.1–2 (2001): 109–10.

[10] Elizabeth Bloch-Smith, "Israelite Ethnicity in Iron I: Archaeology Preserves What Is Remembered and What Isa. Forgotten in Israel's History," *JBL* 122. 3 (2003): 419. Bloch-Smith restricted the "Israel" sites to the central highlands (Dothan, Bethel, Ai, Khirbet Raddana, Tell en-Nasbeh, Giloh, el-Khadr, Beth Zur, and Tel Beersheve).

[11] For example, sites such as Ashdod, Tel Miqne-Ekron, Beth Dagon, Tell el 'Ajjul/Gaza, and Tell Qasile were surveyed. Such sites are commonly within the realm of what is normally associated with the "Philistines."

12 See Joost H. Crouwel, "Chariots in Iron Age Cyprus," *Report of the Department of Antiquities, Cyprus* (1987), 101–18.

13 See Joost Crouwel and Mary Aiken Littauer, "Chariots" in *OEANE*, 485.

14 See Sa-Moon Kang, *Divine War in the Old Testament and in the Ancient Near East* (Berlin: de Gruyter, 1989), 50.

IDOLS IN PRODUCTION AND RITUALS

BY DAVID M. WALLACE

Bronze dragon, sacred animal of Babylonian god Marduk, 700–550 BC.

Idols ate two meals every day because they were hungry, drank water because they were thirsty, and took baths to stay clean. They even sometimes traveled to foreign lands. To the Egyptians, Canaanites, and other neighbors of the Israelites, they were gods fit to be worshipped and to be cared for in every way.[1] Such were the beliefs and practices of ancient cultures in the Near East.

WHAT DOES *IDOL* MEAN?

An idol was an object made by human hands that presented a likeness or image of the god to be worshipped. The Hebrew word translated as "idol" or "graven image" is *pesel*, related to the verb *pasal*, meaning to "hew" or "cut."[2] We learn from both language and archaeology that idols were hewn or carved out of wood or stone.

God instructed the Israelites in Exodus 20:5, "Do not bow in worship to them, and do not serve them; for I, the LORD your God, am a jealous God." Several times the Old Testament repeated this prohibition of idols (Exod. 20:23; 34:17; Lev. 19:4; 26:1; Deut. 4:15–19,25; 5:8). The Hebrews were directed not to worship anything that looked like or represented any type of deity. Isaiah told the people that God was unique, unlike anyone or anything else (Is 40:18–19). No idol made by a craftsman could compare to him.

God instructed the Israelites to make no form or image of any kind with which to worship him (Deut. 4:15–18). Though Israel struggled to remain loyal to God alone, monotheism made Israel's faith unique among the nations, especially among those who lived nearby and against whom they fought. Thus, obeying God's commands against idol worship throughout Old Testament times proved to be a constant challenge for the people of Israel.

HOW WERE IDOLS MADE?

Israel and its neighbors typically made their idols of wood, stone, silver, or gold. The gold and silver made idols more expensive as well as attractive. The more attractive the idol god or goddess, the more people wanted the blessing available to them from that particular idol. Some idols could be held in the palm of the hand; others might be several feet tall. Most idols that were originally sheathed in gold or silver eventually lost their beautiful dazzling covers.

Whenever foreign armies overran a city or nation, they naturally took every possible item made of gold or silver. Houses of worship and temples were among the first places soldiers searched for treasures. Often metals would be melted down to reuse the gold or silver.

When heated to the melting point, both silver and gold are soft and easily formed into objects. Both are capable of being shaped by beating them with a hammer or by the pressure of rollers. Hammers can shape the precious metals into extremely thin sheets that can then be over-laid—one on top of the other—onto most objects, including ancient metals.

When exposed to air, silver oxidizes, so it must be polished. Gold, on the other hand, does not oxidize, even if buried underground or left in a cave or burial vault for hundreds of years.

In the Old Testament era, if not made of wood or stone, idols were first shaped and cast of metal, typically iron or bronze. After cooling, the cast was removed and gold was applied by hand one layer at a time, or the object was dipped into liquid gold. The final product was an idol covered with a gold veneer. This gilding process is still in use today.

HOW IDOLS WERE CARED FOR

The neighbors of Israel believed their images and statues were alive. Their idols had thoughts and feelings. The god

Votive statue of food being offered to the Sumerian god Anu at Uruk.

Stone mold for casting Assyrian idols; dated 1920–1740 BC.

was living in their image or statue. The people cared for their idol because they believed it needed care and attention just like any other living being.

The idols at Uruk temple, for example, received two meals daily. A table was carried in with a bowl of water for cleaning. The idol received a variety of foods. Musicians played at mealtime while the idol ate in private. Afterward, the items were removed and the idol was again provided water with which to clean itself.

In Egypt, idols usually reposed in a dark corner inside the temple where only the priest had access to the idol. The priest was responsible for caring for the shrine that contained the idol. The priest cleaned and perfumed the idol with incense and applied cosmetics. The priest also placed a crown on the idol, identifying it as a deity.[3]

NOTES

[1] Edward M. Curtis, "Idol, Idolatry" in *ABD*, 3:377–78.

[2] Francis Brown, S. R. Driver, and Charles A Briggs, *A Hebrew and English Lexicon of the Old Testament* (Oxford: Clarendon Press, 1980), 820.

[3] Curtis, "Idol, Idolatry," 377–78.

IN THE CITY GATE

BY JOEL F. DRINKARD JR.

View of the gate complex at Dan shows the massive walls of the towers at the entrance. Ruins of benches and a threshold are also located at the gate. Buttresses reinforced the support for the walls at the tower and gate.

Gates in Iron Age Israel (1200–586 BC) routinely had two or more sets of pier walls creating chambers on each side of the gateway. The most common patterns were two, four, or six chambers. The number of chambers does not seem to be related to size of the site, the chronology within Iron Age Israel, or location (Israel or Judah or neighboring states). Instead the number of chambers seems to depend on the topography of the site and the use made of the gate complex. Most gates at major sites in Israel and surrounding lands were made entirely of stone, or had stone lower courses and mud brick above. Pier walls were typically about six feet wide, chambers about nine feet wide and fifteen to eighteen feet deep. And the gates often had towers on either side. At a number of sites, inner and outer gates have been discovered.[1]

Gates were not just entryways into and out of cities and towns, but they certainly did provide entry and egress. The gate complex was at the center of activity for the city. Obviously gates had a defensive purpose of offering protection to the citizens inside. As such, the gate complex often had military installations associated with it. The gate complex included the entryway doors (Neh. 6:1; 7:1), towers (2 Chr. 26:9), and gate bars (Judg. 16:3; 2 Chr. 8:5) that could be put in place to secure the town.

Benches were located in the chambers and immediately inside and outside the gate at many sites including Beer-sheba,[2] Gezer,[3] and Tel Dan.[4] Such benches are often related to biblical texts that speak of "sitting in the city gate" (2 Sam. 19:8). However, these benches

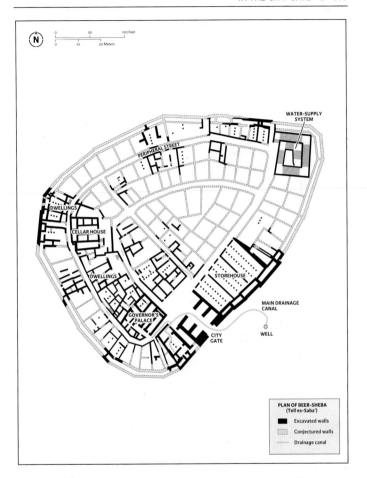

PLAN OF BEER-SHEBA
(Tell es-Saba')

■ Excavated walls

░ Conjectured walls

··· Drainage canal

vary in height from about six inches to more than thirty inches, some too low to sit on, others too high, and others too narrow. In these instances, the bench was probably a shelf on which items could be placed.

In addition, many major business and social activities took place at the gate complex. An open plaza (Hb. *rechob*, "street, square, plaza"; Gen. 19:2; Judg. 19:15; 2 Sam. 21:12) was often located just inside or outside the gate. The plaza was the marketplace where merchants offered their goods, and the people would gather to buy and sell. It was the equivalent of today's mall and farmer's market all in one. Archaeologists have excavated such plazas at Beer-sheba,[5] Tel Dan,[6] and other sites. The market or plaza was a natural gathering place. In such a plaza, Hezekiah spoke to the assembled people to encourage them at the time of Sennacherib's attack (2 Chr. 32:6). Likewise, Ezra read the book of the law to the assembled people in the plaza of the Water Gate of Jerusalem (Neh 8:1,3). Since many benches in gate chambers were unsuited for sitting and the gate chambers were often small, to what did the idea of "sitting in the city gate" refer? Most likely it referred to sitting anywhere in the gate complex, either just inside or just outside the gate but especially in the plaza. Lot was "in Sodom's gateway" (Gen. 19:1), probably in the plaza area, since this is where the angels proposed to spend the night (v. 2). It is also where the Levite sat with his concubine when he was going to spend the night at Gibeah (Judg. 19:15).

Not all such plazas were inside the gate. There is at least one reference to "streets" or "bazaars" (Hb. *chuts*), which were located outside the gate (1 Kgs. 20:34; the basic meaning of *chuts* is "outside"). The late Israeli archaeologist Avraham Biran interpreted such structures excavated outside the gate at Tel Dan as the *chuts*.[7] Again their location close to the gate makes perfect sense. They are the place merchants would offer goods for sale. A location just inside or just outside the city gates is convenient, readily accessible, and also easily kept under the watchful eye of officials to prevent trouble. Another place associated with the gate and just outside the city is a threshing floor. The kings of Israel and Judah held a summit meeting seated on their thrones at the threshing floor at the entrance to the gate of Samaria (1 Kgs. 22:10). Like the bazaars, the threshing floor would be a large open public space, perfect for a public meeting.

The gate complex thus was the place persons gathered and transacted business. Abraham negotiated to purchase the field and burial cave for Sarah (Gen. 23:10–16) at the city gate of Hebron (or Kiriath-arba). Similarly, Boaz negotiated for the purchase of Elimelech's property including the hand of Ruth in marriage (Ruth 4:1–12) at the gate of Bethlehem.

High places or sanctuaries were associated with city gates during the Iron Age. Josiah broke down the high places of the city gate as part of his religious reform (2 Kgs. 23:8). Archaeologists have discovered city-gate sanctuaries at Tel Dan and Bethsaida. The Iron Age gate complex at Bethsaida had at least seven stele, which were worshipped in the high places in the city-gate complex.[8] One just to the right of the gate had a couple of steps leading up to a basalt basin for libation offerings. A stele with a bovine-headed deity sat above the libation area. At Tel Dan, four sets of standing stones (Hb. *matseboth*) have been discovered in the gate complex.[9]

Reconstructed judgment seat in the entrance gate of Dan. The left front base stone is original.

The rebuilt fortress atop a hill overlooking the Canaanite city of Arad. Although Arad dates back to about 4000 BC, the fortress was built in the time of Solomon and David. Characteristically, towers were on either side of the city gate.

Biblical references to "justice in the city gates" refers to justice dispensed in or near the gate complex. Because the gate complex was the place the people gathered for business and socialization, and because it was a place of public assembly for reading the law and encouraging the people, it was also the expected place for holding court. Accusations were made in public, the trial took place in public, and the decision was given in a public place. So also the sentence was carried out in public (Amos 5:15; see Deut. 17:5; 21:18–21; 22:23–24).

In 2 Samuel 19:7–8, the larger context can help readers visualize the gate complex where David was sitting. Before the battle between David's forces and Absalom's forces, David stood "beside the city gate" as the army marched out (2 Sam. 18:4). He was probably standing just outside the gate, reviewing the troops. He then is described as "sitting between the [two] city gates" when a watchman went up to the roof of the gate and saw a runner bringing news of the battle (v. 24). The description suggests Mahanaim had an inner and outer gate, such as ones found at Beer-sheba, Tel Dan, Megiddo, and elsewhere. When David heard that Absalom had been killed, he "went up to the chamber above the city gate" and wept (v. 33). The upper chamber would either be a second story or a rooftop room of the gate complex. Finally, David got up from his mourning and "sat in the city gate"; when the people heard that "the king is sitting in the city gate," all the people came before the king (19:8). So the gate at Mahanaim had an inner and outer gate, a second story or roof room, and a place for the king to sit between the inner and outer gates. At Tel Dan, excavators discovered a platform in the open area between the inner and outer gates. The platform originally had a canopy over it. The excavator suggests that the platform was the location of a seat for the king, a visiting dignitary, or a deity. That reconstructed platform may help people today visualize where David sat for the people to come before him. On a throne in the plaza of Mahanaim, David was reacclaimed as king by the people after the army had successfully put down Absalom's rebellion.

NOTES

1 See drawing, Ze'ev Herzog, "Tel Beersheba," in *NEAEHL*, 1:167.

2 Herzog, "Tel Beersheba," 171.

3 William Dever, "Gezer" in *NEAEHL*, 2:503, 505.

4 Avraham Biran "Dan" in *NEAEHL*, 1:329–30; Avraham Biran, "Sacred Spaces," *BAR* 24.5 (1998): 38–45.

5 Herzog, "Tel Beersheba," 167, 171–72.

6 Biran, "Dan," 329–30; Biran, "Sacred Spaces," 41, 44–45, 70.

7 Biran, "Dan"; Biran, "Sacred Spaces."

8 Rami Arav, Richard A. Freund, and John F. Shroder Jr., "Bethsaida Rediscovered," *BAR* 26.1 (2000): 44–56; Rami Arav, email message, October 15, 2009; and Tina Haettner Blomquist, *Gates and Gods* (Stockholm: Almqvist & Wicksell, 1999), 50–57.

9 Biran, "Sacred Spaces," 44–45; Blomquist, 57–67.

INCENSE IN HEBREW WORSHIP

BY KEN COX

Miniature bronze incense burners, probably for domestic use. From Byblos; first century BC–first century AD.

An altar for burning incense was part of the furnishings of the tabernacle. When Solomon built the magnificent temple in Jerusalem, a golden altar of incense was in front of the curtain in the holy place (2 Chr. 4:19). The incense, composed of four equal parts of rare, expensive ingredients, was to be burned exclusively on the altar.

Priests offered incense by placing burning coals from the bronze altar onto the

Bronze incense shovel; from Israel; dated to the first or second century AD.

incense altar. The priest would place incense ground into powder upon the coals. The fragrant cloud symbolized Israel's prayers rising constantly before the Lord.[1] The perfume of the offering was a pleasing aroma to fill the temple. As kings and honored houseguests were treated with the special aroma of burning incense, likewise the King of kings savored the sweet aroma of the special mixture of incense.[2]

Incense was burned in one other way on the Day of Atonement. The high priest would carry coals on a censer or fire pan into the most holy place and bring the blood of the sacrifice. Upon entering the most holy place, the priest would place incense on the coals, which came from the bronze altar. The result was a cloud that shielded and provided protection for the priest as he came into the consuming presence of God (Lev. 16:12–13).

The improper burning of incense brought immediate punishments. Nadab and Abihu, who were both priests and sons of Aaron, offered "unauthorized fire" in their censers and forfeited their lives (10:1–2).

Incense was to be added to grain offerings that served as fellowship offerings. These "thank offerings" were burned on the altar, the grain and incense together.[3] When grain was presented as a sin offering, incense was not to be added when it was burned. The incense with the thank offerings symbolized the worshipper's gratitude and union with God. The grain the poor offered as a sin offering could not contain incense due to the need of the worshipper to be first restored to communion with God.[4] After the Babylonian exile, the recipe for incense included seven other spices.[5]

In the New Testament, Zechariah, the father of John the Baptist, was the priest who had been selected to offer incense on the altar when he saw the angel that informed him of Elizabeth's miraculous conception. The book of Revelation refers to the smoke of incense as the prayers of God's saints (Rev. 5:8; 8:3).

Bronze incense shovel; from Israel; dated to the first or second century AD.

NOTES

[1] C. F. Keil and F. Delitzsch, "The Second Book of Moses (Exodus)," in *The Pentateuch*, vol. 1 of Commentary on the Old Testament (Peabody, MA: Hendrickson, 1996), 457.

[2] Immanuel Benzinger et al., "Incense" in *Jewish Encyclopedia* (1906), www.jewishencyclopedia.com/articles/8099-incense.

[3] Keil and Delitzsch, "The Third Book of Moses," in *Pentateuch*, 516.

[4] Keil and Delitzsch, "Third Book," 529.

[5] Roland de Vaux, *Ancient Israel: Its Life and Institutions* (Grand Rapids: Eerdmans, 1997), 432; Benzinger, "Incense."

ISTHMIAN GAMES

BY CECIL R. TAYLOR

Starter's pit at the stadium in Isthmia. The Isthmian Games were begun in the sixth century BC by the Corinthians.

Stadium at Delphi, home to the Pythian Games, which were held in year three of the Panhellenic Games cycle.

The games held at Olympia may be the best-known athletic contests from history, primarily because of their modern rebirth. In the world of the first century, many Greek cities offered their own local versions. A set of four of these games came to be known as the Panhellenic ("all Greek") Games because they were open to competitors from any Greek city in the world. These four games ran in a staggered cycle, so individual athletes could compete in all four and in at least one per year. The Olympic Games were held at Olympia every four years in year one of the cycle. The Isthmian Games near Corinth and the Nemean Games near Nemea took place in different months of year two. In year three, the Pythian Games were staged near Delphi. Year four featured the Isthmian and the Nemean Games again. Then the cycle repeated.

Held at the chief religious centers of Greece, these games honored eminent deities. Olympia and Nemea honored Zeus; Delphi honored Apollos; Isthmia honored Poseidon. Far more than sport for participants and spectators alike, these games formed part of the worship of the gods. Each athlete offered his best to the gods both before and during competition. Since Greek society understood that strength, speed, and skill came from the gods, the athletes prayed to them and offered thanks for success.[1]

The festival at Isthmia may have been the most popular of the games for two reasons. First, a visit to Corinth, the wealthy provincial capital of Achaia, was often considered the thrill of a lifetime. Second, held on a site near the eastern coast of the Isthmus of Corinth about eight to ten miles southeast of the city, Isthmia was easily accessible by land and by sea.[2]

BEFORE THE GAMES BEGAN

Rules of the games required every participant to spend at least ten months in strict and regimented training, which involved special diets and serious exercises. Before an athlete could compete, he had to swear a solemn oath that he had obeyed these strict rules. Every major Greek city had training facilities where men could prepare for competition in all

Laver (wash basin) from the temple of Poseidon at Isthmia, which dates from the seventh century BC. Here a person would swear he had kept the rules for nine months, perhaps as part of their purification rite. Poseidon was the patron deity of the Isthmian Games.

events. Many athletes used trainers who coached them in style and technique and also advised them about diet and exercise.[3]

When time came for the Isthmian Games (in the spring of the designated years), competitors and thousands of spectators gathered from cities and colonies all over the Mediterranean world, from Alexandria to Asia Minor to Spain. Only men could compete. Of the major games, Isthmia alone allowed non-Greeks to compete.[4] The festival had the look and feel of a carnival. Vendors sold everything from refreshments to souvenirs to offerings for the gods. Street performers offered musical, theatrical, artistic, and poetic entertainment.[5]

No one knows for sure how many days were given over to the athletic contests, how sacrifices to the honored deity meshed with the sports events, or precisely when the winners received their prizes. The agenda of events, however, was generally the same for all the games.

THE COMPETITION BEGINS

On opening day, contestants solemnly swore before the festival's judges that they had trained for the past ten months and would follow all the rules of the games. The judges also swore to evaluate contests fairly.[6]

Six events formed the core for all the games: foot racing, wrestling, jumping, boxing, javelin hurling, and discus throwing. Competition at Isthmia also included music, dance, drama, debate, chariot and horse races, and even a regatta.[7]

Heralds called participants to each event, giving out the name and city for each contestant, and announced the names of the victors to the crowds.[8] Only the winners got prizes. No awards were given for second or third place finishers. Often the victors' city-states honored them not only with free room and board and theater seats but also with cash. Those honors and awards, however, were less prized than the victor's wreath. Wreaths at Isthmia were circlets sometimes made of pine but more often of withered wild celery.[9]

NOTES

1. Richard Woff, *The Ancient Greek Olympics* (New York: Oxford University Press, 1999), 9; Judith Swaddling, "Olympics BC," *Natural History* 97.8 (1988): 8.

2. Oscar Broneer, "The Isthmian Games," accessed May 15, 2004, http://www.ioa.leeds.ac.uk/1970s/70094.htm; Oscar Broneer, "The Apostle Paul and the Isthmian Games," *BA* 25 (1962): 7.

3. Woff, *Ancient Greek Olympics*, 6.

4. E. Norman Gardiner, *Greek Athletic Sports and Festivals*, Handbooks of Archaeology and Antiquities (London: Macmillan, 1910), 218.

5. Woff, *Ancient Greek Olympics*, 9; Broneer, "Apostle Paul," 23–24.

6. Woff, *Ancient Greek Olympics*, 10.

7. Gordon D. Fee, *The First Epistle to the Corinthians*, New International Commentary on the New Testament (NICNT) (Grand Rapids: Eerdmans, 1987), 433–34, n. 1; Swaddling, "Olympics BC," 8; Woff, *Ancient Greek Olympics*, 12; Broneer, "Isthmian Games," 2–3.

8. See William Smith, "Games" in *Smith's Bible Dictionary* (1884), http://www.ntslibrary.com/PDF%20Books/Smith%27s%20Bible%20Dictionary.pdf, 224.

9. Judith Swaddling, *The Ancient Olympic Games*, 2nd ed. (Austin: University of Texas Press, 1999), 40; Swaddling, "Olympics BC," 8; Broneer, "Apostle Paul and the Isthmian Games," 16–17.

LIONS AS OLD TESTAMENT IMAGERY

BY HARRY D. CHAMPY III

Limestone lion standing over a bull's head, from Damascus, Syria.

The Old Testament writers frequently used lion imagery because the readers and hearers would have readily identified with it. Lions were common in ancient Israel and Judah and remained in the area until early in the fourteenth century AD. Mesopotamia also had lions throughout the Old Testament era and even until the late 1800s AD.[1]

"LIONS" IN THE OLD TESTAMENT

At least seven Hebrew words in the Old Testament refer to a lion: (1) *'ari* or *'aryeh*, a general word; (2) *kephir*, a young lion but covered with a mane; (3) *lebe'*, *lib'ah*, *labi'*, *lebiyya'*, or *libyah*, an older lion or lioness; (4) *layish*, a strong lion; (5) *shachal*, a fierce lion or an old lion; and (6) *gur*, a lion cub. These words occur approximately 150 times in 112 verses.[2] Ezekiel used the words the most (sixteen times), and Nahum has the highest proportional usage by far (ten times in three chapters).

The Pentateuch uses "lions" illustratively and in the context of blessing. For instance, Jacob blessed Judah and spoke of him as a lion cub (*gur*), a lion (*'ari*), and an older lion (*labi'*, see Gen. 49:9). Other examples in the Pentateuch include Moses's blessing of Gad and Dan (Deut. 33:20,22) and Balaam's blessing of Israel/Jacob (Num. 23:24; 24:9).

In the Historical Books (Joshua–Esther), the words often described a lion literally attacking a person (e.g., Samson in Judg. 14). Because of such encounters, people associated lions with fierceness and courage. Saul and Jonathan were reportedly "stronger than lions" (2 Sam. 1:23), and David's mightiest soldiers had "the heart of a lion" (2 Sam. 17:10). Further, artisans even used lions as decorations in the temple and in Solomon's palace (1 Kgs. 10:20; 2 Chr. 9:18–19).

Because a lion could attack suddenly and ferociously, lions became symbolic of judgment, destruction, and punishment. One writer recorded that God sent lions against the people in Samaria (2 Kgs. 17:25). Later the prophets spoke of God's roaring in judgment against his people Israel.

In the Prophets, the writers used lions to picture the wicked who ate the poor as prey (Zeph. 3:3); God's punishment, which comes swiftly and forcefully (Isa. 15:9; Hos. 5:14); impending danger of any kind (Isa. 21:8, see CSB note; Jer. 4:7); and God's deliverance in the messianic age when he will roar and enable the lion to live with the lamb (Isa. 11:6; Hos. 11:10).

ARCHAEOLOGY AND LIONS

Archaeologists have excavated few lion remains because animal remains are limited primarily to domesticated animals, to animals used as food, or to animals used in sacrifices. Lions would not normally fit into any of these categories.

Images of lions appear regularly in artifacts, however. Mesopotamian, Assyrian, and Egyptian reliefs depict lion hunting.[3] A basalt orthostat in a Canaanite temple at Beth-shean illustrates a fight between a lion and a dog.[4] The ivories found in a royal palace in Samaria included lions.[5] A Canaanite shrine at Hazor contained a small figure of a lion.[6] Probably the most famous example, though for its reference to a king rather than for its lion image, is the Shema seal, an eighth-century BC seal from Megiddo with a picture of a roaring lion and an inscription of its owner ("Shema, the servant of Jeroboam").[7]

At Jaffa and Dan, archaeologists have even found evidence of lion sacrifice. At Jaffa, a Canaanite temple contained a lion's skull with an Egyptian scarab in its eye. At Dan, lion bones were found near an altar; the Canaanite name of Dan was Laish ("lion").[8] In 2001, French archaeologists discovered the first mummified lion in an Egyptian tomb; the Egyptians worshipped the lion goddess Sekhmet.[9]

LIONS IN EZEKIEL 19

Ezekiel refers to lions ten times in chapter 19 and only six times elsewhere (1:10; 10:14; 22:25; 32:2; 38:13; 41:19). Chapter 19 is a lament for the princes of Israel, using two separate images: lions (vv. 2–9) and a vine (vv. 10–14). In the lion passage, the mother of the princes is a lioness (*lebiyya'*). She would lie down among the lions (*'ari*) and the young lions (*kephir*). She raised many cubs (*gur*). One cub (*gur*) grew up and became a young lion (*kephir*). He learned to eat prey and even men, but he was trapped and led to Egypt.

With her hope dashed, the lioness took another cub (*gur*) and raised him until he also became a young lion (*kephir*). He then walked about as a young lion (*kephir*) among the other lions ('*ari*). He also learned to eat prey and men. As he roared, the land was made desolate before him, but he was trapped and led to Babylon.

Ezekiel used the two cubs to symbolize the activities of the Israelite princes—the wicked. The two have attacked and killed; they have lived wickedly and have consumed the helpless. Ironically, the lions were objects of God's punishment; the hunters were the hunted and the trapped.

God used Egypt and Babylon as the vehicles of his punishment. Because of these references and because of the date of the prophecies (1:2–3), this lament seems to refer to the historical events of Ezekiel's day. The young lions are the young kings Jehoahaz and Jehoiachin. Jehoahaz was taken to Egypt by Pharaoh Neco, and Jehoiachin was taken to Babylon by Nebuchadnezzar.

Ezekiel used lion imagery to depict God's judgment on these two wicked kings in the occurring political tragedies of his day. The kings who had hunted prey were eventually hunted by God through foreign, conquering kings. In the end all faced destruction.

NOTES

1. W. S. McCullough and F. S. Bodenheimer, "Lions" in *IDB*, 3:136.
2. Twenty-seven of the thirty-nine books in the Old Testament have one of these words; therefore, only twelve books do not have any occurrence (Exodus, Leviticus, Joshua, Ruth, Ezra, Nehemiah, Esther, Obadiah, Jonah, Habakkuk, Haggai, and Malachi). The words are used more than ten times in eight books (1 Kings, Job, Psalms, Isaiah, Jeremiah, Ezekiel, Daniel, and Nahum). Abraham Even-Shoshan, *A New Concordance of the Bible* (Jerusalem: Kiryath Sepher, 1989).
3. Oded Borowski, *Every Living Thing: Daily Use of Animals in Ancient Israel* (Walnut Creek, CA: AltaMira Press, 1998), 197–98.
4. Basalt is a black volcanic stone commonly found in northern Israel. An orthostat is a rectangular stone placed vertically at the base of a wall. "Beth Shean (Tel); Husn (Tell El-)" in *Archaeological Encyclopedia of the Holy Land* ed. Avraham Negev and Shimon Gibson (New York: Continuum, 2001), 83.
5. "Samaria; Shomron; Sebaste" in *Archaeological Encyclopedia*, 447–48.
6. "Hazor (a) (Tel)" in *Archaeological Encyclopedia*, 221.
7. "Seals" in *Archaeological Encyclopedia*, 452; see "Megiddo," 327.
8. Borowski, *Every Living Thing*, 226–27.
9. Stefan Lovgren, "Egyptian Lion Mummy Found in Ancient Tomb," *National Geographic News* (January 14, 2004), www.news.nationalgeographic.com.

LITERACY IN THE ANCIENT NEAR EAST

BY STEPHEN J. ANDREWS

Tablet of administrative archives from a temple of Lagash; dated to about 2370 BC; from Tello at ancient Girsu, which is the earliest known Sumerian site. The tablet is a list of offerings made to the gods.

The earliest "written" documents in the ancient Near East were small clay "tablets" used in southern Mesopotamia around 3500–3000 BC. People incised small tokens of various shapes into the clay to record inventories and possibly economic transactions. When the tablets were baked, or left to dry out, they would harden and thus provide a system of accounting that could be checked repeatedly.

By the beginning of the third millennium BC, Sumerians used the idea of incised shapes to create the basis for the earliest known writing system. The shapes became stylized pictures (pictographs) that were cut into soft clay with a stylus. The pictures or signs could represent a single word (logogram), a concept (ideogram), or a syllable (syllabogram) in the Sumerian language. Several such signs could be placed together to represent the spoken language. The Sumerians used a blunt reed as a stylus that left triangular wedge-shaped marks on the tablets. Consequently, this system has come to be known as cuneiform (wedge-shape) writing.

The Sumerians set up specialized scribal schools to train a small portion of the population to write and read cuneiform script on a tablet. The signs went through several stages of simplification. The cuneiform script contained nearly 1,500 distinct signs, although not all of them were in use at the same place or time. The Sumerians also adapted the cuneiform signs to inscribe on stone monuments, such as the Code of Hammurabi.[1]

The Sumerian cuneiform script was later adapted by the Akkadians, a Semitic people who lived in the northern part of the Mesopotamian river valley, to record their spoken language. The Assyrians and Babylonians also used cuneiform script to record their dialects of the Akkadian language. Archaeologists have discovered hundreds of thousands of cuneiform tablets in excavations at sites in modern-day Syria and Iraq. These texts contain a wide range of societal and cultural records: business documents (sales, inventories, deeds); historical annals (royal chronicles, edicts, letters); and religious writings (myths, epics, hymns, prayers). The Hittites, Hurrians, Urartians, Elamites, and other ancient cultures also adopted the cuneiform script.

EGYPTIAN WRITING

Egyptians had also created their own system of writing by the third millennium BC. They designed this for use primarily on public monuments, tombs, and temples. Their picture-signs (pictographs) could be read as words, as ideas, and as phonetic sounds (phonograms) and came to be known as hieroglyphs or sacred letters.[2] Scribes trained to write this formal script, which contained around a thousand distinctive characters.

The Egyptians contributed to literacy by taking the pith of the papyrus plant from the Nile Delta and creating a thick type of paper for writing. Many copies of the Egyptian magical text, the Book of the Dead, were written on papyrus and placed in coffins.[3] Egyptians later invented two other cursive scripts to simplify the writing process on papyrus for record keeping, inventories, and letters, as well as religious texts and other documents.

The large number of cuneiform and hieroglyph signs restricted literacy to professional scribes who spent considerable time learning their respective systems. The invention of the alphabet early in the second millennium BC changed this situation. The early alphabets were based on consonants only; no vowels were included. Since each letter represented one phonetic unit, each culture needed only twenty to thirty letters

Precuneiform tablet dated about 3300–3200 BC. The tablet was from one of the many administrative archives in the ancient Mesopotamian city of Uruk.

Diorite statue of the Egyptian priest-teacher Ouennefer made to represent a seated scribe; dated to Egypt's Nineteenth–Twentieth Dynasties, about 1295–1070 BC.

In 2008, excavators at Khirbet Qeiyafa, biblical Shaaraim, found an ostracon, an ink inscription on a piece of pottery. This inscription is possibly the earliest evidence of Hebrew writing.

to represent most sounds of their individual language. Eventually, this allowed many people to learn to read and write.

The earliest known alphabetic inscriptions came from three specific areas of the ancient Near East. First, several alphabetic inscriptions were discovered at the ruins of Serabit el-Khadem and in the Wadi Maghara in the Sinai Peninsula. These were labeled proto-Sinaitic. Second, similar inscriptions were found at various sites in the southern Levant (countries on the eastern Mediterranean) and were called proto-Canaanite. Third, more recently two inscriptions were found scratched on limestone walls in the Wadi el-Hol in the Egyptian desert west of the Nile. Scholars have dated these last texts to early in the second millennium BC.

The language of these three inscriptions is Semitic in origin.[4] *Semitic* refers to various ancient people groups who lived in southwestern Asia, including the Akkadians, Canaanites, Hebrews, and others. The name comes from Shem, Noah's oldest son (Gen. 5:32). The texts contained graffiti and short dedicatory texts and were discovered in locations where Semitic peoples served as soldiers, traders, merchants, and slaves. Scholars regard this Proto-Sinaitic alphabet to be the common ancestor of the Paleo-Hebrew and Phoenician scripts and by extension all other alphabets, including the later Hebrew and Greek alphabets used to write the Bible.[5]

Phoenician and paleo-Hebrew scripts include historical texts such as the Mesha and Tel Dan stelae and the Siloam Tunnel Inscription. Additionally, inscribed pottery shards (ostraca) contain letters, dockets, inventories, and numerous other types of inscribed artifacts.[6] The tenth-century BC Khirbet Qeiyafa inscription (from the Old Testament city of Shaaraim; 1 Sam. 17:52; 1 Chr. 4:31) is the earliest inscribed ostracon yet to be discovered within a possible Israelite monarchial context.[7]

IN SCRIPTURE

The Bible presupposes the ability to read and write. God commanded Moses to write down the words of the covenant, among other things (Exod. 34:27; cf. 17:14). Moses may have sat cross-legged on the ground with a writing palette in his lap or in front of a small writing table. Several Egyptian reliefs and statues depict the work of the scribe in this manner. He may have had a writing case (Ezek. 9:2–3,11) containing pens (Ps. 45:1; Jer. 8:8), brushes, small sponges as erasers, black and red inks (Jer. 36:18), and possibly a scribe's knife (v. 23) to trim the papyrus or parchment.

The Bible attests to a high level of literacy.[8] The poems and songs in the Psalms demonstrate sophisticated literary style. History offers no definitive information about the number of people in biblical times who were literate. Most in the Bible who could read and write were leaders or professional scribes and secretaries (Deut. 17:18; Josh. 18:4; 2 Kgs. 10:1; Isa. 8:1).[9] Yet Moses commanded all Israelites to write God's commandments on the doorposts of their houses (Deut. 6:9).

From Egypt's Eighteenth Dynasty, a scribe's wooden writing kit, which includes pens and a palette with wells for red and black pigment. Hieroglyphs record that Egyptians considered serving as a king's scribe a badge of honor. Likely from Thebes, dated about 1550–1525 BC.

NOTES

1 E. Ray Clendenen and Jason Zan, "Hammurabi" in *HIBD* (2015), 697–98.

2 I. J. Gelb, *A Study of Writing*, rev. ed. (Chicago: University of Chicago Press, 1963), 72.

3 Daniel C. Browning Jr., Kirk Kilpatrick, and Brian T. Stachowski, "Egypt" in *HIBD* (2015), 468.

4 Christopher A. Rollston, *Writing and Literacy in the World of Ancient Israel* (Atlanta: Society of Biblical Literature, 2010), 12.

5 John Noble Wilford, "Finds in Egypt Date Alphabet in Earlier Era," *New York Times*, November 14, 1999, nyti.ms/2rhmkdL.

6 See the list in R. Adam Dodd, "Writing," in *HIBD* (2015), 1676–77.

7 Stephen J. Andrews, "The Oldest Attested Hebrew Scriptures and the Khirbet Qeiyafa Inscription," in *The World of Jesus and Early Church: Identity and Interpretation in Early Communities of Faith*, ed. Craig A. Evans (Peabody, MA: Hendrickson, 2011), 153–54.

8 See Dodd, "Writing," 1677–78 for a list of Scripture references. The Bible uses the Hebrew or Greek verbs for "to write" more than 400 times.

9 Dodd, "Writing," 1678.

LIVESTOCK AS WEALTH IN THE OLD TESTAMENT ERA

BY JULIE NALL KNOWLES

Frieze of a dairy scene from Tell al-Ubaid, Egypt. It shows two men transferring liquid from one container to another, probably storing butter. Another man has a large container, presumably containing milk. From about 2500 BC.

SHEEP, GOATS, AND CATTLE

Domesticated near the Caspian Sea, broadtail sheep appear on a bowl of Uruk III (ca 3000 BC) and centuries later on wall reliefs completed for Tiglath-pileser III (ca. 745–727 BC).[1] Sheep became the most important livestock for capital investment in Israel. Job's 7,000 represented great wealth; powerful Nabal had 3,000 to shear in Carmel (1 Sam. 25:2). As well as providing income from food, milk, wool, and felt, sheep were a medium of exchange; for example, Tyre and Damascus traded with wool (Ezek. 27:18); King Mesha of Moab paid Israel tribute with wool and lambs (2 Kgs. 3:4).

Other sheep-rearing tribes probably held grazing rights in Job's "land of Uz." Canaanite and Perizzite herdsmen shared pastures near Bethel and Ai (Gen. 13:7) and could not welcome herds belonging to Abram and Lot. In remote pastures, shepherds corralled livestock at night in rough forts for protection. Sheep held an important role in local economies. Jacob disputed with Laban over wages (31:38–41), using wording of Old Babylonian herding contracts to remind his father-in-law that he owned considerably fewer animals than the 20 percent normally due a shepherd.[2]

Evidence from Jericho dating to about 7000 BC indicated that goats may be the earliest domesticated livestock. On a vase fragment from about 3000 BC found near Baghdad, a person feeds two goats that have curved horns. In fact, the ram-in-the-thicket goat of Genesis 22:13 may have been like one from Ur with horns twisted into a corkscrew.[3] Goats were suited to mountainous territory and hot, dry regions; they provided meat and a steady supply of milk. Merchandise from goat hair and hides included clothing, carpets, tents, and even leather for boats used on rivers.[4]

Agriculture developed in river valleys and with it animal husbandry. With 500 yoke of oxen, what a field Job cultivated! In Mesopotamia, several breeds of cattle—piebald, horned/hornless, and humped zebu from India—served as draft animals. As Job owned more than a thousand head of cattle, his family could have eaten veal, a wealthy indulgence (Amos 6:4). Job probably prospered significantly in cattle trading. A statue found at Megiddo shows a certain Thuthotep with Asian cattle; he may have represented Egypt in shipments of cattle and merchandise.[5] Warriors took cattle as booty; this happened at Ai (Josh. 8:27) and when the Sabeans ravaged Job's fields (Job 1:14–15).

DONKEYS AND CAMELS

Caravan traders, the Sabeans may have seized Job's donkeys as the more valuable plunder. Domesticated in the Nile Valley, donkeys helped transport Abram's entourage from Egypt to the promised land (Gen. 12:16–13:5). Evidence indicates donkeys were being bred at Lahav in southern Israel at the same time trade networks through the region were being developed.[6] Either or both of these occurrences could have links to Abram as he came into Canaan. Also a Twelfth Dynasty Beni Hasan tomb painting shows Israelites entering Egypt with donkeys transporting packs.[7] To own a donkey seemed necessary for minimal existence (Job 24:3); successful merchants used many in their caravans. All Jewish classes—men, women, and children—rode donkeys; rulers chose white donkeys (Judg. 5:10).

Frieze of a dairy scene from Tell al-Ubaid, Egypt. One image depicts a cow being milked. A separate scene (on page 578) shows two men transferring liquid from one container to another, probably storing butter. Another man has a large container—presumably containing milk. From about 2500 BC.

Relief from the palace of King Tiglath-pileser III (744–727 BC) shows sheep and goats, captured during a military campaign, being driven back to the Assyrian camp.

Horse bit with cheek pieces in the form of winged goats.

Perhaps the most amicable animal, its peaceful nature emphasizes the image of Israel's coming Messiah, riding on a donkey (Zech. 9:9). More donkeys were brought from Babylon than any other livestock (Ezra 2:66–67). Some may have been acquired in business, for in the Old Assyrian trade, shares could include donkeys.[8] As described by Herodotus, caravan drivers who brought donkeys to the river enjoyed a rather unique commerce:

The boats which come down the river to Babylon are circular, and made of skins.... Each vessel has a live ass on board; those of larger size have more than one. When they reach Babylon, the cargo is landed and offered for sale; after which the men break up their boats ... and loading their asses with the skins, set off on their way back to Armenia.[9]

The marauders who stole Job's cattle probably took his camels to southern Babylonia, their territory. Domesticated in Arabia, the "ass of the south" had tonic effects on Mesopotamian commerce. A camel's feet accommodate arid soil, and the ability to subsist on little food and water helps camels carry loads over deserts. As slow breeders, however, herds have low growth, which may have given impetus to obtain stock by raiding.[10]

Job did not have an excessive number of camels. Aristotle reported, "Some of the inhabitants of Upper Asia have as many as three thousand camels."[11]

Cuneiform lists and seals show the Bactrian camel (two humped), but caravan travelers preferred the faster dromedary (one humped). Some owners bought goods and sold them again, repeating the process going back. Others arranged to deliver merchandise to another to take farther, the first receiving cargo for return. A merchant's letters might ask that goods be delivered to bearers.

HORSES AND MULES

King Solomon's merchants obtained horses and chariots from Egypt and other horses from Cilicia and traded with Hittite and Aramean states (1 Kgs. 10:28–29). The horses came from those domesticated in northern Persian mountains. Along with chariots, horses (the "ass of the north") reached Egypt during Hyksos domination of the area. During Thutmose III's campaign

Twin pottery jars in the form of bulls. Old Hittite era (1680–1500 BC), from Bogazkoy.

to crush the Hyksos in Israel, a war story tells how an Egyptian commander besieging Joppa asked the defenders to let his horses be brought inside the city, "because outside they are vulnerable." General Djehuty then took Joppa, having saved his horses.[12] This story illustrates the advantage horses gave in military campaigns.

Successive writers regarded the horse as a battle animal. For warfare every kingdom had charioteer corps. For his thousands of horses and chariots King Solomon built stables in "chariot cities" (1 Kgs. 9:19). Although not specifically named as such, Hazor, Megiddo, and Gezer (v. 15) may have been home to both Solomon's chariots and horsemen. The so-called Solomon's stables excavated at Megiddo caused great excitement when discovered. Yet the doorways and aisles are too narrow to easily accommodate horses. So although Megiddo may have been a "chariot city," excavations have yet to unearth Solomon's authentic stables at the site. King Sargon II of Assyria (722–705 BC) found an Israelite royal stable and well-fed horses, and other Assyrian documents mention "king's stables" for horses and mules.[13]

Because crossbreeding was forbidden (Lev. 19:19), the Israelites bought mules (cross of a donkey and a horse). Those ridden by King David's sons (2 Sam. 13:29) may have come from Tyre, which traded in horses and mules with Beth-togarmah in Cilicia (Ezek. 27:14). The art of mule breeding probably developed there, in the Hittites' homeland, which was famous for breeding and training chariot horses. The Hittites also likely bred the superior mules royalty and many wealthy people commonly rode.

On mountain paths mules are sure-footed and can carry much cargo, so mules traveled the northern caravan routes. Of the livestock Jews brought from Babylon, only 3 percent were mules (Ezra 2:66–67). Their owners could have been like the Murashus of Nippur who prospered during the exile[14] and could afford expensive mules. Apparently, the returning Jews did not have sheep, goats, and oxen, but these animals could be bought in Israel.

NOTES

[1] Frederick E. Zeuner, *A History of Domesticated Animals* (New York: Harper & Row, 1963), 173.

[2] J. J. Finkelstein, "An Old Babylonian Herding Contract and Genesis 31:38 f.," *Journal of the American Oriental Society (JAOS)* 88 (1968): 35.

[3]   Zeuner, *History,* 133–39.

[4]   Georges Contenau, *Everyday Life in Babylon and Assyria* (New York: St. Martin's, 1954), 48.

[5]   Amihai Mazar, *Archaeology of the Land of the Bible, 10,000–586 BCE,* vol. 1 in ABRL,187.

[6]   Brian Hesse, "Animal Husbandry and Human Diet in the Ancient Near East" in CANE, vol. 1 (1990), 216.

[7]   Mazar, *Archaeology,* 187.

[8]   Mogens Trolle Larsen, "Partnerships in the Old Assyrian Trade," *Iraq* 39 (1977): 135.

[9]   Herodotus, *Histories* 1.194.

[10] Hesse, "Animal Husbandry," 217.

[11] Aristotle, *History of Animals* 9:50.

[12] T. C. Mitchell, *The Bible in the British Museum* (New York: Paulist, 2004), 38.

[13] Yigael Yadin, "In Defense of the Stables at Megiddo," *BAR* 2.5 (1976): 22.

[14] Contenau, *Everyday Life,* 85.

MEAT SACRIFICED TO IDOLS

BY ALAN BRANCH

Meat market or "Macellum" at Puteoli, which is on the western coast of Italy.

Corinth in Paul's day was a religiously diverse Roman colony that embraced pluralism. Sacrificing to the gods was central to Greco-Roman religion. Although some sacrifices involved the consumption of the entire animal by fire, a standard sacrifice was one in which a worshipper dedicated a portion of the animal to the god or goddess. The rest of the animal was food for the priests, the temple personnel, and/or the worshipper and his family.[1] If the worshipper received part of the meat, he may have taken it home for a private feast. Some of the meat also may have been sold in the marketplace.[2]

Lavish banquets were closely tied to these sacrifices. The portions of the animal not burned to the god or left in the temple were used at social gatherings central to the Corinthian culture. Dining rooms were a common part of ancient temples; people could rent these for social functions (much like today's community centers). For example, one of the most famous temples in Corinth was dedicated to Asclepios, the god of healing. Excavators have discovered three dining rooms at the ancient temple site. Of many religious sites on the Acrocorinth, the sanctuary of Demeter and Kore had been remodeled in Paul's day, and ritual dining was observed outside.[3]

Archaeologists have discovered ancient papyri that were invitations to meals dedicated to pagan gods. These meals were held at various temples or private houses. One example is an invitation to a dinner dedicated to the Greek-Egyptian god Serapis; it says,

In Corinth, the western shops were adjacent to the temple of the imperial cult, which supplied meat for sale locally.

"Chaeremon invites you to dine at the banquet of the Lord Serapis in the Sarapeum tomorrow, the 15th, beginning at the 9th hour."[4] Such feasts in antiquity often included drunkenness and sexual carousing.[5]

People in the twenty-first century have difficulty appreciating the degree to which these "idol banquets" served as a social glue in the Greco-Roman culture. The sacrifices were not just the center of the religious life of a city, but they served as the heart of the social life as well. People associated sacrificial meals with a wedding, a birthday, a funeral, or other important occasions.

Dated AD 150-200, from Thessalonica; a statue head of Serapis (the Hellenized form of Egypt's god of the dead, Osiris). The head was probably from a statue that someone gave as a worship offering. Devotees worshipped Serapis, Isis, and other gods at Corinth.

NOTES

[1] Dennis E. Smith, "Greco-Roman Sacred Meals" in *ABD*, 4:653–55.

[2] Colin Brown, "θύω" in *NIDNTT* (1986), 3:432.

[3] John McRay, *Archaeology and the New Testament* (Grand Rapids: Baker, 1991), 323.

[4] H. Lietzmann, *An die Korinther I–II*, 4th ed. (Tübingen: Mohr, 1949), 49, cited in Robert M. Grant, *Paul in the Roman World: The Conflict at Corinth* (Louisville: Westminster John Knox, 2001), 36, n. 51.

[5] Gordon D. Fee, "εἰδωλόθυτα Once Again: An Interpretation of 1 Corinthians 8–10," *Biblica* (*Bib*) 61.1 (1980): 186.

THE MOABITE STONE: ITS BIBLICAL AND HISTORICAL SIGNIFICANCE

BY R. DENNIS COLE

The numerous caves at Ataroth provided protection and later burial places for its inhabitants.

Ruins at biblical Aroer, which was an ancient Moabite settlement on the north bank of the Arnon River. The inscription on the Moabite Stone says: "I built Aroer and made the highway in the Arnon."

The Moabite Stone, also called the Mesha Stele, stands about forty-nine inches tall and is about thirty-one inches wide and fourteen inches thick.

French missionary F. A. Klein reportedly discovered the Moabite Stone, also called the Mesha stele, in 1868 in the town of Dhiban (equivalent to ancient Dibon). Struggles between the Europeans and local bedouins over the possession of this four-foot tall and two and one-half-foot wide basalt stone inscription resulted in its being broken into several pieces. Eventually the fragments were pieced together and the original text was restored so it could be translated and interpreted.

The Bible records that Moab's King Mesha rebelled against the Israelite overlords after the death of the infamous King Ahab (2 Kgs. 1:1; 3:4–27).

The region of Moab had originally come under the dominion of the Israelites through David's conquests (2 Sam. 8:2; 1 Chr. 18:2). The Israelites seemingly lost control of the territory, however, during the Israelite wars between Jeroboam I and Rehoboam. Several decades later, King Omri restored Israel's dominion over the region of Moab around 880 BC. The Bible does not mention this latter fact. It is directly referenced, though, in the so-called Moabite Stone, the monumental stele (inscribed standing stone) of Mesha, king of Moab. The inscription begins: "I am Mesha, son of Chemosh— … king of Moab, the Dibonite. My father was king over Moab thirty years and I became king after my father."[1] This important archaeological find illuminates these and other facets of the relationship between ancient Israel and Moab.

A vista of Moabite territory near the ancient city of Balu.

Ruins at Dibon, which for a while served as the ancient capital of Moab.

The inscription recounts Mesha honoring Chemosh, Moab's patron god, by building a sacred altar complex in his palace in Dibon. Mesha credited Chemosh for delivering him from his oppressors and giving him victory over all his adversaries. Mesha also tore down the altar erected during the time of King David. The text goes on to recount how, after his successful revolt against Israel and the construction of the worship complex in Dibon, Mesha continued to honor Chemosh through conquests and numerous building projects. The inscription mentions several cities formerly held by Israel and originally allocated to the tribe of Gad, including Dibon, Ataroth, and Aroer (Num. 32:34–36). Against the critics of the Bible and its historical credibility, this text echoes how the biblical account records real geographical information of that era in history. Typical of ancient Near Eastern annals, the Mesha stele records the lofty boasting and exaggeration of a king who perceived his might came from such a god as Chemosh. One should likewise read the records of the Arameans, Assyrians, Egyptians, and Babylonians with a critical eye, discerning the verifiable truth amid the lengthy texts of those periods.

On the Moabite Stone, Mesha reported how Moab had served Israel for thirty years since King Omri conquered this region, a fact not included in 1 Kings.

The writer of Kings downplayed Omri's international fame. Nevertheless, the highly fortified walls and "ivory palaces" of Ahab and the later kings of Israel in Samaria were internationally renowned. Even after Omri, Ahab, and their dynasty had been replaced in the Jehu purge, the kingdom continued to be known as the kingdom of Omri, or *Bit Umri* (house of Omri) in Assyrian documents.

The Mesha stele contributes details to the story of the crucial period in Israel's history after Ahab's death while also confirming the veracity of the biblical account.

A HISTORICAL SNAPSHOT OF ISRAEL AND MOAB THROUGH THE LENS OF SCRIPTURE AND THE MOABITE STONE				
King David gained control over Moab.	Solomon maintained control over Moab, took a Moabite wife, and honored Chemosh, the chief Moabite god.	After Solomon's death and after the kingdom divided, Moab became part of the northern kingdom. Evidently, though, the Moabites eventually broke away.	Israel's King Omri regained control over the Moabites. Omri's son Ahab continued to dominate Moab. Israel dominated Moab for about thirty years.	King Mesha of Moab paid tribute to Ahab. After Ahab died, Mesha led a successful revolt against Israel and gained independence for Moab.
2 Samuel 8:2; 1 Chronicles 18:2	1 Kings 11:1,7		The Moabite Stone	2 Kings 3:4–27 and the Moabite Stone

NOTES

1 Clyde E. Fant and Mitchell G. Reddish, *Lost Treasures of the Bible* (Grand Rapids: Eerdmans, 2008), 99.

MUSIC IN DAVID'S TIME

BY BECKY LOMBARD

The remains of this lyre were found in the king's grave (Tomb 789) located near that of Sub-ad (Pu-abi) in the royal cemetery at Ur.

For Hebrews in the centuries before Christ, music was a vehicle for the worshipper to experience supernatural moments with God (1 Sam. 10:5–6; 16:23; 2 Kgs. 3:14–16).

There were two worship traditions in the Old Testament. First, worship was spontaneous and ecstatic, exemplified in the above passages. Much religious poetry and music was improvised in response to events in the lives of worshippers. After the Israelites were delivered from the Egyptians, Moses and Miriam led in celebration that was poetic, vocal, and instrumental (Exod. 15:1–21). The song they sang was repetitive, involving much physical movement and rhythm.

Worship could also be professional and formal.[1] David led in the organization of worship leader teams who were trained and well skilled at leading and performing music in the temple. The opening ceremony for the temple was a musical spectacular (2 Chr. 5:12–13).

In Hebrew worship of the tenth century, Scripture was not spoken. It was chanted or sung to melody. This was to honor the sanctity of Scripture, setting it apart from the conversations of daily life.[2] Harmony was not used. Voices and instruments performed the same melody, with each performer adding embellishments. There are some indications that drones under the melody might have been common. The spirit was exuberant, and most scholars believe it to have been loud. The instruments used to accompany and help create this heterophonic sound included string (harp, lyre), wind (ram's horn, trumpet), and percussion (tambourine, cymbals, rattles).

A harp from Egypt that was made soon after 1580 BC.

Some implications concerning performance style can be drawn from poetry texts. Many psalms have heading designations that indicate who was to perform the poetry. Several are delineated as repertoire for specific musician guilds that David established (e.g., psalms of Asaph: 73–83). Some headings identify the occasion for which the psalm was intended; others suggest melodic formulas and instruments that were to be part of the performance.[3] Others denote instructions for music leadership and style of performance. The term *selah* occurs throughout the Psalms. Several meanings of this term have been conjectured. The most commonly accepted theory is that it indicated some sort of pause, probably a musical interlude between verses of the text.

One musicological scholar has asserted that the various symbols and marks that appear over and under letters throughout Hebrew Scriptures are a form of musical notation. (Scholars have generally considered these marks to be accent marks or punctuation.) Using the musical

A woman with tambourines or cymbals.

interpretation of these marks, a system of notation has been devised and some transcription and recording of melodies accomplished.[4]

The structure of the poetry is also important in understanding how Israelites worshipped through music. Psalms were written with textual parallelism in which a statement was followed by a restatement of the same idea using different words. This textual style was conducive to musical performance. It allowed for *responsorial* performance where the worship leader sang the first statement and a group of singers responded with the reiteration. Style of writing also allowed *antiphonal* performance where two groups alternated singing the text. Several psalms use a repeated refrain that allowed for a *litany* in which the congregation could respond with each repetition (e.g., Ps. 136).

A ninth-century BC shofar made from a conch shell.

There was no rhyme scheme to Hebrew poetry. The syllable accents within a line were inconsistent and did not allow an even meter as does our music today. There were strong and weak accents within the lines of poetry, and the rhythm of these textual inflections probably guided the rhythm of the music as opposed to any kind of steady beat. The melodic formulas would also have accommodated these irregular poetry lines.[5]

NOTES

[1]   Donald P. Hustad, *Jubilate II: Church Music in Worship and Renewal* (Carol Stream, IL: Hope, 1993), 131–32.
[2]   Andrew Wilson-Dickson, *The Story of Christian Music* (Minneapolis: Fortress, 1996), 23.
[3]   Wilson-Dickson, *Story,* 20.
[4]   Suzanne Haik-Vantoura, *The Music of the Bible Revealed,* trans. Dennis Weber (Berkeley, CA: BIBAL, 1991).
[5]   Wilson-Dickson, *Story,* 21.

"... AND NOT A DROP TO DRINK": WATER'S EFFECT ON CIVILIZATION DEVELOPMENT

BY CLAUDE F. MARIOTTINI

The Nile is life-sustaining for Egypt. Compare the rich farmland and grazing fields at Luxor with the arid mountains beyond.

LIFE IN THE DESERT

Isaac moved throughout the land in search of good pasture for his sheep and goats. During times of drought, seminomadic people moved from place to place, as Isaac did, to find water for their flocks. Drought caused disputes between the inhabitants of the cities and seminomads over water rights because the cities also had meadowlands and flocks that needed water.

In Gerar, Isaac planted crops and had an abundant harvest. Because of God's blessing, he became rich and had a large flock and many servants. The Philistines became hostile toward Isaac and expelled him from their city. Banished from a fertile land, Isaac had to dig wells to provide water for his family and flock.

Gerar was a town in the Negev, a desert region in the southern part of Canaan. Gerar was halfway between Beer-sheba and Gaza. Although the annual rainfall in the Negev is insufficient to sustain much agriculture, it rains enough to allow people to maintain small flocks and to provide cultivation of basic crop plants.

The arid areas of Canaan created a challenge to human settlement and to economic development. The natural water supply was too scarce to meet the demands of settled communities. The arid zones of Canaan experienced occasional dry spells, and the lack of rain extended into long-term droughts (Jer. 14:1–3; Hag. 1:11). During these droughts, people suffered, crops failed, and flocks perished (Jer. 14:1–3; Hag. 1:11).

Because of the harsh climatic nature of arid regions, the need for water is most intense just when water availability by natural precipitation is lacking. This imbalance between water supply and water demand was counterbalanced by the development of other means of providing water, such as wells, cisterns, pools, and water tunnels.

Over the centuries, people settled into the arid and semiarid areas of the ancient Near East and were able to adapt to the harsh conditions of their environment by increasing their water storage capacity and supply. The great civilizations of Mesopotamia and the inhabitants of Canaan and Egypt were able to develop ways of bringing water into their cities. Once water became available beyond the level of subsistence, people built great cities, thus proving that people can build settlements even in areas with extremely dry conditions. In antiquity, the viability of cities depended on their proximity to water sources.[1]

WATER IN THE ANCIENT NEAR EAST

In Egypt, the main source of water was the Nile River, considered the source of life in ancient Egypt. The waters of the Nile allowed the shores of the river to be easily cultivated (Deut. 11:10). The annual flood of the Nile, between July and November, brought a rich silt, called the "black soil," that was deposited on the fields and fertilized the land. Egyptians called this area the Black Land to distinguish it from the Red Land of the desert. The silt the Nile deposited allowed the Egyptians to irrigate the soil and raise different kinds of crops in quantity, including grain (Gen. 42:1–2) and vegetables such as cucumbers, melons, leeks, onions, and garlic (Num. 11:5).[2]

On the other side of the ancient Near East, the Tigris and the Euphrates Rivers provided much of the water that aided the development of the ancient Mesopotamian cultures. The word *Mesopotamia* means the land "between the rivers." This section of the ancient Near East is also known as the Fertile Crescent because of its abundant natural resources and the fertile farmland that made possible an increase in food supply and the growth of cities and villages. The area around the Tigris and the Euphrates was the birthplace of the ancient civilizations of the Sumerians, Akkadians, Assyrians, and Babylonians. The rivers' waters, carried by canals, irrigated agricultural fields in the alluvial lands between the rivers.

WATER IN CANAAN

In Canaan, most towns were built on hills, away from the sources of water. Thus the inhabitants of Canaan depended on rains, the morning dew, springs, wadis, brooks, and other sources to supply the physical needs of people, flocks, and land. The people who lived in Canaan developed several ways of supplementing the amount of water available to them.

Springs—Common throughout much of the Holy Land, springs are a natural source of water. In fact, the land of Canaan is described as "a land with streams, springs, and deep water sources, flowing in both valleys and hills" (Deut. 8:7). The source of most spring water was the rainfall that seeped into the ground. The amount of water available in a spring varied with the time of the year and the amount of rainfall. Springs furnished sufficient water for communities to use for drinking, irrigation, and watering their flocks. Some cities built canals running from the source of water located outside the city that would bring water into the city.

Pools—In the form of natural or artificial reservoirs, pools collected rainwater for use for drinking, irrigation, and watering flocks. The Bible mentions several pools: of Gibeon (2 Sam. 2:13), Hebron (4:12), Samaria (1 Kgs. 22:38), Siloam (John 9:7), and others. Although the pools held an abundant supply of water, their being open meant evaporation worked against long-term water storage.

Water Tunnels—Some cities built tunnels that went from inside the city, under the walls, to a source of water outside the city. Archaeology has confirmed the existence of water tunnels in Jerusalem, Megiddo, Gibeon, and Hazor.

These tunnels were built in a rudimentary fashion by the Canaanites before Israel conquered the land and were vastly improved and expanded during the time of the united monarchy and following. When David became king of Judah, he conquered Jerusalem after Joab used the water shaft to enter the Jebusite city (2 Sam. 5:8; 1 Chr. 11:6). The Jebusites cut the water shaft in the limestone rock in the Late Bronze Age to provide access to the Gihon Spring from within the city. The Gihon was the only perennial source of water in Jerusalem.

When Hezekiah, king of Judah, made preparations for war against Sennacherib, king of Assyria, he dug a tunnel under the hill of Ophel (see 2 Kgs. 20:20; 2 Chr. 32:30). The tunnel served to bring water from the Gihon Spring to a pool inside Jerusalem (Neh. 3:15). After the project was completed, an inscription was carved on the rock marking the completion of the project.

The water shaft of Megiddo was built initially by the Canaanites and was improved many times during the period of Israel's monarchy. During Ahab's time (874–853 BC), workers expanded the water system to include an underground passage that led from inside the city to the spring, which was outside the city wall. This water shaft had a flight of steps that led into a tunnel that continued downward as far as the source of the water. The passage was later expanded and deepened so that water flowed back into it and thus provided the city with an underground reservoir that served as a permanent water source for the citizens.[3]

Wells—Another way people who lived in arid areas tried to obtain fresh water was by digging wells. After Isaac left Gerar, he dug five wells, and all of them produced water

Village women carrying water pots.

(Gen. 26:18–25,32). People dug wells to collect water from a subterranean spring. Some cities built deep wells inside the city walls. The depth of the well dictated the size, as deeper wells required a wider opening at the top to prevent collapse of the walls.

Wells were located near major roads, and the water was sold to travelers (Deut. 2:6,28). People also dug wells in the wilderness (Gen. 16:14), outside a city (24:11), near a city gate (2 Sam. 23:16), in a field (Gen. 29:2), and in a courtyard (2 Sam. 17:18). At Beth-shemesh, the Canaanites dug a well that remained in use until the end of the northern kingdom. At Gezer, a well dated from the second millennium BC was dug by the Canaanites and was still in use by the time of the Israelites. At Gibeon, a large circular well was reached by a flight of steps into a cave where the water dripped from the rock.[4]

Wells were protected by a wellhead (Gen. 29:1–3) or covering (2 Sam. 17:19) to keep people and animals from

Water pot dating to the time of Abraham.

falling in. People used leather containers (Gen. 21:19), jugs (24:20), or buckets (John 4:11) to draw water from the wells. The use of rope and the development of rollers and pulley wheels helped people bring well water to the surface.

Cisterns—Natural sources of water such as perennial rivers and springs are not generally found in most arid areas, and digging for underground water is limited. People who settled in desert areas had to develop the ability to collect and store potable water from runoff during the rainy season. Cisterns provided the solution for storing that rainwater.

Cisterns are artificially constructed reservoirs. Typically bottle or bell-shaped, they differ from wells in that cisterns are filled "by drainage from roofs, streets, or the surface of a slope, or by water channeled from some other source. Wells, on the other hand, might be fed directly from underground springs."[5]

In Canaan, most cisterns were cut into limestone bedrock, which was always porous. Building better cisterns became possible after the discovery during the Early Iron Age (1200 BC) of plasters made of burnt slaked lime that could make the cisterns impermeable. The development of better cisterns contributed to the construction of villages and cities away from the sources of flowing water.[6]

In Canaan, the rainy season, on which the cisterns depended, began in late October and ended in early May. Toward the end of summer, springs and wells either dried up or reduced their flow. When that happened, cisterns and open reservoirs became the only sources of water. Many cisterns were built beside individual houses and fed from roof drainage. These private cisterns were smaller and sunk in the rocks within private boundaries, each owner having his own cistern (2 Kgs. 18:31; Prov. 5:15).[7]

NOTES

[1] Keith Schoville, *Biblical Archaeology in Focus* (Grand Rapids: Baker, 1982), 188.

[2] John Ruffle, "Nile River" in *HIBD*, 1191.

[3] Amihai Mazar, *Archaeology of the Land of the Bible* (New York: Doubleday, 1992), 479–80.

[4] James B. Pritchard, "The Water System at Gibeon," in *Biblical Archaeologist* (*BA*) 19 (1956): 66–75.

[5] Archibald C. Dickie and Dorothea W. Harvey, "Cistern" in *ISBE*, 1:702.

[6] John Peter Oleson, "Water Works" in *ABD*, 6:887.

[7] See "Water Supply" in *The Archaeological Encyclopedia of the Holy Land*, ed. Avraham Negev (Nashville: Thomas Nelson, 1986), 394–96.

OILS, PERFUMES, AND COSMETICS OF THE ANCIENT NEAR EAST

BY GEORGE H. SHADDIX

Two-handled glass perfume flask from Rhodes, Greece; dated late sixth century BC.

The word translated as "perfume" in Song of Songs 1:3 literally means "fat." The word describes the "fat" or oil of the fruit that people used in cosmetics. In Israel, this fruit was for the most part olive oil. The oil of the olive was typically mixed with fragrances to produce perfumes and other cosmetics in the ancient Near East.

Tree owners allowed olives to ripen on the tree and fall to the ground. If needed, people would beat the trees with long poles to make the remaining fruit fall (Deut. 24:20). Once the olives were gathered, those to be pressed for oil were piled up and allowed to ferment. This allowed "a more abundant flow of oil" when pressed.[1] Olive oil was obtained by pressing the olives and straining out the liquid part of the olive. Some of these presses are still used today. At one time, people trampled the olives underfoot as they did grapes (Mic. 6:15).

Once the oil was pressed from the fruit, the oil would be mixed with water. The solid matter would sink to the bottom, and the oil would float on the water. People would skim the oil from the top and store it in earthenware jars or, for larger quantities, in cisterns.

In addition to olive oil, people used oils from other sources to make the base for cosmetics and perfumes in the ancient Near East. For instance, to make skin creams, people used oils from "almonds, gourds, other trees and plants, and animal and fish fats."[2] Olives were in abundance in Galilee, and "only olive oil seems to have been used among the Hebrews."[3] Both men and women used the oil-based cosmetics and perfumes. Men rubbed oil into the hair of the head and beard.[4] This made the hair both stronger and softer (Pss. 23:5; 133:2). Women used cosmetics for personal care and to beautify themselves. These "included eye paint, powders, rouge, ointments for the body, and perfumes."[5]

People have been making and using cosmetics since ancient days. The Bible mentions painting one's eyes (2 Kgs. 9:30; Jer. 4:30; Ezek. 23:40). These eye cosmetics "were minerally based: black often being made from lead sulfate, greens and blues from copper oxide, and reds from iron oxide."[6] People crushed these materials and mixed them with olive oil or some other oil. Fragrances were often mixed as well. Individuals applied eye paint with a finger, stick, or spatula.

People highlighted their cheeks with powder and rouge in reds, yellow, and white. The Egyptians used powder puffs.[7] Mesopotamians colored the palms of their hands and the soles of their feet with red henna. Fingernail and toenail polish was a mixture of henna paint and beeswax.

Craftsmen made these cosmetics. Some ingredients were imported while others were local. "Fragrances came from seeds, plant leaves, fruits, and flowers, especially roses, jasmines, mints, balsams, and cinnamon."[8]

Some cosmetics were used not only for beauty but also for medical purposes. Eye makeup made the eyes look larger. "There may also have been some medicinal value by preventing dryness of the eyelid or discouraging disease-carrying flies."[9]

Perfume was used in ancient times. "The first recorded mention is on the fifteenth century BC tomb of [Egypt's] Queen Hatshepsut who had sent an expedition to the land of Punt to fetch frankincense."[10] In fact, ancient Egyptians especially favored strong scents. During the intertestamental period, Alexandria, Egypt, served as a hub for perfume trade.[11] The Bible mentions several plants that people used when making cosmetics and perfumes. Song of Songs 4:13–14 says, "Your branches are a paradise of pomegranates with choicest fruits; henna with nard, nard and saffron, calamus and cinnamon, with all the trees of frankincense, myrrh and aloes, with all the best spices." All of these "choicest fruits" can produce sweet-smelling fragrances. Proverbs 7:17 also mentions the use of some of these. Scriptures also mention several fragrances people used as perfumes. These "include aloes (Num. 24:6); balm (Ezek. 27:17); cinnamon (Prov. 7:17); frankincense (Isa. 43:23; Matt. 2:11); myrrh (Song 5:5; Matt. 2:11); and spikenard (John 12:3)."[12] Skilled workers (called "perfumer," see Exod. 30:25; Eccl. 10:1) chopped and pressed these raw materials before mixing them with an oil base. "The Israelites mainly used olive oil; in Mesopotamia it was sesame oil; in Ancient Greece it was linseed oil; while the Egyptians used mostly animal fats."[13]

Cosmetics and perfumes were kept in containers made of metal, stone, or glass, or in ceramic jars or boxes (Isa. 3:20; John 12:3). They were sold in the marketplace.

The women of ancient Israel and other countries took pride in their appearance. Living in a hot climate, bathing and adorning the body with oils and perfumes was important. Through the centuries, many traditions have changed. Others, however, are still much the same.

Cosmetic box made of ebony and inlaid with faience plaques and ivory (some ivory inlays have been tinted pink); dated to Egypt's Eighteenth Dynasty, about 1550–1295 BC.

Marble cosmetic container, with inscription marking it as the property of Marduk, god of Babylon; dated about 625–550 BC.

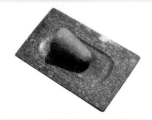

Grinding stone and palette, likely used for making cosmetics and ink dyes. Stone is from Naucratis, in the Nile Delta, and the palette from Semna, which was located farther south, between the regions of Nubia and Cush.

NOTES

[1] James A. Patch, "Oil" in *ISBE* (1952), 2181.

[2] Darlene R. Gautsch, "Cosmetics" in *HIBD*, 351.

[3] "Oil" in M. G. Easton, *Illustrated Bible Dictionary*, 3rd ed. (n.p.: Thomas Nelson, 1897).

[4] Gautsch, "Cosmetics," 350.

[5] Gautsch, "Cosmetics," 350.

[6] Norman A. Rubin, "Perfumes and Cosmetics in the Biblical World," *Anistoriton* 9, March 2005, www.anistor.gr/english/enback/v051.htm.

[7] Martin H. Heicksen, "Cosmetics" in *The Zondervan Encyclopedia of the Bible*, ed. Merrill C. Tenney, rev. ed. (Grand Rapids: Zondervan, 2009), 1:1034–35.

[8] Gautsch, "Cosmetics," 351.

[9] Gautsch, "Cosmetics."

[10] Gautsch, "Cosmetics."

[11] Madeleine S. Miller and J. Lane Miller, *Harper's Encyclopedia of Bible Life*, 3rd ed. (San Francisco: Harper & Row, 1978), 84.

[12] Gautsch, "Cosmetics," 351.

[13] Rubin, "Perfumes and Cosmetics."

PAPYRUS

BY GARY M. POULTON

Papyrus (Cyperus papyrus) is a perennial flowering plant that grows abundantly in the marshes along the Nile. Egyptians processed papyrus, making it suitable as a writing surface; additionally, they used it for making sandals, baskets, and even boats.

One often-overlooked Egyptian invention is the development of a paperlike product that made writing easier. This product was produced from the papyrus plant, from which paper gets its name. Papyrus grew abundantly along the banks of the Nile River. To produce the material, the stem of the papyrus plant was cut into strips. Other strips were placed crosswise on them. They were then pressed together and dried, forming sheets.

These sheets were so well made that a number of manuscripts written more than 5,000 thousand years ago are still intact. The Egyptians used an ink made by mixing water with soot and vegetable gums on a wooden palette. The writing instrument was a simple reed, trimmed at the end into a tiny brush. The writing made with this primitive ink is still legible. Sheets were often formed into books by gumming the right edge of one sheet to the left edge of the next. This would result in a roll. Some of these rolls were forty yards long.[1]

Egyptian paper became one of the main items of Egyptian foreign trade. The Greeks and the Romans later adopted this writing material. "New Testament manuscripts produced before the fourth century were written exclusively on papyrus; after the fourth century almost all New Testament documents were written on parchment."[2]

The abundance of writing materials allowed the Egyptians to develop one of the earliest school systems in history. The youth of the nobility were educated to provide literate public servants for the pharaoh's bureaucracy. Admission to the school was a great honor and to become an educated man was an important achievement. One extant papyrus states, "Behold, there is no profession that is not governed; it is only the learned man who rules himself."[3] The sculpture of a scribe sitting cross-legged with his papyrus on his lap is one of the most common artifacts of ancient Egypt.

NOTES

[1] Will Durant, *The Story of Civilization Part One: Our Oriental Heritage* (New York: Simon & Schuster, 1942), 171.

[2] "Papyrus" in *HolBD*, 1071.

[3] Durant, *Civilization*, 170.

PASSOVER IN JESUS'S DAY [1]

BY G. B. HOWELL JR.

In this early 1900s photo, a man applies blood to the lintel of his home as part of a Passover celebration.

Passover, commemorating the Israelites' deliverance from slavery in Egypt, was the most important of three festivals Jewish men were required to attend each year. Some have guessed that Jerusalem's population doubled for Passover. Merchants and worshippers alike made their way to the city.

Passover officially began on the eve of the fourteenth day of the Jewish month of Nisan (March–April), which was always a full moon (Ps. 81). On the thirteenth, the family would

A Nabatean terra-cotta cup from about the first centuries BC or AD.

completely clean the house and meticulously inspect it for leaven or any leavened product. This inspection would last into the night hours; the family would use oil lamps to complete their work.

On the morning of the fourteenth, the family could still eat products with leaven. When the priest signaled from the temple, the people could eat no more *chametz* (leaven and leavened bread). The priest would offer a second signal, and the families would burn their *chametz*. In the temple, thousands of priests would take their places in the temple before midday.

At midday, the head of each household would bring his sacrificial sheep or goat to the temple. When worshippers arrived at the temple, its doors would be shut. In three waves, the doors of the temple were opened and subsequently shut, allowing worshippers entrance. Once inside, each man would slay his own sacrificial animal. Rather than a clamoring crowd, however, people offered their temple sacrifices in relative quiet. With the sacrificial meat in hand, worshippers would return to their homes.

Houses were filled to capacity. Rich and poor, friend and relative, bond and free assembled freely together. No Jew was to be excluded. Following tradition, the families would cook the sacrificial meat in clay ovens reserved for this particular celebration.

Once the food was cooked, all would recline on sofas, propped up on their left elbows. The head of the house offered a *Kiddush*, which was a blessing said over the first cup. The right hand was ceremonially cleansed and was left free for eating. Worshippers dipped lettuce or celery into a bitter liquid and ate. They broke unleavened bread (called *matzah*), and they ate the Passover lamb (called *Pesach*) with bitter herbs, which they would dip. They also ate *charoset*, a nutty fruit mixture that represented the mortar used by the Hebrew slaves in Egypt.

At the second cup, the son would ask three questions:[2] "Why on all other nights do we dip only once, on this night twice? Why on all other nights do we eat *chametz* and *matzah*, on this night only *matzah*? Why on all other nights do we eat roast or boiled meat, on this night only roast?" The father explained the two dippings; the first referred to the hyssop, used to paint the doorposts; the second emphasized the bitter herbs that made this night different. The *matzah* emphasized the haste with which the Hebrews left Egypt, and roasting was the fastest way to cook an animal. The father would weave details of the Hebrews' enslavement in and exodus from Egypt into his responses.

Afterward, they took the third cup, and the father would sing Hallel psalms (Pss. 113–118). Others joined in, loudly. The father would conclude with a benediction. Participants would consume the fourth cup as they relaxed after the meal.

Children were expected to remain quiet, and the overall mood was reverent. Highlighting the solemnity, no dessert was served. Feasters would eventually parade back toward the temple, with its doors wide open, and join in a night of singing and prayer.

NOTES

[1] The details of Passover in the first century come from Hayyim Schauss, *The Jewish Festivals: From Their Beginnings to Our Own Day* (Cincinnati: Union of American Hebrew Congregations, 1938), 52–55.

[2] Abraham P. Bloch, *The Biblical and Historical Background of the Jewish Holy Days* (New York: Ktav, 1978), 130.

THE PRACTICE OF ROMAN CRUCIFIXION

BY R. D. FOWLER

Assyrian relief from Nineveh's South-West Palace shows captives being impaled. The Assyrians impaled either under a person's rib cage or between his legs. The bodies were put on display as a deterrent to others and to emphasize the brutality of the Assyrian army.

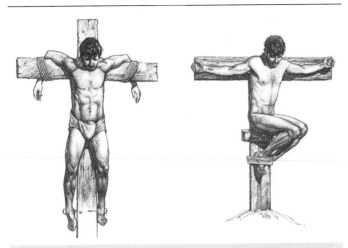

Artist's renderings of first-century crucifixions. A Saint Anthony's cross is on the left and a Latin Cross on the right. The Saint Anthony's has a small wooden block seat.

HISTORY

The precursor to crucifixion was impalement. The Greek word translated as "cross" in the New Testament originally referred to a pointed wooden stake or pole firmly fixed in the ground. Walls of these stakes formed protective palisade fortifications around settlements. Eastern countries, particularly Assyria, developed the practice of publicly displaying the corpses or heads of criminals, traitors, and enemies on these walls as a means of humiliation and intimidation. This practice led to people using the stakes themselves as a means of torture and execution—by impaling offenders on the stake and leaving them to die.[1]

History does not indicate when impalement ceased and crucifixion began, but historians generally agree that crucifixion began among the Persians.[2] The Romans likely adopted it from the Carthaginians.[3] Many ancient texts refer to both impalement and crucifixion but often fail to distinguish between the two and provide little descriptive detail of crucifixion. The Greeks and Romans used crucifixion well before the time of Christ. Alexander the Great used it in the fourth century BC. As early as 250 BC, the Romans were crucifying those they considered deserving. The ancient Romans generally thought of crucifixion as "the slave's punishment." Over time, however, the Romans used it for slaves, thieves, insurgents, and enemies of the empire in general.

People never considered crucifixion to be a Jewish form of punishment, yet Alexander Jannaeus, a Jewish high priest and king who crucified 800 Pharisees in one day, used it in the first century BC as an act of revenge for the Pharisees' rebellion against him. By the first century AD, Rome used crucifixion extensively in the pacification of Judea. Romans also used it throughout the empire as a means of maintaining order and suppressing insurrection. While crucifixion was primarily limited to noncitizens, Roman citizens were not totally free from its terrible shadow. In certain cases, particularly treason, Caesar would issue an edict allowing authorities to crucify even Roman citizens.

Crucifixion took place in public areas outside the city walls—where the bodies were clearly visible. Crucifixion thus punished offenders and intimidated one's enemies. Bodies

Bust of Rome's Emperor Titus, who ruled AD 79-81. Before he became emperor of Rome, Titus distinguished himself as a military commander. One of his campaigns included sacking Jerusalem and crucifying thousands.

on crosses were a common sight in the first century AD. The number of people crucified reached into the thousands. This excessive use, along with its barbaric nature and the religious idea of being cursed, made crucifixion particularly offensive to the Jews (see Deut. 21:22-23).

METHOD

"Crucifixion was a punishment in which the caprice and sadism of the executioners was given full rein."[4] Scourging was the first brutal act related to crucifixion. Roman citizens, though, were exempt from this part of the punishment. The condemned person was stripped of clothing, tied to a post, and beaten with the dreaded Roman flagellum, a whip consisting of leather straps embedded with metal, bone, or rock. Scourging was designed to shred flesh, in some cases exposing both bones and internal organs. Roman law, unlike Jewish law, set no limits on the number of lashes a person could receive. The severity of the scourging was completely at the discretion of the person administering it. In some cases, the scourging caused death; in others, it expedited death. In most cases, though, the scourging merely increased the agony the condemned person experienced on the cross.

Following scourging, the condemned person was clothed and then forced to carry the horizontal beam to the crucifixion site.[5] Typically the Romans hung a sign around the criminal's neck, specifying his offense. Scripture does not mention Jesus wearing the sign Pilate made, though custom dictated that he likely did. At the crucifixion site, the person was again stripped of his clothing and placed on the cross. The sign was also placed on the cross.

Upon arrival at the site, the authorities would secure the person to the cross using ropes, nails—or both. We know Jesus was nailed to his cross; not discounting the theological significance, nothing suggests otherwise. At this point in the process, details vary about how the actual crucifixion took place. Some believe the person was secured to the cross as it lay on the ground; the entire cross was then lifted up and dropped into a hole prepared for it. Others suggest the vertical beam was already in the ground; soldiers attached the person to the horizontal beam and hoisted both up the vertical beam.

Although the Romans had no standard form for the crosses they used, at least four variations were prominent. The Latin cross, likely the form on which Jesus died, had a crossbeam that attached a little below the top of the vertical beam. The second form, a Saint Anthony's cross, looked like a capital T. The third design, the Greek cross, had equal beams and looked like a plus sign. The fourth configuration, the Saint Andrew's cross, looked like the letter X. The variation in crosses, the possibility that crosses could be reused, and the absence of specific details mean that the method of crucifixion could vary—depending on the circumstances and the type of cross. The Latin cross, the Saint Anthony's cross, and the Greek cross each had a small wooden block or seat. This supported the body and prolonged death. Later, after the first century, a footrest was added. After death, bodies were, as a rule, left on the cross to be exposed to the elements and to decay. We know from Scripture this was not the case with Jesus.

This barbaric punishment method continued until the fourth century. Emperor Constantine abolished crucifixion during the later years of his reign. While many details are unclear, one detail is indisputable; crucifixion brought extreme suffering. The tremendous loss of blood, the excruciating pain from the nails, the stretched position, and the exposure to the elements all contributed to extreme suffering prior to death.

NOTES

1   See D. G. Burke, "Cross" in *ISBE* (1979), 825–26.

2   Burke, "Cross," 828.

3   Martin Hengel, *Crucifixion*, trans. John Bowden (Philadelphia: Fortress, 1977), 23.

4   Hengel, *Crucifixion*, 25.

5   Images often depict Jesus carrying the entire cross; however, the weight of both beams would have been close to 300 pounds, making this highly unlikely. The cross beam itself was heavy; carrying it would have been difficult, especially for someone who had been scourged (see Matt. 27:32).

PRECIOUS METALS

BY J. MARK TERRY

Hand- and footholds that allowed miners to descend into the shaft below to retrieve copper; at Timnah, in southern Israel.

Archaeologists tell us that ancient peoples used six different metals: gold, copper, and iron in earlier times and later silver, lead, and tin. Ancient peoples also used three alloys (combinations of metals): electrum (gold and silver), bronze (copper and tin), and later brass (copper and zinc).[1] Each played important parts in ancient cultures, both as a measure of wealth and for their value in making tools, weapons, and utensils. People smelted each of the metals from ore, which meant they searched diligently for ore's sources.

COPPER

Peoples of Bible times prized copper because they could easily fashion it into many different objects. Copper ore was found throughout the Fertile Crescent (the modern Middle East), and its availability led to widespread use. Copper is not hard or durable. Ancient artisans thus combined copper with tin to make bronze. Translators render the same Hebrew word (*nechosheth*) as "copper" or "bronze." Bronze came into such wide use that archaeologists refer to the period from 3150 to 1200 BC as the Bronze Age. The Old Testament refers to bronze doors, fetters, helmets, armor, and swords (1 Sam. 17:5–6; 2 Chr. 33:11; Isa. 45:2).

The New Testament writers mention copper (referring to coins, Matt. 10:9); John used the same Greek word (*chalkos*) to describe "brass" (Rev. 18:12). The Greek

Large roundel with a winged lion in the center. Unearthed at Ecbatana, the capital city of the Medes. Similar objects found in this same area are marked as belonging to Persia's King Artaxerxes II (reigned 404–358 BC), who built a summer palace in Ecbatana.

Lead pipe with stone sleeve sockets that would have joined the pieces of pipe; unearthed beneath the temple of Artemis, the primary goddess of Ephesus.

Hand-operated drill dated about 3150 to 2200 BC, the Early Bronze Age; from Syria. The operator would slide the crossbar up and down the central rotating rod, causing it to spin. The stone weight helped stabilize the drill.

language also used *chalkos* to refer to bronze (9:20). This multiuse of these Hebrew and Greek terms has caused some confusion in English Bible translations about whether the writer was referring to bronze or brass. History helps clarify.

The Romans first began producing brass (an alloy of copper and zinc) about 20 BC, roughly 400 years after the last Old Testament prophet. Strictly speaking, therefore, brass was not known or used in Old Testament times. The King James Version of the Old Testament contains many references to brass. More modern Bible translations use the word *bronze* rather than *brass*. Of course, copper is a common element in both bronze and brass.[2]

GOLD

The Bible refers to gold more than any other metal. The scarcity of gold ore increased its value in ancient times, just as is true today. Peoples of the ancient Near East valued gold for its beauty and luster. Because gold is malleable, goldsmiths of Bible times used it to make jewelry and ornaments. Craftsmen used gold in constructing the tabernacle, Solomon's temple, and many of the utensils used in each (Exod. 35–39; 1 Kgs. 6–7). Biblical texts often use the word *gold* to describe anything beautiful, valuable, or pure.[3]

IRON

The Iron Age (1200–586 BC) followed the Bronze Age. The ancients prized iron because it was harder than bronze, and iron tools and weapons proved more durable. God promised his children that they would find iron in the land of Canaan (Deut. 8:9). This was a demonstration of God's blessing and the richness of the land. The Israelites, like other peoples of the region, used iron to make jewelry; but they especially made plows, axes, picks, swords, and spears from iron. An army with iron weapons had a technological advantage over an enemy using bronze weapons. The Philistines possessed and exploited this advantage over the Israelites, at least for a time (Judg. 1:19; 1 Sam. 13:19–22). Biblical writers used "iron" as a symbol of hardness and judgment (Ps. 2:9; Rev. 2:27).[4]

SILVER

Ancient civilizations knew of and used silver from early times. The Bible often mentions gold and silver together, and both became symbols of wealth (Gen. 13:2; Zeph. 1:18; Hag. 2:8). As the nation of Israel prospered, the amount of silver in use increased. By the time of Solomon, silver was so common that people used it like money. Though the Israelites did not use coins during the monarchy (1050–586 BC), they used weights of silver—shekels, talents, and minas—as units of exchange (Gen. 23:15–16; Exod. 21:32; Neh. 7:72; Isa. 7:23).[5] Determining the exact equivalent weights in modern systems of measurement is difficult, as the weights varied somewhat in ancient times. However, the *Holman Illustrated Bible Dictionary* provides these estimates: A shekel weighed about two-fifths of an ounce; a mina weighed one and one-fourth pounds; and a talent weighed seventy-five pounds.[6] Peoples of the ancient Near East also used silver for jewelry, idols, and items for their temples.

LEAD

Ancient prospectors found lead deposits in Egypt and Asia Minor. Often silver was derived from the smelting of lead (Jer. 6:27–30). The Romans used lead to make water pipes and coins.

TIN

The biblical writers seldom mention tin. The ancients valued it, though, because they could mix it with copper to make bronze (Num. 31:22; Ezek. 22:18,20).

NOTES

[1] W. Gordon Brown, "Minerals and Metals" in *Wycliffe Bible Encyclopedia*, ed. Charles F. Pfeiffer, Howard F. Vos, and John Rea (Chicago: Moody, 1975), 2:1121–22.

[2] Daniel C. Browning Jr., "Minerals and Metals" in *HIBD*, 1131; A. Stewart and J. Ruffle, "Mining and Metals" in *New Bible Dictionary* (*NBD3*), ed. D. R. W. Wood, Howard Marshall, J. D. Douglas, and N. Hillyer, 3rd ed. (Downers Grove, IL: InterVarsity, 1996), 768.

[3] Stewart and Ruffle, "Mining and Metals," 767–68; Browning, "Minerals and Metals," 1131.

[4] Tim Turnham, "Iron" in *HIBD*, 834–35; Stewart and Ruffle, "Mining and Metals," 768.

[5] Browning, "Minerals and Metals," 1132.

[6] M. Pierce Matheney, "Weights and Measures" in *HIBD*, 1666.

PRISONS OF THE FIRST CENTURY

BY BENNIE R. CROCKETT JR.

A model of the Antonia fortress adjacent to the Jerusalem Temple. The Romans would have held Paul here.

CRIMINALS AND PUNISHMENT

Roman prisons and custody in the first century served at least six purposes: protection, remand, awaiting sentencing, execution, coercion, and punishment.[1] Emperor Vitellius used prisons to protect soldiers who had been threatened by fellow soldiers.[2] The Romans also held many people on remand until trials could occur;[3] both John the Baptist (Mark 6:14–29) and Peter (Acts 12:3–11) were such cases.

Those for whom the Romans pronounced a death sentence often died in prison. The bodies of prisoners who died in Rome could be thrown onto the steps of Capitoline Hill, then be dragged with hooks to the Forum, and finally cast into the Tiber River.[4]

The Romans also used prisons to coerce people to reveal guilty colleagues or to extract confessions. Lastly, Roman officers could leave a person in prison for a variety of reasons as a form of punishment.[5] Emperor Tiberius was inhumane toward prisoners, since he extended the life of several people for the purpose of psychological torture, which included a perpetual experience of fear and oppression.[6]

At least four different levels of imprisonment existed: prison, military custody, entrustment to sureties, and release with conditions. Depending on the severity of the charge and the social status of the individual, a prisoner could have chains or not. Military custody was less severe than imprisonment and could include being held in a barracks or camp anywhere in the empire or in someone's home. Custody also covered those going to a provincial capital or Rome for trial or those under watch prior to being sentenced to exile.

Prisoners who had committed less serious crimes were entrusted to sureties, rather than given military custody. Sometimes the Romans entrusted prisoners who were Roman citizens to family members for safekeeping. On rare occasions, a person under military custody could be released on his own pledge to the Roman magistrate. Though technically not in prison, one in military custody (especially a non-Roman) could encounter harsh treatment, but the magistrates sometimes accorded favor to Roman citizens or those with high social standing.

Offenses punishable by imprisonment concerned both capital crimes and lesser offenses. Capital crimes included enemies of war, murder, rape, and treason against the state; these offenses often resulted in execution. Treason had many facets, including initiating civil disturbances and rioting. High treason—which involved betrayal of Rome, the emperor, or any Roman citizen—was cause for automatic imprisonment and execution. Related to treasonous crimes, the authorities judged philosophers and those practicing occult rituals as betraying the state's interests. Other crimes included theft, piracy, mismanagement of money, debt, and desecration of the state's temples. For these crimes, punishments varied from place to place.[7]

A bust of Nero as a child. Nero's persecution of Christians was most likely the cause of Paul's second imprisonment.

CONDITIONS IN THE PRISONS

Custodial situations and the conditions in Roman prisons changed depending on the severity of the crime, the prisoner's social standing, the magistrate's kindness or cruelty, and the location of the imprisonment. Many prisons were underground and dark, accompanied by a shortage of food and sanitary surroundings. One prisoner of Tiberius remarked that prison food gave no satisfaction but also would not permit one to die.[8] Some magistrates allowed prisoners the benefit of care by family or friends (Acts 23:16–17).[9]

Paul's imprisonment at the time of writing 2 Timothy conveys several conditions. He asked Timothy to bring his coat left at Troas, his scrolls, and his parchments (2 Tim. 4:13). Though lacking warmth, Paul had the freedom to read and write. In the same period as Paul, Tacitus reported a man who wrote poetry while in prison and later was executed for doing so.[10] Paul's chains, however, were more serious (Eph. 6:20; Phil. 1:7,13–14,17; Col. 4:3,18), for Roman chains caused wounds, infections, and shame for many prisoners.[11]

On numerous occasions, Roman soldiers raped and abused female prisoners. Suicide rates of men and women in prison were high. Yet irresponsible jailers could be executed for failing in their duty (Acts 12:19).

People greatly feared the prison in Rome, a facility used for serious offenders and those who had no social standing. Later named Mamertine prison, it had a chamber twelve feet underground called the Tullianum. Sallust, the ancient Roman historian and politician, said the Tullianum was an enclosure with walls all around and a chamber above with a stone roof. Its conditions were hideous and fearful because of the neglect of prisoners, the darkness inside, and the putrid smell.[12]

The Romans used the prison in Alba Fucens, a city near Rome, to house enemies of the state. One ancient historian described the prison as an underground dungeon, full of darkness, and noisy because of the large numbers of people condemned on capital charges. The prisoners' food became mixed with the unsanitary conditions of their personal uncleanness. The resulting smell was so offensive that people tried to avoid even going near the prison.[13]

Some prisons were in stone quarries. A person in chains or bonds could be condemned to work in a quarry where walls, functioning as chains, kept one imprisoned. Rome had several such quarry prisons; they were typically reserved for prisoners with higher social status. Despite the grueling work, prisoners preferred the quarry prison over the Tullianum or a dungeon.

NOTES

[1]   Brian Rapske, *The Book of Acts and Paul in Roman Custody*, vol. 3 in *The Book of Acts in Its First Century Setting* (Grand Rapids: Eerdmans, 1994), 10–20.

[2]   Tacitus, *Histories* 1.58.

[3]   Josephus, *Jewish Antiquities* 18.6.5.

[4]   Dio Cassius, *History* 58.1.3; 59.18.3; 60.16.

[5]   Rapske, *Book of Acts and Paul*, 16–20.

[6]   Dio Cassius, *History* 58.3.3–5.

[7]   Rapske, *The Book of Acts and Paul*, 20–46.

[8]   Dio Cassius, *History* 58.3.6.

[9]   Craig S. Wansink, *Chained in Christ: The Experience and Rhetoric of Paul's Imprisonment* (Sheffield: Sheffield Academic, 1996), 82–84.

[10] Tacitus, *Annals* 6.39.

[11] Wansink, *Chained in Christ*, 47–48.

[12] Sallust, *Conspiracy of Catiline* 55.6.

[13] Diodorus of Sicily, *Library of History* 31.9.1–2.

REACHING THE HEAVENS: A STUDY OF ANCIENT TOWERS

BY STEPHEN J. ANDREWS

Watchtower overlooking grain fields near the valley of Lebonah in Israel.

Ruins of ancient Shechem including the temple stone (*matstsebah* or "holy stone") and the standing stone, perhaps the one set upright by Joshua.

The most common Hebrew word translated "tower" is *migdal*. In the New Testament, the Greek word *purgos* occurs four times and refers to a watchtower (Matt. 21:33; Mark 12:1) or a building like the tower of Siloam (Luke 13:4; cf. 14:28).

TYPES OF TOWERS

Remains of ancient towerlike structures are scattered widely over the Middle East. Biblical scholars and archaeologists have assigned a variety of functions to such towers. Not counting the metaphorical use of the term, the biblical text readily identifies four functions.[1]

Agricultural Towers—The Bible closely associates some towers with fields, orchards, vineyards, and winepresses (Isa. 5:2; Matt. 21:33; Mark 12:1). Farmers may have used such towers for storing farming tools and supplies. These towers may also have provided a lookout for protecting the crop from wild animals or thieves. In addition, farmhands could live in these structures while working at a distance from their villages.

A typical tower of this type was made of stone and was circular in shape, nine to twelve feet in diameter. The tower created a platform about three feet above the surface of the ground. This may have allowed shepherds to watch over their flocks in the wilderness (2 Chr. 26:10; metaphorically, Mic. 4:8).

Route Markers and Memorials—Stone towers or monuments marked indistinct paths and roads through the desert (Jer. 31:21). These were often simple heaps of stones that could reach nine to twelve feet in height.[2] Nomadic herders may also have used these along the migration routes as repositories for food and valuables. Apparently, people also used stone towers or pillars as burial monuments (Gen. 35:20; 2 Sam. 18:18; 2 Kgs. 23:17; Ezek. 39:15).

Defensive Towers—Most stone towers were part of a military defense system. Towers served as isolated outposts designed to allow watchmen to forewarn in the event of an enemy's approach (2 Kgs. 17:9; 2 Chr. 14:7; 27:4). These small independent citadels served as

Using more advanced engineering, this tower at Samarra, Iraq, is taller and narrower than the ancient ziggurats that had been common among the Sumerians. The tower dates to the mid-ninth century AD and is about 170 feet tall.

forts or watchtowers from which to oversee traffic along the border roads leading up into the capital (2 Kgs. 9:17; 18:8; 2 Chr. 27:25). Letter four of the Lachish letters and possibly Jeremiah 6:1 indicate the use of fire signals to communicate the activities of the enemy.[3] Those watching for these fire signals may have done so from the vantage point of a defense tower. Such tower fortifications also provided refuge for exposed settlements in times of attack.[4]

Towers were also important parts of the fortifications of a town or city wall (2 Chr. 32:5; Neh. 3; 12:38–39; Isa. 2:15). Psalm 48:12 directs the counting of the towers of Zion; Isaiah 33:18 and 1 Chronicles 27:25 indicate that an officer was in charge of towers. Perhaps due to their function or size, some of the towers of Jerusalem had names (Neh. 3:1; 12:39; Jer. 31:38; Zech. 14:10). These towers were distinct from the gates and most likely reinforced the regular city wall at strategic points (2 Chr. 26:9,15).

Finally, as a defense tower, *migdal* may also refer to a fortified citadel or palace that offered a final place of refuge inside a city. In Judges 9:50–57, Abimelech besieged the city of Thebez and captured it. But the inhabitants fled into the "strong tower" and shut themselves in. The tower of Shechem probably refers to the same type of structure (v. 46). According to the Bible, a citadel also existed at Penuel (Judg. 8:9,17) and Jezreel (2 Kgs. 9:17). Archaeologists have discovered and excavated fortified citadels at Gibeah and Beth-zur.[5]

Place-names and Temple Towers—Some scholars suggest that where the word *migdal* occurs with a place-name it refers to a fortified town with a temple tower (Gen. 35:21; Josh. 15:37; Judg. 9:46–49).[6] Consequently, these towns would owe their names to the temple towers that became their prominent landmark during the Middle Bronze and Late Bronze Ages (2200–1200 BC). However, both biblical and archaeological support for this theory exists only for the tower at Migdal-Shechem (Judg. 9:46–49). As mentioned above, Shechem's tower may have been more like a fortified citadel than a temple tower.

The Chogha Zanbil ziggurat near Susa dates to 1250 BC. It was built under the orders of Elam's King Untash-Gal for the worship of Inshoshinak, the Elamite god of the afterlife.

THE TOWER OF BABYLON

The one case where *migdal* most clearly represents a temple tower is in the famous account of the tower of Babylon (or Babel; Gen. 11:1–9). The central feature of most Mesopotamian cities was the temple complex or precinct. This area contained both a temple where people worshipped the patron deity and a tower called a ziggurat. The type of material used in its construction and the purpose for which it was built clearly suggest that the tower of Babylon is to be equated with the ziggurat temples of the ancient Near East.[7]

People built ziggurats intending them to be artificial mountains containing stairways from the heavens (the gate of the gods) to earth. These square or rectangular stepped pyramids were designed to enable the gods to come down into the temple on certain ceremonial occasions and bring blessings to the city. The structure provided convenience for the god of the city and for the priest who ministered to the needs of the god.[8] The purpose of the ziggurat was to hold a stairway leading up to a small room at the top of the structure.[9] This room was equipped with a bed and a table. The table was supplied regularly with food. The sole reason for this room was for the deity to refresh himself during his descent to the city.

Most ziggurats were made with a sun-dried brick frame filled with dirt and rubble. Kiln-fired brick with bitumen for mortar finished off the structure, making it waterproof and as durable as stone. Unlike a pyramid, a ziggurat had no internal rooms.

The earliest known ziggurat, at Erech (Gen. 10:10), dates to the third millennium BC. It contained a small shrine on a raised platform of clay reinforced with sun-dried bricks and measured 140 feet by 150 feet. The structure was about 30 feet high. The corners were oriented to the cardinal points of the compass. By contrast, the ziggurat at Ur was 200 feet long, 150 feet wide, and 70 feet high, while Entemenanki, the great ziggurat temple of Babylon, was seven stories high.[10]

Builders designed the tower of Babylon to have its "top [or head] in the sky" (Gen. 11:4). In Mesopotamian usage, this phrase was reserved almost exclusively for the description of ziggurats.[11] Ostensibly, the tower of Babylon would have been built for God's convenience to come down and see what humankind had accomplished.

NOTES

[1] E. B. Banning, "Towers" in *ABD*, 6:622.

[2] Banning, "Towers," 623.

[3] W. F. Albright, "Palestinian Inscriptions" in *Ancient Near Eastern Texts Relating to the Old Testament* (*ANET*), ed. James B. Pritchard, 3rd ed. (Princeton: Princeton University Press, 1969), 322.

[4] D. Kellerman, "Migdol," *Theological Dictionary of the Old Testament* (*TDOT*), 71.

[5] Kellerman, 71.

[6] Banning, "Towers," 623–24.

[7] John H. Walton, Victor H. Matthews, and Mark W. Chavalas, *The IVP Bible Background Commentary: Old Testament* (Downers Grove, IL: InterVarsity, 2000), 41–42.

[8] Walton, *IVP Bible Background*, 42.

[9] Photographs of ziggurats may be seen in *The Ancient Near East in Pictures Relating to the Old Testament* (*ANEP2*) ed. James B. Pritchard, 2nd ed. (Princeton: Princeton University Press, 1969), 233–34. An artist's reconstruction of a ziggurat may be found in *Holman Illustrated Bible Dictionary* (*HIBD*, ed. Chad Brand, Charles Draper, Archie England (Nashville: Holman, 2003), 1710.

[10] Edward M. Blaiklock, "Ziggurat" in *The New International Dictionary of Biblical Archaeology* (*NIDBA*), ed. E. M. Blaiklock and R. K. Harrison (Grand Rapids: Zondervan, 1983), 484. A photo of the Ur ziggurat may be found in *HIBD*, 1711.

[11] Walton, *IVP Bible Background*, 42.

ROMAN AGRICULTURE

BY SCOTT A. ANDREW

Almonds became a staple of the Roman diet as the empire expanded.

Italy is a land blessed by rich soil, a mild climate, and abundant rainfall. This was also true in ancient times. Italy's climate "invited possibilities of agriculture on a scale that no other Mediterranean country had ever before been able to attempt."[1] The diets of those living in pre-Roman Italy featured domestic animals, grain, wine, and olive oil. Each of these items were in ample supply.

Grain, oil, and wine—called the "Mediterranean triad"[2]—were the basic food items for the ancient Mediterranean world. As the empire grew, Romans came into contact with new varieties of food. They developed a taste for walnuts, almonds, pistachios, peaches, apricots, pomegranates, cherries, and lemons. When Romans introduced their culture to other lands, they carried with them the fruits, grains, and vegetables they had known at home.

The demand for food grew within the Roman Empire. Merchants discovered that grain could be grown more economically in areas outside Italy. Soon Italy imported all of its grain. By the time of Cicero (106–43 BC), orchards and vineyards covered the Italian countryside. Grapes and olives were Italy's principal farm products.

Olives became increasingly important in the ancient Mediterranean world. Olive cultivation began in Syria as early as 6000 BC. Earthenware tablets from Crete mention the prominence of olives in that culture as early as 2500 BC. After the fall of Crete around 1200 BC, the Phoenicians became masters of trade in the Mediterranean. By the fifth century BC, the Phoenicians and Greeks had distributed olives throughout the Mediterranean world. The Greeks introduced olives to Italy.

Olives became an important part of Roman culture. Though they were grown throughout the Roman Empire, the best olives came from Italy. Olives were prominent in the Roman diet. The economic value of olives came from its oil. Olive oil was irreplaceable in cooking. People anointed their bodies with olive oil after bathing. Romans used it in making perfumes. It fueled lamps throughout the ancient world. Some olive oil was even used as fertilizer.

NOTES

1   Michael Grant, *The Founders of the Western World* (New York: Scribner's Sons, 1991), 142.
2   Kevin Greene, *The Archaeology of the Roman Economy* (Berkeley: University of California Press, 1986), 73.

Olive grove at Tekoa.

ROMAN TRIUMPHAL PROCESSIONS

BY M. DEAN REGISTER

Triumph scene depicting Rome's Emperor Marcus Aurelius, who ruled AD 161-180. The winged figure above the emperor's head represents his divinity.

Roman military victory parades were a spectacle to behold. Well documented in ancient sources, at least 300 times the city of Rome staged a triumphal procession as a demonstration of civic pride, conquest, and power.[1]

DEVELOPMENT OF THE PROCESSION

The Roman practice of the triumphal parade developed gradually. Archaeological evidence from stone inscriptions and ancient paintings suggests the Romans borrowed the concept from Etruscan kings of central Italy who had been influenced by similar ceremonies in Asia Minor. The earliest known triumphal pageant outside Rome was in Asia Minor in the fourth century BC.[2] First-century Roman tablets called the *Fasti Triumphales* record triumphs from the time of the mythical Romulus in 753 BC until the triumph of Balbus in 19 BC. Josephus, the Jewish historian, describes the victory parade of Vespasian and Titus as one of "pompous solemnity" in which both were crowned with laurel wreaths and clothed in purple. The parade carried the two generals before an approving Senate, applauding soldiers, jubilant citizens, and humiliated captives. Furthermore, Josephus's account provides extenuating details regarding the religious aspect of the procession, stressing that the culmination of the parade was located at the temple of Jupiter.[3]

ORDER AND PATH OF THE PROCESSION

Triumphal processions in Rome observed a specific sequence. As one historian has emphasized: "Rome celebrated the triumph and the triumph celebrated Rome."[4] A triumphal procession saturated every aspect of Rome's social, political, and religious life. Although a party atmosphere prevailed, decorum and propriety marked the procession. To heighten the festive mood, organizers carefully choreographed the formality, repetition, and position in the pageant.

On the morning of the parade, the general assembled his victorious army along with the humiliated captives outside the city boundaries at the Campus Maritus (Field of Mars).[5]

Created between the Palatine and Aventine Hills in Rome, the Circus Maximus hosted chariot races, gladiatorial contests, and processions. At its largest, the arena was over 2,000 by 500 feet.

Victory scene showing those conquered bowing to Marcus Aurelius. In the background, banners are raised in celebration of the emperor's victory.

From there, the parade moved through the Porta Triumphalis (Triumphal Arch), the Circus Flaminius (a small racetrack), and the Circus Maximus—the great stadium that could seat up to 150,000 spectators. The parade continued along the Via Sacra and arrived finally at the temple of Jupiter on Capitoline Hill, where a worship ceremony preceded the distribution of the spoils of war to the soldiers and the public.[6]

Scene showing Marcus Aurelius, at the conclusion of the triumphant procession, offering sacrifices to the gods for his victory over the barbarians.

Essential to the procession was the display of painted banners representing battle scenes, victorious slogans, and models of conquered fortresses. This display magnified the victory and exalted the general whom the people lauded as *triumphator*. Following the banner carriers, priests and attendants marched holding censers of burning incense and escorting white sacrificial oxen.[7] Carrying golden saucers the priests would use to catch sacrificial blood, children jumped and skipped behind the oxen.[8] Musicians and dancers accentuated the pageantry by adding mockery to the prisoners on display. Typically the captives were positioned in front of the victorious general's chariot. The conclusion of the parade involved leading some of the captives off for execution, selling some as slaves, and making a sacrificial offering at the temple of Jupiter.

NOTES

[1] Mary Beard, *The Roman Triumph* (Cambridge, MA: Harvard University Press, 2007), 4.

[2] H. S. Versnel, *Triumphus: An Inquiry into the Origin, Development and Meaning of the Roman Triumph* (Leiden: Brill, 1970), 299.

[3] Josephus, *Jewish War* 7.5; Ida Ostenberg, *Staging the World: Spoils, Captives and Representations in the Roman Triumphal Procession* (Oxford: Oxford University Press, 2009), 13.

[4] Ostenberg, *Staging the World*, 13.

[5] Beard, *Roman Triumph*, 81.

[6] David J. Williams, *Paul's Metaphors: Their Context and Character* (Peabody, MA: Hendrickson, 1999), 257.

[7] Williams, *Paul's Metaphors*, 258.

[8] Nigel Rodgers, *The Rise and Fall of Ancient Rome* (London: Anness, 2004), 170.

SABBATH LAW

BY ROBERT E. JONES

Orthodox Jews at the Western Wall in Jerusalem.

To enforce Sabbath law, Jewish rabbis set forth thirty-nine classifications of work. Their action resulted in the developing and systematizing of numerous rules and regulations the rabbis deduced from the Sabbath commandment. The rabbis worked out these Sabbath-day requirements in an increasingly complicated manner with the goal of applying them to every conceivable situation. For example, Jewish Sabbath law prohibited kindling a fire, carrying on trade, treading the winepress, placing a load on an animal, or holding markets. No business activity of any kind or any other activity could occur that might desecrate the Sabbath.[1] Jews, therefore, had to make all necessary arrangements for the Sabbath on the day of preparation so that the day of rest might remain free of all work. Only an urgent obligation or mortal danger could overrule these laws.

A rabbi in the Jewish Quarter of Jerusalem.

NOTES

[1] Eduard Lohse, "*sabbaton*, Sabbath" in *TDNT* (1971), 7:5.

SHIPS AND SHIPPING IN THE NEW TESTAMENT WORLD

BY GERALD L. STEVENS

Block showing inscription that mentions "Tyrdos." The old harbor of Tyre is in the background.

Scene on the first spiral of Trajan's Column in Rome depicts Roman boats being loaded with supplies along the Danube River; a fort and small town are located riverside.

Judea had no deep harbor on its Mediterranean coastline, and Israelite desert nomads who settled in the hill country were not a seafaring people. Philistine Sea Peoples settled the coastal plain. Israelites did not conduct maritime commerce, with the exception of King Solomon, who used alliances with King Hiram of Tyre and harboring facilities at Ezion-geber on the Red Sea, but his sailors were Phoenician (1 Kgs. 9:26–27). Solomon traded gold, silver, and other rare merchandise (10:22). Jehoshaphat constructed a fleet for gold from Ophir, but an east wind in the Ezion-geber harbor wrecked the entire fleet (22:48–49).

Joppa was one of the few Judean ports. Farther north, Herod the Great built a harbor at Caesarea, capitalizing on Roman engineering to harden submerged cement for his breakwaters. Other cities along the Mediterranean coastline such as Tyre, however, were far more legendary for their commercial maritime prowess (Isa. 23:1; Ezek. 27:32–35).

By Roman times, seafaring had become normal for international travel. The main arrangement was by cabotage, the business of sailing near the shoreline and putting in each night, which allowed ancient commercial ship captains to offer individuals short transportation arrangements for hire on the spur of the moment. Other contracts facilitated extended distances. Commercial ports were integral to Paul's journeys, such as Seleucia (Acts 13:4), Troas (16:8), Thessalonica (17:1), Corinth (18:1), Ephesus (19:1), Miletus (20:15), Tyre (21:3), Syracuse (28:12), Puteoli (v. 13), and others with less well-known names, but no less famous in their day.

Shipping was dependent entirely on the seasons. Summer was the best (for steady and dependable trade winds), winter the worst (for ferocious and unpredictable winter northeasters), and spring and fall marginal. The dangerous fall season ran from mid-September to mid-November, and the impossible winter season ran from late November through February. Thus Paul naturally urges Timothy to "come before winter" (2 Tim. 4:21). Sailing in late fall universally was risky and undertaken with caution.

Roman coin; obverse: two cornucopia, Greek inscription: Herod, meaning Herod Archelaus; reverse: galley ship, Greek inscription: Ethnarch.

Delivering crucial goods late in the sailing season could garner significant bonuses. The grain route between Alexandria and Rome of a thousand nautical miles took ten to twelve days eastward, but westward about two to three months, and often required hugging the coastlines of Phoenicia, Asia Minor, and Greece.[1] Accommodations for these voyages were minimal, even for the privileged, who at best could hope for a crowded spot in the cargo hold or a small cabin in the stern. Otherwise, one staked a spot on the open deck, exposed to the weather, but perhaps with a tent enclosure.[2]

Roman grain ships were built with flat hulls for maximum cargo, which meant minimum structural integrity. Cross-lateral movements, such as in stormy weather with assaults of wind and wave, could be devastating. Further, grain cargo was a tremendous liability in storms. Wet grain would swell, adding further stress to watertight seams. A Roman grain ship was the worst ship to be on in a storm at sea.[3]

One of the most detailed accounts of sailing, storm, and shipwreck from the ancient world actually is Luke's account of Paul's voyage and shipwreck in Acts 27–28. Luke's attention to detail, while expressed in layman and not technical terms, is a treasure trove of nautical information, including tackle, winds, topography, and strategies.

NOTES

[1] These estimates follow Lionel Casson's work using references from Pliny, *Natural History* 19.3–4. Casson compiled charts of Mediterranean distance, time, and speed; see Casson, *Ships and Seamanship in the Ancient World* (Princeton, NJ: Princeton University Press, 1971).

[2] Earle Hilgert, "Ships; Boats" in *ISBE* (1988), 4:486.

[3] One of the best resources for understanding the structure of an Alexandrian grain ship is Nicolle Hirschfeld, "The Ship of Saint Paul, Part 1: Historical Background," *BA* 53.1 (1990): 25–30.

SORCERY, WITCHCRAFT, AND DIVINATION

BY JAMES O. NEWELL

Deuteronomy 18:9–18 records the Lord instructing the Israelites about how they were to live once they entered the promised land. Verses 10–11 contain all of the Hebrew words that identified the different methods of foretelling the future and seeking divine guidance

From Nimrud in ancient Babylon, two leaves from hinged writing boards. The fragments of the original wax are inscribed with a cuneiform text of astrological omens. These omens were intended for the palace of Babylon's king Sargon II at Khorsabad.

for making decisions.¹ These actions were the reason the Lord displaced the Canaanites and gave their land to Israel (v. 12). Punishment for these activities was death (Exod. 22:18; Lev. 20:27).

The Bible does not record the origin of sorcery, witchcraft, and divination, nor does it provide descriptions of the practices. The writers assumed the reader would understand the actions behind the terms. Curiosity about upcoming events and circumstances was a constant in the ancient Near East. This caused some men to try to develop skills that supposedly allowed them to see into the future.

Model of a sheep's lung, from Nineveh; terra-cotta. In the ancient Near East, a diviner would commonly pronounce an omen based on his reading of the lungs or liver of a sacrificial sheep. The model's inscription offers instructions for an apprentice who was learning this method of divination.

"The means of divination in the [ancient] Near East are multiple: by prophetic or priestly oracles, dreams, spirits, lots, astrology, the observation of the entrails of a sacrificial animal, the flight of birds, the patterns of oil on water, and the direction of smoke."²

Among the Hittites: "Incantation priests probably most often received their payment in the form of leftover ritual materials. For example, in [one tale,] the *Ritual for the Goddess Wishuriyanza*, the magician is allowed to take with her the pottery and utensils that she has used. This is probably the reason that the rituals often call for [massive] amounts of equipment and foodstuffs."³

Among the Lyceans, some soothsayers relied on fish. "The diviners would observe the movements of fish, their twists and turns, and interpret these movements in accordance with fixed rules. An alternative procedure is recorded for the 'fish oracle' in the bay of Myra. The procedure there called for a sacrifice of calves to be made to the god, whereupon the flesh was then thrown to the fish. If the fish ate the flesh, the omens were good. If they discarded it and cast it on the shore with their tails, this signified that the god was angry."

On the hillside in the distance is the site of ancient En-dor, the home of the medium whom Saul consulted near the end of his life.

Child sacrifice was perhaps the most serious and far-reaching attempt to influence the future by offering such a costly gift to a god in hopes of producing a desired future outcome. The underlying motive of these forbidden practices was the effort "to manipulate or force the 'gods' into certain courses of action."[4]

Mesopotamian divination text gives instructions for studying animal intestines (usually of sheep) to determine the future.

NOTES

[1] C. F. Keil and F. Delitzsch, "Deuteronomy," in *The Pentateuch: Three Volumes in One*, vol. 1 in Commentary on the Old Testament in Ten Volumes (Grand Rapids: Eerdmans, repr. ed. 1975), 3:393.

[2] Jean-Michel De Tarragon, "Witchcraft, Magic, and Divination in Canaan and Ancient Israel," in *CANE*, 2071.

[3] Gabriella Frantz-Szabo, "Hittite Witchcraft, Magic, and Divination," in *CANE*, 2011.

[4] Jack S. Deere, "Deuteronomy," in *The Bible Knowledge Commentary: An Exposition of the Scriptures*, ed. J. F. Walvoord and R. B. Zuck (Wheaton, IL: Victor Books, 1985), 1:296.

SOUND THE SHOFAR!

BY KEVIN C. PEACOCK

Bronze figurine of a trumpeter; from Anatolia; dated eighth–sixth centuries BC.

Of the musical instruments the Old Testament names, the shofar, or ram's horn, is the most frequent. Sometimes translated as "trumpet," the shofar is the only biblical instrument used in synagogues today. Many who hear a shofar have difficulty terming it as a "musical" instrument. Its musical qualities are limited to only two or three harmonic overtones, making it difficult for any melodies, and clear tonality is almost nonexistent. With its high shrill sound, the shofar was ideal as a noise maker.

KINDS OF TRUMPETS

Horns or trumpets in the Bible were of two types, those made of animal horn and those of metal. The Hebrew terms *yobel*, *qeren*, and *shofar* were used interchangeably. *Yobel* ("ram"; Exod. 19:13; Josh. 6:5), usually translated as "horn," refers to a shofar (Josh. 6:4,6; see Exod. 19:13,16). The term *Jubilee* is named after *yobel* (Lev. 25:13), a celebration beginning with sounding of the ram's horn (v. 9). Jubal, the inventor of musical instruments (Gen. 4:21), seems to carry the same name as the ram. *Qeren* ("horn"; 1 Chr. 25:5, CSB footnote) is the literal horn of an animal (Gen. 22:13; Ps. 22:21) from which the musical instrument was made. It is used once as a synonym for shofar (*qeren hayyobel*, "the horn of the ram"; Josh. 6:5). The related Aramaic term *qarna* is in Daniel 3:5,7.[1]

Part of the restored mosaic floor at the synagogue in Hammath Tiberias. The image depicts the Torah ark, menorahs, incense shovels, shofars, lulavs, and ethrogs; dated fourth–fifth centuries AD.

The other type of trumpet was made from hammered metal (Num. 10:1–2), usually bronze, copper, gold, or silver.[2] This *chatsotsrah* was described by Josephus[3] and shown on ancient coins and artwork as a straight tube with a mouthpiece and a flared end. Those used in temple service were always made of silver and were blown by the priests and Levites. These were used in sacrificial ceremony (1 Chr. 15:24), in war (Num. 31:6), and in royal coronations (2 Kgs. 11:14) in much the same way as the shofar.

CONSTRUCTION AND TONES

Shofars are still made today as in ancient times. The horn of any kosher animal except a cow is suitable, but the preferred horn is that of a ram, the animal Abraham sacrificed in place of Isaac (Gen. 22:1–14).[4] Some shofars are left in their natural curved shape, but craftsmen often use steam or heat to soften the horn to straighten it. Then they will bend the wide end, forming a right angle. A hole bored at the point into the natural hollow allows the trumpeter to blow it like a bugle.[5]

The Hebrew Old Testament records two different horn sounds: *teqa'* ("a trumpet blast") and *teru'ah* ("a shout"). Rabbinic tradition defined the *teqa'* as a long sustained lower tone that ended abruptly and the *teru'ah* as a higher trill or series of notes. The rabbis added a third sound comprising three connected short notes, the *shevarim*. These three patterns are combined into sequences, making a phrase of thirty notes that may be repeated several times.[6] This prescribed pattern of different pitches, lengths of tone, and staccato and legato articulation were designed to imitate a sobbing or wailing sound of the human voice.

The Septuagint employed the Greek term *salpinx* ("trumpet") to translate both *chatsotsrah* and *shofar*, making no distinction between the two. The New Testament refers simply to a "trumpet" eleven times, with no differentiation of horn or metal.[7]

NOTES

[1]   Daniel A. Foxvog and Anne D. Kilmer, "Music" in *ISBE*, vol. 3 (1986), 439.

[2]   Foxvog and Kilmer, "Music," 439.

[3]   Josephus, *Jewish Antiquities* 3.12.6.

[4]   Lawrence H. Schiffman, "Shophar" in *Harper's Bible Dictionary*, ed. Paul J. Achtemeier (San Francisco: Harper & Row, 1985), 947.

[5]   J. A. Thompson, *Handbook of Life in Bible Times* (Downers Grove, IL: InterVarsity, 1986), 255.

[6]   Dennis F. McCorkle, "Shofar or Ram's Horn," *The Music of the Bible* (2007), www.musicofthebible.com.

[7]   Foxvog and Kilmer, "Music," 446.

SPICES AND PERFUMES

BY ARGILE A. SMITH JR.

Alabastron (perfume flask) decorated with griffins below a lotus and palmette chain; made in Corinth; dates from 680–650 BC.

PRODUCTION

Almost all of the spices and perfumes used in Israel came from plants, although a few came from animal products. Most of the aroma-producing plants did not grow in Israel. They came to Israel as imports from places such as India, Asia Minor, Arabia, Egypt, and Africa.[1]

Some plants produced leaves or seeds that people used in making fragrant spices. Cumin, for example, was a spice sometimes used in bread. It came from a soft seed that was pulverized before being used in baking. Aloe and mint came from leaves; dill came from seeds as well as leaves. Coriander, which was included in many perfumes, also came from seeds.

Other fragrances were rendered from plant resins. Two of the most popular resins were frankincense and myrrh. Frankincense came from a tree by that name. It produced a resinous gum that was collected by removing the bark of the tree and cutting into the trunk. Similarly, myrrh was gum—collected from a shrub in Africa and Arabia.

Still other spices and perfumes were produced as oils. For instance, nard was an expensive fragrant oil produced from a plant native to India. Once the oil was extracted from the plant, it was preserved in sealed alabaster jars before being exported to Israel.[2]

ACQUISITION

People in Israel often acquired perfumes and spices by means of one of the busy trade routes that traversed through Israel. One of the better-known biblical references to such a route is in Genesis 37; Joseph's brothers sold him to Ishmaelite traders coming from Gilead, their camels loaded with an assortment of "gum, balsam, and resin" (v. 25) from distant places and were on their way to Egypt.

The road that took the Ishmaelites through Dothan was one of several major land routes spice traders commonly used. Another route started in Asia Minor (in modern Turkey) and ended in Israel. Yet another route that ended in Israel began in what is now Iraq and Iran. All of the land routes went through Israel, making the purchase of spices and perfumes possible—albeit expensive.

Another major trade route, this one along the Mediterranean coast, likewise brought spices and perfumes to the country. The Phoenicians controlled the sea route until the Roman era. Ships departed from the ports of Lebanon, made stops at some of the key coastal ports in Israel, and ended in Egypt.[3]

This small glass vessel from Rhodes probably contained scented oil. Rhodes was a center for glass manufacturing; dates from 460–440 BC.

USE

Because of their wide variety of possible uses, spices and perfumes were popular with people in the ancient Near East. The fragrances of the spices and perfumes made

Faience aryballos (perfume flask); probably from Rhodes; dates from 600–550 BC. Greek men used these bottles, which they hung from their wrists, to carry oil for cleaning their bodies after exercise.

them appealing as cosmetics. People would mix spices with oils and rub the ointment on their skin. They would also sprinkle them on garments, couches, and beds to give them a pleasant scent (see Ps. 45:8; Prov. 7:17).

Not only were spices and perfumes enjoyed for their appealing fragrance but also for the social status implied by having them. Since they were imported from so far away, they were typically expensive.[4] When Hezekiah gave a tour of his treasure house to the Babylonians who visited him, he showed them his spices along with his other precious possessions (2 Kgs. 20:13). The wise men presented to Jesus not only gold but also frankincense and myrrh (Matt. 2:11), providing evidence of their value. The nard with which Mary anointed Jesus was valued at the lavish price of 300 denarii (John 12:3–5), indicating the sacrificial nature of her act.

The liturgical role of spices and perfumes was linked to the use of incense in temple worship. Incense was the perfumed smoke that emanated from burning spices blended with other materials.

Burial practices in Israel also demanded a constant supply of spices. Spices were used in burial preparation to provide a pleasant aroma in the otherwise unpleasant environment associated with the decomposition of a corpse.[5]

NOTES

[1]   Claude Mariottini, "Spices" in *HolBD*, 1297.

[2]   "Plants of the Bible" in *The Lion Encyclopedia of the Bible* (Herts, UK: Lion), 15.

[3]   "Trade and Commerce" in *The Lion Encyclopedia of the Bible*, 237–38.

[4]   Victor H. Matthews, "Perfumes and Spices" in *ABD*, 5:227.

[5]   Gerald L. Borchert, *John 12–21*, NAC (2002), 282.

THE TABERNACLE: ITS HISTORY AND USE

BY ALLAN MOSELEY

Replica of the tabernacle, erected at Timnah in southern Israel.

Replica of the table of the Bread of the Presence as it may have appeared in the tabernacle.

As worshippers entered the tabernacle (on the eastern side), the first piece of furniture they encountered was the bronze altar, located in the open space between the entrance to the tabernacle precincts and the entrance to the holy place (Exod. 27:38). The bronze altar was a hollow box made of acacia wood and overlaid with bronze. Horns, or protrusions, were on each corner of the bronze altar. Presumably, priests or worshippers tied animals to the horns to secure the animal before killing. The bronze altar was a place of sacrifice, which is fundamental in biblical theology. Sin leads to death. Sacrifices were offered so the sacrificial animals could die in place of the worshippers.

As worshippers moved from the bronze altar through the open-air court of the tabernacle in the direction of the holy place, they encountered the polished bronze basin (Exod. 30; 38). The bronze, reflecting beneath the water, allowed the priests who washed their hands to observe whether the water was pure. It would also allow them to see themselves and be reminded of their own need for cleansing. Priests were to wash themselves before they entered the holy place, symbolic of the fact that they were to be cleansed from sin before they were qualified to serve. Some have suggested that the bronze altar communicates the idea of justification, and the bronze basin was for sanctification.

As worshippers entered the tent, the golden lampstand was on the left side of the holy place (25:31–40; 37:17–24). The holy place had no windows to allow light to enter, so the lampstand provided light. In the Scriptures, fire and light were evocative of the Lord's presence and direction (3:1–4).

The table of the Bread of the Presence was on the opposite side of the holy place from the lampstand (25:23–30; 37:10–16). The cakes of bread represented the fellowship that God desired to have with all twelve tribes of Israel.

The final piece of furniture in the holy place was the altar of incense (30:1–10; 37:25–29). This altar was on the west side of the holy place, against the curtain that divided the holy place from the most holy place. The horns on this altar presumably were purely ornamental, since no animals were sacrificed on the altar of incense. The smoke of the burning incense, which was to be continual, seems to have represented the prayers of God's people (Ps. 141:2; Luke 1:10; Rev. 5:8; 8:3–4).[1]

The ark of the covenant was the only furniture in the most holy place. The Lord connected the ark to his presence. He said to Moses, "I will meet with you there" (Exod. 25:22). The Lord's presence was associated with a particular space, not a physical object.

God's people constructed the tabernacle and all its furniture in obedience to the Lord's explicit command. He determined where and how he would be worshipped. Pagan religions in the ancient Near East devised worship spaces and rituals that were designed to gain the favor of the gods. However, in the case of the one true God, no person or group has the prerogative to determine how or where he will be worshipped. He commands, and his people worship him accordingly.

NOTES

[1] Walter C. Kaiser Jr., "Exodus" in *The Expositor's Bible Commentary*, ed. Frank E. Gaebelein, vol. 2 (Grand Rapids: Zondervan, 1990), 472–73.

Poles and stakes in the courtyard of the tabernacle replica, which has been erected at Timna in southern Israel.

THE TEN WORDS AND ANCIENT NEAR EASTERN LAWS

BY GARY P. ARBINO

Ruins at the ancient site of Aleppo, in modern Syria.

How does ancient Near Eastern law compare to biblical law, especially those instructions in Exodus 20:1–17—the Ten Words?[1]

TOPICS

Biblical regulations and other ancient Near Eastern codes cover many of the same topics—personal injury, sexual relationships and rape, kidnapping, slavery, restitution, inheritance, livestock, boundaries, and construction. Other topics, however, are not in the Torah: loyalty to king and temple, taxation, commerce, wages, fugitives, and the like.

The Ten Words (more commonly called the Ten Commandments) address some major issues common within the ancient Near East—loyalty, family structure and honor, homicide, adultery, theft, perjury, slander, and possibly inappropriate desires. On the other hand, they contain some unique content: loyalty to one God (rather than the king and his divinity), no idols (a completely unique concept in the ancient world), and the radical proposal of a rest day every seven days (rather than working until the next festival).

Within this broad range of topics, however, ancient text writers made no effort to be comprehensive. Correspondingly, the prescriptions in the Torah also do not specifically address all aspects of ancient Israelite life.

TEXTS

What scholars term "laws" in the ancient Near East actually fall within several types of literature: law codes, edicts, treaties, loyalty oaths, and charters for kingship succession. Currently, some one hundred of these official documents have been excavated and translated. While thirty or so originated in Mesopotamia and northern Syria between the years 2500 BC and 1500 BC, more than half come from the Hittite archives of Anatolia (1500–1200 BC). The remaining texts stem from the mid-first millennium: northern Syria (three documents; ca. 850 BC), the Neo-Assyrian Empire (about fourteen documents, most are fragmentary; dated 820–627 BC), and Neo-Babylonia (one document; ca. 700 BC). Archaeologists and explorers have also discovered hundreds of ancient letters, narratives, and records that illustrate law usage from the ancient world.

The Ur-Nammu Law Code, which is the oldest known law, is from Nippur, Mesopotamia (in modern Iraq). The language is Sumerian; the piece dates to 2112–2095 BC.

PURPOSE

Concern for relationships and seeking to define and govern conduct were the threads connecting these ancient laws. Broadly seen, these relationships are either external, meaning between a king and the people of another land (these called for treaties), or internal, meaning to and/or among the subjects of a king (these called for codes).

The foundational relationship was with the king. Most texts contain an introduction—naming the king, often with his titles, divine descent, attributes, and achievements. These were often in first person: "I am Hammurabi, the shepherd, selected by the god Enlil."[2] Always people understood the king to be the giver of the "law," albeit under the direction and charge of his patron deity or deities. The origin of the Ten Words is different. Unlike other ancient documents, the narrative context of Exodus 19–21 clearly shows that God personally and vocally gave to the assembled people the initial regulations for conduct: "Then God spoke all these words" (Exod. 20:1; see Deut. 5:4).

The chief responsibility of ancient kings was to maintain justice—the right relationships within the kingdom and between treaty partners. Standard in ancient legal presentations was the king's statement that he had established justice. "At that time, I, Ur-Namma [Ur-Nammu], . . . king of the lands of Sumer and Akkad, by the might of the god Nanna . . . I established justice in the land."[3] So essential was this responsibility that ancient kings intentionally depicted themselves presiding over cases. Hammurabi stated: "I have inscribed my precious pronouncements upon my stela and set it up. . . . the judgments that I rendered and the verdicts that I gave."[4] Ancient law documents that scholars term "codes" were thus meant to be seen as the concretized specific case rulings that

The Aleppo Treaty is an agreement between the Hittite king Mursili II and Talmi-sharruma of Aleppo. It regulates future relations between Aleppo and Hatti; dated to 1300 BC.

the king made and that he gathered together. These served as both a model for later cases and as proof of the king's justice. Moses and his colleagues also rendered verdicts that were likely codified (Exod. 18:13–26; 21:1).

Diorite bust from Susa; thought to be either Hammurabi or a prince who reigned before him.

Evidence of lingering influence, dated to about 1,100 years after Hammurabi's original, a fragment of a copy of the Code of Hammurabi from the library of Assyria's King Ashurbanipal.

FORM

The presentation of these codified verdicts is overwhelmingly in the form known as "casuistic" or "case law": If/ When such happens . . . then this is the consequence. The Old Babylonia Laws of Eshnunna (ca. 1725 BC) provide an example: "If an ox gores another ox and thus causes its death, the two ox-owners shall divide the value of the living ox and the carcass of the dead ox. . . . If it gores a slave and thus causes his death, he [the ox owner] shall weigh and deliver fifteen shekels of silver."[5]

Ancient treaties also frequently used this genre for the stipulations by which each party was to abide. A northern Syrian treaty provided a common obligation: "If a fugitive slave, whether male or female, flees from my country to yours, you must seize him and return him."[6]

Regulations also came in a more absolute form, termed "apodictic": You will do this; you will not do that. Used much more commonly in treaties, but present from the earliest times in law codes, these absolute requirements illustrate the nonnegotiables for the two parties involved. A Hittite treaty (ca. 1300 BC) illustrates: "Keep the oath of the king and the hand of the king, and I, My Majesty, will protect you. . . . Do not turn your eyes towards another (land)!"[7] As seen here, sometimes the absolute nature of the apodictic form came with a "rider" that gave either a rationale or a result (here, protection). The Ten Words of Exodus 20 contain both the apodictic form and additional material in four of them (vv. 4,7,8,12).

Both the Covenant Code (20:1–23:33) and the account of Moses's writing the replacement copy of the Ten Words (34:10–26) illustrate that regulations concerning the divine-human relationship (idolatry, festivals, Sabbaths, and sacrifices) and broad standards of social justice for at-risk members of the community (22:21–22; 23:1–3,6–9) are in apodictic form. This makes good sense since the "vertical" and social justice aspects would not usually require additional specificity—no situations existed in which people would allow idolatry or the abuse of a widow.

Although the apodictic form of the Ten Words in Exodus 20 clearly articulates the nonnegotiables of relationships as the people of Yahweh, their placement in the broader context points to a larger structure and intent. They begin with an Introduction of Yahweh and a statement of past benefits (20:2) and stand at the front of a section of mostly casuistic stipulations (21:1–23:19), followed by both promised blessings for adherence and dire warnings for failure (23:20–33) and finally by a ratification ceremony (24:1–11). In addition, witnesses were present (twelve pillars, 24:4; and two tablets—one for each party) and a provision for deposit (in the ark, in the holy of holies/most holy place). Ancient treaties used these structural elements (see "God's Covenant with Abraham" at Gen 17). Importantly, the Ten Words (and what follows) are actually described (Exod. 34:2–28; cf. 24:7–8) as *be'rit* (Hb. for "covenant"), a particular form of a treaty, and (in 34:29) as the "tablets of the *edut*," a Hebrew word that means "witness" or "testimony" or "obligations" and is a cognate of *adé*, the Akkadian word Assyrians used to describe treaties and loyalty oaths.

Carved into this stone wall is a law code discovered at Gortyn on the island of Crete. It dates to the first half of the fifth century BC and is the earliest known European law code.

Thus the Ten Words are much more than laws. They function as the center of relationships—the initial sections of a treaty (covenant) between Yahweh and his people, one in which he is the true and only Sovereign to whom his subjects owe total allegiance and in whose territory there is a correct and nonnegotiable standard for human actions based on divine justice.

NOTES

[1] Unless indicated otherwise, all Scripture quotations are the writer's translation. For a quick reference of various "legal" terms used in the Old Testament, see Psalm 19:7–9.

[2] Martha Roth, "The Codes of Hammurabi," in *Canonical Compositions from the Biblical World*, vol. 2 of *The Context of Scripture* (*COS*), ed. William W. Hallo and K. Lawson Younger (Leiden: Brill, 1997), 336.

[3] From a third millennium code; Martha Roth, "The Laws of Ur-Namma (Ur-Nammu)" in Hallo and Younger, *COS*, 2:411.

[4] Martha Roth, ed., *Law Collections from Mesopotamia and Asia Minor*, 2nd ed., vol. 6 of Writings from the Ancient World (WAW) (Atlanta: Society of Biblical Literature, 1997), 133.

[5] Roth, WAW, 6:67. Notice the similarity to the biblical law in Exodus 21:32,35.

[6] Richard Hess, "The Agreement between Ir-Addu and Niqmepa" in *COS*, 2:330.

[7] Notice both the positive and negative absolutes, also seen in the Ten Words. I. Singer, "Treaty between Muršili and Duppi-Tešub" in *COS*, 2:96.

WEALTH, TRADE, MONEY, AND COINAGE IN THE BIBLICAL WORLD

BY JOEL F. DRINKARD JR.

Sheep in the field. The size of one's flock was an indicator of wealth.

Some persons from civilization's earliest periods in the ancient Near East were wealthy. The wonders of the ancient world spotlight the wealth of some of the ancients. Whether one considers the pyramids of Egypt or the ziggurats of Mesopotamia, these massive structures themselves indicate their builders' wealth. Certainly the rulers of these highly developed societies had to control vast wealth in order to undertake such building projects. Additionally, huge herds and flocks and numerous servants, as in the example of Abraham, were indicators of substantial wealth. Mesha, king of Moab, exhibited his wealth by his annual tribute to the king of Israel: "one hundred thousand lambs and the wool of one hundred thousand rams" (2 Kgs. 3:4). Other indicators of wealth included imported goods, luxury items, gems, and often silver and gold. These imported and luxury goods gave evidence of trade. Neither the empire of Egypt nor Mesopotamia had great stocks of natural resources. Therefore, most metals and luxury goods for these empires came through trade or tribute. Wealth and trade thus usually went hand in hand. Silver and gold were the favorite materials for use in commercial transactions. Other goods such as copper and tin, the ingredients of bronze, were also valuable commodities. All these metals were relatively easy to refine and were easily transportable.

Trade, including long-distance trade, was part of life for even the early inhabitants in the ancient Near East. At Pre-Pottery Neolithic Jericho, excavators have found obsidian tools. Obsidian, a black or banded volcanic glasslike stone, came from Anatolia, about 500 miles away. Its presence at Jericho clearly indicates trade, even international trade. The mechanism of trade from that early time is unknown, but the speculation is that those who lived near the natural resources would trade surplus amounts of their natural resources with nearby communities, who in turn traded with more distant communities, and so forth. One would not have to posit full-blown trade routes and caravans at this early period. Other items indicating trade at Pre-Pottery Neolithic Jericho include turquoise from the Sinai Peninsula and cowrie shells from the Mediterranean coast.

This Tyre shekel (reverse), minted in Jerusalem, shows an eagle.

One of the clearest evidences of international trade is a fourteenth-century BC shipwreck off the coast of Uluburun, Turkey.[1] This Late Bronze Canaanite merchant vessel carried a cargo of more than ten tons of copper and a ton of tin, much of this metal in large ingots each weighing about sixty pounds. The vessel also carried glass ingots, ivory, ebony wood, cedarwood, and terebinth/pistachio resin. In all, the materials and cargo reflect goods from much of the Mediterranean world: Canaan, Egypt, Cyprus, Anatolia, and the Aegean areas. The ship apparently made a circuit to ports in each of these regions, buying and selling goods.

The Beni Hasan tomb paintings from Egypt, dating to about 1890 BC, depict a Canaanite merchant caravan bringing goods to Egypt. The travelers have with them animals, weapons, and perhaps metal

This bronze coin from the time of Herod I (40–4 BC) shows a double cornucopia with a caduceus between.

ingots. The item often described as a bellows carried on several of the donkeys is more likely ingots of copper similar to those found in the Uluburun shipwreck. Also such a caravan is reminiscent of the Midianites/Ishmaelites who, while traveling to Egypt, bought Joseph from his brothers (Gen. 37:25–28).

Trade would require some means of assessing value. Commodities were not of equal value. How would one compare the value of a goat and a donkey? Or, more to the point, the value of a donkey in terms of silver? Obviously some equivalences were needed and even essential. Since precious metals, especially silver and gold, were the favored means of exchange for trade transactions, a system of weights and measures became essential for buying and selling.

Owl stands right with head facing over left shoulder, crook and flail; cable border. From Tyre, about 450–400 BC.

Drachma from Parthia: Phraates IV (38–2 BC); shows a bust on the left and an eagle with a wreath.

The need for weights and measures also produced the need for standards of weights and measure. We do not know the precise equivalent of all the ancient weights and measures, but we can approximate many of them. Several of the measures came from human anatomy. The *cubit* was a standard of length; it was the distance from the elbow to the tip of the middle finger. Similarly, the *span* was the width from the outstretched thumb to the little finger. The *palm* was the width of the hand across the base of the four fingers, and the *finger* was the width of one finger. Four fingers made a palm, three palms made a span, and two spans made a cubit. Some of the weights and measures were originally descriptive: the measure *homer* was the same as the word for "donkey." The homer measure was probably equivalent to a donkey load. Perhaps a *talent* was the measure of a human load. In terms of surface area, a *yoke* was the amount of land a yoke of oxen could plow in a day. Seed was also used as a form of measure: one would describe a field in terms of the amount of seed it would require for planting. Leviticus 27:16 speaks of a field's size in terms of sowing a homer of barley.

The Uluburun shipwreck mentioned above provides evidence of such standards, with several sets of weights and scales included in the wreckage.

The Old Testament shekel was the primary measure for weight, though both larger and smaller weights existed. When Abraham purchased the burial cave for Sarah, at Machpelah, he negotiated the sale with the owner, Ephron the Hethite, in the presence of Hebron's elders. "Abraham agreed with Ephron, and Abraham weighed out to Ephron the silver that he had agreed to in the hearing of the Hethites: four hundred standard shekels of silver" (lit. "four hundred shekels passing to the merchant"; Gen. 23:16).

Clearly coinage was not known at this time; the silver was weighed. Abraham also used a set standard; the shekel was in current use among the merchants. The mention of merchants gives further evidence of trade being common in Abraham's time. Because coins were then undeveloped, pieces of jewelry, metal, and ingots served as the money. Though the exact weight of the shekel from Abraham's era is not known, shekel weights from the monarchy's later period and the weight of shekel coins of the New Testament era show that a shekel weighed about 11.4 grams or two-fifths of an ounce.

The narrative of Jeremiah purchasing the field from his cousin Hanamel shows the continued use of metal weights rather than coins. He purchased the field in Anathoth for seventeen shekels, weighing out the money on scales (Jer. 32:8–9). The low price in comparison to Abraham's price for a field and burial cave may indicate a much smaller field or the reality that the field was virtually worthless, being in land occupied by the Babylonian army.

The mina and the talent were larger weights used for monetary exchange. Fifty shekels made a mina, and sixty minas made a talent. A talent weighed the same as 3,000 shekels. A mina was about one and one-fourth pounds, and a talent was about seventy-five and one-third pounds. But most often even large weights were in shekels. Thus Goliath's body armor weighed 5,000 shekels (ca. 125 pounds) of bronze, and his spearhead weighed 600 shekels (just over fifteen pounds; 1 Sam. 17:4–7).

By the end of the seventh century BC, coinage had developed. Coins were a means of establishing a guaranteed standard for a weight of metals. Kings began to produce standardized weights of silver and gold to guarantee their weight. The earliest coins come from Asia Minor with the kingdom of Lydia certainly being among the first to produce coins. One notable ruler of Lydia was Croesus, known from the proverbial statement "rich as Croesus." Lydia was especially rich in metal ores, silver and gold, in the mid-500s BC and used these metals for coins. But even early coins could be forged. It was possible to make a coin of base metal and plate it with silver or gold. To the casual observer, the coin might well look authentic. So ancients often tested coins, making deep incisions across them; the cut was not to deface the coin but to determine if the coin was pure metal or base metal.

The few Old Testament references to coins are in the latest eras—reflecting the Persian period when coins first appeared. One such coin, the first mentioned in Scripture, the daric (KJV "dram"), was a gold coin about the size of a dime (1 Chr. 29:7; Ezra 2:69; Neh. 7:69–71).

The New Testament mentioned several common coins. The denarius was the most common Roman coin. It weighed about three grams and was about the size of a dime. The denarius was the coin called the tribute "penny" in the KJV. The thirty pieces of silver mentioned as payment to Judas were probably denarii. The Greek drachma was approximately the same weight and value as the denarius.

The tetradrachma (four drachmas) was another common Greek coin. It was basically equivalent to the Jewish shekel in size, weight, and value.

The lepton was the smallest Jewish coin. It is most likely the coin called the widow's mite in the KJV. The prutah was the most common bronze coin in Judea in the New Testament era; it was equivalent to the Greek kodrantes. It was the equivalent of two leptons and in the KJV was called a farthing.

One real problem is trying to determine comparable value today for coins mentioned in the Bible. What was the value of a denarius or talent or lepton mentioned by Jesus? For a talent, the ASV has a footnote on Matthew 18 giving the value as £200 or $1,000. Likewise the NIV notes in Matthew 25 that a talent was worth more than $1,000. These translations agree remarkably on the value of the talent. But these amounts do not communicate the value of a talent well.

Another way to compare the relative value of a talent is to determine its weight and then determine the value of that weight of silver today. The talent was equivalent to 3,000 shekels of silver, each of which weighed approximately 11.4 grams or two-fifths of an ounce. So the talent of silver would weigh seventy-five and one-third pounds. Silver currently (February 4, 2019) is worth about $15 per ounce. On that basis, seventy-five and one-third pounds of silver would be worth $18,072. But I don't think even that communicates best the meaning or value of the talent in Jesus' day.

A better way to determine the equivalent value of a talent today is to look at the relative earning power or buying power of the talent in that day and consider a comparable earning power or buying power today. The talent was equivalent to a weight of 3,000 shekels, and that would be equivalent to 12,000 denarii. The denarius was a day's wage or salary for the common laborer. In Matthew 20, the owner of the vineyard agreed with the day laborers to the pay of a denarius for a day's work. A denarius was also probably the wage for a soldier. In today's earning power or buying power, a day's wage for a laborer is based on the minimum wage of $7.25 per hour. Typically, unskilled workers earn more than the minimum wage, perhaps $8 or $8.50 per hour. If we take $8 per hour as a typical wage for a laborer, then an eight-hour day would earn $64—that's what a denarius would have meant in Jesus's day translated into a day's wage for us today. The master of the household in the parable of talents gave one servant five talents, another two talents, and another one talent. Remember that a talent was 12,000 denarii, so it was 12,000 days' wages. Again, based on the equivalence of value today, a talent would be $768,000! The master of the household was putting a fortune in the hands of each servant. Following our buying equivalent using today's funds:

5 talents = $3,840,000
2 talents = $1,536,000
1 talent = $768,000

Moving from a massive fortune to the minuscule, Jesus pointed out to his disciples a poor widow who put into the treasury "two tiny coins worth very little" (Mark 12:41–44). The Greek text says the poor widow put in two lepta, which make a kodrantes. It took 336 lepta to equal a denarius. This widow put into the treasury $1/168$ of a day's wage. Using the same buying power equivalence as above, two lepta would be thirty-eight cents; in terms of two coins, it would be less than two quarters.

NOTES

1   Cemal Pulak, "Shipwreck: Recovering 3,000-Year-Old Cargo," *Archaeology Odyssey* 2.4 (1999): 18–29, 59.

WEARING PURPLE

BY DARRYL WOOD

Ruins overlooking the Mediterranean at Tyre.

Fondness for the color purple existed for centuries. As a clothing color, it was available primarily to the wealthy. Let's consider the background and significance of wearing purple in the first century AD.

PURPLE DYE

Purple dye has a long history of coming from the sea.[1] The ancients extracted purple from a mollusk (*Murex trunculus* or *Murex brandaris*) found along the Mediterranean coast. The Phoenician coast, especially, contained large quantities of these mussels. Tyre and Sidon ranked among the central cities for processing this dye. Manufacture of the mussels produced varying shades of purple. Violet, crimson, or blue might result. The shade of the dyed fabric depended on the mussels' species, the strength of the dye, and other factors in the process. Pliny, the first-century Roman historian, described the manufacturing method.[2] After entrapment and extraction from the sea, workers broke the shells. They removed slimy glands and heated them in salt water. This routine required many laborers and proved to be difficult work. A sickening smell resulted from the process. Modern excavations at Sidon revealed large heaps of discarded shells from these factories.

EARLY USE OF PURPLE

The earliest evidence for the use of purple dye dates to the second millennium BC. Murex shells discovered near Ugarit in northern Syria support that date. Trade relationships between Ugarit and the Phoenician cities suggest that purple dye existed that early in Phoenicia as well.

Mold-blown purple vessel from Sidon with relief decorations; approximately three and one-half inches tall.

Purple products proved to be of great value to the Phoenician economy, as illustrated on coins from Tyre dated to the fifth century BC. Some coins from that period carried an image of the *Murex*. Apparently the Phoenicians dominated trade in purple. They extracted *Murex* in such great quantities that it is rarely found in the area today. A location near the sea enhanced the ability of those who manufactured purple to trade those products in places far from their homeland. Dyed fabrics, enhanced by embroidery, found their way to distant parts of the world. The Greek poet Homer wrote about the beauty of robes the Sidonian women made.[3]

In the Hellenistic culture of the first millennium BC, some vassal kings wore purple.[4] Pliny records that Romulus, one of the mythological founders of Rome, dressed in a purple cloak. Further, Rome's third king, Tullus Hostilius (seventh century BC), wore a purple striped robe after he defeated the Etruscans.[5] References to purple cloth appear frequently in the Old Testament (Exod. 26:1,31; 28:6; Judg. 8:26; 2 Chr. 2:14; Esth. 8:15; 3:14; Song 3:10; Ezek. 27:16; Dan. 5:7).

Limited sources, difficulty of production, and the requirement that it be shipped likely restricted availability of purple fabric. These factors drove up the price. Access to purple cloth, then, remained with the religious elite, royals, and wealthy in ancient times.

Scene on the Arch of Titus at the Roman Forum shows General Titus riding victoriously in a chariot.

FIRST-CENTURY USE

Knowing first-century-AD uses of purple fabrics enhances our understanding of their significance in Jesus's time. The societal elite dressed in purple clothing in first-century Roman culture. Roman historians noted its costliness. Pliny comments on the high price of "double-dyed Tyrian purple."[6] The Roman Senate practiced a tradition in which a victorious general might be proclaimed *imperator*. He paraded into the city riding a chariot and was received by the public with great fanfare. The general wore the triumphal dress of the day, which included a purple robe embroidered in gold.[7] Although this practice originated earlier, it remained a staple of first-century Roman culture.

Purple clothing highlighted the influential status of the wearer. Roman senators wore it to distinguish themselves from other nobility. Priests, who offered religious sacrifices, donned purple garments to gain approval from the gods.[8] Men and women alike believed purple clothing complemented their appearance and made them beautiful. Many associated the color purple with luxury.[9] The cost of purple clothes probably confined access to the wealthy or privileged.

References to purple clothing in the New Testament reflect its prominence and value. Lydia, a leader in the formation of the church at Philippi, dealt in purple fabrics (Acts 16:14). The book of Revelation states that merchants would mourn the fall of Babylon and the loss of a market for their fine products, including purple (18:12,16). In the parable of the rich man and Lazarus, the rich man's purple clothing (Luke 16:19) and sumptuous living pointed to his elevated status in life.

NOTES

[1] See 1 Maccabees 4:23 and Josephus, *Jewish War* 5.5.4.

[2] Pliny, *Natural History* 9.60.124–64.141.

[3] Homer, *The Iliad* 6.285–95.

[4] First Maccabees 10:20,62; 11:58; 14:43–44.

[5] Pliny, *Natural History* 9.63.136–37.

[6] Pliny, *Natural History* 9.63.137.

[7] Dio Cassius, *Roman History* 6; Livy, *Livy* 10.7.9–10; T. E. Schmidt, "Mark 15.16-32: The Crucifixion Narrative and the Roman Triumphal Procession," *New Testament Studies* (*NTS*) 41.1 (1995): 2–3.

[8] Pliny, *Natural History* 9.60.127.

[9] Pliny, *Natural History* 9.65.139–41.

WHAT KIND OF TAMBOURINE? FROM "MIRIAM: ALL WE KNOW"

BY MARTHA S. BERGEN

After the destruction of the Egyptians in the Red Sea, Miriam took up a tambourine and led the women of Israel in celebration: "Sing to the LORD, for he is highly exalted; he has thrown the horse and its rider into the sea" (Exod. 15:21). What kind of tambourine, though, did she use? Was it the freehanded instrument with rows of cymbals, or was it more like a hand drum?

Hebrew uses two different words to describe the two instruments. A *sistrum* typically accompanied ritual ceremonies and was associated with the Egyptian goddess Hathor. Small discs, each with a hole in the middle, hung from the rods. Although these were common in Egypt, this was not the instrument Miriam played.

Miriam played a *toph* (Hb. for "tambourine" or "timbrel"), which is thought to have been a wooden or metal hand drum, covered on at least one side with ram or goat skin. A *toph* evidently had no cymbals or discs that jangled. The Hebrew term is onomatopoetic, imitating the instrument's sound. *Toph* drums were the most common musical instruments in ancient times.[1]

Shown are an Egyptian *sistrum* dated 2500 BC and a terra-cotta figurine of a woman playing a *toph*, dated to the ninth century BC.

NOTES

[1] "Musical Instruments," in *Tyndale Bible Dictionary*, ed. Walter A. Elwell and Philip W. Comfort (Wheaton, IL: Tyndale House, 2001), 925; Ronald F. Youngblood, "[*toph*]," in *TWOT*, 2:978.

WITH HARP AND LYRE: MUSICAL INSTRUMENTS IN THE OLD TESTAMENT

BY BECKY LOMBARD

Close-up scene on the Standard of Ur. A singer and a man playing the lyre are entertaining the king, who is banqueting with his friends (not shown).

The Israelites understood that God both ordained and enabled music. They viewed music as coming from the Lord and longed for their music to return to him as the fragrance of the incense.

Music was formational in the life, work, and worship of the Israelite community. After the parting of the Red Sea, Miriam took up her tambourine and sang of the Lord's rescue and strength (Exod. 15). Joshua and those he led used music to topple the walls of Jericho (Josh. 6). Deborah and Barak sang of God's victory in battle (Judg. 5). Saul's life changed when he met prophets accompanied by men playing harps, tambourines, flutes, and lyres (1 Sam. 10).

Lists of musical instruments appear regularly in the Old Testament narrative. The first appears in Genesis 4:21, which introduces Jubal, "the first of all who play the lyre and the flute." Some ensemble listings are small groups, like that in Psalm 92—"with a ten-stringed harp and the music of a lyre" (v. 3). Others are quite extensive. David's appointed orchestra of Levites included harps, lyres, cymbals, trumpets, and ram's horns (1 Chr. 15:16–16:5). Old Testament passages often pair the harp and lyre, which had wide usage in the ancient Near East (1 Kgs. 10:12; 1 Chr. 13:8; Pss. 81:2; 108:2; 150:3).

Clay plaque depicting a musician; from Mesopotamia. Music was a regular part of temple rituals, burial ceremonies, and festival celebrations. Individuals also played music for entertainment.

Old Testament instruments fall into three major categories—string, percussion, and wind. Though we have no original instruments through archaeological studies, we can look at pottery, drawings, and clay figures from the biblical era in Israel and surrounding areas.

STRINGED INSTRUMENTS

Harp—The harp's construction resembled an archer's bow. Strings stretched across a curved wooden frame or across two pieces of wood joined at a right angle. Each string sounded a single pitch and was larger than the strings of the lyre. According to the Talmud, harp strings were made with sheep intestines and sounded louder than those of the lyre.

Lyre—The lyre was the most common stringed instrument of biblical times. Though today we typically think of David as a harpist, he actually played a lyre. Its wooden construction was typically a sound box with two upright arms attached. Strings stretched from a crosspiece and spanned the arms to the sound box. A fingerboard made it possible for strings to play multiple pitches.[1] The lyre was always an instrument of joy. When the occasion for joy ceased, the lyres were put away and remained silent (Ps. 137:2). Prophets warned that if the people continued in sin, they would be punished, and the lyre would no longer be heard (Ezek. 26:13).

From the general region of the Holy Land, drawings remain that show Semitic people playing the lyre. One of these drawings shows captives playing the lyre under the eye of the Assyrian guard. In this instance the players are using their hands to play. Evidence indicates people used their hands when playing instrumental pieces but used the plectrum (a pick made of wood or bone) when accompanying voices.[2]

PERCUSSION INSTRUMENTS

Bell—Bells were attached to the hem of Aaron's priestly robe (Exod. 28:33–35). The bells of biblical times likely resembled small rattles with a pellet or clapper. Archaeologists have found many bells of that description, made of bronze, in sites in Israel.

Cymbal—Cymbals first appear in Scripture during the time of David, in the procession that moved the ark to Jerusalem. They were the only percussion instruments included in the temple instruments that David specified (1 Chr. 15:16). David appointed Heman, Asaph, and Ethan to sound the cymbals, a Levitical position of much distinction and privilege. Cymbals were probably used to accompany singing with other instruments, to draw God's attention to the worshippers, and to signal the beginnings of singing in services of worship.

Made of bronze, the twin cymbals were shaped like saucers. The centers were pierced for finger rings made of iron or wire. Questions remain as to whether they were used horizontally or vertically. They were sounded by striking one against the other or by touching their rims together. Depending on the performance method, the sound of cymbals ranged from light tinkling to a dull clash.[3]

Tambourine—The tambourine was probably a small hand drum. Archaeologists think it probably did not have the "jingles" attached like our modern tambourine. In Scripture, women often played this instrument as they sang and danced with joy. Many clay figures holding the small hand drum date from biblical time.[4]

WIND INSTRUMENTS

Flute—Scholars have varied opinions about the words that most English Bibles translate as "flute." Some use the word "pipe" to describe the flute. Early models were hollow reed pipes with finger holes. With the larger ensembles of temple music, the "pipe" used was probably a stronger-toned reed. These louder instruments probably consisted of two pipes strung together creating a double pipe, each fingered by a different hand. Bronze and clay artifacts from Israel and likely from the Old Testament era portray individuals playing these instruments.[5]

Basalt relief showing musicians playing tambourines and lyres. From the palace of the Hittite King Barrekup at ancient Zinjirli-Sam'al (in modern southeastern Turkey); dates from the late Hittite period, eighth century BC.

From Thebes, Egypt, restored wooden harp with a spade-shaped sounding board. Such harps were in use in Egypt from the time of the Old Kingdom (2700–2160 BC); this one probably dates from the New Kingdom (ca 1300 BC).

Bronze wheeled stand dated to the thirteenth or twelfth century BC. Decorated with scenes that depict a seated harp player approached by a musician and a serving boy; on the back, a winged sphinx. From Cyprus.

Trumpet—Trumpets of Old Testament times were fashioned of straight tubes of metal with bell-shaped ends. People used bronze trumpets in secular settings and silver ones for sacred occasions. Unlike our modern trumpets, these had no valves. This limited to three or four the number of tones the instrument could make. The sound they emitted was probably not very lovely but, in the minds of the people, it was loud enough to bring the attention of God in heaven down to man on earth.

Trumpet players generally performed in pairs or larger groups. In 2 Chronicles 5:12–13, when the Levites brought the ark of the covenant into the temple from the city of David, priests blew 120 trumpets, joining singers, more trumpets, cymbals, and other instruments. Only the priestly descendants of Aaron could play trumpets for sacred occasions (Num. 10:8) and in war (2 Chr. 13:12). Players sounded trumpets for numerous events in Old Testament life: to summon Israelites to the tent of meeting, to signal to Israelites to break camp, as a remembrance of God's presence among his people, to sound an alarm in warfare, on holidays and at the beginning of the new moon, over sacrifices and burnt offerings, when the ark was moved to Jerusalem, at the dedications of the first and second temples, and to join other instruments of praise.[6]

Shofar—English Bibles often translate the Hebrew term *shofar* as "trumpet" to refer to an instrument made from the ram's horn. Some scholars believe the significance of the ram's horn was rooted in the importance of the sacrificial ram that God provided Abraham as he obediently began to offer Isaac. The shofar was a ritual and warfare trumpet. It was used to signal and give commands, as well as sound the alarm. When the Israelites blasted the shofar and shouted, the wall of Jericho tumbled. It is the only biblical instrument still in use today in its original form.[7]

Musical instruments of the Old Testament are many and varied. Our understanding and knowledge of them is also widely dispersed and varied. Though we have no sound or musical notation from the era to narrow our understanding, what we can piece together is an understanding of the character of the sound, the symbolism of the music as it sounded, and something of the cultural setting in the biblical world.

NOTES

1. Richard Leonard, "Musical Instruments in Scripture" in *The Biblical Foundations of Christian Worship*, vol. 1 in The Complete Library of Christian Worship, ed. Robert E. Webber (Peabody, MA: Hendrickson, 1993), 237.
2. Ovid R. Sellers, "Musical Instruments of Israel," *BA* 4.3 (1941): 38–39.
3. Ivor H. Jones, "Music and Musical Instruments" in *ABD*, 4:935; Alfred Sendrey, *Music in the Social and Religious Life of Antiquity* (Rutherford, NJ: Fairleigh Dickinson University Press, 1974), 99, 205–6.

4   Jeremy Montagu, *Musical Instruments of the Bible* (Lanham, MD: Scarecrow Press, 2002), 16–18.
5   Montagu, *Musical Instruments*, 47.
6   Sendrey, *Music*, 189–91.
7   Montagu, *Musical Instruments*, 19–23.

Holman Bible Publishers is grateful to the following persons and institutions for the graphics in the *Ultimate Guide to the Holy Land*. Where we have inadvertently failed to give proper credit for any graphic in the Bible, please contact us (customerservice@ lifeway.com), and we will make the required correction in subsequent printings.

BIBLICAL ILLUSTRATOR PHOTOGRAPHS

Biblical Illustrator, Nashville, Tennessee: pp. 12; 14; 16; 26; 42; 56; 57; 60; 163; 199; 206; 213 (top); 271; 276; 283 (both); 337; 347; 369 (bottom); 381; 389; 425; 431; 469 (top; British Museum); 496 (right; British Museum); 499; 508 (bottom); 510 (top); 514 (both); 517 (bottom); 528; 550 (British Museum) 551 (both; British Museum); 552 (top; British Museum); 555; 573 (British Museum); 574; 595; 600; 627; 628 (top); 630 (top); 633 (bottom); 643 (bottom; British Museum); 650 (bottom).

British Museum, London: pp. 27; 28 (both); 32; 43 (top); 54; 55; 82; 83; 84; 85 (top); 88 (bottom); 92; 108; 127; 128 (top); 143 (both); 144; 152; 184 (top); 202; 205; 298; 299; 300; 364; 365 (top); 421 (both); 424; 427 (top); 460; 473 (bottom); 512; 526; 560; 632; 637 (top).

FreeIsraelPhotos.com: p. 440.

LifeWay/Fon Scofiled Collection: p. 107.

Matson Photo Collection, Library of Congress: p. 137 (top).

Morton-Seats Collection, Midwestern Baptist Theological Seminary: pp. 35.

Jerry Vardaman Collection: pp. 94; 195; 235 (Mike Yarber); 263; 594.

Anderson, Jeff: p. 326.

Borgan, Joy: p. 19 (National Museum of Roman Art).

Bruce, Brent: pp. 51 (Metropolitan Museum of Art, New York); 63 (both; top, Walters Art Museum, Baltimore; bottom, Oriental Museum of Chicago); 79; 88 (top; Ashmolen Museum, Oxford); 100 (top); 123 (bottom; Metropolitan Museum of Art, New York); 128 (bottom; Ashmolean Museum, Oxford); 149; 160 (bottom; Walters Art Museum, Baltimore); 179; 184 (bottom; Metropolitan Museum of Art, New York);

201; 212; 214; 219 (bottom); 284 (Ashmolean Museum, Oxford); 301 (St. Louis Museum of Art); 342; 343; 351; 359; 362; 384; 488 (bottom); 513 (top; Ashmolean Museum, Oxford); 522 (top; University of Pennsylvania Museum of Archaeology and Anthropology); 547; 572 (Lynn H. Wood Archaeological Museum, Southern Adventist University, Collegedale, TN); 628 (bottom); 640; 651.

Eddinger, Terry: p. 548.

Hiller, Kristen: pp. 78; 99; 102 (top); 120 (both); 138 (Eretz Israel Museum, Tel Aviv); 145; 146; 194; 339; 340; 344; 383; 392; 393; 398 (both); 437; 443; 556 (Eretz Museum, Tel Aviv).

Hooke, Tom: pp. 183; 302; 386; 605 (bottom).

Howell Jr., G.B.: pp. 52 (top; The Louvre); 85 (bottom; The Louvre); 102 (bottom); 103 (both; top, Museum of Fine Arts, Boston; bottom, Oriental Museum, Chicago); 105 (The Louvre); 133 (Cincinnati Museum); 141; 142; 159 (The Louvre); 161 (both; top, Art Institute of Chicago; bottom, The Louvre); 163 (Thessaloniki Archaeological Museum); 168 (The Louvre); 169; 186; 191 (Delphi Aracheologica Museum); 203 (North Carolina Museum of Art, Raleigh); 213 (bottom); 221; 226 (top; Cincinnati Museum); 249; 250; 303; 307; 312; 313; 321; 327 (bottom; Thessaloniki Archaeological Museum); 332; 353; 361; 372; 469 (bottom; The Louvre); 508 (top; Oriental Institue Museum of Chicago); 522-23 (bottom; Chicago Field Museum); 535 (Corinth Archaeological Museum); 558; 570 (The Louvre); 571 (The Louvre); 576 (top; The Louvre); 580 (bottom; Thessaloniki Archaeological Museum); 592; 605 (top; Oriental Museum, Chicago); 629 (The Louvre); 630; 640 (both; The Louvre).

Hughes, Randy: p. 334.

Kandros, Micah: p. 377.

Maeir, A.: p. 295; 296 (both); 297; 542.

McLemore, James: pp. 2; 3; 5; 66; 73; 89 (bottom; Istanbul Archaeological Museum); 218; 228; 238; 273; 289; 331; 388; 439; 442; 496 (middle, Jerry Vardaman Collection; right).

Rogers, David: pp. 9 (The Louvre); 15 (both;

bottom, Callaway Collection, The Southern Baptist Theological Seminary); 22 (British Museum); 23 (University Museum, University of Pennsyvlania); 40; 46 (both, Jewish Museum, New York); 52 (bottom; British Museum); 62 (Museum of the Ancient Orient, Istanbul); 80 (Metropolitan Museum of Art, New York); 87 (British Museum); 90 (both; top, University Museum, University of Pennsylvania; bottom, Adana Archaelogical Museum, Adana, Turkey); 111; 113 (top); 115 (British Museum); 117 (Metropolitan Museum of Art, New York); 123 (top; Metropolitan Museum of Art, New York); 125 (Museum of Fine Arts, Boston); 137 (Jewish Museum, New York); 150 (British Museum); 160 (top; Metropolitan Museum of Art, New York); 176 (both; top, Archaeological Museum, Antakya, Turkey; bottom, The Louvre); 180 (Callaway Collection, The Southern Baptist Theological Seminary); 181 (Jewish Museum, New York); 182; 187 (top; Archaeological Museum, Istanbul); 208; 209 (The Louvre); 234; 245 (British Museum); 260 (Museum of Art and Archaeology, University of Missouri, Columbia); 264; 282 (top); 283 (bottom; British Museum); 294; 315 (Archaeological Museum, Ankara, Turkey); 327 (top; British Museum); 329; 330 (both; bottom, Archaeological Museum, Ankara, Turkey); 369 (top; British Museum); 373 (Oriental Institute, University of Chicago); 375 (The Louvre); 379 (Archaeological Museum, Ankara, Turkey; 380 (Archaeological Museum, Ankara, Turkey); 411 (top; Museum of Art and Archaeology, University of Missouri, Columbia); 470 (both; top, Museum of Fine Arts, Boston; bottom, Joseph A. Callaway Archaeological Museum, The Southern Baptist Theological Seminary); 493 (Joseph A. Callaway Archaeological Museum, The Southern Baptist Theological Seminary); 497 (Ephesus Museum); 498 (University Museum, University of Pennsylvania); 509 (British Museum); 510 (Museum of Fine Arts, Boston); 515 (University Museum, University of Pennsylvania); 520(both; bottom, British Museum); 538 (top; British Museum); 556 (top); 585 (University Museum, University of Pennsylvania); 590 (both; bottom, University Museum, University of Pennsylvania); 639 (top; Museum of the Ancient Orient, Istanbul); 650 (top; British Museum); 652.

Rutherford, Mike: pp. 217; 219 (top).

Schatz, Bob: pp. 8 (both; top left, Musuem of the Ancient Orient, Istanbul); 10; 18; 30; 49 (National Museum of Damascus); 58; 61; 71; 72; 75 (Istanbul Archaeological Museum); 76; 89 (middle two); 91; 96; 108; 112 (Royal Ontario Museum, Toronto); 116 (Istanbul Archaeological Museum); 119; 122 (Shahba Museum, Philippopolis, Syria); 130; 131; 134; 136; 139; 151 (Cairo Museum); 165 (Istanbul Archaeological Museum); 167; 174 (Museum of the Ancient Orient, Istanbul); 175 (Hatay Archaeological Museum); 187 (bottom); 193; 196; 207; 225; 226 (bottom); 227; 229; 230; 231; 235; 237; 239; 244; 253; 255 (Nof Ginnosar Museum, Israel); 256; 262; 263 (bottom); 266; 267; 268; 278; 281; 282 (bottom); 286; 287 (top); 292; 293; 304; 306; 308; 309; 310; 316 (Capitoline Museum, Rome); 336; 346; 349; 350; 352; 354; 355; 356; 358; 368; 371; 376; 387; 391 (both); 404 (both; bottom, Greco-Roman Museum, Cairo, Egypt); 403; 406; 411; 414; 416; 417; 419; 431 (bottom; Capitoline Museum, Rome); 432; 449; 450; 452; 457 (top; Roay Ontario Museum, Toronto); 459; 461 (both; bottom, Anatolian Civilizations Museum of Ankara); 472; 481; 482; 486 (The Egyptian Museum, Cario); 487; 489; 521 (National Museum of Damacus); 525; 533 (Istanbul Archaeological Museum); 534; 540 (Ancient Corinth Museum); 538 (bottom; Hatay Archaeological Museum); 541; 545 (Anatolian Civilzations Museum of Ankara); 564; 569; 570 (Archaeological Museum in Isthmia); 567 (National Museum of Damascus); 576 (bottom); 579; 587 (Hazor Museum, Israel); 588; 591; 598 (Department of Antiquities in Jordan Archaeological Museum, Amman, Jordan); 606; 608; 611; 616; 618; 619; 620; 621; 624; 642; 647; 648 (both; top, Royal Ontario Museum); 653 (Museum of the Ancient Orient, Istanbul).

Severance, Murray: p. 154.

Smith, Audrey: pp. 223; 430; 580 (top).

Smith, Louise Kohl: pp. 7; 34; 104; 147; 189; 248; 252; 258; 259; 463; 613; 641.

Tolar, William: p. 1735.

Touchton, Ken: pp. 6 (Israel Museum); 48; 124

(Capitoline Museum, Rome); 132 (National Maritime Museum, Haifa); 456; 491; 527;
Veneman, Justin: pp. 317; 318 (both); 333; 623 (both).

OTHER PHOTOGRAPHS

Jupiter Images: p. 597.
Public Domain Images: p. 473 (top).

MAPS, ILLUSTRATIONS, AND RECONSTRUCTIONS

Biblical Illustrator, Nashville, TN: p. 488 (bottom).
Holman Bible & Reference: pp. 20; 37; 43 (bottom); 64; 89 (top); 97; 215; 272; 422; 539.
Latta, Bill: p. 113 (bottom).
Linden Artists, London: pp. 100 (bottom); 222; 254; 385.

*STILL WANT MORE OF THE HOLY LAND?
CHECK OUT THE CSB HOLY LAND
ILLUSTRATED BIBLE.*

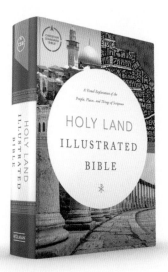

This unique Bible offers over 1,200 images, maps, illustrations
and articles showing the Holy Land in the context of
the people, places, and events of Scripture to create a study
experience that will deepen your understanding of the Bible.